INTERNATIONAL HANDBOOK OF HIGHER EDUCATION

Springer International Handbooks of Education

VOLUME 18

International Handbook of Higher Education

Part Two: Regions and Countries

Edited by

James J.F. Forest
U.S. Military Academy,
West Point, NY, USA

and

Philip G. Altbach
Boston College,
Chestnut Hill, MA, USA

 Springer

A C.I.P. Catalogue record for this book is available from the Library of Congress.

ISBN-10 1-4020-4011-3 (HB)
ISBN-13 978-1-4020-4011-5 (HB)
ISBN-10 1-4020-4012-1 (e-book)
ISBN-13 978-1-4020-4012-2 (e-book)

Published by Springer
P.O. Box 17, 3300 AA Dordrecht, The Netherlands.

www.springer.com

Printed on acid-free paper

Printed in the Netherlands.

TABLE OF CONTENTS

PART ONE: GLOBAL THEMES AND CONTEMPORARY CHALLENGES

PART TWO: REGIONS AND COUNTRIES

PREFACE TO VOLUME TWO

A primary objective of *The International Handbook of Higher Education* is to provide a rich resource for expanding our understanding of higher education worldwide. A comparative perspective of important social institutions—including the university—helps us identify phenomena that, while framed by different political and social arrangements, leads to a better understanding of a complex world and our place within it. In the study of higher education, we are so often bound by the constraints of national thinking that a comparative perspective become especially valuable, because academic institutions worldwide stem from common traditions, and the issues facing higher education around the world have many common characteristics. Together, these two volumes compliment each other in highlighting important themes and issues that transcend the many differences in history, culture, and experience that occur among nations.

Volume One of this *Handbook* addressed important themes in a mostly international and comparative perspective. The chapters of this second volume provide a more detailed analysis of many countries and regions, adding greater qualitative depth to the comparative perspectives offered in the first volume. The volume also provides a significant amount of geographic diversity: all the major regions of the world are covered in these chapters, and each country represented in this volume has a well-developed system of higher education. Also, by limiting the number of countries covered in this volume, we have been able to provide greater depth in exploring key issues and challenges within each country chapter.

We invited authors to explore the themes addressed in Volume One in greater detail within the context of a particular regional or national experience. Each author was given full autonomy in organizing their chapters, although we asked that they include in their discussion a few important topics such as the history of the nation's higher education system and policy; increasing demands for access, expansion and accountability; economic and financial issues; differences between public and private institutions (including their respective governance models, student bodies, etc.); challenges facing the academic profession; graduate education; and the impact of the "brain drain" phenomenon on the country's workforce development needs. The results of their efforts, we are convinced, offer useful comparative insights into the world of higher education.

These regional and country chapters allow the reader to contextualize the general themes and interpretations of higher education represented in Volume One.

James J.F. Forest and Philip G. Altbach (eds.), International Handbook of Higher Education, xi–xii.
© *2006 Springer. Printed in the Netherlands.*

Further, studying the cross-national similarities and differences described in both volumes helps us better understand and appreciate our own system of higher education. Even when scholars enhance our understanding of a single nation and its uniqueness, this is often best understood through comparison with other national contexts.

SECTION 1

Regional Perspectives

20

HIGHER EDUCATION IN THE ARAB WORLD

Linda Herrera
Institute of Social Studies, The Hague

Higher education in the Arab region has been witness to a prolific history. Long inter-twined with major religious, intellectual, political, social, and economic movements, institutions of higher learning have occupied a central place in Arab societies. The university in the contemporary Arab world can be conceptualized as a global, universal institution located within a region with particular histories and cultures of learning.

The Arab region, which contains 5% of the world's population and consists of 22 member states of the League of Arab States, spans the Southern Mediterranean, Northern and Central Africa, and Western Asia. Arabic is the dominant—albeit not the only—language in the region, and Islam is the majority religion for some 90% of the population, with Christianity accounting for much of the remaining 10%[1] The region contains a great deal of diversity, yet despite significant differences, a number of features—including the prominence of numerous pan-Arab political and economic organizations, a shared language, majority religion, political systems, common history, and experience of regional politics—allow for a coherent treatment of the Arab region.

Legacies of Higher Learning in Arab Societies[2]

The indigenous institution for higher learning, the *madrasa*, has been a mainstay of Arab institutional life since the emergence of Islam in the seventh century. With the ascendancy of Islamic civilization and the subsequent rise of the "Arabic sciences" to global eminence during the Abbasid and Umayyad dynasties, the madrasa and other institutions involved in the transmission and production of knowledge, profoundly in-fluenced practices of higher learning across place and time. The madrasa specialized largely in "religious sciences," at the heart of which was Islamic law and the Arabic language, the language of sacred revelation. Among the most renowned and endur-ing madrasas have been the Azhar in Cairo, the Qarawiyyun in Fez, and Zaytuna in Tunis. Historian George Makdisi persuasively demonstrates how certain common fea-tures of the contemporary university—such as the conferring of master's and doctoral degrees, protections for academic freedom, inaugural lectures, the wearing of robes and holding of "chairs"—originated with the madrasa (Makdisi, 1990, pp. 26–38). He similarly establishes a connection between the madrasa-based intellectual movements

James J.F. Forest and Philip G. Altbach (eds.), International Handbook of Higher Education, 409–15.
© *2006 Springer. Printed in the Netherlands.*

of scholasticism and humanism and similar movements of the much later university of the Christian West. Scholasticism refers to a highly sophisticated method of legal disputation used in the teaching of the Islamic legal sciences that came to be used in the "exact" sciences. This method traveled to Spain and Persia and—through a series of translations and borrowings—came to be known as the "scientific method" (Makdisi, 1981, p. 131). Humanism, which evolved out of the madrasa from as early as the 7th century, refers to a methodological approach to Arabic language and literature based on imitation of the classics known as *studia adabiya*, which is linked to *studia humanitatis* of the Italian Renaissance (Makdisi, 1990, p. xxi).

Whereas religious science was the domain of the madrasa, the "foreign" or "pagan" sciences of mainly ancient Greece—as well as Persia, India, Egypt and China—flourished largely outside the madrasa in spaces for learning and experimentation such as observatories, hospitals, private homes, and libraries, which were also known as "academies." The foreign sciences spread both through the flow of scientists, scholars, travelers, merchants, and students across the fluid borders that made up the Islamic empire, and through vigorous endeavors by the learned and powerful to acquire and translate the written works of the ancients. Among the earliest and most notable academies was the *Bait al-Hikma* (House of Wisdom) of Baghdad, where scholars from diverse geographic, religious, and linguistic backgrounds assembled to consult and translate manuscripts and hold scholarly seminars.

The pursuit of translation within a context of pluralistic communities in urban centers of learning—especially Baghdad, Cairo, Damascus, Fez, Cordoba, Sicily, and later Istanbul—contributed to staggering advances in the "Arabic" sciences.[3] From the 9th to the 15th centuries, and possibly as late as the 19th century, fields as varied as mathematics, trigonometry, algebra, geometry, optics, medicine, chemistry, physics, astronomy, philosophy, agriculture, navigation, cartography, architecture, and music flourished in the Arab-Islamic lands (Hogendijk & Sabra, 2003, p. vii). The Arabic sciences reached Europe via the western reaches of the Islamic empire in Sicily and Andalusia. Arabic works were translated into Latin and (eventually) vernacular European languages, and penetrated Christian Europe at the dawn of the Italian Renaissance (Cobb, 1963).

In the wake of the European Renaissance and Industrial Revolution, and with the emergence of Europe as a global economic and imperial force (within the context of Russian imperial expansion) there rose an urgency among the leaders of the Islamic empire—now dominated by the Ottomans whose seat of power was Istanbul—to modernize their armies and supporting institutions, including educational institutions. Higher educational models from Europe and to some extent Russia were viewed as containing the formula for achieving power, economic success, and scientific advancement in the new world order. As early as the 1720s, official state delegations from the Ottoman Empire traveled to Europe to visit and study their institutions of learning. As Ekmeleddin İhsanoğlu notes, one of the first attempts to "set up an Ottoman intellectual institution without an organic structure" occurred during the reign of Ottoman Sultan Ahmet III, when scholars were assembled in 1720 for the purpose of translating works of history and philosophy from European languages into Turkish and Arabic (1996, p. 165). By the first decades of the 19th century, states were more systematically supporting exogenous knowledge institutions for modernizing reforms.

The figure most often credited with setting up foreign inspired institutions of higher learning was the viceroy Mohamed Ali Pasha, based in the Ottoman province of Egypt (r. 1805–1849). In 1809, he sent a group of students on an educational mission to Europe and over the next decades established numerous schools in Egypt—roughly equivalent to vocational high schools and technical colleges—that specialized in military sciences, medicine, agriculture, veterinarian medicine, midwifery, pharmaceutics, chemistry, engineering, and translation (Heyworth-Dunne, 1968 [1939]). With the exception of the School of Midwives, all schools were the exclusive domain of men. The institutes, which represented a mix of Arabic, Turkish, Persian and European curricula and staff, for the most part did not survive beyond Mohamed Ali's reign, although they set a precedent for successive rulers. The more enduring institutions of learning were those founded by foreign missions, governments, and organizations.

New forms of schooling had been spreading among the non-Muslim minority (*millet*) and foreign communities since the 18th century. Foreign missions throughout the Middle East catered largely to minority sects and exerted great influence over the native Arab Christian and Jewish populations through their extensive networks of primary and secondary schools. The 1907 census of Egypt indicates that non-Coptic Christians and Jews made up the highest percentage of literate groups, followed by Coptic and Muslim boys, presumably because of their high participation in the foreign schools and, in the case of Muslim boys, their involvement in *kuttabs*, the Quranic primary schools.

Literacy among Muslims girls, who also attended kuttabs but in far lower numbers than boys, and for whom participation in the foreign schools was considered culturally taboo, was by far the lowest (Herrera, 2002). A mere two out of every 1,000 Muslim girls was literate, compared to 78 per thousand Muslim boys and 313 per thousand Jewish girls.[4] The foreign schools provided a natural pool of students for the early new universities in the region, which included the Syrian Protestant College, later named the American University of Beirut (est. 1866); the University of Saint Joseph, also located in Beirut and founded by French Jesuits (est. 1874); and the American University in Cairo (est. 1920). These foreign universities served as models of sorts for the nascent national universities, and played pioneering roles in areas such as women's education.[5]

In the decades leading up to the breakdown of European colonial rule, strong nationalist anti-colonial movements spread throughout the Arab region. In Egypt, the Levant, and the Maghrib—the foreign schools, symbols of European power—became bitterly contested. Nationalist reformers advocated control over their countries' educational institutions and endeavored to build their own national models of primary, secondary, and tertiary education. They pursued policies of school expansion with the aim of not only taking control over their institutions—and, as such, the socialization of their youth—but for the purpose of cultivating a Muslim middle class that would be able to compete with the prosperous segments of foreign and minority communities in matters of trade and other commercial endeavors. The economic success of non-Muslim groups in the Ottoman territories was attributed in part to the legal privileges afforded them by the capitulations, but also to the skills, languages, and other competencies they acquired through their participation in the new schooling. The new educational paradigms, in other words, were considered to provide the necessary training, socialization, credentials, and social capital needed for mobility and employment in the new professions, bureaucracies, and economies of the emerging nation-states.

Nationalization and the Expansion of Higher Education

In the post-World War I and II period the Arab region, in keeping with education trends globally, experienced prodigious growth of what can be called, with some caveats, "westernized" higher education. In 1939, a total of 10 universities existed in the Arab world; by 1961, the number increased to 20, and by 1975, 47. By the year 2000, over 200 universities were operating in Arab states, more than a quarter of which had opened during the 1990s. In addition to universities, the region has also witnessed the prolific growth of a variety of higher education institutes specializing in a range of professional and technical studies, as well as distance education universities (UNESCO, 2003, p. 7).

The post-colonial expansion of higher education, while it has undeniably contributed to multiple aspects of social and political development, has also engendered a great degree of tension and debate.

The nascent national education systems—of which the university represented a prominent symbol—played a critical role in forging and solidifying new national identities and in leading countries towards achieving national and regional development and political autonomy. Governments made it a priority to establish national universities, either by reorganizing and reforming already existing institutions—as was the case in Iraq, Tunisia, and Morocco—or by founding new universities from scratch, as occurred in Libya, Lebanon, Saudi Arabia and Jordan (Waardenburg, 1966, p. 35). In many cases, national universities were founded even before the expansion of national secondary schooling took root. In Lebanon, for example, a mere three government secondary schools—albeit scores of foreign missionary schools—were in operation at the time the first national university, the Lebanese State University, was founded in 1952. It was as if, in the words of a chronicler of the period, ". . . independence and sovereignty would not be complete without a state university to symbolize them" (Bashshur, 1964, p. 72).

Egypt asserted itself early on as the regional leader in national higher education. Its King Fouad the First University—later named the Egyptian University and, finally (in 1952), Cairo University—was conceived by nationalists under the leadership of Saad Zaghlul Pasha in 1906, while Egypt was still under British mandate rule. Initially a private university staffed by visiting foreign professors, it was nationalized in 1925.

Women initially participated in university life in a limited way until gaining full participation as faculty and students throughout the course of the ensuing decades.[6] The university represented the "liberal ideal" until the early 1950s, when it underwent an intensive process of Arabization, Sovietization, and expansion during the presidency of Gamal Abdel Nasser (1956–1970) (Reid, 1990).

Egyptians played a vital role in advancing national higher education throughout the Arab region by providing a national university model for emulation, by supplying other Arab universities with staff and expertise, by opening branches of its universities in other Arab cities—such as Khartoum and Beirut—and by admitting students from other Arab countries to its programs. The Egyptian national university has variously combined elements of French, British, Arab, Islamic, Soviet, and American influences, mirroring the political and social shifts in the country and region.

The Egyptian influence in Arab higher education began to wane following the 1970s oil boom in the Gulf countries. With the flow of oil, the countries of the Gulf—particularly Saudi Arabia—assumed a position of region-wide dominance and geopolitical strategic importance.

Close economic and geopolitical alliances with the United States contributed to the choice of the American model with its credit-point system as the prevailing higher education model in the Gulf (Mazawi, 2004).

The expansion of mass higher education, particularly since the 1970s, has led to major shifts in the ways in which knowledge and knowledge institutions have come to be located in larger power structures.[7] Although the modern university has overtaken the madrasa in many respects, the madrasa—and religious authorities trained therein—are far from obsolete.[8] Not only has the madrasa remained intact, but it has witnessed a revival in past decades. Such a revival speaks partly to the enduring affinity of Arabs and Muslims with indigenous Islamic institutions, particularly in times of crisis, yet it may also be indicative of the university's inability to achieve the widespread reach, legitimacy, and societal transformation for which reformers, policymakers, intellectuals, and ordinary members of society have long hoped for it.

Challenges Facing the Contemporary Arab University

When Egyptian born and educated Ahmed Zewail was awarded the Nobel Prize in Chemistry in 1999 for his work in femtochemistry (the branch of chemistry that studies ultrafast elementary chemical reactions as they occur), the first Arab to win such a scientific tribute in the contemporary period, Arabs rejoiced. Yet the honor was bittersweet, for Zewail's accomplishments—by his own admission—would not have been possible had he not left his position at an Egyptian national university and taken up a post abroad. As Zewail relates in his autobiography *Voyage through Times: Walks of Life to the Nobel Prize* (2002), unlike the hierarchical, bureaucratic, and inflexible system of Egyptian and other such national higher education systems that thwart innovative research initiatives (especially by junior faculty), the academic culture at the prestigious and financially endowed California Institute of Technology (Caltech) allowed him tremendous possibilities. By providing him autonomy in decision making, collegial support, high caliber graduate students to assist him, and generous financial backing, Zewail was able to develop his Nobel-recognized work in a mere ten-year period. In his acceptance speech in Sweden, Zewail recalled those towering figures of Arabic science of the past and hoped his award would "inspire the young generations of developing countries with the knowledge that it is possible to contribute to world science and technology" (p. 255). Yet he has not been able to solve the question of how Arab youth—given the current state of Arab higher education with its problems of governance, resources, and freedom—could make the type of contribution to world science and knowledge that he envisions.[9]

The Arab university has been undergoing a period of crisis, transition, expansion, and introspection for several decades. In the widely debated Arab Human Development

Reports of 2002 and 2003, the authors, a group of reform-minded Arab intellectuals, posit that the Arab region suffers from a serious "knowledge deficit." They argue that the relative stagnation in knowledge production has been due, at least in part, to an inward-looking nativism that has hindered Arab intellectual culture. Unlike the prodigious rate of translation that occurs in countries such as Japan and Korea that have successfully, in their assessment, made the transitions to knowledge societies in the past half-century, the translation movement in the Arab region remains "static and chaotic" (United Nations Development Program (UNDP), 2003, p. 3). While precise figures on the current number of translations are not available, it appears evident that in the fields of the social and physical sciences, humanities, and arts, translation has been exceedingly paltry at best. The region's research output in science and technology represents a mere 1% of global output, and research funding is among the lowest in the world (UNDP, 2002, pp. 65, 71). Despite a number of noteworthy faculties and programs in Arab national universities in Morocco, Egypt, Sudan, Egypt, Palestine, Lebanon, and Tunisia (to name just a few), the scientific quality of most faculties in national universities across disciplines has been mixed at best. Limited financial resources translate not only to low scientific output, but to substandard equipment, low salaries, limited scholarships, few international scholarly exchanges, and deteriorating facilities—all of which present daunting impediments to academics, especially in the poorer Arab countries.

In the area of governance, the prevalence of oftentimes cumbersome, authoritarian, and sometimes absurdly bureaucratic institutional structures seriously hinder the university's ability to prosper. Arab governments have variously carried out purgings of "undesirable" faculty. Heavy-handed and security-oriented administrations often interfere in academic life in areas such as student admissions, faculty and student research, student conduct, travel of faculty, choice of curricular materials, and topics of conferences. In most Gulf countries, for example, scholarly research on social, religious, cultural, and ethical issues remains severely restricted (Morsi, 1990, p. 44). An Algerian professor, when questioned about the state of academic freedom in Arab universities, explained, "In Arab universities, instead of academic freedom, there are different levels and types of academic oppression" (quoted in Taha-Thomure, 2002, p. 75). The current restraints on freedom cause particular bitterness for intellectuals who take pride in their region's historical contributions to world culture. An Arab professor of political science disparagingly remarked that unlike the past, when Arabs contributed to the advancement of learning and sciences, the contribution of Arabs to academic culture in the contemporary period is its "academic police." He lamented, "If the West has borrowed our sciences, scientific methodology and academic institutions in the past, I doubt that our invention of 'academic police' can be adopted by the West . . . [M]ay be it is exportable to Latin America. This market might be interested in such a police force" (quoted in Sabour, 2001, p. 120).

The situation appears even more complicated when we consider how universities have long been battlegrounds between governments and political oppositional forces, in which divergent ideologies—including Arab nationalism, communism, Islamism, and secularism—have competed for supremacy. The Arab world holds the inauspicious distinction of being home to some of the world's most contentious and bloody conflicts on local and international scales. Military conflict and political instability—whether through civil war, foreign occupation, or internal power struggles—clearly take heavy tolls on the quality and ability of higher education to prosper.

Since the 1970s, intensive Islamization—which has taken both socio-cultural and militant forms—has influenced university cultures in countries such as Algeria, Sudan, and Egypt. Islamists have attempted, and succeeded in many cases, to censure the ideological content of courses, forcibly implement practices such as sex-segregation and Islamic dress codes (especially for female students and staff) and—in the case of the more militant wings—harass, intimidate, and sometimes even target intellectuals and students for assassination. Iraq under United States occupation offers the most recent example of militant political Islamization of universities; increasing testimonies from Iraq's universities report student violence and harassment, pressure being put on female students to don an Islamic uniform and, most alarming, a spate of assassinations—including beheadings—of Iraqi academics, presumably because of their association with the foreign occupiers (Watenpaugh, 2004).[10] The combination of authoritarian governmental regimes and oppressive oppositional forces, both of which tend to use educational institutions as figurative and literal battle grounds, bodes especially poorly for the prospering of free and productive academic cultures.

Another example of the effects of political instability and occupation can be found in the West Bank and Gaza Strip where colleges and universities struggle under persistent assaults by the Israeli military on people and property, which has included the destruction of two ministries of education. Nevertheless, Palestinian higher education has witnessed significant expansion since 1971, where, for a population of 3.5 million, there exist five universities and 26 community colleges. Civil society advocate Fouad Moughrabi observes, "So strong is the belief in the positive value of education that most students would brave checkpoints, curfews, and life-threatening restrictions in order to arrive at their schools . . . [M]ost faculty would also put up with tremendous difficulties to meet their classes. Simply attending school and meeting classes become major acts of defiance, turning universities and schools into sites of resistance" (2004). Indeed, education constitutes one of the more powerful—albeit least reported—sites of struggle for Palestinians.

Among other inroads achieved in higher education have been the high participation of women in higher education in Arab states, a cause for cautious optimism. Early in the 20th century, Arab women struggled for the right to join universities as full members. In the year 2000, the enrollment of women in colleges, higher institutes, and universities throughout the region was proportionally high. In Egypt, Lebanon, and Iraq, women have made up half or more of the students in several faculties—including, at times, prestigious and traditionally "male" faculties such as medicine. In the Arab Gulf countries of Saudi Arabia, Qatar, and Kuwait, women make up more than half of the undergraduate student populations, in part because men from the Gulf are more likely to study abroad. However, female students do not have access to the full range of faculties open to their male counterparts. In Saudi Arabia, for example, in keeping with the conservative tenets of Wahhabi Islam, schooling is segregated and separately administered beginning with the primary level. Female students tend to be tracked to colleges for "female" professions, such as teaching and social work, which are under the administration of the Presidency General for Girls' Education. Women, however, do have limited access to the predominantly male universities under the Ministry of Higher Education, yet their numbers remain extremely small.[11] These women, while chiefly members of the urban middle to upper classes (Mazawi, 1999), nevertheless represent a highly significant cohort in higher education in the Gulf. Although women have made tremendous strides in higher education, at present the attainment of university degrees does not translate into comparable participation in the political arena and the labor force. However, the trend towards increased female attainment of higher education is likely to gradually lead to broader changes towards greater gender equity.

While a great deal of educational reform and innovation occurs within the Arab region, certain basic conditions of stability and peace are needed to ensure that reforms will be more far-reaching and lasting.

In light of the effects of regional and international conflicts on educational quality, the authors of the above mentioned UNDP reports call for more international scholarly exchanges, regional cooperation, reform of knowledge institutions towards more flexibility, and pursuit (as in the past) of more translations of scholarly and literary works into Arabic, because "openness, interaction, assimilation, absorption, revision, criticism and examination cannot but stimulate creative knowledge production in Arab societies" (UNDP, 2003, p. 8). At the same time, they recognize how difficult international exchanges have become since the terrorist attacks of September 11, 2001 (UNDP, 2002, 2003). Arab scholars are regularly denied visas to international conferences and visiting academic positions in North America and elsewhere. Within one year following the 9/11 attacks on the United States, the number of Arab students studying in the United States dropped 30% (UNDP, 2003, p. 2). In the post-9/11 era, when the need for exchange, openness, self-reflection, and criticism are more essential than ever, opportunities for Arabs to engage in knowledge exchanges—especially in the West—seem to be rapidly diminishing. The lack of political stability, compounded by restrictions on academic freedom, bleak economic opportunities, military conflict, and social and political instability, represent some of the more salient reasons why the region as a whole continuously loses many of its valuable human resources to brain drain. At the end of last century, some one million "highly qualified" Arabs were estimated to have been working in countries belonging to the Organization for Economic Cooperation and Development (OECD). In 1995–96 alone, 25% of the region's 300,000 first-tier graduates from Arab universities emigrated, as did more than 15,000 doctors in the two-year period from 1998–2000 (Zahlan, quoted in UNDP, 2002, p. 71; UNDP, 2003, p. 10). In light of the current situation, a number of attempts are being made, particularly by way of regional cooperation and international investment and involvement, to fortify Arab higher education.

Pan-Arab Cooperation

A number of inter-governmental, non-governmental, and international organizations have accelerated efforts in recent years to organize research, training, funding, accreditation, and cooperation for region-wide joint programs in higher education.

Among the more visible and active organizations are the Association of Arab Universities, the Arab Federation for Technical Education, the Arab Federation of Councils for Scientific Research, UNESCO's Regional Bureau for Education in the Arab States, the World Bank, the UNDP Regional Bureau for Arab States, the Arab League Educational Cultural and Scientific Organization (ALESCO), the Arab Bureau of Education for the Gulf States (ABEGS), the Arab Network for Open and Distance Education, the University of the Middle East Project (UME), and the Islamic Educational, Scientific and Cultural Organization (ISESCO).

Educators and policymakers have also responded to pan-Arab needs by expanding distance learning. Open universities provide flexibility and access to higher learning to populations for whom conventional classroom study would prove difficult, such as women restricted by family obligations or conservative cultural attitudes, working students, and populations in conflict-ridden or war-torn regions where physical travel to and from campuses could prove hazardous. Some of the better-known examples of pan-Arab open universities include Al-Quds Open University (QOU), The Arab Open University (AOU), and the Syrian Virtual University. The QOU grew in response to the difficulties faced by Palestinians who wished to pursue higher education under conditions of occupation and economic hardship.[12] A more recent initiative, the AOU, was established in 1999 and relies primarily on curricular resources and programs from the United Kingdom's Open University.[13] Similarly, the Syrian Virtual University, established in 2003, works largely in cooperation with North American universities to provide Arab students opportunities to earn accredited degrees through distance learning. A number of other universities located in both the North and South offer distance learning to students located in the Arab world.[14] Each program differs with regard to their offerings and curricular materials. While the QOU produces its own textbooks and other audio and visual materials through its in-house media center, the programs at the AOU and the Syrian Virtual University rely largely on pre-fabricated curricular materials from the U.K. and North America. The latter two programs, while successful in many respects, have been criticized for not adequately addressing local needs or advancing local knowledge production (UNESCO, 2003, p. 8).

Privatization of Higher Education

From the 1990s, all education sectors—including higher education—have experienced extensive privatization, a trend which corresponds to more general changes stemming from neoliberal economic reforms. The private university boom has been most pronounced in Jordan, and began in the early 1990s when Palestinians of professional migrant worker families returned to Jordan from Kuwait following the first Gulf War of 1991. In the decade of the 1990s alone, 12 new private universities opened in Jordan, seven in Lebanon, six in Egypt, and several more in Yemen and Sudan, with plans in all countries for more. Many of the new private universities have been established in cooperation with North American and European universities; they are highly profit-driven and oriented largely towards professional training. Some of the more financially lucrative universities even own their own secondary schools, ensuring a steady flow of paying students from one educational stage to the next.

It was largely thought in development and policy circles that privatization of higher education could potentially alleviate states from the burden of supplying the vast majority of higher education to their populations, provide more flexibility in the delivery of education, and address the growing demands of the international labor market by providing the necessary types of education and training for new generations. Yet the new private universities appear to be falling far short of the many hopes placed on them.

In its report on Higher Education in the Arab Region, UNESCO takes a guarded view towards the growing privatization of higher education, cautioning: "[T]here is as yet no evidence that these new universities have succeeded in lifting the strain and alleviating the pressure on the higher education system in the region. Nor is there any evidence, with few exceptions, that they have provided students with more diversity or are succeeding to meet the needs of students, society, the labor market and the requirements of the global economy" (2003).

With the market-driven privatization of higher education, certain principles once embedded in the educational endeavor such as citizenship building, ethics, community responsibility, are apparently being replaced to a large degree by individual interest and economic rationality. The new private universities, therefore, raise serious questions about equity in education and the role of the university in the production of an educated citizenry capable—developmentally, technically, and ethically—of serving local, regional, and global needs.

Towards Humanism and Freedom

Higher education confronts a host of challenges, many of which seriously impede the Arab university's ability to realize its greater potential. Arab societies have historically placed a high value on knowledge and formal learning. The primacy of the sciences and arts during much of Islamic civilization, the proliferation of pluralistic polities, and notions of justice and social development have all drawn to a great extent on principles embedded in cultures of learning. Yet the rich cultural and ethical educational Arab heritage, in all its syncretism, appears to be increasingly under threat due to a combination of factors including the persistence of political and military conflicts in the region, the lack of democratic governance, and the short-sightedness of educational reforms that are largely market driven. Meaningful reforms in higher education, and institutions of knowledge more generally, have the potential to contribute to the forging of societies in which peace and freedom can prevail. Clearly, higher education plays a potentially decisive role in cultivating the type of educated person needed to confront and address challenges in the current era of intensified social and political conflicts and struggles for greater democratization and social justice.

Notes

1. The 22 nations that make up the Arab region and which are all member states of the League of Arab States are The Hashemite Kingdom of Jordan, United Arab Emirates, Kingdom of Bahrain, Republic of Tunisia, Democratic and Popular Republic of Algeria, Republic of Djibouti, Kingdom of Saudi Arabia, Republic of Sudan, Arab Republic of Syria, Republic of Somalia, Republic of Iraq, Sultanate of Oman, State of Palestine, State of Qatar, Federal Islamic Republic of Comoros,

State of Kuwait, Republic of Lebanon, Socialist People's Libyan Arab Republic, Arab Republic of Egypt, Kingdom of Morocco, Islamic Republic of Mauritania, and Republic of Yemen.

2. A portion of this section has been previously published by the author in the *Encyclopedia of the Modern Middle East and North Africa*, 2nd edition, in the entry entitled, "Education and Social Transformation in the Middle East" (2004).

3. The extraordinary body of scientific work I refer to here falls under the rubric of both "Islamic" and "Arabic" science. I use the term "Arabic" science because, although a number of the leading scientists were neither originally from "Arab" lands, nor native Arabic speakers, but from Persia, Afghanistan, and India, the common language of communication and scholarship among scientists and scholars throughout the Islamic empire was Arabic.

4. According to the 1907 Egypt census data, out of a Muslim population of 10,269,445, a total of 402,090 males and 10,579 females were literate. Among the Coptic population of 706,322, a total of 67,256 males and 5,765 females were literate, and among the Jewish population of 38,635, a total of 11,024 males and 5,910 females were literate. By far the highest literacy rates were among the "other" groups which included native and non-native Egyptians of other Christian denominations. Among a total of 175,576 others, 68,299 males and 38,399 females were literate (Landau, 1969, p. 71).

5. Also note that early in the 20th century new scientific organizations such as the Tangier based Mission Scientifique au Maroc (est. 1904) and the Cairo based *Soci'et'e d'Economie Politique* (est. 1909), both founded by the French, played important roles in forming transnational professional research communities in the Arab region and in the development of Middle East area studies programs in Europe and North America (Mitchell, 2003, pp. 4–6).

6. The first Arabic lectures were delivered in the Women's Section by Malak Hifni Nasif and Nabawiyya Musa before it was temporarily suspended in 1912. In 1929 Zainab Kamael Hasan became the first woman to be employed by the Faculty of Science as a full-fledged member of the teaching staff, opening the way for like positions by other women (Elsada & Abu-Ghazi, 2001, pp. 71–73, 115).

7. As Andr'e Mazawi cogently puts it, the transition in the Arab world from indigenous schooling to the "new" schooling "is not merely 'modernization,' structural change,' or 'transition.' Rather, it expresses a more basic, often radical, and certainly conflict-loaded transformation of the existing social bases of power; the determination of new sources of authority (both political and social); and the definition of what valid (and therefore politically connoted) knowledge is" (2000a).

8. As Dale Eickelman observes, "the social networks of influence and patronage formed in part through . . . mosque universities [which] have remained remarkably intact in many countries, and the 'cognitive style' conveyed by Islamic education retains a popular legitimacy" (1981, p. 237).

9. Ahmed Zewail attempted to found world-class state of the art university in Egypt by the name of University of Science and Technology (UST) (Zewail, 2002, p. 266). Due to a number of bureaucratic, political, and financial barriers, the project never came to fruition as he envisioned it.

10. See also Nabil Al-Tikriti (2005) for an assessment of the state of higher education in Iraq since March 2003.

11. For example, in the 2000–2001 academic year, only 643 out of 23,000 students enrolled at the Imam Muhammad bin Saud Islamic University were female (http://www.saudinf.com/main/j44.htm).

12. The UNESCO–PLO initiative dates to the mid-1970s, although it was not until 1991 that the university assumed full-scale operations and considerably expanded. The student enrollment increased from roughly 400 in 1991 to over 35,000 in 2001. Its branches are currently located in Palestine, Jordan, Saudi Arabia, and the United Arab Emirates, with plans for further extension to other countries (Al-Quds Open University website: http://www.palestine-net.com).

13. The Headquarters of the AOU is in Kuwait, and its branches are currently located in Egypt, Lebanon, Bahrain, Jordan and Saudi Arabia.

14. The Indira Gandhi National Open University of India, for example, has since 1997 been offering courses in a number of Arab Gulf countries where high numbers of Indian expatriate workers reside (Mazawi, 2000b).

References

Al-Quds Open University Website. Available online at http://www.palestine-net.com/education/quo. Retrieved September 9, 2004.

Al-Tikriti, N. (2005). From showcase to basket case: Education in Iraq. *ISIM Review, 15*, 24–25. Available online: http://www.isim.nl.

Bashshur, M. A. (1964). *The role of two Western universities in the national life of Lebanon and the Middle East: A comparative study of the American University of Beirut and the University of Saint-Joseph* (p. 361). Ph.D. dissertation, Department of Education, University of Chicago.

Cobb, S. (1963). *Islamic contributions to civilization.* Washington, DC: Avalon Press.

Eickelman, D. (1981). *The Middle East: An anthropological approach.* Englewood Cliffs, NJ: Prentice Hall.

Elsada, H. & Abu-Ghazi, E. (2001). *Significant moments in the history of Egyptian women, (vol I).* Cairo, Egypt: National Council for Women.

Herrera, L. (2002). The soul of a nation: Abdallah Nadim and educational reform in Egypt (1845–1896). *In Mediterranean Journal of Educational Studies, 7*(1), 1–24.

Herrera, L. (2004). Education and social transformation in the Middle East. In P. Mattar, C. E. Butterworth, N. Caplan, M. R. Fischbach, E. Hooglund, L. King-Irani, & J. Ruedy (Eds.), *Encyclopedia of the modern Middle East and North Africa* (2nd ed.). New York: MacMillan

Heyworth-Dunne, J. (1968 [1939]). *An introduction to the history of education in modern Egypt*, (2nd ed.). London: Frank Cass.

Hogendijk, J. P. & Sabra, A. I. (2003). *The enterprise of science in Islam: New perspectives.* Cambridge, MA: The MIT Press.

İhsanoğlu, E. (1995/1996). Genesis of learned societies and professional associations in Ottoman Turkey. *In Archiuum Ottomanicum, 14*, 160–190.

Landau, J. (1969). *Jews in nineteenth century Egypt.* New York: New York University Press.

Makdisi, G. (1981). *The rise of colleges: Institutions of learning in Islam and the West.* Edinburgh, Scotland: Edinburgh University Press.

Makdisi, G. (1990). *The rise of humanism in classical Islam and the Christian West.* Edinburgh, Scotland: Edinburgh University Press.

Mazawi, A. E. (1999). Gender and higher education in the Arab states. *International Higher Education, 17*(Fall). Retrieved on September 4, 2004 from http://www.bc.edu/bc org/avp/soe/cihe/newsletter/News17/text1 1.html.

Mazawi, A. E. (2000a). A special focus: Aspects of higher education in the Arab states. *International Higher Education, 18* (Winter). Retrieved on September 4, 2004 from http://www.bc.edu/bcorg/avp/soe/cihe/newsletter/News18/text9.html.

Mazawi, A. E. (2000b). Crossing the distance: The Open University in the Arab states. *International Higher Education, 18* (Winter). Retrieved on September 4, 2004 from http://www.bc.edu/bcorg/avp/soe/cihe/newsletter/News18/text14.html.

Mitchell, T. (2003). The Middle East in the past and future of social science. In *The politics of knowledge: Area studies and the disciplines.* University of California International and Area Studies Digital Collection. Available online: http://repositories.cdlib.org/editedvolumes/3/3.

Morsi, M. M. (1990). *Education in the Arab Gulf states.* Doha, Qatar: Educational Research Center, University of Qatar.

Moughrabi, F. (2004) Palestinian universities under siege. *International Higher Education, 36* (Summer). Retrieved on September 4, 2004 from http://www.bc.edu/bc org/avp/soe/cihe/newsletter/News36/text005.html.

Reid, D. M. (1990). *Cairo University and the making of modern Egypt.* Cambridge: Cambridge University Press.

Sabour, M. (2001). *The ontology and status of intellectuals in Arab academia and society.* Aldershot, UK: Ashgate.

Taha-Thomure, H. (2002). *Academic freedom in Arab universities: Understanding, practices and discrepancies.* Lanham, NY: University Press of America, Inc.

UNESCO Regional Bureau for Education in the Arab States. (2003). *Higher education in the Arab region: 1998–2003*. Paris: UNESCO.

United Nations Development Program (UNDP). (2002). *Arab human development report 2002: Creating opportunities for future generations*. New York: United Nations Publications.

United Nations Development Program (UNDP). (2003). *Arab human development report 2003: Building a knowledge society*. New York: United Nations Publications.

Waardenburg, J. (1966). *Les universit'es dans le Monde Arabe actuel, (The universities of the Arab world) (vol I)*. Paris: Mouton & Co.

Watenpaugh, K. (2004). Between Saddam and the American occupation: Iraq's academic community struggles for autonomy. *Academe* 4. Available online: http://www.aaup.org/publications/Academe/2004/04so/04sowate.htm. Retrieved on September 14, 2004.

Zewail, A. (2002). *Voyage through time: Walks of life to the Nobel Prize*. Cairo, Egypt: The American University in Cairo Press.

21

HIGHER EDUCATION IN CENTRAL AND EASTERN EUROPE

Peter Scott

Kingston University, UK

Central and Eastern Europe offers a diversity of higher education systems—ranging from "post-Soviet," in the sense that specialized higher education institutions often subject to non-education ministries are still prominent and traditional universities play a less dominant role, to "market" systems, with increasingly significant private sectors. The region also offers a diversity of institutional types—from traditional (often, very traditional) universities through specialized universities and quasi-industrial "monotechnics" to highly entrepreneurial private institutions. In addition, the region offers a range of academic and organizational cultures—from the "scientific" and "public" to the "applied" (or vocational) and "market." As a result of this diversity it is difficult to make valid generalizations that can be applied to Central and Eastern European higher education as a bloc.

Two interlinked frames of reference can be used to describe the reform of higher education in Central and Eastern Europe since 1989. The first is that the unity of Central and Eastern Europe is an artifice, contingent on half a century of Communist rule. The nation-states that occupy the region (bounded on the west by the Elbe and the mountains of Bohemia, on the east by the plains of Russia, and on the north by the Baltic Sea, and which stretches south towards the Adriatic and Aegean Seas) are as heterogeneous as the nation-states that occupy Western Europe (stretching from the Arctic to the Mediterranean). Central and Eastern Europe is both part of a larger whole—Europe—and subdivided into many regions. Its institutions, including its universities, reflect that variety. Almost certainly, despite their common experience of Communism, universities in Central and Eastern Europe have less in common with each other than, for example, universities in Latin America.

The second is that, because Central and Eastern Europe is an artifice (and also because the impact of Communism was both more nuanced and less totalitarian than is commonly supposed), higher education in the region—like society at large—has been going through a period of transition rather than of transformation. The preferred vocabulary is revealing; "transition" suggests a much less radical process than "transformation." Within this larger (but perhaps also more limited) context there are two

James J.F. Forest and Philip G. Altbach (eds.), International Handbook of Higher Education, 423–441.
© 2006 *Springer. Printed in the Netherlands.*

contrasting accounts of the development of higher education in Central and Eastern Europe in its first post-Communist decade. The first insinuates that it has been released from a totalitarian time-warp, and consequently is engaged in a process of catching up with the West (a process that has been difficult, and is still incomplete). The second account suggests that higher education in Central and Eastern Europe, because it has had to cope with the collapse of values and structures associated with Communist rule, has been both free and forced to flirt with privatization and other radical remedies that have been resisted by higher education in the West, certainly in Western Europe—and, as a result, has the potential to create new models of higher education in the 21st century.

Both are true—and both are exaggerated. There has been an element of catching-up because most Central and Eastern European higher education systems had tended to stagnate during the last two decades of Communist rule; scientific productivity declined, for example, and rates of expansion slowed, while in the West they accelerated. It is also broadly true that the immediate response after 1989 was to reassert a classical—even elitist—ideal of the university that was inimical to the wider engagement with state, economy and society that is characteristic of the evolution of Western European higher education systems. Little attempt appears to have been made—at any rate, initially— to harness higher education to the urgent task of the transition to a post-Communist society (in marked contrast with, for example, South Africa, where higher education reform and the building of a new multi-racial nation have been intimately associated).

A key difference is that post-1989 reforms have been largely organizational. Although the patina of crude Marxism-Leninism has been rubbed away, the scientific foundations of the system have remained almost intact. Indeed, these foundations have been strengthened by the removal of the (political) barriers to scientific intercourse with the West. Central and Eastern European universities aspire to—and do—contribute to "metropolitan" scientific and broader intellectual cultures, rather than challenging these cultures from the "periphery." Even during the Communist period this was essentially true.

Of course, there has also been a radical—even experimental—element in the post-1989 reconstruction of higher education. The collapse of Communist-era control systems and the inadequacy of state support forced many higher education institutions to adapt or die. This is apparent at many levels. In some Central and Eastern European countries radical restructuring has taken place, although sometimes as a result of institutional collapse rather than on a planned basis; the natural sciences and engineering, which dominated many Central and Eastern European universities between 1945 and 1989, have been displaced by business and management and information technology; private institutions have proliferated (where the legal regime permitted such developments); and public institutions have behaved in increasingly entrepreneurial ways (which critics have regarded as verging on the piratical). However, more recently enthusiasm for free-market and neo-liberal prescriptions has waned—and, as a result, the pressure on Central and Eastern European higher education to provide a test-bed for radical-right reform has decreased.

Any assessment of higher education in Central and Eastern Europe at the beginning of the 21st century must incorporate elements of both accounts—catching-up and radical experiment—but must also avoid the danger of over-emphasizing either. Both accounts must be related to the wider frames of reference—first, that Central and Eastern Europe is an artifice, which has been progressively deconstructed during the past decade, and secondly, that the key motif of post-1989 higher education reforms (as of wider socio-economic reforms) has been transition rather than transformation (Hüfner, 1995). Based on a study of higher education reform in Central and Eastern Europe undertaken by the author on behalf of CEPES, UNESCO's European Center for Higher Education in 1999–2000 (Scott, 2000), this chapter begins with a brief historical overview, followed by an analysis of five major themes of importance to the study of Central and Eastern European higher education. The discussion concludes with a review of the two standard views of higher education in the region—exceptionalism (the idea that higher education in the region is categorically different from other parts of the world) and underdevelopment (higher education in the region has lagged behind the West, which provides the only model of development)—noting that since neither of these is satisfactory, alternate accounts merit consideration and further research.

The Historical Context

In 1945, there were important differences within Central and Eastern Europe. Some, notably the Czech Republic, already possessed advanced industrial economies similar to those of the most advanced Western European countries; others remained predominantly agrarian in their economic structures. Social structures reflected these economic differences; in some countries sophisticated middle-classes already existed, while in others divisions between landowners and peasants were still predominant. Two countries—Bulgaria and Romania—had become independent in the 19th century; the others had only achieved independence with the break-up of Imperial Russia and Austria-Hungary (and the reduction in the territory of Prussia-Germany following 1918). Some had fought on the side of the Axis powers in World War II; others had been defeated and occupied by the forces of Nazi Germany. In nearly all of these countries, substantial ethnic and national minorities existed, despite the destruction of European Jewry during the Holocaust.

Although Communist rule tended to suppress, and even to reduce, these national differences, they were not eliminated entirely. The imposition of planned economies, accompanied by forced industrialization and (on a more limited scale) the collectivization of agriculture, led to a process of both leveling-up (in the case of the "peasant" economies) and eventually leveling-down (in the case of "advanced" economies). As a result, economic differences in the region were reduced, although they have tended to re-emerge since 1989 as countries have been more, and less, successful in managing the transition to "market" economies. Social differences may also have been reduced during the period of Communist rule, as previously favored social groups lost their privileges and/or were eliminated, although this social leveling was significantly reduced by the emergence of a *nomenklatura* under the aegis of the Communist Party.

Since the fall of Communism these differences have been partly re-established in some Central and Eastern European countries, and income differentials have been widening since 1989. Political divisions within the region were also reduced and suppressed by enforced membership of the Soviet-dominated Warsaw Pact. Again, eligibility for membership of the European Union or NATO has introduced new divisions since 1989. Ethnic differences were also overlaid by the imposed uniformity of Communist rule, with the important exception of the former Yugoslavia, and ethnic homogeneity was promoted by the expulsion of German minorities in the immediate post-war period. But, again, these differences have tended to re-emerge since 1989, exposing once again the multi-ethnic and multi-religious character of many Central and Eastern European societies.

In the 1990s, understandably, there was an overwhelming temptation to regard the Communist period as a deviation, or historical cul-de-sac. But this proved to be neither possible nor perhaps sensible. First, there are no black holes in history. The Russian Revolution of 1917 was as much a world event as the French Revolution of 1789. Opponents and supporters are equally subject to its long-term significance. Second, the Communist era was not monolithic. There were important temporal differences, as post-war "liberation" was succeeded by Stalinist terror, then the post-Stalin "thaw," followed by the "normalization" (or neo-Stalinism) of the Brezhnev period and the final crisis of the Communist system. Third, there were also important spatial differences; in Hungary the period of the thaw persisted despite Brezhnevism, while in Romania neo-Stalinism lasted until the (bitter) end when the Ceausescu regime was overthrown. These differences have persisted into the post-Communist period, shaping both political cultures and administrative competences. Fourth, the two halves of the continent were not entirely disconnected during this period. All parts of Europe went through processes of modernization during this half-century, some sophisticated perhaps and others crude, which nevertheless transformed social conditions; both were subject to similar global forces. Their political and economic systems may have been different but they inhabited the same world.

It may be dangerous to over-estimate the exceptionalism of the experience of higher education in Central and Eastern Europe under Communist rule. It developed particular—and, on the whole, negative—characteristics during this period. However, these characteristics did not abolish the important differences between universities across the region that existed before 1945; nor should the significance of these characteristics be exaggerated at the expense of other more generic influences which affected all European higher education systems. This is important in two aspects. First, it leads us to question the ahistorical interpretations of higher education that have grown up in Central and Eastern Europe since 1989. Continuity may be more considerable than we care to admit—not only in the sense that developments during the Communist period cannot simply and sensibly be ignored (these developments were—and are— real, not least in terms of the continuity of personnel), but also in the sense that the Communist regimes that ruled the region between 1945 and 1989 were never able to exclude (although they were able to distort) external influences, which played an important role in shaping higher education in Central and Eastern Europe during this half-century.

Even during the Stalinist period, Communism was never able either to suppress the ideal and operation of an autonomous civil society completely, or to exclude external influences entirely. Josef Jarab has offered a salutary corrective in the case of (what was still then) Czechoslovakia: "In the sweeping political rejections of the former regime, its ugly and dehumanizing objectives were taken as results truly and generally achieved. But fortunately, they had in fact never accomplished their goals to the extent they might have thought. Due to inefficient bureaucracy and rather lukewarm attitudes of many people working within the system, especially after 1968, the totalitarian educational project could not and did not fully succeed. It is also worth remembering and reminding ourselves and our Western colleagues that good teaching did not completely disappear from our schools with the introduction of Communist ideology" (Jarab, 1993).

Second, questioning the notion of exceptionalism is important because it suggests that it is misleading to regard universities in the region as, in any but the most superficial economic sense, underdeveloped. They have always been fully "European" before 1945 and after 1989—but also, crucially, during the years between. Until the stagnation of the Communist regimes in the 1970s, higher education systems in Central and Eastern Europe (and, in particular, in the former Soviet Union) had been able to produce remarkable achievements—both in terms of growth of student numbers (and so an expansion of social opportunities, sadly unaccompanied by the development of a truly democratic culture), and in terms of research, notably in the mathematical and physical sciences and engineering.

Statistical Portrait

If the former constituent parts of the Soviet Union (apart from the Baltic States) are excluded—the Russian Federation itself with almost 6 million students, Ukraine with 2.3 million, Belarus with 337,000 and Moldova with 110,000—there were 4,364,395 students in Central and Eastern Europe in 2002–03. This is probably an underestimate because of the significant number of students in private institutions and also due to different methods of data collection. The number of students per 100,000 inhabitants ranged from 5,102 (in Latvia) to 1,420 (in Albania); the average for the region was just over 3,000. Although lower than in Western Europe and, in particular, North America, there have been substantial gains in participation since the collapse of Communism in the region (see Table 1).

There are significant variations in the number and size of institutions. In particular, many recently established private institutions have had small numbers of students, but it is also true that the average size of universities is much smaller than in Western Europe or North America. Outside the former Soviet Union there are few universities comparable in size to Italian, French or German universities. There are also significant variations in student/faculty ratios, although these figures need to be treated with particular caution because of different definitions of teaching staff (see Table 2).

The impression that emerges from this statistical portrait of higher education in the region is of a two-way split. On the one hand, there is a number of predominantly smaller and medium-sized countries where the main influence appears to be "European"—in the sense that they have comparatively small numbers of private institutions (and even smaller proportions of private students). Slovenia and the Czech Republic are examples of this first group (both, significantly or not, were part of Austria-Hungary until 1918). On the other hand, there is a number of (typically larger) countries where the main

428   Scott

Table 1.   Total Enrollment and Proportion in Private Institutions

Country	Total Number of Students	% in Private Institutions
Albania	43,700	0.2%
Bulgaria	230,513	13.4%
Croatia	140,731	2.7%
Czech Republic	248,756	3.2%
Estonia	63,625	20.3%
Hungary	381,560	14.2%
Latvia	118,944	22.9%
Lithuania	145,784	4.5%
FYR Macedonia	49,275	3.5%
Poland	1,800,548	29.4%
Romania	596,297	23.3%
Slovak Republic	141,805	0.4%
Slovenia	101,458	2.9%
Bosnia and Herzegovina	101,399	—

Source: Scott, P. (2000). Ten years on and looking ahead. In *Review of the transformations of higher education in Central and Eastern Europe*. Bucharest: CEPES Studies on Higher Education.

influence since 1989 appears to have been "American"—in the sense that they have much larger numbers of private institutions and students and sometimes less generous student/faculty ratios, which may be evidence of a more entrepreneurial approach. Poland and Hungary are examples of this latter group.

Table 2.   Diversity of Institutions and Staff/Student Ratios

Country	Public Institutions	Private Institutions	Student/Faculty Ratios
Albania	11	1	19.6:1
Bulgaria	37	14	13.9:1
Croatia	84	14	24.1:1
Czech Republic	28	27	18:1
Estonia	13	22	15.1:1
Hungary	30	36	16.5:1
Latvia	20	17	21.7:1
Lithuania	30	13	13.3:1
FYR Macedonia	31	5	16.4:1
Poland	125	252	22.3:1
Romania	55	70	20.1:1
Slovak Republic	22	1	11.8:1
Slovenia	62	17	24:1

Source: Scott, P. (2000). Ten years on and looking ahead. In *Review of the transformations of higher education in Central and Eastern Europe*. Bucharest: CEPES Studies on Higher Education.

Key Themes

Five major themes emerged from the CEPES study on which this chapter is based: the scale and scope of Central and Eastern European higher education; the diversity of higher education across the region; the sequencing of successive phases of higher education reform since 1989; the balance between continuities and discontinuities; and structural reforms, or the creation of new legal, administrative and academic frameworks.

Expansion

All higher education systems, East and West, experienced rapid growth during the post-war period culminating in the spectacular expansion of the 1960s. It was only in the last two decades of Communist rule that growth rates diverged, as higher education in Western Europe experienced a second wave of expansion and Central and Eastern Europe stagnated politically and economically. In the ten Central and Eastern European countries covered by the CEPES study (referenced earlier), the number of students enrolled in higher education institutions increased from 1,284,509 in 1989 to 2,137,997 in 1996 (an increase of two-thirds in seven years), and then to 3,829,290 by 2002 (an even more impressive growth rate of almost 80%). The rate of growth is equal to that which has occurred in any other higher education system since 1945, and provides a measure of the quantitative transformation of higher education in Central and Eastern Europe.

However, within this overall expansion, there have been some significant trends. To begin with, in 1989 almost 40% of students were studying natural sciences; by 1996 the proportion had dropped to only 10%, although there has subsequently been a mild recovery. During the same period, the number of humanities and social studies students increased almost three-fold—from 27% of the total to 43%. The numbers of students in education, medicine and engineering have remained stable and grown more slowly. Also, the number of graduates increased by only 45%, despite the 66% increase in student enrollments between 1989 and 1996. In some countries there was almost no increase, and in one an absolute decline. This suggests that non-completion rates have risen across the region, which can largely be attributed to the overall growth in student numbers and the shift towards the humanities and social sciences (but may also reflect a relaxation of the social disciplines imposed by the Communist state).

Further, the number of tertiary-level teachers increased by an even smaller amount, only 27%, between 1989 and 1996. However, by the standards of Western Europe and North America, student/faculty ratios were still favorable; the ratio was 8:1 in 1989 and nearly 11:1 in 1996. Since then, there has been a further deterioration in staff/student ratios. Although the Slovak Republic still enjoys a highly favorable student/faculty ratio of roughly 12:1, in Poland—the largest higher education sector in the region—it has risen to a challenging 22:1. The arrival of mass higher education in the region (and also the disappearance of other special factors, such as the privileged status of some specialized higher education institutions during the Communist period) has led to a convergence of staffing levels between the two halves of Europe.

Diversity or Commonality?

A major theme which emerged from the CEPES report was the balance to be struck between emphasizing the common characteristics of higher education systems and institutions in the region and highlighting their differences. A further complication arises from the fact that some of these common characteristics are retrospective, because they reflect the uniformity imposed during the Communist era (and therefore might be expected to diminish in significance), while others are prospective, because they relate to the demands to which all higher education systems in the developed world are subject (and presumably are likely to intensify). A still further complication arises because this dilemma between commonality and difference in Central and Eastern Europe is overlaid by the wider debate about whether higher education systems are converging or diverging.

The case for emphasizing difference has already been discussed. Before 1945, universities across the region had little in common with each other, and certainly no more (or less) than with universities in other parts of Europe. They included some of Europe's oldest universities—Prague (1347) and Cracow (1364)—which long predated the development of nation-states or nationalist consciousness. But the first Romanian university was not established until 1860 and the first Bulgarian university in 1904; in both cases the links with nation-building were explicit. It was only as a result of their forced subjection to Communism that common characteristics emerged; with the collapse of Communism, not only are these original differences based on traditional orientations re-emerging but new ones are being created by the different rates of change and directions taken by post-Communist developments. Some universities have been much more successful than others at adapting to the new environment of political pluralism and market engagement—in some cases because they are (literally) new foundations, in others because they have greater room for maneuver, and in others again because their national governments have embraced change with more enthusiasm and/or success.

The case for emphasizing commonality, therefore, is two-fold. First, higher education in nine of the ten countries covered by the study on which this chapter is based were subject for almost half a century to Communist regimes which were animated by a common ideology, created analogous state structures and, ultimately, had a single reference point in the sense that they were subordinate to the will of the Soviet leadership. The Conference of Ministers of Higher Education in Socialist Countries was influential in formalizing this orthodoxy. Only Slovenia, as a republic in the former Yugoslavia, was an exception because the Titoist principle of self-management was also applied to higher education. Second, during the period 1945–1989 all European systems exhibited similar trends, including expansion of student numbers and consequent massification, subordination to socio-economic requirements and greater accountability to political interests.

The collapse of Communism apparently removed the first imperative for commonality, but arguably, only to introduce another—the common dilemmas created by the transition to a post-Communist society across the region. So even after Communism ceased to exist, it continued to promote homogeneity. Of course, the Europe-wide—even global—trends were intensified by the collapse of Communism and its replacement by democratic-capitalist regimes. As a result, universities throughout the region have had to develop policies for retraining inappropriately qualified staff and to rebalance their portfolios of academic programs to reflect new political and social conditions, both of which are examples of post-Communist adaptation, and also to develop courses in business, management and information technology—an example of the wider impact of global forces.

Jan Sadlak has attempted to conceptualize these transitions in terms of three models of higher education in Central and Eastern Europe—pre-Communist, Communist, and post-Communist—within an analytical framework that emphasizes commonalities rather than differences (Sadlak, 1995).

Sadlak's broad framework (see Table 3) emphasizes the general characteristics of higher education in Central and Eastern Europe during these three periods. There are, of course, exceptions to the rule. Peter Darvas' argument that "if there is anything peculiar about the region [Central and Eastern Europe], it is the level of complexity of changes that may exceed that which can be observed globally" may help to reconcile this apparent contradiction (Darvas, 1998). Higher education in the region has followed a broadly similar post-Communist trajectory, but one characterized by increasing differentiation.

Sequences of Reform

The third theme is that the reform of higher education systems in Central and Eastern Europe has already gone through three main stages. The first stage was characterized by two imperatives. The first imperative was a desire to disengage the academic system from the very tight association with, and subordination to, the economic system that had prevailed during the Communist period. The second imperative was to liberalize academic structures as part of a wider liberalization of political structures, with the former being largely a contingent effect of the latter.

The conclusion of a so-called Transatlantic Dialogue organized by the Pew Charitable Trusts in 1991–92 and involving both American university and college presidents and European rectors from both Eastern and Western Europe was clear: "Autonomy is the first of many steps needed to restore the university in Central and Eastern Europe to its former vitality." The author of this chapter was a participant in the three seminars—at Trento, Olomouc and Madison—which formed the Dialogue, and derived an equally clear impression: "The Central and Eastern European participants insisted on a ringing restatement of this idea [of the liberal university] in the purest, even absolutist, terms. The need, as the Eastern Europeans saw it, was to re-establish free universities—like free parliaments and free courts . . . In many debates during the Dialogue, its Central and Eastern European members seized the high moral ground, while their Western European and American colleagues were prepared to settle for the life of 'market' and state accountability" (Scott, 1993).

However, by the mid-1990s it had become clear that this disengagement of the academic system from the economic system and the bestowal of (formally) unrestricted autonomy on higher education had led to significant difficulties. First, because of the strains produced by the transition from centrally planned to market economies in most

Table 3.   Attributes of Central and Eastern European Higher Education Systems

	Pre-Communist Implicit and Self-regulatory	Communist Centrally-regulated	Post-Communist Explicit and Self-regulatory
Main traits	Confidence in values of particular academic freedom	Aims, tasks and resources in teaching and research defined by the Communist Party and allocated by the State	Competition for students, funding; importance of institutional/program, academic standing; multiple forms of self-representation; adherence to academic freedom
System-wide regulation	Minimal	Compulsory and detailed party/state regulation	Preferably within a broad regulatory role of the State
Planning/system approach	None or very limited	Comprehensive: an instrument of political control	Particularly important at institutional level
Accountability	Limited mainly to own constituency	Mainly to political authorities (Communist Party)	Accountability towards multiple constituencies
Autonomy	Yes—but its parameters were also differently defined from nowadays	Hardly any—or at the discretion of the political authorities	Determined by the degree of accountability to specific constituencies
Incentives	Reliance on intrinsic motivation in learning and research	Achievement of goals set by the party and state	Well-being of the institution and its principal constituency
Financing and budgeting	Heavily tuition-dependent; input-oriented line-item budgeting	Totally state-dependent but relatively 'worry-free'/rigid line-item budgeting	Multiple sources and instruments of financing and budgeting
Relation to labor market	Minimal and only indirect	Close coordination with state-set manpower planning	Significant but indirect; a result of interaction of multiple constituencies
Internal governance and structure	Federation of relatively independent sub-units—'chairs'	Externally determined and politically controlled (*nomenklatura*)	Concentration of administrative power; diversity of structure
Strategic planning	Occasionally at sub-unit level/not essential for governance	Almost none at institutional and sub-unit level	Essential for survival and/or well-being of the institution; important approach in governance

Source: Sadlak, J. (1995). In search of the "post-Communist" university—the background and scenario of the transformation of higher education in Central and Eastern Europe. In K. Hüfner (Ed.), *Higher education reform processes in Central and Eastern Europe*. Frankfurt: Peter Lang.

Central and Eastern European countries—strains which were particularly intense in the public sector—it was not feasible to maintain this disengagement. In a negative sense, higher education was affected by the erosion of its resource base, which undermined its effective autonomy. In a positive sense, universities clearly had a key role to play in the process of economic transition. This role was explicitly recognized by the World Bank in the 1993 loan it made to Hungary, which placed particular emphasis on the development of human capital.

Second, the autonomy granted to universities was used—or perceived to be used—to block reform. Although substantial structural changes were made in all higher education systems in the region during the 1990s (including important staffing changes), few other Central and Eastern European higher education systems experienced the radical reconstruction experienced by the East German system following German re-unification. It has been estimated that almost half of the higher education teachers in the former German Democratic Republic lost their jobs, compared with fewer than 10% in the rest of Central and Eastern Europe.

Third, the liberalization of academic structures undertaken in the immediate after-math of the collapse of Communism proved in some cases to be impractical. New higher education laws were sometimes utopian in their formulations—and difficult to implement against a background of substantial continuity of personnel and a significant erosion of resources. For example, rectors were granted formal powers which, in practice, they were often unable to exercise. Issues of governance and management were left undetermined.

As a result, the second phase of post-Communist reform—from the mid-1990s onwards—attempted to remedy these weaknesses. Universities retreated from what could be called the "liberal absolutism" of the years immediately after 1989, when both opponents of the former Communist regimes and their passive supporters had insisted on a high degree of institutional autonomy, although for different reasons. Autonomy, initially seen largely in terms of an absence of state power, was gradually replaced by new notions of civic and market accountability. The importance of higher education in terms of economic development as well as political and cultural renewal was more readily acknowledged, as the emphasis switched from the subordination to the manpower needs of planned economies to engagement with a "knowledge society," albeit in the context of post-Communist transition. More practical attention was paid to issues of institutional governance and management.

This second stage, therefore, was one of emerging pragmatism. After the first stage—characterized by utopianism and dominated by politico-cultural issues—which lasted in most countries until 1992 or 1993, the emphasis switched to the need to expand and diversify higher education to meet new socio-economic demands. The mid-1990s were dominated by these efforts. More recently, in a third stage of development, attention appears to have switched again to issues of structure—and thus back to governance and management (but in much more pragmatic terms). It is now much more readily recognized that systems and institutions need to be sufficiently robust to cope with a) the practical implications of the institutional autonomy and academic freedom granted in the immediate aftermath of 1989, and b) the strains of expansion and diversification that took place in the mid-1990s. This third stage, therefore, can be regarded as a period of normalization—but in two senses. The first is that the structures (and mentalities) needed to systematize and institutionalize post-Communist reforms are now being built; the second is that the agendas of higher education in both parts of Europe, East and West, are rapidly converging.

The Lure of the West?

Several of the institutional case-studies used in the CEPES report emphasize the importance of Western European (and North American) models in shaping the reconstruction of higher education in Central and Eastern Europe. Academic and administrative staff with a strong orientation to the West or with direct experience of higher education in the West are identified as among the most consistent supporters of reform, while those whose experience had been confined to Communist-dominated systems are identified as being passive, skeptical or even resistant to reform. In some countries in the region, Western "returners" have played an important role. (The other side of the coin, of course, is that all Central and Eastern European higher education systems have suffered from "brain drain" to the West, currently estimated to be 15% of teachers and researchers).

The reasons for this orientation are easy to understand. First, during the Communist period the West had been the "other"—and consequently a focus for the hopes of those who opposed or resisted the former regimes. When the "iron curtain" was removed, it was natural that this longing for the West should be expressed through admiration and imitation of its values. Second, more concretely, the West provided examples of free institutions which actually operated—including, of course, universities. So it was equally natural that these institutions provided templates for the reform of the totalitarian structures inherited from the Communist period. This was particularly necessary in the development of business schools—which had not existed in pre-1989 universities, except in the stilted form of faculties of economics—and of private higher education institutions which, of course, were not permitted during the Communist period.

Third, the drive to the West was an attempt to reconnect Central and Eastern European universities to what is now called in the wake of the 1999 Bologna Declaration "the European space in higher education." The emphasis on internationalization in many Central and Eastern European universities is a concrete expression of this aspiration. However, this focus is very much on building stronger links with Western Europe and North America; as such, it is very different from the meaning attached to internationalization in universities in the West, which is already shading into something very different, globalization (Högskoleverket, 1997). Fourth, the West was seen as a source of the funding needed for reconstruction (which is another reason for the rather narrow focus of internationalization). This funding was provided not only by Western governments and supra-national agencies (prominent among which was the European Union), but also by private foundations such as the Soros Foundation and the Volkswagen-Stiftung.

However, this identification with the West has encountered certain difficulties. The first, and most obvious, can be summed up in a simple question—which West? There are several models of higher education in Western Europe (which are derived from the traditional taxonomy of Humboldtian, "Napoleonic" and Anglo-Saxon models described earlier in this chapter, but substantially readjusted by recent massification). There are also many different types of institutions—university and non-university—in most Western European systems (Britain and Sweden are the only two countries with, even approximately, unified higher education systems). The second is that the Western model of higher education is not only increasingly pluralistic; it is also highly volatile. Significant reforms have taken place during the 1990s. To take just two examples: in England, the former polytechnics became universities in 1992, and later in the decade *fachhochschulen* (along the German model) were developed in Austria out of a plethora of trade and craft schools.

Accordingly, as the engagement between Central and Eastern European higher education and Western European (and North American) universities has deepened, it has also become more complex. In the immediate post-Communist period, higher education in the West offered a stylized—and perhaps idealized—model. Its subordination to political authority, not simply in terms of administrative structures and funding regimes, but increasingly in terms of quality-assurance and other performance measures as the state redefined itself as an important customer; its accountability to public opinion, which forced universities to "manage" their reputations with growing professionalism; its exposure to market influences; its (on the whole) willing engagement with society—such characteristics were little noticed at first. Today, a more nuanced relationship with the West can be observed, which can partly be explained by the continuing, even increasing, influence of neo-communist parties and the backlash against the "shock therapy" of radical privatization and marketization in parts of Central and Eastern Europe, but can mainly be attributed to a better understanding of the real circumstances of higher education in the West. Normal service has been resumed.

At a more practical level universities in Central and Eastern Europe have been enthusiastic supporters of the development of the Bologna process and also of national quality assurance and accreditation systems. There seem to be two main reasons for the region's support for the idea of creating a "European Higher Education Area" (despite its implicit agenda of transatlantic competition, which might have been expected to appeal to those systems and institutions that have been most influenced by American models). One is that by joining in Bologna, Central and Eastern European can reassert their "European-ness" after four decades of Communist rule. The second is that, because their structures have been in a state of flux since 1989, it has been easier for them to adapt the two-cycle bachelor's-master's pattern that is at the heart of the Bologna reforms. Their enthusiasm for quality assurance and accreditation, in sharp contrast to the skepticism expressed by many Western European (especially U.K.) institutions, reflects a belief that peer-review based systems represent a liberation from stifling state regulation.

Restructuring Higher Education in the Region

The fifth and last major theme is the scale and complexity of the restructuring of higher education systems in Central and Eastern Europe (Aaviksoo, 1997). Higher education in the region has had to be reconstructed on a scale, and at a speed, never attempted in Western Europe. Adjustments that have required long gestation in the West have had to be accomplished within four or five years. For example, in the West complex issues such as the relationship between universities and other higher education institutions and between higher education and research have been managed by a lengthy process of reform and negotiation stretching over several decades; in Central and Eastern Europe, such issues had to be immediately resolved after 1989.

In some countries reconstruction has been total, and has had to proceed from first principles. Not only did the legal framework in which higher education institutions operate have to be entirely rewritten, the fundamental mission of institutions and their articulation within wider systems also had to be reconsidered. In other words, institutional restructuring has taken place against a background of normative uncertainty, which has never been experienced in the West.

Standard solutions that could be applied across the region have not been available. Not only have the different countries in Central and Eastern Europe been more or less successful in their attempts at economic reform (which have determined their capacity to fund and manage higher education reform), and taken up different stances to their Communist pasts (which have influenced their willingness to undertake reform), institutional patterns and administrative processes have varied across the region. For example, in some countries the need has been to strengthen the university at the expense of its constituent parts; in others, to decentralize power and decision making. So, even where common objectives have been pursued, different solutions had to be found (EURYDICE, 1997, 1999).

In all parts of the region, staffing has been a major issue. As previously noted, only in the eastern *länder* of Germany has there been a substantial turnover of academic and administrative staff. Elsewhere, universities have struggled to cope with staff who were inappropriately qualified (because the subjects they taught were no longer in demand among students) and/or were insufficiently skilled in teaching methods. (The debates about learning and teaching styles, course design and student assessment that have occurred in most Western European higher education systems did not take place on a significant scale in Central and Eastern Europe during the Communist period). They now face an urgent need to renew their staff, either by retraining or replacement, in order to refresh their portfolios of academic programs. Another problem is that low salaries mean that many academic staff have more than one job.

With the exception of a minority of institutions—which either have received generous financial support from outside the region and/or have been able to charge high fees because they concentrate on courses in subjects like management and information technology—higher education in Central and Eastern Europe has been chronically under-funded (Dinca & Damian, 1997). This under-funding has constantly hampered attempts at institutional renewal. Although there are signs in a few countries in the region that the transition to a market economy has been (relatively) successfully accomplished, and during the 1990s the region had an economic growth that substantially exceeded that in Western Europe, across the region as a whole economic restructuring is far from complete (and there are particular difficulties with regard to reconstituting a modern and viable public sector, which embraces most elements within higher education systems). One result has been that public institutions have become semi-privatized by depending increasingly on income from fees; the "private sector" is within, not without.

Higher education systems in Central and Eastern Europe have also been subject to substantial reshaping since the collapse of Communism. At the system level, three general features may be particularly significant. The first is that in some countries a significant private sector has developed (which is much larger as a proportion of student numbers than in nearly every Western European country). The private sector is seen by some as more dynamic and flexible than publicly-funded higher education. It is not clear whether the private sector will expand, in line with a global trend towards privatization in higher education, or contract, because if or when publicly-funded institutions become more flexible and better resourced, private institutions will lose their comparative advantage. The largest number of private institutions is in Poland (252 private institutions, compared to only 125 public institutions in 2002, although the former enrolled less than a third of the total number of students). In other countries in the region there has been much greater resistance to the development of private higher education. In Slovenia, for example, only 2.9% of students are enrolled in private institutions, and in the Czech Republic the proportion is only a little higher (3.2%). In the early years after 1989, the growth of private higher education was a hectic and largely uncontrolled process, but more recently greater regulation has been introduced.

The second feature is the integration of research institutes (once managed separately by Academies of Science or central ministries) into universities, thus producing a better relationship between teaching and research and also releasing additional teaching staff resources. However, although a general phenomenon, this trend towards incorporation is also uneven. The extent to which true integration has been achieved is often unclear. (It is worth noting that this is not an exclusively Central and Eastern European problem; attempts to produce greater synergy between German universities and Max Planck institutes have also produced difficulties). As a result, the place of research within higher education continues to be unstable in contrast to the better-understood and accepted relationships between research and teaching characteristics of Western European and North American systems.

The third feature is that efforts have been made to create more systematic binary systems. During the Communist era, non-university higher education was best described as pre- or proto-binary. Advanced education outside the universities typically took two forms: a) specialized monotechnic institutions (often administered by other Ministries apart from the Ministry of Education—or of Higher Education); and b) higher technical schools, which were often closer in spirit to secondary education. During the 1990s, many Central and Eastern European countries decided, if not to integrate monotechnic institutions into multi-faculty universities outright, then to develop common planning frameworks. Decisions were also made to upgrade higher technical schools (which sometimes, as in Hungary, involved mergers to create larger institutions). Nevertheless, the survival of many "Soviet-era" specialized higher education institutions and the comparative weakness of what might be called the "generalist" university tradition have influenced the form of restructuring in Central and Eastern European higher education systems.

Conclusion

The two standard accounts of Central and Eastern European higher education are exceptionalism (the idea that higher education in the region is categorically different— either in a negative sense, because of the debilitating experience of Communist rule, or in a positive sense, because it has been able to undertake radical reforms impossible in the West) and underdevelopment (i.e., Central and Eastern European higher education has lagged behind higher education in the West, which provides the only model of development). However, neither is satisfactory. Both capture only those elements of Central and Eastern European higher education that were most directly touched by the experience of Communist rule—elements which are diminishing in significance—at the expense of the totality.

Exceptionalism

Clearly, between 1945 and 1989 the development of higher education in Central and Eastern Europe was decisively shaped by the experience of Communist rule. However, that influence was qualified in three ways:

1. The experience of Communist rule varied between the different countries in the region and between different periods of time;
2. Higher education in Central and Eastern Europe was not hermetically sealed from external influences; and
3. The imperatives of modernization shaped higher education in both East and West.

Prospective and positive assertions of exceptionalism are just as problematic as historical and negative ones. The picture that emerged from the CEPES study was of a purely European higher education system—indeed, of a system that in crucial respects is more purely European than higher education in Western Europe. There, the development of higher education has been significantly influenced by the evolution of the American system, by the currents of globalization and by the heterogeneous nature of Western societies (most apparent in terms of multi-ethnicity). Because of Communist rule, these influences were—and still are—weaker in Central and Eastern Europe. Thus, the Humboldtian university exists in a purer form east of the Elbe (in its original homeland, of course).

Underdevelopment

The second account, that higher education in Central and Eastern Europe is under-developed, is equally unsatisfactory. Of course, there are some (limited) respects in which notions of underdevelopment may be useful. The most obvious is the slower rate of growth in student numbers after 1970, which, arguably, meant that in a quantitative sense, higher education in Central and Eastern Europe was less mature than in Western Europe and North America. As observed earlier, there was little difference between growth rates in the East and the West before 1970. Only with the stagnation of the last two decades of Communist rule did a gap open up. Although Central and

Eastern Europe experienced the first post-war wave of higher education expansion, in most countries in the region the second wave was delayed until after the collapse of Communism in 1989.

Arguably, slower growth rates after 1970 meant that institutions had less incentive to innovate, and may have contributed to the underlying conservatism of higher education in the region (which, of course, was also a product of the political cultures and social systems that prevailed until 1989). But even the argument about the developmental effects of delayed expansion has to be treated with care. Within Western Europe, there were important variations in the timing of the second wave of post-war expansion. In France and Germany, it was a phenomenon of the 1970s. But in Britain, the second wave did not occur until the later 1980s and 1990s, only marginally before the resumption of growth in Central and Eastern Europe.

The issues that preoccupy higher education in Central and Eastern Europe today are broadly similar to those that preoccupy higher education in Western Europe or North America—the balance within institutions between central administration and faculties, schools or departments; the relationship between research and teaching; "distributed" delivery of higher education programs (often linked to a regional agenda); the tension between systemic planning and institutional initiative; the maintenance of institutional diversity within increasingly "volatile" systems; new patterns of funding, in which student fees and the commercial exploitation of intellectual property (in its widest sense) are more important and state funding less important; and the renewal of the academic profession (in terms of both recruitment and retraining).

Alternative Accounts?

Two alternative accounts of Central and Eastern European higher education appear to be more promising than either exceptionalism or underdevelopment. The first account emphasizes the importance of spatial dimensions and has two distinct aspects. To begin with, although there is not enough research evidence to contrast the experiences of "big" countries (such as Poland or Romania) with those of "small" countries (such as Lithuania or Slovenia), studies in other countries suggest that size may produce a significant effect. For example, a recent study of educational policymaking in England, Scotland, Wales and Northern Ireland (the constituent parts of the United Kingdom) highlighted the importance of scale in generating appropriate policy communities, shaping leadership cadres and influencing policy transfers (Raffe et al., 1999). It can be argued that reforms and other policy initiatives are more likely to emerge in "big" countries because the plurality of interests produces a more creative environment. On the other hand, one can argue that they are easier to implement in "small" countries because of the greater intimacy of political and administrative networks.

Another aspect of the spatial dimension is that the coherence of Central and Eastern Europe was contingent on its incorporation in the Communist bloc. Thus, the artificiality of viewing this as a coherent region has been exposed by the collapse of the Communist system. First, older affinities are re-emerging—particularly around the Baltic, in the Balkans and even the old 19th century concept of *Mitteleuropa*. Second, wider groupings are emerging, or being extended; the best examples are the European Union and, more controversially, NATO (as well as the idea of a "European Higher Education Space"). Third, the impact of globalization is becoming more intense throughout the continent. Taken together, these three trends are producing significant changes in national (and individual) identities and in the orientation of all socio-economic systems, including higher education systems.

The second alternative account of higher education in Central and Eastern Europe emphasizes the developing relationship between postsecondary learning and the so-called "knowledge society." None of the three main strands within the European university tradition—Humboldtian, "Napoleonic" or Anglo-Saxon—is perhaps truly compatible with a mass higher education project of the kind that has been attempted in the United States. All retain elements that may inhibit the full engagement of higher education with the knowledge society. Higher education in Central and Eastern Europe and in Western Europe are alike in this respect. The knowledge society, of course, is a hybrid phenomenon—or, more accurately, a set of interlocking phenomena. Most frequently emphasized is the growing importance of information and communication technologies and the increasing power of round-the-clock, round-the-globe markets—along with the apparent triumph of neo-liberal ideology. However, other phenomena are equally (or more) important—notably, worldwide resistance to global markets, the so-called "risk society" (with its baleful effects on the authority of "experts") and, of particular significance to higher education, new and more distributed patterns of knowledge production (Gibbons et al., 1994; Nowotny, Scott, & Gibbons, 2001).

In some respects, Central and Eastern European higher education may be at an advantage. For example, the decay of state authority and financial exigency may have reduced the barriers to privatization at an operational level, although at a normative level nostalgia for a classical ideal of the university may be an inhibition. In other respects, Central and Eastern European higher education may be at a disadvantage. For example, its exposure to globalization is comparatively much less than in Western Europe or North America, and distributed knowledge production systems are less developed. But the sum of these comparative advantages and disadvantages is likely to balance out— and, in any case, is a minor consideration judged against the larger social, economic, political and cultural challenges that all higher education systems face.

Neither of these alternative accounts is sufficiently developed to challenge some of the presumptions made about higher education in Central and Eastern Europe—which, despite the evidence, often still reflect notions of exceptionalism and underdevelopment. But both deserve further elaboration. The first (spatial) interpretation would better explain the differences that are emerging in the region (and which existed, in a suppressed form, throughout the Communist period). The second interpretation might offer a better explanation of the inhibitions—even occasionally conservatism—of higher education in the region by emphasizing not the particularities of the Communist experience but the commonalities within a European university tradition that may be mass in scale and structure but elitist and hierarchical in its fundamental values (certainly in contrast to the more open American higher education system).

If either (or both) of these interpretations are seen as having any substance, the challenges facing higher education in Central and Eastern Europe appear in a different light—not as "catching up" with higher education in Western Europe—a limited (and perhaps self-limiting) and finite project—but as part of a wider enterprise to re-orient the whole of European higher education by reaching out beyond the elites (old and new, cultural or technical) into the diverse communities that constitute modern Europe, and by realizing the potential of the new synergies between knowledge and society and the economy, identity and culture.

Acknowledgments

The analysis in this chapter is mainly based on a study of higher education reform in Central and Eastern Europe undertaken by the author on behalf of CEPES, UNESCO's European Center for Higher Education in 1999–2000 (Scott, 2000).

References

Aaviksoo, J. (1997). Priorities for higher education in Central and Eastern European Countries. *Higher Education Management, 9*(2), 19–27.

Darvas, P. (1998). The future of higher education in Central-Eastern Europe: Problems and possibilities. *European Review, 6*(4), 489–503.

Dinca, G., & Damian, R. (1997). *Financing of higher education in Romania*. Bucharest, Romania: Editura Alternative.

EURYDICE: The Information Network for Education in Europe. (1997). *Supplement to the study on the structures of the education and initial training systems in the European Union: The situation in Bulgaria, the Czech Republic, Hungary, Poland, Romania and Slovakia*, Brussels, Belgium: EURYDICE.

EURYDICE. (1999). *Supplement to the study on the structures of the education and initial training systems in the European Union: The situation in Estonia, Latvia, Lithuania, Slovenia and Cyprus*, Brussels, Belgium: EURYDICE.

Gibbons, M., Limoges, C., Nowotny, H., Schwartzman, S., Scott, P., & Trow, M. (1994). *The new production of knowledge: Science and research in contemporary societies*, London: Sage.

Högskoleverket. (1997). Central and Eastern Europe. In *National policies for the internationalization of higher education in Europe*. Stockholm, Sweden: Högskoleverket (National Agency for Higher Education).

Hüfner, K. (1995). Higher education reform in the context of rapidly changing societies. In K. Hüfner (Ed.), *Higher education reform processes in Central and Eastern Europe*. Frankfurt, Germany: Peter Lang.

Jarab, J. (1993). Higher education and research in the Czech Republic. *Policy Perspectives, 5*(1), 7B–11B.

Nowotny, H., Scott, P., & Gibbons, M. (2001). *Re-Thinking science: Knowledge and the public in an Age of uncertainty*. Cambridge, UK: Polity Press.

Raffe, D., Brannen, K., Croxford, C., & Martin, C. (1999). Comparing England, Scotland, Wales and Northern Ireland: The case for "home internationals" in comparative research. *Comparative Education, 35*(1), 9–25.

Sadlak, J. (1995). In search of the "post-Communist" university—the background and scenario of the transformation of higher education in Central and Eastern Europe. In K. Hüfner (Ed.), *Higher education reform processes in Central and Eastern Europe* (pp. 43–62). Frankfurt, Germany: Peter Lang.

Scott, P. (1993). Reflections on the transatlantic dialogue. *Policy Perspectives, 5*(1), 1B–5B.

Scott, P. (2000). Ten years on and looking ahead. In *Review of the transformations of higher education in Central and Eastern Europe* (pp. 341–407). Bucharest, Romania: CEPES Studies on Higher Education.

22

HIGHER EDUCATION IN DEVELOPING COUNTRIES

David E. Bloom and Henry Rosovsky
Harvard University, USA

Social and economic inequalities are among the most striking features of the modern world. Per capita income is more than 60 times higher among the wealthy industrial countries than it is among low-income economies.[1] The absolute income gap between these country groups was $29,000 in 2002, triple the level of 1960. Disparities in health, education, and the relative status of women have been, and continue to be, pervasive. Huge numbers of people live under conditions of extreme insecurity, raising a complex set of moral, political, social, and economic issues.

In the last century, possessing, accessing, and being able to apply knowledge has become an increasingly vital determinant of national wealth. But during this period, the industrial world has had a virtual monopoly on knowledge generation and a disproportionate share of individuals with higher education. For example, while only 15% of the world's population lives in the industrial countries,[2] those countries account for more than 90% of patents granted[3] and the vast majority of Nobel Prize winners. And while, as of 1995, more than a quarter of the population over age 25 in industrial countries had at least some higher education, the corresponding figure in developing countries was just 6% (Task Force on Higher Education and Society, 2000).

Higher education is the primary engine through which advanced knowledge (as opposed to training) is produced and imparted. Policymakers have tended to view higher education as relatively unimportant compared with other development imperatives such as primary education and health. Yet most developing countries are being buffeted by new powerful forces, including democratization, rapid demographic change, the knowledge and information technology revolutions, and the process of globalization. A central premise of this chapter is that expanding and strengthening their systems of higher education represents a major channel through which developing countries can address these and other global forces, promote their economic and social development, and narrow a wide range of development gaps.

This chapter reviews and assesses the higher education scene in developing countries. It also discusses selected factors that seem to be impeding developing countries from capturing the benefits that higher education can provide.

James J.F. Forest and Philip G. Altbach (eds.), International Handbook of Higher Education, 443–459.

Three caveats deserve mention at the outset. First, higher education is not destiny: it is just one set of institutions whose contributions to development are mediated by many other contextual factors. Second, the beneficial effects that can result from rethinking and repositioning higher education will not appear suddenly. The full benefits of any reform initiative will likely take a long time to become evident. Finally, there is considerable heterogeneity among developing countries with respect to their higher education institutions and systems, as well as their social, economic, and political conditions, and their cultures and histories. Notwithstanding these sources of heterogeneity, this generalized examination will focus on higher education issues affecting *most* developing countries.

Characteristics of Higher Education in Developing Countries

This section reviews salient features of the recent history of higher education in developing countries and describes the current range of institutions. It then provides brief surveys of public expenditures on higher education, physical infrastructure conditions, and student demographics.

Historical Overview: The Expansion of Higher Education

Until the disintegration of the major colonial empires in the aftermath of World War II, and for some time after, higher education in developing countries had an elite focus, with students typically pursuing training for positions in the civil service or a few lucrative professions. Aspirations to undertake higher education have, however, expanded in recent decades, and that is closely connected to the expansion of primary and secondary education and rising incomes. Analysis of recent enrollment trends in higher education shows that:

- From 1980 to 1999,[4] the gross enrollment rate for higher education grew from 35% to 60% in industrial countries, but only from 8% to 14% in developing countries.[5] Four regions that were particularly far behind (East Asia and the Pacific, the Middle East and North Africa, South Asia, and sub-Saharan Africa) showed major improvements, but in terms of percentage point increase, the change was largest in the Middle East and North Africa (moving from 11% to 22%) (World Bank, 2003).[6]
- Tertiary attainment rates among the population aged 25 and over have increased sharply over time. Among the high-income countries, they increased from 8% to 26% between 1965 and 1995; among low- and middle-income countries, they increased from 1% to 6%. Nevertheless, as of 1995, only 2% of the population of sub-Saharan Africa (ages 25 and over) had received some higher education. For East Asia and the Pacific, the corresponding figure was only 3%.[7]
- From 1992 to 2002, enrollment in tertiary level institutions is estimated to have grown by 5% per year in developing countries.
- From 1980 to 1994, the share of women enrolled in higher education in the developing world increased from 35% to 40%. From 1990 to 1994, women's enrollment

grew at an average rate of 9.9% per year in sub-Saharan Africa and 6.7% in Eastern Asia and Oceania, compared with only 2.2% in the industrial countries (where more women were enrolled to begin with). Female enrollment is driving much of the increased demand for higher education in developing countries.

Demographic change. During the last 50 years, many countries have been undergoing substantial demographic change, including rapid population growth, changes in the age structure of the population, and declining family size. An examination of current demographic trends permits estimates of the future size and structure of national populations. Information about demographic change, when combined with data on sharply increasing primary and secondary school enrollment rates, indicates that the demand for higher education will increase substantially in developing countries during the next few decades (Task Force on Higher Education and Society, 2000). From 1992 to 2002, the population age group most likely to seek higher education—20–24 year olds—increased by 3.2% per year in sub-Saharan Africa, 1.8% in Asia, and 1.1% in Latin America.

Declining family size is a particularly important determinant of the demand for higher education because families with fewer children typically invest more resources in each child. Although private expenditures on higher education will increase, there will be considerable pressure for increases in public expenditure as well, because otherwise a rapidly growing number of children raised with the expectation of access to higher education will not be able to afford it.

Expansion of secondary education. The gross enrollment ratio for secondary education in low-income countries increased from 18% to 46% between 1970 and 2000; it increased from 27% to 75% among middle-income countries (World Bank, 2004). For those students who manage to overcome all the obstacles that make completion of secondary school difficult, higher education appears to offer a once-in-a-lifetime opportunity: the chance to gain credentials, connections, and skills that will be useful throughout their lives and might lead to a higher income. Increases in secondary school completion have therefore led to a natural, salutary, and unavoidable increase in the demand for higher education.

Other considerations related to expansion. As tertiary enrollments increase, higher education institutions are unlikely to be able to maintain quality without a concomitant expansion in resources. They will need more teachers for the tertiary level and will have to renovate and expand their facilities. Even assuming that such measures are politically and financially feasible, quality may still suffer: since some of the most effective resources and people may already be employed in the higher education system, new additions to the education system may not be as productive as existing resources.

Types of Higher Education Institutions

Institutions of higher education can be categorized according to their level, goals, and funding sources. In developing countries, the apex consists of research universities, whose academic professionals typically view scholarship as equal to, or more important than, teaching. Students at these institutions, which are usually publicly sponsored, few in number, and prominent as symbols of national achievement and pride, have generally attained the highest academic standards. At the same time, private universities, which are generally not-for-profit and sometimes also of high quality, have also thrived.[8] The next (and wider) rung consists of provincial or regional institutions, where there is somewhat less emphasis on research and more on teaching. The widest rung of the higher education ladder consists of community colleges and polytechnic and vocational institutions. In addition, professional schools at various rungs of the ladder span a wide range of quality, as do postsecondary vocational schools. At the very bottom of the ladder are the so-called "garage universities," which have proliferated in many developing countries in response to the rapidly growing demand for higher education credentials. These institutions—which operate on a private, for-profit basis—are low-quality, unsupervised, transient, and exploitative.

With regard to funding, universities have traditionally been seen as a province of the state, which had responsibility for funding and operations. Although recent years have witnessed a proliferation of for-profit institutions, the absence of quality standards and the financial impulse that drives such institutions have led to severe quality problems in many cases.

Governments face a huge challenge in responding to this often chaotic array of institutions, many of which are new and completely unregulated. Accreditation—whose purpose is to confer public approval of the offerings, method of operation, and results obtained by an educational institution—is a particularly thorny issue that, if left unaddressed, could lead to surfeits of low-quality "degree"-granting organizations and of "graduates" who have not acquired significant new knowledge or mastered new skills.

Public Expenditure

In developing countries, public expenditure on higher education is a contentious issue. The perception that tax revenues emanating from the entire tax base are benefiting only a narrow segment of the populace often provokes opposition to high levels of public spending on a country's universities. Nevertheless, the political power of those with resources has in many cases meant that countries actually spend significant resources on their public systems of higher education.

In sub-Saharan Africa, East Asia and the Pacific, and South Asia, public expenditures on higher education were just 2–3% of gross domestic product in 1995. This is less than other regions (i.e., Eastern Europe and Central Asia, Latin America and the Caribbean, the Middle East and North Africa, and the industrial countries) where the corresponding figure was 5%.[9]

Interestingly, across developing regions, public current spending on higher education as a fraction of total public current spending on education is 16%, with little cross-regional variation. This figure is only slightly below the 18% spending share among high-income countries. However, as total spending on education is much lower among developing countries, it follows that they spend much less on higher education than the high-income countries.

Since 1980, public spending on higher education worldwide has grown at roughly 5% annually. The rate of increase has varied considerably, from nearly 7% in East Asia to only about 1% in Eastern Europe and Central Asia.

Physical Infrastructure

The fragile physical infrastructure of most universities in developing countries impedes research and student learning.[10] Frequently, buildings are crumbling and too small, electricity and telecommunications services are unreliable, laboratories are severely underfunded and antiquated, and libraries lack recent titles. Poor coordination between capital and operating budgets creates problems as funds are allocated for the construction of new facilities, but not for their operation and maintenance. This problem is especially important with respect to new technology for information sharing and communication, as it is estimated that operating costs represent up to three-fourths of the total life-cycle costs of technology investment (World Bank, 2002).

Students

Approximately 71 million university students, nearly 65% of the world's total, are enrolled in universities in the developing world. A little more than half of these are in East Asia and the Pacific, Eastern Europe, and Central Asia. Most of the rest are roughly evenly divided between Latin America and the Caribbean and South Asia.[11] Not surprisingly, developing countries with larger populations tend to have higher enrollment figures. For example, the largest tertiary enrollment figures are for China (12.1 million), India (9.8 million), Indonesia (3.2 million), and Brazil (3.1 million).[12] (For comparison, note that both France and the United Kingdom have just over two million higher education students, and Denmark has 0.2 million.)

In developing countries, those who are not poor have much greater access to primary and secondary education: the number of years of schooling completed decreases at lower ends of the socioeconomic spectrum. For similar reasons, urban university students are much more likely to complete secondary education than rural university students. Consequently, the pool of young people most likely to enter an institution of higher education is disproportionately rich and urban. Compounding the wealth issue are the out-of-pocket costs of a university education and the "opportunity costs" of higher education—i.e., the income that would have been earned while a student is in school instead of working.

Figure 1 shows that gross enrollment ratios in high-income countries dwarf those in developing countries, with sub-Saharan Africa the furthest behind.

Among low- and middle-income countries as enrollment data are available for 2000, the top five countries were Russia, Latvia, Estonia, Belarus, and Poland, with gross enrollment ratios ranging from 64% to 56% (World Bank, 2003), clearly reflecting the considerable emphasis the former Soviet bloc placed on education. At the other end of the scale, gross enrollment ratios of 1% in 2000 are found in Burundi, Djibouti, Mozambique, Niger, and Tanzania. These figures are consistent with the overall low level of resources and human development in sub-Saharan Africa.

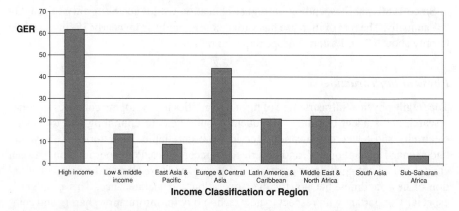

Figure 1.   Tertiary gross enrollment ratio (GER) by region.
Note: Data are for 2000 or most recent year. The regional classifications do not include any high-income countries.
Source: World Bank (2003).

Figure 2 plots each country's gross enrollment ratio in the year 1980 (horizontal axis) and the year 2000 (vertical axis). Points on the 45 degree line indicate countries with static enrollment ratios. Points above (or below) the 45 degree line represent countries for which enrollment ratios have increased (or decreased) over time. As the

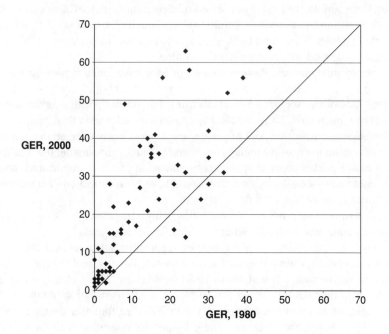

Figure 2.   Trends in gross enrollment ratio (GER).
Source: World Development Indicators (2003).

preponderance of data points sit above the 45 degree line, Figure 2 clearly shows that the great majority of developing countries (for which there are data in 1980 and 2000) have improved their gross enrollment ratios over time.

Contemporary Issues

Developing countries face a number of formidable challenges with respect to their higher education institutions and systems. Some of these arise because of external changes such as the world's knowledge and technology revolutions and the process of globalization. Others are more closely connected to internal issues, such as management and organization, curriculum reform, educational finance, and the rapidly growing demand for higher education. This section reviews a number of these issues and considers their implications for higher education in developing countries.

The Knowledge and Technology Revolutions

Technical and scientific knowledge is growing more rapidly than at any other time in human history. For obvious reasons, developing countries have not played a major role as creators of this type of knowledge; at best, they have been successful adaptors. The process of adaptation places a premium on individuals who are able to work in a knowledge-technology centered environment: people with higher education. Their scarcity may mean that low-income countries will fall further behind economically advanced countries. The industrial revolution created the first and deeply entrenched income gap between nations. The knowledge revolution may increase this gap.

Besides creating a greater need for trained individuals, the knowledge explosion has other consequences for higher education. The most obvious is that in most fields, students must learn much more than ever before; many will be pushed to narrow their studies so they can study particular areas in greater depth. New information and communication technologies have the potential to facilitate this process by improving communication among students, teachers, and researchers, and by easing their access to quality educational materials. Videoconferencing, for example, is becoming more accessible, and it is often an inexpensive and adequate substitute for conference travel.

The Internet will increasingly serve as an information repository and teaching aid. It is accessible in more than 180 countries and links more than 30 million host computer systems. However, the Internet access and participation gap between developing and industrial countries is wide and growing (Khalil, 2003).

In combination with radio and television, new technologies can replace or complement traditional methods for delivering higher education and may prove especially valuable in meeting the demand for expanded access to high-quality higher education. The use of such technologies could lower the cost of teaching students, especially when considering distance education. However, the net benefits should not be overstated. Information technologies require not just the appropriate hardware and software, but the associated infrastructure along with specially designed curricula and qualified instructors.

Rural populations, which account for some 55% of the developing world, stand to gain much from the capacity of new information technologies to overcome their isolation. While infrastructure costs do present a barrier, rural residents could benefit from higher education once electrification and telecommunications infrastructure reach these areas and make distance learning an option. This may prove to be more cost-effective than building traditional schools in isolated regions.

New information technologies could also improve the quality of higher education. Not only can good instructional materials be updated frequently, but the best teachers can easily reach more students than in the past. The technologies might also permit more active student participation.

While little systematic evidence is available to support the view that new technologies promote better educational outcomes, as these continue to be developed and disseminated, researchers will likely provide empirical evidence that demonstrates their utility. Nevertheless, some words of caution are necessary. The use of new technologies will require planning and resources to ensure satisfaction of bandwidth requirements, electricity supply needs, and the burgeoning demand for Internet access points. The difficulty of financing infrastructure investments in many developing countries raises a familiar question: will new technologies simply widen the existing gap in access to higher education between developing and industrial countries?

Technological change encompasses more than the well-known advances in telecommunications and information technology. Production methods are changing rapidly; new techniques, materials, and management methods are constantly reshaping industry; and new practices are changing the face of agriculture. Many of these changes require broadly educated, well-trained people to manage new processes and to work effectively in revamped industrial contexts. Countries whose citizens are unable to adapt relatively quickly to the ever-changing demands of both the local and the global economy will find themselves falling further behind.

The rapid growth of the knowledge economy means that new technologies are continually making old ones obsolete. Thus workers' skills can quickly become less useful, and they need to be able to acquire new proficiencies. However, higher education in developing countries does not currently equip students with this flexibility, since it tends—too often—to focus on rote learning instead of rewarding creativity and curiosity. Incorporating technology in instruction holds the promise of making learning more focused on exactly what each student needs. Such incorporation can include everything from the adaptation of online lesson plans for local use to highly interactive, computer-based instructional methods.

One of the advantages of incorporating technology into education is that students become accustomed to the types of tools that businesses use. The best example of this is in the use of the basic set of word processing and spreadsheet computer programs and the Internet. Students' daily use of this technology will inevitably enhance their abilities to function in a world that is increasingly dependent on such skills. However, two difficulties arise in incorporating technology in this way. First, academic staff may be more reluctant than students to shift their style to be more technologically oriented. Second, many countries' universities simply do not have enough computers to ensure that most students have sufficient access to carry out all their assignments using a computer.

Financing Higher Education

Many developing countries have faced significant struggles over the extent to which the government should finance higher education. Some segments of the population see such funding as a right akin to the state's more widely accepted responsibility for primary and secondary education. Others point out that as the well-off constitute most of the student population, state funding is regressive and unjustified. The policies that a country ends up following will ultimately be dictated, in part, by social and political pressures.

The question of whether a country should have a general subsidy for higher education has been debated at length. For decades, economists analyzing issues of public funding relied on rate-of-return analyses that sought to clarify who—individuals or society as a whole—gained from investments in higher education. These analyses typically took into account only the higher earnings that accrued to individuals who received higher education and did not consider the broader societal benefits—some of which are economic—that a society receives when its people are more educated. Taking into account these broader benefits can tilt the case toward the justification of public funding.[13]

Even with such a tilt, however, the case for a *general* subsidy for higher education would still rely on several conditions that may or may not be met. First, the social net benefit from the investment must be positive; that is, the gains for society as a whole must outweigh the costs of such an investment in higher education. Second, individuals, on their own, must lack sufficient incentive or ability to undertake the socially desirable level of investment themselves. And finally, the subsidies under consideration must have a higher social net benefit than other competing investments (Bloom & Sevilla, 2004).

Whatever policies a country adopts, state financing will inevitably be limited given developing countries' overall financial constraints and the high and rapidly growing demand for higher education. Countries are unlikely to be able to count on state financing to provide all the funds needed for higher education.

Substantial funds for higher education already come from students and their families. In many countries and for some groups of students this is perfectly reasonable, because the beneficiaries have access to sufficient resources to pay a sizable share of their own higher education. State subsidization would amount to a transfer from poor and middle-income households to the rich. Even though the middle class often attempts to resist paying for any part of a university education, governments will most often insist that those who have the resources pay a significant share of the costs. However, state financing can accompany private provision; for instance, the state can provide scholarships to promising students who attend a private university.

Democratization, Decentralization, and Globalization

For the first time in history, more than half the world's population is living in countries with democratic political systems, and the numbers are rising. This trend affects both the possibilities for social and economic development and their inherent challenges.

The allocation of public resources to higher education is more transparent in a democracy, and the public is more heavily involved. The latter could lead to pressure for more scholarships and greater accountability, and ultimately to beneficial innovations in higher education. Also of significance is the role of higher education in opening up space for public discourse regarding societal values. Finally, academic freedom undoubtedly is greater in democratic societies.

Accompanying the expansion of democracy is the trend to decentralize public services from the national level to provincial or municipal levels. If extended to higher education, such decentralization could promote quality by enhancing autonomy for universities over spending allocations, academic standards, and personnel matters; greater inter-provincial competition could also promote quality. However, decentralization could also prove detrimental if higher education institutions do not have sufficient numbers of well-trained administrators to take over this function from government administrators.

While decentralization moves forward within countries, national economies have become increasingly integrated in the last decade through international trade and international movements of labor, capital, and ideas. Higher education has considerable potential to make an impact on both the positive and negative aspects of globalization. Higher education can help developing countries thrive as a result of globalization—for example, by putting countries in a better position to reach and implement informed decisions about how to manage their integration into regional and global economies. Countries with a larger proportion of highly educated people tend to be more competitive in world markets, because a higher skill level complements capital-intensive production and acts as a magnet for the attraction of direct foreign investment. On the other hand, globalization also increases access to gaining higher education abroad, and offers many college graduates from developing countries easier opportunities to earn higher incomes by leaving their home country. Globalization thereby magnifies the vexing problem of "brain drain," although this problem is partially offset by migrants' economic and social remittances.

Higher education also affords opportunities to deal with many of the large and growing economic and social deficits and disparities that seem to be accompanying globalization. Many of these disparities are reflected in the United Nations' Millennium Development Goals. These include eradicating extreme poverty and hunger, ensuring universal primary and secondary education, empowering women, and reducing child mortality. All of these goals are potentially addressed through the widening and deepening of higher education systems, either directly—by increasing knowledge and skill (and therefore individual productivity and income)—or indirectly, by strengthening national and global institutions.

Challenges for Public Universities

Public universities have an important role to play in national development insofar as they are frequently the only universities with research potential. As part of the public sector, however, these universities suffer from many of the same challenges as other state-owned enterprises. Resources are not well used because there is resistance to change, and employees in state-run institutions lack the motivation to serve the public good efficiently. In universities, rules about decision making, tenure, workloads, and research may hobble potential advancements. The typically low levels of funding available to public universities help to push many academic professionals into taking second jobs at other academic institutions, thereby making them less available to students. Heavy tuition subsidies at public universities also make them a coveted first option for prospective students who lack economic means. Unfortunately, many such students lack access to secondary schools that are of sufficient quality to secure their admission to public higher education institutions.

For-profit private universities face a different constraint that can make them ineffective as a means of providing adequate education: the need to make a profit. Since many students are seeking a degree but not necessarily a true education, private institutions can all too easily be tempted to ignore quality. Students get their degree, but may not acquire a *bona fide* body of knowledge and skills.

Curriculum Reform

Curricula need to be relevant to current issues and technologies. The flexibility required by a rapidly changing world economy highlights the need for a corps of well-rounded individuals whose education has explored a wide range of areas—meaning that liberal (or general) education will have an increasingly central role to play in a revamped curriculum. In the end, curriculum reform is both a technical and a political problem; a failure to recognize its political aspects can doom even the most technically worthy efforts.

For-profit universities may have less control over curricula and educational quality than public universities due to the need to conform to market demand. This is obviously not the case with not-for-profit private institutions, but in many countries (including some industrial countries) standards for all institutions (private and public) are not well spelled out and are not enforced. Accreditation is a huge problem, because government authorities may lack the competence or motivation to ensure that universities are actually offering a useful education to students. And as noted earlier, many students, in turn, care about little more than receiving a credential.

The adoption of a top-down committee approach is responsible for the collapse of many reform efforts. Stakeholder participation appears to be essential to curriculum design and reforms, and preventing those interested in and affected by reform from participating can doom it from the outset. Teachers, students, administrators, employers, donors, and other interested parties must be encouraged to voice their views, and academic professionals in particular must be handled carefully, because they are often the ones who feel the most threatened by curriculum change.

Liberal education. Western civilization is home to a long tradition of liberal education, defined as an emphasis on the broad development of an individual and not just training for an occupation. By offering students a range of courses that goes well beyond those required by any one specialty, liberal education emphasizes individuals' ability to think, communicate, and learn; to adopt a comparative and international perspective; and to provide a basis for further, more specialized study. The beginnings of this philosophy can be traced back to ancient Greece and to the *trivium* (grammar, rhetoric, and logic) and *quadrivium* (arithmetic, geometry, astronomy, and music) of medieval times. That tradition has continued, and today liberal education is an important component of higher education in a number of industrial countries.[14]

The contrast with developing countries is stark. Since achieving independence, many developing countries have viewed liberal education as a luxury. This is reflected in the curricula of both secondary and higher education institutions, which tend to favor vocational training. Governments shun liberal education on the grounds that it is elitist, emblematic of the values of Western colonialism—indeed, that it would be an inheritance of colonial systems, and too expensive. While these attitudes may be changing, most developing countries still do not recognize the benefits of a liberal or general education. There are exceptions, however, reflected by programs in Bangladesh, China, and Pakistan.

Developing countries could benefit from the introduction—or in a few cases, the expansion—of high-quality general education. Liberal education can promote responsible citizenship and civic virtue, and foster an understanding of the differences among groups in a society. While such an education is not appropriate for all students, countries can benefit if there is a significant group of citizens who can operate at a high intellectual level in rapidly changing times—whether to perform such unusual functions as negotiating with international aid donors, deciding whether to import generic AIDS drugs, or developing a fair electoral system, or more prosaically to run and participate in organizations and businesses with international links.

The content of general education curricula will vary from country to country, and the process of designing such curricula allows nations to assess what matters to their particular society given its history, culture, and values. Rather than blindly adopting models from elsewhere, countries can review lessons learned in other places and adapt them to suit their own requirements.

Nevertheless, many developing countries perceive liberal education as an expensive frill that does not fulfill any of their genuine needs and may find that justifying students' "dabbling in" literature, philosophy, history, and the arts is not possible when their needs are so stark. Moreover, the diversified instructional staff required to impart a liberal education complicates running a university. Adding to the perception of liberal education as impractical is the fact that interactive liberal arts courses are best taught in smaller groups, placing extra financial demands on a university. Worse yet, liberal education courses might extend the period during which students attend university. Finally, those with a stake in the status quo may perceive liberal education as a threat, because students with this kind of background are more likely to question orthodoxy of all types.

Science education. Science and technology present some unique challenges for universities. First, basic scientific inquiry often requires large investments to deliver long-term, but highly uncertain, benefits. The free market is not good at funding basic research, especially if the poor are more likely to reap benefits than the rich. Consider, for instance, the low priority given to finding a cure for malaria: most of the victims are poor; since they would not be able to pay the likely high cost of new drugs, companies have little incentive to develop such remedies. Second, the way that scientific knowledge is produced is changing rapidly. Individual scientists working alone in their laboratories have largely become a thing of the past. Today, scientific research tends to transcend organizational and disciplinary boundaries, involve public and private sector participation, and employ teamwork.

Providing education in science and technology at the university level requires a significant investment in physical resources, including laboratories and libraries. With funds scarce in all developing countries, such investment will be difficult. A more careful sharing of resources within and among institutions might alleviate this problem somewhat, but more resources will undoubtedly be needed if science education is to advance rapidly.

Improving and expanding science education will also require new, well-trained, dedicated academic professionals who can communicate effectively with large numbers of students. The problem here is twofold: first, past deficiencies in producing scientists and teachers who are well-trained in science mean that the pool of available people to draw from is small; and second, highly qualified scientists often enjoy well-paid or otherwise appealing employment opportunities abroad or outside the education sector.

Management and Delivery

The manner in which tertiary education is organized and administered has a significant effect on the results achieved by a country's system of higher education. A system-wide perspective—one in which the structure and operation of institutions of higher education are considered in concert—addresses the place of various institutions in relation to each other and their links to the rest of the education system and to society as a whole. It naturally leads to the development of a rational, stratified system of higher education—i.e., one with a range of different types of institutions with different objectives. Links to higher education institutions in other countries are also becoming increasingly important.

Governance. Governance—the formal and informal arrangements that allow higher education to function—is a key determinant of the effectiveness of institutions. Academic freedom, autonomy, monitoring and accountability, and meritocratic selection of teachers and students are among the essential and proven principles of good governance. Tools for converting these principles into action range from specific mechanisms for hiring and promoting academic professionals and administrators, to boards of trustees, academic councils, institutional handbooks, and visiting committees.

An institution's governance structure sets the stage for everything that occurs within its walls. Institutional performance is generally improved when practices and procedures established by the governing authorities are stable and transparent.

Too many universities in developing countries—and elsewhere—are governed as participatory democracies, that is, department or faculty chairs elect deans and rectors, who must periodically run for re-election. This situation makes senior administrators vulnerable to pressures coming from academic professionals in any area where they have to make hard choices. As a result, in order to keep their posts, administrators must listen and respond to the wishes of academic professionals, whether or not those wishes serve the greater interests of the university. By contrast, top-down governance, with effective faculty consultation, is less fractious and more efficient than participatory democracy and might serve developing countries well.

Role of the state. The state can provide clarity and guidance concerning the role and functioning of institutions of higher education. In the case of public institutions, the state is also the primary source of funds. In most developing countries, public universities are a source of great national pride. Citizens have an interest in ensuring that these universities produce graduates who have the knowledge and skills that are relevant to the country's development, and they also have an interest in ensuring that public funds are wisely spent in achieving this goal. The state is responsible for promoting these legitimate interests. To do this, it must typically promulgate broad rules and a framework within which public institutions of higher education must operate. By contrast, many believe that the state's role in a university's *internal* governance should be quite circumscribed.

As mentioned earlier, the state also has an important role to play in regulating private universities, especially in relation to accreditation.

Academic staff. With the salaries of academic professionals almost invariably low in developing countries, teaching staff face strong temptations to work outside the university. Such work may take the form of adjunct teaching at another institution or employment in a non-academic institution. On the one hand, this is entirely understandable and difficult to prevent. On the other hand, the university community must realize that cohesion—which can help inspire both academic professionals and students to maintain higher academic standards, and can be an essential ingredient in bringing about a stimulating academic atmosphere—will suffer when academic professionals view the university as just one of several sources of employment.

Brain drain. The brain drain issue can pose obstacles to the reform of the higher education sector. As noted earlier, even if a developing country does manage to produce more highly trained academic professionals, they are more mobile (in the context of an increasingly globalizing world) and may be more readily tempted by higher salaries in other countries. Similarly, students who are skilled in the development and acquisition of knowledge, and might therefore become good academic staff, are tempting targets for firms, governments, and international development organizations.

The existence of brain drain makes arguing the case for investment in higher education more difficult. If a sizable number of a country's best students—whose education has been funded out of the public purse—emigrate as soon as they have graduated (and do not send home significant remittances), what benefit has the country reaped from its investment? Unless a country takes brain drain into account during policy development, it may complicate decisions about investment in higher education, and could provoke strong political opposition. Developing good institutions—both in education and the workplace—can help stem brain drain. International organizations that place conditions on overseas scholarships requiring recipients to return can also make a difference. Of great importance, obviously, are wages for those who are well educated, since higher earnings will deter some people from emigrating, or entice them to return to their original country. In addition, political stability greatly increases the likelihood that well-educated individuals will want to live in their home country.

Conclusion

The United Nations' Millennium Development Goals (MDGs) represent the central imperatives of contemporary international development efforts. These eight goals, which were endorsed by over 180 heads of state in 2000, are intended to point the way toward improving living standards among the world's most vulnerable people, with a focus on the estimated 1.2 billion people living on less than one dollar per day. In addition to the goal of poverty reduction, the MDGs focus on such items as child and maternal health, combating infectious diseases, environmental sustainability, the status of women, and access to primary education.

Conspicuous for its absence among the MDGs is any mention of higher education. This omission is surprising given the intrinsic benefit of higher education in enabling many people to live a fuller life. It is even more surprising given the potentially large instrumental benefits of higher education in moving developing countries onto higher and more sharply rising development trajectories and mitigating cross-country disparities in living standards.

Notwithstanding higher education's absence from the MDGs, expanding access to higher education and improving its quality represent both basic goals and instruments of development progress. Moving forward to reform higher education institutions and systems in developing countries will require considerable financial and human resources. It will also take vision and committed, long-term leadership, as the payback period for investments in higher education reform is more naturally measured in decades than years. Despite these obstacles, developing countries would do well to keep in mind the words of Lao-Tsu, Chinese philosopher and founder of Taoism: "A journey of a thousand miles begins with a single step."

Acknowledgments

Phil Altbach provided useful comments and Larry Rosenberg provided helpful assistance in preparing this chapter.

Notes

1. The figure refers to GDP per capita measured in constant US$ for the year 2002. If measured in international dollars (adjusted for purchasing power parity differences across countries), the disparity was 13 in 2002.
2. By industrial countries we mean those identified as high-income countries by the World Bank: the United States, Canada, the countries of Western Europe, Slovenia, Israel, Kuwait, Qatar, United Arab Emirates, Brunei, Hong Kong-China, Japan, Singapore, South Korea, Taiwan-China, Australia, New Zealand, and several small island countries. All other countries are considered "developing countries." This includes Africa, much of Asia, most of the Middle East, nearly

all of Latin America, and all parts of the former Soviet Union. By this definition, developing countries encompass nearly 85% of the world's population.

3. In relation to patents, see http://www.southcentre.org/publications/ecommerce/ecommerce-09.htm

4. 1998 data are used when that is the latest year available.

5. The gross enrollment ratio is the ratio of total enrollment, regardless of age, to the population of the age group that officially corresponds to a particular level of education. For tertiary education, the gross enrollment ratio is expressed as a percentage of the population in the 5-year age group following the official secondary school leaving age, which varies somewhat by country.

6. Throughout, we use regional definitions supplied by the World Bank, with industrial countries treated as an entirely separate category, as noted above. Sub-Saharan Africa encompasses all of what has traditionally been considered East, Southern, and West Africa. The Middle East and North Africa encompasses the remainder of Africa and the Middle East as far east as Iran. Latin America and the Caribbean includes, of course, Mexico and Central America. Eastern Europe and Central Asia includes all of what was traditionally considered Eastern Europe, as well as all of the countries of the former Soviet Union, including Russia. South Asia stretches from Afghanistan to Bangladesh. East Asia and the Pacific includes all other Asian countries and the islands of the Pacific. China, of course, is the dominant factor in the data for this region.

7. The figure for "East Asia and the Pacific" includes China, which, with a 2% attainment rate, mostly determines the regional average. Of note, the corresponding figures are 19% for South Korea and 22% for Japan.

8. Universidad de los Andes (in Colombia) is one example of a longstanding, high-quality, private institution. More recently, other top-level private universities, such as the Lahore Institute of Management Sciences, have been founded.

9. The surprisingly low figure for East Asia is due to the fact that China, which spends little compared to GDP, dominates the figures for that region.

10. There are, of course, important exceptions to this general picture, such as the Aga Khan University in Karachi, Pakistan, the Indian Institutes of Technology, the University of Cape Town in South Africa, and a number of institutions in the former Soviet Union.

11. These figures are based on an analysis of data from the UNESCO Institute for Statistics website. The largest country for which data are missing from this source is Pakistan. Country categorization into regions is based on World Bank (2003).

12. UNESCO Institute for Statistics website.

13. A longer discussion of these issues appears in Task Force on Higher Education (2000) and Bloom and Rosovsky (2004). Also, please see the chapter by Bloom, Rosovsky and Hartley in Volume 1 of this *Handbook*.

14. The European tradition of elite-based higher education placed liberal education into the academic preparatory secondary schools. That is changing as Europe's higher education systems reorient themselves toward mass education.

References

Altbach, P. G. (1998). *Comparative higher education.* Norwood, NJ: Ablex.

Bloom, D. E., & Rosovsky, H. (2004). 'Higher education in developing countries: Peril and promise'— Has it made a difference? *Comparative Education Review, 48*(1), 78–81, 85–88.

Bloom, D. E., & Rosovsky, H. (2003). Why developing countries should not neglect liberal education. *Liberal Education, 89*(1), 16–23.

Bloom, D. E., & Sevilla, J. (2004). Should there be a general subsidy for higher education in developing countries? *Journal of Higher Education in Africa, 1*(2), 137–150.

Castro, C. M., & Levy, D. C. (2000). *Myth, reality, and reform: Higher education policy in Latin America.* Washington, DC: InterAmerican Development Bank.

Khalil, M. (2003). The wireless Internet opportunity for developing countries. Paper presented at the World Summit on Information Society, Geneva, Switzerland (December). Washington, DC: The World Bank.

Task Force on Higher Education and Society. (2000). *Higher education in developing countries: Peril and promise.* Washington, DC: The World Bank.

UNESCO Institute for Statistics. Website: www.uis.unesco.org/TEMPLATE/html/Exceltables/ education/enrol_tertiary.xls

World Bank. (1994). *Higher education: The lessons of experience.* Washington, DC: The World Bank.

World Bank. (2002). *Constructing knowledge societies: New challenges for tertiary education.* Washington, DC: The World Bank.

World Bank. (2003). *World development indicators 2003.* Washington, DC: The World Bank.

World Bank. (2004). *World development indicators 2004.* Washington, DC: The World Bank.

23

EUROPEAN INTEGRATION IN HIGHER EDUCATION: THE BOLOGNA PROCESS TOWARDS A EUROPEAN HIGHER EDUCATION AREA

Hans de Wit

University of Amsterdam, the Netherlands

In discussing European integration in higher education, one has to keep in mind that Europe is not a homogeneous region; still less is its education homogeneous, as the rationales behind the Bologna Declaration on the European space for higher education of 1999 make manifest. This implies that when analyzing the regionalization of higher education in Europe, one has to take account of several important issues, such as national and regional differences, diversity of languages, different educational traditions and systems, diversity of stakeholders, and the co-existence of universities and a strong non-university sector.[1]

The Bologna process directed to the realization of a "European Higher Education Area" by 2010, although recognizing this diversity, implies a substantial reform of higher education, beyond the borders of the 25 countries of the European Union. The Bologna Declaration was signed on June 19, 1999, in Bologna, Italy, by the ministers of education of 29 European countries, who based their declaration on the following understanding: "A Europe of knowledge is now widely recognized as an irreplaceable factor for social and human growth and as an indispensable component to consolidate and enrich the European citizenship, capable of giving its citizens the necessary competences to face the challenges of the new millennium, together with an awareness of shared values and belonging to a common social and cultural space. The importance of education and educational cooperation in the development and strengthening of stable, peaceful and democratic societies is universally acknowledged as paramount, the more so in view of the situation in Southeast Europe" (Bologna Declaration, 1999).

By 2005, the number of signatory countries had increased to 45, including Russia. All higher education institutions in the signatory countries are supposed to be organized in conformity with the declaration by 2010, even though the declaration is voluntary and not binding for the countries and their institutions.

The declaration can be seen in connection with another ambitious process, agreed upon by the members of the European Council at their meeting in Lisbon in March

James J.F. Forest and Philip G. Altbach (eds.), International Handbook of Higher Education, 461–482.
© 2006 *Springer. Printed in the Netherlands.*

2000, "to become the most competitive and dynamic knowledge-based economy in the world, capable of sustainable growth with more and better jobs and greater social cohesion" (European Council, 2000), and to the Copenhagen process, launched in 2002, on enhancement of European cooperation in vocational education and training.[2] Together, these processes—but in particular the Bologna process—are the foundation for a reform agenda that not only requires more transparency and the removal of obstacles for internal labor and student mobility, but also must make education and research more competitive in the context of the global knowledge economy.

Following a review of past efforts to internationalize and Europeanize higher education, this chapter will address contemporary trends and challenges of European integration. Although reference will not be made exclusively to the European Commission's policies for Europeanization, the historical analysis presented here coincides with the phases noted by Brouwer (1996, p. 516):

- 1951–1972, the phase of incidental cooperation;
- 1972–1977, the preparatory phase of European cooperation in education;
- 1977–1986, the first phase of implementation of educational programs, mainly based on intergovernmental cooperation;
- 1986–1993, the second phase of implementation, mainly based on action by the EU; and
- 1993 onwards, the first phase of implementation of the EU Treaty for EU cooperation.[3]

During the first three stages (between 1951 and 1992), the role of the European Commission (EC) in education was limited by claims of sovereignty by the member states, and the growth of its role was slow, although steady. After 1992, with the inclusion of education in the Maastricht Treaty, its role could become more proactive. Brouwer's analysis stops in 1995, but one can extend his last phase until 1998. As described in this chapter, a new phase began in 1999, through which cooperation and harmonization will meet in a more coherent European education policy, stimulated by the Bologna Declaration.

The 1950s and 1960s: *Laissez-Faire*[4]

To understand the present European situation, it is essential to place current developments in a historical perspective. Macro-historical changes affecting the international dimension of Europe's higher education were: the emergence of nation-states in the 19th century and earlier; Europe's historical role in the world, in particular its role in colonization and in the process of de-colonization; the impact of higher education in countries such as France, Germany and the United Kingdom on higher education in the rest of the world; recent trends in European integration; the collapse of the former Soviet Union and associated East–West rapprochement; recession and financial constraint; "massification" of higher education; and the dissolution of some structures and blocs and the emergence of others.

Confining discussion to the macro-level and the post-World War II period, the 1950s and 1960s in Europe are not seen today as a period of internationalization, but it would be entirely wrong to believe that international student mobility was absent then. In general, the period 1950–1970 was, according to Baron (1993, p. 50), characterized by a "foreign policy" among receiving countries of "benevolent *laissez-faire*," providing open doors to foreign students—students who to a large extent came from the former (and, at that time, still existing) French and British colonies. Some elements of this are still seen in the patterns of student flow to these countries, although (especially in the British case) the impact of more recent policies has largely transformed the picture.

Guy Neave (1992) sees massification of the student flow and its bipolar nature (i.e., the dominance of the United States in the Western bloc and of the former Soviet Union in the Communist bloc) as the main characteristics of the international dimension of higher education in the 1960s and 1970s. The open-door and *laissez-faire* policy and the one–way dimension of foreign student flow were the other characteristics of the process of internationalization of higher education, at a global level and in Europe in particular. The universities themselves played a mainly passive role as receivers of foreign students.

Gisela Baumgratz-Gangl (1996) gives the following characteristics of internationalization in Europe before the introduction of the European programs: historical ties with former colonies (usually combined with cultural and linguistic ties); political considerations; the presence of political refugees; economic considerations; educational demands; research cooperation in the natural sciences; top-level postgraduate study; migration of "guest workers;" increasing foreign language competence at the secondary school level; traditional links between disciplines (mainly philology); traditional mobility of elites; improvement of transport and communication and expansion of tourism; cooperation at the postgraduate level between Western Europe and the U.S.; and mobility of Third World students and staff to Western Europe (also known as the brain drain phenomenon).

Although this list looks impressive, the effects of these factors on higher education cooperation within Europe were marginal. International activity was mainly oriented towards the cooperation of European higher education with the U.S. (outward mobility) and with the Third World (inward mobility). A European policy for internationalization did not exist, and the same applies to the institutional level. At the national level, international cooperation and exchange was included in bilateral agreements between nations and in development cooperation programs, driven by political rationales. Institutions were passive partners in these programs.

The 1970s: The First Steps to Policies of Europeanization

In the 1970s, this changed. In 1972, Sweden set up a program emphasizing internationalization as a means to promote international understanding, cooperation and peace, a program in which the universities should play an active role as change agents. The program included measures to internationalize the curriculum, credit transfers and exchanges (Hans Löwbeer, 1977). Germany also shifted around that time from a foreign affairs policy of internationalization to a more regulative and differentiated approach. Outgoing mobility was given more emphasis than the previous open-door policy for foreign students. The establishment of an "Integrated Study Abroad" program, administered by the German Academic Exchange Service (DAAD), is an illustration of that change. A change in pattern from South-North mobility to North-North mobility accompanied these changes (Baron, 1993; Kehm & Last, 1997).

In 1976, the Council of European Communities adopted an action program for education. This was the first such move, since the Treaty of Rome did not mention education as an area for community action. The 1963 Treaty of Rome (signed by Belgium, France, Germany, Italy, Luxembourg and the Netherlands) only included the principles of common vocational training, not other areas of education. Action was limited mainly to information exchange and exchange of young workers. Other initiatives—such as cultural, scientific and technological cooperation, the creation of European schools and a European university, and mutual recognition of diplomas— were (although linked to and inspired by the cooperation among the six countries that signed the treaty) not a formal part of the treaty, owing to political motives and related delays in decision making (Brouwer, 1996).

The Commission therefore had to justify its action program by non-educational, mainly economic criteria. As Field (1998, p. 85) notes, the European Community (EC)—and also later its successor, the European Union (EU)—tends to use other areas of activities to pursue its plans when its policy thinking exceeds the limits of the competency of the Treaty. Brouwer (1996, p. 58) gives four reasons why the European Community was reluctant to give priority to actions in the field of education until 1972: its emphasis on economic integration; a legal dispute on the limitations of the EC for actions in the field of education; the political context that limited the role of the EC in areas that the member states saw as their own competency; and the differences in national educational systems and the national orientation of these systems.

The action program of 1976 was a result of the first meeting of the Ministers of Education of the European Community, convened in Brussels, November 16, 1971. The basis for that meeting was established at the conference of heads of states of the European Community in December 1969 in The Hague, where cooperation in the area of education was advocated as part of further political integration. The 1971 meeting recognized the importance of broadening European action from vocational training to other areas of education—and particularly higher education—because of its economic significance.

The extension of the EC from six to nine countries (with the inclusion of Denmark, Ireland and the United Kingdom) as of January 1, 1973 coincided with a period of stagnation due to economic and political problems.[5] For education, though, new initiatives were taken as a follow-up to the 1971 meeting of education ministers. In 1973, the creation of a Directorate for Education, Research and Science (DG XII) under the responsibility of the first Commissioner for Science and Education, Ralf Dahrendorf, not only institutionalized education within the Commission structure but also linked EU policies for education and research. With this, the Commission was able to move away from having to base its rationales for an education and research policy on non-educational arguments—economic rationales primarily—to a proactive and integrated policy in these fields.[6]

Brouwer (1996, p. 86) gives seven rationales for the legitimization of European cooperation in the area of education:

- the importance of training and education for the process of European cooperation and integration (both from the perspective of quality improvement of education and from the point of mutual understanding);
- the need for more harmonization between the different national systems;
- the need for the creation of solutions to challenges resulting from the free movement of persons (including foreign languages, education for children of immigrants, and recognition of diplomas and qualifications);
- closer cooperation between national policies for education and actions of the EC in other fields;
- more involvement of European youth in the building of Europe;
- the need for a systematic exchange of information; and
- the need for linking European actions with other intergovernmental bodies, such as UNESCO, OECD and the Council of Europe, as well as the incorporation of education in development cooperation.

In these rationales we recognize the first signs of issues that are still dominant in the European policy for education: harmonization, Europeanization and globalization.

In 1974, the ministers of education of the European Community adopted the principles for an "Education Action Program" that was launched in 1976. It was composed of three main categories: mobility in education, education for children of immigrant workers and the intention to implement a European dimension in education. The action program included three measures for higher education: "Joint Study Programs," "Short Study Visits" and an educational administrators program.

Although important in itself, the impact of the action program was marginal (Field, 1998, p. 32). In that sense, the period 1972–1985 can be seen as a period of stagnation. In comparison to the "Integrated Study Abroad" program of Germany, the scope of the European programs was limited. But for other European countries who lacked a national policy and action program, at least it was something. The reasons for this stagnation, according to Brouwer (1996, p. 121), were the financial crisis of 1971, the energy crisis of 1973 and the resulting global economic crisis of the 1970s that stagnated economic and political integration and focused attention on national solutions.

The 1980s: The Great Leap Forward

The 1980s produced four distinct changes: first, the open-door mobility of individual students; second, the development of a research and development policy for the EC; third, student mobility as an integrated part of study; and fourth, the widening of scope to other regions, including countries within Western, Central and Eastern Europe as well as countries outside Europe, particularly in concert with development aid programs.

Individual Mobility

With respect to the individual mobility of students, the European nations and universities began changing their benevolent *laissez-faire* policy to a more controlled reception and, in some cases, the active recruitment of fee-paying foreign students. At first, this applied nearly exclusively to the case of the United Kingdom, with the British decision in 1979 to introduce full-cost fees for foreign students. Higher education as an export commodity quickly became dominant in the U.K. For the U.K., this created a conflict with the development of the European mobility programs. Gribbon (1994, p. 24) refers in that respect to the dilemma of British institutions in reconciling their interest in these programs (focused on European partners) with their interest in export, mainly outside Europe.

For most people on the European continent, considering the education of foreign students as an export commodity was still an anathema at that time. On the European continent, the reception of foreign students was (and in most cases still is) based more on foreign policy arguments than on considerations of export policy. Often, it can be claimed in all fairness that foreign students cost more than they bring in, owing to the subsidization of higher education. This is also the case in the former Communist countries such as the Soviet Union, where students were received for ideological reasons, but after the collapse of Communism were no longer welcome for a number of years because of the high costs to their hosts' faltering economies.

At the end of the 20th century, the international movement of students as an export commodity had spread over the European continent and became a more important element of higher education policy than it had been in the past, both at the national and institutional level. Examples of this new focus can be seen, for instance, in the Netherlands. Policy documents of the Dutch government declare the recruitment of foreign students to be a policy issue. This is a significant change from the previous two decades, when national policy aimed at discouraging foreign students from study in the Netherlands.[7] Similar trends can be observed in France, Germany and Scandinavia, although in these cases the rationale of status and indirect, long-term economic effects is more important than direct income, which is the driving rationale in the United Kingdom.[8]

The Research and Technological Development Programs

The internationalization of research is a phenomenon that is generally accepted worldwide. International joint ventures of research groups are not exceptional, and there is a long tradition of conferences, seminars, workshops and congresses for academic exchange of ideas and findings. In addition, the technological needs of modern society demand very expensive research projects that individual research groups, institutions of higher education, companies or even national governments cannot finance alone. Therefore, a logical role exists for the European Commission in stimulating international cooperation in science and research in the Union: to stimulate those activities in which European cooperation offers major advantages and generates the maximum beneficial effects. Another rationale was the challenge posed by new technologies and related competition with the U.S. and Japan.

A research and development (R&D) stimulation policy was in existence several years before the moves took place to establish a general education policy in the EC. In the period between the 1960s and 1983, cooperation in this field was mainly intergovernmental and the role of the EC was still marginal and concentrated on coal, nuclear energy, and steel. In 1974, it expanded to other areas, in particular based on the establishment of a Committee for Scientific and Technical Research (CREST). In 1979, a stimulus towards an R&D policy was given with the establishment of the European Strategic Program for Research and Development in Information Technology (ESPRIT), followed by programs such as RACE (communication technology), BRITE (industrial technology), SPRINT (innovation and technology transfer) and ECLAIR (linkages between agriculture and industry).

According to Preston (1991), the objectives of the European R&D policy were:

– to establish a European research and technology community;
– to increase the capacity of European industry to develop its own technological capability through research and innovation;
– to strengthen the international competitiveness of the European economy;
– to establish uniform rules and standards where these were needed; and
– to improve the quality of life and living.

As is clear from these objectives, Europeanization, harmonization and globalization are central elements in this policy.

Since 1984, most of the programs have taken place within so-called Framework Programs, the first running from 1984 to 1987, the second from 1987 to 1991, the third from 1990 to 1994, and the fourth from 1995 to 1999. In 1994, a program for "Training and Mobility of Researchers" was approved. Larédo (1997) sees the development of public-private networks of research institutes with industry, based on the public initiative of the European Union, as an extremely valuable result of the Framework Programs. These programs promoted a new structural arrangement whereby large European firms gained access to new technologies, stimulated industrial competitiveness, and were geared towards innovation in "collective goods."

The EC Mobility Programs

During the late 1970s and early 1980s, the notion of "study abroad"—in the sense of sending students to foreign institutions of higher education as part of their home degree program—became an issue on the continent that overshadowed the developments in individual mobility of students. Since the 1980s, student mobility as a one-way, individual process stimulated by political and/or economic considerations has (with the exception of the United Kingdom) lost prominence as a policy issue. It has been marginalized by the greater attention given to student mobility within the framework of exchange programs, which have been among the top priorities in higher education policies of the 1980s and 1990s. Before this period, organized programs for the exchange of students and staff did exist, but these programs were limited in both funding and scope, stimulating mainly unrelated exchanges at the postgraduate level.

The 1976 "Joint Study Programs" scheme of the EC aimed at the promotion of joint programs of study and research between institutions in several member states. The focus of this experimental program was primarily the stimulation of academic mobility within the EC. The program grew gradually from 32 projects in its first year

(1976–77), to 200 in 1983–84, with a budget of 700,000 European Currency (ECU). In 1984, the Commission added a budget line for student grants into the Joint Study Programs Scheme. This scheme was replaced in 1987 by its successor, the European Action Scheme for the Mobility of University Students (ERASMUS).

The action program of 1976 was the basis for future activities in academic cooperation and exchange within the European Community. The member states limited the role of the European Community in the field of education, however, to complementary measures, decided only with the authorization of the Council of Ministers. Education would remain the exclusive task of the national governments, although from 1982 onwards, social and economic factors gave the Commission more room to extend its role in this area (Brouwer, 1996, pp. 202–205). The objectives that the EU policy for education sought to achieve in that period were: a multicultural Europe; a Europe of mobility; a Europe of education for all; a Europe of expertise; and a Europe open to the world (ibid, p. 252). One can observe in these objectives a more pragmatic and less ambitious approach. Pluralism and complementarity are more dominant than harmonization and Europeanization.

Ironically, the lack of a legal basis for action in the field of higher education gave the European Commission a great deal of freedom for creative programmatic action in the field of education in the period after 1982—a freedom and creativity that would have been less within a more formal legal structure. The launch of COMETT in 1986 (a program for cooperation between higher education and industry) and of ERASMUS in 1987 (a program for cooperation within higher education) were followed by several other education programs.[9]

Wächter et al. (1999, p. 63) call ERASMUS "the Community's flagship program," which— although it might be perceived as such in the higher education community— is an exaggeration of its importance. Since the implementation of the ERASMUS program in 1987, however, significant results have been achieved in cooperation and exchange within higher education in the European Union. Thanks to ERASMUS, between 1987 and 2003 more than a million students have been exchanged. In 1991, the European Free Trade Agreement (EFTA) countries were allowed to take part in the ERASMUS program, and when Austria, Finland and Sweden joined the EU in 1995, Norway (which stayed out of the EU) was allowed to continue its participation.[10] Switzerland, which had also decided not to join the EU, did not get that privilege, because of disagreement on other issues. This country established a separate budget to continue participation in ERASMUS activities on a bilateral basis. In 1998–1999, the SOCRATES program[11] was gradually opened to countries from Central and Eastern Europe, including Bulgaria, the Czech Republic, Hungary, Poland, Romania, Slovakia and Slovenia, as well as the Baltic States (Estonia, Latvia and Lithuania) and Cyprus, even before (with the exception of Romania) they became members of the EU in 2004. Romania and (as of 2004) Turkey continue to take part in the EU programs.

In the 1990s, the creative and informal period of educational policy of the European Community came to an end. The Maastricht Treaty—signed in 1992 and ratified on November 1, 1993—included education for the first time. This decision was, according to Brouwer, (1996, p. 229) influenced by the following factors: the existing practice of cooperation in education; a recognition of the important contribution of education to the realization of the objectives of the treaty and related policies; existing jurisprudence of the Court of Justice in Luxembourg (since 1985) in the field of education; the need to expand the responsibilities of the community as a result of the decisions on European Monetary Union (EMU) and European Political Union (EPU); and changing opinions on the role of the European institutions and national governments among the member states.

In preparation for the changing role of education under the Maastricht Treaty, the European Commission presented two memoranda, one on open distance education and one on higher education. The first one expanded the role of the Commission to a new important area of education; the second confirmed the new role of the Commission with respect to higher education.

In 1991, the EC published the "Memorandum on Higher Education in the European Community." This document was the basis for an intensive debate on the role of the European Union in education and on the future of the educational programs. The "added value" of EU action in the sphere of education is significant, according to the EC and in the words of its president, Jacques Delors: "The mutual integration and opening up to each other of general education and professional training systems are an economic issue, in terms of maintaining competitiveness, and a political issue, in terms of defending democracy and human rights."[12]

Although in general it was well received, critical comments were made by the educational sector on the one-sided focus by the EC on economic and political criteria at the expense of a broader cultural and academic approach.

The importance of strengthening the European dimension in education was placed high on the agenda. The programs should contribute to the realization of this dimension and its four objectives (Brouwer, 1996, p. 262):

- preparation of young people for their involvement in the economic and social development of the European Community;
- improvement of their knowledge of the historical, cultural, economic and social aspects of the union and its member states, the European integration process, daily life in other member states, and the relation of the EU with other countries;
- improvement of their opinion in the advantages of the EU, the challenges of its greater economic and social space, the European identity, the value of European civilization and the foundations for its present development; and
- strengthening of their image of Europe as a Europe of citizens and improvement of the knowledge of its languages.

Related issues that were also given attention were the development of a European Credit Transfer System (ECTS) as part of ERASMUS/SOCRATES,[13] recognition of diplomas, and the development of an open European space for cooperation in higher education. All together, these new measures redirected step by step the scope of the debate to harmonization, integration and Europeanization, moving gradually away from the previous direction of pluralism and complementarity, but without stating that explicitly as such. The end of the 1980s also saw the development of the EC's relationships and involvement with other parts of the world.

The Involvement of the EC with the Rest of the World

The role of the European Commission in higher education has not been limited to educational mobility and exchange within the European Union.

Cooperation within Central and Eastern Europe. The opening up of Central and Eastern Europe has had an enormous impact on higher education in this region and on cooperation between institutions of higher education in Western, Central and Eastern Europe. As Denis Kallen (1991) makes clear, academic cooperation and exchange already existed before this opening up and was developing rapidly in the 1980s, in particular with Poland and Hungary. Cooperation concentrated mainly on staff exchanges and far less on student exchanges. From the point of view of the regimes in these countries, academic cooperation was mainly a political issue and little institutional or personal autonomy was possible.

Although, as Ladislav Cerych (1996) states, the opening up of Central and Eastern Europe had a global effect, the increase in academic mobility with Western Europe was quantitatively greater than with any other area. Regional proximity and the political push by national governments and the European Commission formed the basis for this strong inner-European academic cooperation. The EC, through its so-called PHARE program[14] for European enlargement, opened the way in 1989 for several forms of cooperation, both in R&D and in education. An example is the "Trans European Mobility Program for University Studies"—the TEMPUS scheme. Its general objective was to contribute, as part of the overall PHARE program, to the general economic, social and humanitarian reforms in Central and Eastern Europe, and to their transition to a market economy and multi-party system. Its specific objectives (Brouwer, 1996, p. 300) were to:

- simplify the coordination of support in the area of exchange and mobility of students and staff;
- contribute to the improvement of the quality of higher education;
- stimulate cooperation with EC partners;
- extend opportunities for foreign language study; and
- extend opportunities for study and internships.

In summary, the program provides support for the development of education by way of mobility grants for students and faculty as well as through infrastructural support. In the second phase, 1993–1996, the specific objectives were more oriented toward national needs (and strengthening the development of higher education systems) than to mobility and economic aid.

Thanks to TEMPUS and other programs supported by national governments and other international private and public organizations, a rapid improvement in the educational infrastructure and of the quality of education in Central and Eastern Europe has been achieved. One of the main problems still to be solved is the brain drain of qualified faculty and students. But although this and many other important problems remain to be solved, an important step forward in bridging the gap between higher education in Western and Central and Eastern Europe has been made. Also, in the area of R&D, the situation in Central and Eastern Europe is better than it was 15 years ago, thanks to the support of the EC and national governments. Now, most of these countries have become members of the EU or at least are accepted as participants in the EU programs. Further, all the countries (including, since 2003, Russia) have signed the Bologna Declaration and are taking part in its development process.

Cooperation with Countries Outside Europe. The cooperation programs of the EU also go beyond Europe. For example, a program was launched in 1990 to promote cooperation in higher education with the Maghreb countries around the Mediterranean Sea (MEDCAMPUS).[15] In 1994, a similar program called *América Latina–Formación Académica* (ALFA) was set up to stimulate cooperation with Latin American universities. The activities funded by this program include the development of academic and administrative management; measures to facilitate recognition, development and adaptation of curricula; cooperation between institutions of higher education and companies; innovation and systematization of education; institutional assessment; joint research projects; and the mobility of students (Wächter et al., p. 1, 1999, p. 65). In 2002, an additional program was established: *América Latina–Bolsas de Alto Nível* (ALBAN), a joint scholarship program for Latin American postgraduate students and professionals who need to improve their professional knowledge or skills in any European higher education institution or center of research. The creation of the European, Latin American and Caribbean Space for Higher Education in 2004 (in Guadalajara, Mexico) in connection with the meeting of heads of states of the three regions, is intended to strengthen even further the cooperation in higher education between these regions.

In Asia, the EU launched several bilateral projects and programs, of which the most important are the EU–China Higher Education Cooperation Program of 1996 and the EU–India Cross-Cultural Program of 1997, both of which were intended to stimulate the development of European Studies degrees and centers and to provide professorships, fellowships and grants for study and training.

In North America, the introduction of a program for cooperation in higher and vocational education between the European Union and the U.S. in 1993 (formalized in 1995) and a similar program for cooperation with Canada in 1995 were intended to confirm to the transatlantic partners that the process of "Europeanization" is not intended to create a "Fortress Europe." In October 1995, an official EC/US scheme for cooperation in higher education was established. The U.S. counterpart of the EC for the pilot phase and the final program is the Fund for the Improvement of Post-Secondary Education (FIPSE). One month later, a similar EC/Canada program was launched. The Canadian counterparts of the European Commission DG XXII are Human Resources Development Canada (HRDC) and the Department of Foreign Affairs and International Trade (DFAIT).[16]

The early fear on the part of some governments and academics outside Europe of the emergence of a "Fortress Europe" in international education has been proved to be unfounded by a booming number of exchange agreements and programs of cooperation, linking institutions of higher education in Europe with counterpart institutions all over the world. Guy Haug (2000, p. 28) predicts that, in the future, when the European internal market is more or less established, there will be an even stronger emphasis on exchange and cooperation between Europe and the rest of the world.

This is reflected in the creation of the new ERASMUS Mundus program, starting in 2004 and intended to create high level joint degree programs between EU institutions and those from elsewhere in the world. The rationales for this program, according to Gonzales (2002, pp. 30–31) include the desire to:

- provide a response to the growing internationalization of higher education;
- ensure that the United States of America and Australia are not the sole poles of attraction for international students;
- ensure that Europe retains the leading edge of educational development by sharing best practices and experiences with third-country institutions;
- encourage better recognition around the world of Europe's role as a center of educational excellence; and
- ensure that future world leaders have a better understanding of Europe's culture and history, and of its contributions and potential, particularly in higher education.

These initiatives may have been launched by the EC or national governments, but others have developed independently of such funding, and are based instead on the growing awareness in higher education that the world of science is not limited to Europe.[17]

Linkages with Development Aid Programs. Support to the Third World in general—and to higher education in the South in particular—has received significant attention throughout Western Europe. The European Commission in the 1990s became one of the international funding organizations for development cooperation in the educational field, alongside national governments, international organizations such as the World Bank, foundations and institutions of higher education themselves. Although cooperation in education with the developing world was already mentioned in the early 1970s as a potential area for the EC, the role of the EC remained marginal as development cooperation was seen as a national responsibility. In the so-called "Report Janne of 1973" (on EU policy for training), cooperation with developing countries is mentioned as one area of concern. In the same year, Commissioner Dahrendorf confirmed this in his work program (Brouwer, 1996, pp. 76–78). Activities in this area took place mainly in the scope of R&D action programs (such as Life Sciences and Technologies for Developing Countries).

Complementarity is one of the main objectives of the EC in this area, together with the strengthening and development of democracy; durable economic and social development; integration in the world economy; and the fight against poverty. In 1994, the role of the EC in education and development cooperation was recognized. But given the sensitive relationship between national and EC responsibilities, the activities of the Commission in this area are developing only gradually (ibid., pp. 475–477).

The Present Decade: Towards Harmonization of Systems and Structures

This overview of the development of higher education Europeanization between the 1960s and 1990s illuminates how these developments have culminated in a broad range of recent programs and activities to stimulate a European dimension in higher education. The main focus lay in the Europeanization of higher education with an emphasis on R&D, mobility of students and staff, curriculum development and network building. As the Director for Education of the European Commission, David Coyne, noted in a 2004 interview (EAIE Forum, p. 13), the EU academic mobility programs—ERASMUS in particular—have "created an indispensable foundation for the European Higher Education Area."

At the turn of the century, Europe prepares for a big step forward in Europeanization, manifested in the Bologna Declaration on the European Higher Education Area. The groundwork for what is already widely known in higher education as the "Bologna Declaration" was laid by the "Sorbonne Declaration," signed on May 25, 1998 in Paris by the ministers of education of France, Germany, Italy and the United Kingdom on the occasion of the anniversary of the University of Paris. In this "Joint declaration on harmonization of the architecture of the European higher education system," the ministers of the four dominant countries of the European Union foresee that Europe is:

> Heading for a period of major change in education and working conditions, to a diversification of courses of professional careers, with education and training throughout life becoming a clear obligation. We owe our students and our society at large, a higher education system in which they are given the best opportunities to seek and find their own area of excellence. An open European area for higher learning carries a wealth of positive perspectives, of course respecting our diversities, but requires on the other hand continuous efforts to remove barriers and to develop a framework for teaching and learning, which would enhance mobility and an ever closer cooperation (Sorbonne Declaration, May 25, 1998).

The Sorbonne Declaration was a French initiative based on the Attali report *Pour un Modèle Européen d'Enseignement Supérieur*, which compares the French system with other European systems of higher education as the basis for a reform of the French system. The declaration came as a surprise—not only to the higher education community but also to the European Commission and the ministers of education of the other member states. It seemed rather unlikely that four countries with fundamentally different higher education traditions would be willing to lead the way to harmonization. In 1993, as part of the Maastricht Treaty, education did become an area in which the European Commission could take action, but only as a subsidiary focus. Thus, joint European action on higher education was not high on the agenda of the European Council of Ministers.

It appears that the ministers of education of the four countries acted deliberately as representatives of their national governments, outside the context of the European Commission. Perhaps they saw this as a way to maintain control over the necessary process of harmonization. Such a proposal would have been far more difficult to sell if presented by the Commission, by one of each of the four larger countries, or by the smaller countries.[18] Thus, the U.K. needed France, Italy and Germany to convince the British public of the advantages of a joint initiative to harmonize European higher education with the British system. The Germans, for their part, needed the support of the other countries to sell a plan at home to introduce the bachelor's and master's degree structure.[19] And the French and Italians needed the others to convince their peoples of the need for reform of their higher education systems, something that had previously been blocked by massive protests.

Of course, intensive debates followed. However, the Sorbonne Declaration was surprisingly well received, both in the political arena and in the higher education community of the four countries, as well as in the rest of Europe. Andris Barblan (1999) gives the following explanations for this positive reception:[20]

- The process was initiated from unexpected quarters, the European role of the Commission being taken over at the national level by ministers of education: "Four Ministers were calling the European tune."
- Political decision makers were urging the development of a process they had entrusted earlier to those people first responsible for higher education—academics.
- The discussion at the Sorbonne was an extremely rare constellation of users, providers and political leaders. "The declaration was itself part of a learning process aiming at a long-term goal, the European space of higher education—still to be defined."

This positive reception of the Sorbonne Declaration set the stage for a broader initiative. On the invitation of the Italian minister of education, a meeting took place in Bologna, Italy. The debate was based on the Sorbonne Declaration and on a study prepared by the Association of European Universities (CRE) and the Confederation of European Union Rectors' Conferences on "Trends in European Learning Structures" (Haug et al., 1999). The study showed the extreme complexity and diversity of curricular and degree structures in European countries. Whereas the Sorbonne Declaration spoke of harmonization, both the study and the resulting Bologna Declaration avoided this word—owing largely to the potential negative interpretations. Instead, the study speaks of "actions which may foster the desired convergence and transparency in qualification structures in Europe."

It is important to observe that above all, the Bologna process reconfirmed trends under way in Germany, Austria and Denmark to introduce a bachelor's and master's degree structure. Second, it has stimulated similar movements in countries such as the Netherlands, where several universities had already started to develop bachelor's and master's degrees and where the minister of education had paved the way for allowing them to do so. The declarations, in themselves an attempt to keep a political grip on developments in the higher education sector, serve as a catalyst for reform of higher education throughout Europe. There is still a long way to go. Radical reforms in higher education traditionally spark massive protests, and even more so when such a reform—as David Crossier (2004, p. 14) observes—"is often simplistically and mistakenly portrayed as moving European higher education systems closer to Anglo-Saxon traditions."

On June 19, 1999, in Bologna, Italy, the ministers of education of 29 European countries signed the Declaration on the "European Higher Education Area." The wide support for this declaration beyond the member states of the European Union is unique and has attracted broad international attention. In the declaration, the ministers outline their intentions of achieving the following objectives:

- adoption of a system of easily understood and comparable degrees, including the adoption of a Diploma Supplement;
- adoption of a system essentially based on two main cycles, undergraduate and graduate;
- establishment of a system of credits—such as the European Credit Transfer System (ECTS)—as a means of promoting student mobility;
- promotion of mobility by overcoming obstacles to the effective exercise of free movement;
- promotion of European cooperation in quality assurance; and
- promotion of the European dimension in higher education.

The creation of a European space for higher education, the prime objective of the Bologna Declaration, should be completed in 2010. A set of specific objectives has been formulated to make this possible:

- a common framework of understandable and comparable degrees;
- undergraduate and postgraduate levels in all countries;
- ECTS-compatible credit systems;
- a European dimension in quality assurance; and
- the elimination of remaining obstacles to mobility.

Every two years, the Bologna process is monitored in order to assess its progress. The second meeting took place in 2001 in Prague, Czech Republic. The number of participating countries increased from 29 to 33, and the ministers confirmed their commitment to the six steps outlined in the declaration, while adding three new areas:

- lifelong learning, as a means to help European citizens to become more competitive by allowing them to learn new technologies;
- inclusion of higher education institutions and students, recognizing and further encouraging the active involvement of the higher education institutions and student organizations in the Bologna process; and
- promoting the attractiveness of the European Higher Education Area.

The third meeting took place in 2003 in Berlin, Germany. The number of signatory countries increased to 40, the most important addition being Russia. Two new actions were added in the Berlin document:

- creating the European Higher Education Area and European Research Area—two pillars of the knowledge based society, recognizing the close link between education and research, and including the doctoral level as the third cycle in the Bologna process; and
- stocktaking midway through the process (by a series of reports on the progress), in particular with respect to quality assurance, the two-cycle system and the recognition of degrees and periods of studies.[21]

The fourth meeting took place in 2005 in Bergen, Norway, and assessed the progress of the process mid-term. The preparation was in the hands of a Follow-up Group, composed of the representatives of all members of the Bologna process and the European

Commission, with the Council of Europe, the European University Association, the European Association of Institutions in Higher Education (EURASHE), the National Unions of Students in Europe (ESIB), and the European Center for Higher Education of UNESCO (UNESCO-CEPES). The composition of the Follow-up Group is an illustration of the active involvement of the different stakeholders in higher education, and in particular a recognition of the importance of involving the student unions, even though they may have different views on certain aspects and potential implications of the process.[22]

Both the European University Association (EUA) and ESIB over the past several years have organized events to discuss their views and input regarding the Bologna process, including the Conventions of European Higher Education Institutions in Salamanca, Spain, in 2001, and in Gratz, Austria, in 2002 (initiated by EUA), as well as a meeting of national student unions in Göteborg, Sweden, in 2001. The Salamanca Convention emphasized as necessary conditions the European tradition of higher education as a public good (rather than as a mere commercial commodity), university autonomy, and the crucial role of quality assurance mechanisms. In Gratz, the convention agreed upon a declaration in which the higher education institutions urged for:

- maintaining universities as a public responsibility;
- consolidating research as an integral part of higher education;
- improving academic quality by building strong institutions;
- furthering mobility and the social dimension;
- supporting the development of a policy framework for Europe in quality assurance; and
- pushing forward the Bologna process (EUA, 2003).

The students gathered in Göteborg put emphasis on the social dimension of mobility, cultural diversity, and in particular, free and equal access to all levels of higher education. The main concern of ESIB is the strong focus on the economic role of education and the strong focus on competition, noting that "One of the main dangers is that the structural reforms towards greater transparency of European higher education make this education tradable on a global market."[23]

The call for more emphasis on quality assurance mechanisms in the course of the process has come more to the forefront than at the start. As Guay Haug (2003) states, "in spite of the hesitation of many institutions and systems and the active resistance of some, an organized answer at the European level is necessary in quality assurance/accreditation." The European Network for Quality Assurance (ENQA) plays an active role in initiating discussions and actions to provide such an answer. In the area of accreditation for continental Europe, a new phenomenon linked directly to the Bologna process—the creation of a European Consortium for Accreditation in Higher Education (ECA) by 13 accreditation organizations in eight European countries (Austria, Ireland, Germany, Flanders, Norway, Spain, Switzerland and the Netherlands)—is another manifestation of the growing attention given to this issue. The objective of ECA is to achieve mutual recognition of each other's accreditation decisions by the end of 2007.[24]

The Bologna Declaration not only looks at the internal implications for higher education, but also explicitly refers to the need to increase the international competitiveness of European higher education and to make it more attractive to students from other continents (Van der Wende, 2000). In that sense, the declaration follows the pattern visible everywhere, with competitiveness becoming a driving rationale for the internationalization of higher education. As Van der Wende (1997, p. 227) observed in her study on national policies for the internationalization of higher education, one can see a shift in dominance of rationales (from political to economic rationales) in Northwestern Europe over the past ten years. In a more recent study, she described this as a shift in paradigms from cooperation to competition (Van der Wende, 2001, p. 249). The creation of a European identity and the development of competitiveness (vis-à-vis the rest of the world) are the key motivators for the political initiatives in education put forth by the European Commission.

If we try to understand the rationales from those countries that are tuition-free or charge rather low tuitions—in other words, continental Europe—from a national point of view, the driving rationales for an international market approach include: economic growth and competitiveness, national and regional identity, and profile/status. In those countries, the stakeholders—which are the driving forces behind this orientation on marketing—seem to be national governments, in particular, Ministries of Economic Affairs. They have found their justification in the appeal from the Bologna process to make higher education in Europe more competitive, and in the incorporation of education in the General Agreement on Trade in Services (GATS) (Knight, 2002).

Van Vught et al. (2002, p. 117) though, in answering the question of whether the Bologna process is an adequate European response to the wider challenges of globalization, comes to the conclusion, that "in terms of both practice and perceptions, internationalization is closer to the well-established tradition of international cooperation and mobility and to the core academic values of quality and excellence, whereas globalization refers more to competition, pushing the concept of higher education as a tradable commodity and challenging the concept of higher education as a public good." And Cerych (2002, p. 123) states that "the Bologna process represents a more or less traditional inter-governmental process, relatively flexible, respectful of university autonomy and automatically supportive of diversity of higher education." In that respect, it would be a simplification to see the Bologna process as merely a response to globalization; more accurately, it can be seen as a form of internationalization and Europeanization of higher education at a new level, moving from ad hoc initiatives towards systematic effort, and in the end from disconnected and specific actions to an integrated internationalization of higher education (Teichler, 1999, pp. 9–10).

As mentioned before, the Bologna Declaration should be seen in connection to another ambitious process, agreed upon by the members of the European Council at their meeting in Lisbon in March 2000, "to become the most competitive and dynamic knowledge-based economy in the world, capable of sustainable growth with more and better jobs and greater social cohesion." Its rationale is based on the fact that according to the European Council, "The European Union is confronted with a quantum shift resulting from globalization and the challenges of a new knowledge-driven economy.

These changes are affecting every aspect of people's lives and require a radical transformation of the European economy. The Union must shape these changes in a manner
consistent with its values and concepts of society and also with a view to the forthcoming enlargement" (European Council, 2000).

The Lisbon Strategy is among others directed to the development of a European
Research Area. "Research activities at national and Union level must be better integrated
and coordinated to make them as efficient and innovative as possible, and to ensure
that Europe offers attractive prospects to its best brains. The instruments under the
Treaty and all other appropriate means, including voluntary arrangements, must be
fully exploited to achieve this objective in a flexible, decentralized and non-bureaucratic
manner. At the same time, innovation and ideas must be adequately rewarded within
the new knowledge-based economy, particularly through patent protection" (European
Council, 2000).[25] The link between the two processes, as we have seen, was established
at the Berlin meeting in 2003, where the close link between education and research
was confirmed.

The Lisbon Strategy is more ambitious than the Bologna Declaration, but at the
same time less concrete in its actions.[26] The European Commission in 2004 confirmed
doubts expressed by politicians and the higher education sector that its objectives will
not be reached by 2010 as was originally planned, but nevertheless holds to its agenda.
Together, the two processes will strive to create a European Higher Education, Research
and Innovation Area.

Will higher education in Europe in 2010 be more innovative, homogeneous and
transparent? David Crossier (2004) states that "the nature of the reform process—with
each country moving in its own way towards a common, but somewhat elusive, goal—
has understandably sometimes generated confusion and thrown up contradictions. In
terms of core reforms, such as the introduction of a two-cycle degree system, debate and
discussion on the direction of reform of course reflects the diversity of national systems,
cultures and traditions. Hence, reforms which are intended to improve transparency by
using common terminology may sometimes inadvertently muddy the picture" (Crossier,
2004, p. 14). National agendas at this stage of implementation appear in many cases
to be more important than the common agenda of the Bologna Declaration—in the
implementation of credit points, in the lengths of the two cycles, in the choice between
a binary or one single higher education system, in the way quality assurance and
accreditation are organized (institutional and/or by program), etc. In the end, there will
be more transparency in terminology and generic frameworks (e.g., the use of bachelor's
and master's, accreditation, credit points, etc.). But under that broad transparency, a
more diverse higher education will evolve. In that respect, it will not differ from the
American higher education culture, which is also based on a common terminology
and generic frameworks, but heterogeneous in the way the institutions operate. The
innovation agenda is more challenging and requires more commitment and investment
at the national and regional level than at present is the case. In sum, the Bologna process
and the Lisbon Agenda link reform of higher education with a joint effort to improve
R&D—a necessary and unavoidable process to prepare European higher education for
future competition and cooperation, both within the European Higher Education Area
as well as with the rest of the world.

Notes

1. For an overview and analysis of European higher education systems and structures, see Haug, et al. (1999), "Trends in Learning Structures in Higher Education."
2. See of the Lisbon Strategy for instance http://europa.eu.int/comm/education/policies/2010 /et_2010_en.html; and for the Copenhagen Process http://europa.eu.int/comm/educaiton /policies/2010 /vocational_en.html.
3. These phases are more or less the same as those presented by Field (1998, p. 25–26), who speaks of four stages: 1957–1973, when education and training received relatively little interest; 1974–1985, development of some interest but mainly in vocational training; 1986–1992, education becomes a significant area of policy for the EU; 1992 onwards, development of a more radical approach seeking to promote the concept and practice of the learning society.
4. The following sections of this chapter draw from chapter 3, *The International Dimension of Higher Education in Europe*, of de Wit (2002), *Internationalization of higher education in the United States of America and Europe. A historical, comparative and conceptual analysis.* Westport, CT: Greenwood Press.
5. In 1981, Greece would become the tenth member. In 1986, Spain and Portugal were included; in 1990, the former DDR, as part of Germany; and in 1995, Sweden, Finland and Austria.
6. See for instance Wächter, et al. (1999, p. 62), and Brouwer (1996, p. 74).
7. With the exception of students from developing countries, provided with fellowships to be trained at specialized International Education Institutes.
8. The change from political to economic rationale as the dominant rationale in Northern European internationalization strategies is clear from the reports in Kälvermark and Van der Wende (1997), although less for Southern European countries as the Greek report illustrates.
9. EURTECNET, a scheme for the development of professional education and information technology, in 1985; PETRA, a program to promote cooperation and exchange in further education, in 1987; DELTA, a scheme for learning technologies, in 1988; IRIS (later NOW), a scheme to promote professional education for women, in 1989; LINGUA, a scheme for the promotion of the learning of European languages, in 1989; and FORCE, a scheme for continuing education of workers, in 1990 (Brouwer, 1996; Wächter, 1999).
10. In 1989, the Nordic countries, Norway, Sweden, Finland and Denmark, created their own program for cooperation and exchange in education: Nordplus. This program continues to be active, even after the inclusion of Sweden, Finland and Norway in the European programs in 1991.
11. SOCRATES is not an acronym, and is often used interchangeably with Socrates. Like Erasmus, the program is named after the philosopher.
12. Delors, Jacques (1994), interview in *Le Magazine.* European Commission, summer 1994, Issue 2, Brussels.
13. ERASMUS is not an acronym, and is often used interchangeably with ERASMUS. Like SOCRATES, the program is named after the philosopher.
14. PHARE is not an acronym, and is often used interchangeably with Phare.
15. In 1996 this program was frozen, but it is in the process of being restarted.
16. For a critical analysis, see de Wit, 2004.
17. See for instance Laureys (1992, p. 110). ERASMUS has also been the inspiration for similar regional plans without involvement of the European Union, for instance in Asia and the "Program for North American Mobility in Higher Education" between the U.S., Mexico and Canada, in the framework of NAFTA.
18. In reality, some smaller countries such as Denmark were already further on their way towards accomplishing what the Sorbonne Declaration intended.
19. A structure that was introduced into Germany in 1998, parallel to the present structure.
20. Andris Barblan, Secretary General of CRE, presentation to the XII Santander Group General Assembly, April 17, 1999 on "The Sorbonne Declaration: follow-up and implications, a personal view."
21. Stocktaking already has been an important part of the process from the beginning, in the form of Trends reports, prepared by the European University Association:

- Trends I, Trends in Learning Structures in higher Education, 1999
- Trends II, 2001
- Trends III, Progress towards the European Higher Education Area, 2003.

22. For more information on the Bologna Process see for instance: http://www.eua.be:8080/eua/en/policy_bologna.jsp ; http://www.wes.org/ewenr/bolognaprocess; http://www.bologna-berlin 2003.de; http://www.bologna-bergen2005.no; and http://www.enqa.net/bologna.lasso.
23. See http://www.esib.org/policies/esibbologna.htm.
24. That the British accreditation organization has not yet joint the ECA is caused by the difference in approach to accreditation: in the United Kingdom by institution, in the other countries by program.
25. The European Research Area is described by the European Commission as follows: "Europe has a long-standing tradition of excellence in research and innovation, and European teams continue to lead progress in many fields of science and technology. However our centers of excellence are scattered across the continent and all too often their efforts fail to add up in the absence of adequate networking and cooperation. In the past, collaborative actions have been initiated at European and Community level, but now is the time to bring our endeavors together and to build a research and innovation equivalent of the "common market" for goods and services. That structure is called the European Research Area and is regrouping all Community supports for the better coordination of research activities and the convergence of research and innovation policies, at national and EU levels" (http://europa.eu.int/comm/research/era).
26. Blank and Lopez-Claros (2004) identify eight dimensions in the strategy: creating an information society for all; developing a European area for innovation, research and development; liberalization (completing the single market, state aid and competition policy); building network industries (in telecommunications, in utilities and transport); creating efficient and integrated financial services; improving the enterprise environment (for business start-ups, in the regulatory framework); increasing social inclusion (returning people to the workforce, upgrading skills, modernizing social protection); and enhancing social development. They see a mixed performance on these eight dimensions, with the Nordic countries scoring well and southern Europe scoring less well. The EU as a whole receives lower scores than the U.S. in seven out of the eight dimensions, the exception being sustainable development, but with a quite small margin (ibid., 12).

References

Barblan, A. (1999). The Sorbonne Declaration: Follow-Up and Implications: A Personal View. Presentation to the XII Santander Group General assembly, 17 April, 1999.

Baumgratz-Gangl, G. (1993). Cross cultural competence in a changing world. *European Journal of Education, 28*(3), 327–328.

Baron, B. (1993). The politics of academic mobility in Western Europe. *Higher Education Policy,* 6(3).

Blanke, J., & Lopez-Claros, A. (2004). *The Lisbon review 2004: An assessment of policies and reforms in Europe.* Cologny/Geneva: World Economic Forum.

Brouwer, J. (1996). *De Europese gemeenschap en onderwijs. Geschiedenis van de samenwerking en het communitaire beleid op onderwijsgebied (1951–1996).* Baarn, The Netherlands: BKE-Baarn.

Cerych, L. (1996). East–West academic mobility within Europe: Trends and issues. In P. Blumenthal, C. Goodwin, A. Smith, & U. Teichler (Eds.), *Academic mobility in a changing world: Regional and global trends* (contributions to the Wassenaar Colloquium, 1992). London, UK: Jessica Kingsley.

Cerych, L. (2002). Sorbonne, Bologna, Prague: Where do we go from here? In J. Enders & O. Fulton (Eds.), *Higher education in a globalizing world. International trends and mutual observations. A Festschrift in honor of Ulrich Teichler* (pp. 121–126). Dordrecht, The Netherlands: Kluwers Academic Publishers.

Crosier, D. (2004). Progress towards the European higher education area: what the "Trends" reports are telling us. *EAIE Forum*, 6(1), 14–15. (Spring).

de Wit, H. (2002). *Internationalization of higher education in the United States of America and Europe. A historical, comparative and conceptual analysis.* Westport, CT: Greenwood Press.

de Wit, H. (2004). A decade of transatlantic cooperation. *International Higher Education*, 35 (Spring), 3–5.

EAIE Forum. (2004). (Brian Frost Smith) In conversation with David Coin. *EAIE Forum*, 6(1) (Spring).

European Council. (2000). *Presidency conclusions, Lisbon European Council, March 23–24, 2000.* Available online at http://europa.eu.int/comm/lisbon_strategy.

European University Association (EUA). (2003). *Graz Declaration 2003—Forward from Berlin: The role of the universities.* Geneva, Switzerland: EUA.

Field, J. (1998). *European dimensions: Education, training and the European Union.* Higher Education Policy Series no. 39. London: Jessica Kingsley.

Gonzales, A. (2002). The contribution of the European Community to enhancing the global profile of higher education in Europe. In M. Dhondt & B. Wächter (Eds.), *Marketing education worldwide. Papers presented at a Seminar of the Academic Cooperation Association (ACA), Dijon, 2002.* Brussels, Belgium: Academic Cooperation Association.

Gribbon, A. (1994). Idealism or a marriage of convenience? An examination of internal relationships in international exchange programs. *Higher Education Management*, 6(1), 23–31.

Haug, G. (2000). National exchange agencies in the process towards a European space for higher education. *Journal of Studies in International Education*, 4(2), 21–32.

Haug, G. (2003). Quality assurance/accreditation in the emerging European higher education area: A possible scenario for the future. *European Journal of Education*, 3, 229–241. (September).

Haug, G., Kirstein, J., & Knudsen, I. (1999). *Trends in learning structures in higher education.* Project report prepared for the Bologna Conference on 18–19 June 1999 on behalf of the Confederation of European Union Rector's Conferences and CRE. Copenhagen: Danish Rector's Conference Secretariat.

Kallen, D. (1991). Academic exchange in Europe: Towards a new era of cooperation. In *The open door: Pan-European academic cooperation—An analysis and a proposal.* Bucharest, Romania: CEPES/UNESCO.

Kälvermark, T., & Van der Wende, M. (1997). *National policies for the internationalization of higher education in Europe.* Stockholm: Högskoleverket Studies, National Agency for Higher Education.

Kehm, B., & Last, B. (1997). Germany. In T. Kälvermark & M. Van der Wende (Eds.), *National policies for the internationalization of higher education in Europe.* Stockholm: Högskoleverket Studies, National Agency for Higher Education.

Knight, J. (2002). Trade talk: An analysis of the impact of trade liberalization and the General Agreement on Trade in Services on higher education. *Journal of Studies in International Education*, 6(3) (Fall), 209–299.

Larédo, P. (1997). Technological programs in the European Union. In H. Etzkowitz & L. Leydesdorff (Eds.), *Universities and the global knowledge economy: A triple helix of university-industry-government relations.* Science, Technology and the International Political Economy Series. London: Pinter.

Laureys, G. (1992). Mobility has come to stay: Management strategies to meet the demands of internationalization in higher education. *Higher Education Management*, 4(1), 108–120.

Löwbeer, H. (1977). Internationalization of higher education—Sweden: A case study. In A.S. Knowles (Ed.), *The international encyclopedia of higher education.* San Francisco, CA: Jossey-Bass.

Neave, G. (1992). *Institutional management of higher education: Trends, needs and strategies for cooperation.* Unpublished International Association of Universities (IAU) Document for UNESCO, Paris.

Preston, J. (1991). *EC education, training and research programs: An action guide.* London, UK: Kogan Page.

Teichler, U. (1999). Internationalization as a challenge of higher education in Europe. *Tertiary Education and Management*, 5, 5–23.

Van der Wende, M. C. (1997). International comparative analysis and synthesis. In T. Kalvermark & M. Van der Wende (Eds.), *National policies for the internationalization of higher education in Europe*. Stockholm: Hogeskoleverket Studies. National Agency for Higher Education.

Van der Wende, M. C. (2000). The Bologna Declaration: Enhancing the transparency and competitiveness of European higher education. *Journal of Studies in International Education*, *4*(2), 3–10.

Van der Wende, M. C. (2001). Internationalization policies: About new trends and contrasting paradigms. *Higher Education Policy*, *14*(3) (September), 249–259.

Van Vught, F., Van der Wende, M., & Westerheijden, D. (2002). Globalization and internationalization: Policy agendas compared. In J. Enders & O. Fulton (Eds.), *Higher education in a globalizing world: International trends and mutual observations* (pp. 103–120). *A Festschrift in Honor of Ulrich Teichler*. Dordrecht, The Netherlands: Kluwer Academic Publishers.

Wächter, B., Aaro, O., & Brigitte, H. (1999). Internationalisation of Higher Education. In B. Wächter (ed.), Internationalisation in Higher Education: A Paper and Seven Essays on International Co-opration in the Tertiary Sector (pp. 11–92). ACA Papers on International Co-operation in Education. Bonn: Lemmens.

24

HIGHER EDUCATION IN FRENCH-SPEAKING SUB-SAHARAN AFRICA

Juma Shabani
UNESCO Harare Cluster Office, Zimbabwe

The establishment of higher education institutions in French-speaking African countries began in 1896, but it is during the first decade after the independence of these countries that the higher education sector experienced a major development. At that time, the mission assigned to higher education institutions was primarily related to the preparation of human resources needed for operations of the civil service and the development of the education sector.

In French-speaking African countries (also known as Francophone Africa), higher education institutions started facing problems during the 1970s, such as a rapid increase in student enrollments, the insufficiency of financial resources allocated to the higher education sector and the implementation of policies which allocated a significant share of the resources to student scholarships and various subsidized social services provided to students. This trend, which continued at least until the end of the 1980s, led to a significant deterioration of staff working conditions, the degradation of infrastructure and facilities and a lack of teaching materials. Together, these resulted in a major decline in the relevance and quality of higher education offered in these countries.

At the beginning of the 1990s, the decline in relevance and quality of higher education had reached such an alarming level that several French-speaking countries decided to undertake major reforms of their higher education systems in order to enable them to respond more effectively to the challenges of sustainable human development. Towards the end of the 1990s, all the major stakeholders in higher education in Africa had agreed that there was an urgent need for revitalizing higher education in Africa. This support was clearly affirmed at the 1998 UNESCO World Conference on Higher Education and in several subsequent publications, in particular a 2002 World Bank policy document entitled *Constructing Knowledge Societies: New Challenges for Tertiary Education*.

This chapter analyzes the development, challenges and opportunities of higher education in French-speaking African countries during the period from 1960 to 2004. The analysis encompasses the major stages of higher education development in French-speaking countries, covering systems, students and staff issues, research, inter-university cooperation, funding policies and reforms undertaken in selected

James J.F. Forest and Philip G. Altbach (eds.), International Handbook of Higher Education, 483–502.
© *2006 Springer. Printed in the Netherlands.*

countries for revitalizing their higher education systems and institutions. The discussion also includes two examples of opportunities offered to higher education institutions through the implementation of a New Partnership for Africa's Development (NEPAD) initiative and efforts to improve the use of communication and information technologies.

Major Stages of Higher Education Development in Francophone Sub-Saharan Africa

Higher Education Before National Independence

The development of modern higher education in French-speaking Africa goes back to 1896, when the medical institute of Tananarive in Madagascar was established. Not long thereafter, France established the William Ponty Teacher Training School in 1903, on Gorée Island in Senegal, and the Dakar Medical Institute in 1918, also in Senegal.

Beginning in 1941, France established higher education centers in some of its African colonies. These centers—which were affiliated with French universities—were gradually developed into national universities. Until the 1970s, these national universities kept close administrative links with universities in France—in practice, these institutions were virtually certified copies of their French counterparts. France was thus closely involved in the funding and management of national universities in Africa.

In the former Belgian colonies—namely, the Democratic Republic of Congo, Rwanda and Burundi—the history of higher education goes back to 1949, with the establishment of the university center of Lovanium in Kinshasa, which was developed into a full-fledged university in 1954. A second university was established in 1956 in Lubumbashi. In Burundi and Rwanda, higher education started in the early 1960s. The higher education system in these countries was then composed of two major institutions—namely, the Institute of Agriculture and the Faculty of Sciences (Shabani, 2003). As was the case for the former French colonies, the development of higher education in the former Belgian colonies closely followed the Belgian model.

Higher Education After National Independence

After the independence of African countries during the 1960s, the development of higher education in French speaking countries was strongly influenced by the various models of economic development suggested by the World Bank. Today, it is generally agreed that the development of higher education in Africa went through three major stages, which are briefly analyzed below.

First Stage: 1960–1970. At the time of most African countries' independence during the early 1960s, it was agreed that the primary mission of higher education institutions was to prepare human resources as needed for national development, in particular for the operations of the civil service and the development of the educational system. This mission was achieved thanks largely to the support received from bilateral and international cooperation agencies, including the World Bank.

Second Stage: 1970–1990. During this period, several factors contributed to the deterioration of higher education in Africa. Indeed, this period was characterized by economic and financial constraints, which resulted in a reduction in public recurrent expenditure per student from $6,300 in 1980 to $1,500 in 1988 (World Bank, 1995). This decline was more pronounced in French-speaking countries (Samoff & Caroll, 2004). Several countries also experienced dramatic social changes and unrest, which resulted in several arrests and killings of students, frequent closures of university campuses, political repression of academic staff, and persistent brain drain. Many governments became hostile to universities, as they considered them as threats to political stability. During the 1970s and 1980s, the World Bank published four education policy documents, including one focusing on education in sub-Saharan Africa (World Bank, 1988). These documents criticized higher education's role in promoting development and its "over-expansion" in the poorest countries (Samoff & Caroll, 2004), particularly in sub-Saharan Africa. The 1988 policy paper on sub-Saharan Africa emphasized the need for giving more priority to basic education. The major argument for redirecting resources to basic education was based on research studies showing that social rates of return for investments in education were higher for basic education than for higher education. African governments were therefore compelled to give more priority to investment in basic education. They were also challenged to reduce public recurrent expenditure per higher education student, to increase registration and tuition fees, and to promote private higher education.

The priority granted to basic education was reaffirmed during the World Conference on Basic Education for All, held in 1990 in Jomtien, Thailand. The increase of support for basic education may have come at the expense of higher education. Indeed, widening access to basic education required significant resources. But during this period, most African countries did not have the resources needed in order to increase their education budgets. This situation was mainly due to increases in the foreign debt and the payment of debt servicing, the decline in prices of raw materials and agricultural products, the devaluation of national currencies and the implementation of structural adjustment policies. This situation resulted in a further decline in the recurrent expenditure per student, which had already dropped significantly during the period 1980–1988. By 1995, it had fallen to $1,241 (UNESCO, 1998a).

Third Stage: 1990–Present. At the beginning of the 1990s, several French-speaking countries began to develop strategies needed to revitalize their higher education systems. This was the case in Burundi, where the government decided to undertake an institutional and financial audit of the University of Burundi in 1993, and in Senegal, where a national consultation was convened in 1993 in order to reach a consensus on the agenda for the reform of the higher education system.

In 1995, the World Bank published another document, entitled *Higher Education: The Lessons of Experience* (World Bank, 1995), which took stock of activities implemented by the World Bank in developing countries in order to identify the strategies required for the revitalization of higher education in those countries. In the case of sub-Saharan Africa, several strategies had already been proposed in another World Bank document, *Universities in Africa: Strategies for Stabilization and Revitalization* (Saint,

1992). The 1995 document identified four major areas of reform for the revitalization of higher education in developing countries. These include differentiation of institutions, promotion of private institutions, modification of funding policies, redefinition of the role of government and promotion of quality and equity.

During the mid-1990s, at least four factors were used to justify the need for revitalization of higher education in Africa: the advanced stage of deterioration of higher education institutions; the promotion of a holistic approach to the development of the education sector; the need for involving higher education institutions in developing the capacity to achieve Education for All goals (mainly through teacher training programs); and the recognition of the significant role that African universities are expected to play in the process of sustainable human development in the knowledge and information society.

In October 1996, during the annual meetings of the World Bank and the International Monetary Fund, the African Ministers of Finance and the President of the World Bank agreed to work together in order to revitalize African universities. Following this agreement, the Association of African Universities and the World Bank produced a report in 1997, in collaboration with several stakeholders, outlining the strategies and guidelines required for revitalizing African universities. The guidelines are directed at the universities, the African governments, the donor community and the World Bank.

The need for revitalization of higher education in Africa was reaffirmed during the World Conference on Higher Education held in 1998 in Paris (UNESCO, 1998b), and in two major publications: *Higher Education in Developing Countries: Peril and Promise* (UNESCO/World Bank, 2000) and *Constructing Knowledge Societies: New Challenges for Tertiary Education* (World Bank, 2002).

Therefore, today the international environment is very supportive of efforts to revitalize higher education in sub-Saharan Africa, and French-speaking countries should seize this historic opportunity. In reality, several French-speaking countries are already successfully implementing various reforms geared towards the revitalization of their higher education systems.

Higher Education Systems

As indicated earlier in this chapter, the development of higher education in French-speaking Africa was closely modeled along the French and Belgian systems. In almost every country, higher education systems began with the establishment of a center for higher education which was later developed into a full-fledged national university. Following the model of France, in addition to national universities, French-speaking Africa also established schools of engineering, teacher training schools (generally with the assistance of UNESCO) and higher education professional training institutions, supervised by government ministries other than the ministry of higher education. Beginning in the 1990s, the French-speaking countries of Africa also strongly encouraged the establishment of private higher education institutions. However, there are a few exceptions to the process described above. In the former French equatorial African countries—which included Central African Republic, Congo Brazzaville, Gabon and Chad—the higher education system established in the early 1960s consisted of a network of five institutions distributed throughout the four countries (Mintsa mi-Eya, 2003). During the early 1970s, this network broke down because each country decided to establish its own national university. Similarly, in the late 1960s, Togo and Benin established a joint higher education institution with a campus in each country. This arrangement was abandoned in the early 1970s when each country decided to create its own university (Guedegbe, 2003). In Mali, the development of the higher education system began with the establishment of several specialized institutions which were merged in the early 1990s to form the University of Mali, currently known as University of Bamako (Bagayoko & Diawara, 2003). Similarly, the first university in Madagascar was established by merging the independent faculties of law, arts and science and technology and the school of medicine (Stiles, 2003).

Following the rapid increase in student enrollments and the various problems that it generated, French-speaking countries decided to create new university centers in order to reduce enrollments in national universities. This was the case in 1977 in Cameroon, with the establishment of four new university centers, and in 1993 in Côte d'Ivoire, where it was decided to split up the national University of Côte d'Ivoire into three university centers. Later, these centers were developed into independent universities. Several other countries established new universities during the 1990s and at the beginning of 21st century, including Benin, Burkina Faso, Gabon, Madagascar, Senegal and Togo. Furthermore, in order to improve the geographical distribution of higher education institutions, the French-speaking countries established centers of higher education and university colleges, and encouraged the establishment of private universities in selected provinces beginning in 1993. In the Democratic Republic of Congo, 263 private higher education institutions had been established by 1996 throughout the various provinces (Lelo, 2003).

Generally, each French-speaking country also hosts one or more regional specialized schools known as *écoles inter-états*, a campus of the African Virtual University and a campus of the Francophone Virtual University. At the beginning of the 1990s, French-speaking sub-Saharan Africa had already established more than 20 regional specialized schools.

In April 2004, the higher education system of Senegal was composed of two public universities, 15 higher education professional training institutions (of which 12 were supervised by government ministries other than the ministry of higher education), a regional/provincial university center and 42 private higher education institutions. Senegal was also host to several regional specialized schools, a campus of Suffolk University (whose headquarters are in Boston, U.S.), a campus of the African Virtual University and a campus of the Francophone Virtual University. Several other French-speaking countries have similar higher education systems.

It is also worth mentioning that some countries are investing increasingly in distance education, mainly in order to widen access to higher education, raise the quality of education and improve opportunities for lifelong learning. In Madagascar, the National Center of Tele-teaching, established in 1992, offers degree and non-degree courses in 22 regional study centers. In 1997, over 8,000 students were enrolled in university study programs at the Center. By 1999, the Center had already awarded more than 3,900 degrees (Stiles, 2003). In Mauritius, distance education is provided in at least three institutions—the Mauritius College of the Air, the University of Mauritius and the Mauritius Institute of Education (Baichoo, Parahoo, & Fagoonee, 2003).

In order to improve the geographical distribution of higher education institutions and to effectively address the increasing demand for higher education, the government of Senegal is planning to establish in the near future a polytechnic university, two regional university centers and the *Université du Futur Africain,* intended for postgraduate studies. This university, which will be opened to researchers and postgraduate students of other African countries, will operate in close partnership with universities in developed countries.

Higher education systems in French-speaking countries are made up of three levels of studies—the first and second levels consist of two years each, and a third level offers postgraduate education, leading to four different types of degrees:

- Degree of Advanced Studies, which is equivalent to a master's degree. This degree can be obtained after one year of training and research, and prepares students for doctoral programs;
- Postgraduate Degree of Professional Studies, which can also be obtained after one year of professional training;
- Doctorat de 3ème Cycle, which can be obtained after two years of training and research following achievement of the Degree of Advanced Studies; and
- Doctorat d'état, which can be obtained after two to three years of research following achievement of the Doctorat de 3ème Cycle.

In 1987, France decided to abolish the two types of doctoral degrees mentioned above and to introduce a new doctoral degree equivalent to a Ph.D. Some French-speaking African countries (like the Benin Republic) adopted this reform, whereas other countries (like Senegal) are still maintaining the former system. However, it is worth noting that Senegal is in the process of modifying its degree structure, and will eventually offer only three degrees corresponding to the bachelor's, master's and Ph.D. degrees.

Students

In universities throughout the former French colonies, there is no selection for admission into faculties. The only requirement is the diploma of baccalauréat (secondary school leaving certificate), which is equivalent to the A level in the British system. However, in addition to the baccalauréat, candidates to schools of engineering should also pass an entrance examination. In some countries like Burundi, the Democratic Republic of Congo and Guinea, there is also an entrance examination for admission to the faculties. In Guinea, for example, only one-third of the candidates who sit for the entrance examination are admitted into universities (Sylla, Ez-zaïm, & Teferra, 2003). In Madagascar, the government introduced in 1993 a selective admissions process which helped to reduce student enrollment in the universities from 33,202 students in 1993 to 18,945 in 1997 (Stiles, 2003).

This policy of open door access to faculties has led to a rapid increase in student enrollments. In all the French-speaking universities, the capacity of infrastructure and laboratories has largely been exceeded, and the student-staff ratios have steadily declined. This development, combined with the reduction in public resources allocated to higher education, has resulted in high failure rates and a decline in the quality of education. In Benin, it is estimated that a student needs an average of eleven years to complete a four-year program of study (Guedegbe, 2003). However, it is worth mentioning that in French-speaking countries, a high rate of failure occurs at all levels of the education systems. In Gabon, for example, since 1973 the rate of failure in primary education has ranged between 30% and 40%. In 2000, the rate of failure at the secondary school leaving certificate examination was as high as 61.6%, and in the seventh year of the Faculty of Medicine of Omar Bongo University, the rate of failure was 50% (Mignot, 2002). In Madagascar during the period 1996–1998, the rate of failure at the leaving certificate examination ranged between 68% and 75% (Stiles, 2003).

Contrary to the faculties, the enrollments in schools of engineering are quite stable, since admission policies take into account the real capacity of the institutions. In some professional institutions, like the teacher training schools, enrollments are even decreasing. For example, during the period 1987–2000, enrollments in teacher training schools (*écoles normales supérieures*) dropped from 1,500 to 200 students in Côte d'Ivoire (Houenou & Houenou-Agbo, 2003) and from 537 to 264 students in Senegal (Dieng, 2003); similarly, enrollments dropped from 230 in 1998 to 185 in 2000 in Mauritania (Kharchi, 2003).

In French-speaking universities, the bulk of the students are registered in the first two years as well as in the Faculty of Arts and Humanities. For example, in 1997, 53% of the students at the University of Ndjamena in Chad were enrolled in the Faculty of Arts and Humanities (Al Habo, 2003). During that period, students enrolled in the first two years at the University of Dakar in Senegal represented 68.2% of the total student population (Dieng, 2003).

Academic Staff

According to the African and Malagasy Council for Higher Education (CAMES), a sub-regional body in charge of the promotion of academic staff in several French-speaking African countries, the scale of regular academic staff ranks should comprise the following four levels: lecturer, senior lecturer, associate professor and full professor. This classification is different in CAMES member states using national mechanisms for staff promotion like in Burundi and Cameroon. Indeed, in Cameroon academic staff ranks comprise only three levels (Government of Cameroon, 1993), whereas in Burundi this scale is made up of six levels (Shabani, 2003). In general, appointment to each of the above regular positions is made through a presidential decree, following a proposal from the Minister for Higher Education. In addition to the regular academic staff positions, all the universities employ various categories of staff on a contractual basis.

This section of the chapter reviews the conditions for staff recruitment, as well as the benefits, obligations and criteria for staff promotion and academic careers. Usually, these conditions are defined in a Presidential Decree on Higher Education Academic Staff. In each French-speaking country, candidates to the rank of lecturer should hold a postgraduate degree at least equivalent to the Doctorat de 3ème Cycle. In most countries, assistant lecturers are recruited for a period of two years, renewable twice. If they do not manage to get tenure at the end of the six-year period, they are then put at the disposal of the civil service for a new posting. In Burundi, the rank of assistant lecturer is part of the regular academic staff positions. As in the case of student distribution per faculties, there is an unequal distribution of the academic staff per faculties and departments as well as among academic ranks. It is also worth mentioning that in most countries the rapid increase in student enrollment during the 1990s resulted in a significant decrease in student-teacher ratios. However, this was not always the case— for example, the student-teacher ratio in Cameroon improved from 38:1 in 1993 to 34:1 in 1999 (Gaillard & Zink, 2003; Njeuma, 2003). During the period 1993–1997, the government of Madagascar introduced a policy which helped to reduce the student population in the universities by 43%, and at the same time increased the academic staff by 26%. As a result of the implementation of this policy, the student-teacher ratio improved from 47:1 in 1993 to 22:1 in 1996 (Stiles, 2003).

The teaching load roughly ranges between 120 hours per year for full professors to 200 hours for lecturers and 250 hours for assistant lecturers. Statutory remuneration is composed of basic wages and various types of allowances, in particular allowances for administrative assignments, research allowances and overtime for teaching assignments.

During the 1990s, the academic staff conditions of service steadily deteriorated in almost all the countries. Indeed, in all French-speaking countries using the CFA Franc currency, the devaluation of the currency by 50% significantly reduced the purchasing power of the staff. In addition to this, some countries experienced further cuts in staff salary. In Côte d'Ivoire, for example, it is estimated that between 1992 and 2000 the salaries of the various categories of academic staff were reduced by anywhere between 64% and 76% (Houenou & Houenou-Agbo, 2003). In Cameroon, the staff salaries were reduced by 66% in 1993 (Njeuma, 2003). In August 2000, delays in the payment of staff salaries in the Central African Republic had reached 17 months (N'guerekata, 2003).

Regarding academic staff, it is also worth mentioning that during the 1990s, several countries lost a sizeable number of their academic staff because they were either killed in wars or went into exile. This is the case in Rwanda—where thousands of skilled personnel and professionals were killed during the 1994 genocide—as well as Burundi and the Democratic Republic of Congo, each of which experienced a massive brain drain due to political instability and wars. Recently, several countries have taken appropriate measures in order to improve the working conditions of academic staff. For example, in Côte d'Ivoire the new government decided in June 2001 to realign academic staff salaries to their 1992 level, while in Senegal the government has built new staff offices and apartments for staff accommodation.

Research

Like in most African countries, the establishment of modern research institutions in French-speaking Africa goes back to the colonial era. As indicated earlier, during the

1960s it was agreed that higher education institutions should focus on the development of human resources. Consequently, during this period, research was carried out mainly by French researchers in research centers established by France during the colonial period. The operation of these centers was funded by France.

Beginning in the mid-1970s, the French-speaking countries have invested significantly in research development. Indeed, for the period 1970–1985, the public financial resources allocated to research increased sevenfold and the number of researchers and scientific publications grew by a factor of ten. In 1985, Africa contributed almost 1% of the scientific production cited in international bibliographic databases, compared to 3% for Asia and 1.5% for Latin America (Waast, 2004). In 1987, the government of Cameroon funded between 85% and 95% of research activities, including staff salaries (Gaillard & Zink, 2003).

In sub-Saharan Africa, research is undertaken in three types of institutions: universities, national research centers (supervised by government ministries other than the ministry of higher education), and regional and international centers funded by bilateral and international cooperation agencies. Private research is very weak except in South Africa, where the private sector contributes almost 50% of the research budget.

A study carried out recently on the state of research in Africa at the dawn of the 21st century led to the following results (Gaillard & Waast, 2001):

- There are major regional disparities between the various sub-regions of the African continent. Indeed, the study shows that two countries—South Africa and Egypt—produce 50% of scientific publications in Africa, while another four other countries—Morocco, Tunisia, Nigeria and Kenya—produce 25%.
- Senegal, Côte d'Ivoire and Cameroon are the three major producers of science in French-speaking Africa.
- The English-speaking countries of Africa suffered more from the reduction in public resources allocated to research and the deterioration of research facilities. For example, for the period 1989–1999, Nigeria (which occupied the third place in research publications in Africa, after South Africa and Egypt) lost almost half of its research capacity.
- The number of publications produced by French-speaking African countries increased by 30% during the period 1990–1997. In the case of Cameroon, despite the various problems encountered by the research community, the number of publications was increased by a factor of three during the period 1987–2001 (Gaillard & Zink, 2003).
- The publications produced in sub-Saharan Africa mainly focus on the fields of medicine and agriculture.

The study was conducted over a two-year period. It analyzed publications produced between 1989 and 1999 and recorded in two major international bibliographic databases, as well as a questionnaire completed by 1,500 researchers living in 43 African countries, and data collected during field visits to 15 countries.

As was the case for higher education generally, in 1985 the public resources allocated to research started to decrease. Since then, research has been mainly carried out thanks to financial contributions received from bilateral and international cooperation agencies.

In Cameroon, for example, the government portion of funding for research decreased from 95% in 1987 to 60% in 1993, while funding from external sources increased to 40% over the same period (Gaillard & Zink, 2003). In Burkina Faso, more than 90% of the research undertaken by the University of Ouagadougou in 2003 was funded from external sources (Traoré, 2004). The other challenges facing French-speaking countries in the field of research include the limited number of postgraduate programs, qualified researchers and research support staff, isolation of researchers, inadequate research facilities and the low priority given by universities to research activities (Seddoh, 1993).

Since the mid-1990s, the importance of research in aiding sustainable human development has been widely recognized at the African, regional and international levels. Indeed, the revitalization of research in French-speaking Africa is strongly supported by the New Partnership for African Development (NEPAD) and the Economic and Monetary Union of West Africa (UEMOA), through their programs for developing regional research centers of excellence, and through various research funds provided by the Francophone University Agency.

French-speaking countries of Africa also benefit from the contribution of regional research centers funded by bilateral and multilateral cooperation agencies. In West Africa, regional research centers focus their activities in the fields of rice, food crops, solar energy, groundnut and oilseeds, endemic and parasitic diseases, physics and mathematics (Traoré, 2004).

Since 1994, the Francophone University Agency has set up a special fund intended to promote research in sub-Saharan African French-speaking countries. In 2003, the agency funded six major research programs in Burkina Faso and 10 research units in Central and West Africa and in the Indian Ocean (Traoré, 2004).

Thus, as seen in the case of higher education more broadly, the current international environment is very supportive to the revitalization of research in Africa, and French-speaking Africa should take advantage of this opportunity. In reality, some countries have already initiated several activities to encourage the revitalization of research. In Senegal, for example, the University of Dakar is reviving and strengthening its postgraduate programs, and the government is in the process of establishing a national center for scientific research (Sock, 2004). In Cameroon, the government established a special fund in 1999 to support university research, and in 2002 it recruited 278 young researchers, mainly in the fields of agricultural and medical research (Gaillard & Zink, 2003).

Inter-University Cooperation

Inter-university cooperation in French-speaking Africa goes back at least to the establishment of the University of Dakar in 1957, which was designed to be a regional university and was expected to serve all the countries of the former French West Africa. In 1961, higher education in the former French Equatorial Africa was organized in the form of a network of institutions distributed throughout four countries: Gabon, Chad, the Central African Republic and Congo Brazzaville.

The following section of this chapter provides a brief analysis of three major experiences in inter-university cooperation in French-speaking Africa: two initiatives launched by the African and Malagasy Common Organization—specifically, the African and Malagasy Council for Higher Education (CAMES) and the regional specialized schools known as *écoles inter-états*—and the experience of the Francophone University Agency.

The African and Malagasy Council for Higher Education (CAMES)

The CAMES was created in 1968 by the Common African and Malagasy Organization (*Organisation Commune Africaine et Malgache*, or OCAM) to harmonize and coordinate the implementation of higher education and research policies in French-speaking countries of Africa. Currently, CAMES is made up of 16 member states,[1] and implements the following four programs (CAMES, 2002; Kiniffo, 1993; Ouiminga, 1998):

- Recognition of higher education degrees (a program established in 1972). In 2002, the CAMES had already organized 20 meetings of experts to review 637 applications for the recognition of degrees and diplomas. 518 requests were granted recognition.
- The African pharmacopeia and traditional medicine. This program was created in 1974 to promote regional cooperation in this field. In 2002, CAMES had already organized 11 research seminars, where 333 research papers were presented.
- The Inter-African Consultative Committees. This program was established in 1978 to review applications submitted by academic staff and researchers for promotion. In 2002, the various technical Consultative Committees had already evaluated 6,188 applications. 62.4% of these applications were recommended for promotion. It is worth mentioning that some CAMES member countries like Burundi and Cameroon have established national mechanisms for staff promotion.
- For some academic fields like medicine, law, economics and management, the criteria for staff promotion include a high level competitive examination known as "aggregation." By 2002, CAMES had organized 21 such examinations.

The Francophone University Agency

The Francophone University Agency (*Agence Universitaire de la Francophonie*, or AUF) was established in 1989 to replace the Association of Francophone Universities (which had been founded in 1961 to promote North–South and South–South inter-university cooperation and solidarity between institutions of higher education that use French as a working language). Currently, AUF is a network of more than 520 institutions of higher education and research. The agency operates in more than 35 countries, through its sub-regional offices, virtual campuses and training institutions. Its headquarters are located at the University of Montreal in Canada. In order to achieve its objectives, the AUF is implementing the following four major programs (Mve Ondo, 1998; 2002):

- *The International Fund for Inter-University Cooperation*: This fund was established in 1967 to support the following activities: a staff exchange program, encouraging the mobility of academic staff and researchers within French-speaking universities in Africa; the reinforcement of North–South inter-university cooperation in teaching and research activities; the development of databases and directories; staff exchanges between personnel of departments of French studies; and in-service training of French teachers.

- *The Francophone Research Fund*: This fund was established in 1993 to support the following activities: capacity building of research centers in developing countries; research projects jointly carried out by researchers from developing and developed countries; projects by young researchers; and the development of national research policies.
- *The Networks*: The agency has established two types of networks: institutional networks and thematic research networks. Currently there exist at least 11 institutional networks involving more than 700 Deans of Faculties, and 18 thematic research networks working in priority areas of human resources development identified by the summits of Heads of Francophone Countries. The priority areas include biotechnologies, HIV/AIDS, entrepreneurship, demography and environment law.
- *The Francophone Information Fund*: Since 1989, this fund has supported the operations of several centers that were established in order to provide access for researchers to international databases and to the Internet. The fund also enables the agency to contribute to the programs of the UNISAT (University Through Satellite) initiative, launched in 1992 to offer postgraduate programs in collaboration with French Universities using distance education and virtual learning techniques.

Regional Specialized Schools

The regional specialized schools known as *écoles inter-états* were established during the 1960s by the African and Malagasy Common Organization (OCAM). Each school operates under the overall supervision of an executive board made up of representatives of all the member state signatories to the legal instruments establishing the school. The schools offer training and provide research opportunities in various areas, including veterinary medicine, insurance, journalism, rural development, town planning and management, demography, informatics and railways. The budgets of the schools are made up of financial contributions received from member states represented on the executive board, as well as other contributions from donors. In 1988, French-speaking African countries had already established more than 20 regional specialized schools (Tedga, 1988). However, it is worth mentioning that some schools have closed down mainly due to financial problems caused by arrears in the payment of membership subscriptions.

Financing

As indicated earlier, since the mid-1970s the public financial resources allocated to higher education in sub-Saharan Africa have steadily declined. In Cameroon, for example, during the period 1991–1999, student enrollments in universities increased by a factor of 1.4, whereas the budget allocated to universities was reduced by a factor of 10

(Gaillard & Zink, 2003). Such cuts result in a sharp decline in public recurrent expenditure per student. Indeed, in sub-Saharan Africa the recurrent expenditure per student decreased from $6,461 in 1975 to $1,500 in 1988 and $1,241 in 1995 (World Bank, 1995; UNESCO, 1998a, 1998b; Samoff & Carroll, 2004). In several French-speaking countries, the decline in financial resources also resulted in reductions of the wages for academic staff. For example, in 1992, the government of Côte d'Ivoire decided to reduce the salaries of new lecturers by 50%. In Cameroon, the staff salaries were reduced by 66% in 1993. In all the French-speaking countries, the staff lost considerable purchasing power in 1994 following a devaluation of the common currency by 50%. These decisions led to a significant deterioration of staff working conditions and to a decline in the quality of education, since the academic staff had to spend more time on other jobs than on student supervision.

In 1988, several donors, including the World Bank, affirmed that higher education in sub-Saharan Africa was still very expensive. These assertions were based on a comparison of the public recurrent expenditure per higher education student to that of a primary school pupil and to the gross national product per capita. Indeed, whereas at that time the public recurrent expenditure per higher education student ranged between 30% and 100% of the GNP in the rest of the world, in Africa this figure ranged between three times the GNP in Congo and 38 times in Mauritania (Orivel, 1996).

In French-speaking sub-Saharan Africa, a significant share of the higher education budget is allocated to scholarships and various other social services provided to students. Indeed, while in 1995 this expenditure accounted for only 6% of higher education budgets in Asia and 14% in the OECD countries, it represented 55% of higher education budgets in French-speaking sub-Saharan Africa, compared to 15% in English-speaking Africa (World Bank, 1995).

In 1973, the government of Gabon granted scholarships and special allowances to all secondary school and higher education students. In 1992, almost 58% of the budget allocated to the two public universities in Gabon was spent on scholarships and other social services provided to students (Mve Ondo, 1993).

However, during the 1990s, due to the rapid increase in student enrollments and the reduction of higher education budgets, several countries were not able to sustain these kinds of grants for students. In 1993, Cameroon decided to terminate the scholarships system and to introduce substantial registration fees (Njeuma, 2003), while Côte d'Ivoire introduced a student loan scheme in 1996 (Houenou & Houenou-Agbo, 2003). In 2002, Gabon was providing scholarships to 50% of its higher education students (Mignot, 2002). In Burkina Faso, during the period from 1995–2001, the percentage of students at the University of Ougadougou benefiting from public scholarships decreased from 30% to 16% (Guenda, 2003). However, some countries are still spending a lot of money on providing assistance to students. In Guinea, the resources allocated to student scholarships increased from 34% of the higher education budget in 1995 to 55% by the end of 1990s (Sylla et al., 2003). In Madagascar, the percentage of students receiving scholarships increased from 51% in 1994 to 74% in 1997 (Stiles, 2003).

Revitalization of Higher Education

Since the 1990s, several countries have undertaken various types of reforms in order to revitalize their higher education systems. The cases of Côte d'Ivoire, Cameroon, and Senegal illustrate the primary trends seen throughout French-speaking Africa.

The 1992 Reform in Côte d'Ivoire

This reform was initially conceived in 1977, but was not implemented until 1992. The major objectives of the reform included the following (Touré, 1998): improvement of the relevance and quality of higher education, widening access through diversification of the higher education system, and redefinition of relationships between higher education institutions and the government and civil society.

In 1992, the National University of Côte d'Ivoire was split up into three university centers that were developed in 1996 into full-fledged universities. The reform also made it possible to gather six schools of engineering with very low enrollments into one national polytechnic institute, and to grant accreditation to 37 private higher education institutions (Houenou & Hoeunou-Agbo, 2003). Currently, the government allocates 11.3% of the higher education budget to private institutions. The reform also led to the establishment of a student loan scheme, and currently the government allocates 24.3% of the higher education budget to the implementation of that scheme. In order to improve the staff working conditions, in June 2001 the new government decided to realign academic staff salaries to their 1992 level. Unfortunately, the current civil war in Côte d'Ivoire promises to undermine most of these higher education reform efforts.

The 1993 Reform in Cameroon

In 1991–1992, Cameroon had one university (the University of Yaoundé) and four university centers (which had been established in 1977). The University of Yaoundé had an enrollment of more than 32,000 students, in facilities initially designed for 5,000 students, while the four university centers were largely under-utilized. In addition, the low levels of higher education funding did not make it possible to continue granting scholarships and other social services to the students. This situation framed the origins of the 1993 reform.

In 1993, the government decided to establish six universities. The government also introduced some innovations like the semester and credit transfer systems, terminated the scholarship system, introduced a substantial registration fee (to be paid by students) and adopted a policy intended to facilitate the promotion of private higher education institutions. In 2002, there were at least 16 private higher education institutions in Cameroon (Njeuma, 2003).

The implementation of this reform was undermined by a decision to reduce higher education budgets by 74% during the period 1992–1994. Despite this substantial budget cut, the reform achieved significant results in the following areas (Njeuma, 2003):

- more effective use of the university centers, which helped relieve overcrowding at the University of Yaoundé;

- improved access to university education and better geographical distribution of universities across the country;
- improvement in the student-teacher ratios, which dropped from 37:6 in 1993 to 33:8 in 1999; and
- abolition of scholarships and the introduction of more substantial registration fees.

The 1993 Reform in Senegal

This reform was implemented through two major projects: the Project for the Improvement of Higher Education (PAES) and the rehabilitation of the University of Dakar. The PAES was implemented between October 1996 and June 2003, thanks to a loan from the World Bank of US$30.9 million. The PAES has now been integrated into the higher education component of the country's ten-year plan for education and development (2000–2010). The major objective of the PAES was to develop a cost-effective higher education system capable of adequately addressing the issues of quality, relevance and equity. The project was carried out through the following actions:

- reinforcement of the capacity of the library of the University of Dakar;
- improvement of teaching and research; and
- reinforcement of management capacities, including the reorganization of student social services.

The reform also envisioned a gradual reduction of student enrollments from 24,000 in 1996 to 17,500 in 2002, mainly through the establishment of new university colleges and private higher education institutions. Unfortunately, following strong opposition from the university students' association to the reduction of enrollments, the university had to cancel this decision during the 1997–1998 academic year. In January 2004, although the Ministry of Education had already accredited 42 private higher education institutions, student enrollments at the University of Dakar had reached 35,000 students (Dieng, 2003).

To improve the academic staff conditions of service and the quality of teaching and learning at the University of Dakar, the government has recently built two new lecture halls, several classrooms and offices, a new library with advanced information and communication technology facilities, and more than 200 apartments for the accommodation of academic staff. Another batch of 140 apartments is under construction (Dieng, 2003; Sock, 2004). Moreover, to address the issue of overcrowding at the University of Dakar, the government is developing both short-term and long-term plans for the establishment of a polytechnic university and a university college in each of the provinces of Senegal.

Future Prospects for Higher Education in Francophone Africa

Universities in French-speaking countries of Africa should take advantage of the opportunities offered by programs of NEPAD and the various applications of information and communication technologies (ICTs), in particular virtual learning, virtual libraries and regional and international databases. This section of the chapter explores the many benefits that universities can obtain through the implementation of the NEPAD program of action, as well as the opportunities offered by the Virtual Institute for Higher Education in Africa (VIHEAF), which is jointly managed by the UNESCO Harare Cluster Office and the National Universities Commission of Nigeria.

The New Partnership for African Development (NEPAD)

NEPAD is a program of the African Union, developed by African leaders and based on a common vision and a shared conviction that they have the duty to eradicate poverty and to place African countries—both individually and collectively—on a path of sustainable growth and development. NEPAD's long-term objectives include the eradication of poverty in Africa; an end to the marginalization of Africa that has resulted from globalization; and the promotion of women's participation in all activities. To achieve these objectives, NEPAD has developed a program of action that covers all the seven priority areas[2] of human development identified by the African heads of state. Universities can play a major role and actually benefit significantly from collaboration with NEPAD in the areas of education and sciences.

It is now agreed that scientific research and technological innovation play a major role in achieving sustainable development in the knowledge-driven global economy. NEPAD explicitly recognizes in its program of action that "Africa's economic renewal and sustainable development will not be achieved without investment in science and technology." In order to respond to this challenge, NEPAD is committed to establishing networks of centers of excellence in science and technology.

NEPAD has also identified four major science and technology areas for the promotion of African growth and development: bioscience, information and communication sciences, geosciences and environmental sciences. In its efforts to establish networks of centers of excellence, NEPAD has launched three initiatives: the African Institute of Space Science; the Bioscience Facility for Eastern and Central Africa; and the African Laser Center. French-speaking universities should join these initiatives and even develop new initiatives (related to the four NEPAD areas of priority in sciences), which could be implemented as part of the NEPAD program of action.

The Virtual Institute for Higher Education in Africa

The Virtual Institute for Higher Education in Africa (VIHEAF) is a collaborative project between the UNESCO Harare Cluster Office and the National Universities Commission (NUC) of Nigeria. It is an online (Internet-based) training program that targets basic and higher education teachers in sub-Saharan Africa. The VIHEAF has the capacity of managing 20,000 learners simultaneously. The major objectives of the project are:

- To build and strengthen the capacity of teachers and other personnel in educational institutions throughout sub-Saharan Africa in critical areas of national and regional needs, as identified through the machineries of the African Union, the conferences of African Ministers of Education, and NEPAD;

- To provide Internet-based training on various areas of capacity-building for teachers at all levels of the education system. For higher education, the proposed courses include higher education pedagogy and the development of learning materials for distance education. Other courses could be offered at the request of higher education institutions in Africa.
- To share experiences among staff in institutions of higher learning—within the context of the 1998 World Conference on Higher Education (WCHE) and the African Network for Innovations in Higher Education (ANIHE)—on best practices in higher education teaching.

All staff of the educational institutions in sub-Saharan Africa—including primary and secondary schools, universities, polytechnics/technikons, and colleges of education—are eligible to participate in these training programs, which are offered free of charge.

The programs currently run 24 hours a day, seven days a week in three-month cycles, and are conducted in English. The development of website courses for French and Portuguese-speaking learners will be completed shortly. Each learning module provides students with exciting lessons embedded with video and audio support. Participants also contribute to discussion forums, carry out a project and take periodic online tests. A virtual graduation ceremony caps the end of the module. Agreements are being finalized through NUC to ensure that VIHEAF programs are credit-earning and lead to diplomas awarded by the University of Abuja, Nigeria. Similar arrangements will be signed with Francophone and Lusophone universities for programs delivered in French and Portuguese, respectively.

A number of other initiatives also deliver training to Africans using open and distance learning strategies, including the African Virtual University and Open Universities in several African countries. The comparative advantage of VIHEAF over these initiatives will include its wider reach and affordability of its programs, as they are offered free to participants. Also, VIHEAF programs (unlike others) will be offered in English, French and Portuguese. Most importantly, the tailoring of its programs to UNESCO's mandate and focus of operations is a unique comparative advantage. All the modules of VIHEAF address UNESCO's focal areas. No other institute of its kind in Africa or elsewhere delivers similar programs via a virtual learning environment.[3]

Conclusion

In sum, higher education in French-speaking African countries have experienced a spectacular expansion—particularly since obtaining their national independence during the 1960s—in terms of increases in the number of public and private institutions and in student enrollments. It is generally recognized that higher education institutions in French-speaking countries have successfully achieved their initial goal of developing the human resources needed for the operations of the civil service and the growth of the education systems. During the 1970s, these institutions were beset with several problems that were primarily caused by the rapid increase in student enrollments, the insufficiency of financial resources allocated to the higher education sector and the implementation of policies which allocated significant resources to the various subsidized social services provided to students.

Since the 1990s, several countries undertook reforms which made it possible to slightly improve the relevance and quality of higher education. It is anticipated that in the current regional and international environments—characterized by a renewed support for the development of higher education—and the emergence of new opportunities, in particular those related to the implementation of the NEPAD program of action and the improvement of access to ICTs, the ongoing and new reforms of higher education in French-speaking Africa will lead to a major revitalization of higher education in those countries.

Notes

1. The 16 members of CAMES are Benin, Burkina Faso, Burundi, Cameroon, Chad, Central Africa Republic, Congo, Gabon, Guinea, Ivory Coast, Madagascar, Mali, Niger, Rwanda, Senegal, Togo.
2. The NEPAD priority areas are:

   1. conflict prevention, management and resolution;
   2. political and economic governance including capacity building and peer review mechanism and code of conduct;
   3. market access—promotion of intra-African trade and increased access to markets of industrialized countries;
   4. development of agriculture;
   5. human resource development;
   6. provision of key infrastructure to facilitate sub-regional and continental integration-information communication technology ICT, energy, transport and water sanitization; and
   7. increase capital flows.

3. Further information on the project can be obtained at the Institute's website (http://www. viheaf.net).

References

African and Malagasy Council for Higher Education (CAMES). (2002). *Results achieved during the period 1972–2002.* Available online at http://www.cames.bf.refer.org/htm/realis.htm.

Al Habo, M. A. (2003). Chad. In D. Teferra & P. G. Altbach (Eds.), *African higher education: An international reference handbook.* Bloomington, IN: Indiana University Press.

Bagayoko, D., & Diawara, M. M. (2003). Mali. In D. Teferra & P. G. Altbach (Eds.), *African higher education: An international reference handbook.* Bloomington, IN: Indiana University Press.

Baichoo, R., with S. K. A. Parahoo, & I. Fagoonee. (2003). In D. Teferra & P. G. Altbach (Eds.), *African higher education: An international reference handbook.* Bloomington, IN: Indiana University Press.

Dieng, M. M. (2003). *Education policies: The case of Senegal.* Dakar, Senegal: Ministry of Education, Department of Higher Education.

Gaillard, J., & Waast, R. (2001). *Science in Africa at the dawn of the 21st century.* IRD.

Gaillard, J., & Zink, R. (2003). (In collaboration with Anna Furo Tullberg). *Scientific research capacity in Cameroon.* Stockholm, Sweden: International Foundation for Science.

Guedegbe, C. M. (2003). Benin. In D. Teferra & P. G. Altbach (Eds.), *African higher education: An international reference handbook.* Bloomington, IN: Indiana University Press.

Guenda, W. (2003). Burkina Faso. In D. Teferra & P. G. Altbach (Eds.), *African higher education: An international reference handbook.* Bloomington, IN: Indiana University Press.

Government of Cameroon. (1993). Decree no. 93/035 of January 19, 1993 on a special statute of the Higher Education Academic Staff. Yaoundé, Cameroon.

Houenou, P. V., & Houenou-Agbo, Y. (2003). Côte d'Ivoire. In D. Teferra & P. G. Altbach (Eds.), *African higher education: An international reference handbook*. Bloomington, IN: Indiana University Press.

Kharchi, A. (2003). Mauritania. In D. Teferra & P. G. Altbach (Eds.), *African higher education: An international reference handbook*. Bloomington, IN: Indiana University Press.

Kiniffo, H-V. T. (1993). How to reform the CAMES in order to improve its efficiency? In J. P. Tedga (Ed.), *Ten measures to revitalize the African university*. Paris, France: T. B. Conseils.

Lelo, M. (2003). Democratic Republic of Congo. In D. Teferra & P. G. Altbach (Eds.), *African higher education: An international reference handbook*. Bloomington, IN: Indiana University Press.

Mignot, A. (2002). *Report on higher education in Gabon*. Libreville, Gabon: Ministry of Higher Education, Research, and Technological Innovation.

Mintsa mi-Eya, V. (2003). Gabon. In D. Teferra & P. G. Altbach (Eds.), *African higher education: An international reference handbook*. Bloomington, IN: Indiana University Press.

Mve Ondo, B. (1993). Scholarships policies in Africa. In J. P. Tedga (Ed.), *Ten measures to revitalize the African university*. Paris, France: T. B. Conseils.

Mve Ondo, B. (1998). The association and networks of Francophone universities. In J. Shabani (Ed.), *Higher education in Africa: Achievements, challenges and prospects*. Harare, Zimbabwe: UNESCO-BREDA.

Mve Ondo, B. (2002). Higher education in sub-Saharan Africa: The example of the programs of the Francophone University Agency. In J. Shabani, P. Okebukola, O. Jegede, & A. Kanwar (Eds.), *Development and management of open and distance higher education in Africa*. Harare, Zimbabwe: UNESCO-Harare Cluster office.

N'guerekata, G. M. (2003). Central African Republic. In D. Teferra & P. G. Altbach (Eds.), *African higher education: An international reference handbook*. Bloomington, IN: Indiana University Press.

Njeuma, D. L. (2003). Cameroon. In D. Teferra & P. G. Altbach (Eds.), *African higher education: An international reference handbook*. Bloomington, IN: Indiana University Press.

Orivel, F. (1996). French-speaking universities in sub-Saharan Africa: A critical impasse. In Z. Morsy & P. G. Altbach (Eds.), *Higher education in an international perspective: Critical issues*. UNESCO International Bureau of Education. New York & London: Garland Publishing.

Ouiminga, R. M. (1998). The African and Malagasy Council for Higher Education. In J. Shabani (Ed.), *Higher education in Africa: Achievements, challenges and prospects*. Harare, Zimbabwe: UNESCO-BREDA.

Saint, W. (1992). *Universities in Africa: Strategies for stabilization and revitalization*. Washington, DC: World Bank.

Samoff, J., & B. Carroll. (2004). Conditions, coalitions and influence: The World Bank and higher education in Africa. Paper prepared for presentation at the Annual Conference of the Comparative and International Education Society. Salt Lake City, UT, March 8–12, 2004.

Seddoh, K. 1993. Revitalizing research. In J. P. Tedga (Ed.), *Ten measures to revitalize the African university*. Paris, France: T. B. Conseils.

Shabani, J. (2003). Burundi. In D. Teferra & P. G. Altbach (Eds.), *African higher education: An international reference handbook*. Bloomington, IN: Indiana University Press.

Sock, O. (2004). Higher education and scientific research policy in Senegal: Current situation and future prospects. Paper presented at Fifth Annual Global Development Conference, New Delhi, India, January 2004.

Stiles, J. (2003). Madagascar. In D. Teferra & P. G. Altbach (Eds.), *African higher education: An international reference handbook*. Bloomington, IN: Indiana University Press.

Sylla, S., with H. Ez-zaïm & D. Teferra. (2003). Guinea. In D. Teferra & P. G. Altbach (Eds.), *African higher education: An international reference handbook*. Bloomington, IN: Indiana University Press.

Tedga, P. J. M. (1988). *Higher education in Black Africa: The disaster?* Paris, France: L'Harmattan.

Toure, S. (1998). Strategies for improving the relevance of higher education: The experience of Côte d'Ivoire. In J. Shabani (Ed.), *Higher education in Africa: Achievements, challenges and prospects*. Harare, Zimbabwe: UNESCO-BREDA.

Traore, A. S. (2004). Relationships between research programs and bilateral and multilateral development policies in sub-Saharan Africa. Paper presented at the 5th Annual Global Development Conference. New Delhi, India, January 2004.

UNESCO. (1998a). Higher education statistics for the period 1980–1995. Document prepared for the World Conference on Higher Education, Paris, France.

UNESCO. (1998b). *Final Report of the World Conference on Higher Education*. Paris, France.

UNESCO/World Bank Task Force on Higher Education and Society. (2000). *Higher education in developing countries: Peril and promise*. Washington, DC: The World Bank.

Waast, R. (2004). Letter of the Coordination Committee of *Tomorrow Africa* 11.

The World Bank. (1988). *Education in sub-Saharan Africa: Strategies for adjustment, revitalization and expansion*. Washington, DC: The World Bank.

The World Bank. (1995). *Higher education: The lessons of experience*. Washington, DC: The World Bank.

The World Bank. (2002). *Constructing knowledge societies: New challenges for tertiary education*. Washington, DC: The World Bank.

25

LATIN AMERICAN UNIVERSITY TRANSFORMATION OF THE 1990s: ALTERED IDENTITIES?

Marcela Mollis

University of Buenos Aires, Argentina

In times of difference, plurality and fragmentation there is a strong tendency to assume that one important trend can be taken as constitutive of the whole. The 1990s were marked by the presence of a neo-liberal regime of truth that was driven by a clearly defined universalistic ambition. Although produced and practiced inside societies of the North, the most detrimental effects of neo-liberalism have been felt in the South, particularly by its higher education systems. This chapter presents a theoretical and practical critique of ongoing trends and outcomes of Latin American university reform, with special focus on the Argentine and Brazilian cases, and provides elements and values of what could be an alternative model for the future of universities in the region.

Latin American Higher Education: A General Overview

Although the Latin American countries are similar in languages and religion, they have many differences—such as population, ethnic composition, GNP per capita and comparative inequality in income distribution. Their social models range from socialism in Cuba to strongly market-oriented Chile, which has attained certain successes in the context of economic globalization. From colonization through independence to modernization, post-colonialism and whatever lies beyond, no two countries have necessarily followed the same path nor are their stages of development directly associated with one another. While development may appear outwardly to be quite similar, differences in cultural, geographic and historical circumstances yield highly varied rates and outcomes of development.

Having recognized the different context of each country in the region, there is a common pattern of educational enrollment expansion in Latin America, from the second half of the 20th century to the present. Overall, the growth rate of higher education in Latin America in the post World War II period has been remarkable. In 1950, there were approximately 1.5 million students in higher education; in 1995, more than eight million. In 1950, there were 105 universities in Latin America, and by the 1990s there were

James J.F. Forest and Philip G. Altbach (eds.), International Handbook of Higher Education, 503–515.
© 2006 *Springer. Printed in the Netherlands.*

over 700, among more than 2,500 institutions of higher learning, including teacher colleges, technical institutes and junior colleges (Albornoz, 1993, p. 136). Even so, in the past three decades the average enrollment ratio has been only 17% of the relevant age group—well below the advanced countries. Of course, there is much variation. According to Carmen García Guadilla (2001), Argentina has reached a 39% participation rate, approaching "universal access" as defined by Martin Trow (1974). Twelve countries are at "mass level": Bolivia, Colombia, Costa Rica, Cuba, Chile, Ecuador, El Salvador, Panama, Peru, Dominican Republic, Uruguay and Venezuela. Seven countries are in the "elite phase": Brazil, Honduras, Mexico, Nicaragua, Guatemala, El Salvador and Paraguay. The expansion of Latin American higher education was accompanied by diversification, with an increase in the role of non-university providers and of the private sector. Some countries now have more than one million students (Argentina, Brazil, and Mexico). Columbia, Peru and Bolivia have between 500,000 and one million students, while Bolivia, Cuba, Chile and Ecuador enroll between 150,000 and 500,000. Costa Rica, El Salvador, Guatemala, Honduras, Nicaragua, Panama, Paraguay, Dominican Republic, and Uruguay each enroll less than 150,000 students (García Guadilla, 2001, p. 30).

Although countries such as Chile and Mexico began to reform their systems in the 1980s, discussions on transformation became common only in the 1990s. The discourse included alternative financing options; closer relationships with the productive sector; institutional efficiency; and evaluation and accreditation mechanisms. Approaches to reform have differed considerably. According to Carmen García Guadilla (2001, pp. 30–31), some countries moved to change the legal framework first. Others pressed ahead with reforms. For example, in 1981 Chile approved a new education law containing the elements of the transformation model that the World Bank subsequently propagated as exemplary modernization. In the 1990s, seven countries approved new laws: Argentina in 1995, Brazil in 1996, Colombia in 1992, El Salvador in 1995, Nicaragua in 1990, Panama in 1995 and Paraguay in 1993. The international agenda for the transformation of higher education in the region was also put into practice through the establishment of national institutions for the accreditation and evaluation of universities. Argentina, Brazil and Mexico have placed priority on evaluation systems, while Chile and Colombia have placed priority on accreditation. Sub-regional associations such as MERCOSUR, Central America and NAFTA are pressing for accreditation models as the best means of facilitating academic interchange.

Latin American Universities and Their Historical Identity

The universities of Latin America have a long tradition. Many were established more than two centuries before their counterparts in North America, and most were state institutions, including Catholic universities during the Spanish period. From the very beginning, Spanish conquerors were concerned with educating the individuals who would govern the state and the Catholic Church, which at that time were combined as a single institution in Latin America. The first Latin American university was founded in 1538, only 45 years after the arrival of Christopher Columbus on Santo Domingo.

Universities were established in 1540 in Mexico, in 1551 in San Marcos, Perú, and in 1613 in Cordoba, Argentina. In contrast, the first Brazilian university, Lavras, was founded in 1908. The universities have played a unique role in Latin America, different from the rest of the world. In addition to postsecondary teaching and research, they have assumed such social responsibilities as preparing political leaders, fostering ideological discussion, promoting social change, safeguarding tradition, and retaining and spreading the local culture.

In order to interpret the idea of "university" which underlies Latin American universities, many references have been made to the model of university proposed by Napoleon Bonaparte in the 19th century. However, the so-called Napoleonic university does not reflect the particularity of university institutions in Latin America. Following the break with colonial Spain, secular professional knowledge came to characterize the Latin American university model by the end of the 19th century; this is what the German historian Hans Steger (1974, p. 32) described as the "university of lawyers." Luis Sherz (1968) recognizes a predominantly secular, pragmatic, and state-oriented conception in the professional university, which has the mission of shaping citizens, professionals, and public administrators. The same author also affirms that this model adapts to relatively static social systems and keeps a close link to the state, which recognizes privileges and rights to the university while financing it. Such universities appear as official state institutions. Under the Ministry of Education funding, the state had become the "teaching state," and as such, the administrator and inspector of the whole educational system, and situated as an "exclusive sovereign in educational matters" (Scherz, 1968, p. 107).

Lawyers who graduated from these institutions since the end of 19th century became the statesmen and public officers who created the instruments of political control within the state institutions (i.e., courts, prosecution offices, police headquarters, etc.). Through the schools and the press, they carried out other activities which allowed them to widen the expression of the hegemonic classes, whether as writers, poets, or educators. "This group gave rise to a bureaucratic elite and a political class with a formalistic and pompous style which adapted perfectly to the interests of the dominant classes" (Scherz, 1968, p. 109).

Consequently, the Latin American university of the 19th century—recognized as a "university of lawyers"—shared or controlled political power, exerted a significant influence on the field of ideas, and had an increasing weight on the system of cultural institutions (Mollis, 1990). On the one hand, foreign examples in the 20th century had a relevant organizational influence: the German emphasis on research, the English development of institutional diversity, the French Napoleonic conception of the relationship between state and university, and the North American model of autonomy, funding and private institutions. On the other hand, the academic model of Latin American universities is derived from the European one—specifically, the University of Paris, which had a strong influence in Latin America and is still alive in the more traditional institutions. In this model, the curricula are organized by professional programs, the universities have strong linkages with the state and (despite academic autonomy) the state provides the funds and has indirect control over the institutions. For this reason, these institutions met the demands of the ruling social class (mainly, their political and cultural demands). Professional training has thus been seen as the central task to be accomplished by the Latin American universities from the 19th century to the present.

The International Trends to Reform Higher Education in the 1990s

Literature on the restructuring of higher education systems in many developed and underdeveloped economies in the late 20th century (Altbach, 1999; Mollis, 2003a; Marginson & Considine, 2000; Velloso et al., 1999) indicates a number of common trends converging into a new orthodoxy about the value of higher education and how it should be managed. According to Mala Singh (2001, pp. 24–25), some key trends include:

- The requirement of higher education to demonstrate efficiency, effectiveness and value for money through external quality assurance systems and other account-ability frameworks.
- Declining amounts of public funds to subsidize student fees and service costs, and the requirement to satisfy the incremental demand for higher education with less public investment.
- The requirement to run public universities according to private sector princi-ples, and the dominance of managerial and entrepreneurial approaches to higher education.
- The requirement to diversify sources of funding, thus reducing the primary re-sponsibility of the state for public education.
- The privatization of higher education (either component parts of public institutions, like cleaning services and even specialized fields of study, or through encouraged competition with public institutions).
- Market-responsive curriculum reforms, a shift from basic to applied research, in-creased emphasis on academy/industry links, and greater concern over issues of intellectual property rights and the prioritization of research for product develop-ment and commercialization.

The implementation of structural adjustment policies to liberalize the economies of Latin America and integrate them more tightly into the world capitalist system has pro-voked a number of crises throughout the region. In diminishing the role of state in the provision of basic social services—part of the cost-cutting policies recommended by the World Bank and the IMF—the social safety net provided for the most marginalized populations has been effectively removed. The distance between the wealthy and the poor is increasing. Moves to decentralize and privatize economies are paralleled by initiatives to dismantle centralized ministries of education and charge fees for educa-tional services that were once provided free to all (Arnove, Franz, Mollis, & Torres, 1999, pp. 323–324).

A recent report of The Latin American Studies Association (LASA) Task Force on Higher Education examines the functions, financing, and governance of tertiary education as well as efforts to privatize and professionalize it. The report concludes that although democratization has often rescued higher education from government neglect, market orientations have not produced a coherent reform agenda. It furthers notes that the reform agenda is highly polemical, with supporters arguing that neo-liberal reforms have not been sufficiently implemented and opponents arguing that it brought to institutions nothing but an alteration of the social, political and scientific identity of the universities (Mollis, 2003b). The following features describe the consequences of the implementation of the international agenda to reform Latin American higher education in the 1990s:

- Promulgation of higher education laws to regulate higher education within contexts of traditional autonomy.
- Institutional diversification (the creation of new tracks that changed the historical Latin American double-track system into a division of university and non-university tertiary institutions); transformation of the structures of higher education systems (the creation of new institutions like "university colleges" and "university institutes;" and the creation of short-term courses to grant vocational certificates within the university system (charging fees).
- Diversification of financial sources (charging users fees instead of providing free service, and establishing services-for-profit partnerships).
- Strategic alliances between international agencies and governmental decision makers, as well as strategic alliances among the corporate sector, the public sector and the universities.
- Incremental private investment in higher education; marketization of non-accredited (and unsupervised) private tertiary institutions (non-university sector), along with incremental growth of new providers like financial foundations, banking system, corporations, etc.
- New policies for accountability, institutional and program evaluation, and university and graduate program accreditation (combined with the establishing of national and central agencies for accreditation and institutional evaluation).
- New types of institutional coordination—national, regional and inter-campus coordination, supported by new institutional regulations and agreements.
- Strong differentiation among faculty members through the implementation of incentive policies to award productivity based on performance indicators.
- Academic and curricular reforms, including: shortening of university professional programs; granting certificates for short-term courses at the university level; new learning models based on the "training of professional skills and competences;" and expansion of professional graduate courses (at the master's level).
- New methodologies for the dissemination of knowledge, such as the dominant presence of information technologies and electronic distance learning, that shift the traditional teaching role to remote tutorial activities (Mollis, 2003a).

The above trends and consequences of the implementation of the global and international agenda for reforming higher education systems are bringing universities in line with other social arrangements designed to position national economies for global competitiveness. According to Mala Singh (2001), "the new policy framework for the restructuring of higher education in developed economies is functioning as a powerful and influential global paradigm, shaping higher education policies and practices in many developing countries' economies, despite huge social, economic and historical differences" (p. 25).

The most recent document on higher education published by the members of the Task Force on Higher Education and Society (World Bank & UNESCO, 2000) starts by saying:

> The world economy is changing, as knowledge supplants physical capital as the source of present (and future) wealth. Technology is driving much of this process, with information technology, biotechnology, and other innovations leading to remarkable changes in the way we live and work. As knowledge becomes more important, so does higher education. Countries need to educate more of their young people to a higher standard—a degree is now a basic qualification for many skilled jobs. The quality of knowledge generated within higher education institutions, and its accessibility to the wider economy, is becoming increasingly critical to national competitiveness. This poses a serious challenge to the developing world (p. 9).

The Task Force's observations highlight the worldwide desire to help developing countries become aware of the economic imperative which justifies the transformation of higher education systems. Other sections of the report also convey the relevance of reforms linked to an economic imperative: "There are notable exceptions, but currently, across most of the developing world, the potential of higher education to promote development is being realized only marginally" (World Bank & UNESCO, 2000, p. 10). What we see in all of this is the tendency for the geopolitics of knowledge and power to divide the world into countries that consume "knowledge" produced by the countries which dominate globalization both economically and culturally, and countries which reassign the economic function of training human resources to university institutions located in the periphery.

The International Agenda for Transforming Latin American Universities: Privatization and Marketization in Argentina and Brazil

Most of the private universities and postsecondary institutions in Latin America were created in the second half of the 20th century, and they are for all practical purposes new inventions. Before the 1950s, there were only 14 private universities in Latin America. By the 1970s, they had increased to 50, and by the 1990s there were 197 private universities (García Guadilla, 1996, p. 26). Two possible explanations can be posed to interpret this significant expansion. First, governments are aware of the difficulties in satisfying the increasing demands for higher education with the current state institutions, given organizational and financial constraints. Second, neo-liberal policies in the region resulted in the reduction of public funding and in the transfer to the private sector of numerous activities. Philip Altbach (1999) also points out that not only has demand overwhelmed the ability of governments to pay, but there has been a significant change in the way that higher education is considered. The idea of an academic degree as a "private good" that benefits the individual rather than a "public good" for society is now widely accepted. The logic of today's market economies and an ideology of privatization have contributed to the resurgence of private higher education and the establishment of private institutions where none existed before (Altbach, 1999, p. 1).

Although Latin American higher education has grown faster than primary and secondary education, and its growth rate is the highest for any region of the world—approximately 3% annually between 1975 and 1990—it is the private sector that registered the most dramatic gains. In the 1970s, approximately 5% of higher education students were enrolled in private institutions; today over than 30% attend private universities and colleges. Enrollment in private universities in Brazil is the highest in Latin America—at 61.5% of the country's enrollment, it is double the average figure for Latin America. There are, of course, deep differences in public and private higher education from country to country throughout the region.

In Argentina, for instance, there were 149 students per 10,000 inhabitants in 1980, compared to 478 students in 2000. Currently, more than 1,700,000 students—representing 15.6% of the total enrollment in the education system—attend institutions of higher education. Here, the higher education system is divided into two tracks: the university and the non-university track, which consists of primary and secondary school teacher training institutions and vocational technical training institutions. In 2000, roughly 75% of the students in the higher education system were on the university track, while 25% were on the non-university track.

The growth in the number of private universities and tertiary institutions during the 1990s is striking. There was a widespread perception that traditional universities were not meeting the needs of the lifelong learning cohort, and subsequently new providers—like elitist private universities—entered the field to meet market demands. In contrast to the 11 public universities created in the last decade, there were 27 private universities created in the same period. At present, there are 91 universities and colleges in Argentina. Though public universities enroll the bulk of higher education students, there was an increase of 369% in enrollments in the non-university private track from 1980 to 2000, in contrast to a 226% increase in the university track (Mollis, 2003, p. 22).

In addition to the expectation that the universities in Latin America will generate new sources of funding from the private sector, they participate in evaluation and accreditation processes as well. Universities also face the challenge of responding to an increased demand for higher education. Only a few years ago, it was almost impossible to think about evaluation and accreditation for the traditional universities because they were very powerful institutions, totally independent of all external authority and strongly resistant to any kind of public control, given that they had been established as autonomous institutions. Consequently, the institutional reforms of the 1990s made the traditional autonomy responsive to the international agenda and to local economic demands.

The discourse of international agencies is neither uniform nor homogenous. In the case of Argentina there was considerable agreement between the statements of the World Bank and those of the Inter-American Development Bank (IDB) (Mollis & Bensimon, 1999). However, there was one important variation. The World Bank maintained that quality was impoverished in Argentina's higher education system, and attributed this impoverishment to the autonomy and the state subsidizing of universities.

It suggested constant monitoring of student performance, restricted admission to the university, and the payment of tuition. Free access was linked to the squandering of resources and the politicization of the university (World Bank, 1993, p. 89). By contrast, the IDB rejected the use of homogenous and generalizing instruments to measure quality. It suggested initiatives that would be "innovative" and aspire to achieve change, as well as partnerships in initiatives between the state, provincial governments and the private sector (Mollis & Marginson, 2002, p. 316).

Although the terms privatization and marketization are frequently used (sometimes interchangeably) to describe recent changes in welfare provision, they are loosely defined, according to Whitty and Power (2000, pp. 93–107). Both terms are not intrinsically linked, though one can lead to the other. As Simon Marginson (1993) points out, "while privatization does not in itself constitute market relations, it creates a potentially favorable environment for market activity" (Marginson, 1993, p. 178). Whereas theories of modernization assume that all countries of the Latin American region wish to be modern in the same Northern conceptions of development, the neo-liberal underpinning of globalization suggests that all the countries will profit equally from reliance on the market.

The market-driven reform is based on the idea that the market will compensate for the withdrawal of public funds from the public educational system. However, early results of these policies do not bode well for the institutional development of the universities. One of the most visible consequences of these market-driven policies is the proletarianization of researchers and faculty members as a result of salary cuts, dismantling humanistic programs and the public disinvestment in research and technology development. The "marketization" process is economically driven not only by the global dominance of the market but mainly in response to the third sector—the service sector—of Latin American economies, which is the sole dynamic sector in a recessive labor market in an unindustrialized capitalistic economy (Mollis, 2002, p. 22).

Brazil in 1998 had 169 million people and nearly 1.7 million tertiary-level students, which represented an enrollment of 11% of the 20–24 year-old cohort. There were 851 postsecondary institutions, of which 218 (26%) were public and 633 (74%) were private. Among them there were 127 universities (53.5% were public and 46.5% were private), 91 research universities, and 724 non-university institutions (21% of them public and 79% private) (García Guadilla, 1996, p. 25; Gonzalez, 1999, p. 78).

Luis Eduardo González (1999) points out that the higher education system of Brazil falls under the jurisdiction of the Ministry of Education through the Federal Council of Education (CFE). Undergraduate programs must be accredited by the CFE, with reaccreditation every five years. As a result, there is no well established system for evaluating undergraduate programs (such as that which exists for the graduate programs). Rather, the accreditation of undergraduate studies has consisted basically of establishing "input" criteria for assigning resources and determining some factors, such as the student/faculty ratio or the cost of teaching, among others (González, 1999, p. 79).

From an analysis of current higher education policies in Brazil, several authors—such as Helgio Trindade (2000) and Denise Leite (2001)—point out that recent trends are associated with a neo-liberal project aimed at minimizing the state. These policies try to adapt the highest level of formal education to market demands and to the national state reconfiguration process. Dias Sobrinho explains:

"At present, a significant concern is to verify that diversification and differentiation policies under way in the country are based on four fundamental suppositions of neo-liberalism: a) they try to favor competition and the satisfaction of different demands and clients; b) they try to "naturalize," even more, individual differences through the gradual establishment of a meritocratic system, where each individual will have access to the kind of higher education that he or she "may" afford; c) they increase the subordination of higher education to the market, particularly training and the privatization of activities and services; and d) they explain the method of operation of the system rather than its social purposes" (Dias Sobrinho, 2000, p. 58).

Another aspect of the new identity of the Brazilian university is related to the change in the curricula. The importance of graduate course curricula began to grow after the start of the higher education reform in 1995. Some of the elements which had a bearing on the matter include Law 9131/95; national and international discussions on professional standards and competences; the process started by the Secretariat of Higher Education in 1997; and the position adopted by the *Foro de Pró-Reitores de Graduaçao* for institutional evaluation and accreditation. The Ministry of Education intends to adapt university curricula to the changes in the labor market on the basis of the following principles: flexibility for the curricular organization, adaptation to job market demands, integration of graduate and postgraduate courses, emphasis on general training, and development of general skills. The neo-liberal labor market requires individuals to acquire multiple skills and flexibility. Other Brazilian authors (Leite, 2001; Trindade, 2000) have also come to the conclusion that higher education in Brazil is being adapted to processes associated with the "academic capitalism" well described by Slaughter and Leslie (1997), meaning that institutions adopt a mercantile rationality for the benefit of enterprises, rulers, and hegemonic classes (Catani & Ferreira de Oliveira, 2000, p. 48).

Denise Leite (2001) describes the impact of extrapolating values from the market and infusing them into some Brazilian university campuses: "'Entrepreneurial professors' are the result of such extrapolation: they sell their courses—i.e., they make their curricular offerings more attractive in search of student-clients. They adapt their conferences and papers to the sales codes of canned knowledge: efficiency and productivity indicators, evaluation of results, and leadership to win. The international agencies hire entrepreneurial professors as expert technicians in pre-established descriptions subject to the adjustment of theories and concepts" (Leite, 2001, pp. 23–26). Overall, privatization and marketization are having a major impact throughout the higher education systems of this region.

Evaluation and Accreditation in Latin American Universities: Some Remarks

In the last decade, the assessment of universities (including quality assurance) has become a major focus of regulation, a pattern that is structured globally in ways that contribute to convergence across countries. Quality assurance policies emerged and developed in the 1990s as part of a neo-liberal agenda for university modernization, an agenda framed by the intersecting relations between global, national and institutional agencies. The struggle over assessment varies depending on the universities' size, age, mission, and whether they are public or private. In a context of negotiation that tends to be more political than academic, the discourse and practices of international agencies, central government and university actors are often at odds. University assessment is not a neutral search for universal, quantifiable "total quality;" it is constituted through conflict and the exercise of power. The university does not independently establish its own parameters, yet neither can the government set assessment parameters without regard for the university. The field of assessment, then, is a shifting interplay of university autonomy and governmental heteronomy (Mollis & Marginson, 2002, p. 312).

Although there is not yet a sufficient body of experience or data to support conclusions about the impact of evaluation and accreditation in the region, there is some empirical evidence to support the following observations, mainly elaborated by the regional expert on evaluation and accreditation, Luis González (1999, p. 91):

- there is a lack of adequate information to ensure transparency of the market and of the governmental policymakers for establishing the national agencies for accreditation;
- demand for postsecondary education is increasing, influenced by popular trends and the promotion of certain careers that is not necessarily socially congruent with demands of the labor market;
- there exists a delay between the reporting of specific labor market needs and the availability of trained professionals to satisfy these needs, which impacts regional and local economic development; and
- the evaluation system was created by the state as part of the neo-liberal policies for the region and not for the institutions themselves; this fact does not necessarily lead to a positive impact in terms of improving institutional quality.

In the last 10 years, economic globalization has underpinned experiments in university assessment and control within the neo-liberal framework. Governments are re-engineering their systems to monitor and control academic life. Simultaneously, in many countries there has been a reaction among universities and intellectuals with a history of autonomy, demanding forms of accreditation and assessment independent of government and oriented toward improving the quality of teaching, learning and research. The new governmental heteronomy has subordinated institutional autonomy without abolishing it. In Latin America—and probably all around the world—the terms of autonomy have shifted from an education-centered and participatory culture (especially in Argentina) to the culture of self-managing corporate institutions led by professional managers or administrative bureaucracy. In the practices of assessment in most of the countries, there appears to be a weakening of specifically pedagogical objectives, as assessment takes the form of institution-wide approaches controlled by managers or bureaucrats—depending on private or public administration—rather than discipline or course-based approaches shaped by teachers and students (Mollis & Marginson, 2002, p. 326).

Conclusions

The 1980s was a decade of "structural adjustments," and represented the deployment of the neo-liberal doctrine through the imposition of a new scheme of financial discipline and modernization of the state. Since then, as in the case of other major social institutions, Latin American universities have been undergoing dramatic reorganizations in a context that takes the global economy rather than the nation-state as its point of departure. This "common sense" was built in the 1980s and definitely took shape late in the 1990s, acknowledging the social value of higher education but emphasizing its role in meeting labor market demands and enhancing national competitiveness.

The idea of a Latin American public university during the 20th century (either publicly or privately managed, such as the universities managed by religious orders) implied scientific quality, social importance, pertinence, and equity. Clearly, the 21st century's idea of a corporate university differs from the former in that it appeals to profit in favor of public interests, and contributes to social segmentation while placing the interests of ruling elites and capitalist ambitions at the center.

At present, the altered identities of at least the Argentine and the Brazilian universities lead these institutions toward the homogenization of knowledge and shape them in the interests of international banking agencies and for the service sector's needs. It is necessary and urgent to decontaminate the concept of quality from the connotations of total quality; to separate the notion of financial logic from financial return; and to dissociate efficiency from academic excellence, demanding instead that the university fulfill its social responsibility to its beneficiaries. There is an urgent need to recover the social, ethical, and humanistic significance of educational quality. The university does not only produce the technical and scientific knowledge necessary for the development of the country; above all, it must produce the knowledge necessary for a democratic, just, and more equitable construction of society.

The Latin American university must invent knowledge not conditioned by the codes of profit; it must reconstruct its identity for the benefit of our societies, which are unprotected from possessive individualists who deny the value of culture because it is not listed on the stock exchange. If the Latin American university is considered as a market entity, then there is no space for real and significant criticism. Institutional evaluation and assessment must be directed toward the deepening of the conditions of criticism at the university, promoting public debates—acting as a mediator among actors, sectors, and institutions—and must be developed as a collective action focused on the criticism of the institution itself, both internally and in its relations with the larger society.

This chapter supports the idea that the efficient administration of a Latin American public university should not be based on profit earning, but on the sense of its social function. Some necessary missions in responding to the global challenges of our impoverished societies include the need to train independent and creative professionals as active citizens and future leaders; to foster epistemological diversity and disagreement; to turn single-sided thinking into a plurality of alternative ways of thinking; to enrich the cultural heritage; and to make science sensitive to social needs. Also, the expansion of scientific and cultural fields—and the production of scientific, technological, and cultural assets—creates wealth and strengthens the economic development of the peripheral countries about which the international agencies are so much concerned. Clearly, higher education has an important role to play in Latin America throughout the foreseeable future.

References

Aboites, H. (1999). *Viento del Norte (Winds of the North)*. Plaza and Valdés Editores (Editors: Plaza & Valdés). México D. F.: UAM (Autonomous University of Mexico).

Altbach, P. (1999). *Private prometheus: Private higher education and development in the 21st century*. Chestnut Hill, MA: Center for International Higher Education.

Arnove, B., Franz, S., Mollis, M., & Torres, C. (1999). Education in Latin America at the end of the 1990s. In *Comparative education: The dialectic of the global and the local* (pp. 305–329). Oxford, UK: Rowman & Littlefield Publishers.

Catani, A. M., & Ferreira de Oliveira, J. (2000). A reforma da educação superior no Brasil nos anos 90: Diretrizes, bases e ações (*The Brazilian higher education reform of the 90's: Orientations, bases and actions*). In A. M. Catani, (Ed.), *Reformas educacionais em Portugal e no Brasil* (*Educational reforms in Portugal and Brazil*). Belo Horizonte, Brazil: Autentica.

Dias Sobrinho, J. (2000). Avaliação e privatização do ensino superior (Evaluation and privatization of higher education). In H. Trindade (Ed.), *Universidade em ruinas: Na república dos profesores* (*University in ruins: A republic of professors*). Rio Grande do Sul, Brazil: Vozes, Petrópolis/CIPEDES.

García Guadilla, C. (1996). *Situación y principales dinámicas de transformación de la educación superior en América Latina* (*Balance and dynamic principles of transformation of Latin American higher education*). Caracas, Venezuela: CRESALC/UNESCO.

García Guadilla, C. (2001). Globalization, regional integration and higher education in Latin America. *International News, 46* (November), 28–33.

González, L. E. (1999). Accreditation of higher education in Chile and Latin America. In P. Altbach (Ed.), *Private prometheus: Private higher education and development in the 21st century*. Chestnut Hill, MA: Center For International Higher Education

Leite, D. (2001). *Avaliacao institucional e democracia. Posibilidades contra-hegemónicas ao re-desenho capitalista das universidades* (*Institutional evaluation and democracy: Counter-hegemonic alternatives or capitalistic reshaping of universities*). Paper presented at the 20th General Assembly of CLACSO, Guadalajara, Mexico, November 21–24.

Marginson, S. (1993). *Education and public policy in Australia*. Cambridge, UK: Cambridge University Press.

Marginson, S., & Considine, M. (2000). *The enterprise university: Governance and reinvention in Australian higher education*. Cambridge, UK: Cambridge University Press.

Mollis M. (2001). Higher education systems in transition in the era of globalization: A view from Argentina. *International News, 46* (November), 32–34.

Mollis, M. (2002). Higher education in transition. *International Higher Education, 26* (Winter), 21–23.

Mollis, M. (Ed.). (2003a). *Las universidades en América Latina: Reformadas o alteradas?* (*Latin American universities: Altered or reformed?*) Buenos Aires, Argentina: ASDI-CLACSO.

Mollis, M. (2003b). A decade of reform in Argentina. *International Higher Education, 30* (Winter), 24–26.

Mollis, M., & Bensimon, M. (1999). Crisis, calidad y evaluación de la educación superior desde una perspectiva comparada: Argentina y Estados Unidos (*Crisis, quality and evaluation of higher education. A comparative perspective of Argentina and the U.S.*). In H. Cardiel & R. Rodríguez (Eds.), *Universidad y contemporánea. Política y gobierno* (*Contemporary university. Policy and government*). Tomo II CESU, México: Porrúa Grupo Editorial.

Mollis M. & Marginson, S. (2002). The assessment of universities in Argentina and Australia: Between autonomy and heteronomy. *Higher Education, 43*(3), 311–330.

Singh, M. (2001). Re-inserting the public good into higher education transformation. *International News, 46* (November), 24–27.

Slaughter, S., & Leslie, L.L. (1997). *Academic capitalism: Politics, policies, and the entrepreneurial university.* Baltimore, MD: The Johns Hopkins University Press.

Trindade, H. (Ed.). (2000). *Universidade em ruinas: Na república dos profesores (University in ruin. A republic of professors).* Rio Grande do Sul, Brazil: Vozes/CIPEDES.

Trow, M. (1974). Problems in the transition from elite to mass higher education. In *Policies for higher education,* from the General Report on the Conference on Future Structures of Postsecondary Education (pp. 55–101). Paris, France: OECD.

Velloso, J., Cunha, L. A., & Velho, L. (Eds.). (1999). *O ensino superior e o Mercosul (Higher Education and the MERCOSUR—Common market of the South).* Brasilia, Brazil: UNESCO-Garamond.

Whitty, G. & Power, S. (2000). Marketization and privatization in mass education systems. *International Journal of Educational Development, 20.*

World Bank. (1993). *Argentina: From insolvency to growth. A World Bank country study.* Washington, DC: World Bank.

World Bank & UNESCO. (2000). *Higher education in developing countries: Peril and promise.* Washington: The Task Force on Higher Education.

26

HIGHER EDUCATION IN SCANDINAVIA

Evanthia Kalpazidou Schmidt
University of Aarhus, Denmark

With the emergence of the knowledge-based society, higher education in Scandinavia[1] has undergone substantial reforms. Socio-economic restructuring and the globalization of markets have influenced infrastructure and development, while international trends in higher education have inspired policies. Similarities in history, cultural and political conditions in the Scandinavian states underscore common features in higher education, although there are many differences as well. This chapter focuses on the development, structure and policy of university systems. Part I discusses general characteristics of the Scandinavian countries, highlighting recent changes and future perspectives, while Part II provides individual country descriptions.

General Characteristics of Higher Education in the Scandinavian Countries

Access and Participation

According to a recent OECD (2003a) study, Scandinavian countries are among those that invest the most public resources in education. Denmark, Norway and Sweden spend the highest amount on educational institutions per student. Denmark, Finland and Sweden (together with the U.S. and Canada) are countries with the highest total expenditure on tertiary education institutions (public and private) as measured by percentage of GDP budgeted for research, educational and ancillary services. In fact, public support for students and households accounts for about 30% or more of public tertiary budgets in Denmark and Sweden.

From this, it comes as no surprise that access and enrollment rates are among the best in the world. Rates of participation in higher education are over 60% of young people in most Scandinavian countries, and students can expect to receive at least 3 years of tertiary education during their lifetimes. Iceland and Sweden have the largest subsidies in terms of student loans, and also have high rates of access to tertiary education. Finland does not have a publicly funded loan system. Despite this, Finland has the second highest tertiary participation rates among the OECD countries (OECD, 2003a). Extensive student exchange programs exist throughout Scandinavia. Sweden

James J.F. Forest and Philip G. Altbach (eds.), International Handbook of Higher Education, 517–537.
© *2006 Springer. Printed in the Netherlands.*

and Denmark received the highest proportion of foreign students in Scandinavia in 2001 (7.3% and 6.5%, respectively) while many Icelandic and Norwegian students (20.5% and 5.1%) studied in a foreign country (OECD, 2003a).

Research and Development

The level of research and development (R&D) in Scandinavia is among the highest in the OECD. Among the EU top 10 R&D performers (as measured by the amount and impact of faculty publications) are higher education institutions in Denmark, Finland and Sweden. Indeed, compared to the OECD average, all the Scandinavian countries show impressive publication rates, with significant growth—particularly in Finland—during the 1990s. In comparative measurements of technological performance and patents per capita, Finland and Sweden achieved marks as high as 156 and 214, respectively, compared to the EU mean of 80 (OECD, 2003b).

There are similarities among the research policies that have been implemented throughout Scandinavia during the last several years. University education and research are currently perceived within the framework of R&D and innovation policy, and quality of outcomes is assessed on the basis of societal relevance (a transition from Mode 1 to Mode 2 research).[2] Cooperation with the private sector has been given particular attention, and hence external funding has increased considerably (Kalpazidou Schmidt, 2003). Simultaneously, with a higher proportion of research funds allocated by means of competition, the share of public funding granted directly to institutions is decreasing. Implications include changes in organizing and distributing funding, in organizing research environments, and in the strategic direction of institutional governance.[3]

Another trend in Scandinavia is greater state intervention in research policy, along with increased emphasis on strategic planning and government monitoring. A strengthening of the research councils has taken place in Denmark, Iceland, Norway and Sweden, creating a more flexible funding system that encompasses strategic research directions and promotes interdisciplinary approaches. Centers of excellence have been established (in Denmark, Finland, and Norway) together with new foundations based on public funding (in Denmark, Norway and Sweden)—all of which focus on problem-oriented research and user-oriented postgraduate programs (cf. Kaiser et al., 2003; European Commission, 2003).

Among the Nordic countries, Sweden (4.3%) and Finland (3.4%) invested the most in R&D in relation to GDP within the OECD (2003b). Corresponding figures for the other countries of the region are 2.4% in Denmark, 3% in Iceland and 1.6% in Norway. While differences in R&D investments between Denmark, Finland and Norway were minor in the beginning of the 1980s, differences became pronounced in the 1990s. Finland's spending grew the most as a result of investments in the electronics industry, while Norway's grew the least, with limited investments in industry. Of the total spending on R&D, the industrial sector amounted to 78% in Sweden, 71% in Finland, 69% in Denmark, 60% in Norway, and 59% in Iceland. Meanwhile, public higher education spending on R&D was 26% in Norway, 22% in Denmark, 19% in Sweden and Iceland, and 18% in Finland.

Human Resources

With regard to human resources, Finland, Sweden and Iceland (together with Japan and the U.S.) lead the OECD in terms of the number of researchers relative to the population. Finland and Sweden reflect the highest number of researchers per 1,000 members of the labor force in the EU (higher than the U.S. and second only to Japan). Further, between 1995 and 1999, the number of researchers grew by 50% in Finland, 19% in Sweden and 16% in Denmark. In 2001, Finland and Sweden had the greatest share of human resources per capita in R&D (0.57% and 0.56% respectively), with 0.48% in Denmark and 0.32% in Norway. The proportion of the workforce involved in R&D is highest in Finland (2.03%), with only Japan achieving higher rates. Corresponding figures are 1.62% in Sweden, 1.48% in Denmark and 1.13% in Norway. Aside from these impressive figures, however, a large number of academic staff in Scandinavia will be retiring in the near future, causing increasing concern about the future of higher education and R&D in this region (OECD, 2003b; Kim, 2002).

A comparative look at the production of new Ph.D.s in science and technology also reflects favorably on the Scandinavian countries; for every 1,000 inhabitants, 1.24 new doctorates were awarded in Sweden, 1.01 in Finland, and 0.49 in Denmark—all of which are higher than comparable figures in the U.S. (0.41) and Japan (0.25). Overall, the number of Ph.D.s in Scandinavia doubled during the 1990s. The fastest growth has been observed in Finland, which (together with Korea, Germany and Switzerland) led the OECD in production of university level graduates in the natural sciences and engineering (as a share of total graduates) in 2001 (OECD, 2003b). Finland and Sweden (together with Switzerland and Germany) recorded the highest numbers of doctoral graduates per capita. In Denmark and Norway, the corresponding figures were below the EU average, but above the OECD mean. In Sweden, the flow of doctoral students has declined due to financial restrictions introduced in 1998. In Denmark, figures increased in the beginning of the 1990s (due to the introduction of the 3-year Ph.D. program) but recent entrance figures indicate stagnation. In Norway the population of doctorates has been traditionally low, but the government intends to increase the number of doctoral students by up to 60% in the coming years. A future challenge for Scandinavian higher education is thus to further build the human resources and make use of all existing potential in order to develop the knowledge-based economy (NORBAL, 2004).

From a Scandinavian perspective, Denmark has the strictest professional advancement system and thus the lowest numbers of full professors per capita. In Denmark, Finland and Norway, non-essential restructuring of the academic advancement system has been initiated during the last several years. In Sweden, a promotion reform in 1999 raised the number of professors, although the professoriate is still smaller than in Finland. Norway enjoys the highest number of professors in Scandinavia (Kalpazidou Schmidt, 1996; 2004).

Most Nordic countries have developed initiatives to encourage women to apply for positions and thus make use of their countries' full human resource potential. From this perspective, an interesting observation is that dynamic research environments[4] have a larger share of female staff than others. In Finland, targeted long-term measures in the 1980s increased the number of women in higher education and research (50% of

Ph.D. graduates are female). Norway has taken similar initiatives, but without achieving similarly positive results. In Sweden, an affirmative action-like approach is expected in recruitment for higher education positions, and the issue of female under-representation is currently being discussed in Denmark (Ståhle, 1999; Kalpazidou Schmidt, 2004).

Regional Cooperation

All Scandinavian countries participate in the EU schemes SOCRATES/ERASMUS (for students) and Marie Curie Fellowships (for researchers), both of which aim to increase academic mobility throughout Europe. In addition, there are Nordic regional cooperation schemes based on agreements from 1971. Nordic Ministers of Education and Research regularly meet within the framework of the Nordic Council of Ministers. In 1995, it was decided to create a common Nordic area for education and research. Approximately 26% of the Council's budget is allocated to education and research. Other priorities of the Council include the establishment of networks with the Baltic States, Northwest Russia and the Barents Sea region.

In 1989, Nordic exchange programs for students and teachers (NORDPLUS) were established. The Nordic Academy for Advanced Study also provides research funding to students and researchers with an aim to promote mobility in the region. Recent initiatives include distance education and the establishment of Nordic e-networks among schools and higher education institutions, and a program for Nordic Centers of Excellence. A Southern Scandinavian regional cooperation initiative is the Øresund University, involving 12 universities on both sides of the Øresund Strait (i.e., the countries of Denmark and Sweden). This project aims to strengthen interregional relations between existing education and research institutions.

Scandinavian Models: Changes and Perspectives

One could ask whether there is a Scandinavian model for higher education. There is no simple answer to this question, as it depends on the point of view (national or international) and the topic in focus. However, seen from an international perspective one can identify some common features.

In Scandinavia, higher education is perceived as a public service and as such is in principle tuition free. Education has traditionally been state controlled and funded by central governments or other public authorities. However, decentralization and institutional autonomy are gaining ground. Increased autonomy goes along with new modes of institutional governance. Stronger institutional governance has been implemented, with enlarged responsibility for leadership and new managerial models based on hierarchies. The introduction of external members on university governing boards has increased the number of stakeholders and, in some cases, weakened the authority of professors. Universities have been given a third responsibility (in addition to education and research) of contributing to regional and national socio-economic development. Increasing concentration on this third mission has influenced the organization, content and governance of institutions (cf. Kalpazidou Schmidt, 2005; Kim, 2002; Tjeldvoll, 1996).

Meanwhile, the state has reduced its financial support, making universities more accountable for education and research outcomes and responsible for identifying new external funding sources. Demands on legitimating activities have increased, meaning that issues such as efficiency, strategic planning, control at the institutional level and international competitiveness have been given more attention. Innovation, efficiency and competitiveness dominate the agenda. National agencies have been established to perform systematic evaluations in order to receive better counseling and enhance institutional development. In some cases, evaluations have been used for control and resource allocation (cf. Kalpazidou Schmidt, 1996; Kalpazidou Schmidt, Graversen, & Langberg, 2003; Kalpazidou Schmidt & Siune, 2003).

International trends such as the transition to a mass system (widening access and expanding higher education, often without additional funding), increased mobility, internationalization of education and research, and cooperation across borders have influenced higher education systems throughout Scandinavia. The market for higher education has been opened up with new institutions, programs and competition, as well as with new modes of cooperation. Efforts to integrate the European Research Area and the European Higher Education Area are indicative of the development towards the Europeanization of systems and harmonization of degrees.[5]

However, differences exist within a range of issues. There are differences in pace, strength and the chronological introduction of reforms in the Scandinavian countries. Governments have been setting the aims and strategies for higher education and research, but the intensity of change has varied. One important success factor is the political consensus on goals for science policy and investments in education. Sweden and Finland have, as a consequence of economic recession, undergone the most dramatic changes, adopting the "triple helix"[6] concept and involving external agents in governance. Denmark has moved in the same direction, while Norway has been more moderate in its reform policy and implementation pace.

These are among the most important trends and policy challenges that transcend several Scandinavian higher education systems. Obviously, a closer scrutiny of each country reveals individual challenges and key trends which may further improve our understanding of higher education in this region.

Brief Country Descriptions

Denmark

Knowledge institutions in Denmark include universities, governmental research institutions, university hospitals, technological service institutions, centers of tertiary education and business academies, and science parks. There are 12 universities that differ in terms of history, capacity and size, academic profile and scope. The University of Copenhagen was founded in 1479; the University of Aarhus, in 1928; and the newest—IT University of Copenhagen, established in 1999—became the 12th university in 2003. With an eye toward decentralization, three universities were founded in Odense (1966), Roskilde (1972) and Aalborg (1974). In 2001, 44% of young people entered university programs, which is a low number compared to the rest of

Scandinavia. Today, there are roughly 110,000 university students and 10,000 university teachers and researchers (UVM, 2002).

Recent years have seen a separation of responsibilities for higher education outside the universities—which falls under the jurisdiction of the Ministry of Education—and universities and research, which are the responsibility of the Ministry of Science, Technology and Innovation. The Ministry of Culture is responsible for an additional 20 higher education institutions which specialize in the fine arts, music, and architecture, among other such fields. In 2003, Parliament approved a University Act that changed the legislative framework and economic conditions for universities. In accordance with the new act, external board members are now appointed and universities have gained a greater degree of self-governance and institutional autonomy. One important change is the appointment, rather than election, of institutional leaders (rectors, deans of faculties and heads of department) and the abolition of collegial bodies. Moreover, the new act extends the role of the universities in the exchange of knowledge and competencies with other agents, including the private enterprise sector. The strategic selection of research and education activities is another priority. The act also aims to reduce the number of dropouts, increase international mobility and interaction, and introduce a modular structure for all bachelor's and master's programs (Ministry of STI, 2003; 2004; cf. Kalpazidou Schmidt, 2005).

Structure of higher education. The Danish higher education system is based on three types of programs that differ with regard to duration and level: *Short-cycle programs* (of $1^1/_2$–$2^1/_2$ years), offered in vocational colleges (technical and business) and specialized institutions (colleges of education, engineering, etc.); *medium-cycle programs* (of 3–4 years) offered at specialized vocational institutions and universities, and leading to professional diplomas; and *long-cycle programs* (a 3-year bachelor's and 2-year *candidatus* program or a 5-year continuous program leading to a *candidatus* degree) offered at the universities. Ph.D. programs are also offered at all universities.

Two types of higher education institutions exist: colleges and universities. Colleges (CVUs) are professionally oriented and comprise more than 150 specialized institutions, offering short-cycle and medium-cycle professional programs. Colleges are increasingly merging and transforming into larger, more diverse units. Some colleges with short-cycle programs are evolving into business colleges, and others with medium-cycle programs have formed one of the now 23 centers for higher education.

Of the 12 universities in Denmark, five are multi-faculty and four are mono-disciplinary universities (specializing in engineering, education, pharmacy, agriculture and veterinary science). An additional mono-faculty university—the Technical University of Denmark—focuses on technological training and research. Two of the multi-faculty universities (Roskilde and Aalborg) give attention to project-based learning, while three universities (Copenhagen, Aarhus, and Southern Denmark) have traditional multi-faculty structures. Finally, there are two business schools with university status in Aarhus and Copenhagen.

In 1992, a 3 + 2 (long-cycle) program was introduced to make the system compatible with international degrees. The Ph.D. program was also reformed in 1993 resulting in an expansion of the number of students. However, in recent years (due to stagnation in enrollments), the number of degrees awarded has stabilized. A number of doctoral schools have been set up within nearly all disciplines, aiming to ensure the continued development of dynamic environments.

Access and enrollment. As a rule, there is free admission to higher education, but taking into consideration three elements: centrally determined rules which specify admission requirements, such as qualifying exams; determination of the capacity of the annual intake; and admission control to match the number of applications with institutional capacity. Studies are tuition free with the exception of students enrolled in the Open University courses or courses in part-time education tailored for employees in the private enterprise sector. Also, the government has recently proposed tuition fees for students from non-EU countries (Ministry of STI, 2004).

In the early 1990s, a joint admission system for higher education introduced two quotas regulated by central rules. *Quota I* gave admission according to the average grade in the qualifying exam of students, while *quota II* was based on criteria specified by the institutions that allowed for individual assessments with regard to work experience, other education or study abroad. A reform in 1995 allowed institutions of higher education to determine their own admission procedures, but in 1999 the central determination of quotas for each level of education was reintroduced. Nowadays, all universities adhere to the coordinated application scheme that distributes student places according to centrally decided access criteria (UVM, 2002).

The number of degrees awarded by the newer universities has grown significantly since the 1980s, while the number of degrees awarded by the traditional universities (Copenhagen and Aarhus) has remained constant over time. However, recent stagnation in enrollment figures seems to reflect a decline in the numbers of young people.

Financing. Higher education in Denmark is funded mainly by public means at a rate higher than in other Scandinavian countries (with the exception of Norway). Sources of university funding include direct appropriations provided by the annual Appropriations Act; targeted research grants provided by the research councils, the EU, and foundations; and private donations. University *basic research grants* (approximately 60% of the research budget) are not targeted toward specific research, while *subsidies* (approximately 40% of the research budget) are attached to specific programs and projects. In recent years, a portion of the grants has been activity dependent—i.e., reliant on student production, training of researchers and the ability to attract external funds. In addition to direct funding to the institutions, the Danish government allocates substantial resources (the highest among OECD countries) to student grants. Most university grants for educational purposes are directly linked to the number of "full-time equivalent students" who are successfully passing annual exams (Ministry of STI, 2004).

Quality assurance. In 1999, development contracts between universities and the Ministry of Science, Technology and Innovation were introduced. A university development contract is a letter of intent stating strategic areas in which the university intends to focus. The *first-generation university development contracts* (2000–2004) focused on education and research, quality assurance, internationalization, IT-based learning and innovation. The *second-generation contracts* focus on the strengthening of links with society, national and international cooperation (also with businesses), quality assurance, research and benchmarking with foreign universities (Ministry of STI, 2004).

The external quality assurance of a university's education and teaching consists of (i) a nationwide body of external experts in the assessment of quality and relevance of education, and (ii) members of the Danish Evaluation Institute. Bottom-up evaluations of education are also undertaken by the universities, and other quality development instruments are used. Accreditation is an acknowledged quality assurance tool in Denmark (cf. EURYDICE, 2005; Kalpazidou Schmidt, 2003).

Academic positions. Staffing comprises the following full-time positions: professor (tenured), associate professor (tenured) and assistant professor (untenured). The total number of full professorships is determined at a central level. Professors' assignments comprise teaching, research and administration. There is also a number of term-limited or part-time academics within research or teaching.

Danish universities have approximately 1,300–1,350 full professorships—a low number compared to other Scandinavian countries, especially Norway and Finland. Even though the number of full professors has recently increased, there are at present 200–250 vacant professorships. The age of scientific staff implies high annual retirement among staff in tenured positions by 2010–2015. University expansion during the late 1960s and early 1970s created a high number of positions for associate professors and researchers, but this was followed by a time of stagnation in recruitments. Stricter qualification requirements introduced in 1984 increased the average age of staff in tenured positions. Young academics are usually employed in untenured positions. Internal and external mobility of scientific staff is modest. However, the government intends to introduce the concept of "super professors" with the aim to attract the best Danish and foreign researchers and build internationally competitive research environments.

Internationalization and mobility. Internationalization of higher education has expanded in recent years, and a growing number of institutions offer programs in English. Danish students increasingly include study visits abroad as part of their education, and a growing number of students earn their entire degree abroad. Half of these study in either the UK or another Scandinavian country. Students may obtain a state education grant for a maximum of 4 years, provided that they enroll in publicly recognized education programs. Students participate in exchange programs or bilateral exchange arrangements that usually last between one and two semesters. With the introduction of the EU program SOCRATES/ERASMUS, student mobility out of Denmark has doubled, while mobility into Denmark has improved by a factor of four. In 2001, more than 7,000 Danish students studied abroad (4% of the country's total student population); most studied in another EU country, with more than 900 in Scandinavia and a similar number in non-EU countries. Internationalization of education and research training is part of the university development contracts. Ph.D. programs must include visits at other primarily international institutions. In 2000, 5,000 Ph.D. students enrolled at Danish universities; 9% of them were foreign students. At the same time, 5% of all Ph.D. students obtained a degree abroad. Denmark provides tax incentives to the recruitment of foreign experts (UVM, 2002).

Finland

In comparison with other OECD countries, Finland has done outstanding in terms of R&D and innovation. Higher education has played a key role in this process, as more than 72% of young people enter tertiary education (OECD, 2003a, 2003b). Higher education in Finland consists of universities and polytechnics, Open University and Continuing Education. The first university was founded in Turku in 1640. In the beginning of the 19th century it was moved to Helsinki and remained Finland's only institution of higher education until 1908, when the Helsinki University of Technology was founded. Later a Finnish- and Swedish-language university was established in Turku. In the 1950s and 1960s, institutions within economics and technology were founded. The scope of higher education was narrow and geographically concentrated in Southern Finland. In the 1960s and 1970s, higher education expanded due to demands for educated labor and regional equality, with the establishment of universities in Eastern and Northern Finland (Ministry of Education, 2002a; 2002b).

Parliament approved its first Higher Education Development Act in 1966. The purpose was to ensure a steady growth of resources for universities and increase capacities in technology, natural sciences and medicine as well as to ensure international compatibility. A new act approved in 1987, with additional funds for universities, prepared for reforms and a shift towards steering by results. In the 1990s, a binary system was introduced with the establishment of the polytechnics network.

In 1999, a Development Plan for Education and Research (1999–2004) was adopted. It focused on improving quality through evaluation and competition, educational equality, lifelong learning and a public commitment to maintaining a high level of funding. Higher education institutions were encouraged to improve (i) regional responsiveness, through cooperation with their local society, and (ii) internationalization at every level; in one strategic objective, approximately one-third of all students are expected to study abroad for at least part of his or her degree. Today, significant achievements in these areas have become a hallmark of Finnish higher education. Also, the Finnish technological infrastructure is considered one of the best in the world, and engineering is strongly represented in higher education institutions—in this regard, the Finnish system differs from many of its European counterparts (Ministry of Education, 2001; 2002a).

In recent years, authority has been transferred from the Ministry of Education to the institutions, and the system of steering by performance is nowadays based on well developed evaluation procedures. Universities and the ministry formulate objectives for each institution and make agreements on funding or the number of students to be enrolled (as is the case for polytechnics). According to the University Act, universities are autonomous and entitled to accept external representatives (businesses and otherwise) as board members. The Polytechnics Act, ratified in 2003, acknowledged the role of social partners to formulate objectives for the polytechnics.

Structure of higher education. In Finland there are ten multi-faculty universities, six specialized universities and four art academies, all public and engaged in education and research. In addition, there are 29 polytechnics awarding professional degrees.

In 1995, a system of researcher schools was established to supplement traditional postgraduate education. At present, 24 polytechnics are given permission to award up to 300 postgraduate degrees. The polytechnic degree is designed to respond to requirements of the labor market.

The university degree system has regularly been reformed based on evaluations carried out by the universities and the Council for Higher Education. Lower academic degrees are first degrees of the bachelor's level and consist of 3 years of studies. Higher academic degrees are second-cycle master's degrees and consist of a total of 5 years, or a bachelor's plus 40–60 credits (Ministry of Education, 2002a; 2002b).

Access and enrollment. Entrance examinations are a key element in the selection process for enrollment in higher education. During the last decade, the number of undergraduate students has risen by nearly 40%, and similar growth has been seen among the number of master's and doctoral students. The Finnish matriculation examination determines general eligibility for university education, and is equivalent to international certificates. A 3-year vocational qualification also provides admission to university studies. Universities may also admit applicants who have completed Open University studies. Selection procedures are based on matriculation examinations, school-leaving certificate and entrance tests. As such, there is no national entrance examination common to all universities. Admission to polytechnics is based on a joint national system for application administered by the National Board of Education. Polytechnics determine their own entry requirements. Entrance to polytechnic postgraduate programs requires a minimum of 3 years work experience after completion of higher education studies.

Financing. In general, higher education in Finland is publicly funded. However, external funding as a percentage of overall funding is rising. The Academy of Finland and the National Technology Agency are the main funding agencies. Public university budgets are allocated according to a formula that has been gradually implemented since 1997, and implies that universities are granted resources primarily according to target numbers for master's degrees and doctorates. Lagging behind the targets has an impact on funding. The research budget for universities is also based on the number of doctoral degrees produced, although Finland recently announced its intentions to increase public research spending between 5% and 13% for major research agencies (universities, polytechnics, the Academy of Finland and the Technology Center of Finland). Polytechnics are also financed mainly by the government (57%) and by local authorities (43%), with additional funds granted on a performance basis (Research Nordic 2003; Ministry of Education, 2002a; 2002b).

Quality assurance. Universities and polytechnics have extensive self-evaluation procedures, and performance evaluation is an integral part of university and polytechnic operations. Evaluation is both external and internal, and includes several councils and boards. Institutions are assisted in their evaluations by the Higher Education Evaluation Council, established in 1996, and evaluation of research is conducted by the Academy of Finland.

Academic positions. Academic positions in Finland consist of professors, senior assistants, assistants and lecturers. There are full-time untenured positions as well, although declining in numbers. There are approximately 8,000 teaching positions, of which 2,200 are full professorships. Polytechnics employ principal lecturers with a licentiate or doctoral degree and lecturers with a master's degree. Both categories require a minimum of 3 years work experience. There is an ongoing debate in Finland on who is qualified to serve as a lecturer at the polytechnics.

Internationalization and mobility. Internationalization has been a main goal of Finnish educational policy and is regarded as a crucial factor in quality assurance. A virtual university was launched in 2001, linking national and international education. Cooperation with institutions abroad was extended in the 1990s and resulted in increased student exchanges. The policy target by the end of the 1990s was that (as a minimum) 6,000 higher education and 8,000 polytechnic students (nearly one-third of all new students) should complete part of their study abroad. Currently, more than 80% of Finnish students in foreign countries are enrolled at European institutions. However, the number of outgoing exchange students is slowing down.

Meanwhile, approximately 4,000 foreign students (1,400 postgraduates) were enrolled at Finnish universities in 2002, with another 2,600 studying at the polytechnics. However, the overall percentage of foreign students in Finland is low by international standards (namely 2.3% at the universities and polytechnics).

By the end of the 1990s, funds were earmarked to enhance researcher mobility. Key cooperation partners were the U.S., Canada, China, Russia, Germany, the UK and Sweden. However, university researcher exchanges have not increased at the same level as student exchanges. The mobility of teachers is limited, and Finland has taken initiatives to encourage the repatriation of Finnish postdocs and scientists working abroad (Ministry of Education, 2001; 2002a).

Iceland

In Iceland, higher education is relatively homogeneous, mainly organized within the public sector and for a long time has been dominated by the University of Iceland (established in 1911). There are ten higher education institutions, eight of which have university status. A new Higher Education Act was adopted in 1997, providing changes in areas of organization and governance. A unitary system with minor internal differentiation was introduced on this occasion. The autonomy of institutions increased and representation of academic staff on boards was weakened (two external members are appointed). In 2003, institutions were asked to establish formal internal quality systems (Jonasson, 2002).

Structure of higher education. Most degrees in Iceland are of the 3-year bachelor's type. A significant proportion of master's and Ph.D. students moved to the U.K., U.S. and Canada, influencing the development of Icelandic higher education in an Anglo-Saxon direction. Recent growth in the number of enrollments has been seen, and doctoral studies are now offered in the faculty of arts at the University of Iceland.

Access and enrollment. Universities are responsible for the student selection process, and admission requirements consist of passing a matriculation examination. Applicants with work experience, but without completing a matriculation examination, may also be admitted. Except for the University of Iceland, all admissions are based on a competitive selection. In 2001, approximately 14,000 students were enrolled in higher education— more than 60% of the college-age population—with two-thirds of them enrolled at the University of Iceland. Another 2,000 students were studying abroad.

Financing. Higher education in Iceland is primarily funded by block grants from the national budget. However, due to a rise in student numbers, public higher education institutions are considering the introduction of tuition fees or new restrictions on admission.

Quality assurance. Iceland has no tradition of program or quality evaluation in its higher education system. However, the Ministry of Education, Science and Culture has recently initiated a new system for the evaluation of programs and particular subject areas.

Academic positions. Academic positions are comprised of teaching positions (professors, associate and assistant professors) and research positions (scientists, scholars and specialists, mainly in the natural and medical sciences). The majority of staff hold teaching positions and only a small proportion hold research positions.

Internationalization and mobility. Internationalization has been a feature of the Icelandic higher education system throughout the last century. It is estimated that up to 40% of all students at the university level study abroad, primarily in the Nordic countries.

Norway

The first academic institution in Norway was founded in Trondheim in 1760 (Royal Norwegian Society of Science) and the first Norwegian university was established in Oslo in 1811. Other universities followed after World War II—in Bergen (1946), Trondheim (1969/1996) and Tromsø (1972). There are also many specialized higher education institutions—established between 1897 and 1972—with study programs in science and technology, teaching, agriculture, medicine, business administration, architecture, physical education/sports and music (EURYDICE, 2005; Ministry of Education and Research, 2001).

   A loan fund was introduced in 1947 to provide support for students as part of a policy to promote equal opportunities in higher education. Structural reforms in the late 1960s resulted in a growth in the number of institutions, many with small numbers of students. Through a higher education reform in 1994, many regional and vocational colleges merged into university colleges in order to raise academic standards and prioritize resources. Until recently, colleges were acknowledged as *state colleges,* and their designation as *university colleges* reflects their upgrading. Nowadays, Norwegian colleges offer programs at higher levels of study and employ more staff holding doctoral degrees.

All higher education in Norway is subject to the Universities and Colleges Act of 1995, which was revised in 2002 to address the accreditation of institutions and systems for internal quality assurance. In connection with the Quality Reform of Higher Education Act (2000), which aimed towards greater equality between public and private institutions, the degree structures in Norway were revised in accordance with the Bologna Declaration. These reforms increased institutional autonomy, linked financial incentives to outcomes, and introduced a system of quality assurance and formal accreditation (Ministry of Education and Research, 2001; 2003; Ot. prp. nr. 79, 2003–2004).

Structure of higher education. Norway offers higher education at 38 publicly funded and 31 privately funded institutions. There are four universities and six specialized university-sector higher education institutions, 26 university colleges and two colleges/academies of arts and crafts. With the implementation of the Quality Reform in 2003, the constitution of university boards was changed to ensure increased external representation. Institutions are obliged to collaborate with community and industry, and boards are requested to draw more than one-third of their members from their local community. A new higher education reform has been proposed (but not yet approved by Parliament), which could bring substantial changes in the status and operating environment of universities and colleges, introducing self-governance with a majority of external board members. (The Competence Reform, Report No. 42 to the Storting, 1997–1998; Ministry of Education and Research 2005).

Universities and specialized institutions offer degrees at different levels. University colleges in Norway are more research-oriented than in other countries and offer postgraduate education as well. Some private higher education institutions offer postgraduate education at the doctoral level. The degree system is the same for all public higher education, which facilitates mobility between universities and university colleges.

Access and enrollment. As of 2001, approximately 200,000 students were participating in some form of Norwegian higher education, with the vast majority (more than 90%) attending state institutions. Following a significant increase in the number of students during the 1980s and 1990s, there has been a drop in student intake. Today, more than 62% of the college-age population are enrolled in programs at the tertiary level.

Entry to tertiary education is regulated by the capacity of institutions. The minimum requirement for admission is successful completion of upper secondary education. Since 1997, the Upper Secondary School Leaving Certificate has been based on 13 years of schooling. Admission to a university may also be achieved with other qualifications recognized as being equivalent to the general matriculation standard. Some fields of study have additional entrance requirements. Admission can also be granted on the basis of a combination of formal, informal and non-formal qualifications.

Financing. Higher education is funded by the government by means of framework allocations. The total amount granted directly to the institutions is determined by Parliament as part of the annual budget. Since 1996, the demands on financial management and control have increased. Following the reform of 2003, institutions disburse funding allocations internally, but the amounts are decided on the basis of past performance and indicators such as credits and degrees awarded, research outcomes, international activities and publications.

Research funding is also part of the annual framework allocations to institutions. Public funding dominates the research financing at universities and colleges (88% in 1999), while institutions may also apply for additional funds from the Research Council and other agents. Universities are the main agents in public R&D, with 78% of the country's total R&D funds being allocated to these institutions in 2001.

Quality assurance. Institutions are responsible for quality assurance. In 2004, an internal system of quality assurance was established, in compliance with national criteria. The main task of the Norwegian Agency for Quality Assurance in Education (established in 2003) is quality assurance at the national level, which involves accreditation and evaluation of each institution's internal quality assurance system by means of audits.

Academic positions. In 2000, the number of academic staff in higher education was approximately 11,600, of which 34% were women. In addition to the traditional full, associate and assistant professors (3,000)—employed mainly at universities—other scientific staff include lecturers (3,500), "høgskoledosent" (50), "secondary positions" (200), and "scholars" (2,200). Norway has the highest ratio of full professors per capita in Scandinavia, but despite policy initiatives to address gender issues, almost 90% of full professors are male. As in other Scandinavian countries, Norway will soon face problems with a decrease in teaching and research staff due to retirements.

Internationalization and mobility. The reform of 2003 has put increased emphasis on internationalization. Universities and state colleges have been obliged to focus on this issue. Students are entitled to studies abroad as part of their Norwegian degree, and institutions are encouraged financially to facilitate mobility and increase their intake of foreign students. To further stimulate internationalization, a center for international cooperation in higher education has been established (NIFU, 2001).

In 2001, about 16,000 Norwegians studied abroad, of which 2,000 students were participating in student exchange programs. Loans and grants are portable and additional funding is awarded to students abroad. Compared to other Scandinavian countries, Norway has a small number of foreign students but the number is increasing, in particular with student intake from Central and Eastern Europe and developing countries.

Sweden

In Sweden, higher education expanded significantly during the second half of the 20th century. The greatest expansion occurred in the 1960s and 1990s. More than 70% of young people enter tertiary education. In 2002, there were 330,000 students in undergraduate education and 18,600 postgraduate students; the number of doctoral degrees awarded that year was over 2,400 (Swedish Universities and University Colleges, 2003).

The first university in Sweden (and Scandinavia) was founded in Uppsala (1477) and the second in Lund (1666). In the mid-1940s, higher education was offered at the universities of Uppsala and Lund, the university colleges of Stockholm and Gothenburg, and at specialized institutions of medicine, economics and technology. In the late 1950s, the university colleges of Stockholm and Gothenburg became universities. As a result of the growth of students during the 1960s and 1970s, university branches and university colleges were established throughout the country.

Reforms in 1977 and 1993 have reshaped the higher education landscape in Sweden. With the 1977 reform, all postsecondary education became integrated into a single system. At the same time, free admission was abolished. In 1993, a new Higher Education Act and Higher Education Ordinance came into force, which reduced the influence of the central government and introduced decentralization of decision making, while also making new demands on institutional efficiency and control of outcomes. According to the act, institutions would determine admissions on the basis of general guidelines. A new system for allocating resources to undergraduate education was introduced in 1993, based on the number of students and assessments of performance, rather than on the planned volume of education. The selection of academic leaders was modified and a new "third role"—serving the local community—was given to institutions.

Massification, institutional autonomy and quality have become key issues, together with efficiency, innovation and competitiveness. Recently, issues of governance and leadership have dominated the agenda, and national agencies in higher education have been reformed. An agency for higher education was re-established in 1995 to oversee quality assessments, reviews and analysis. In 2001, two new authorities were established—the National Science Council and an Agency for Research, Development and Innovation (Kim, 2002; Kim & Mårtens, 2003; Trow, Henkel, House, Kristensen, & Neave, 2002).

Structure of higher education. There are 50 public and private higher education institutions in Sweden, including 11 state-run universities (in addition to the Karolinska Institute and the Royal Institute of Technology), seven independent colleges of art, and 16 university colleges. The Chalmers University of Technology, the Stockholm School of Economics and the University College of Jönköping each have private governing bodies. A number of smaller private institutions also have the authority to award undergraduate degrees. Institutions are run by a governing board; the chair and a majority of members are appointed by the government, while staff and students are represented as well. Institutions are granted university status based on an assessment by the government; the same holds true for institutions who seek to establish so-called "areas of research," giving them the right to award postgraduate degrees. (cf. EURYDICE, 2004; 2005)

Access and enrollment. The number of students in Sweden increased from 16,000 in 1950 to 330,000 in 2002. Recent higher education policy aims to increase enrollments so that 50% of an age cohort enters higher education by the age of 25, compared with the current level of 46%. In Sweden (as in Denmark and Iceland), more than half the students enter a university after the age of 22. This reflects the flexibility of programs as well as the Nordic view of the value of work experience for studies.

The number of new enrollments in postgraduate programs has recently increased to 3,600 after a period of stagnation. Postgraduate degrees more than doubled between 1990 and 2002, and the number of doctorates increased by 90%. The proportion of women with postgraduate degrees has also risen to 44% (2002).

The general eligibility requirement for admission to undergraduate studies is the completion of upper secondary school. Students without formal qualifications may enter if they are more than 25 years old and have a minimum of 4 years work experience. There are in most cases course eligibility requirements as well. Additional requirements are often tied to various study programs and courses. A selection process takes place whenever the number of qualified applicants exceeds the number of seats, and competition for entrance is often intense.

Financing. Allocation of resources is based on results (number of students and performance) and is annually determined by the government. Research and postgraduate training are funded by special grants. Government grants for undergraduate education and research/postgraduate training account for 65% of total expenditures. Other external resources for research come from contractual work granted by research councils, sectoral agencies, local authorities and the private sector. Over a 20-year period, funding of research has undergone important changes. At the beginning of the 1980s, two-thirds of the research was funded by the government. In 2002, just over 55% of research and postgraduate programs were funded by external resources (including research council funds).

Quality assurance. Sweden was the first Nordic country to use audits as a means to ensure quality. Institutions have the responsibility for quality control, and the government is responsible for accreditation. The National Agency for Higher Education is responsible for evaluations, audits and monitoring. In 2002, the second and final round of audits of quality assurance was completed. The agency is in the process of evaluating undergraduate and postgraduate programs.

Academic positions. Since 1985, the number of staff in higher education has increased by 34%. In 2002, a total of 51,500 persons (full-time positions) were employed at higher education institutions. This figure accounts for roughly one-quarter of the total number of state employees. From 2001 to 2002 the number of professors increased by 7% and postgraduate students by 8%. The number of full professors has risen constantly since 1985 (to 4,000 in 2003), with the largest increases in the last few years. This was mainly due to a 1999 promotion reform that allowed qualified senior lecturers to advance to full professor positions. Even the number of senior lecturers has increased as a result of the reform. The number of postdoctoral research appointments doubled in the 1980s but has declined in recent years.

Teaching and research staff include professors, postdoctoral fellows, senior lecturers and junior lecturers, and part-time and visiting teachers. The number of academic staff expected to retire in the near future is rising, with retirements projected to take place at the same time as an increase in the student cohorts entering higher education (2008–2013).

Internationalization and mobility. Internationalization of higher education has been an issue in Sweden for almost three decades. In the late 1980s and early 1990s, internationalization grants were integrated into the funding of universities. From 1989, mobility was further enhanced as Swedish students became eligible to use grants for studies abroad. Sweden provides tax incentives to facilitate the recruitment of foreign experts.

During the academic year 2001–02, nearly 27,500 Swedes studied abroad. Most followed undergraduate programs for one or two semesters, a large majority of them in Europe. Today, the U.S. is host to the largest number of Swedish students (4,600). A large number of Swedes also study in Denmark (1,000). With regard to exchange programs, ERASMUS accounts for over half (4,500) of all exchange students. Since 1998–99 there have been more incoming students than Swedes studying abroad. The same trend is seen in countries like Finland, Norway, the Netherlands and the U.K.

Conclusion: Recent Changes and Future Perspectives

In Denmark, a national strategy was introduced in 2003 aimed at strengthening higher education training and research and creating new science framework conditions. At the same time, the university system, the public research institutions and the research councils were reformed to respond to greater socio-economic demands for enhanced competitiveness. A number of recent reforms have been implemented, including a quality-promoting evaluation system and a research budgeting model.

In general, the Danish higher education system is characterized by flexibility and life-long learning schemes that facilitate mobility between its parts. Future challenges include the development of institutional structures and the effective functioning of university boards that were introduced by a new University Act, as well as improving relations with industry. One key issue is the sustainability of many small institutions in a changing environment of increased internationalization, interdisciplinary approaches, demands on quality performance and cooperation with industry. Another issue involves the need to adjust programs within the humanities and social sciences (which are the largest university faculties) to better meet labor market demands; currently only 50% of graduates in the humanities (and only 66% of social sciences graduates) successfully enter the labor market upon graduation.

The Finnish higher education system is characterized by competitiveness and innovation. A "management by results" principle was adopted to increase accountability. Universities have been granted higher autonomy and research councils have been reorganized to better respond to socio-economic demands and interdisciplinarity. A key issue in Finland is the strengthening of university autonomy and a balanced development of the binary system of universities and polytechnics. The high level of unemployment in Finland will most likely continue to pose a challenge to education, as will the expectations that regional and other stakeholders have for institutions to contribute to socio-economic development. In the future, performance-based funding will be increased, taking into account employment rates of graduates. The education equality principle and lifelong learning approach will continue to be on the higher education agenda, as well as the organization of graduate degree studies.

In the Icelandic scientific research community, many small institutions have merged with larger universities, thus limiting the diversification of research. However, the domination of higher education by the University of Iceland is declining, as other institutions (including privates) enroll an increasing number of students. Also, the system of scientific research has recently been reorganized. Major changes include restructuring of the Icelandic Research Council and the establishment of two funding agencies—one for research and one for development and innovation—which aim to enhance science-industry relations. Traditionally, graduates and researchers have been state employees, but this is changing as a consequence of the private sector's increasing investments in R&D. The introduction of tuition fees, distance education and lifelong learning are contemporary issues on the Icelandic higher education agenda.

Norwegian higher education focuses on competence development and coordination. There is currently a reform process underway in Norway which aims to improve quality; increase institutional autonomy; develop a more results-oriented higher education funding system; establish a continuous evaluation system; improve students' financial support; and increase internationalization. Reforms—which were met with significant opposition from academia—were initiated in order to strengthen innovation, user-oriented programs and interdisciplinary approaches. Meanwhile, demand for higher education seemed to decrease in Norway, resulting in policies meant to stabilize student enrollments. Other key issues in Norway include the need to improve links between higher education and industry, and to develop institutional structures and reorganize university boards with representation of different stakeholders.

The Swedish higher education system focuses on integration, uniformity and equal distribution. Major changes have recently occurred in the structure of funding— 11 councils and agencies were transformed into three research councils and one research and technology agency. The main tasks of these bodies are to support fundamental research and promote a renewal of the science system, giving special attention to young academics and faculty mobility. Issues on the country's higher education agenda include increased decentralization and institutional autonomy; continued quality improvement; increased focus on interdisciplinarity; cooperation with societal agents; further expansion; and reducing the level of inequality in student recruitment (with respect to social background). Academic leaders must also grapple with the crucial issue of building human resources in academia. Finally, it remains to be determined whether the uniformity of the Swedish system is feasible in the long run—growing differences between the different segments of the higher education system in almost every aspect (institutions, staff, students, research and resources) highlights the difficulty of maintaining a uniform system.

Prospects and Challenges

Universities in Scandinavia, as in other parts of the world, develop within a contextual framework that requires constant reconsideration of their role, structure and financing. Some current and future policy challenges include the need to:

- build up "new higher education intelligence" and further develop strategies to meet challenges of the knowledge-based society;
- expand the higher education systems in ways that encompass diversity of missions (e.g., education, research and innovation, regional and national development) and introduce diversified structures (based on identification of strengths and promotion of core competencies) to increase these institutions' capacity for meeting socio-economic demands;
- enhance the autonomy of institutions, consolidate new institutional structures and improve governance through the training and professionalization of university leaders and managers (in particular in Denmark and Norway, where management in its present form is a relatively new responsibility) while at the same time safe-guarding the authority of the faculty;
- improve mechanisms to attract additional funds from diversified sources, and manage finances in a way that leaves space for basic research and fields or disciplines that may not attract high amounts of external resources;
- further develop dynamic frameworks that continue to promote the "third mission" (i.e., university-industry relations) without compromising scientific excellence;
- maximize the utility of (and stakeholder involvement in) quality assessments and accountability efforts in education and research, emphasizing the self-improvement benefits of evaluation, benchmarking and monitoring;
- develop higher education systems that balance continued expansion of universities with increasing quality requirements;
- balance the public and private investments in basic and market-oriented research, and further develop environments that enable the fertilization of ideas across sectors and disciplines (i.e., interdisciplinarity and multidisciplinarity);
- enhance the role of higher education institutions as regional actors, and improve knowledge transfer and dissemination to society;
- improve the attractiveness of the academic profession and researchers' careers, particularly in Denmark (where they also face an important issue of limited numbers of professors in the country), Norway and Sweden, while paying particular attention to gender issues;
- reinforce opportunities for the mobility of students and researchers (particularly in Norway and Finland, where the number of foreign students is limited), and improve the standardization of accreditation procedures in ways that can further stimulate mobility (an important consideration for Denmark); and
- emphasize the role of universities as a critical voice in society. Universities are the most reflective part of society and the only place where thinking—including critical thinking—is institutionalized and recognized as a vital characteristic of democracies.

These are among the policy challenges that most commonly transcend several Scandinavian higher education systems. How the systems respond to these challenges will clearly determine the nature of higher education's future throughout the region, and will require innovation, flexibility, and thoughtful, long-term strategies.

Notes

1. The term Scandinavia is used for easy reference instead of the more correct Nordic countries, the latter referring to Denmark, Finland, Iceland, Sweden and Norway. Finland and Iceland are not a part of Scandinavia but included in the chapter due to effective policy and significant results (Finland in particular).
2. The transition from Mode 1 to Mode 2 research has been described by Gibbons, Limoges, Nowotny, Schwartzman, Scott, & Trow (1994). According to theory, knowledge in Mode 2 is generated in the context of application and is directly influenced by societal needs.
3. Implications of policymaking on institutions are described in Kalpazidou Schmidt (1996); Kalpazidou Schmidt, Graversen, & Langberg, (2003).
4. Kalpazidou Schmidt, Graversen, & Langberg, (2003); Graversen, Kalpazidou Schmidt & Langberg, (2005).
5. See the chapter by Hans de Wit in this volume.
6. Interaction between university, industry and government (cf. Etzkowitz & Leydesdorff, 1997; 2000).

References

European Commission (2003). *Third European report on science & technology indicators, 2003.* Brussels: European Commission, Community Research.

Etzkowitz, H. & Leydesdorff, L. (1997). Introduction to special issue on science policy dimensions of the Triple Helix of university-industry-government relations. *Science and Public Policy, 24* no. 1, 2–6.

Etzkowitz, H. & Leydesdorff, L. (2000). The dynamics of innovation: from national systems and "Mode 2" to a triple helix of university-industry-government relations. *Research Policy, 29* no. 2, 109–123.

EURYDICE (2004). Focus on the structure of higher education in Europe 2003–4: National trends in the Bologna process. DG for Education and Culture. http://www.Eurydice.org Accessed June 2004.

EURYDICE (2005). Database on education systems in Europe. http://www.Eurydice.org. Accessed May 2005.

Gibbons, M., Limoges, C., Nowotny, H., Schwartzman, S., Scott, P. & Trow, M. (1994). *The new production of knowledge. The dynamics of science and research in contemporary societies.* Thousand Oaks, CA: Sage Publications.

Graversen, E. K., Kalpazidou Schmidt, E. & Langberg, K. (2005). Dynamic research environments— a development model. *The International Journal of Human Resource Management.* 16:8 August, 1503–1516, Routledge.

Jonasson, J. T. (2002). Higher education reforms in Iceland at the transition into the 21st century. In I. Fägerlind & G. Strömqvist (Eds.), *Reforming Higher Education in the Nordic Countries. Studies of change in Denmark, Finland, Iceland, Norway and Sweden* (pp. 137–188). Paris: International Institute for Educational Planning.

Kaiser F., et al. (2003). Higher education policy issues and trends. An update on higher education policy issues in 11 Western countries. *CHEPS—Higher Education Monitor, 2003.*

Kalpazidou Schmidt, E. (1996). *Research environments in a Nordic perspective: A comparative study in ecology and scientific productivity.* Acta Universitatis Upsaliensis. Uppsala Studies in Education 67.

Kalpazidou Schmidt, E. (2003a). *Science and society—Building bridges of excellence. Perceptions on the interaction between public research and enterprises.* The Danish Institute for Studies in Research and Research Policy.

Kalpazidou Schmidt, E. (2003b). *The use of evaluations in Europe. Evaluation and science policy.* The Danish Institute for Studies in Research and Research Policy.

Kalpazidou Schmidt, E. (2004). *Research and higher education in the Nordic countries. A comparison of the Nordic Systems.* The Danish Centre for Studies in Research and Research Policy.

Kalpazidou Schmidt, E. (2005). Management of Knowledge and Organizational Changes in Higher Education: The new Danish University Act. Paper presented at the Fifth International Conference on Knowledge, Culture and Change in Organisation. University of the Aegean, Rhodes, Greece, 19–22 July 2005. Forthcoming in the *International Journal of Knowledge, Culture and Change Management*, vol. 5, 2005.

Kalpazidou Schmidt, E. & Siune, K. (2003). *The use of R&D evaluations in European science policy*. The Danish Institute for Studies in Research and Research Policy.

Kalpazidou Schmidt, E., Graversen, E. K. & Langberg, K. (2003). Innovation and dynamics in public research environments in Denmark: A research policy perspective. *Science and Public Policy, 30*(2), (April), 107–116.

Kim, L. (2002). Alike but different: A comparative study of higher education and research in the Nordic countries. *National Agency for Higher Education*.

Kim, L. & Mårtens, P. (Eds.) 2003. *The wild growing higher education. Studies in research, environments and knowledge pathways*.

Ministry of Education (2001). An international strategy for higher education. Finland. http://www.minedu.fi. Accessed June 2004.

Ministry of Education (2002a). Finnish universities. Finland. http://www.minedu.fi. Accessed June 2004.

Ministry of Education (2002b). Higher education policy. Finland. http://www.minedu.fi. Accessed June 2004.

Ministry of Education and Research (2005). OECD Thematic review of tertiary education, Country Background Report for Norway.

Ministry of Education and Research (2003). Ryssdal committees report, "New act on universities and higher education," September 23, 2003. Norway.

Ministry of Education and Research (2001). Fact sheet U01.016. Reforms in higher education—a more open system. Summary of government bill 2001/02:15, November 2001. Norway.

Ministry of Science, Technology and Innovation (2003). General notes to the draft bill on universities (The University Act). Ministry of STI, Denmark.

Ministry of Science, Technology and Innovation (2004). Reviews of national policies for education: University education in Denmark. Examiner's report (pre-publication version, 6 January 2004). Ministry of STI, Denmark.

NIFU (2001). Internationalization of Research and Higher Education. Proposal for a Strategic Institute Programme (SIP)-A, Summary.

NORBAL (2004). Statistics on awarded doctoral degrees and doctoral students in the Nordic and Baltic countries. http://www.nifu.no. Accessed June 2004.

Norwegian Parliament. The Competence Reform Report No. 42 to the Storting (1997–1998).

Organization for Economic Cooperation and Development (OECD) (2003a). *Education at a glance*. Paris: OECD.

OECD (2003b). *Governance of public research. Toward better practices*. Paris: OECD, Science and Technology.

Ot. prp. No. 79 (2003–2004) om lov om universiteter og høyskoler. Norway.

Research Nordic (2003). Helsinki pushes ahead with spending increases. August 18, 2003.

Ståhle, B. (1999). *Age, gender and recruitment in Danish university research*. Copenhagen, Denmark: UNI-C.

Swedish Universities and University Colleges (2003). *Annual report 2003*. Stockholm: The National Agency for Higher Education.

Tjeldvoll, A. (1996). Recent developments in Scandinavian higher education. *International Higher Education*.

Trow, M., Henkel, M., House, E., Kristensen, B. & Neave, G. (2002). *The national reviews of Swedish higher education*. Report by the International Advisory Committee to the National Agency for Higher Education in Sweden.

UVM (2002). *Facts and figures, education indicators Denmark 2002*. Ministry of Education, Denmark.

27

HIGHER EDUCATION IN SOUTHEAST ASIA IN THE ERA OF GLOBALIZATION

Molly N.N. Lee
UNESCO Bangkok, Thailand

Southeast Asia consists of ten countries as reflected by the member states in the Association of Southeast Asian Nations (ASEAN)—Brunei, Cambodia, Indonesia, Laos, Malaysia, Myanmar, the Philippines, Singapore, Thailand, and Vietnam. These countries have marked differences in terms of size, economic wealth, political ideologies, and educational traditions. Brunei and Singapore are very small states as compared to Indonesia, which has a huge population and a wide geographical area. Singapore, Malaysia and Thailand are newly industrialized countries and Brunei is an oil-rich country. Cambodia, Myanmar, Laos and Vietnam are in a state of transition—moving from a centrally planned economy to a market economy, from an agricultural economy to an industrial economy, and from a socialist regime to a more democratic system. All these countries except Thailand have a colonial history, and their education systems have been very much influenced by their colonial heritage.

Despite the diversity, higher education systems in Southeast Asia face similar problems and challenges. All these systems have budgets to balance, standards to maintain, faculties to satisfy, and social demands to meet (Postiglione & Mak, 1997). Among the less developed countries, the higher education systems are chronically under-funded but face escalating demand for access; further, the faculty are under-qualified, the curricula are under-developed, and the students are poorly taught (World Bank, 2000). Many of these systems are undergoing restructuring under the influence of global trends in higher education reforms in the areas of funding, resources, governance and curriculum development.

This chapter will analyze the historical development of higher education in Southeast Asia and examine the trends and policy challenges in a comparative perspective. It will explore issues relating to access, funding, and accountability as well as the changing academic profession and regional cooperation. The development of higher education in this region can be broadly divided into three main periods, namely: (i) the colonial period, (ii) the early independence period, and (iii) the contemporary period. It is argued that higher education is greatly influenced by its historical past, nation-building efforts, and current global trends. The analysis of the realities and challenges facing higher

James J.F. Forest and Philip G. Altbach (eds.), International Handbook of Higher Education, 539–555.

education in this region will show that there is an interplay between national needs and global trends.

Historical Development

During the pre-colonial days, only a few countries in this region had some form of higher education, usually established by religious bodies. In Vietnam, education in Confucianism was established at the Temple of Literature (Huong & Fry, 2004), while in Indonesia, non-formal Islamic education was carried out in the mosques (Buchori & Malik, 2004), and in Thailand, higher learning took place in the palace, temples and communities (Sinlarat, 2004). However, higher education in its modern form is a Western implant brought to the shores of Southeast Asian countries by colonial rulers—with the exception in Thailand, where it was voluntarily adopted (Altbach & Selvaratnam, 1989).

Western influences on higher education in this region are complex and varied, involving the Dutch in Indonesia; the British in Brunei, Singapore, Malaysia, and Myanmar; the French in Indochina; and the Spanish (and later the Americans) in the Philippines. Thailand is the only country that has maintained its independence from colonial rule; however, its rulers were strongly influenced by Western ideas and have voluntarily adopted Western models of higher education. The Soviet model of higher education was very influential in Vietnam and Cambodia during the 1960s and 1970s. In the contemporary period, it is the North American (and to an increasing degree, Australian) influence that is becoming more dominant in this region. According to Watson (1989), Western models of higher education can be divided into four types:

   (i) the West European Model—government controlled and funded, with selective, competitive and elitist institutions, and admissions based on merit;
  (ii) the Centralized Model—also government controlled, selective and competitive, but highly political in course content, with admissions based on political and social class requirements;
 (iii) the North American Model—encouraging both the development of both public and private sectors of higher education, and promoting open access to all who have successfully completed secondary level education; and
 (iv) the Combination Model—bearing the hallmark of flexibility and embracing different features of the other models.

It is important to note that the influence of a particular model may be strong during a nation's colonial period, and that over the years many countries have adopted different models at different points in time. A study of the development of higher education in Malaysia and Singapore shows that what exists today is a hybrid of British and American models (Lee, 1989; Tan, 2004). In Thailand, the French and British models were closely followed until World War II, after which the American influence became particularly strong (Watson, 1989). In Vietnam, it was the French influence during the period from 1945 to 1954, the Soviet influence from 1954 to 1975, and American influence in the period after 1975 (Huong & Fry, 2004).

Despite these and other important variations, it is possible to make some broad generalizations when tracing the development of colonial higher education in Southeast Asia. First, the colonial language was used in universities. Second, the governance structure, the organization of the academic profession, the research system, the curricula and textbooks were all based on Western academic models. Third, many of the academic staff were from the metropolitan regions of the country. Fourth, except for the Americans, all the other colonial powers were initially reluctant to set up higher education institutions in the colonies because of their subversive potential. It is worthy noting that "the colonial universities were the seedbeds of the downfall of colonialism and of the emergence of independent nations" (Altbach, 1989, p. 9). However, due to local pressure and the need to train professionals to support the colonial administrations, higher education institutions were established to cater to the elites in each of the colonies. These elements of colonial heritage shaped the development of higher education in this region. Even in Thailand, the Western impact has been strong (although it is not an impact based on a colonial relationship). Thai rulers were strongly influenced by Western ideas as they strove to modernize Thailand. The decision to develop the first university, based on the French model, was taken by the Thai monarchy as a means of training people for government service (Watson, 1989).

After gaining political independence, all the ex-colonies tried to adapt and further develop the higher education systems that they inherited to meet local needs and national aspirations. A major reform has been to gear higher education toward "nation-building" and similar concepts. In nearly all the countries, there were attempts to break away from colonial influence through indigenization efforts as well as broadening the search for alternative models of higher education. One of the first tasks in this area was to replace expatriate staff with local staff; thus began the Malayanization, Filipinization, and Indonesianization of the civil service as well as the academic profession. With the exception of Singapore and Brunei, all the countries of this region began to use their own national languages in their higher education institutions. There has also been a strong move against cultural imperialism by indigenizing the curriculum and using textbooks written by local scholars. Overall, a variety of attempts were made to adapt university education more appropriately to local culture and ensure its relevance to local needs.

A case in point is Indonesia, which managed to break away from the Dutch model of higher education by using Bahasa Indonesia as the medium of instruction in universities, recruiting local staff instead of foreign staff, expanding its higher education system (even at the expense of quality), developing relevant programs, and developing a harmonious relationship with the state (Cummings & Kasenda, 1989). Immediately after gaining its independence in 1945, the Indonesian government established Balia Perguruan Tinggi Gajamada (Gajamada Center of Higher Learning) and the Indonesian Islamic University (UII) in Yogyakarta. The establishment of UII marked the beginning of the modernization of Islamic education in Indonesia. Today, Islamic tertiary educational institutions are a characteristic feature of higher education in Indonesia, enrolling about 15% of the total number of tertiary students in the country (Buchori & Malik, 2004). Similarly, the development of Islamic universities in Indonesia, Malaysia and Southern Philippines is part of the outcome of the continuing search for alternative models of higher education that are more appropriate to local cultures.

The Soviet model of higher education was adopted at one time to suit the socialist ideologies that prevailed in Vietnam, Cambodia and Laos. The key feature of the Soviet model is the establishment of specialized institutions by separate ministries to train personnel to serve its respective ministry. This model suited the central planning system, incorporating a tradition of guaranteed post-graduation jobs. In the more recent period, the North American model has proven more popular and has been adopted by many countries in this region. Examples include the establishment of a land grant university in the Philippines (Gonzales, 2004); the use of a modular system for undergraduate courses and the North American nomenclature for academic job titles in Singapore (Tan, 2004); the introduction of the semester system, credit system, and continual assessment in Malaysia (Lee, 1997); and the establishment of graduate schools in several countries, including Singapore, Malaysia, Thailand and Vietnam.

Unlike the academic traditions in the West, the governments in Southeast Asian countries have considerable power over higher education. With the exception of Indonesia and the Philippines, the government is the main provider of higher education. In many countries, higher education is under the jurisdiction of the Ministry of Education (e.g., Brunei, Singapore, Thailand) or the Ministry of Higher Learning (e.g., Malaysia), and there is strong government control over higher education throughout most of the region. For example, the Singapore government plays a dominant interventionist role in controlling and directing major policy decisions concerning their higher education institutions, giving predominance to economic considerations in higher education planning and policymaking (Tan, 2004). In the case of Indonesia, not only does the government consider the role and function of higher education to be a means to support national development, but academics are expected to work harmoniously with the nation's leaders (Cummings & Kasenda, 1989). It is a common practice for university presidents and vice chancellors to be appointed by their respective governmental ministry.

Throughout the region, the state has taken a keen interest in the university because higher education has been called upon to fulfill a great variety of roles. Higher education is often seen as providing future leaders of politics, bureaucracy, the armed forces and the economy; stimulating economic growth and social development; promoting national unity and social cohesion (particularly in multi-ethnic societies); and developing and preserving cultural heritage and traditions (Lee & Wong, 2003).

The traditional roles of universities include teaching, research and service, but in reality many of the universities found in this region are only teaching institutions, and for those that do research the research productivity is very low when compared to their Western counterparts. As Gonzales (1989) points out, "nothing foreign can be transferred without adapting itself to the local environment. Often, form but not substance remains, but the dynamics are altogether indigenous" (p. 117).

In particular, the quality of higher education in countries with a large private higher education sector (like Indonesia and the Philippines) is highly questionable, with institutions of varying standards. At one end of the quality spectrum, there are prestigious universities like the University of the Philippines and De La Salle University in the Philippines, and Universitas Indonesia and Gajamada University in Indonesia. At the other end, there are many sub-standard higher education institutions which do not produce much new learning, and instead focus on a repetition of subject matter already learned and demand little from their students other than rote memorization of notes (Gonzales, 2004). There is very little quality control, and the quality of the graduates ranges from near zero competence in their specialization to a level of global competitiveness, depending on which higher education institutions they graduate from.

In the past several decades, Southeast Asian countries have witnessed a rapid expansion of higher education, resulting in a deterioration in average quality, under-funding, poor and overcrowded facilities, under-qualified academic staff, curricula lacking relevance, the absence of research, and inequitable access. For example, Indonesia and the Philippines now have systems of higher education serving two million or more students, and Thailand and Vietnam each enroll over one million students (World Bank, 2000). In Malaysia, only about 26% of the faculty in public institutions of higher learning have a Ph.D. degree (Hussien, Jantan & Ansari, 2002), whereas among the faculty of 93,884 in the Philippines, only 32% have at least a master's degree, and of this group only 7% have doctorates (Gonzales, 2004). As a result of the increasing number of graduates, graduate unemployment is a common feature in countries like Indonesia, Philippines, Thailand and Malaysia. There is a mismatch between economic needs and university output, resulting in underemployment and brain drain. Every year thousands of Filipino and Indonesian graduates leave their countries to seek employment abroad, especially in the Middle East. Many medical doctors and health service workers from the Philippines work abroad, and few of those with advanced degrees earned abroad return to the Philippines. Despite the rapid expansion of higher education in many countries, there are major imbalances between urban and rural areas, rich and poor households, men and women, and among ethnic groups within these countries.

In view of the current situation, there are both internal and external pressures to change and reform higher education. Local social, political and economic pressures, demographic pressures, the growing demands of a globalized knowledge economy, and the need to meet international standards are all instrumental in pressuring various governments to restructure their higher education systems to suit local needs and priorities. The restructuring of higher education is a worldwide phenomenon, and it is possible to identify some common trends in the restructuring process that took place in many developed countries during the 1990s (Singh, 2001). First, higher education institutions are increasingly being required to demonstrate efficiency, accountability and productivity from various quarters, notably from the state (which is usually the major source of funding for higher education). Second, there has been a decline in the amount of public funds available, requiring institutions of higher learning to diversify their sources of funding by adopting entrepreneurial approaches to higher education and improving cost-efficiency by institutionalizing corporate managerialism. In many countries, higher education has been privatized either by allowing private institutions to be established or by permitting public institutions to engage in revenue-generating activities. All these global trends are influencing Southeast Asian countries in areas related to access, equity, funding, accountability, and quality assurance. New developments and reforms in each of these specific dimensions warrant special attention in order to gain a full understanding of the recent evolution of higher education in Southeast Asia.

Table 1.   Gross Enrollment Ratio at Tertiary Level by Country and Year

Country	1965	1975	1985	1995	2000
Brunei	n/a	n/a	n/a	7	14
Cambodia	n/a	n/a	n/a	2	3
Indonesia	3	2	7	11	n/a
Laos	n/a	n/a	n/a	2	3
Malaysia	2	3	6	11	23
Myanmar	1	2	n/a	6	8
Philippines	19	18	38	30	30
Singapore	10	9	12	34	n/a
Thailand	2	4	20	20	32
Vietnam	n/a	n/a	n/a	4	10

Source. (UNESCO, 2002) and (World Bank, 2000).
n/a = data not available.

Widening Access

As mentioned earlier, higher education in Southeast Asia has undergone massive expansion due to ever-increasing social demand stemming in part from population growth, the democratization of access to secondary education and the growing affluence of many countries in this region. At the individual level, higher education is perceived as an avenue for social mobility, while at the national level, higher education is seen as an instrument for human capital development and for sustaining economic growth, restructuring society, and promoting national unity. In addition, many countries stress the important role of higher education institutions in maintaining their national competitiveness in the globalized knowledge economy.

The rapid and impressive growth in tertiary student enrollments throughout Southeast Asia from 1965 to 2000 can be seen in Table 1. The countries can be broadly divided into three groups with high, medium and low gross enrollment ratios (GERs). Countries with a high GER (30% or more) are Singapore, Thailand and Philippines; countries with a medium GER (10–25%) are Malaysia, Brunei Indonesia and Vietnam; and countries with a low GER (below 10%) are Myanmar, Cambodia and Laos. The most impressive growth occurred between 1995 and 2000 in countries like Brunei, Malaysia, Thailand and Vietnam. In the Philippines and Indonesia, the absolute number of tertiary students may have increased substantially, but this is not adequately reflected in the GER because of high population growth rates in these countries.

The increased access to higher education is accompanied by a widening of access, which means higher education is being made increasingly available to socially disadvantaged groups such as ethnic minorities, women, indigenous people and people with disabilities. Several countries use explicit quotas to provide higher educational opportunities to underrepresented groups. Until 2002, Malaysia had an ethnic quota system (in favor of the Malays and indigenous people) for admission to public universities;

Vietnam gives preference to enrollment in subject areas such as science, technology, agriculture, and teacher training, and to applicants from remote and mountainous areas (Huong & Fry, 2004); and in Thailand, a quota system was introduced in the provincial universities whereby a percentage of the places at the local university were reserved for local or regional students (Watson, 1989). With the exception of Malaysia and the Philippines, access to higher education is a significant challenge for young women. In Cambodia, female students in higher education institutions comprise only about 22% of the total enrollment (Chamnan & Ford, 2004), and in Singapore, the proportion of female students in the National University of Singapore medical faculty has been kept at about one-third as a result of a deliberate government policy (Tan, 2004).

The widening access of education has also brought about a differentiation of higher education institutions. Differentiation can occur vertically and horizontally (World Bank, 2000). Different types of higher education institutions have proliferated vertically, with the traditional research universities being joined by polytechnics, professional schools, technical institutes and community colleges. These different types of higher education institutions have different purposes and cater to the different needs of diverse groups of students. Horizontally, there are different types of higher education providers, including private providers run by for-profit corporations, nonprofit organizations and religious groups. For example, in the Philippines there are chartered and non-chartered public institutions, stock and non-stock private universities and colleges, and sectarian and non-sectarian institutions (Gonzales, 2004). Open universities and regional universities were established in many countries to make higher education more accessible to the people, especially working adults and those staying in rural areas. Thailand has three open institutions of higher learning, including Ramkamhaeng University and Sukothai Thammarthirat Open University, which enrolled about half of the total number of tertiary students in the country (Sinlarat, 2004).

Another new development is the emergence of various forms of trans-border education. Globalization in higher education is truly reflected in the growth of new information and communication technologies, increased trade in educational services, and the emergence of borderless education. Many countries in this region are importers of cross-border education from advanced countries like Australia, United Kingdom and the United States. Cross-border education can take different forms, such as the mobility of institutions, programs, students, and distance education. A very illustrative case is Malaysia, which is both an importer and exporter of cross-border education. To date, four foreign universities have established branch campuses on Malaysian soil. Private colleges in Malaysia have formed partnerships with foreign universities to offer various kinds of transnational education initiatives, such as twinning programs, credit transfer agreements, external degree programs and joint-degree programs (Lee, 2004). Besides being an importer, Malaysian private colleges also export higher education by recruiting foreign students and establishing a commercial presence in neighboring countries like Thailand and Indonesia.

The rapid and massive expansion of higher education in this region brings with it a whole host of problems, such as strains on public funding and increasing concern with regard to the quality of courses, facilities, staff, and graduates. To overcome some of these problems, many countries have initiated higher education reforms to address issues related to financing higher education and pursuing accountability, efficiency and productivity in higher education institutions.

Financing Higher Education

The widening access to higher education and rising unit costs have caused tremendous strain on national budgets, resources and infrastructure for higher education. Therefore, many governments have no choice but to restructure their higher education systems and seek alternative sources of funding for higher education. In this respect, quite a number of the Southeast Asian governments have adopted the neo-liberal ideologies that gained popularity during the Thatcher-Reagan period of the 1980s. Neo-liberalism seeks to increase corporate earnings and economic efficiency by privatizing public institutions, reducing state regulation and taxation, and rolling back the "costly" welfare state (Carl, 1994). Neo-liberals espouse the superiority of the market, instead of the state, as the allocator of resources. Based on these ideologies, the restructuring of higher education in many countries involves the privatization of higher education, the corporatization of public universities, and implementation of cost-recovery mechanisms.

While private higher education has a long tradition in the Philippines and Indonesia, it is comparatively new in other countries like Singapore, Malaysia, Thailand and Vietnam. The Philippines has 85% of its tertiary enrollment in the private sector— the highest figure in the world—and Indonesia ranks fifth with 62% (World Bank, 2000). In other countries, the state has been the main provider of higher education until recent years, when new private providers have entered the scene. In Malaysia, private higher education has expanded tremendously in the last two decades—the proportion of tertiary enrollments in the private sector rose from 9% in 1985 to 43% in 1999 (Lee, 2004), and the number of private universities has increased from zero in 1995 to 16 in 2004. In Thailand, the Private Higher Education Institution Act was passed in 1979, allowing the private sector to offer degree programs. By 2000, there were 50 private higher education institutions, and most of them were established in the 1980s and 1990s (Ministry of University Affairs, Thailand, 2000).

After the introduction of *doi moi* (economic renovation) in 1986, private higher education institutions (or more commonly known as people-founded higher education) began to appear in Vietnam. By the year 2000, there were 22 people-founded universities and colleges, enrolling 11.4% of the total number of tertiary students in the country (Loc, 2002; Huong & Fry, 2004). The privatization of higher education in this region has helped to ease the budgetary constraints faced by national governments in their effort to widen access to higher education. This move is also aligned with the global trend of commodification and marketization of higher education.

Another significant recent trend has been the reduction of public funding for higher education, as reflected by budget cuts in public universities. This practice was very obvious during the 1997 Asian economic crisis, when the International Monetary Fund (IMF) and World Bank required countries to cut public spending before being provided any loans. Consequently, public universities have been required to seek diverse sources of revenue and engage in market-related activities. The global trend has been to change universities into self-sustaining enterprises and to develop the corporate culture and practices that will enable them to compete in the marketplace. One can find this trend throughout Southeast Asia, exemplified by the "corporatized universities" in Malaysia, "entrepreneurial universities" in Singapore, and "autonomous universities" in Indonesia and Thailand.

In 1998, five public universities were corporatized in Malaysia. After being corporatized, these universities have been run like business corporations. In the effort to create "profit-making centers," these universities have been engaged in recruiting full-fee paying students, seeking research grants and consultancy, franchising educational programs, renting out university facilities, and investing in other business ventures (Lee, 2004). In the case of Singapore, universities were given block grants instead of annual budgets, and in 1991, a University Endowment Fund was established for encouraging the two public universities to attract philanthropic donations as alternative sources of income apart from government grants and tuition fees. The Singapore government pledged to give S$3 (US$1.73) to every dollar raised by the universities. The ultimate goal here has been to lower the government's share of the universities' operating budgets from 75% to 60% (Lee & Gopinathan, 2003).

The Asian economic crisis hastened higher education reforms in Thailand, where privatization or corporatization of government projects and agencies was part of the IMF's US$17.2 billion bailout package. As a result, all public universities in the country were to become autonomous in financial and administrative terms by 2002, implying diminishing levels of financial support from the central government (Atagi, 1998).

In 1999, two important laws were passed in Indonesia addressing changes in the administration of higher education institutions, in an effort to move toward greater institutional autonomy. By 2000, four public universities had been selected to function as "guides" for other universities in Indonesia in developing greater academic and financial autonomy, which involved changes in university funding—such as introducing block funding mechanisms and charging increased tuition fees (Beerkens, 2002). In all these reforms, the state tightens its purse strings and loosens its tight control by allowing higher educational institutions to gain more autonomy.

Besides these major reforms, there is also a worldwide trend toward the introduction of (and increase in) fees in public higher education. Because of financial stringency, the global shift in policy has been from fee-free to fee-paying and the provision of support schemes to students in the form of grants and loans. The rationale behind this policy shift is cost-recovery and cost-sharing. In Singapore, for example, tuition fees in the arts and social sciences were expected to increase to 25% of the recurrent cost (Bray, 1998). In Cambodia, the government has allowed public universities to accept fee-paying students above their quota of non fee-paying students (Chamnan & Ford, 2004). The Malaysian government offers scholarships and loans to students who cannot afford to study in the universities. The government, under the Eighth Malaysian Plan (2001–2005), allocated a sum of US$684.2 million to the National Higher Education Fund which provides financial assistance to students (Lee, 2004).

Distance higher education is also very popular in many Southeast Asian countries because it is seen as a cheap mode of delivery. New forms of distance education have been developed with the advancement of information and communication technologies, such as e-learning, web-based learning, video-conferencing, and virtual libraries.

The Southeast Asian region has a large number of adult learners attending distance teaching universities, and there are a few mega-universities which enroll several hundred thousand students each—including the Universiti Terbuka in Indonesia and Sukothai Thammathirat Open University in Thailand. Many of these distance-teaching universities use both a conventional method—involving printed materials, audio and videocassettes, radio and TV, and face-to-face tutorials—as well as e-learning programs with online instruction.

This overview demonstrates how Southeast Asian countries, like countries in other parts of the world, have sought different ways of financing higher education to fuel the expansion of access. In general, there is a wide variety of higher education institutions throughout the region—in terms of public or private—as well as a mix of conventional and distance learning universities. Public universities have gained more institutional and financial autonomy, but at the same time they are held more accountable and are expected to be more transparent, efficient and productive in their day-to-day management. With this proliferation of private higher education and distance education, there is growing concern over quality assurance, quality assessment and quality management.

Pursuing Accountability

The role of the state in higher education has changed over the years. In nearly all the Southeast Asian countries, the state has expanded its role as a provider to include new protector and regulator roles. As a provider, the state allocates resources to higher education institutions, and as a protector, it takes on the function of consumer advocate by improving access to higher education and by formulating policies to promote social equality. As a regulator, the state monitors the quality of academic programs and oversees the development of higher education institutions through accreditation and program licensing.

With the expansion of private higher education and the emergence of cross-border education and distance education, there is a growing concern about the quality of higher education among stakeholders. Assuring the quality of education is a fundamental aspect of gaining and maintaining credibility for programs, institutions and national systems of higher education worldwide (Middlehurst & Campbell, 2003). This is particularly true in Southeast Asia, as quality assurance has been one of the prime concerns in many countries throughout the region. Quite a number of countries have used legislation to regulate the development of their higher education system and establish quality assurance frameworks to monitor their higher education institutions and programs, although countries like Brunei, Laos, and Myanmar still do not have any quality control mechanisms.

Malaysia uses both legislation and quality assurance frameworks to regulate its higher education system. The Malaysian legislature passed four bills in 1995 and 1996 which have direct impact on the higher education system in the country (Lee, 2004). The 1996 National Council on Higher Education Act put in place a single governing body to steer the direction of higher education development in the country. The 1995 amendment of the 1971 Universities and University College Act lays the framework for the corporatization of public universities, requiring them to be more accountable in the spending of public funds. The 1996 Private Higher Education Institutions Act defines the government's regulatory control over all private institutions in the country, and the 1996 National Accreditation Board Act led to the establishment of the National Accreditation Board which oversees the accreditation of all educational programs offered by private higher education institutions.

A study by Stella (2004) shows that external quality assurance in most countries of the region is of relatively recent origin. Countries that have a quality assurance framework include the following:

- Cambodia: the Accreditation Committee of Cambodia (ACC), established in 2000;
- Indonesia: the National Accreditation Board for Higher Education (BAN), established in 1994;
- Malaysia: the National Accreditation Board (LAN), established in 1996;
- the Philippines: the Accrediting Agency of Chartered Colleges and Universities in the Philippines (AACCUP), established in 1989, and the Philippines Accrediting Association of Schools, Colleges and Universities (PAASCU), established in 1957;
- Thailand: the National Educational Standards and Quality Assurance (NESQA), established in 2000; and
- Vietnam: the Quality Assurance Unit, established in 2002.

Quality assurance initiatives may be related to a particular program, an educational institution or the entire higher education system. There are three basic approaches to quality assurance: accreditation, assessment and academic audit. Whatever their basic approach, the quality assurance frameworks found throughout Southeast Asia have several common core elements, such as: (i) evaluation based on pre-determined and transparent criteria; (ii) a process based on a combination of self-study and peer review; (iii) a final decision made by the quality assurance agency; (iv) public disclosure of the outcome; and (v) validity of the outcome for a specific period of time (Stella, 2004). Despite these common elements, there are many variations in quality assurance practices that are designed to serve unique national contexts. However, research has shown that there is very little quality assurance and accreditation criteria for transnational education and e-learning in the region (Jung, 2004).

At the institutional level, higher education institutions throughout the world have been under increasing pressure for greater accountability and cost-efficiency from various quarters, notably the state. These external pressures have led to the adoption of corporate managerialism by higher education institutions to improve accountability, efficiency and productivity (Currie, 1998). Many universities and colleges have implemented management practices from the private sector, such as mission statements, strategic planning, total quality management, ISO certification, rightsizing and benchmarking. Faculties and research units are expected to operate as cost centers and are required to carry out strategic planning and prepare business plans. Cost centers and programs that are not considered viable have been closed down. All these changes in management practices can be seen as a trend of central university authorities acquiring a more powerful role in resource management and in orienting and controlling department activities. Changes in university management have also brought about changes in the working conditions for the academics—the main actors in all universities.

The Changing Academic Profession

As universities expand, the direct power of academics over the structure of governance has been limited by a new layer of professional bureaucrats who have significant power in the day-to-day administration of the university (Altbach, 1991). The emphasis on accountability has required academics to submit to more fiscal control, pressure to increase productivity, and more rules and regulations as well as rigorous assessment procedures. For example, in Singapore academics are compensated on a performance basis rather than on seniority, and in Malaysia the academic staff are required to sign "personal performance contracts" with their respective heads, with annual salary increments based on performance. The penetration of the corporate culture into higher education institutions has required academics to behave like entrepreneurs and to market their expertise, services and research findings. The corporate culture may have brought about increases in institutional autonomy, but it also demands more accountability on the part of the academics. It places increasing emphasis on performance and competition. This can cause a cleavage between academics in the natural and applied sciences (who are constantly subjected to the pressure of being engaged in entrepreneurial activities) and those in the social sciences and humanities, who perceive the social value of their research being undermined by university authorities. As a consequence, the academic culture loses its collegiality and becomes more bureaucratic and hierarchical, with a concentration of power at the top (Lee, 2002).

The academic culture is quite weak in this region, for there is hardly any research going on in many of the universities in the Philippines, Indonesia, Cambodia and Laos—in each case, for various reasons. First, the academic staff is either bogged down with teaching or they lack the facilities and resources to carry out research. Second, many of the academics do not have a postgraduate degree, so they are not trained to do research. Third, the academics are so poorly paid by their institutions that many of them have to take on a second job in order to survive economically. However, in the more developed countries like Singapore, Malaysia and Thailand, there have been significant scientific research contributions in some specific areas, including marine biology, forestry, tropical medicine, and agricultural crops such as rubber, cocoa and rice.

Academic freedom in some countries—like Singapore and Malaysia—is quite limited when compared to other countries, with restrictions on what can be researched and what the academic community can express to the public. There have even been cases of censorship of research findings which are deemed to be politicaly sensitive by the powers that be. For example, the Malaysian government has used legislation to gag both the dons and students from participation in shaping public discourse and national debates (Lee, 2002). As for academics teaching in the cross-border education programs, they have even less academic freedom because what they teach is not determined by themselves but by their counterparts overseas.

In the past, academics in this region have had both tenure and civil service status, but with the restructuring of higher education, academics were removed from the civil service in some countries like Thailand and Indonesia. It is common to find appointments of academic staff on a contractual basis, lacking the job security and prestige of the traditional professorship. In general, academic remuneration in this region is comparatively lower than developed countries—with the exception of Singapore, which has a very competitive salary scheme to attract global talent to work in the country. There is some inter-country flow of academics in this region, like Burmese medical doctors teaching in Malaysian universities, Malaysian academics teaching in Brunei, and Indonesian academics working in Malaysia. This inter-country flow of academics is one of several examples of regional cooperation that can be observed throughout Southeast Asia.

Regional Cooperation

The amount of regional cooperation in higher education in this region is quite extensive, as reflected by the number of international bodies and inter-governmental organizations that were established for this purpose. First, there is the Southeast Asian Minister of Education Organization (SEAMEO), founded in 1965 as a chartered international organization with the purpose of promoting cooperation in education, science and culture throughout the region. Under SEAMEO, the Regional Center for Higher Education and Development (RIHED) was established in Bangkok, Thailand to provide programs in training, research and development, information dissemination and policy analysis in higher education among member countries.

The UNESCO Regional Bureau of Education for the Asia and Pacific region is also based in Bangkok, Thailand, and has established a network of networks in the region, linking up cooperative entities such as the University Twinning and networking scheme (UNITWIN), the Associated School Project Network (ASP Net), the Asia-Pacific Network for International Education and Values Education (APNIEVE), and the International Project on Technical and Vocational Education (UNEVO). One of its main roles is to ensure quality and standards in higher education through capacity building and standard setting. UNESCO is very active throughout the region in providing professional training on quality assurance approaches and methods and in facilitating mutual recognition of degrees, diplomas and certificates among countries in the region.

Another Asia-Pacific regional body is University Mobility in Asia and the Pacific (UMAP), established in 1993 under the initiative of Asia-Pacific Economic Cooperation (APEC) countries to increase the exchange of university students and staff through cooperation among countries in the region. UMAP's objectives are: (i) to identify and overcome impediments to student mobility; (ii) to move beyond bilateral to multilateral arrangements; and (iii) to develop and maintain a system of granting and recognizing academic credit (Smith, 2004).

Besides these inter-governmental organizations, there are also a number of non-governmental organizations that were established by universities and academics themselves. The oldest, the Association of Southeast Asian Institutions of Higher Learning (ASAIHL), was founded in 1956 to foster the development of member institutions and to cultivate a sense of regional identity by providing regular opportunities for the discussion of academic development and general university development. Over the years, ASAIHL has established various types of fellowships and academic exchange programs, and has expanded to include universities outside the Southeast Asia region—including countries like Hong Kong (China), Australia, Canada, Japan, New Zealand, Sweden and the U.S. (ASAIHL, 2004). Some of the more recently established non-governmental organizations include the Association of Universities of Asia and the Pacific (AUAP), the ASEAN Universities Network (ANU), the Asia Pacific Distance and Multimedia Education Network (APDMEN), and the Asia Pacific Higher Education Network (APHEN). Much of the regional cooperation is focused on facilitating the mobility of university staff and students, research collaboration, and the exchange of ideas on institutional management and development.

Future Trends and Challenges

Globalization is a key force behind many of the future challenges facing this region. Indeed, the concept of globalization is a theme which has gained wide currency among educators, policymakers, scholars and professionals as they examine how education systems in different countries have evolved over time. Educational changes in any country are not only affected by its own socio-economic and political development but are also influenced by the process of globalization. Globalization is a multi-dimensional process with economic, social, political and cultural implications for education. This is particularly so for higher education in a globalized knowledge society. Higher education plays an important role in knowledge production and dissemination, and it is often recognized as an essential driving force for national development in many countries. In the context of globalization and knowledge economies, countries need a highly skilled workforce to increase their national competitiveness. There is also the belief that higher education can help make societies more democratic, alleviate poverty, and strengthen citizenship participation and human rights.

The specific elements of globalization that stand to affect higher education directly or indirectly include the growing importance of the knowledge economy, the perception of higher education as a marketable commodity, the increasing trade in educational services, and educational innovations related to information and communication technologies (UNESCO, 2003). All these developments have implications for higher education in terms of quality, access, diversity and funding. However, globalization affects each country in different ways due to each country's history, traditions, culture, resources and priorities.

The future trends in the development of higher education in this region will be quite similar to other parts of the world with continuing expansion, continuing search for different sources of funding, and continuing diversification of higher education institutions. There will also be increased calls for institutional autonomy, financial diversification and quality control in higher education as well as increasing demands from different social groups for access. The global trends will include movement towards a mixed funding model, innovative use of new information and communication technologies, and better management and deployment of limited physical and human resources. As for curriculum development, there will be increasing pressure for relevance, flexibility and adaptability to changes in the society as a whole and in the workplace in particular.

Universities throughout the world, including those in Southeast Asia, face the challenge of no longer being the sole producer of knowledge. At the beginning of the 21st century, there are multiple sites of knowledge production—including corporate universities established by big commercial firms, non-university institutes, research centers, government agencies, industrial laboratories, think tanks, and various kinds of consultancies. According to Gibbons (1998), "the parallel expansion in the number of potential knowledge producers on the supply side and the expansion of the requirement for specialist knowledge on the demand side are creating the conditions for the emergence of a new mode of knowledge production" (p. 33). The key issue is the relevance of higher education in the context of changing knowledge production and changing demands of the workplace, as more Southeast Asian countries become industrialized and move towards a knowledge economy and post-Fordist production. A major challenge for the universities is to carry out teaching and research which is transdisciplinary, ensure flatter hierarchies, and become more socially accountable and reflexive through an expanded system of quality control (Gibbons, 1998). Furthermore, universities are called upon to produce knowledge workers who are problem identifiers, problem solvers, and problem brokers. The challenge is how to apply knowledge that may have been produced anywhere in the world to work in a particular local situation.

A major impact of globalization on higher education is the delinking of the university from the nation-state. It has been argued that "the university is no longer linked to the destiny of the nation-state by virtue of its role as a producer, protector, and inculcator of an idea of national culture" (Readings, 1996, p. 3). The modern university as derived from the Humboldtian philosophy is an ideological arm of the nation-state which develops and transmits national culture to its citizenry. Culture in this context is seen as the sum of all knowledge that is studied, as well as the cultivation and development of one's character as a result of that study. It is the idea of culture which ties the university to the nation-state. However, the link between the university and the nation-state no longer holds in the era of globalization. The contemporary university has been transformed from an ideological arm of the state into a bureaucratically organized and relatively autonomous consumer-oriented corporation. Therefore, with the declining role of the nation-state and the increasing power of globalization, questions have been raised about the role and social mission of contemporary universities (Kwiek, 2001). According to Johnstone (2001), the challenge is for the university to provide a counterweight against the "de-culturing" and "de-nationalizing" forces of globalization by continuing to play its indispensable role in promoting an inclusive multiculturalism and universal values. Universities in Southeast Asia will have to face these multiple challenges by redefining and reinventing themselves to suit the changing societal needs in the era of globalization.

References

Altbach, P. G. (1989). Twisted roots: The Western impact on Asian higher education. In P. G. Altbach & V. Selvaratnam (Eds.), *From dependence to autonomy: The development of Asian universities* (pp. 1–21). Dordrecht: Kluwer Academic Publishers.
Altbach, P. G. (1991). The academic profession. In P. G. Altbach (Ed.), *International higher education: An encyclopedia* (pp. 25–45). New York: Garland Publishing.

Altbach, P. G. & Selvaratnam, V. (Eds.). (1989). *From dependence to autonomy: The development of Asian universities*. Dordrecht, The Netherland: Kluwer Academic Publishers.

Altbach, P. G. & Umakoshi T. (Eds.). (2004). *Asian universities: Historical perspectives and contemporary challenges*. Baltimore: John Hopkins University Press (*in publication*).

Association of Southeast Asian Institutions of Higher Learning (ASAIHL). (2004). Online at: http://www.asaihl.org. Retrieved March 15, 2004.

Atagi, R. (1998). Economic crisis accelerates the reform of higher education in Thailand. *International Higher Education, 11*, 9–10.

Beerkens, E. (2002). Moving toward autonomy in Indonesian higher education. *International Higher Education, 29*, 24–25.

Bray, M. (1998). Financing higher education in Asia: Patterns, trends, and policies. *International Higher Education, 13*, 12–14.

Buchori, M. & Malik, A. (2004). Evolution of higher education in Indonesia. In P. G. Altbach & T. Umakoshi (Eds.), *Asian universities: Historical perspectives and contemporary challenges*. Baltimore: John Hopkins University Press.

Carl, J. (1994). Parental choice as national policy in England and the United States. *Comparative Education Review, 38*(3), 294–322.

Chamnan, P. & Ford, D. (2004). Cambodian higher education: Mixed visions. In P. G. Altbach & T. Umakoshi (Eds.), *Asian universities: Historical perspectives and contemporary challenges*. Baltimore: John Hopkins University Press.

Cummings, W. K. & Kasenda, S. (1989). The origin of modern Indonesian higher education. In P. G. Altbach & V. Selvaratnam (Eds.), *From dependence to autonomy: The development of Asian universities* (pp. 143–166). Dordrecht, The Netherland: Kluwer Academic Publishers.

Currie, J. (1998). Globalization practices and the professoriate in Anglo-Pacific and North American universities. *Comparative Education Review, 42*(1), 15–29.

Gibbons, M. (1998). Higher education relevance in the 21st century. Paper presented at the UNESCO World Conference on Higher Education, Paris, France, October 5–9, 1998.

Gonzales, A. (2004). Past, present, and future dimensions of higher education. In P. G. Altbach &T. Umakoshi (Eds.), *Asian universities: Historical perspectives and contemporary challenges*. Baltimore: John Hopkins University Press.

Huong, P. L. & Fry, G. W. (2004). Higher education in Vietnam. In P. G. Altbach & T. Umakoshi (Eds.), *Asian universities: Historical perspectives and contemporary challenges*. Baltimore: John Hopkins University Press.

Hussien, S. A., Jantan, M., & Ansari, M. A. (2002). *Enhancing the proportion of faculty composition with Ph.D. in public universities in Malaysia*. Kuala Lumpur, Malaysia: Ministry of Education.

Johnstone, D. B. (2001). Globalization and the role of universities. Online at: http://www.gse.buffalo.edu/FAS/Jonston/RoleofUniversities.html. Retrieved January 8, 2001.

Jung, I. (2004). Quality assurance and accreditation mechanisms of distance education for higher education in the Asia-Pacific region: Five selected cases. Paper presented in the Workshop on Exporters and Importers of Cross-Border Higher Education, Beijing, China, March 20–22, 2004.

Kwiek, M. (2001). Globalization and higher education. *Higher Education in Europe, 26*(1), 27–38.

Lee, M. H. & Gopinathan, S. (2003). Hong Kong and Singapore's reform agendas. *International Higher Education, 32*, 14–15.

Lee, M. N. N. (1997). Malaysia. In G. A. Postiglione & G. C. L. Mak (Eds.), *Asian higher education: An international handbook and reference guide* (pp. 173–197). Westport, CT: Greenwood Press.

Lee, M. N. N. (2002). The academic profession in Malaysia and Singapore: Between bureaucratic and corporate cultures. In P. G. Altbach, (Ed), *The decline of the guru: The academic profession in developing and middle-income countries* (pp. 173–206). Boston: Center for International Higher Education, Lynch School of Education, Boston College.

Lee, M. N. N. (2004). *Restructuring higher education in Malaysia*. Monograph series no. 4/2004. Penang, Malaysia: School of Educational Studies, Universiti Sains Malaysia.

Lee, M. N. N. & Wong, S. Y. (2003). University education for national development. In J. P. Keeves & R. Watanabe (Eds.), *International handbook of educational research in the Asia-Pacific region* (pp. 1207–1220). Dordrecht, The Netherland: Kluwer Academic Publishers.

Loc, N. (2002). Non-public or people-founded higher education in Vietnam. In *Report of the second regional seminar on private higher education: Its role in human resource development in a globalized knowledge society* (pp. 129–136). Bangkok, Thailand: UNESCO PROAP and SEAMEO RIHED.

Middlehurst, R. & Campbell, C. (2003). Quality assurance and borderless higher education: Finding pathways through the maze. The Observatory on Borderless Higher Education. Online at http://www.obje.ac.uk. Retrieved August 1, 2003.

Ministry of University Affairs, Thailand. (2000). *Thai higher education in brief*. Bangkok, Thailand: Ministry of University Affairs, Thailand.

Postiglione, G. A. & Mak, G. C. L. (Eds.). (1997). *Asian higher education: An international handbook and reference guide*. Westport, CT: Greenwood Press.

Readings, B. (1996) *The university in ruins*. Cambridge, MA: Harvard University Press.

Singh. M. (2001). Re-inserting the "public good" into higher education transformation. *Society Research in Higher Education (SRHE) International News, 46* (November 2001), 24–27.

Sinlarat, P. (2004). Thai universities: Reflection of social change. In P. G. Altbach & T. Umakoshi (Eds.), *Asian universities: Historical perspectives and contemporary challenges*. Baltimore: John Hopkins University Press.

Smith, B. (2004). UMAP: A model of access to quality higher education exchange. Paper presented at the International Conference on Access to Higher Education, Manila, Philippines, March 23–24, 2004.

Stella, A. (2004). Quality assurance frameworks for traditional providers in higher education in the Asia-Pacific region. Paper presented in the Workshop on Exporters and Importers of Cross-Border Higher Education, Beijing, China, March 20–22, 2004.

Tan, J. (2004). Singapore. In P. G. Altbach & T. Umakoshi (Eds.), *Asian universities: Historical perspectives and contemporary challenges*. Baltimore: John Hopkins University Press.

UNESCO. (2002). Gross enrollment ratio at tertiary level by country and gender for the academic years 1998/1999 and 1999/2000. Online at: http://www.uis.unesco.org. Retrieved October 21, 2002.

UNESCO. (2003). *Higher education in a globalized society*. Paris: UNESCO Education Position Paper.

Watson, K. (1989). Looking West and East: Thailand's academic development. In P. G. Altbach & V. Selvaratnam (Eds.), *From dependence to autonomy: The development of Asian universities* (pp. 63–95). Dordrecht, The Netherland: Kluwer Academic Publishers.

The World Bank (2000). *Higher education in developing countries: Peril and promise*. Washington, DC: The World Bank.

28

HIGHER EDUCATION IN SUB-SAHARAN AFRICA

Damtew Teferra
Boston College, USA

Higher education in sub-Saharan Africa, in the form and shape we recognize today, is a young and nascent phenomenon. Since its inception (through the incarnation of the educational systems of colonial powers), higher education in sub-Saharan Africa has made significant strides, but also faced major challenges. Higher education in sub-Saharan Africa has emerged from virtual nonexistence some four decades ago to an enterprise that enrolls several million students and recruits hundreds and thousands of faculty and staff.

The number of institutions in sub-Saharan Africa has increased from half a dozen in the 1960s—when most of the nations in the sub-region declared independence—to over 300 in 2003 (Teferra & Altbach, 2003). However, as impressive as these developments are, the systems and the institutions face a plethora of problems and challenges. This chapter provides an overview of the state of higher education in the sub-continent, covering historical and contemporary challenges, and concludes on a guardedly optimistic note.

Historical Perspectives

Higher education in sub-Saharan Africa is as ancient as the obelisks of Ethiopia and the Kingdom of Timbuktu in present-day Mali. While Africa can claim an ancient academic tradition, the fact remains that traditional centers of higher learning in Africa all but disappeared; most were overshadowed or destroyed by colonialism (Teferra & Altbach, 2003). It should be fiercely argued, however, that even though these ancient institutions have very little influence (if at all) on current developments in African higher education, the notion that Africa lived in "dark ages" prior to colonialism is without much ground (Lulat, 2003).

Overall, the colonial powers were non-committal toward (if not deliberately thwarting) the development of higher education in the continent—they were fearful, but rightfully, that an educated society would not tolerate (and therefore challenge) unjust establishments like colonialism. Emerging nearly from scratch some four decades ago,

James J.F. Forest and Philip G. Altbach (eds.), International Handbook of Higher Education, 557–569.
© *2006 Springer. Printed in the Netherlands.*

universities have now grown to around 300, in addition to many other forms of post-secondary institutions such as teacher training institutions, professional schools, and vocational schools.

The profound legacy of colonialism in sub-Saharan Africa perpetuates in the colonial languages that continue to dominate, without competition, the landscape of the sub-continent's scholarship, business, and government. Much of the legacy—in terms of curriculum, organization of academic programs, and administrative culture—still looms large in the sub-continent. As described in the following sections of this chapter, major expansion and remarkable growth, accompanied by crisis, mark much of the history of the continent's higher education development.

Enrollment

Sub-Saharan Africa has the lowest tertiary education enrollment rate in the world. An estimated 2 to 2.5 million students are currently enrolled in tertiary institutions across the sub-region. Despite remarkable growth in enrollment in the sub-region, the actual participation figures still remain rather dismal for a population estimated to be around 700 million. Overall, the enrollment rate for the sub-continent hovers around 3%, although sizeable differences exist among countries. For example, Nigeria and South Africa dominate the sub-region in terms of absolute figures, together accounting for 1.5 million students. And yet Ethiopia, Tanzania, and Uganda (for example) have enrollments below 2% of their respective populations.

Major enrollment disparities by gender, economic status, regional setting (rural/urban), academic programs, ethnicity, and race abound. These are common issues throughout the sub-continent, and a variety of efforts—both national and international—are underway to address them.

Except for a few exceptions, the percentage of female students in all sub-Saharan African institutions is quite low, from 20% in Ethiopia, Tanzania, and Togo, to just over 50% in Swaziland and Lesotho. Gender disparity grows even more severe in the hard sciences, where males dominate. The socio-cultural milieu and the socioeconomic realities in the sub-continent have considerable influence not only on the enrollment of female students but also on their subsequent progress. Mama (2003) notes that enrolling women is only the first hurdle in a much longer process, and it may well be where the greatest gains have been made, quite simply because access has been the main focus of advocacy group efforts to date. However, as she observes, "What do women achieve once they get into the university? What proportions of those who enter come out with degrees, or continue into postgraduate studies or academic careers?"

In addition to gender, considerable differences in enrollment exist by economic status and regional settings. While in many countries, students from well-off families (usually based in major cities and the best schools) dominate the institutions of the sub-region, in other countries students from rural areas and disadvantaged economic backgrounds dominate. Reports on recent higher education developments in some countries, tracking the impact of new fees and tuition, note that these new schemes favor enrollment of students from better-off backgrounds.

Funding

Funding higher education institutions remains a universal issue of concern around the world. This is particularly so at higher education systems in sub-Saharan Africa, where social, economic, and political turmoil continues to challenge the sub-region. With the culmination of the euphoria that resulted from nation-building (following independence), and the intensification of proxy wars by Cold War adversaries in the sub-continent, much of the infrastructure of the region collapsed and developmental schemes were obliterated. Inflation, economic collapse, civil strife, natural disaster and structural adjustment programs took their toll on the development of Africa's social, economic and cultural institutions. These institutions in much of the sub-continent simply collapsed under the heavy weight of complex problems. Higher education was not spared; in fact it became one of the first hard-hit institutions.

External forces, such as the World Bank, tendered higher education in sub-Saharan Africa its final deathblow by withholding support from it. Based on the infamous—and yet erroneous and now quietly disregarded—study on rates of return, it shifted the lending policy of the World Bank away from higher education, and as a consequence dismantled it. The impact of this study is much deeper and profound, as it not only withdrew World Bank support for higher education in the sub-continent, it also prompted other multilateral and bilateral agencies to follow suit. The governments of the sub-region, under pressure from multilateral agencies, simply obliged by withdrawing their support to higher education, purportedly in favor of primary education.

Virtually all sub-Saharan African countries carry a heavy burden of providing free higher education to their citizens. In these countries, the states provide upwards of 90% of the support for higher education. Until recently, higher education in the region has been virtually a public enterprise, in which citizens expected and demanded its free delivery. The perception has, however, shifted significantly as external pressure mounted, existing institutions became unable to accommodate the burgeoning need, and many private institutions have sprung up in the sub-continent over the last decade.

The pervasive neo-liberal policies, the harsh structural adjustment programs, and increasing "liberalization" of the global market have pushed many public institutions—including higher education—to curtail their financial dependence on the state. As a result, higher education institutions have engaged in a host of resource revenue diversification and contentious cost-shifting initiatives (Johnstone & Teferra, 2004). A growing number of institutions have imposed fees on a number of services or completely dropped them, adopted outsourcing (i.e., privatized certain non-core activities) and/or levied tuition fees. They have also expanded their entrepreneurial efforts by attracting contractual research, engaging in consultancy, leasing property and initiating new, attractive, and marketable programs.

Higher education is an expensive enterprise—way too expensive compared to other forms of education. And yet much of the existing discussions seem to either ignore or overlook this obvious fact when they deliberate in the context of African higher education. Numerous studies, which analyzed educational expenditure within the contested terrain of "rate of return," seem to have been preoccupied with an emphasis on the high cost of higher education without a sound and persuasive *raison d'etre*. It should be underscored that higher education is a costly venture, as it involves not only knowledge dissemination at the highest level but also knowledge creation. Knowledge creation is a very expensive undertaking, and higher education as its manufacturing industry simply needs massive resources.

Higher education in sub-Saharan Africa, a continent of 48 nations, is an enterprise of around four billion dollars. Nigeria and South Africa make up the largest share of this figure. By all accounts, the funding of higher education remains dismal, and many calls have been made for major increases and shifts in resources.

Private Higher Education

Private higher education is a rapidly growing educational development throughout much of the sub-continent. As the demand for higher education escalated and the capacity of existing public institutions to address local need has drastically dwindled, private institutions have emerged as an important safety net. In many countries, private institutions outnumber their public counterparts. While their number is larger, their enrollment figures remain rather small. It is important, however, to note that the rate of private provision in tertiary education has grown significantly in recent years, and therefore may conceivably match—if not exceed—enrollment in the public sector.

Overall, many of the private institutions are for-profit, even though in some countries sectarian nonprofit ones have emerged. In Ghana, for example, the major private institutions are dominated by religious sects from different Christian persuasions. In some other countries, Islamic private institutions have also been established through the support of rich Muslim countries in the Middle East.

Most of the programs of study in these institutions share common features—they tend to be market oriented, revenue focused, and narrow in their scope. Across the sub-continent, the programs of study—especially for the profit-driven institutions—appear to be very common and normally include secretarial science, business management, accounting and finance, computer science/IT, tourism and hotel management. For-profit private institutions have a very limited footing in those fields which seem to have poor job prospects. Virtually all the private institutions are focused on the undergraduate market.

Some aspects of private higher education have crept into public institutions in what is now generally described as "privatization of public institutions." Serious discussions and debates are underway to restore the public dimension of the university in Africa within the domineering milieu of liberalization and privatization (Sall, Lebeau, & Kassimir, 2003).

Quality of Education

As the continent confronted a plethora of social, political and economic upheavals, the state and quality of virtually all civil service institutions, including tertiary institutions, have suffered seriously. The enrollment rates in virtually all African countries have escalated without commensurate resources; the physical plants have dilapidated, in some cases, beyond repair; the laboratories have halted their regular activities for lack of supplies and chemicals; the libraries have cancelled virtually all paid acquisitions; highly skilled personnel—both faculty and staff—have left for better living and working conditions both abroad and internally (i.e., in sections of the local economy outside higher education); and many of the universities have been disrupted by frequent closures that in some cases spanned more than a year.

The combination of these factors has significantly impacted the provision of quality education in the continent. The quality of teaching and learning has as a consequence suffered. Research and publishing in many cases have been relegated to the status of luxury items which the institutions felt that they could live without.

As private higher education becomes an increasingly important feature of the sub-region's higher education landscape, so is the issue of quality control. In many countries today, the significant growth of private higher education has triggered a need to police these institutions by either establishing accreditation bodies or developing operational guidelines. While it may be arguable and even controversial to impose some of the regulations on private institutions that the public ones cannot uphold, this trend is nonetheless gathering momentum, in response to the emergence of some dubious and fraudulent institutions. It is important to note that the frenzy of distance and virtual education has not yet caught up in the sub-continent largely due to economies of scale, financial and infrastructural issues such as a lack of reliable phone lines, power supply, and Internet access.

Needless to say, much of the private institutions in sub-Saharan Africa are home-grown and have not yet attracted much international attention, except in South Africa, where a large market and sound infrastructure are available. However, thanks to increasing cross border activities—due to globalization—certain African-based "accrediting" institutions and "teaching" institutions of questionable quality (if not completely bogus) have sprung up. One relevant example is a Liberian-registered institution, Saint Regis University, which is considered by U.S. accreditation agencies to be a "diploma mill," granting diplomas (including a doctorate) based almost totally on "life experiences" and "little or no course work" (Chu, 2004). In fact, it has become a routine exercise for online users to delete spam emails that promise diplomas without having to do much work, using such contemptible sale pitches as "University degrees for sale!", "Get your bachelor's, master's, or doctorate in days!", and "Get the job you deserve with a university degree—no need to go to school." The sanctity of academic fortresses has thus come under threat, as unscrupulous elements are sneaking in under the guise of market liberalization and so many "fly by nights" have mushroomed, largely fostered by the power of the Internet.

While Third World countries, including those of Africa, may not fairly and equitably compete with developed countries in cross border education, it is conceivable that they might serve as global centers of diploma incubators that can provide bogus credentials. Though marginal, these trends of private higher education may have some effect on the developed world, which pursues aggressive positions in international agreements (such as the GATS) in pushing tertiary education as part of the "free" trade regime.

Research and Publishing

Research and publishing capacities of African institutions have deteriorated precipitously over the years. As enrollments escalated, teaching loads have increased significantly, consequently chipping away the requisite time and commitment available for research. The lack of earmarked funding for research, the provision of supplies, and requisite current journals and other publications have negatively impacted research. Governments have also not helped the situation, as they have for decades either directly cracked down on universities, or indirectly suppressed critical voices by implicitly fostering self-censorship. The departure of too many seasoned and competent faculty—leaving behind an overworked, overcrowded, poorly paid and demoralized faculty—dealt a final blow to an already shaky situation.

Funding expenditures for research and development in sub-Saharan Africa have remained way below the 1% mark that was pledged by African countries in many major regional and international meetings. As a consequence, the region remains the least knowledge producing in the world.

In many African countries, public universities remain the sole national hub for research and publication. Any crisis or constraints in these institutions directly reflects on the output of research and publication of a nation.

A viable and reliable means of disseminating new knowledge and perspectives is also woefully lacking. Journals are often irregular in their issue, few in number, broader in scope and also poor in quality (Teferra, 2003). Hence, major findings and breakthroughs continue to be published in reputable international journals, relegating the home-based and regional-based journals as second-class citizens of the global information resource networks.

The lack of regular, relevant, widely distributed, and reliable local journals necessitates publishing in overseas journals—forums that are often neither sympathetic nor caring, nor are they unbiased towards African academia and scholarship. As local journals decline in quality, quantity and influence, researchers are naturally gravitating towards overseas journals, submitting to their cumbersome, Eurocentric and increasingly idiosyncratic guidelines. This tendency has serious ramifications on the sub-continent's knowledge discourse and affects the perception of others towards the body of research published in such forums that unfairly dominates the policy environment affecting the continent.

Stacks of unpublished reports often occupy large offices and lab spaces of many African faculty who either lack the time to turn them into published papers or simply do not fully recognize their benefit as more than promotional tools. While it appears that many in Africa feel that their promotion depends on publishing (Teferra, 2004a), all indications are that productivity has dwindled over the years, under the heavy weight of too many constraints and challenges.

Another scenario has also surfaced; as universities have deteriorated, to the extent of failing to pay salaries in some countries, their faculty are engaging in extensive "moonlighting" to make ends meet. A few (but rather productive) members of the research community have intensely engaged in developing a lucrative consultancy practice, often for international and multilateral organizations and corporations. The terms and decisions with regard to publications that emanate from such works and their intellectual property rights are often regulated by these institutions. For sure, these have deep ramifications for the sub-continent.

While the state of research remains dismal, some efforts are underway to provide better access to published sources—especially journals—largely through electronic delivery initiatives (Teferra, 2001). It should be noted, however, that even though the delivery of up-to-date knowledge and information is one prerequisite for the development of research, building a sound research infrastructure requires far more long-term effort and commitment.

Academics

The academic system remains largely a male-dominated enterprise. Women are often less represented, occupy low ranks, and hold low administrative and academic positions. They also tend to have a higher proportion in the "soft" sciences and to be less involved in research and publication activities.

As tertiary education is slowly expanding and the number of academics is increasing, and as the salaries and benefits of academic work have dwindled over the years, these trends have eroded the social status of the faculty. However, while declining in its social value, the academic profession still garners a considerable reputation throughout much of the sub-continent.

There is a growing concern that senior African academics are aging and that a new, competent generation is not replenishing them quickly enough. According to a recent study, the majority of Ghanaian faculty are in their late 50s, and recruitment has not kept up to counterbalance the trend. The problem of aging faculty is indeed widespread, and encompasses universities in Mozambique, Tanzania, and Uganda (Sawyerr, 2004).

Migration of Expertise: The "Brain Drain" Phenomenon

One of the most serious challenges currently facing capacity building efforts in particular, and socio-economic development in the sub-continent as a whole, is the exodus of high-level personnel from the continent. It may not be surprising that a region fraught with upheavals and dwindling resources generates such massive waves of one-way migration.

As salaries and compensation have dwindled over the years (particularly when compared to inflation rates), and as institutions failed to provide the most basic facilities and services for teaching and research, faculty sought employment opportunities elsewhere. As the crisis in the continent mounted, it escalated the flight of high-level experts to an attractive market with a favorable and liberal immigration policy.

Brain drain is a common and serious phenomenon throughout the world, with particular implications for the African sub-continent. Many Ethiopian, Nigerian, and Zambian academics are employed in the southern part of Africa—particularly in Botswana, Namibia, and South Africa—while a significant number of highly-talented South Africans have migrated to Canada, the United Kingdom and the United States for better pay, working conditions and living environments. In a certain region of Canada, for example, South Africans make up 20% of the migrant population of medical doctors (Teferra, 2004b). In 2003, according to the U.K. General Medical Council, over 7,400 South African and 1,900 Nigerian registered doctors were working in the United Kingdom alone (Dovlo, 2004). In 2003, more than 1,300 nurses from South Africa arrived in Britain, with another 500 coming from Nigeria (BBC, 2004).

Brain drain is most often used to mean the physical mobility of experts from one place to another, typically overseas. And yet "onsite" brain drain—in terms of poor utilization of existing expertise at home—has not yet attracted the attention it deserves. Severe financial and logistical constraints have hampered the productivity of those academics who remained behind. Even those who left for better remuneration in other areas or businesses hardly put their full expertise into practice.

Several national and international initiatives have been launched to curb the exodus of high-level expertise, but with little success so far. Some of the initiatives have been rather restrictive, while others have been cumbersome and poorly implemented. Some of the initiatives were simply ineffective and had to be scrapped and reinvented. Overall, we have yet to see an effective mechanism to replenish migrant talent.

There is, however, a growing interest in involving migrant African experts in academia, research, and business. The initiatives of the African Union to engage the intelligentsia of the African Diaspora in the socio-economic development of the region comprise one such important development. A number of ministerial meetings have recently taken place and a major conference, expected to foster the contribution of the Diaspora for African development, took place near the end of 2004. Moreover, the recently established Pan-African Parliament of the Union has slated seats for African Diaspora representatives.

HIV/AIDS

HIV/AIDS has emerged as one of the most serious health hazards of the 21st century, and seriously confronts the African continent. According to a recent United Nations report (UNAIDS, 2004), in 2003 alone an estimated three million people in the region became newly infected, and in some countries—such as Botswana, one of the richest countries of the sub-region—40% of certain age groups are reported to have been infected by the disease.

Universities often tend to offer a "liberal" and "open" environment for interaction between members of the opposite sex—more so than is common in a typical African cultural setting. A young, energetic and sexually matured population moves freely around and often lives together as dorm-dwelling students, far from the close scrutiny of parents, relatives and their immediate community. Such an environment creates a conducive situation for spreading the disease affecting the community both within the campus and beyond.

The impact of HIV/AIDS on higher education is tremendous. The sickness and death of a member of the university community is a direct drain on university resources, from providing health care to finding a substitute or replacement. Absence and ineptitude that emanate from associated ailments affect students, staff, and academics directly or indirectly. Often academics and staff bear the burden of covering for ailing colleagues without compensation or extra benefits. Administrators are often reluctant to terminate the employment benefits of ailing colleagues, while they are also unable to make temporary replacements.

Overall, universities have not played a leading role in addressing this serious human catastrophe of major social, political, economic and cultural consequence. Though slow in their reaction, many universities have more recently recognized the depth and magnitude of the problem and initiated ways to mitigate it. What remains for universities across the continent is to ensure that the recommendations and initiatives from organizations like the Association of African Universities (AAU), the Association of Commonwealth Universities (ACU), and the South African Universities Vice Chancellors' Association (SAUVCA) are translated into vibrant action programs. Doing so will accelerate the transformation of traditional, piecemeal and somewhat cosmetic reactions to HIV/AIDS into dynamic, fully integrated, comprehensive, and proactive institutional responses (Kelly, 2003). Ottala (2004), however, observes that virtually all Francophone and Lusophone tertiary institutions still lack formal HIV/AIDS policies.

Academic Freedom and Autonomy

Sub-Saharan Africa remains one of the last bastions of government dictatorship and authoritarianism. The region is also known for its endless cycle of violence and civil conflict. More than 40% of the world's armed conflicts regrettably take place in the continent (Regher, 2004). Hostile environments such as these are not fertile ground for knowledge creation and knowledge dissemination.

When one speaks of universities in Africa, one is actually often referring to public institutions—although a considerable growth in private higher education has been recorded in recent years. The autonomy and governance of public institutions are thus generally determined and dictated by the goodwill of governments, which often provide more than 90% of their income.

University professors are known to be fired, imprisoned, tortured, or even killed for their points of view. Atrocities are committed not only by those agents acting on behalf of governments but also by fringe groups that consider academia a threat. In many countries, censorship—both self-imposed and sanctioned—reigns supreme, nurtured by fear of persecution, and as a consequence constraining the capacity for knowledge creation and free expression in the region.

The end of the Cold War and the winds of liberalization and democratization in the sub-continent have created a more favorable environment for academic freedom, as academicians are more openly expressing themselves within and outside their academic confines. The growth of opposition political parties and civil societies in the sub-continent has certainly moderated the long-standing stature of universities as barracks of opposition, monitors of social injustice, and agents of social transformation.

Sizeable ground gained through political reform has been lost, however, to heavy economic deprivation that confronted much of the sub-continent's higher education systems. The forces of political and economic liberalization, which appear to have given more space to academic freedom, also had another sinister side, which constrained its engagement with the new global, regional, national, and institutional realities.

It is tempting to confine the analyses of academic freedom to institutional and ideological constraints posed by the state and the universities themselves. In the African context, the discourse ought to be more expansive, for it is quite evident that the pursuit of academic freedom involves not only struggles against the authoritarian predilections and practices of the state, civil society, and the academy itself, but it is also an epistemological one against paradigms, theories, and methodologies that inferiorize, misrepresent, and oversimplify African experiences, conditions, and realities (Zeleza, 2003).

Information and Communication Technologies

African institutions have benefited significantly from unprecedented developments in information and communication technologies (ICT). Before ICT development in the sub-continent became the main agenda focus of foundations, multilateral organizations, NGOs and private businesses, it was conceived and grown in the wombs of universities. Levey (2002) points out that, despite numerous hurdles, the major factor that catalyzed the development of ICT in the continent (especially e-mail), was the great thirst and enormous need for academic and scholarly communication in the land of forbidding cost and extremely poor communication services. Even though Africa and its institutions remain far behind the rest of the world in ICT access and development, the strides made and the benefits gained in the continent are tremendous (Teferra, 2003). In fact, the highest growth rate in connectivity is recorded in Africa, simply because existing infrastructure is woefully lacking.

ICT initiatives that relate to higher education institutions in Africa can be generally grouped into three broad categories: individual institutions' initiatives aimed at expanding access to ICT, as part of an institutional or national education network; regional initiatives that cover most countries or universities; and initiatives aimed at increasing the flow of content in higher education (Adam, 2003).

These initiatives have had a visible impact on teaching, learning, and research activities—and moreover, on the most chronic problem of African academics: communication with the outside world. Faculty have used the Internet to download materials and track the frontiers of their disciplines. They have used ICT to launch collaborative initiatives, instruct remotely, publish their papers, and engage in dialogue with colleagues around the world. ICT has also been widely acknowledged for easing the feeling of academic isolation (Teferra, 2003).

All is not that rosy though. A complex set of issues confronts the effective utilization of ICT in the sub-continent's higher education institutions. The most important challenge remains infrastructural: the phone lines, the power supply, the capacity to maintain and upgrade systems and machines, and narrow bandwidth are all issues of concern. While access to international knowledge sources using ICT has been encouraged and supported—and as a consequence some ground has been broken—the effort to create, develop and package knowledge in the sub-continent remains largely inadequate (Teferra, 2001).

A New Era of Higher Education in Africa

A new era of higher education in Africa began in the late 1990s, as leading think tank institutions and major donors elevated the status of higher education (which had been hitherto downgraded for over two decades, based largely on the account of a sloppy study) to a major policy and resource agenda item. The World Bank study, which in effect downplayed the importance of higher education for over two decades, now resurrected it in another report (World Bank, 2002), rather tacitly recognizing it as a critical element of development in which developing countries must build in earnest if they are to progress in an information age that feeds on knowledge and breeds on competition. In this seminal work, the World Bank stresses higher education as "more influential than ever in the construction of knowledge economies and democratic societies" (p. 1), in essence emancipating higher education in the sub-region from the shackles of decades of neglect.

However, long before this position paper was published, some positive developments were already emerging. The Partnership for Higher Education in Africa, a consortium of four major U.S.-based foundations, is probably the most notable one. This consortium—which comprises the Ford, MacArthur, and Rockefeller Foundations and the Carnegie Corporation of New York—earmarked $100 million for strengthening higher education in Africa. These foundations, along with others—such as the Swedish Agency for International Development (SIDA)—have currently redirected their support toward the development of African higher education institutions.

Many conferences on African higher education have been organized recently, both in Africa and overseas. Research on higher education has also become a growing (albeit still small) activity of a number of institutions. In terms of publications, three visible initiatives are especially worth mentioning: the most comprehensive book on the subject available today, *African Higher Education: An International Reference Handbook* (Teferra & Altbach, 2003); the launching of a dedicated journal, the *Journal of Higher Education in Africa*; and a series of publications by the Partnership for Higher Education in Africa. A number of institutions have also launched a variety of initiatives in African higher education that include the Association of African Universities (Ghana), the Center for International Higher Education (Boston College), the Council for the Development of Social Science Research in Africa (CODESRIA, Senegal), the Organization for Social Science Research in East and Central Africa (OSSREA, Ethiopia), and the United Nations Economic Commission in Africa (Ethiopia). Other institutions, such as the Center for the Study of Higher Education (University of the Western Cape, South Africa), have in fact launched graduate programs in higher education administration and management. The launching of the International Network for Higher Education in Africa (http://www.bc.edu/inhea) and the effort to establish the Society for Higher Education in Africa are some of the ongoing efforts to enhance research, analysis, advocacy, and publication on higher education in the continent.

Reform initiatives and strategic planning to overhaul higher education institutions at national and institutional levels in many countries have also become commonplace. Numerous countries have undertaken strategic planning, often prompted by domestic imperatives and international pressure, which led to major reforms. The interest and focus of overhauling the higher education system in Africa will not, hopefully, fade away under the weight of numerous competing priorities and the often quickly shifting interests and agendas of funding and donor institutions.

Conclusion

In the 21st century, higher education in sub-Saharan Africa faces numerous challenges. Escalating enrollments, declining resources, high outflow of academics (brain drain), equity and quality balance, and the scourge of HIV/AIDS are just some of the complex issues which confront the system. In this information age, where knowledge creation and dissemination are critical for socio-economic progress, the sub-region cannot afford to ignore these challenges.

Certain developments, however, call for some guarded optimism. Favorable national and international policies, increasing support from bilateral and multilateral donor and funding institutions, rising private higher education providers, expanding technologies in information and communication (that enhance onsite teaching, enable distance learning, and foster academic research), a growing trend in strategic planning, and other reform initiatives call for some optimism.

What is even more comforting is that the research community interested in African higher education is growing. Research, publishing and conferences on African higher education, inside and outside the sub-region, have grown visibly. One only hopes that these endeavors will in effect maintain the momentum in revitalizing higher education and development in the sub-continent.

References

Adam, L. (2003). Information and Communication Technologies in Higher Education in Africa: Initiatives and Challenges. *Journal of Higher Education in Africa*, *1*(1), 195–221.

BBC News. (2004). Nurse poaching crackdown launched. Online at: http://news.bbc.co.uk/go/pr/fr/-/1/hi/health/3598806.stm. August 25, 2004.

Chu, L. (2004). GA [Georgia, U.S.] Teachers' case sheds light on use of "diploma mills." *Boston Globe*. Online at: http://www.boston.com/news/education/higher/articles/2004/05/08/ga_teachers_case_sheds_light_on_use_of_diploma_mills/. May 8, 2004.

Dovlo, D. (2004). The brain drain in Africa: An emerging challenge to health professionals education. *Journal of Higher Education in Africa*, *2*(3), 1–18.

Johnstone, B. & Teferra, D. (2004). Introduction. *Journal of Higher Education in Africa*, *2*(2), 1–5.

Kelly, M. (2003). The significance of HIV/AIDS for universities in Africa. *Journal of Higher Education in Africa*, *1*(1), 1–23.

Levey, L. A. (2002). Is the glass half full or half empty: ICT in African universities. In L. A. Levey & S. Young (Eds.), *Rowing upstream: Snapshots of pioneers of the Information Age in Africa* (pp. 55–68). Johannesburg, South Africa: Sharp Sharp Media.

Lulat, Y. (2003). The development of higher education in Africa: A historical survey. In D. Teferra & P. G. Altbach (Eds.), *African higher education: An international reference handbook* (pp. 15–31). Bloomington, IN: Indiana University Press.

Mama, A. (2003). Restore, reform but do not transform: The gender politics of higher education in Africa. *Journal of Higher Education in Africa*, *1*(1), 101–125.

Ottala, B. (2004). Institutional policies for managing HIV/AIDS in Africa. In W. Saint (Ed.), *Crafting institutional responses to HIV/AIDS: Guidelines and resources for tertiary institutions in sub-Saharan Africa* (pp. 17–32). Washington, DC: World Bank.

Regher, E. (2004). Introduction. In *Armed conflicts report 2004*. Ontario, Canada: Project Ploughshares, Institute of Peace and Conflict Studies, Conrad Grebel College. Online at: http://www.ploughshares.ca/content/ACR/ACR00/ACR04-Introduction.html

Sall, E., Lebeau, Y., & Kassimir (2003). The public dimensions of the university in Africa. *Journal of Higher Education in Africa, 1*(1), 126–148.

Sawyerr, A. (2004). African universities and the challenge of research capacity development. *Journal of Higher Education in Africa, 2*(1), 213–242.

Teferra, D. (2001). The knowledge context in African universities: The neglected link. *International Higher Education, 25*, 23–25.

Teferra, D. (2003). *Scientific communication in African universities: External assistance and national needs*. New York, NY: RoutledgeFalmer.

Teferra, D. (2004a). African intellectual nomads in the information wonderland. *International Association of Universities Newsletter, 10*(1–2: January–February), 1–3.

Teferra, D. (2004b). Mobilizing the African Diaspora. *International Higher Education, 35*, 20–22.

Teferra, D. & Altbach, P. G. (2003). Trends and perspectives in African higher education. In D. Teferra & P. G. Altbach (Eds.), *African higher education: An international reference handbook* (pp. 3–14). Bloomington, IN: Indiana University Press.

UNAIDS. (2004). Report on the global AIDS epidemic, July 2004. Online at: http://www.unaids.org/bangkok2004/GAR2004_html/GAR2004_00_en.htm

World Bank. (2002). Constructing Knowledge Societies: New Challenges for Tertiary Washington, DC: The World Bank.

SECTION 2

National Perspectives

29

ARGENTINA

Ana M. García de Fanelli
National Commission of Scientific Research and Technology, Argentina

The University of San Carlos, the earliest Argentine higher education institution, was founded in 1613. First built as a novitiate of the Society of Jesus, it later became the National University of Cordoba, following its incorporation by the national government during the mid-19th century. In 1821—a decade after national independence—the University of Buenos Aires (UBA) was founded in the wealthiest city of the country. The UBA has continued to be the largest higher education institution and the model for other Argentine universities. By the late 1950s, only nine universities had been established, mostly located in the main cities around the country. All were funded by the national government and were formally autonomous.

Autonomy has been zealously defended since the 1918 student movement in Cordoba City gave rise to "the Cordoba 1918 Reform." This movement quickly spread throughout the country and to other Latin American countries. Student leaders criticized university control by a committee of professors and called for a self-governing university with the participation of students, professors, and alumni on university councils.

Another historical event that shaped the current Argentine higher education system originated from the Catholic Church's contested pressure to foster the creation of private institutions, which concluded with the 1958 law that authorized their functioning under the regulation of the national government. This law promoted the expansion of private universities, especially in the City of Buenos Aires and other important cities in the country. The growth of the private sector has gone hand in hand with an increase in the number of public and private non-university tertiary institutions, mainly since the 1970s. These tertiary institutions comprised technical and vocational schools and teacher training colleges offering short-cycle programs.

The evolution of the Argentine higher education system in the last 20 years has produced a more complex and diverse structure. Throughout the 1980s and 1990s, the system became more heterogeneous. National and private universities now differ enormously in size, scope and range of studies, commitment to research, and their status in society. In spite of the diversity, these universities share a strong professional orientation and student concentration in only a few professional fields (such as law, public accountancy, medicine, the media, and psychology).

James J.F. Forest and Philip G. Altbach (eds.), International Handbook of Higher Education, 573–585.
© 2006 *Springer. Printed in the Netherlands.*

Enrollment Expansion

Compared to other Latin American countries, the Argentine university sector developed well before the rest. As a consequence, Argentina now has the highest higher education gross enrollment rate in the region—48% in 1999–2000—and a top female tertiary gross enrollment ratio of 60% (UNESCO, 2004).

In the 20th century, the average annual growth rate of higher education enrollment averaged 6.7% (see Table 1), but with significant fluctuations owing to the country's political and economic instability.

Between 1930 and the restoration of democracy in 1983, elected governments alternated with military dictatorships. The admissions policies under military regimes were determined by the central government and generally included entrance examinations. Under democratic governments, and at autonomous national universities, the admissions policy was determined by each institution or even by the individual schools. After the experience in restricted access under military governments, the authorities at national universities—in particular bowing to the pressure of student movements—regarded the open admissions policy as a symbolic opposition to the previous system. As shown in Table 1, the number of students in national universities expanded strongly under the democratic governments in place during 1952,[1] 1973, and 1983. Since then, the national university growth rate has stabilized at 6%, while the total population increased at less than 1.5% on average.

Fluctuating enrollment rates also reflected the evolution of the economy. Early higher education expansion from 1880 to 1930 was strongly linked with the country's economic affluence. Throughout this period, economic growth was led by the strong increase in agricultural exports, which integrated Argentina with international markets. Under these conditions, the fiscal revenues coming from sustained growth enabled the

Table 1.   The Expansion of Argentine Higher Education, 1906 to 2000

Period	Average Annual HE Enrollment Rate of Growth	Average Annual National University Enrollment Rate of Growth
1906–2000	6.7%	7.0%
1906–1918	11.4	13.2
1918–1930	6.6	7.4
1930–1952	7.3	7.4
1952–1955	11.5	12.1
1955–1966	5.0	3.8
1966–1973	6.7	6.0
1973–1975	19.5	23.9
1975–1983	−.03	−4.4
1983–1984	16.7	26.8
1984–2000	4.1	6.3

Source: García de Fanelli, A. (2004). *Universidad Pública y Asignación de Fondos (Public University and the Allocation of Funds)*. Buenos Aires, Unpublished.

state to develop a good quality, cost-free public service to satisfy the demand of the newly developing middle class.

The disarticulation of international trade flows generated by the crisis of the 1930s interrupted the expansionist process. Faced with the challenge of introducing radical changes into its development model, Argentina—along with most Latin American countries—adopted a new strategy based on import substitution. This growth model relied much more heavily on fiscal resources than the previous export-oriented model. Constrained by rising social demands and costly industrial development strategies, the Argentine government began to suffer systematic fiscal crises beginning in the 1950s. In particular, 1975–84 marked a period of stagnation, de-industrialization, high inflation, and dramatic foreign indebtedness (Fanelli et al., 1992).

During the 1990s, the Argentine economy experienced major structural changes as a consequence of privatization, market deregulation, and macroeconomic instability. After a phase of high growth between 1990 and 1998, the economy suffered a significant slowdown that ultimately resulted in economic depression and crisis. In 2001–2002, the financial sector and the exchange rate system (the so-called Convertibility Plan) collapsed. As a consequence, labor market conditions worsened substantially, income distribution became much more skewed, and the Argentine global socio-economic situation deteriorated.

The macroeconomic volatility throughout the 1980s and 1990s had dramatically affected the level of higher education expenditure. Under these circumstances, the impact of the open-admission and the cost-free policies that facilitated the access of newly-integrated social groups to national universities completely differed from pre-1930 experiences. Increasing enrollment within a context of scarce financial resources led to a gradual deterioration in teaching and research conditions, especially in the more solicited professional programs.

Finance

In light of the economic cycles, the real value of higher education expenditures failed to grow during the hyperinflationary period of 1989–90 and the Convertibility Crisis of 2001. However, it rose throughout the growth period of 1993–98. As the enrollment rate increased during this period by an average of 6%, the expenditure per student fell dramatically. Some data estimate that the expenditure per student in the national university sector decreased by 32.6% between 1980 and 2003 (Becerra et al., 2003).

Public expenditure as a percentage of GDP also reveals sustainability problems in the Argentine higher education system. In 1998, public higher education expenditures were 0.59% of GDP and the public expenditure per student was barely 22% of per capita GDP (García de Fanelli, 2002). Moreover, while the higher education system has been expanding, it has received little funding for research and development (R&D). Total investment in R&D in Argentina (0.44% in 2002) fell far below the levels in industrialized countries, and even in other Latin American countries like Brazil (1.05% in 2000) and Chile (0.57% in 2001) (SECyT, 2002).

The federal government provides most of the financial support that national universities receive in the form of a block grant. Amounts are allocated mainly through a mechanism based on the institution's previous share and its lobbying activity in Congress. Since 1990, new mechanisms to fund the higher education system have been introduced to improve efficiency and equity (García de Fanelli, 2002). First, since 1992, public universities have enjoyed greater institutional autonomy thanks to their freedom to negotiate pay scales within government thresholds. However, this policy has not been implemented at the largest and most important national universities due to political obstacles related to wage scale bargaining, especially in a context of stringent funding and growing enrollment. Second, an increased proportion of public funding between 1995 and 2000 was allocated through contracts on a competitive basis—for example, via the Fund for the Improvement of Quality in Universities (FOMEC). FOMEC was a mechanism that sponsored both the reform process and the betterment of public university quality. The distribution of resources was carried out through competitive procedures designed to support proposals embracing government-established goals (Marquís et al., 1999). Third, in 1994, the Secretary of Higher Education launched an incentive program for faculty who both teach and conduct research. The Program of Incentives for Research-Teachers prompted the comprehensive development of academic commitment and the increase in full-time posts. Fourth, the Secretary of Higher Education also implemented the use of formula funding to allocate a small proportion of public funds for national universities. As a test case, a formula was used to distribute a very low proportion of the budget in 1997, 1998, and 2003. Its implementation was interrupted between 1999 and 2002 as a consequence of scarce financial resources, political opposition, and technical problems in determining the input and output indicators used in the formula. In 2003, national government authorities and the National Interuniversity Council (CIN)—comprised of the national university presidents—negotiated the terms of a new formula for allocating public funds for national universities.

The Structure of the Higher Education System

In total, there are 94 public and private universities and university institutes[2] and 1,754 non-university tertiary institutions (see Table 2). In both sectors, private institutions outnumber public ones.

With 1.2 million students, the public university tier or "national university sector" is by far the most important in terms of student enrollment, academic staff, political visibility, social prestige, and functions. It is also the only educational sector under the jurisdiction of the national government. All other public institutions at the primary, secondary, and tertiary levels were transferred via a decentralization policy from the national government to the provinces between 1970 and 1990.

Within the national university sector, we find a widely differentiated university system, ranging from a few research-intensive schools (mostly in the basic sciences) in some traditional national universities to primarily teaching institutions in schools or universities devoted mainly to professional training.

While the average enrollment of national universities is around 30,000, the amount of students at each university varies considerably. There is one mega-university: the University of Buenos Aires (UBA). UBA, located in the wealthiest city of the country, accounts for 26% of Argentina's total enrollment, with nearly 326,000 undergraduate

Table 2.   The Argentine Higher Education System: Institutions and Enrollment, 2002

Sector	Number of Institutions	Undergraduate Enrollment	Graduate Enrollment
University	94	1,422,433	40,902
Public	42[b]	1,263,842	32,643[d]
Private	52[c]	158,591	8,259[e]
Non-University[a]	1,754	413,965	26,199
Public	760	243,600	10,431
Private	994	170,365	15,768

Source: MECyT (2002, 2004).
[a]Non-university data correspond to the year 2000.
[b]Thirty-six public universities and 6 university institutes.
[c]Forty-one private universities and 11 university institutes.
[d]Author's estimation. Data correspond to the year 2000.
[e]Data correspond to the year 1997.

students. There is also a large *Universidad Tecnológica Nacional* (national technical university), with almost 64,000 students and branches throughout the country. At the other end of the spectrum, some universities located in the provinces and other recently created ones have fewer than 4,000 students (MECyT, 2004). The diversity in the size of institutions is due to both the concentration of the population and economic activities in the metropolitan area of Buenos Aires City and Greater Buenos Aires,[3] together with the government's policy in the early 1970s to establish at least one public university in each province regardless of the size of the population. Also, during the 1990s, new universities were created in several different locations throughout Greater Buenos Aires.

The increasing number of private universities has also contributed to the heterogeneity of the new structure of the Argentine higher education system. Although private universities outnumber public ones, undergraduate enrollment in the former is scarcely 11% of the nation's total (see Table 2).[4] This is a consequence of four factors: (1) the public undergraduate level is tuition-free; (2) some national universities are more prestigious and offer a greater variety of programs than other private ones; (3) no public financial aid exists for students attending private institutions; and (4) the admissions process in the public sector is not very restricted—in fact, admission to public universities is granted to all high school graduates. Some universities or schools apply entrance examinations or require students to take specific courses—in particular, medical schools (Trombetta, 1999).

Like the public sector, the private university sector is also quite varied, and includes both secular and religious institutions. Using Levy's typology (Levy, 1986), there are demand-absorbing and elite institutions in the secular sector. Of the 52 private universities and university institutes, only a few probably fit the elite type (with high expenditures per student, full-time professors and full-time students, research activities, high-quality facilities, and good libraries). There are also some confessional private universities—mainly associated with the Catholic Church—that incorporate religious perspectives into their objectives. Some of them are trying to compete with secular universities in the academic market niche of the demand-absorbing type, while others are trying to improve the quality of their educational programs in order to contend for a place in the elite niche of the academic market. Private universities depend almost entirely on private funding (donors, the Church, firms, etc.) and student tuition and fees. However, some private institutions have recently received public institutional grants as research centers, and their professors compete for public research funds at the national research agencies.

The non-university tertiary tier embraces such institutions as teacher-training institutes and technical and semi-professional schools, including those training para-medical personnel, social workers, artists, and technicians.[5] This highly heterogeneous sector has been under the direct control and financial supervision of the provincial governments since the 1992 decentralization policy. The private non-university tertiary tier is also regulated by the provincial governments, but it depends financially on tuition and fees.

Undergraduate and Graduate Programs in the University Sector

The undergraduate level of education includes both the *"licenciado"* degree—following an average of 5 years of study—and professional degrees, generally with a longer duration, in fields such as medicine, engineering, public accountancy, architecture, psychology, and law. Compared with public universities, private ones show a greater concentration in the social sciences and a shorter duration of undergraduate programs (Balán & García de Fanelli, 1997).

Both the public and private sectors have not only shown important institutional growth but also a greater diversity of programs. The two main features of this expansion have been the increasing concentration in social sciences and humanities degrees, and the growth of short-cycle programs. As shown in Table 3, the majority (42%) of newly-admitted students at public universities study social sciences programs, while only 4% take basic sciences courses (biology, physics, mathematics, and chemistry). In

Table 3.   Student Intake and Graduates at National Universities by Field of Study, 1990–2000

Field of Study	Student Intake		Total Graduates	
	1990	2000	1989	1999
Social Sciences	62,712	117,573	12,559	14,300
Humanities	20,015	40,573	3,822	5,068
Applied Sciences	55,114	71,268	8,667	9,374
Health Sciences	27,845	37,128	7,005	8,566
Basic Sciences	6,714	11,195	1,090	1,163
Total	172,400	277,737	33,143	38,471

Source: MECyT (2002).

addition, the enrollment trend by field of study shows a steadily increasing proportion of students and graduates in the social sciences, especially in business administration, public accountancy, and law. The growing supply of social sciences programs is directly related to student demand.

In terms of enrollment, the undergraduate level in Argentina is quite developed, while graduate education is radically underdeveloped (García de Fanelli, 2001). Several institutional and financial conditions help explain the current situation of graduate programs. First, only about 20% of those who enter national universities graduate within six years, and many of them eventually drop out. Second, unlike the undergraduate level at public universities, graduate education is almost totally financed by students and their families. The tuition level is determined by the total cost of the program and has to cover a professor's fees as the labor market dictates. Third, the few available scholarship programs target young, full-time students, yet most of the graduate students are in their 30s and study part-time.[6] Finally, neither the doctorate nor the master's degree was a requirement for entry into (or promotion within) the academic profession until the 1995 Higher Education Act. As a result of these trends, the graduate academic market is very young, and clear public policies are necessary to foster its growth.

Governance and Quality Assessment

The 1995 Higher Education Law established a common framework for public and private institutions in both university and non-university tiers. The purpose of this was to help set the conditions for the formulation of policies to coordinate the system as a whole. Nonetheless, the real ability of the national government to coordinate higher education policy has been very limited owing to the autonomy of national and private universities and the control of the tertiary non-university sector by provincial governments.

The Argentine Constitution recognizes the autonomy and administrative autarchy of national universities which is enshrined in their individual charters or statutes. Collegial and executive bodies govern national universities, and the assembly is the highest authority. The assembly, composed of the executive and collegial bodies, is in charge of the construction of, approval of, and amendments to the university statute, as well as the election of the president or rector of the university. Members of the university councils are elected by professors, students, and alumni. Although the administration is controlled by the university president or rector and staff members, the university council rules over national universities (Balán, 1993).

The majority of Argentine universities are organized into professional or academic-based schools or *facultades* that enjoy considerable autonomy. Schools are run by the school council—comprising representatives from professors, students, and alumni—which also elects the dean of the school. Within each school, chairs are the main teaching units and the chair-holder enjoys considerable autonomy to design the curricula of the course and to manage the chair. One characteristic of these council representatives at public universities has been their ties with major national political parties. Consequently, there has been an element of partisanship about the way votes from the constituencies have been cast.

Unlike the national university sector, private universities are more hierarchical in their organization. This means that collegial bodies participate less in the decision-making process. Private university presidents are elected by university boards, whose composition reflects the orientation of the founding organization (for example, religious or business orientation). Faculty representation is very limited, and university presidents appoint deans and other administrative staff.

The higher education system is also composed of a large number of tertiary institutions that fall legally under the responsibility of the provincial government. Like primary and secondary level institutions, tertiary institutions are not autonomous and are vertically governed by the provincial authorities.

Although the 1995 Act recognizes university autonomy, it also encourages accountability in the use of public funds. In particular, the 1995 Act promotes the institutional assessment of all universities and the periodic accreditation of some professional programs (e.g., medicine, engineering, law, public accountancy, and psychology) and all graduate studies. The National Committee of University Assessment and Accrediting (CONEAU) is in charge of all these activities with the help of peer reviewers. The Ministry of Education, together with the Council of Universities,[7] establishes the standards for the accreditation process. This policy is important, as CONEAU could influence the curricula by defining minimum criteria for program quality or standards. In addition, graduate programs can volunteer to accept to be accredited and to be graded as: excellent ("A"), very good ("B") and good ("C"). Although the quality assessment review is not directly linked to the allocation of funds, there is a modest relationship—the distribution of some funds has been indirectly related to CONEAU's results.[8] CONEAU's quality assurance is also quite important as a market signal of product quality. Accreditation and evaluation processes contribute to certifying educational quality and, by doing so, give more transparency to the academic market. CONEAU also monitors private universities during their period of provisional authorization. If the steering reports indicate that the university is performing well after 6 years, the institution will become autonomous (Fernández Lamarra, 2003).

In sum, the Ministry of Education does not have direct authority over the higher education sector and, in fact, cannot design the public policies that are to be automatically implemented within it. Public and most private universities are autonomous and public policies oriented to reforming the tertiary non-university sector must meet with the approval of provincial governments. In this context, a public policy to promote the improvement of the system and to encourage institutional innovation depends on negotiation. It must achieve a consensus among the main actors on new instruments that can indirectly steer the system via financial or quality assessment measures.

Teaching, Learning, and Research Activities

The positions of the Argentine academic profession generally comprise two broad categories: professors (full, associate, and assistant) and junior teaching staff (senior and assistant); they can be hired on a full-, half- or a part-time basis.[9]

To cope with the issues of demand pressure resulting from an open admissions policy and a context of public financial stringency, the public university has adopted a policy of hiring more part-time and volunteer staff, especially—but not only—for the lowest academic positions (junior teaching staff).In 2000, full-time faculty represented only 14% of the total. Many of these faculty members are sometimes called "taxicab" professors because they work at several higher education institutions simultaneously and accumulate teaching hours at different schools or universities. This practice is quite prevalent among graduate programs (García de Fanelli, 2001).

Most of the national universities' statutes establish that "regular" or "ordinary" faculty are appointed on the basis of periodic, openly competitive procedures.[10] These statutes also stipulate that the authorities can make special and exceptional 1- or 2-year appointments with the institution. Professors and junior teaching staff hired under these conditions are called "interim." In spite of the legal framework that determines the institutional conditions for the development of permanent ("ordinary" faculty) and non-permanent ("interim" faculty) labor contracts, the social practices deeply deviate from these formal arrangements. Some reports on the external evaluation of national universities and data from the Ministry of Education reveal that more than half of the faculty are interim and that many are under de facto permanent contracts without a periodic performance evaluation.

As a consequence, although the openly competitive contest is the best-known instrument for the appointment of professors, there is a clear perception among different academic members that it does not actually seem to be a workable procedure. The failures of the open competitive contests can be attributed to a fragile financial scenario, with increasing demand and open-admission policy, the lack of incentives to sit ad-honorem on a jury, the lengthy bureaucratic procedures, the rigidity of the chair system, and corporative and political vested interests.

Like interim and fixed-term contracts at national universities, the appointment procedure at private universities does not usually follow an openly competitive contest mechanism. The decision is generally taken by the governing board upon the recommendation of the faculty, based on the candidate's academic and professional qualifications and personal contacts. Contracts are generally designed on an hourly basis, although there are some private institutions—mainly of the "elite type"—that hire their professors under a stable wage relationship.

Transnational education is also instituting new trends in higher education. In Argentina, this process has mainly targeted the graduate level, and takes the form of "branch campuses" or "joint programs." The first corresponds to those universities that set up branches in other countries to offer one or more programs. This is the case of Bologna University in Argentina.[11] With respect to "joint programs," some Argentine private universities and a few public ones have signed formal agreements with foreign universities to offer a joint degree at the graduate level, mainly in the social science fields. Both types of transnational programs hire faculty on an hourly basis and under self-employment of service contracts. As a consequence, employment relations in the transnational education programs follow the same structure as other local graduate programs: unstable, fixed-term contracts.

Like most faculty members, about half of the students at public universities attend part-time as they work and study at the same time. This and other factors related to the students' academic background at the secondary level explain the very low entry-graduation ratio: only about 20% of incoming students graduate within 6 years, and those who graduate take at least 50% more time to complete the formal duration of their program (MCyE, 2000).[12]

Although public universities and a few private ones carry out some research activities, most publicly funded research is organized by specialized research agencies, outside the universities. The most important of these agencies is the *Comisión Nacional de Investigaciones Científicas y Tecnológicas* (CONICET). CONICET supports research through subsidies, fellowships, and especially via the so-called research career. In 2004, over 3,575 researchers held positions at CONICET, most of whom are also professors at national universities (CONICET, 2004). Research activity at public universities is conducted by their full-time academic staff. Nonetheless, as was already mentioned, the proportion of full-time staff is quite small.

Although no exact statistics exist on the total number of professionals and scientists that have emigrated from Argentina to industrialized countries, some data confirm that the brain drain issue negatively impacts on the recovery of human capital investment. Many students that have studied abroad, especially in the United States, have not returned after their graduation. United States data offer some clues as to the dimension of the problem. There are approximately 7,000 Argentine researchers living abroad. Argentine scientists represent 9.5% of the total Latin American scientists that conduct R&D activities in the United States. This figure is only higher among scientists from Mexico (17%), Cuba (12.5%) and Colombia (10%) (Albornoz et al., 2002).

One public policy implemented in 2004 to improve research and teaching conditions—and, in so doing, reduce or prevent the brain drain—has been to raise the wages of CONICET researchers and full-time national university professors. CONICET has also increased the number of research scholarships available for Ph.D. training and for postdoctoral training. In addition, the Ministry of Education has launched a scholarship scheme to promote the study of engineering and other degrees that are considered relevant to the economic competitiveness of the country.

Conclusion

The Argentine higher education system has undergone a rapid and an unplanned expansion, both in institutional and enrollment terms, and in a context of financial volatility and political instability. In the early 21st century, two of the most important problems have been the lack of sustainable financing to develop an internationally competitive higher education system and the vertical and horizontal disarticulation.

Regarding the funding issue, it is often said that were it possible to increase public funds allocated to higher education, the main problems would still persist. Clearly the expansion in the amount of funds is not a sufficient condition for improvement and innovation, but it seems to be a necessary one for:

- increasing research activity, both in public and in private universities;
- changing the distortions in the present wage scale and improving the wage levels and labor conditions of the faculty;

- fostering the coordination role of the government via program-based contract and formula funding to allocate new resources throughout public universities—in this way, the government could develop an incentive structure to promote consensus among the main actors and foster an innovative university; and
- promoting equal opportunity through scholarships or loan programs.

Debates about the weaknesses of Argentine higher education also stress the system's inflexibility regarding student transfer from one institution to another, and even from one program to another within the same institution. The National Commission for the Betterment of Higher Education, comprised of academic and professional experts, recommended several areas of curricular reform in 2001–2002: shorten the length of the undergraduate programs; create a common 2-year first cycle in related fields within a group of universities; and articulate the university and the non-university forms of tertiary education. The discussion has also examined both the establishment of a credit system as a means to facilitate student mobility between programs, and the articulation between the first degree and the graduate level (specialization, master's, and doctoral programs). In brief, the betterment of the Argentine higher education system requires more funds for the design of new decision and incentive structures, and structural reforms to increase student mobility between institutions and programs.

Notes

1. Enrollment increased, in particular, when the Peronist government suppressed entrance exams and tuition and fees in 1952.
2. Since the 1995 Higher Education Act was ratified, a new type of university institution has developed: the "University Institute." These institutions specialize in only one field of study, for example, health care, engineering, or law.
3. Argentina is an urban country (in 2001 89% of its 36,260,130 inhabitants lived in urban areas), with most of the population (31.6%; around 12 million) concentrated in the metropolitan area of Buenos Aires City and Greater Buenos Aires (INDEC, 2004).
4. The number of students in public universities could be overestimated and underestimated in private universities. The main factor is that public university authorities seldom exclude inactive students and the private sector does not give accurate and updated information to the Ministry of Education. According to the 2001 Census of the National Population, 904,919 students attended public universities and 220,338 attended private universities. That is, one in five attended private universities (INDEC, 2004).
5. See Trombetta (1998), *Alcances y dimensiones de la educación superior no universitaria en la Argentina.* Buenos Aires: Unpublished Master's thesis.
6. Admission to doctoral and master's degree studies is based on the successful completion of a university program obtained after more than five or six years of study. Available statistics on the average length of study suggest that it is closer to nine. By the time students obtain their undergraduate degrees, they are about 27 years old. This can be explained by the fact that many students combine study and work.
7. The Council of Universities is comprised of the National Interuniversity Council (CIN) and the Council of Private University Presidents (CRUP).
8. For example, from 1995 to 1999 the graduate level received special funds through the Fund for Quality Improvement in Universities (FOMEC). Specifically, some graduate programs obtained funds to provide scholarships and to hire professors from abroad. To qualify for these grants, graduate programs should have an "A" or, at least, a "B" mark. Also, the National Council

for Scientific and Technological Research (CONICET) has established a system of fellowships addressing candidates in graduate training programs. It is a requisite that the programs must be accredited with an "A" or "B" qualification.

9. Most of the information about the Argentine academic profession is based on García de Fanelli (2004b).

10. This Argentine academic labor contract is similar to the Anglo-Saxon "tenure" contract. It is effective for seven years and is then renovated every seven years through a new competitive contest process.

11. CONEAU requires all foreign universities to follow the same approval procedure as Argentine private universities before they can operate in the country.

12. The author estimates that the dropout rate could be much lower, perhaps 50%. The difference can be attributed to the fact that students who have applied to the university, but have never actually passed any courses, cannot truthfully be considered "students;" further, there is often double counting, due to changes a student makes in their degree program, school, or university they attend. See García de Fanelli (2004a).

References

Albornoz, M., Fernández Polcuch, E., & Alfaraz, C. (2002). *Hacia una estimación de la "fuga de cerebros" (Toward an estimate of the "brain drain").* Buenos Aires: REDES (Documento de Trabajo no. 1).

Balán, J. (1993). Governance and finance of national universities in Argentina: Current proposals for change. *Higher Education, 25*(1), 45–60.

Balán, J. & García de Fanelli, A. M. (1997). El sector privado de la educación superior (The private sector and higher education). In R. Kent (Ed.), *Los temas críticos de la educación superior en América. Los años 90. Expansión privada, evaluación y posgrado (The main issues in Latin American higher education),* (Vol. 2, pp. 9–93). Mexico City, Mexico: Fondo de Cultura Económica.

Becerra, M., Cetrángolo, O., Curcio, J., & Jiménez, J. P. (2003). *El gasto universitario en la Argentina (University expenditure in Argentina).* Buenos Aires: World Bank.

CONICET. (2004). Comisión Nacional de Investigaciones Científicas y Tecnológicas (National Commission of Scientific Research and Technology). Buenos Aires: CONICET. http://www.conicet.gov.ar.

Fanelli, J. M., Frenkel, R., & Rozenwurcel, G. (1992). Growth and structural reform in Latin America. Where we stand. In *The market and the state in economic development in the 1990.* Amsterdam: North-Holland.

Fernández Lamarra, N. (2003). *La educación superior argentina en debate (The debate over Argentine higher education),* Buenos Aires: EUDEBA-IESALC.

García de Fanelli, A. M. (2001). Los estudios de posgrado en la Argentina: una visión desde las maestrías de ciencias sociales (Graduate programs in Argentina: a view from the social sciences master's programs). In A. M. García de Fanelli, et al., *Entre la academia y el mercado. Posgrados en ciencias sociales y políticas públicas en Argentina y México (Between the academy and the market: Graduate programs in social sciences and public policies in Argentina and Mexico)* (pp. 129–196). Mexico City, Mexico: ANUIES.

García de Fanelli, A. M. (2002). Financiamiento universitario y política pública en Argentina: la asignación de fondos públicos y la generación de recursos privados en los años noventa (University funding and public policy in Argentina: The allocation of public funds and the generation of private sources in the nineties). *Revista de la Educación Superior, 31*(3), 47–67.

García de Fanelli, A. M. (2004a). Indicadores y estrategias en relación con el abandono y la graduación universitarios (Indicators and strategies in relation to university dropout and graduation). In C. Marquís, (Ed.), *La agenda universitaria (The university agenda).* Buenos Aires: Universidad de Palermo.

García de Fanelli, A. M. (2004b). *Academic employment structures in higher education: The Argentine case and the academic profession in Latin America.* Geneva: International Labor Organization (ILO).

INDEC (2004). Instituto Nacional de Estadísticas y Censos (National Institute of Statistics and Census). Buenos Aires: http://www.indec.gov.ar.

Levy, D. (1986). *Higher education and the state in Latin America: Private challenge to public dominance.* Chicago: The University of Chicago Press.

Marquís, C., Riveiro, G., & Martínez Porta, L. (1999). El FOMEC: Innovaciones y reformas en las universidades nacionales (Innovation and reforms in national universities). In E. Sánchez Martínez (Ed.), *La educación superior en la Argentina* (Higher Education in Latin America) (pp. 95–109). Buenos Aires, Argentina: Ministerio de Cultura y Educación.

MECyT (Ministerio de Educación, Ciencia y Tecnología de Argentina). (2004). *Anuario de estadísticas universitarias* (Argentine Ministry of Education, Science and Technology. *Yearbook of university statistics*). Buenos Aires, Argentina: http://www.me.gov.ar.

MECyT. (2002). Comisión Nacional para el Mejoramiento de la Educación Superior, Informe final (National Commission for the Betterment of Higher Education. Final report). República Argentina: MECyT.

SECyT. (2002). *Indicadores de ciencia y tecnología* (*Science and technology indicators*). Secretaría de Ciencia, Tecnología e Innovación Productiva, Ministerio de Educación, Ciencia y Tecnología de la Argentina (Science, Technology and Productive Innovation, Argentine Ministry of Education, Science and Technology).

Trombetta, A. (1999). El ingreso en las universidades nacionales argentinas (Access to Argentine national universities). In *Sistemas de admisión a la universidad. Seminario internacional (University admission models. International seminar),* (pp. 121–149). Buenos Aires, Argentina: Ministerio de Cultura y Educación.

UNESCO. (2004). *Statistical Yearbook.* Paris: UNESCO.

30

AUSTRALIA

Simon Marginson
Monash University, Australia

Australia is an island continent in the southern hemisphere of 7.7 million square kilometers and a population of 20 million (2004) clustered in coastal centers with high urban concentration. It has a stable polity and developed economy, producing 1.4% of the world's GDP (2003). Australia originated in six separate British colonies established after 1788 on the basis of the dispossession, cultural destruction and partial genocide of the indigenous inhabitants. The federated colonies were granted "dominion" status by Great Britain in 1901. Though the British monarch is still head of state and Australia inherited British common law, most constitutional ties with the U.K. have been abolished. In terms of economics, military-strategic matters—and to some extent culture—Australia is now closer to the United States than the U.K. Nevertheless, Australia is a Westminster-style democracy, and its institutions—including higher education—are still marked by their British origins. Even in recent years, policy changes in Australian higher education have paralleled British developments more closely than those of any other nation. At the same time, like New Zealand (but unlike other English-speaking nations) Australia is located near East and Southeast Asia, has a closer relationship with China than does the U.S., and has extensive economic and educational ties throughout the Asia-Pacific region.

Australia is a federation of six states and two territories, plus islands to the north and in the Pacific, Indian and Southern oceans. The Commonwealth (Australian or national) government dominates military and international matters, tax and economic policy, and welfare payments. Publicly-supported education and health services are largely provided by state and territory governments, but the national government leads higher education policy. Australia's GDP of US$518.4 billion (2003) ranks as 13th largest in the world. Gross National Income per capita was $28,290 in purchasing power parity; 20th in the world, though Australia ranks second behind Norway on the UN Development Index (measuring broader living standards) (World Bank, 2004). Australia is a major minerals exporter, and has a technology-intensive agribusiness sector, though there are serious problems of land and water degradation in this driest and most ecologically fragile continent. Elaborately transformed manufacturing is weaker than in most OECD economies, as well as in the East and Southeast Asian nations that absorb most Australian trade. In the information and communications technology

James J.F. Forest and Philip G. Altbach (eds.), International Handbook of Higher Education, 587–611.
© 2006 *Springer. Printed in the Netherlands.*

(ICT) sector, Australia has the highest deficit in international trade of any OECD nation (OECD, 2003). However, Australia has a robust finance sector, is a strong exporter of transport, tourism, education and business services, and has certain strengths in research.

As a British settler state, Australia was formed by migration and sustains a higher rate of migration and population increase than most OECD nations, despite internal tensions about immigration and refugee policy. Migration modifies—though it does not eliminate—the trends of low fertility and an aging population. The majority of Australians originated from Britain and Ireland, with some via New Zealand or South Africa. But Australia also has continuing indigenous traditions, and since World War II has received waves of people from Northern, Central and Southern Europe; the Middle East; most nations of Asia; the Pacific islands; and the Horn of Africa. Large segments of the population are descendants of Greek, Italian, Vietnamese and Chinese settlers; in the two largest cities of Sydney and Melbourne, almost one in ten are Asian born, and Melbourne contains the second largest city population of Greeks in the world after Athens. Recent policy has favored skilled, professional and business migrants, often from Asian nations, many first entering Australia as foreign students. Australia combines these diverse starting points within homogenizing economic, educational, legal and political institutions, so that stable Anglo-American monoculture triumphs over complexity. Anglo-Irish descendants still lead business and dominate politics and the professions. The sole public language is English. At the same time, Australia practices a policy of "multiculturalism" which, though contested, encourages tolerance and some expression of cultural diversity, while normalizing economic, social and educational opportunities for non Anglo-Celtic settlers. While there are some inter-cultural tensions, especially in relation to indigenous people and in rural areas, open racism is no longer acceptable in the principal urban centers, and inter-cultural marriage is common.

Educational institutions have been important in cultural mixing. Australians of non-Anglo-Celtic origin generally outperform the majority in the first or second generation after arrival, with exceptions among some Middle Eastern families. On the other hand, there is less support for historically-derived legal, political and cultural rights of in-digenous people than in the other British settler states of New Zealand and Canada. Indigenous people are severely disadvantaged in incomes, employment rates and health indicators, and have relatively low participation and success rates in tertiary education. The education system has been unsuccessful in connecting positively to indigenous traditions or providing an untroubled space for self-determining indigenous programs and institutions.

Australia shares with the U.K., Canada and New Zealand the British tradition of state-founded, self-governing and self-accrediting universities, organized in a national system, with broadly distributed research activities and doctoral qualifications as the faculty norm. Australia's national higher education system, which includes only degree-level institutions, consists of 36 public universities and 13 smaller public and private institutions. Together they enrolled 929,952 students in 2003 (DEST, 2004) and pro-duced 2% of the world's scholarly publications. In 2003, 54% of higher education students were women.

In addition to the national higher education system, there were a further 30,000 students in government-accredited degree-level courses in 79 private institutions (Watson, 1999), which are ineligible for most forms of government research funding. Higher education institutions provide bachelor's, master's and doctoral degrees, plus shorter diplomas and certificates. Bachelor's degrees are three to four years, except some professional courses such as medicine (five to six years). Bachelor's-level students often enroll in combined degree programs. Some master's courses are only one year long, but 18 months or two years are more common. Fully commercial (full-cost tuition) programs are largely deregulated, and the duration and content is subject to much greater variation than with subsidized programs. The separate Vocational Education and Training (VET) sector included over 1.7 million students at sub-degree level in 2003, mostly part-time (NCVER, 2004). Several universities, mostly in Victoria, are "cross-sectoral" institutions, offering both VET and higher education. All higher education and VET programs are subject to the Australian Qualifications Framework, which specifies standards and equivalence. Articulation between VET and higher education is well established only in engineering, information technology and business studies. Less than 10% of beginning higher education students are from VET.

The rate of graduation from tertiary education in Australia (42% in 2001) is above the OECD country average of 30%. Spending on tertiary education is also higher than the OECD country average. Public spending on tertiary education was 0.8% of GDP in 2000, below the OECD average of 1%, but private spending at 0.7% is more than double the OECD level of 0.3% (OECD, 2003). Like other British-influenced systems, since the 1980s Australian higher education has been shaped by neo-liberal economic policies. It has shifted from state-funded higher education—largely free of direct tuition charges—to mixed public and private funding of entrepreneurial institutions competing for students and revenues. The system has become more status-differentiated, commercial ventures are growing and new private institutions are emerging. Students and families provide on average one-third of institutional revenues. Almost one student in four is a fee-paying foreign student.

History

Until World War II, Australian institutions were small, under-developed and isolated from their communities. Participation rates were very low. In 1939, only two Australians in every thousand attended a university. The sons (rarely the daughters) of affluent families often went to Britain for university education. For their part, the universities drew on British and European intellectual traditions rather than the emerging industries, democratic institutions and embryonic public cultures of the settler state. Higher education consisted of the universities founded in the six original colonies. The University of Sydney began in 1851 and the University of Melbourne in 1852, followed by Adelaide (1874), Tasmania (1890), Queensland (1909) and Western Australia (1911). Later, local university facilities were opened in the small national capital of Canberra (1930) and at Armidale (1938), under the supervision of the Universities of Melbourne and Sydney respectively. When Sydney and Melbourne were founded, there were four universities in England, four in Scotland and one in Ireland. The Australian universities drew more from the Scottish model of daytime lectures and vocationally grounded courses than from the Oxford and Cambridge approach of personal development among leisured aristocratic scholars in residential colleges. In its first three decades, Sydney had more money and Melbourne more students, but both struggled to survive, handicapped by the attractions of more rapid methods of colonial advancement and the slow development of upper secondary education, which achieved mass character only in the 1950s. Initial degree programs in the classics, humanities, mathematics and natural sciences were soon joined by the professional disciplines of medicine and law, which established the premier status that they still enjoy in the utilitarian system today. The first woman graduate was Bella Guerin at Melbourne in 1883. Though research received little funding, there were surprisingly strong beginnings in the physical sciences, medicine, geology, biology and anthropology (Selleck, 2003). Nevertheless, until the 1960s most of the best research conducted by Australians, and most of the Ph.D. training, took place abroad.

In 1939, there were 10,354 degree students (less than a third were women) and just 81 students in graduate degree programs. Australia's contemporary mass higher education system had its origins in the World War II (1939–1945) and postwar reconstruction policies of the national government.

Government Formation of a Segmented National System

Constitutionally, education was the responsibility of state governments. In 1939, 45% of university revenues derived from state governments and 32% from student fees. The Australian government played a minor role only, primarily in research. But during the war, the government began to view the population as a "human capital" resource to be harnessed in the national interest—though the phrase was not heard until the 1960s—and in 1942, when it acquired from the states the sole power to levy income taxes, it secured the capacity to expand its role. Student numbers were shaped by wartime "manpower planning;" the government secured a constitutional amendment allowing it to provide benefits to students; and after 1945, places were provided for returned services personnel, temporarily doubling student numbers.

In 1946, the government founded the Australian National University (ANU) to conduct research and postgraduate training in the physical sciences and engineering, including nuclear physics; medical sciences; social sciences; and Pacific and Asian studies. ANU was to become Australia's best-funded and most internationally-focused university. In 1950, the national government agreed to contribute one-quarter of the operating costs of state universities, but this was not enough. In the long economic boom of the 1950s and 1960s, demand for university graduates expanded while the supply of students from secondary education grew dramatically. With the inescapable pressures to expand higher education, state financing of higher education became more inadequate, and reluctantly, the national government was drawn into the financing and planning of a national higher education system.

The key moment was a three-month inquiry into the universities in 1957, appointed by Liberal Party/Country Party Prime Minister Robert Menzies, and led by Sir Keith Murray, the Chairman of the U.K. University Grants Committee. The Murray

Committee found that the universities were short-staffed and poorly equipped, with high failure rates and weak postgraduate schools. It led to a Grants Committee (along U.K. lines), and an expanded national role in operating grants and capital funding. Student numbers began to grow sharply and new universities opened, led by the University of New South Wales (NSW) in Sydney in 1949, and Monash University (in outer-suburban Melbourne) in 1957.

Meanwhile, higher education had begun to play an important role in Australian foreign policy in Asia. In 1950, Australia initiated the Colombo Plan, supported by other English-speaking countries, to provide degrees and technical training for students in developing nations from Southeast and South Asia. It was designed as a neo-colonial alternative to communism. By opening an educational passage between Asia-Pacific nations and Australia, the Colombo Plan normalized the presence of Asian students at a time when Asian immigration was blocked by the White Australian policy. They congregated at the newer institutions: the ANU, the University of NSW and Monash University. The Colombo Plan students were followed by private students from Asia, who paid partial-cost fees and were subject to quotas.

During an economic recession in 1960, the government became concerned about the potential costs of university expansion, and established an advisory committee of the Australian Universities Commission, chaired by Leslie Martin, to create a second, cheaper and explicitly vocational segment of higher education as the main avenue for future growth. Though the committee extolled the benefits of liberal education, it was enamored of human capital theory and discussed education in explicitly economic terms. The colleges of advanced education (CAEs) were expected to provide sub-degree programs and liaise closely with industry. They were not expected to conduct research. Funding, administration and planning were shared by the state and national authorities, while the states managed teacher training and technical education, and provided bursaries for teachers-in-training. The national government took the main policy and funding role in the universities and funded university scholarships. Australia had committed itself to a binary system of mass higher education along British lines (DEET, 1993, pp. 1–13), grounded in a rather awkward national/state division of responsibilities. The burgeoning popular demand and growing cost of funded places—as well as the "credential creep" of the CAEs and teachers' colleges into degree programs—soon became destabilizing elements.

Between 1960 and 1978, student enrollment increased from 53,391 to 312,943 (see Table 1), with postgraduate enrollment rising from 2,630 to 19,836—the greatest expansion in Australian history (Marginson 1997, pp. 9–73). Amid strong demand for staff, academic salaries relative to other professions reached an historical high in 1973. Shortages were alleviated by recruiting in the U.K., U.S. and central Europe. Between 1969–70 and 1975–76, national spending on higher education almost quadrupled in constant price terms. In 1974, the Labor Government (led by Gough Whitlam) assumed full national responsibility for funding universities, advanced education and teachers' colleges (Marginson, 2003), so that the national government funded almost 90% of all institutional income.

Though the government claimed its abolition of tuition fees would abolish all financial barriers to entry, at the time only 20% of students in higher education paid fees, and

592   *Marginson*

Table 1. Number of Students, Australian Higher Education, 1950–2000

	Number of Students	Proportion (%) That Were Women
1950	30,630	21.6%
1955	30,792	21.9%
1960	53,633	23.1%
1965	110,250	24.0%
1970	161,455	27.1%
1975	276,559	40.6%
1980	329,523	45.3%
1985	370,016	47.6%
1990	485,066	52.7%
1995	604,176	53.9%
2000	695,485	55.2%

Source: DEST (2004). Basis of calculation of student numbers differs from comprehensive calculation over full year that is used in Tables 2 and 3. Using same basis as those tables, total number of students in 2000 was about 805,000.

tuition was only 5% of institutional income. However, fee abolition had an important symbolic role, enabling many more Australian families to aspire to a university education, while grants for living costs received by two-thirds of students provided more substantial economic help. Between 1974 and 1980, private foreign students were also not required to pay tuition fees, though places continued to be limited by quota.

By 1978, there were 19 universities with a common mandate to conduct research and doctoral programs. Research activity was largely supported from federal operating grants, plus targeted research projects funded by the Australian Research Grants Scheme. Though some Ph.D.s continued to be earned offshore, for the first time most academic disciplines could reproduce themselves within Australia. The newer universities were founded in "greenfield" sites on the edge of the major cities, combining cheap real estate with the benefits of scholarly retreat. Some followed the example of the British University of Sussex (and others) in developing radical initiatives in cross-disciplinary programs, area and problem-focused studies, ecological research, student-centered learning, progressivist assessment and participatory internal government; Latrobe, Flinders, Murdoch and Griffith Universities were notable innovators. Along with the more orthodox modernist foundations preceding them, they attracted high quality young staff who welcomed the opportunity to work in more democratic institutions with a less Anglophile and traditional air than the older "sandstones" (Queensland, Sydney, New South Wales, Melbourne, Monash, Adelaide, Western Australia and ANU). It often seemed the postwar universities would eclipse their predecessors. There were also more than 100 CAEs, ranging from large institutes— focused on engineering, applied sciences and business—to small teacher training and specialist art and agricultural colleges. The policy authority of the states in advanced education was increasingly overshadowed by Canberra. The federal government also established a national inquiry into technical and further education (TAFE)—the Kangan committee—leading to the declaration of a nationally coordinated TAFE system and shared federal-state funding. Federal policy and funding advice were coordinated by specialist commissions in each of the university, CAE and technical education sectors, under the overall authority of the Commonwealth Tertiary Education Commission (CTEC). The Commission was chaired by economist and statistician Peter Karmel, the most influential of all the public figures in a notable system-building period.

A Unified National System Based on Mixed Public-Private Funding

Following the oil shock of 1974 and the shift to a monetarist fiscal policy, federal funding was frozen in 1975 and the planned open university and extended TAFE funding were shelved. The expansion of universities was halted; the last institution founded during this period—Deakin University in Victoria—enrolled its first students in 1977. The period until the mid-1980s was a quiet time, marked by an initial decline in demand from secondary school graduates, expanded mature age entry in newer universities and the CAEs, aging staff, and mounting pressures to control costs. The large institutes of technology stepped up their degree enrollments, placing pressure on the arbitrary binary divide. Smaller teachers colleges were rationalized by closure or merger. After 1981, student retention through the end of secondary school began to rise, foreshadowing another wave of system expansion, but with a different political economy. In 1984 and 1985, a new policy consensus about higher education—inspired by the Thatcher government in the U.K.—developed in the Treasury and the Prime Minister's office. It was believed that while participation rates should be increased sharply, Australia could no longer afford free tertiary education. The way forward was to install mixed funding and market competition for tuition revenues and industry support, to create an export market as in the U.K., and possibly to create private universities. In 1985, a full-fee market for foreign students was announced; and in 1986, a Higher Education Administration Charge of $250 per full-time domestic student was introduced. The CTEC was seen as too close to the institutions, and an obstacle to policy change; it was abolished in 1987, and in 1988 Labor Minister John Dawkins announced a wholesale reconstruction of the system and its financial base. Dawkins proved remarkably successful as a minister, and his policies were implemented in full.

Dawkins announced that participation rates would be increased close to North American levels, facilitating a massive increase in supply and (in effect) demand; between 1985 and 1995, the number of students rose from 370,016 to 604,177. This growth was partly financed by students themselves. Dawkins introduced a Higher Education Contribution Scheme (HECS), a uniform annual charge paid to the government (not the university), fixed initially at 25% of the average cost of courses and repaid through the tax system on an income contingent basis. At the time of its introduction, repayment of the HECS was deferred until a graduate's income reached the national average weekly earnings; later, this repayment threshold was eroded by inflation. The HECS was an innovative policy and attracted considerable international attention. It did not satisfy those neo-liberal reformers who wanted direct buyer-seller relations between students and institutions, but it provided fiscal relief—between 1986–87 and 1989–90, public funding per student fell by 38.0% (Marginson, 2001, p. 206)—while minimizing the negative effects on access. In the early years, before HECS levels and repayment rates were increased and the repayment threshold was eroded, the deterrent effects were mild and near neutral by socio-economic background. At the same time, the policy rhetoric attending the HECS was to pave the way for future system marketization. Dawkins argued that because students secured private benefits from higher education, this should be mirrored in its cost structure, in which the private and the public components were treated as zero-sum. Because the private benefits could be identified by rates of return analysis, while the public benefits of higher education were essentially determined by policy assumptions—and because in a low tax environment, government had a vested interest in minimizing public spending—future reductions in spending were all too readily justified by the notion of higher education as a private benefit.

The changes to institutional identity and system structure were also profound. Dawkins reworked a cooperative system of two vertically segmented sectors into a unitary system of universities in which all institutions competed for teaching and research resources "on the basis of institutional merit and capacity" (Dawkins, 1988, p. 28)—a system grounded in formal equality but differentiated by market competition. In 1988, the Minister announced that full funding would be provided only to comprehensive universities with over 8,000 students. This triggered a process of mergers and institutional restructuring—assisted by state governments controlling the acts governing universities—in which many universities became multi-site institutions. Most existing universities made substantial acquisitions from the former CAE sector, and 18 new public universities emerged, doubling the total number. Two new private universities also gained recognition, though at first they received no funding and were out-competed by the public institutions with lower cost HECS-based places. The main new sources of funds were private fees from foreign students and postgraduate vocational students, and government funds allocated on a competitive basis. Part of the government's operating grants were now allocated on the basis of research performance, instilling a performance culture in all institutions, while national research funds open to competition became the principal mechanism for funding research activities. There were wholesale changes in leadership, missions and internal cultures, facilitating administrative modernization and the creation of more economically autonomous institutions as favored by the government. The newly empowered layer of executive leaders were expected to build territory, activity and status in entrepreneurial fashion. Traditional academic cultures were placed under pressure and struggled to take root in the newer universities (Marginson & Considine, 2000).

After Dawkins, the government envisioned universities as competitive firms whose bottom line was comprised of their own resources and competitive position. The notion of the university as an independent quasi-firm suited the older sandstone universities, which had never been comfortable with national system building and the capacity of the government to use its funding power to intervene. At the same time, the system outcome was less egalitarian than Dawkins had hoped. The oldest universities, benefiting from concentrated research capacity and the long-term accumulation of social support and prestige, were best placed to compete for public funds and leverage market revenues off their positional status. The new universities were expected to conduct research and doctoral training, but were never funded at a level sufficient to establish basic research infrastructure in all disciplines, as their pre-1987 predecessors had been. They were forced into a predominantly applied research orientation and to focus more on chasing immediate dollars than on building long-term scholarly capacity.

Government Formation of a Buyer-Seller Undergraduate Market

The Dawkins reforms were followed by a series of policy changes enhancing the role of private costs and market competition, especially after a Liberal-National Party government was elected in 1996. Government-source funding per unit of student load, which after 1995 was only partly indexed for cost increases and was specifically reduced from 1997, fell from US$7,160 in 1990 to $5,220 in 2001 (in constant 2000–2001 dollars; DEST, 2004). Between 1995 and 2000, public spending per tertiary student declined by 30%, the largest such decline in any OECD member, while the average OECD nation increased public spending per student by 5% (Vincent-Lancrin, 2004). The decline in public funding triggered strong incentives to raise market-related incomes and transformed university cultures and priorities. Foreign student fees were fully deregulated and scholarships de-emphasized (1988); postgraduate fee arrangements were extended (1987–1995); and later, income-contingent loans were introduced to facilitate domestic investment in those postgraduate programs (2001). HECS was differentiated into three levels according to field of study, and average HECS charges rose by two-thirds (1997). Meanwhile, the threshold for HECS repayment dropped to just over half average weekly earnings. These changes enhanced deterrent effects and fell more heavily on poorer students than others (Aungles, Buchanan, Karmel, & MacLachlan, 2002).

Resources were partially shifted from teaching and research, being increasingly targeted to revenue-generating activities, and the enhancement of institutional competitiveness. Areas of expenditure growth included marketing and management functions, new buildings, offshore recruitment and offshore branch campuses. In 2003, only 38% of effective full-time university staff worked predominantly in academic roles. The decline in the capacity to sustain teaching and basic research affected all universities and disciplines, but was most strongly felt in the post-1987 universities—particularly in the basic sciences, social sciences and humanities, disciplines viewed as less attractive to fee-paying students than business and information technology (IT). Resources for teaching and research declined, while the average student/faculty ratio rose from 14:1 in 1993 to 21:1 in 2003 (AVCC, 2004). The Canberra-driven installation of quality assurance in the early 1990s—and regular quality audits (principally for global consumption) by the Australian Universities Quality Agency after 1999—provided techniques for concealing the effects of resource decline while promoting a "customer focus." Though the undergraduate core of higher education still consisted of HECS-based places subject to uniform charges, deepening resource problems and intensified competition—and particularly, tensions between the open-ended growth of foreign students and the constraints on publicly-funded domestic student places—were continued sources of instability, laying the basis for another major system change.

The government made three attempts to establish a buyer-seller market. First, the West inquiry (1997) floated a voucher model; however, the inquiry committee was politically inept, and the proposed reform had little attraction within the sector. Second, then-Minister David Kemp prepared proposals for undergraduate fees supported by a loans scheme (1999), but after these were leaked prematurely there was a public backlash and the scheme was dropped. Finally, a new minister (Brendan Nelson) crafted a national review and introduced a package of marketization reforms that promised higher incomes to the strongest universities. The package was driven by the national Treasury, the most powerful department, continuing its long interest in the creation of market competition in higher education. These reforms were piloted through the national parliament in December 2003.

The Nelson reforms brought three changes. First, though the HECS remained a payment from students to the government covering only part of the average cost of student places (with the balance funded by government), it was moved closer to a market fee. Individual universities were permitted to vary the HECS up to 25% above current levels, or downwards to zero, a range of $0–5,140 per annum in 2005. Most universities announced that they would opt for the maximum charge. There was little regard for the goal of maximum access with minimum deterrence that had underpinned the original HECS. Second, universities were permitted to charge direct tuition fees at any level, to up to 35% of the domestic students enrolled in each undergraduate course. Third, fee-paying students in both public universities and accredited private institutions were made eligible for a new system of income-contingent loans entitled FEE-HELP. As with HECS, there was to be no real interest rate on income contingent student debts, though students taking FEE-HELP loans would pay an annual surcharge of $2,000, and there would be a $50,000 ceiling on FEE-HELP debts. Further, in the longer term the government could reunify the tuition charging system as a buyer-seller market by lifting the caps on HECS levels and FEE-HELP loan debt and abolishing the $2,000 surcharge.

Under the new regime, many students could be expected to opt for fee-paying places in prestigious universities and courses rather than HECS places in less desired courses. Further, the cost gap between HECS places in public universities and fee-charging places in private institutions was narrowed: together with the FEE-HELP mechanism in private institutions, this made a large-scale private sector viable for the first time. Because income contingent loans with no interest rate entailed public subsidy, via both the interest regime and the non-repayment of part of student debt, in the future these loans could be expected to place downward pressures on the direct public funding of institutions, and over time shift funding into a voucher regime.

There were two compensatory policies: scholarships of up to $16,000 per course for a small number of students from low socio-economic or geographically isolated backgrounds; and the lifting of the income threshold for income contingent repayment to an indexed $35,000 per year (not incidentally, this made the full-fee market economically accessible). Individual universities began to extend their own scholarship schemes. The Nelson reforms brought both the cost and culture of Australian universities closer to the U.S. They closed the gap between an Australian HECS place and an American in-state public place, and by creating high-priced prestigious Australian degrees, encouraged Australian investment in American degrees.

Growth, Participation and Access

The Dawkins reforms broadened the mass higher education system, so that between 1993 and 2003 the proportion of the labor force with degrees rose from 12 to 21%—a further 33% held sub-degree tertiary qualifications—while the earnings of bachelor's-level graduates dropped from 100% to 90% of average weekly earnings (Gallagher, 2004). Private rates of return to bachelor's degrees declined by more than 1% after the cost of HECS rose in the mid-1990s (Chapman & Ryan, 2002). However, earnings levels for secondary school graduates also trended downwards, and the rate of unemployment for graduates was half the national average, so demand for university entry was maintained. Nevertheless, from 1995 to 2000, funded domestic student load was tightly constrained, rising by only 7.5% to 599,878. At the same time, foreign students—determined by market supply and demand, and constrained only by visa policy—increased by 107% to 95,607. In 2003, there were 719,555 Australian and New Zealand students and 210,397 foreign students (a data series break prevents precise comparison with the earlier years), with foreign students reaching a record 22.6% of all students. Between 2002 and 2003, foreign student enrollment rose by 13.7%, while domestic enrollment rose by only 0.9%.

In terms of level of study, the main growth areas were fee-paying vocational postgraduate programs (for both domestic and foreign students) and foreign student enrollments at the bachelor's level. The number of students entering master's programs, mostly in business studies and IT, rose by 122% in the decade after 1993, while the number of higher degree research (mostly doctoral) students rose by only 5% (Gallagher, 2004). In terms of field of study, the main growth in both higher education and VET was in business-focused programs (such as marketing, management and IT), followed by health studies. From 1988 to 2000, the proportion of all students enrolled in business, management and economics rose from 19% to 26%. The proportion in humanities and social sciences, the second largest group, was constant. During the early years of the new millennium, following shifts in labor markets, student demand for places in IT training leveled off and applications for teacher training increased. Participation by older students is high by international standards—in 2003, 29% of all students were at least 30 years old, many of them seeking a second qualification.

In sum, since the early 1990s national policy has shaped participation so that expansion has occurred in the market-driven areas, while domestic access from school into HECS-based undergraduate places has been restricted. Between 1996 and 2003, entry following secondary school completion fell by 13%, while entry scores rose sharply, particularly in Victoria and Queensland. The proportion of qualified young people applying for entry to degree programs but not offered a place reached 28% in 2004. Correspondingly, the number of young people commencing sub-degree programs in the VET sector has risen.

Reduced domestic access may become a main policy issue for the national government. Between 2000 and 2015, the Australian population aged 15–19 years is projected to rise by 2%, while the average OECD country will experience a decline of 9% (OECD, 2004). It remains to be seen whether full-fee places supported by low cost loans will increase access after 2005. Many such places will be taken up not by students who would otherwise have failed to secure entry, but by those upgrading participation to a more prestigious institution and/or more attractive fields of study. Whether this opens up more participation in less prestigious institutions for a new layer of secondary school graduates depends on the attractiveness of those less prestigious institutions (which, in an increasingly stratified system, is likely to diminish), the effects of the rising private cost of those places, and whether government funding is maintained in the longer term.

The creation of a buyer-seller undergraduate market may undermine participation among already under-represented social groups, especially in the prestigious institutions where they will be increasingly crowded out by full-fee paying students, but also overall. Here, Australia has a mixed recent record. Between 1994 and 2003, domestic students from "low socio-economic status" districts as a proportion of total enrollments was almost constant at 14.5% in 2003, while domestic students from non-English speaking backgrounds dropped from 5.1% to 3.5%. Indigenous students remained almost constant at 1.2% of the student body in 2003, about two-thirds of the indigenous share of the Australian population. They were concentrated in the non-science disciplines, with low graduation rates. Meanwhile, the representation of women in non-traditional courses improved; by 2003, women constituted two-thirds or more of enrollments in education, health studies, creative arts, humanities, and social sciences, and half in business, agriculture and the basic sciences. They were still only one-third of architecture students, less than a quarter of students enrolled in information technology, and 16% in engineering and related technologies (DEST, 2004). Women remain severely under-represented in manufacturing and construction industry-related vocational training.

Internationalization

Australia educates 10% of all cross-border students and is the third largest exporter of degree-level programs after the U.S. and U.K. Education is Australia's third largest services export, generating US$3 billion in tuition revenues and foreign student spending in 2003. That year, 74% of the 210,397 foreign students studied directly in Australia (as opposed to an overseas location), and 85% were from the Asia-Pacific region (Nelson, 2003; DEST, 2004). After commercial marketing was installed as the framework of supply in 1988, all universities became active providers of foreign education. There was extraordinary growth, fueled on one hand by middle-class Asian demand for English-language education (and migration status) and on the supply side by financial incentives, aggressive entrepreneurship by institutions, and coordinated marketing by the government's Australian Education International (AEI) and the university-financed International Development Program (IDP Australia). Australia also benefited from geographic proximity to Asia, a favorable climate and a reputation for being safer than the U.S. Further, for most of this time the average per student cost of tuition and living expenses was less than two-thirds of that in the American state universities and the U.K., a significant cost advantage.

Table 2. Students by Nation of Permanent Residence,
Australian Higher Education, 2002 and 2003

	2002	2003
Australia*	705,873	714,089
New Zealand	5,690	5,466
Singapore	29,956	29,878
Hong Kong China	26,956	29,169
Malaysia	23,725	27,267
PR China	19,956	27,020
Indonesia	11,981	11,865
India	8,390	11,133
U.S.	8,325	9,418
Thailand	5,202	5,815
Taiwan	3,977	4,410
Norway	3,868	3,991
other nations	42,722	50,431
*All foreign students***	*185,058*	*210,397*
All students	896,621	929,952

Note: *includes students who were not Australian citizens
but had permanent residence (31,9778 in 2003). **does not
include New Zealand students who occupy an intermediate
status.
Source: DEST (2004).

Almost two thirds of Australia's foreign students are enrolled in business studies
and IT, followed by engineering and related technologies, and health sciences. Most
are at the bachelor's level, with 28.2% enrolled in master's programs. There is little
subsidization of foreign research degrees. In 2002, the ratio of full fee-paying places to
scholarship places was 61:1 (DEST, 2004), and in 2003 doctoral degrees comprised only
7,821 of total foreign enrollments (i.e., 3.7% of all foreign students). Unlike the U.S.,
foreign students do not play a strong role in research and graduate teaching, narrowing
the potential of internationalization. The main importing nations are Singapore (29,878
students in 2003), Hong Kong China (29,169), Malaysia (27,267), the People's Republic
of China (27,020), neighboring Indonesia (11,865), India (11,133) and the U.S. (9,418)
(see Table 2). Australia enrolls more students from Southeast Asia than do American
universities, but is a lesser provider to China, Korea, Japan, and Taiwan, and the Indian
subcontinent (though numbers from China and India have grown rapidly in recent
years).

In 2002, there were 13 Australian universities with more international students than
the University of Southern California, the largest American provider of international
education in 2002–03 with 6,270 students (IIE, 2003; DEST, 2004). The largest foreign
student enrollments were at Monash (15,996), Royal Melbourne Institute of Technology University (RMIT) (14,024), Curtin University of Technology (13,624), and NSW
(10,179). Central Queensland University had 8,916 foreign students on seven campuses,

including Fiji, accounting for 40.3% of all its students (DEST, 2004). Internationalization has had a major impact on student services provision and campus atmosphere, but less dramatic effects on teaching methods and classroom discourse. There has been little change in curricula, and the level of cultural mixing between local and foreign students disappoints many foreign students (Smart, Volet, & Ang , 2000). Many universities are active overseas in franchising and twinning programs with local partners, especially in Singapore, Malaysia, Hong Kong and China. Some of the Asian-based partners work with several universities from Australia or the U.K., offering a choice of English-language degrees. A small number of Australian universities have overseas campuses—for example, Monash in Malaysia and South Africa, Curtin in Malaysia, and RMIT in Vietnam. These initiatives bring the Australian universities closer to Asian cultural and educational norms and in the longer term may stimulate a deeper internationalization.

Institutional Stratification

Australian higher education is divided into distinct segments with varying capacities and potentials. The establishment of the unified national system in 1988 closed one form of stratification (university/advanced education), but the new emphasis on competition and private income-raising opened others. In education markets, institutions with the most prestige and resources are best placed to compete. Over time their relative position is strengthened.

Table 3 provides details of the major segments of Australian higher education. The elite sandstones or Group of 8—Queensland, Sydney, New South Wales, Melbourne, Monash, Adelaide, Western Australia and ANU, all relatively early foundations—are identified as top choices by recent secondary school graduates as measured by entry scores, as well as research prestige and performance. The national Institutional Grants Scheme (IGS), allocated competitively on the basis of research performance, provides another useful indicator of elite status (Nelson, 2003, p. 103–104). In 2003, all sandstones received at least $15.3 AUD million in IGS grants. The next highest recipients were Tasmania and Wollongong, pre-Dawkins universities with medical faculties, both of which received $7.0 million AUD. Sydney, Western Australia and Melbourne enjoy what are in Australian terms high incomes from donors and private investments, partly insulating them from government intervention and commercial forces. The large universities of technology enroll many domestic and foreign students, but are weak in research funding per staff because they lack basic research capacity.

Until 2005, it was difficult for private universities to compete with the public institutions because of their fee structure. This also inhibited their capacity to build critical mass in research, though after 1996 some private institutions were made eligible for research grants. However, as noted earlier, the Nelson reforms render private institutions economically competitive for the first time, by establishing a system of tuition loans identical to that operating for full-fee places in the public system, and the national government has signaled its intention to encourage private sector development. The first major beneficiary is likely to be Notre Dame Australia, which in 2003 was granted a government-funded medical school in Sydney. The government also indicated that

Table 3. Segments of Australian Higher Education, 2002 and 2003 data

	Med	Total Students 2002	Student-Faculty Ratio 2002	Research Student Share 2002 (%)	International Student Share 2002 (%)	Flexible Delivery Share 2002 (%)	Total Income 2002 ($ million)	Non-current Assets 2002 ($ million)	Institutional Grants Scheme 2003 ($ million)
Sandstones									
U. Melbourne	Y	39,378	18.1	9.9	19.9	3.0	856.3	2,612.4	29.8
U. Queensland	Y	37,498	18.8	9.8	14.9	7.5	814.5	1,416.6	28.3
U. Sydney	Y	42,305	17.0	8.2	17.4	3.9	816.3	2,698.2	27.1
U. New South Wales	Y	42,333	19.3	6.3	24.4	10.1	701.5	1,273.3	25.4
Monash U.	Y	52,010	19.0	5.6	27.9	23.8	735.4	1,218.0	19.3
Australian National U.	Y	11,979	17.8	12.5	16.8	0	461.7	1,364.2	16.6
U. Western Australia	Y	15,885	16.2	11.5	16.0	0	360.4	1,134.9	16.1
U. Adelaide	Y	16,188	16.5	9.3	15.3	7.5	334.2	661.4	15.3
Other Pre-1987									
U. Tasmania	Y	13,750	19.7	7.5	9.1	10.9	199.7	269.8	7.0
U. Wollongong	N	18,764	20.9	5.5	35.0	1.1	210.1	392.8	7.0
La Trobe U.	N	24,930	18.6	5.5	13.3	0.7	314.0	593.5	6.3
Macquarie U.	N	27,239	26.2	3.8	24.2	17.5	295.9	812.8	6.2
Griffith U.	Y	30,969	19.7	4.1	17.3	7.5	350.7	801.4	6.1
U. Newcastle	Y	23,502	19.1	5.3	12.8	7.5	256.9	709.3	5.4
James Cook U.	Y	13,189	21.1	5.1	10.5	17.0	173.5	387.1	4.9
Flinders U.	Y	13,644	17.0	6.6	12.1	10.9	177.2	242.5	4.5
Murdoch U.	N	12,734	19.5	6.0	17.4	24.1	156.0	312.5	4.3
U. New England	N	18,202	22.5	4.5	6.7	81.9	148.3	338.8	3.8
Deakin U.	N	33,033	24.9	2.7	12.9	54.7	325.8	665.3	2.9

Continued

Table 3. *Continued.*

	Med	Total Students 2002	Student-Faculty Ratio 2002	Research Student Share 2002 (%)	International Student Share 2002 (%)	Flexible Delivery Share 2002 (%)	Total Income 2002 ($ million)	Non-current Assets 2002 ($ million)	Institutional Grants Scheme 2003 ($ million)
				U. Technologies					
Curtin U. Technology	N	33,240	20.6	4.8	34.0	11.5	360.9	623.6	5.2
Queensland U.T.	N	39,192	25.7	2.8	12.9	15.1	365.2	516.1	4.9
U. South Australia	N	30,627	22.5	5.7	29.0	22.0	286.1	618.0	4.5
Royal Melbourne I.T.	N	38,280	23.0	4.8	34.9	3.7	478.2	1,224.4	4.5
U. Tech. Sydney	N	29,290	19.2	3.1	17.9	0	287.7	730.1	3.6
				Other Public Universities					
U. Western Sydney	Y	35,361	22.1	2.7	21.6	4.5	296.7	639.8	3.2
U. Canberra	N	10,419	22.6	2.5	17.7	[0.04]	105.8	178.4	1.7
Swinburne U.T.	N	14,404	24.2	3.7	22.2	[0.01]	233.2	398.1	1.7
Victoria U. Tech.	N	19,475	16.1	3.4	23.5	1.9	277.8	632.6	1.7
Edith Cowan U.	N	23,829	20.9	3.5	16.0	24.4	202.9	487.3	1.4
Northern Territory U.	N	5,612	19.8	3.8	6.1	26.3	91.6	150.5	1.2
Southern Cross U.	N	11,961	22.4	3.8	14.1	52.9	89.7	172.4	1.2
Charles Sturt U.	N	39,776	33.4	1.1	20.9	83.4	187.4	337.1	1.2
Central Queensland U.	N	21,763	38.3	1.5	42.2	40.9	210.6	182.9	1.0
U. Southern Queensland	N	24,271	20.2	1.3	26.4	81.0	118.6	154.4	0.9
U. Ballarat	N	6,615	23.8	2.8	31.9	0	106.9	216.5	0.5
U. Sunshine Coast	N	3,947	27.5	1.6	10.5	11.3	32.5	57.3	0.1

				Private Universities				
Austral. Catholic U.*	N	11,894	18.9	2.8	8.1	8.9	104.4	176.8	0.5
U. Notre Dame Aust.	Y	2,832	n.a.	1.0	18.7	1.7	20.2	38.6	0.1
Bond U.	N	n.a.	n.a.	n.a.	n.a.	n.a.	n.a.	n.a.	0.1
Minor Sites									
[various]	–	6,250	–	–	9.6	–	69.4	233.1	0.4
TOTAL	–	896,621	20.4	5.1	20.6	19.2	11,614.1	25,496.2	277.6

Note: *Private university funded as public universities. Med = Medicine Faculty (Y = Yes, N = No). Dollar amounts in AUD, current prices. Research student share = research students as proportion of all students. International student share = fee-paying international students as proportion of all students. Flexible delivery share = proportion of students external (distance) students or multi-modal students, distinct from internal (wholly campus-based) students. Student-teacher ratio = ratio of effective full-time students to effective full-time academic staff designated teaching only or teaching/research, including casual staff. Institutional Grants Scheme awarded competitively on research performance: formula is 60% research grants, 30% research students, 10% publications count.

Sources: DEST (2004); Nelson (2003); Australian Vice Chancellors' Committee (2002).

it might facilitate the entry of foreign providers, possibly by negotiating with the state governments a loosening of the legal definition of "university."

Policy, Governance and Accountability

All Australian governments have agreed that for an institution to use the title "university" it must fulfill certain conditions, including an independent governing body, academic freedom, teaching and research across a range of disciplines, and financial viability. These conditions normalize large comprehensive research-intensive universities and seal off the title from small specialist institutions, emerging would-be private providers, and foreign for-profits. However, some institutions have gained access to the title "university" without fulfilling all conditions. As noted, there are pressures to loosen the criteria, which at the time of this writing were under review.

There are 39 designated universities, and some non-university institutions, established under mostly state government legislation as self-accrediting institutions. These are also designated by Commonwealth legislation as part of the national higher education system and are eligible for national research funding. These designated institutions enroll more than 95% of higher education students. More than 93% of all students are enrolled in public institutions, which are required to report regularly to the government and are held accountable for the discharge of their purposes as specified in the legislation, including the prudential supervision of investments and the monitoring of commercial entities owned by the university. The governing council or senate of each university—some of whose members are nominated by the government—is responsible for performance and the supervision of executive officers.

From the Dawkins reforms onwards, the national government has encouraged smaller governing bodies, a diminished role for staff and student representatives and an enlarged role for external members from business and industry. Governing bodies do not always possess complete information about commercial entities, and practical operational control rests with university executives; much depends on the latter, particularly the vice chancellor. Accountability works less well in relation to partnerships than wholly-owned assets. Within this legal framework, individual universities have as high a degree of operational autonomy as in the U.K. They determine missions and developmental strategies, priorities and activities, control budgets, build buildings, appoint and manage staff, and determine programs of study, subject to the Australian Qualifications Framework and registration by relevant professional associations. Major site acquisitions and alterations may require state approval, and institutions have a restricted capacity to leverage their public assets to raise loan funds. Private entities such as Notre Dame Australia have more limited public responsibilities and a greater freedom in managing assets and composing governing bodies.

Prior to the Dawkins reforms, the national government exercised a detailed supervision of operating budgets and capital works through its financial power. Governmental influence is now secured more by positioning institutions as self-managed corporations and steering them from the distance. Likewise, the policy culture has shifted, from an often detailed specification of expectations about the contribution of universities to national purposes, to the assumption that competition for funds and prestige, structured as the government determines, will drive efficiency, force accountability to industry and student "clients," and secure production of public goods. The appropriate Enlightenment metaphor is not so much that of Adam Smith's "invisible hand", but the government as clock-maker. Once set in place, the clock seems to tick under its own momentum.

While universities enjoy unprecedented administrative and financial autonomy, the national government now shapes the university "product" via the performance-based funding of research and research training; innovation funds, which are subject to competitive bidding; the conditions governing the receipt of grants; standardized data collection; and the homogenizing effects of quality assurance systems. The government also controls the number of HECS-based places, and requires universities to meet a small number of direct targets in areas stipulated in the legislation covering grants—for example, the number of indigenous students enrolled. Quality assurance (QA) has become a standard organizational reflexivity. Within institutions, it takes a generic form, more manager- than discipline-driven, encouraging homogenization and the use of QA data for marketing purposes. Nationally, the Australian Universities Quality Agency (AUQA) conducts five-year audits of all self-accrediting institutions (including their offshore operations), and also audits the state/territory accreditation agencies. The creation of AUQA in 1999 was designed to strengthen the global reputation of Australian universities, following the emergence of similar national agencies in the U.K. and New Zealand.

In addition to the self-accrediting higher education institutions, a further group of private sector entities—normally designated as "colleges" or "institutes"—provide degree programs in specialist areas such as theology. Both institutional accreditation and the accreditation of each specific program are subject to periodic review by relevant state/territory governments. The autonomy of VET institutions is more limited than that of higher education institutions. They conduct their own commercial activities, but funded VET programs are supervised by state and territory governments, and are often subject to the authority of industry-training bodies.

Financing and Management

Between 1996 and 2002, the proportion of total university funding derived from public sources fell from 58% to 44%, while funding from students rose from 19% to 32%, half from the HECS. Revenue from foreign student fees increased from US$389 to $941 million (142%), while total fee income from domestic students in degree and diploma courses was less significant but almost tripled over the period. By 2002, more than one dollar in five was drawn from explicitly commercial activities, designed to create a surplus: foreign student education; vocational education provided to postgraduates; continuing professional education; commercial research and consultancy; and other services such as merchandising and the hiring of facilities. Whereas in 1996 foreign students provided 6.6% of total university funding, Table 4 shows that by 2002 the level of dependence on this source had reached 12.5% (DEST, 2004).

The rapid and major growth of market revenues and corporate expenditures has been accompanied by significant changes in internal organizational cultures, more obvious

Table 4.   University Revenues by Source, Constant Prices, 1990, 1996 and 2002

Source of funding	Total Funding from This Source			Proportion of All Funding by Source		
	1990 ($ million)	1996 ($ million)	2002 ($ million)	1990 (%)	1996 (%)	2002 (%)
Government	2,684	3,422	3,326	68.4	58.1	44.1
HECS from students	261	683	1,191	11.8	11.6	15.8
International student fees*	114	389	941	2.9	6.6	12.5
Postgraduate student fees	10	66	147	0.3	1.1	2.0
Undergraduate student fees	0	0	46	0	0	0.6
Continuing education fees	38	58	66	1.0	1.0	0.9
All other sources**	614	1,275	1,825	15.7	21.6	24.2
Total	3,922	5,893	7,542	100.0	100.0	100.0

Note: Constant 2000–01 prices, USD. $1.00 AUD = $0.67 USD. *includes international students at all levels of study **includes payments for contract research, donations and bequests, investment income, etc.
Source: DEST (2004).

in newer universities than the sandstones (where inherited academic cultures are resilient). Nevertheless, in all institutions the role and power of vice chancellors has been enhanced; the practical authority of their deputies and of full-time executive deans with resource powers has partly displaced that of part-time disciplinary leaders; and performance management and internal competition for resources have become entrenched. In many universities, peer assemblies of tenured academic staff now play a relatively minor role. Instead of academic decisions tending to determine resource flows, resource decisions tend to shape the academic landscape. Whereas research centers with income-earning capacity enjoy the autonomy of quasi-firms, in mainstream faculties and schools the content of teaching and research is increasingly affected by market demand, cost incentives, standardized accountability and management systems. Australian universities are distinctive in the extent to which business models of organization and internal marketing shape the campus environment (Marginson & Considine, 2000). They are also strong users of ICTs. Most teaching programs incorporate at least some online resource provision; many are provided in both face-to-face and full online delivery mode; and routine student administration such as enrollment is normally available via the Internet.

The Academic Profession

The academic profession is structured along British lines. The career grade for permanent staff is senior lecturer, equivalent to associate professor in the U.S. In Australia, the levels of associate professor and professor are reserved for superior performance—especially (but not only) superior performance in scholarship and research—as well as for executive roles such as Faculty Dean. Tenure is granted after varying procedures and periods: there is no normalized pathway as in the U.S. Like academic appointments, tenure is more an administrative decision driven by financial and labor market considerations than a determination by scholarly peers on academic grounds, though scholarly achievement is part of the administrative consideration. Tenured posts are mostly linked to teaching: there are few tenured research-only staff outside the ANU's four research schools. Across the Australian higher education system, the rapid growth of student-faculty ratios has been associated with the mushrooming of untenured academic employment, much of it taking the form of "casual" or "sessional" teaching paid on an hourly basis, and the replacement of small tutorial groups by large classes. Conditions of work, largely regulated on a local university basis, are subject to industry-wide standards in specific areas (for example, the procedures governing the dismissal of permanent staff) supervised by the national Industrial Relations Commission. Academic pay is no longer centrally determined, but the National Tertiary Education Union has been able to control the university-by-university bargaining process so as to maintain parity across institutions and fields of study within a band of 10% or so, aside from additional clinical loadings in medicine and related fields, and at the professorial level, where a wide variety of arrangements apply and incentive and reward payments are common.

In exchange rate terms, the value of 12 months' salary and remuneration at the professor and senior lecturer levels in Australia is about two-thirds of the level of American salaries and average remuneration for the 9–10 months outside the summer period. It is widely perceived that there is a "brain drain" problem in Australia, but it is difficult to quantify. In terms of salaries and research infrastructure—and perhaps also in academic workloads and in opportunities for scholarly development—Australian universities are less attractive than Cambridge, Oxford, or the leading American doctoral universities. On the other hand, migration brings additional doctorally qualified personnel into Australia. In aggregate terms, Australia appears to gain qualified staff overall, but it loses some of its best researchers either at the postdoctoral stage or mid-career. The Australian government provides a small number of Federation Fellowships designed to keep world-class researchers in Australia and encourage expatriate researchers to return. In the coming years, the quality problems created by "brain drain" may be exacerbated by a quantity problem determined by demographics. Universities are about to undergo a phase of wholesale retirement and replacement. Although there is no mandatory age of retirement, withdrawal at ages 60–65 years is common: in 2003, 13,801 (38.5%) of the 35,867 full-time and fractional full-time staff with academic classifications were aged 50 years or higher (DEST, 2004). Though the position will vary greatly by field of study, it is unlikely that the number of Australians with doctoral qualifications will be sufficient to fill all vacancies. There may be substantial opportunities for foreign staff: given relative salaries, it is likely that many of these opportunities will be filled by faculty from China, Southeast Asia and South Asia. It is also likely that there will be major changes in the balance between different fields of study. University managers will take the opportunity presented by the large-scale withdrawal of staff from tenured positions to align numbers in different fields more closely to the map of student demand and revenue-raising opportunities.

Research and Graduate Studies

Most full-time academic staff are categorized as "Teaching/Research," and are expected to be involved in scholarship and publishing. However, research with significant funding support tends to be concentrated in the older and stronger universities and among a minority of staff. Of the funding allocated in 2003 under the Research Training Scheme (RTS), more than half went to six sandstone universities, while only about one-fifth of applications for Australian Research Council (ARC) Discovery Grants were successful. The main forms of national government support for research include grants allocated by the ARC and the National Health and Medical Research Council (NHMRC) for projects, fellowships and research infrastructure; project funding from government departments; the component of operating funds allocated to universities on the basis of research performance under the Institutional Grants Scheme; grants for research training places and infrastructure under the RTS; and scholarships for postgraduate research students. In 2003, there were 1,550 new Australian Postgraduate Awards and 330 new International Postgraduate Research Scholarships. ARC and NHMRC allocate funding on the basis of the excellence of proposals and past researcher performance; the IGS and RTS allocations are performance-related; and project funding is client- and purpose-driven. The strengthening of industry funding and of university-industry links has been a principal objective of research policy, but only about 5% of the support for research in Australian universities comes from this source, due primarily to the weakness of local industry. Industry R&D inside and outside universities is below the average for OECD nations, while government spending on university research is above the OECD average. Donor and philanthropic funding supports a small number of research chairs and projects, but at a lower level than in the U.S.

Prior to the 1980s, research was conducted autonomously in academic disciplines, some (particularly the natural sciences) comprised by global networks and others more locally referenced. Though disciplines and cross-disciplinary centers remain primary sites of organization, designated research activity is now closely shaped by the systems of funding and management. National research funding is allocated primarily on the basis of past performance. In measuring this, income for research plays a much larger part than scholarly publications, so that research is viewed by some as a quasi-economy in which past resources generate future resources. Performance-related research funding tends to encourage concentration, and also augments the status of the most successful universities, encouraging institutional stratification. The other main development in recent years has been the growing role of international collaborations, and within that, the trend towards large-scale cross-country projects with multiple national funding. About 40% of ARC-funded projects involve international collaborations. Patterns of collaboration favor North America, the U.K. and Western Europe, though research linkages in Japan, Singapore and China are growing. Australian researchers have developed areas of global strength—as measured by publications, citation rates and quality indices in (for example) the chemical sciences, certain fields of engineering and technologies, geology, agriculture, veterinary and environmental sciences, areas of medicine, and some humanities (such as philosophy). The Australian government has earmarked four areas for future development as global strengths: complex and intelligent systems, genome-phoneme research, nano- and bio- materials, and photon science technology.

The ANU is the strongest research university in Australia, with a high rate of international collaborations and concentrated strengths in the physical sciences and engineering, medical sciences, social sciences, and in Asian and Pacific studies (where it is considered a world leader). It has perhaps the largest group of academic experts on China and Indonesia anywhere outside those countries. In a 2004 survey of the research performance of the world's universities, conducted by the Shanghai Jiao Tong University Institute of Higher Education (SJTUIHE, 2004), ANU ranked 53rd, with the University of Melbourne (which has strong medical research institutes) at 82nd. The Universities of Queensland and Sydney were positioned among the world's top 150 research universities, and the Universities of New South Wales and Western Australia were among the top 200. Adelaide and Monash were ranked among the top 300. A further six Australian institutions were ranked among the top 500—Flinders, La Trobe, Macquarie, Murdoch, Newcastle and Tasmania. The Jiao Tong survey rankings indicate a somewhat disappointing view of Australian research, in terms of both the quality and spread of research capacity. As well as being eclipsed by larger nations such as the U.S., U.K., Germany, Japan, France and Canada, Australia's leading universities were clearly outranked by the smaller systems of Switzerland, the Netherlands and Sweden. By comparison, the closest international peer nation (Canada) had 23 universities in the top 500, compared to Australia's 14. None of the universities created by the Dawkins reforms of 1987 (or afterwards) had developed sufficiently so as to figure in the world's top 500 research institutions.

Conclusion

While the nation's mass higher education system had for many years been publicly funded and administered, over the last two decades Australia has dismantled that system by degrees, replacing it with a mixed-funded set of self-managed, corporate-style universities with unusual dependence on (and sensitivity to) short-term market signals. This has not noticeably improved the industry-university synergy, as was hoped, but it has rendered the universities quick to secure business opportunities in Asia, and developed their competence in marketing and financial management. The Nelson reforms introduced in 2004 took the process a step further by creating full-scale price competition in undergraduate education. Initial limits on the number of places subject to full fees are likely to be lifted. Viable comprehensive private institutions (as well as a plethora of specialist private institutions) will emerge, with the support of government subsidized loans for tuition. An increasing proportion of the remaining public funds for higher education will be absorbed by the subsidization of loans and the provision of the scholarships necessary to counter-balance the regressive social effects of full-price tuition. This is consistent with longer term trends across Australian social policy as a whole, away from the public funding of institutions and in favor of funding individuals as quasi-consumers (and voters). However, in higher education this structural change has placed severe pressure on basic research capacity. Growing reliance on market-generated incomes has retarded the development of basic research capacity, which in Australia (as elsewhere in the world) had always been government-dependent.

Australia's relative standing in research was probably greater in the mid-1980s than the mid-2000s. With leading universities in Singapore, Taiwan and China strengthening their research at a rapid pace, there is a danger that Australia will miss the opportunity to maximize research synergies in the Asia-Pacific region, despite Australia's extensive regional activity in teaching programs. However, rather than reverse the shift to private funding, the Australian government has boldly placed more faith in the vision of Milton Friedman—that a freer play of market forces, in which student and industry beneficiaries of higher education pay the costs, will eventually enrich higher education overall. The outcome is a system more dependent on student funding than the U.S. Australia is a test case of whether Friedman was right.

The outcome is as yet unknown, but one thing is clear and universally agreed: the post-Nelson system will generate a more pronounced institutional stratification. The lesser universities will struggle. They will remain relatively accessible, but there is an obvious danger that mass higher education will become tied to price cutting, endemic quality problems will be only partly concealed by marketing and quality assurance, and research capacity will stagnate or decline. The more marketized system has two potential upsides: fiscal savings, and the potential to create a layer of stronger universities. The sandstone universities will use domestic fee-charging to improve their resource position, recruit more high-cost faculty, and raise their global profiles (while reducing their direct dependence on foreign students). The questions yet to be resolved are the extent to which the new private incomes, generated through teaching degrees, will transfer into long-term basic research capacity; whether the leading universities can adequately replace their senior research staff, who originated in the period of high public funding; and whether their global research performance will improve overall. If Australia can leverage an improved basic research capacity primarily on the basis of market-generated revenues, rather than government or philanthropic funding, it will be the first nation in the world to do so.

References

Aungles, P., Buchanan, I., Karmel, T., & MacLachlan, M. (2002). *HECS and opportunities in higher education: A paper investigating the impact of the Higher Education Contributions Scheme (HECS) on the higher education system.* Research, Analysis and Evaluation Group, Department of Education, Science and Training (DEST). Canberra, Australia: DEST.

Australian Vice Chancellors' Committee, AVCC. (2004). Statistical data. Available online at http://www.avcc.edu.au/policies_activities/resource_analysis/key_stats/index.htm.

Australian Education International. http://www.aeo.us.

Chapman, B. & Ryan, C. (2002). *Income contingent financing of student charges for higher education: Assessing the Australian innovation.* Centre for Economic Policy Research (CEPR), Australian National University. Canberra, Australia: CEPR ANU.

Dawkins, J. (1988). *Higher education: A policy statement.* Canberra, Australia: Australian Government Publishing Service.

Department of Employment, Education and Training (DEET). (1993). *National report on Australia's higher education sector.* Canberra, Australia: Australian Government Publishing Service.

Department of Education, Science and Training (DEST). (2004). Statistics relating to higher education. Available online at http://www.dest.gov.au/highered/statinfo.htm.

Gallagher, M. (2004). *Which way past the crossroads? Reflections on Australia's policy directions for tertiary education and research*. Canberra, Australia: Australian National University Policy and Planning Office.

Institute for International Education (IIE). (2003). Data on foreign student education in the United States. Available online at http://www.iie.org/Content/NavigationMenu/Research_Publications/Study_Abroad_Statistics/Study_Abroad_Statistics.htm

Marginson, S. (1997). *Educating Australia: Government, economy and citizen since 1960*. Cambridge, UK: Cambridge University Press.

Marginson, S. (2001). Trends in the funding of Australian higher education. *The Australian Economic Review, 34*(2), 205–215.

Marginson, S. (2003). The Whitlam government and education. In J. Hocking & C. Lewis (Eds.), *It's Time Again: Whitlam and modern Labor* (pp. 244–272). Melbourne, Australia: Circa.

Marginson, S. & Considine, R. (2000). *The enterprise university: Power, governance and reinvention in Australia*. Cambridge, UK: Cambridge University Press.

National Council for Vocational Education Research (NCVER). (2004). Statistics. Available online at http://www.ncver.edu.au/statistic/index.html?PHPSESSID=8bfa7c6cafafcc7f4488a8a2a0aff83d.

Nelson, B. (2003). *Higher education: Report for 2003 to 2005 Triennium*. Commonwealth Minister for Education, Science and Training. Available online at http://www.dest.gov.au/highered/index1.htm.

Organization for Economic Cooperation and Development. (2003). Statistical data on science and technology. Paris: OECD. Available online at http://www.oecd.org/statisticsdata/0,2643,en_2649_33703_1_119656_1_1_1,00.html

Organization for Economic Cooperation and Development. (2004). *Education at a glance*. Paris: OECD.

Selleck, R. (2003). *The shop: The University of Melbourne 1850–1939*. Melbourne, Australia: Melbourne University Press.

Shanghai Jiao Tong University Institute of Higher Education (SJTUIHE). (2004). *Academic Ranking of World Universities–2004*. Available online at http://ed.sjtu.edu.cn/ranking.htm.

Smart, D., Volet, S., & Ang, G. (2000). *Fostering social cohesion in universities: Bridging the cultural divide*. Paper prepared for Australian Education International, DEST. Available online at http://www.dest.gov.au/highered/repts.htm.

Vincent-Lancrin, S. (2004). Building future scenarios for universities and higher education: An international approach. *Journal of Policy Futures in Education, 2*(1).

Watson, L. (1999). *Survey of private providers in Australian higher education 1999, 2000–04*, Evaluations and Investigations Program, Higher Education Division. Canberra, Australia: DEST. Available online at http://www.dest.gov.au/archive/highered/eippubs/eip00_4/survey.pdf.

World Bank. (2004). Data and statistics. Available online at http://www.worldbank.org/data.

31

BRAZIL

Simon Schwartzman
Institute for the Study of Work and Society, Brazil

Brazilian institutions of higher education were, from the beginning, part of a peculiar project of modernization launched by imperial Portugal at the end of the 18th century, transplanted to colonial Brazil with the Portuguese Court in 1808 and continued after political autonomy in 1822. It was led by Sebastião José de Carvalho Melo, the Marquis of Pombal, who was a minister of King D. José I from 1750 to 1777, known for the expulsion of the Jesuits from the Portuguese empire and the renovation of the traditional University of Coimbra in Lisbon.

Pombal hoped to free Portugal from the grips of Catholic restoration and conservatism, allowing it to share the benefits of the spreading scientific and industrial revolution without, however, incorporating new sectors in the ruling circles or allowing any major change in society or the economy. The Portuguese experience should be contrasted with that of other Western European countries, where the evolution of higher education was part of a much broader process of social and political modernization, mediated by different sorts of new professional groups—lawyers, the military, engineers, university professors, and scientists responsible for the progressive rationalization and institutionalization of the new social order. Portugal and Spain did not participate in the great religious and cultural transformations marking the end of the European Middle Ages, and never developed the strong professional, academic or religious corporations and movements that were present (to various degrees) in societies like Britain, France or the German states.

Brazil's enlightened elites, like their counterparts elsewhere in Latin America, entered the independence years of the early 19th century admiring and copying the French opposition to all forms of corporatist arrangements and privileges, including those of the Church and of the traditional universities. Once free from colonial rule, different versions of the Napoleonic system of higher education were created, taking away from the Church most of its role in providing elite education. When the first Brazilian professional schools were established in 1808, they were meant to prepare cadres for public administration—the military forces, the engineering corps, the hospitals and the handling of legal affairs—but lacked professional and scholarly traditions upon which truly modern institutions could be developed. They also lacked the pressures for performance and competence that would be required in conditions of intense competition

James J.F. Forest and Philip G. Altbach (eds.), International Handbook of Higher Education, 613–626.
© *2006 Springer. Printed in the Netherlands.*

for social mobility. Latin America's enlightened elites could speak French and handle French concepts, including the democratic and rationalist ideals; their societies, however, remained restricted by the limits of their economies, based on a few export products, large pockets of traditional or decadent settlements, one or two major administrative and export centers, and in Brazil, a slave system lasting almost to the end of the 19th century. This double jeopardy led to the general lack of intellectual and institutional vigor typical of most scientific and higher education institutions in the region throughout the 19th century.

The first higher education institutions were established in Rio de Janeiro (for military engineering, and medicine), Salvador (medicine), Recife and São Paulo (law). After 1850, under Emperor D. Pedro II, Brazil entered a sustained period of political stability and economic growth, which allowed for the gradual expansion of its educational institutions and the consolidation of a few scientific centers, like the National Observatory, the National Museum and the Imperial Geological Commission. At the end of the 19th century, following the expansion of coffee plantations and the arrival of several million European immigrants to the Brazilian southern states, the old Imperial regime was replaced by a federated republic, and dozens of "faculties"—as well as a few new research institutions—were created in the state of São Paulo and in other regions. However, Brazil's first university—the University of Rio de Janeiro—was not established until 1920; created by the federal government as a loose federation of previously existing professional schools, it remained Brazil's only university for many years (Schwartzman, 1991).

The institutional and intellectual framework of contemporary Brazilian higher education institutions was established during the 1930s, with a major overhaul in 1968. The Getúlio Vargas period (1930–1945) was a time of growing political and administrative centralization, culminating in the fascist *putsch* of 1937. Political events in Italy, including the 1923 Giovanni Gentile education reforms, were permanent sources of inspiration both for the reform of secondary education and the organization of universities, all under close ministerial supervision. In 1931, the new government established a Ministry of Education and Health, and legislation was introduced defining the framework for the country's university system, which was to combine a faculty of philosophy, sciences and letters (responsible for basic research and teacher education) with independent professional schools in law, medicine, engineering, pharmacy and others. The curricula for all careers were to be defined by law and would be mandatory for all, while a National Council of Education would supervise and give stability to educational policies.

In 1934, the Vargas regime sealed a political pact with the conservative Catholic Church, granting it control over education policy and institutions. In 1939, the University of Rio de Janeiro was reorganized according to the 1931 legislation. With the creation of its *Faculdade de Filosofia* (Faculty of Philosophy), to be led by Catholic intellectuals, and a new name—the University of Brazil—these changes were meant to provide the model for all other higher education institutions in the country. However, the political and economic elites in the state of São Paulo, already the country's economic hub, maneuvered to keep their autonomy, and in 1934 had created their own university—the first to follow the letter of the 1931 legislation, but remaining under local control. Its *Faculdade de Filosofia,* fully staffed with European academics, became Brazil's first university to conduct research as a permanent and recognized activity, and the first to grant advanced degrees (Schwartzman, Bomeny, & Costa, 2000).

Political centralization, authoritarianism and enthusiasm with European fascism receded in the early 1940s, particularly after Brazil joined the allies in World War II. However, the centralizing and bureaucratic tendencies of the 1930s would remain in the years to follow, less for ideological choice than for institutional inertia. A network of federal universities developed after 1945, in large part through the federalization of several state universities created in the 1930s and 1940s, and later by the notion that each state in the federation was entitled to at least one federal university. The state of São Paulo kept its tradition of regional independence and self-sufficiency, and developed its own system of public higher education. The Church and State pact of 1934 left its imprint, but receded with political liberalization, and the early 1940s saw the establishment of the Pontifical Catholic University in Rio de Janeiro, the first of several. Isolated faculties continued to be created both privately and by the federal, state and local governments in the following years, leading to the current *de facto* diversification of Brazilian higher education: a network of federal universities, a large state system in São Paulo, and a variety of smaller state and local institutions in other regions.

Growing demand for higher education since the late 1960s has led to a rapid and uncontrolled expansion of private institutions. Most recently, higher education in Brazil expanded dramatically during the 1990s, going from 1.5 to about 3.5 million students by 2002—still small, considering the country's population of about 180 million. Most of this growth was due to the expansion of the private sector, which today accounts for about three-fourths of total student enrollment. Postgraduate education has also expanded, and Brazil today offers the largest collection of master's and doctoral programs in Latin America (Balbachevsky, 2004; Durham, 2004).

Context

Higher education in Brazil was traditionally a channel of elite education and reproduction within a highly stratified, regionally unbalanced and unequally developed society. As education expanded, access to culture and expert knowledge provided new grounds for claims to social and political leadership, which changed in character as the number and social origins of the student body also evolved. In Brazil, as elsewhere in Latin America, political activism has been a permanent feature of university life. Political leadership, social mobility and, more recently, professional credentials and job security have frequently overshadowed the acquisition of professional skills required by the job markets as the main motivations for higher education.

In the past, most people lived in the Brazilian countryside; today, more than 70% are urban, leading to serious problems of housing, transportation, overcrowding, violence and other manifestations of urban decay. Modern industry is concentrated in São Paulo and other southern states, while large, capital-intensive rural enterprises dominate extensive parts of the land, including some of the largest frontier and demographically sparse states. The densely populated northeastern states, dominated since the 17th century by sugar cane plantations, have remained in a state of chronic poverty for centuries, and have been a source of steady population migration to the southern and urban regions (Schwartzman, 2000).

Population growth was extremely high between 1940 and 1960, going from 41.2 to 70.1 million; two decades later, the 1980 census registered 119 million, a similar rate of increase. By 2004, Brazil had an estimated population of 178 million, but with falling birth rates, the expectation is that population growth will cease within a few decades.

Important ethnic differences are also apparent. Racial mixing is very high, but afro-descendants are still at the bottom of the social pyramid, in terms of education, employment and wealth. The native population that existed during the colonial period was either decimated or fully assimilated, except for small pockets of a few hundred thousand in some areas. There is only one spoken language, Portuguese, but socially unrecognized linguistic differences exist not only among regions but mostly among social strata, a condition presumably accounting for serious learning difficulties of lower class students in public schools. Italian, German and Japanese immigrants were forced to close their mother tongue schools in the 1930s, and it is still forbidden in Brazil to provide basic education except in Portuguese, except for a few private foreign schools providing bi-lingual education in the main cities. There are no higher education institutions organized along linguistic, ethnic or cultural lines.

When asked, most Brazilians declare themselves Catholic. Yet, Catholicism coexists with different forms of African and spiritualist cults, and some forms of Protestant fundamentalism have made substantial inroads among the poorer strata. The Catholic Church has traditionally been very active in educational matters, and still runs about a dozen universities, as well as many secondary and fundamental schools. There are also a few Protestant higher education institutions, but none related to the Afro-Brazilian religions.

Brazil is formally a federation of states, further divided into thousands of municipalities and local districts. The 1988 Constitution leaned toward decentralization, but except for the state of São Paulo, most regions are heavily dependent on federal transfers. Public subsidies, public employment and special access to privileged business opportunities are still the main source of living for the upper strata of the country's poorer or economically decaying regions. Economic transfers to the poorer sectors, however, have not been significant, owing to a lack of motivation, administrative incompetence or a sheer lack of resources.

Education closely mirrors this picture. Although access to first-year, public basic education is now generally available, the quality of educational services is very unequal. Repetition and dropout rates are very high, and strongly correlated with socioeconomic conditions. For the population older than 18, the average number of years of schooling for Brazil as a whole was as low as 6.5 years in 2002; in rural areas it was 3.4, and in the northeastern region, 5.1 years. Assessments carried out by the Ministry of Education and international comparisons confirm that large segments of the student population remain functionally illiterate after several years of schooling. Instead of investing in the solution to this qualitative problem, Brazilian society has moved toward the quantitative expansion of preschool, secondary and higher education, leading to increasing gaps in access to good quality education (Oliveira, 2004; Soares, 2004).

Institutions

Brazilian higher education is formally unified along two lines: one (more traditional) related to the public regulation of professions, and the other (more modern) oriented toward the organization of knowledge in academic disciplines. These two unifying principles are not recognized as different, and their uneasy coexistence helps to understand the deep contradictions, differentiation and contrasts among higher education institutions that occur in practice.

The 1931 university legislation reinforced the traditional Napoleonic notion that higher education institutions were schools licensed by the state to teach and certify for the established professions. Each teaching institution was a *faculdade*, in the sense that they were granted the faculty, or franchise, to act on the State's behalf in providing education and extending legally binding professional credentials. This franchising system worked both for public and private institutions, leading to several important consequences. Since all institutions had to provide the same qualification, there was little room for academic autonomy. Education credentials acquired a value that was fairly independent from their knowledge content, increasing the demand for formal education with an incentive to do it as easily and cheaply as possible. Carriers of diplomas in new fields of knowledge and education—like economics, journalism or administration—lobbied to create their own market segments, and therefore brought their courses under the same principle of national uniformity and federal regulation; there was no place nor incentives for research or non-professional degrees, and no role—except a ceremonial or a purely bureaucratic one—for a unified university authority and administration.

An elaborate structure was set in place to keep this system under control. Each profession was to be controlled by professional councils, elected by their peers under ministerial supervision, and responsible for keeping standards, protecting the market against uncertified persons, and helping to draft the mandatory basic curricula for professional education. All teaching institutions were supposed to provide the same core curricula, with some room to add options and special emphasis. In practice, given the link between courses taken and professional privileges, the mandatory curricula often occupied the whole four or five years of study for each profession. This complex system was to be further controlled by a National Council of Education and its state counterparts, which were supposed to authorize the establishment of new institutions and care for their quality and reliability.

This system generated a large bureaucratic web of rules and regulations for student admissions, curricular change and degree registration, all to be inspected by the Ministry of Education and supervised by the education and professional councils. The public universities, as part of the civil service, were also subject to the administrative and financial regulations emanating from the central administration and the government's accounting offices. Most of this control, however, dealt with formalities. In practice, once an institution received authorization to teach, it would almost never be revoked, and the basic equivalence of skills to be provided by the different institutions throughout the country was never achieved. Moreover, as the higher education system expanded, differences in quality tended to increase, and to become publicly recognized.

A 1968 reform bill sought to reorganize the traditional Napoleonic system along the North American model, centered on academically defined departments geared toward research and postgraduate education. The traditional chair system, led by prestigious part-time lawyers, medical doctors and engineers, was replaced by full-time academics organized in departments and research institutes. A two-year, college-like "basic cycle" was to precede professional education in all careers. Students were supposed to fulfill the educational requirements for their professional careers by picking their credits among different departments. Career programs were supposed to be coordinated by interdepartmental committees, with the disappearance of the traditional *faculdades*. Isolated and independent professional schools were supposed to disappear or be absorbed into university structures along the new framework. This whole conception was to be helped by the building of integrated campuses on the outskirts of Brazil's main cities, to replace the old faculties' buildings scattered in downtown areas. From the beginning, this reform faced at least three serious obstacles: the overall political climate in which it was implemented, the explosion of demand for higher education, and resistance from the traditional *faculdades*.

The year of 1968 was almost everywhere a time of political mobilization and youth protest, which in Brazil took the shape of huge student demonstrations against the military government that had seized power in 1964. Repression followed, and between 1969 and the mid-70s urban guerrillas clashed with the military in a climate of political repression and fear that was particularly hard on academic institutions. The implementation of a university reform law in such a context could only be perceived as part of the government's repression against the students and the liberal academic community, and thus be taken with suspicion. That the innovations introduced by the reform had been copied from the United States only contributed to this perception. Nevertheless, the placement of research at the core of the universities, the end of the chair system and the establishment of postgraduate studies had been central to the aspirations of many who now faced confrontation with the military authorities, and remained in place since then.

The 1968 reformers failed to perceive the explosion of demand for higher education that was already taking place in Brazil as well as elsewhere in Latin America and the Western world. Admittance to Brazilian universities has always been arranged through entrance examinations, and in 1968 the large number of candidates denied access for lack of places became a political embarrassment for the government, which decided to increase the number of openings in public institutions and to ease the requirements for the creation of private and isolated *faculdades*. These new institutions were mostly low-cost teaching schools staffed with part-time and not well-qualified professors (working mostly in the evenings) and catering to students that could not meet the university's entrance requirements, usually because of the low quality of their secondary education. Thus, while the reform postulated a gradual convergence of higher education toward a unified university model, it immediately began to diverge into a strongly stratified system, with free, more prestigious and usually better public sector institutions at the top and an extended, low quality and paid private system at the bottom (Schwartzman & Klein, 1993).

The traditional faculties of law, medicine, engineering, dentistry and a few others were fairly successful in resisting the new legislation. They often kept their old buildings downtown, never moving to the new campuses. When introducing the department structure and the credit system, they did it in their interior, while resisting disciplinary unification with other careers and discipline-based departments and institutes. The chair system was often replaced by oligarchies of full professors. The traditional faculties also resisted the introduction of full-time employment, and were slow in establishing postgraduate programs. They kept almost everywhere, in short, the dominance of professional over disciplinary identity. The traditional professions' ability to resist occurred because the new legislation did not change the rule, or the general assumption, that each higher education career was supposed to lead to a nationally valid professional entitlement. As the system expanded, new professions were added to the old ones, each striving to get its own legal status and protection: pharmacists, veterinarians, psychologists, librarians, nutritionists, education supervisors, nurses, journalists, social workers, statisticians, geologists, economists, and so forth.

In spite of these difficulties, the new legislation led to the creation of discipline-based departments and institutes coming out of the old *Faculdades de Filosofia, Ciências e Letras* (Faculty of Philosophy, Sciences and Letters), which became responsible for the education of secondary school teachers and for postgraduate education and research (the two-year introductory basic cycle proscribed in the 1968 legislation was never implemented except in very few places). They also took charge of professional education in the new professions, alone or in cooperation with other departments. As the teaching load increased, the departments expanded very quickly, often by hiring young teachers without postgraduate degrees for full-time teaching tasks. Postgraduate education, however, expanded rapidly, supported by the Ministry of Education, the Ministry of Science and Technology, and state institutions such as São Paulo's *Fundação de Amparo à Pesquisa* (FAPESP). Thanks to this combined effort, Brazil now has the largest postgraduate education establishment in Latin America. In 2001, 6,000 students received their doctoral degrees and 30,000 their masters. This segment is heavily subsidized, and most courses are in public institutions. In 2002, the higher education census conducted by the Ministry of Education identified 242,000 teaching positions in Brazilian higher education, 21% of which were filled by doctoral degree holders. In public institutions, this proportion was 36%, compared with only 9.5% in the much larger private sector.

The end result of these developments is an extremely differentiated system of higher education, which is made particularly difficult to understand because the differences are not formally acknowledged. Ideally, there should be only research universities, or institutions evolving toward this model. In practice, there are profound regional inequalities: traditional professional schools, postgraduate programs with strong research components, low quality graduation courses in the "soft" disciplines, a large private sector with evening courses and lax admittance requirements, and a few highly prestigious public and private institutions.

Governance

In 1988, after 20 years of military authoritarianism, Brazil adopted a new Constitution reinstating the unity of higher education around the research university model, and granting full academic, financial and administrative autonomy to universities. The Constitution also guaranteed that public education should remain free of charge, and forbade any kind of public subsidy to the private sector, except for research projects or for "community" institutions. Many issues were left unresolved—including the true extent of "autonomy," the regulation of non-university institutions, the role of the federal and state councils of education, and the legal status of universities and professors regarding the civil service. A comprehensive education bill was approved by Congress in 1996, recognizing for the first time the existence of university and non-university higher education institutions, and requiring periodic assessment of their academic quality and status.

The new legislation did not change the ways public and private institutions are managed. Brazilian public *faculdades* have been traditionally ruled by their schools' "congregations," or academic senates, made up of full professors and token representation from students and lower rank faculty. Appointments for the main executive positions—rectors and the schools' directors—were usually made by the federal or state government from short lists produced by the institutions. The 1968 reform had strengthened the powers of the rector's office (and the government's control), and required universities to produce a list of six nominees (instead of the traditional three) from which they would choose to fill the position of university rector. Political liberalization after 1985 opened the way to pressure from students, teachers and employees' associations, who sought equal weight in one-man-one-vote elections for executive posts at all levels in the public universities, equal representation in all deliberative bodies, and (after 1988) recognition that the universities were free to choose their authorities internally, without consulting any kind of external body or public authority. Most public universities adopted these procedures in one way or another, and the government usually appointed the most voted-for candidate for rectorship in the lists coming from the universities, therefore keeping the formalities of the law without conflicting with the universities. Private institutions, at the other extreme, tend to be ruled as proprietary institutions, without any degree of autonomy regarding their owners or controlling institutions.

Quality assurance has been a concern for many years, and Brazil has an important tradition of regular assessment of its postgraduate programs, carried on regularly by CAPES (*Coordenação de Aperfeiçoamento de Pessoal de Nível Superior*, an agency within the Ministry of Education) through the use of peer review committees and information on scientific and academic outputs. Each postgraduate course is rated on a seven-point scale every two or three years, with the higher grades given to courses considered of international quality. The ratings are used by CAPES to allocate fellowships and to provide other kinds of support to the postgraduate programs. Because of their reputation and reliability, CAPES' evaluations are routinely used by other government and non-government institutions in their dealings with the country's university research and postgraduate education programs.

For first-degree courses, the Ministry of Education started with a program to provide support for institutions willing to carry on self-evaluations, and in the 1990s moved to create two new mechanisms. One was the assessment of the material and human resources available for students, to be conducted by committees of specialists in the different academic fields. The other was the National Assessment of Courses, a procedure through which students completing their graduation degrees must take a national exam related to their chosen career field, leading to a national ranking of all professional course programs in the country while preserving the privacy of individual results. Except for extreme cases, there are no benefits or punishments associated with these assessments, but their publication has created a competition for perceptions of quality higher education which had not existed before.

Regardless of the legislators' intentions, sectoral differentiation will continue and increase in the near future. Besides the known differences between the public and the private sectors, regional initiatives are likely to grow and to find their own solutions to the problems of governance and financing. In 1988, the São Paulo state system, formed by the University of São Paulo, the University of Campinas and the State University of São Paulo, was granted full administrative and financial autonomy vis-à-vis the state government, and a fixed percentage of the state's main excise tax was provided for their expenses. The state council of rectors took the responsibility for the distribution of resources among the universities, and also for the definition of salary levels. This decision freed the state government from the constant pressures to ensure salary increases for teachers and administrative personnel, and placed them fully in the rectors' hands. It also placed a limit on the percentage of the state's budget that can be allocated to higher education. Another significant regional experience is that of the southern state of Santa Catarina, which developed a network of small community universities throughout the state's territory. This pattern partially comes from the fact that Santa Catarina is a small state with multiple urban centers, modern agriculture and industries and a fairly highly educated population, which could not count on either federal or state resources to attend to their educational needs. The state's community universities and schools are run by a combination of local authorities, business groups and the Church.

Public resources for higher education in Brazil grew steadily until the early 1980s, and then stabilized, with abrupt yearly variations due to the high inflation rates and general economic depression. Access to Brazilian public universities has been traditionally provided free of charge, and they are fully maintained by the federal or state governments. Most of the money goes toward salaries, which account for 80 to 90% of current expenses. Salary levels and privileges for professors and administrative employees in the public sector have been defined through bargaining between the government and the teachers and employees' association, leaving little latitude for the universities' internal decisions on salary levels, promotion rules and alternate allocation of salary money. Resource allocations are supposed to be done once a year in the federal and state budgets. However, high inflation has required many ad-hoc decisions on budgetary supplements, leading to uncertainty about the future and deteriorating conditions. Money for research, student fellowships and out of the ordinary projects have to be sought outside the regular budget. The National Research Council, the *Financiadora de Estudos e Projetos* and São Paulo's *Fundação de Amparo à Pesquisa* are the usual sources of support for university research, while student fellowships for postgraduate studies can also be obtained from CAPES. In addition, universities can establish cooperative agreements with public corporations and some branches of the government, and also with the private sector. Foreign foundations and intergovernmental organizations are also available. Some departments in some universities have become extremely skillful in tapping these external sources (Schwartzman & Schwartzman, 2002).

Tuition can be charged in the private sector, but is limited because of the usually lower social origin of its students, and is often controlled by the government. The alternative for the private sector is to provide the cheapest possible type of education for the largest possible number of students. One strategy has been to concentrate in fields not requiring expensive equipment and teaching materials; another has been to hire only part-time teachers, which are sometimes full-time professors in a public institution nearby. A third strategy is to press for public subsidies, which were never very high, and were strongly limited by the 1988 Constitution. The only major kind of public support for the private sector that remains is a system of student loans, which is much smaller in the early years of the new millennium than it was in the late 1990s, due to high levels of non-performance, supporting less than 10% of the students in private institutions. More recently, a new sector of high quality, elite private institutions has begun to emerge, providing expensive degree programs in law and business-related fields.

Teaching, Learning and Research

Institutional and sectoral diversification in Brazilian higher education led to profound differences in the teaching and research staff, as well as in the quality of educational experiences the students receive. We can summarize these differences into three general categories, organized hierarchically (Schwartzman & Balbachevsky, 1996). At the top, there is an elite of about 28,000 faculty with doctoral degrees or equivalent titles, and about 100,000 students in M.A. and Ph.D. programs in the best public universities, mostly in the southern part of the country. Professors are endowed with reasonable salaries and can complement them with fellowships, research money and better working conditions; postgraduate students are selected from among the best graduates of public universities, do not pay tuition and usually get a fellowship for two or more years.

The middle strata is comprised of about 92,000 faculty in public universities, attending by about one million undergraduate students. Faculty teaching postgraduate courses in public institutions are also required to teach undergraduate students, and the academic qualifications of this group have been growing steadily—in 2001, 36% had a doctoral degree, and 30% a master's. Most of these academics have full-time contracts and civil service status, meaning job security and significant fringe benefits. However, their real salaries have been gradually deteriorating, and only those more active in research are able to complement their salaries with research or contract money. Formal regulations notwithstanding, many full-time academics also work in their professions, do consulting work or teach in private institutions.

Courses and facilities at this level are uneven, with the best in the central-southern region and in the traditional professions, and the worst in public universities of the northeast and in the social science fields. Students in public universities have access to almost free restaurants and a few other facilities, but lodging is very rare, and physical installations, laboratories, research materials and teaching aids are scarce. Students in the most competitive public institutional programs (like medicine, dentistry, engineering, law and journalism) usually come from the best private secondary schools (which typically means middle- to upper-class families) and often pay for courses to prepare them for the university's entrance examinations—an industry by itself. As the educational system expands, these students are faced with increasingly serious problems of unemployment, in spite of the relative quality of their education. Entrance to the least competitive academic programs—mostly teacher preparation in letters, history, geography and pedagogy, or in the social sciences—is very easy, and the expansion of evening courses for these areas in recent years has led to an increase in students coming from lower socioeconomic backgrounds to public institutions.

Finally, at the bottom of the quality hierarchy there are around 150,000 lecturers serving about 2.5 million students in private institutions. Most of these teachers work part-time, are not well qualified, and have to take on a large teaching load in several institutions—or a combination of jobs—in order to survive. In 2002, 11% had a doctoral degree, and another 38% a master's; 16% had full-time contracts, and 56% did not have any permanent contract at all, working on a per-class basis. Some of these lecturers have full-time appointments in public universities, and moonlight in private schools; others are retired from the public sector. They are not organized, and do not reproduce the teachers' associations that prevail in the public sector. Tuition in these institutions is usually low; however, the students can barely afford them. Facilities and teaching materials are minimal or nonexistent. Courses are mostly in the "soft" fields, particularly in administration and law. Most students are already employed, and look for education as a means for job improvement or promotion; they are often more interested in credentials than in knowledge for its own sake.

This picture has been changing in recent years, as public institutions suffer from budget limitations and come under pressure to open up to students from lower socioeconomic backgrounds, including the establishment of racial quotas for black students or students coming from public secondary schools. Access for low-income students to public institutions is growing, and a niche is emerging for high quality private institutions in fields like economics, law, business and marketing, and in intensely disputed fields like dentistry. Today, although most students in higher education still come from middle- and upper-level social strata, the socioeconomic profiles of students in the public and private sector are similar, with most of the stratification taking place in terms of career choices and opportunities (Schwartzman, 2004).

These differences combine with profound regional imbalances between the southern states, and more specifically between the state of São Paulo and the rest of the country. São Paulo is Brazil's biggest and most industrialized state, encompassing about one-fifth of its population and one-third of its postgraduate enrollment. This is also the region where the dual nature of Brazilian higher education developed more fully. There is proportionally lower enrollment in public universities than in other regions, but the universities are usually better, while the private sector is much more complex and differentiated than elsewhere. There are few federal institutions in the state, which contrasts with the country's poorest region, the northeast, where more than 70% of the students are enrolled in federal universities, with few alternatives in local institutions or in the private sector.

Career paths vary greatly throughout this diversified system. At the University of São Paulo, a doctorate is the minimum qualification for admittance to the academic career; in other public universities, a postgraduate degree is not an absolute requirement for a first-level position. Regular appointments are made after an elaborate and formalized process—including written exams, public lectures and evaluation of the candidate's credentials. Promotion to the higher ranks—to associate and full professorship—also requires similar procedures. Many Brazilian universities still accept the institution of *livre docente*—an adaptation of the old German *privatdozent*, which in practice is obtained through public examination and the presentation of an academic dissertation, and assures an academic status immediately below full professorship. In the past, *livre docência* was a mechanism to assure academic quality; today, it is most often a mechanism to avoid the doctoral degree requirement for admission and promotion, except again at the University of São Paulo, where the *livre docência* remains a required step, after the doctorate, in the path toward full professorship.

Once admitted at any level in a public institution, tenure is assured in practice except for extreme cases of misbehavior. Brazilian public universities are part of the civil service, and professors are hired as civil servants, which means (among other things) employment stability, generous retirement and other benefits. Recent legislation has reduced the retirement benefits for incoming or recently hired personnel, but did not change their stability. In the private sector, on the other hand, the rule is the absence of career structures and tenure mechanisms. Professors are hired as lecturers when needed, and dismissed at will.

The rigidity and formality of appointment and promotion procedures in the public sector have led to the search for alternate mechanisms. The University of São Paulo, for instance, can appoint professors by invitation for limited periods; however, their admittance to the regular career requires a formal examination. In the past, and mostly in the federal universities, similar mechanisms have led to the admittance of large numbers of people who were later granted the rights of stability and career promotion through ministerial decrees or judiciary decisions. One consequence was the low academic level of many institutions; the other was their inability to hire new and supposedly more qualified personnel, for lack of academic slots. Another feature of this system is that mobility between universities is almost nonexistent, since jobs and ranks are not transferable between institutions, even within the same system.

Academic power within Brazilian public universities is usually in the hands of two groups: academic units (schools, "faculties," or institutes), within the limits set by the government, and the professors' and employees' associations and unions. Curricula for the legally recognized professions and careers are established by the National Council of Education, and can only be expanded or interpreted locally. Universities are free, however, to establish new courses and careers, and have no limitations regarding their postgraduate programs, except the periodic evaluation by CAPES. Non-university institutions, even in the private sector, can only be created or offer new degrees with the formal authorization of the Federal Council of Education. The government has the power to establish salary levels and the availability of slots in the public sector, and to regulate tuition prices in private institutions.

Academic power in the public sector is also influenced by the universities' teacher associations, which are nationally organized (as the *Associação Nacional de Docentes do Ensino Superior*, or ANDES) and affiliated with the country's more militant central union, the *Central Unica dos Trabalhadores.* ANDES' militancy since the 1980s has been instrumental in assuring the salary levels and job stability of university professors, but has also helped to paralyze the government's initiatives in terms of university reform, and has led to the rigidity of rules and procedures of the public universities in matters of academic careers, placing a clear limit to the universities' formal autonomy. The employees' associations are a relatively new phenomenon in Brazilian universities, and have followed a general pattern of political and union organization of Brazilian civil servants. These associations have been active in several strikes at the federal and state levels, and participate wherever direct elections for executive offices in public universities are held.

Conclusion

The challenge of Brazilian higher education for the turn of the millennium is whether it will be able to accommodate the country's growing educational demands while fulfilling its role as centers for academic excellence and scientific research. The current situation—in which better quality education is provided free in the public sector, while low quality, mass schooling is only available privately—is changing, as the public sector comes under increasing pressure to broaden its coverage, and the private sector becomes more clearly proprietary and looks for quality niches. The educational role to be fulfilled by Brazilian universities is not limited to their current or prospective students. Basic and secondary education in Brazil today is plagued by an acute lack of qualified teachers, and it is not clear how the universities can recover their traditional role of teacher education, given the low prestige of the teaching profession and the poor educational background of those willing to join its ranks. The universities will also have to play a growing role in the continuous education for all professions, and in providing non-conventional courses for those who want to learn more but are unable or unwilling to attend the regular courses given along the traditional curricula.

These challenges will have to be met within a context of economic constraints. The Brazilian public sector is not likely to increase the share of the national budget going to education in the near future (which is already beyond 5% of GNP) nor the share of higher education vis-à-vis other educational levels. Pressures for evaluation, administrative efficiency and accountability are likely to increase, together with a growing movement toward new sources of income, including cost recovery from the better-endowed students. The full administrative, patrimonial and academic autonomy granted to the Brazilian universities by the 1988 Constitution and the 1996 Education Law, if properly implemented and coupled with a robust assessment system, could become a precious instrument in this search for a broader and more diversified role and a larger and more equitable financial basis. On the other hand, autonomy can also provide more traditional and shortsighted elements within the universities with a weapon for retrenchment, isolation and resistance to the realities of the external world. This is the dilemma for the future.

References

Balbachevsky, E. (2004). Graduate education: Emerging challenges to a successful policy. In C. Brock & S. Schwartzman (Eds.), *The challenges of education in Brazil*. Oxford, UK: Triangle Journals.

Durham, E. R. (2004). Higher education in Brazil—Public and private. In C. Brock & S. Schwartzman (Eds.), *The challenges of education in Brazil*. Oxford, UK: Triangle Journals.

Oliveira, J. B. A. (2004). Expansion, inequality and compensatory policies. In C. Brock & S. Schwartzman (Eds.), *The challenges of education in Brazil*. Oxford, UK: Triangle Journals, Ltd.

Schwartzman, J. & Schwartzman, S. (2002). O ensino superior privado como setor econômico (Private higher education as an economic sector). *Ensaio - Avaliação e Políticas Públicas em Educação (Public Evaluation and Politics in Education)*, *10*(37), 411–440.

Schwartzman, S. (1991). *A space for science the development of the scientific community in Brazil*. University Park, PA: Pennsylvania State University Press.

Schwartzman, S. (2000). Brazil, the social agenda. *Daedalus, 129*(2), 29–53.

Schwartzman, S. (2004). Equity, quality and relevance in higher education in Brazil. *Anais da Academia Brasileira de Ciências, (Annals of the Brazilian Academy of Sciences)*, *26*(1), 173–188.

Schwartzman, S. & Balbachevsky, E. (1996). The academic profession in Brazil. In P. G. Altbach (Ed.), *The international academic profession: Portraits of fourteen countries* (pp. 231–280). Princeton, NJ: Carnegie Foundation for the Advancement of Teaching.

Schwartzman, S., Bomeny, H. M. B., & Costa, V. M. R. (2000). *Tempos de Capanema (Times of Campanema)* (2nd ed.). São Paulo, Rio de Janeiro, Brazil: Paz e Terra; Editora da Fundação Getúlio Vargas.

Schwartzman, S. & Klein, L. (1993). Higher education policies in Brazil 1970–1990. *Higher Education, 25*(1), 31–35.

Soares, F. (2004). Quality and equity in Brazilian basic education: Facts and possibilities. In C. Brock & S. Schwartzman (Eds.), *The challenges of education in Brazil*. Oxford, UK: Triangle Journals.

32

CANADA

Glen A. Jones
Ontario Institute for Studies in Education, University of Toronto, Canada

The second largest nation on earth, Canada has a population of 32 million and a population density slightly higher than Australia. The vast majority of its institutions of higher education, like its citizens, are situated within 200 kilometers of the southern border with the United States. This relatively narrow strip of land running east-west contains the core financial and industrial infrastructure that positions Canada as one of the G8 industrial nations. The population dwindles as one moves north, especially in central and western Canada, until one reaches Canada's three northern territories. The Canadian Artic is one of the most sparsely populated areas on earth, and its citizens maintain many of the cultural traditions that have been associated with those lands for centuries.

Describing Canadian higher education is almost as difficult a task as defining the nation itself. Like its neighbors to the south, Canada boasts one of the highest participation rates in higher education in the world, and a number of its universities are frequently ranked among the very best. At the same time, the Canadian policy approach to higher education has been—and continues to be—unique, reflecting many of the complex social and economic factors that differentiate this country from its western, developed peers. The objective of this chapter is to provide a broad description and analysis of higher education in Canada, beginning with an overview of the institutions and structural arrangements, followed by a review of the historical development of higher education in Canada with a particular emphasis on federal and provincial government policy, and concluding with a brief discussion of key issues.

Overview

Canada is a federal state composed of ten provinces and three territories. Under the Canadian constitution, education is a provincial responsibility and the provinces have legislative and regulatory authority over higher education. This decentralized approach has led to substantive differences in higher education policy arrangements and institutional structures by province (cf. Jones, 1997). While the provinces have come to assume the central role in postsecondary education policy and the direct funding of public institutions, the federal government continues to play a role in higher education

James J.F. Forest and Philip G. Altbach (eds.), International Handbook of Higher Education, 627–645.
© *2006 Springer. Printed in the Netherlands.*

through a range of initiatives viewed as justifiable under other areas of constitutional authority, especially in terms of skills training for employment, student financial assistance, research and development, and issues of national culture. There is little doubt that Canada's federal arrangement has had an enormous impact on Canadian higher education (Cameron, 1991), a topic that will be discussed in more detail later in the chapter.

Canadian higher education has been traditionally defined in terms of two broad institutional types: universities and non-degree postsecondary institutions (frequently captured under the umbrella term "community colleges"). However, this categorization has tended to ignore a range of postsecondary institutions and activities that fall outside the mainstream "public" sector, and Statistics Canada is currently experimenting with a far more inclusive classification system that more clearly illuminates the diversity of institutional structures and arrangements (Orton, 2004). Under this emerging classification system, Canadian postsecondary institutions are divided into five major types: universities and degree-granting institutions; colleges and institutes; school boards that operate adult and postsecondary programs; government institutions; and career colleges.

There are over 190 university and degree-granting institutions in Canada. The vast majority of students are enrolled in publicly supported, relatively autonomous universities, though there are now a handful of small private universities. The more traditional university sector includes 45 universities that offer primarily undergraduate programs, 15 comprehensive universities, and 15 medical/doctoral universities. In addition, there are three degree-granting institutions that have a specific mandate to address the needs of First Nations and Métis populations. The largest number of institutions in this grouping (116) are specialized, the majority of which have degree-granting authority, limited to the provision of religious and theological education, though there are also special purpose institutions focusing on art, music, and other field-specific programming. All of these institutions focus on degree programs.

The primary objective of colleges and institutes, in contrast, is to offer certificate and diploma programs that are three years or less in length. There are over 300 colleges and institutes, most of which are publicly-supported institutions operating under direct provincial government regulation. Over 30 colleges also have the authority to grant specialized degrees (often associate or applied degrees) in areas related to their core technical/vocational mission. Roughly 120 colleges and institutes offer a comprehensive range of postsecondary diploma programs, while 145 offer only a limited range of programs in specialized areas. Ten have a specific mandate related to Canada's First Nations.

Career colleges are the largest category of postsecondary institutions in Canada. There are over 550 such colleges registered by the provinces, and—given differences in the regulatory environment by province—many others that operate without the need for provincial licensure or recognition. Career colleges are private businesses that offer certificate and diploma programs, frequently focusing on specialized occupations or vocations. In addition, federal and provincial governments directly operate 27 different institutions designed to facilitate apprenticeship programs or provide specialized training related to public-sector careers, including police, coast guard, and air traffic control.

Finally, a range of adult (and, in some cases, postsecondary) education programs are offered by school boards. The vast majority of these initiatives focus on adult learning, language programming and basic-level employment skills.

National statistics on enrollment have tended to focus on the data collected from publicly supported institutions, but even with this limitation Canadian participation rates are very high in international terms. In 1998–99, Canadian universities enrolled over 580,000 full-time and almost 256,000 part-time students in degree programs. Colleges enrolled over 400,000 full-time and 91,000 part-time students in postsecondary programs. Junor and Usher (2002) note that if students in trade and vocational programs are included, the total number of Canadians enrolled in postsecondary programs in 1998–99 was 1.65 million (p. 35).

Canada has two official languages, English and French, and while federal government services are provided in both languages, there are substantive provincial and regional differences in language utilization and access to postsecondary education by language. New Brunswick is the only officially bilingual province, though many provinces have postsecondary institutions that offer programs in both languages, or offer programs to serve the needs of minority language populations.

Colonial Roots

Canada is a nation founded as a federation of colonies, and there is little doubt that this early colonial history influenced later developments in higher education. The French colonial regime lasted for a century and a half, beginning with the founding of Quebec by Champlain in 1608 and ending with the Treaty of Paris in 1763. The population of New France grew slowly; there were still only 65 residents by 1628 and, even after more active attempts at expansion, the figure rose to only 6,705 by 1673 (Philips, 1957).

The Roman Catholic Church assumed the core responsibility for education, though the earliest initiatives—primarily associated with the Jesuits and Recollets—focused on attempts to convert, school and generally "civilize" the neighboring native populations. Such an objective, with frequent variations, would underscore Canadian policy toward the education of Canada's First Nations for the next three centuries. The first secondary school was founded by the Jesuits in 1635, and the classical program of studies that had emerged by 1655 would continue to play an important role in secondary education in Quebec until the reforms of the 1960s. More advanced courses were gradually introduced in mathematics and theology (Audet, 1970).

The effective end of the French colonial period concluded with the capture of Quebec by the British in 1760. Britain now controlled a colony dominated by French culture and language, and while the new regime destroyed many of the institutions associated with New France, it was generally tolerant of the educational work of the Roman Catholic Church. Dual educational systems eventually emerged, with Roman Catholic schools serving the Francophone population and distinct educational structures serving the Anglophone population.

In some respects, it was the American Revolution that had the most direct impact on the emergence of higher education institutions during this period. The revolution was, in some respects, a civil war, and the victory of those seeking to sever the relationship with colonial authority led to the migration north of those who wanted to live under the protection of the crown. These Empire Loyalists also brought with them expectations of the social and cultural institutions that should be associated with a civilized British colony. Unlike the far more developed and densely populated jurisdictions that they had left behind, they would arrive to find that there were no institutions of higher education in any of the northern colonies, a serious omission for those who feared the spread of American republicanism.

A handful of colleges emerged within the British colonies in the late 1700s and in the first decades of the 19th century. Colonial legislatures awarded charters to King's College in Windsor in 1789 (Nova Scotia) and the College of New Brunswick in Fredericton in 1800, both based on the institutional model of King's College in New York (Bailey, 1950; Muir, 1994; Vroom, 1941). The estate of James McGill provided the financial support for the creation of McGill College (Montreal) under a royal charter awarded in 1821. Land endowments were associated with the royal charters awarded to the King's Colleges at York (Toronto) and Fredericton, both of which also included innovative governance structures and assigned the role of president to the local Anglican Archdeacon (Jones, 1996).

The response from other Protestant denominations, beginning in the 1840s, was to create their own institutions of higher learning. Queen Victoria granted charters for Queen's College in Kingston (Presbyterian), Victoria College in Cobourg (Methodist) and Acadia College in Horton (Baptist) in 1841. Created and supported by specific church organizations, denominational colleges became the dominant institutional model in the modest expansion of higher education during the rest of the century.

It is important to recall that these were all extremely small, financially struggling institutions; the fact that some colleges had access to public support through the revenues associated with crown endowments while others did not became the topic of considerable debate. In the case of King's College at York, the view of many Loyalists that a British institution supported by the crown should naturally be affiliated with the Church of England was in direct conflict with those who viewed the arrangement as unfair and discriminatory. A political solution emerged only after greater authority was delegated to the colonial legislatures under the rubric of "responsible government," and King's College at York was transformed into the secular, provincial University of Toronto in 1849. The University of New Brunswick assumed a similar role in 1858.

Confederation to 1945

The Dominion of Canada was created under the British North America (BNA) Act of 1867, a piece of British legislation governing the federation of colonies that became the provinces of Ontario, New Brunswick, Nova Scotia and Quebec. Higher education was far from a central issue in the discussions that led to federation, in part because there was so little of it to talk about. At the time of confederation there were only 1,500 students in the entire nation, and only five institutions could claim enrollments of 100 or more (Cameron, 1992).

The importance of the BNA Act to the development of higher education in Canada is difficult to overstate. The Act not only created Canada, it prescribed a federal governance arrangement that continues to be a component of the Canadian constitution. One of the lessons drawn from the enormous bloodshed of the American civil war was the need to create a strong central government. The new federal government was assigned responsibility for trade, in order to ensure economic stability, and defense, in order to address the recurring threat of American imperialism. The provinces were assigned responsibility for minor, local issues, including hospitals and education.

The fact that the BNA Act assigned responsibility for education to the provinces is neither unique in the broader context of federal states, nor surprising given the diverse local needs of the original colonies. Almost all federal state arrangements assign education to the local jurisdiction, and in Canada the notion of some form of uniform approach to education could never have addressed the needs of both the primarily French-speaking, Catholic population of Quebec and the largely Protestant, English-speaking population of Ontario. The uniqueness of the Canadian constitutional approach to higher education was not that it was delegated (under the rubric of education) to the provinces, but rather that the federal government has never been able to negotiate a clear, direct role in this policy arena. Canada may be the only nation in the developed world that has never had a national university or higher education act, or even a government minister assigned responsibility for higher education. The federal government does play an important role in higher education policy, but it is a role that has evolved through the dance of federal-provincial relations to the frequently discordant tune of Canada's constitutional debate.

While four provinces were created through confederation in 1867, the BNA Act also provided a framework for expansion, and over the next 80 years other colonies would join the Dominion and new provinces would be carved out of the western territories. In the central and eastern provinces, many universities were already in place at the time of federation and the new provinces simply inherited the modest higher education infrastructure (and the frequently less-than-modest problems) associated with the colonial period. In Ontario, the new provincial government decided to avoid the politics of denominational disputes by declaring that public funds would only be available to secular institutions. In most provinces higher education was not regarded as an important policy issue; few institutions received government grants, and the level of support (when available) was small.

In the western provinces, in contrast, the new governments moved to create new provincial universities, in part to avoid the potential denominational battles experienced in the east, but also with a conviction that institutions of higher education would play a role in the social, cultural, and economic development of the jurisdiction. Each of these four provinces created a single, secular, provincial university. Manitoba became a province in 1870 and the University of Manitoba was created, essentially as an examining body, in 1877, though the charter was revised in 1917 to more closely parallel the provincial universities of other western provinces. British Columbia became a province in 1871 and an initial attempt to create a provincial university was made in 1880, though limited interest and a shortage of provincial revenues postponed the creation of the University of British Columbia until 1908 (Harris, 1976). Alberta and

Saskatchewan became provinces in 1905, and both provinces moved quickly to establish provincial universities: the University of Alberta was created in 1906 and the University of Saskatchewan was created in 1907.

These four institutions were also influenced by the emergence of the American state university model (Campbell, 1978). Service to the broader community became an important component of institutional activities, often through distinct units focusing on "extension" programming. They also quickly established degree programs in applied fields directly related to local needs, such as agriculture.

While western universities were influenced by the University of Wisconsin's notion of "Our campus the state," a number of eastern universities became increasingly interested in the emerging model of the American research university. Given Canada's colonial history, there was a natural tendency for the major Anglophone universities to look to Oxford and Cambridge as the shining examples of what universities could and should be, but the rise of the German model—and its translation at Johns Hopkins into research-based doctoral programs—was difficult to ignore. Canadian students began to pursue doctoral programs in the United States, and A. H. Young noted that "In the one case they are lost to their native land; in the other they propagate views which, if not hostile to England, are at least far from being friendly to her" (Friedland, 2002, p. 177). Queen's College introduced a Ph.D. program in 1889; the University of Toronto followed suit in 1897, and McGill in 1906 (Friedland, 2002).

As publicly supported universities began to emerge in each province, institutions began to struggle with two questions: the relationship between the university and the state, and the appropriate structure for university governance. There was little common agreement on the role of government, and a range of different approaches to institutional governance had emerged in corporate charters. In Ontario, political interference in the work of the University of Toronto—including cases of political leaders making university appointments without consulting the president—led to the creation of a royal commission charged with the responsibility of reviewing both university-government relations and university governance arrangements.

The 1906 report of the Flavelle Commission established a model that was gradually adopted in many parts of Canada, and it clearly influenced the governance structures of the new western universities. The recommendations of the Commission were based on a central conclusion:

> We have examined the governmental systems of other state universities upon this continent and have found a surprising unanimity of view upon the propriety of divorcing them from the direct superintendence of political powers (Alexander, 1906, p. 276).

This "divorce" would be accomplished through the delegation of state authority over the university to a corporate board composed largely of members appointed by government. The governance structure would be bicameral: a corporate board composed of lay members would oversee the administrative affairs of the university, but the senate—the academic governing body composed of representatives of the faculties, colleges, alumni and the administration—would be retained and assigned executive authority over academic issues. As Ross (1976) has noted, the senate followed in the English tradition and was remarkably similar to the structure adopted by the University of Manchester in 1870. The draft University of Toronto Act, appended to the Commission's report, was quickly approved by the Ontario Government with few amendments (Wallace, 1927). While other institutions had already experimented with bicameral governance structures, the Flavelle Commission provided a rationale and a governance framework that was gradually adopted by almost every English-speaking university in Canada (Cameron, 1991; Harris, 1984; Jones, Shanahan, & Goyan, 2001).

The universities that emerged during this period were largely autonomous institutions, at least in terms of their relationship to government. The majority of universities were affiliated with a particular religious denomination, with most French-language institutions linked to the Roman Catholic Church and most English-language institutions affiliated with Protestant denominations. The level of Church influence on the affairs of the universities varied by institution, but provincial governments seldom interfered with the work of these privately supported and funded institutions. The relatively small number of publicly supported universities were also chartered as private nonprofit corporations, and while governments clearly took a greater interest in their affairs, the university-government relationship generally focused on annual decisions on the level of government grants, with little regulation or interference in university decision making. Institutional autonomy was a component of the Anglo-Saxon model of the university that the English-speaking institutions inherited from their British colonial roots (Amaral, Jones, & Karseth, 2002), but it is also true, as Neatby (1987) has argued, that there was considerable consensus on the mission of the university:

> Universities trained the children of the political elites; they served as a finishing school for their daughters and prepared their sons for admissions to the liberal professions. These social functions were understood by governments and by university officials; there were no major confrontations over admissions, over course content or over student discipline because both groups shared the same social values. Cabinet ministers and members of the Board of Governors might belong to different parties, but they were all men of substance with similar views of the social order (p. 34).

The provincial governments had constitutional responsibility for education, but higher education was far from an important area of public policy. Governments provided modest annual grants to a limited number of institutions that were generally viewed as public, and these institutions expanded slowly. Most private institutions were struggling denominational colleges relying on donations and church support to supplement tuition revenues. Canadian universities received little public or political attention, a situation that would change dramatically following World War II.

1945 to 1970: Higher Education as Public Good

The federal government's involvement in higher education was extremely minor until the creation of the veterans benefit program following World War II. However, two government initiatives had an important and direct impact on the sector. First, in 1874 the Government of Canada established a Royal Military College in Kingston as a function of the central government's responsibility for defense. There was no opposition from the provinces, though a century later the College would require the approval of the Government of Ontario in order to award degrees in that province. The second government initiative of importance was the creation of the Advisory Committee for Scientific and Industrial Research, later known as the National Research Council, in 1916 (Neatby, 1987). Noting the ways in which German scientists had revolutionized manufacturing processes in several industries, and following the lead of the British government, the Council was conceived as a mechanism for encouraging applied industrial research in order to promote economic development. While the original emphasis was on industry-based research, many of the Council members were professors, and the Council soon began to sponsor the work of a small number of university scholars and support graduate students in the sciences (Thistle, 1966).

The decision to provide qualified veterans with higher education benefits following World War II brought the federal government directly into the higher education policy arena. The terms of the benefit program had involved considerable discussion with the National Conference of Canadian Universities, a national association of university administrators and faculty that had been formed in 1911 (Pilkington, 1974). Under the arrangement, the government would pay the tuition for each veteran who qualified to attend a university, and the institution would receive a grant of $150 per enrolled veteran (Cameron, 1991).

The program was enormously successful. Canadian university enrollment increased by 46% in 1945–46, when 20,000 veterans decided to pursue higher education. In 1946–47, the number increased to 35,000. As the doors of the universities opened to veterans, other citizens began to demand access, and a new generation began to view higher education as an achievable goal. Even excluding the veterans, total university enrollment increased by close to 70% between 1941 and 1951 (Cameron, 1991). Given this dramatic increase in demand, and the fact that the veterans program was only a short-term measure, universities turned to both the national and provincial levels of government for assistance.

The arguments for increasing government support for higher education were increasingly premised on the assumption that higher education was a public good. Canada's postwar economic and industrial transition had been enormously successful, and the economic boom brought with it a new sense of national identity and purpose. Higher education became increasingly viewed as an important component of Canada's economic, cultural and social development. The final report of the Royal Commission on National Development in the Arts, Letters and Sciences recommended that the Government of Canada provide direct grants to universities based on provincial population. Acknowledging that they were provincial institutions, the Commission concluded that universities must become part of the national agenda since "theirs must be regarded as the finest of contributions to national strength and unity" (Royal Commission, 1951, p. 132). Human capital theory would later provide support for the Economic Council of Canada's conclusion that funding higher education should be regarded as the highest priority of government (Economic Council of Canada, 1965).

There is little doubt that by the early 1950s it was clear to both the federal government and the provinces that access to higher education in Canada should be expanded, and that this expansion would require a substantive investment on the part of the federal government; the challenge was to find an approach that satisfied all parties. As the veterans benefit program began to conclude, the Government of Canada decided to continue providing direct grants to universities based on enrollment and provincial population, in order to sustain (though not to further expand) enrollment levels. The provinces of Ontario and Quebec responded by accusing the federal government of interfering in provincial constitutional territory. Ontario's primary concern was that the new grants would be given to all universities even though provincial policy limited university grants to secular institutions. Quebec strongly advised universities not to accept federal support, and then increased provincial grants to universities in order to compensate for this lost revenue.

In 1958, Prime Minister St. Laurent announced a new funding program designed to support a massive expansion of university enrollment. The initiative was a direct response both to increasing demand as well as statistical projections of the future demand for higher education associated with the postwar baby boom (Bissell, 1957). Instead of direct government grants to universities, federal government funds would be routed through a new Canadian Universities Foundation (essentially operated by the National Conference of Canadian Universities). The new arrangement did not appease the concerns of Quebec, which continued to advise provincial universities to refuse grants and then once again increased the level of provincial grants. Funds for Quebec universities were initially held in trust by the Foundation, and then later transferred to the provincial government.

A third federal government approach to funding the expansion of postsecondary education was announced at a federal-provincial conference in 1966. Explicitly acknowledging that education was an issue of provincial jurisdiction, but asserting that the expansion of higher education was an issue of national importance, the federal government announced that direct grants to universities would be replaced with transfers to the provincial governments. The new mechanism involved three major components: a transfer of tax revenues from the federal government to the provinces; an equalization formula designed to address inequities in provincial revenues; and a guarantee that the federal transfers would fund no less than half of the operating expenses of the university sector. The federal government would no longer be in the business of providing direct operating grants to universities.

The federal government's role in financing the expansion of postsecondary education was not limited to operating grant support. The government initiated a range of programs dealing with capital construction, research funding, and cooperative housing and residence construction. In 1964, the federal government announced the creation of the Canada Student Loans Program, a federal program that—in typical Canadian fashion—was administered by the provinces and integrated with provincial loan and grant programs.

The 1966 federal funding arrangement reinforced the central role of the provinces in terms of regulating and funding postsecondary education, but most provinces had already taken steps to plan for the expansion and assumed core responsibilities for coordinating growth. In some respects, each province developed its own unique plan for expansion in response to local needs, but there were at least three common elements: the movement toward a secular, public university sector; the creation of new institutions and institutional forms; and the development of new coordinating arrangements and structures.

Each of the four western provincial universities had been assigned a public monopoly over the ability to grant university degrees, and this notion of controlling degree-granting authority—while providing public support only to secular institutions—also underscored provincial policy in other jurisdictions (Skolnik, 1987). When Newfoundland joined Canada, becoming the tenth province in 1949, the new provincial government transformed Memorial College into Memorial University—a provincial, secular university with a bicameral governance structure and monopoly authority, similar to the "one university" concept in the west. In 1868, Ontario's government determined that public grants would only be provided to secular universities, and many denominational universities began to reconsider their future direction in the new era of expansion, significant government grants, and increasing demand. The vast majority of these institutions decided to either become independent secular universities or enter into federation or affiliation arrangements with public universities, in order to retain their religious ethos in the broader scholarly community of a secular institution. The major reforms in Quebec shifted the role of the Roman Catholic Church and repositioned the state as the major entity responsible for Francophone education and higher education. By the early 1970s, Canadian universities were essentially viewed and defined as public, secular institutions.

Provincial governments also took steps to review the current state of higher education and consider how best to meet the economic, social, and human resource needs of the jurisdiction. Managing and coordinating the growth of higher education became the subject of provincial task forces that offered advice on the development of new coordinating structures and institutions. It was quite clear that existing universities needed to expand, but most provinces also decided to create new universities, and all ten provinces took steps to create new types of postsecondary institutions.

The "one university" concept was gradually abandoned in all four western provinces, either through the granting of independent university status to what had previously been campuses of colleges of the provincial university, or through the creation of completely new institutions. In British Columbia, Victoria College became the independent University of Victoria, and the new Simon Fraser University was created in 1963. The Calgary campus of the University of Alberta became the independent University of Calgary in 1966, while the provincial government created the University of Lethbridge and (in 1970) Athabasca University, specializing in distance education and open-access programming. Two colleges of the University of Manitoba (Brandon and United) were transformed into Brandon University and the University of Winnipeg in 1967. The Regina campus of the University of Saskatchewan became the University of Regina in 1974.

The exact opposite situation occurred in Prince Edward Island. Faced with two universities that refused to coordinate activities, the government decided to merge them to create the new University of Prince Edward Island. PEI and Newfoundland would become the only provinces to have a single, provincial university.

The expansion in Ontario included the creation of new institutions (such as Brock, Trent, and York), the transformation of denominational universities into secular, publicly supported institutions, and a shift in the legal status and mission of former government institutes or colleges (for example, the creation of the University of Guelph). Following the recommendations of the Deutsch Commission, New Brunswick began to consolidate its activities into one French-language university (the Université de Moncton) and two English-language universities (the University of New Brunswick and Mount Allison University).

By far the most dramatic reforms took place in the province of Quebec, largely because the reorganization of higher education was viewed as an important component of a much broader socio-political transformation frequently referred to as the "quiet revolution." The rise of nationalist sentiment, the growing recognition of social and economic inequities based on language, and the shift in the role of the Roman Catholic Church within Quebec society combined to underscore the need for significant change. The responsibility for redesigning Quebec's entire educational system was assigned to the Royal Commission of Inquiry on Education, chaired by Alphonse Parent, and the recommendations of the Parent Commission were revolutionary in scope and impact (Henchey & Burgess, 1987). The entire school curriculum was redesigned to replace the former classical curriculum, and secondary school would end at Grade 11. Following secondary school, students moved to one of the new *colleges d'enseignement general et professional* (CEGEPs). Created in 1967, these new colleges offered two-year pre-university programs as well as vocational education programs. Students could then apply to attend one of the existing universities or—beginning in 1968—one of the campuses of the new Université de Québec system. Until the University of Toronto moved to a tri-campus model in 2002, Quebec was Canada's only multi-campus university system with both campus-level and system-level governance arrangements.

The CEGEP was not the only non-degree institutional form to emerge as a function of provincial government expansion of higher education. The need to increase access and address the new postsecondary training and educational requirements of industry had been highlighted in every provincial review and task force. The common solution was to create a new type of institution to complement the existing university structure, though the mission and structure of these institutions varied substantially by province. In British Columbia and Alberta, the new community colleges were designed to increase access to university education (by offering university transfer programs) as well as offer a wide range of technical/vocational diploma programs. In Ontario, the new Colleges of Applied Arts and Technology did not have a transfer function, but would offer a comprehensive range of vocation-oriented programs, including diploma programs ranging up to three years in length. Generally speaking, all of these new colleges and institutes were high-access institutions subject to higher levels of government regulation than their university peers; in fact, the New Brunswick college system was essentially an office of the provincial ministry.

The final common component of provincial reforms involved the emergence of provincial coordinating structures. The new colleges were generally coordinated and regulated by government, but there was a perceived need to find a mechanism to coordinate the activities of the university sector while respecting institutional auton-omy. Every province except Newfoundland eventually experimented with a coordinat-ing body or commission for the university sector, frequently named after (but seldom resembling) the University Grants Committee of the United Kingdom. In the three maritime provinces (New Brunswick, Nova Scotia, and Prince Edward Island) these provincial bodies were later replaced by the regional Maritime Provinces Higher Edu-cation Commission, which provided advice to all three provincial governments. These intermediary bodies were later abandoned in Alberta, British Columbia, Saskatchewan, and, more recently, Ontario. Two provinces now have councils that provide the govern-ment with advice on both the university and non-university sectors: the Newfoundland and Labrador Council on Higher Education, created in 1992, and Manitoba's uni-versity coordinating body, which was transformed into a postsecondary council in 1996.

By the early 1970s, Canada had made the transition from elite to mass higher ed-ucation. Both levels of government were involved in funding what was now largely regarded as a public higher education system: the federal government, through transfers to the provinces and through the direct funding of research, skills training, and a range of other targeted initiatives; and the provincial governments, through the provision of operating and capital support. New institutional types—commonly referred to by the umbrella term "community colleges"—had been created in every province, with the goal of increasing access and addressing the new educational needs of an increas-ingly diverse and specialized labor force. While the features and functions of these colleges varied dramatically by province, Canadian universities had become far more homogeneous during this period. All Canadian universities were now publicly funded, secular degree-granting institutions, with missions that included both teaching and research.

1970 to 2004: From Structural Stability to Major Reforms

The expansion of higher education did not end with the reforms of the 1960s; in fact, enrollment in postsecondary education continued to increase until the mid-1990s, although the political and economic environment shifted dramatically. The recession of the early 1970s led to a significant decline in provincial tax revenues, and governments at all levels began to look for ways of moderating—if not reducing—expenditures. There were no wholesale moves to restructure or substantively reform higher education in any Canadian province during the next two decades, and in many respects the approach of all governments was to simply stabilize or reduce the level of per-capita student grants in order to create greater efficiency, encourage increased levels of accessibility, and provide new targeted funds to encourage institutions to address particular priorities. The basic system-level structure of Canadian higher education remained relatively stable between (roughly) 1970 and 1990.

The new economic environment meant that universities could no longer count on huge annual grant increases, and they began to look for ways of reducing costs, fur-thering efficiencies, or increasing income. Given that faculty salaries represented by far the largest component of university expenditures, faculty began to look for ways of protecting their rights and working conditions. Both faculty and students had success-fully advocated for reforms in university governance arrangements during the 1960s, and most governing boards included both faculty and student representation (Jones & Skolnik, 1997). Faculty senates had been expanded to include student members, and the senate and board meetings at most universities were more open and transparent (Jones, 2002). While these changes had created more participatory governance processes, they did little to reassure faculty in the face of government cuts. Thus, beginning in the early 1970s, a number of faculty associations turned to unionization and collective bargaining as a means of protecting faculty interests. As Tudivor has noted, "by the mid-1980s, the landscape was transformed, with over 50% of faculty unionized on 29 campuses" (1999, p. 85). There was a second, minor wave of unionization in the 1990s. Today, even for those institutions where there is no faculty union, there is usually a contractual agreement between the faculty association and the university governing the salary negotiation process and the procedures associated with appointments, tenure, and promotion.

Enrollment in Canada's community colleges continued to expand, and many colleges began to be actively engaged in the provision of specialized training programs spon-sored by the Government of Canada—through targeted skills training initiatives—or by private industry. While the colleges in some provinces had an explicit university trans-fer function, in others—such as Manitoba and Ontario—questions began to emerge concerning the appropriate relationship between the college and university sectors. In the case of Ontario, the two sectors were essentially distinct, with little articulation at either the system or institutional levels.

Given the changing economic climate, the federal government—like its provincial counterparts—searched for new ways of controlling expenditures on higher education. Over time, the 1966–67 arrangement had lost its political luster. The provinces con-tinued to be concerned that the grants were essentially "conditional," since they were linked to provincial expenditures. From the federal government's perspective, the 50% guarantee—the condition that concerned the provinces—also meant that the federal government's level of expenditures was increasing at a rate determined by the other level of government.

A new fiscal arrangement was introduced in 1976–77. Established Programs Fi-nancing (EPF) linked a number of federal-provincial funding arrangements—including health care and postsecondary education—into a transfer envelope allocated on the ba-sis of a new formula. Tax point transfers to the provinces were increased, and cash transfers were based on a population-based formula including an equalization com-ponent. Transfers for higher education under EPF were unconditional. Funds were transferred to the provinces, which had complete discretion in determining how these funds would be spent.

Arguing about the terms of the EPF arrangements soon became a major Canadian political pastime (Cameron, 1991). Within a few years, the Government of Canada began to argue that transfer payments were being spent on roads and bridges when they should be directed to postsecondary education, an argument disputed by the provinces and logically facile given the "unconditional" nature of the EPF arrangement. By the early 1980s, the argument was inverted, and provinces began to complain that EPF transfers no longer provided the level of support needed given the rising costs of health care and postsecondary education.

Under the (Progressive Conservative) Mulroney government of the late 1980s, the federal government began to unilaterally tinker with the EPF formula. Cash transfers to the provinces were reduced in order to help reduce the federal deficit. The government also reduced expenditures in a number of targeted areas with implications for higher education, including the budgets of the research councils.

It was the (Liberal) Chretien government, however, that essentially transformed the financial arrangements underscoring Canadian higher education through two types of initiatives, roughly five years apart. In its 1995 budget, the Government of Canada combined EPF with the Canada Assistance Plan to create a new, expanded transfer envelope called the Canada Health and Social Transfer. It then slashed the level of support associated with the combined programs. As David Cameron noted, "rather than the 4.4% cut claimed by the Minister of Finance, the real cut amounted to some 37%" (1997, p. 27).

This sudden, dramatic decrease in a critical source of university funding had significant implications. Many of the provinces were already reducing grants to postsecondary education as a function of their own deficit reduction programs, and the sudden decrease in federal transfers simply exacerbated the situation. The second implication is that in many respects the 1995 budget signaled the political death of federal transfers as a major source of support for postsecondary education. The Canada Health and Social Transfer program continues to exist, but there is little doubt that Canadian voters have been far more concerned with the need to adequately support the increasing costs of health care than they have been with the level of cuts to postsecondary education. The current political discussion of provincial transfers focuses almost exclusively on health care.

The second type of federal initiative that had enormous implications for postsecondary education involved the emergence of a range of new programs focusing on research and development. The federal government had long been the major funding source for university-based research, primarily through the work of three granting councils that administered peer-reviewed research funding programs as well as graduate and postdoctoral fellowship programs. Given the federal government's contribution to institutional operating support under EPF, these councils only supported the direct costs of research projects. The overhead or indirect costs associated with research, including physical infrastructure, the costs associated with administering the grants, and the salaries of principal investigators were never supported. In other words, federal funding mechanisms assumed that universities were obtaining the necessary overhead support through provincial transfers.

Some provinces also operated research funding mechanisms, though only Quebec operated a peer review-based granting council. Ontario operated a matching grant program to encourage university-industry cooperative research ventures, and devoted considerable resources to supporting a number of provincial Centers of Excellence— research centers linked to both universities and industry focusing on areas of study viewed as being of strategic importance to the provincial economy. These programs were not insignificant, but the federal government continued to play the key role in research funding.

Under the Mulroney (Conservative) Government, funds to the research councils had been reduced, but new programs focusing on strengthening the linkages between university and industry-based research were initiated. While each of the granting councils continued to support curiosity-based research, new "strategic" granting programs were created. The Government also created a federal Centers of Excellence program designed to link researchers from different universities in different regions with related industries.

Investing in Canada's research and development infrastructure was a priority for the Chretien (Liberal) government, and while its attention was initially focused on deficit reduction, the movement toward a balanced budget (and eventually a surplus) provided a political foundation for a series of initiatives designed to address Canada's poor record of national expenditures on research and development compared with other OECD nations (Wolfe, 2002). The largest of these initiatives was the Canada Foundation for Innovation, which provided massive infrastructure funding for research programs linked to private sector support.

A second major initiative was the creation of the Canada Research Chairs program in 2000. Allocated largely on the basis of prior institutional success in research council competitions, the program provided salary and some infrastructure support for the creation of 2,000 new research chairs at Canadian universities.

The Canada Research Chairs program was designed to strengthen the research capacity of Canadian universities, but it was also a response to growing concerns about a possible "brain drain" to the United States. At the apex of the dot.com phenomenon, stories of Canadian information technology professionals moving to high paying positions south of the border were commonly featured in the Canadian press. Statistics Canada studies noted that, in reality, only a small trickle of well-educated Canadians migrated to the United States, while Canada actually attracted a much larger number of knowledge workers from other countries (Zhao, Drew, & Murray, 2000). In terms of the professoriate, there was little doubt that major American research universities were able to offer salary packages beyond the means of their Canadian counterparts. With this in mind, the Canada Research Chairs initiative was designed to help universities attract leading international scholars and to retain leading Canadian professors.

The federal government also increased the budgets of the three granting councils. More recently, the government has taken steps toward providing institutions with support for the overhead costs associated with government-funded research.

These initiatives have signaled a dramatic shift in the role of the Government of Canada, and they have enormous implications for Canadian higher education. While Slaughter and Leslie (1997) suggested that Canada was the "odd country out" in terms of their analysis of "academic capitalism," the recent trends of decreasing government operating support, combined with new investments targeted toward research as a means of furthering economic development, suggest that Canadian higher education policy is now paralleling trends in some other Anglo-Saxon jurisdictions. While there has never been an explicit institutional hierarchy within the Canadian university sector, these new initiatives are undoubtedly increasing the level of diversity within the sector based on research intensity. Finally, the reduction in provincial transfers and increased new support focusing on research in targeted areas has important regional implications;

generally speaking, universities in the Atlantic and prairie provinces have not been major beneficiaries.

There have always been differences by province in how higher education is funded, coordinated and regulated (Jones, 1997), and the mammoth decrease in unconditional federal transfers to the provinces simply exacerbated these differences. Neo-liberal government policies in Alberta, Ontario and, most recently, British Columbia involved substantive increases in tuition, decreases in operating grant support, the creation of performance funding mechanisms in Alberta and Ontario (though these mechanisms are associated with only a minor component of total operating grants), and initiatives designed to strengthen market-like forces within the higher education sector and increase linkages between institutions of higher education and private industry (cf. Jones & Young, 2003; Young, 2002). All three provinces have also expanded the range of institutions that can offer degrees, including community colleges (which in Ontario and Alberta now have the authority to offer applied degree programs), specialized colleges (such as the Ontario College of Art and Design and the Emily Carr Institute of Art and Design), and, subject to provincial review, private universities. The traditional binary divisions between the university and non-university sector are blurring. At the same time, other provinces—such as Quebec and Manitoba—have maintained low tuition policies as a mechanism for encouraging accessibility, and have not pursued neo-liberal reform agendas. Quebec CEGEPs do not charge tuition, and Quebec universities have quite modest fees.

Substantive tuition increases in some provinces, especially British Columbia, Ontario, and Nova Scotia, have raised important questions concerning the degree to which higher education in Canada can continue to be viewed as a "public" entity. Concerns about the impact of tuition on accessibility and the level of student debt led to a number of federal government initiatives, including the creation of the Canada Millennium Scholarship Foundation (which provides modest grants to supplement what is largely a loan-based Canadian student financial assistance system) and several tax/grant incentives designed to encourage families to save for postsecondary education. The government has recently announced that maximum loan levels under the Canada Student Loans program will be increased and that a new initiative will be available to support students from low-income family backgrounds. In general terms, however, Canada's student financial assistance arrangements have not been reformed to address rising tuition fees and student maintenance costs, and they involve a far-from-transparent labyrinth of federal, provincial and institutional support mechanisms.

Higher Education in Canada: Issues of Balance

In many respects, higher education in Canada is in transition, and there are far more questions than answers concerning the impact of recent policy reforms and the future direction of the increasingly complex web of institutions, federal and provincial government policy arrangements, and coordinating structures that constitute postsecondary education in this country. The transition from elite to mass higher education in Canada, in contrast to the American experience, was largely accomplished through the creation of a network of relatively homogeneous, secular universities and new non-university, government-regulated institutions that varied dramatically by province in terms of their form and mandate (Skolnik, 1986). The homogeneity of the Canadian university sector can no longer be assumed, in part because major sources of new government funding favor research intensive institutions that have the capacity to focus on research activities viewed as strategic to the knowledge economy, but also because of the increasing emergence and recognition of new degree-granting institutions. This increasing diversity of arrangements has led to the development of an entirely new classification system for Canadian postsecondary institutions, and there is little doubt that this new way of counting and classifying institutions will have an impact on future discussions and policy arrangements.

Canadian higher education continues to be defined in part by the highest levels of participation in the world—participation rates that might seem surprising given the public policy emphasis on supply rather than the demand side of the market equation—and decreasing levels of per-student operating support. Enrollment in Canada's universities and colleges increased steadily from 1945 until the mid-1990s, leveled off, and then began to increase again during the early years of the new millennium. Depending on one's point of reference, Canada's publicly supported universities and colleges can be regarded as either increasingly efficient or underfunded in comparison with their American counterparts, though it is important to note that their degrees and diplomas are widely accepted in international terms, and a number of Canadian universities are frequently included in rankings of the best institutions in the world. High participation rates do not, of course, imply equality of access. Canada's record of addressing the postsecondary educational needs of First Nations populations has been abysmal, and increasing tuition fees in some jurisdictions without significant reforms to Canada's student financial assistance mechanisms are raising increasing concerns about accessibility for low-income families and other traditionally under-represented groups.

It is important to recognize that there has never been a Canadian "system" of higher education, and even the provinces have seldom developed the coordinating arrangements and planning mechanisms that one would normally associate with a "system" of postsecondary education. To some extent, Canada's decentralized approach can be explained by the unique historical development of the political federation, but it is also a function of provincial government policy approaches that have favored steering autonomous universities through targeted funding and regulation rather than more heavy-handed restructuring and reform. Canada's universities continue to have considerable autonomy compared with many other jurisdictions (Anderson & Johnson, 1998), but it is an autonomy that is exercised by an increasingly complex institutional navigation through market-like policy approaches, private sector linkages, and a range of frequently uncoordinated federal and provincial government initiatives. Decentralization has also provided the foundation for the increasing diversity of institutions in what had previously been viewed as the non-university sector, including degree-granting colleges, public colleges that continue to focus on providing highly accessible technical/vocational programs, and a range of private providers. To what extent can this decentralized, autonomous approach be sustained in the face of increasing institutional diversity and differentiation without some form of national accreditation mechanism?

Perhaps the most important questions facing higher education involve issues of balance in the face of increasing—and often competing—demands. Regardless of how one defines the term, Canadian higher education is less "public" than it was two decades ago, and there is little agreement on the appropriate balance between public and private interests or objectives. The decline in operating support combined with new, massive investments in research and development may impact the balance between teaching and research within universities, and the fact that most of this research investment focuses on only a subset of disciplines and fields may have an impact on everything from faculty renewal and faculty workloads (by discipline) to the role of Canadian universities in the broader critical discussion of Canadian society. Canadian higher education is in transition, but it is a transition in which there is little clarity in terms of the overall direction or objectives, little analysis of what may be lost as a function of reform, and little sense of how the various components of this increasingly complex puzzle fit or do not fit together.

References

Amaral, A., Jones, G. A., & Karseth, B. (2002). Governing higher education: Comparing national perspectives. In *Governing higher education: National perspectives on institutional governance* (pp. 279–298). Dordrecht, The Netherlands: Kluwer Academic Publishers.

Anderson, D. & Johnson, R. (1998). *University autonomy in 20 countries*. Technical report. Canberra, Australia: Department of Employment, Education, Training and Youth Affairs.

Audet, L. (1970). Society and education in New France. In J. D. Wilson, R. M. Stamp, & L. Audet (Eds.), *Canadian education: A history*. Scarborough, Canada: Prentice-Hall.

Bailey, A. D. (1950). *The University of New Brunswick memorial volume*. Fredericton, Canada: University of New Brunswick.

Bissell, C.T. (Ed.). (1957). *Canada's crisis in higher education. Proceedings of a conference held by the National Conference on Canadian Universities*. Toronto, Canada: University of Toronto Press.

Bouchard, B. (2000). University education: Recent trends in participation, accessibility and returns. *Education Quarterly Review, 6*(4), 24–32.

Campbell, D. (1978). Western Canada. In E. Sheffield (ed.), *Systems of higher education: Canada*. New York: I.C.E.D.

Cameron, D. M. (1991). *More than an academic question: Universities, government, and public policy in Canada*. Halifax, Canada: Institute for Research on Public Policy.

Cameron, D. M. (1997). The federal perspective. In G.A. Jones (Ed.), *Higher education in Canada: Different systems different perspectives* (pp. 9–29). New York: Garland Publishing.

Economic Council of Canada. (1965). *Second annual review: Towards sustained and balanced economic growth*. Ottawa, Canada: Queen's Printer.

Finnie, R., Lavoie, M., & Rivard, M-C. (2001). Women in engineering: The missing link in the Canadian knowledge economy. *Education Quarterly Review, 7*(3), 8–17.

Friedland, M. L. (2002). *The University of Toronto: A history*. Toronto: University of Toronto Press.

Harris, R. S. (1976). *A history of higher education in Canada 1663–1976*. Toronto: University of Toronto Press.

Henchey, N. & Burgess, D. (1987). *Between past and future: Quebec education in transition*. Calgary: Detselig.

Jones, G. A. (1996). Governments, governance, and Canadian universities. In J. C. Smart (Ed.), *Higher education: Handbook of theory and research* (Vol. 11, pp. 337–371). New York: Agathon Press.

Jones, G. A. (Ed.). (1997). *Higher education in Canada: Different systems, different perspectives*. New York: Garland Publishing.

Jones, G. A. (2002). The structure of university governance in Canada: A policy network approach. In A. Amaral, G. A. Jones, & B. Karseth (Eds.), *Governing higher education: National perspectives on institutional governance* (pp. 213–234). Dordrecht, The Netherlands: Kluwer Academic Publishers.

Jones, G. A., Shanahan, T., & Goyan, P. (2001). University governance in Canadian higher education. *Tertiary Education and Management, 7*, 135–148.

Jones, G. A. & Skolnik, M. L. (1997). Governing boards in Canadian universities. *Review of Higher Education, 20*(3), 277–295.

Jones, G. A. & Young, S. J. (2003). "Madly off in all directions": Higher education, marketization and Canadian federalism. Paper presented at the conference on "Markets in higher education: Mature economies," Douro River, Portugal, October.

Junor, S. & Usher, A. (2002). *The price of knowledge: Access and student finance in Canada.* Montreal, Canada: The Canada Millennium Scholarship Foundation.

Muir, W. R. (1994). Canada's public university system: Cultural inevitability or historical accident. Unpublished paper presented at the Annual Meeting of the Canadian Society for the Study of Higher Education, Calgary, Alberta, June.

Neatby, H. B. (1987). The historical perspective. In C. Watson (Ed.), *Governments and higher education: The legitimacy of intervention.* Toronto, Canada: Higher Education Group, Ontario Institute for Studies in Education.

Orton, L. (2004). A new understanding of postsecondary education in Canada. Presentation at the Annual Meeting of the Canadian Society for the Study of Higher Education, Winnipeg, May 31.

Philips, C. E. (1957). *The development of education in Canada.* Toronto, Canada: W. J. Gage.

Pilkington, G. (1974). A history of the National Conference of Canadian Universities: 1911–1961. Unpublished doctoral dissertation. Toronto, Canada: University of Toronto.

Ross, M. G. (1976). *The university: Anatomy of academe.* Toronto: McGraw-Hill.

Royal Commission on National Development in the Arts, Letters and Sciences. (1951). *Report.* Ottawa, Canada: King's Printer.

Skolnik, M. L. (1986). Diversity in higher education: The Canadian case. *Higher Education in Europe, 11*(2), 19–32.

Skolnik, M. L. (1987), State control of degree granting: The establishment of a public monopoly in Canada. In C. Watson (Ed.), *Governments and higher education: The legitimacy of intervention* (pp. 56–83). Toronto, Canada: Higher Education Group, Ontario Institute for Studies in Education.

Slaughter, S. & Leslie, L. (1997). *Academic capitalism: Politics, policies and the entrepreneurial university.* Baltimore: John Hopkins.

Thistle, M. (1966). *The inner ring: The early history of the National Research Council.* Toronto, Canada: University of Toronto Press.

Tudivor, N. (1999). *Universities for sale: Resisting corporate control over Canadian higher education.* Toronto, Canada: James Lorimer and Company.

Vroom, F. W. (1941). *King's College: A chronicle 1789–1939.* Halifax, Canada: The Imperial Publishing Company.

Wallace, W. S. (1927). *A history of the University of Toronto 1827–1927.* Toronto, Canada: University of Toronto Press.

Wolfe, D. (2002). Innovation policy for the knowledge-based economy: From the Red Book to the White Paper. In G. B. Doern (Ed.), *How Ottawa spends 2002–2003* (pp. 137–150). Toronto, Canada: Oxford University Press.

Young, S.J. (2002). The use of market mechanisms in higher education finance and state control: Ontario considered. *Canadian Journal of Higher Education, 32*(2), 79–102.

Zhao, J., Drew, D., & Murray, T.S. (2000). Brain drain and brain gain: The migration of knowledge workers from and to Canada. *Education Quarterly Review, 6*(3), 8–35.

33

CHILE

José Joaquín Brunner* and Anthony Tillett†
*Universidad Adolfo Ibáñez, Chile; †Anthony Tillett, Santiago, Chile

Chile has not escaped the multiple pressures facing higher education across the world (Brunner, 2003). All countries face the urgent task of refocusing higher education through more flexible and adaptive institutions as a way of maintaining their social and educational relevance. Moreover, for developing countries, present choices require that higher education address an historic deficit—ensuring greater equity of access and opportunity—as increasing numbers of students achieve satisfactory primary and secondary education levels, thus leading to increasing demand among qualified applicants to higher education.

Any analysis of the response of Chile's higher education to the historic deficit and future needs must be broadened to include the history, policy and approaches of the institutions themselves. When compared to many European countries, for example, Chile's higher educational institutions are strongly autonomous and the role of the government consequently weaker. Indeed, there is no overall planning for the sector and government policy is limited to specific financial support (and, increasingly, persuasion). There is, however, a growing opinion that higher educational institutions play a key role in supporting greater economic competitiveness, crucial for Chile's open economy, and this recognition is creating a consensus about the value and importance of higher education among government, economic groups and the public at large.

Chile's response is shaped by the move, over the last 30 years, from a predominantly state-controlled to a market system in providing higher education (Brunner, 1997). Costs and funding have become the predominant issues, together with two characteristic market issues—economies of scale and regulation. Higher education in Chile today is shaped less by relations with the government than by interactions between the component institutions. Even so, there is a healthy recognition among policymakers and university leaders that educational excellence, based on international norms, must be a principal goal for higher education. For a market higher education system, where the units are autonomous, quality presents a formidable challenge. As government funding is limited, both as a matter of economics and policy, public policy relies on competition to provide these changes. Hence, the challenge of building a solid consensus about the value of higher education and its future role goes hand in hand with providing greater

James J.F. Forest and Philip G. Altbach (eds.), International Handbook of Higher Education, 647–666.

opportunities to overcome the historic deficit and adjusting to competition for students and funds by higher education institutions.

Current Structure and Rules

The present structure of higher education in Chile consists of three types of institutions: universities, professional institutes (*institutos profesionales* or IPs), and technical training centers (*centros de formación técnica* or CFTs).[1] Universities can be subdivided into public and private; the former are supported by state funds and belong to the Council of University Rectors (CRU),[2] while the others are private corporations and do not have access to state institutional funding. Although the institutional map is unlikely to change in the next few years, the size and scope of the different components—and the relationship of one to the other—is altering quickly.

The current institutional pattern is provided in Table 1. Although university, professional and technical education implies a hierarchy of knowledge and prestige, there are important differences within (and increasingly between) the components, and the table illustrates three such features. First, the distinction between the CRU and private universities has a profound impact on the overall structure—far beyond ownership—principally because of funding. In fact, universities work under two general regimes: public (belonging to the CRU) and private universities. Those that belong to the CRU are described as "public" because the state guarantees part of their funding. However, within the CRU there are both old and new state and private universities, notably those of the Catholic Church.[3] In contrast, private universities are corporations or foundations constituted under civil law as nonprofit institutions. Second, branches or local campuses reflect the reach of the different components across the regions. And finally, an important distinction comes from the way that higher education is evolving, with more

Table 1. Higher Education Institutions: Number and Branch Campuses, 2003

			Number	Branch
	Institutions			
Universities	CRU	Traditional	8	30
		"Derived"*	17	101
	Private	Autonomous	24	87
		Non-autonomous	14	20
IP			52	111
CFT			113	183
Total			228	532

Note: *refers to universities which were originally branch campuses of the eight universities that made up the system to 1980 and from which they evolved or "derived."

Source: Ministerio de Educación, Compendio de Educación Superior, 2004. http://www.mineduc.cl and Comisión Nacional de Acreditación de Pregrado (2003).

and more institutions achieving autonomy and greater authority to make independent decisions.

While there are principles common to all higher education institutions, the differences (enshrined in law) determine behavior. The differences are in terms of the degree of autonomy, including legal rights and obligations; what can be taught; and how the different components are financed.

- *Autonomy:* All CRUs are autonomous by law, while private universities and IPs earn their autonomy after a period of 6 to 11 years of supervision by the Higher Education Council. CFTs are established under the supervision of the Ministry of Education and become autonomous by ministerial decision once the legal requirements are met.
- *Degree subjects:* Chile distinguishes between professional and technical qualifications and academic degrees. Academic degrees—*licenciaturas* and higher degrees such as the M.A. and Ph.D.—are reserved only for universities, as are 17 professional titles that require a *licenciatura.*[4] IPs have the right to grant professional titles excluded from the reserve list and that do not require a *licenciatura.* And CFTs provide short (up to 3 years) technical certificate courses in vocational areas.
- *Financial support:* Whereas CRU universities receive institutional support from the government, private universities, IPs and CFTs have to rely on their own resources—principally fees, services and, with the exception of CFTs, donations. The government's principal transfer payment is the Direct Financial Contribution (AFD) delivered to the CRU, with 5% reserved as a competitive fund for excellence between members. The government also distributes funds according to the number of good students that higher education institutions can attract,[5] known as the Indirect Financial Contribution (AFI). Other funds, notably for physical infrastructure and student loans, are reserved for the 25 CRU members.

Expanding Dimensions of the System

Between 1990 and 2004, higher education enrollment increased from 249,000 to 567,000 undergraduates, consistent with growth at the secondary education level. From 1980 to 2003, the percentage of the population between 18 and 24 years participating in higher education increased fourfold (see Table 2).

The number of university graduates has been growing accordingly, from 18,000 to 58,000 between 1980 and 2003. The total stock of professional and technical personnel in 2002 has been estimated at 522,000, of which around 17% received their degree after 1995, 20% are less than 29 years old, and 42% are between 25 and 34.

Policy Inheritance

Chile's higher education landscape is a combination of continuity and change. Continuity rests principally with the key role exercised by the eight "traditional" universities—those established during the 19th century (Universidad de Chile and Universidad Católica de Chile) and the other six established before 1960.[6] Born of three different

Table 2.   Higher Education: Total Enrollment, 1980–2003

Institutions	1980	1985	1990	1995	2000	2003
Universities	118,798	118,079	131,702	231,227	319,089	403,370
CRU		113,128	112,193	161,850	215,284	246,750
Private		4,951	19,509	69,377	103,805	156,620
Professional Institutes		32,636	40,006	40,980	79,904	101,674
Public		18,071	6,472	0	0	0
Private		14,565	33,534	40,980	79,904	101,674
Technical Education Centers		50,425	77,774	72,735	53,184	62,070
Total Institutions	118,798	201,140	249,482	344,942	452,177	567,114
Participation rate (18–24 year-olds)	7.4%	11.5%*	14.2%	19.7%	25.7%	30.5%

Source: Ministerio de Educación, Compendio de Educación Superior, 2004. http://www.mineduc.cl.
(*) estimate.

trends—the state's commitment to professional education, knowledge as a civilizing instrument, and later, engineering and technology; the Catholic Church's rivalry with the state and concern about moral values in education; and provincial universities, founded by local elites to meet local economic and social demands—by 1960 these eight universities were all recognized by the state and thus were publicly funded, did not charge fees, and are estimated to have enrolled around 20,000 students in 1957, of which around 35–40% were female. Their main task was to educate professionals, although there was an incipient commitment to research. Their profound influence and continued importance is all the more remarkable because of three radical policy processes in the second half of the 20th century: the student-led reform process of 1967; the re-organization of higher education by the military regime (1973–1990); and the recent emergence of a higher education market.

The historic inheritance has inspired policy and continues to determine present choices and influence future paths. The sequence—tradition, control and market— is useful shorthand for understanding the development of Chile's contemporary higher education system.

During the period 1967–1973, Chilean universities underwent an intense period of reforms, first triggered from within by the student movement, and later conditioned from outside by the political process that deeply divided society between supporters and opponents of President Allende's socialist government (1970–73). The achievements of the reform period were not trivial. Student enrollment grew to 146,000; the number of courses at the graduate, undergraduate and extension levels was expanded; and the educational role of universities, in terms of their staffing and curriculum, was redefined. For the first time, an academic profession emerged and research as a modern enterprise was established in some of the oldest universities. Although in many aspects the rhetoric did not match achievements, discussion took place in an atmosphere of pluralism, which ended with the 1973 military coup.

The military brought with them a deep resentment of student and faculty politics and a general suspicion of higher education (Hunneus, 2002, p. 42). Even though most rectors had been critical of the UP government, the *junta* appointed retired and serving officers to these positions, who began the process of vetting and dismissing staff for political views, closing departments and research centers (particularly associated with the social sciences), and ending any possible discussion that did not support their position.

Until 1980, the military government's higher educational policy was limited to control and repression. But starting in 1980, a profound and far-reaching reform was launched with the aim of creating a higher education market with public and private providers, changing the funding structure of state-supported universities, and encouraging the differentiation of the higher education system into three different institutional levels (i.e., universities, IPs, and CFTs).

Policies During the 1990s

Chile's current higher education system is a modified product of the military government's reform of 1980. In fact, with the return of democracy in 1990, higher education's status quo was widely recognized as unsatisfactory. Teachers and staff were demoralized, financial resources had been declining, the CRU and research were underfunded, and too few middle class and lower income students had opportunities to obtain degrees. A higher education policy was urgently needed. In response, the government took a number of key decisions: first, a commitment was made to concentrate on educational equity to benefit the majority of Chileans—in other words, primary and secondary education—which was reflected in the distribution of public funds;[7] second, the government sought to build an inclusive consensus about the value of higher education, and appeal to the institutions, researchers and staff; and third, a decision was made to use and modify the inherited institutional framework.

A key step in this reform process was the formation in 1990 of a commission (*Comisión de Estudio de la Educación Superior*, Higher Education Research Commission), 1990) with a broad representative membership and which reported to the President in March 1991. Their report made six policy recommendations: consolidate the institutional base of higher education; develop teaching and student quality; assure the system's equity and quality; support scientific research and cultural activities; increase and diversify higher education finance; and improve the legislative framework.

The government has used three general approaches to implement these recommendations and adapt them to changing conditions: first, ensuring that an independent body—the Higher Education Council (*Consejo Superior de Educación*)—uses clear and public criteria for granting recognition and autonomy to private universities and IPs; second, using rational self-interest of both public and private institutions to improve quality by a formal (although voluntary) process of accreditation,[8] and making

Table 3. Higher Education: Public Financial Support, 1990–2003 (thousands of millions of 2003 pesos)

	1990	1995	1996	2000	2001	2002	2003
				CRU only			
Direct Public Funds (AFD)	60.6	85.7	89.9	100.4	101.7	105.3	105.3
Institutional Development Fund	–	9.2	13.7	24.6	26.7	29.6	34.2
Student Support	n/a	n/a	n/a	n/a	n/a	n/a	n/a
Student Loan Fund	27.7	19.0	22.3	41.9	43.6	47.3	49.2
Scholarship Funds	–	13.2	13.1	18.8	20.5	21.0	20.6
Total Student Support	27.7	32.2	35.4	60.7	64.1	68.3	69.8
Other	–	8.5	7.3	6.1	6.5	6.6	6.2
Total to CRU	88.3	135.6	146.3	191.8	199.0	209.8	215.5
				Mixed			
Indirect Public Support (AFI)	19.6	19.7	19.6	17.5	17.4	17.5	17.0
University Teachers Instruction Fund	–	–	–	2.4	3.1	0.3	0
New Millennium Scholarships	–	–	–	–	–	–	2.4
Science Research Council (CONICYT)	10.4	24.9	30.3	34.1	37.0	41.2	41.0
Subtotal Mixed Funds	30.0	44.6	49.9	54.0	57.5	59.0	60.4
Subtotal—State Funds (CRU & Mixed)	118.3	180.2	196.2	245.8	256.5	268.8	275.9
Donations (50% tax support)	2.4	7.1	8.9	10.2	12.9	12.3	12.0
Total	120.7	187.3	205.1	256.0	269.4	281.1	287.9

Source: Adapted from González (2004, p. 101).

the entrance examination more consistent with the current secondary school curriculum and a broader range of learning skills; and third, increasing the amount, mechanisms and scope of financial support for higher education.

Finance is one of the government's strongest weapons and yet, as private higher education continues to grow, there are bound to be continued calls for a more equitable distribution of resources between components. For many observers, the difference between public and private universities is less their legal status than their receipt of government funds. As Table 3 shows, 74.6% of all public funds went exclusively to the CRU in 1990, a figure that grew to 78% in 2003. Mixed funds are open to both public and private institutions, and donations are important for both.[9]

In sum, the democratic government's success has been, ironically, to develop higher education using (and gradually changing) the rules inherited from the military government.

Student Demand and Access

Contemporary higher education reflects both Chile's economic dynamism and deep social changes—its policy inheritance—of the last 30 years. These features fuel one another as the economy demands more knowledge-based skills, more students complete secondary education and smaller families have the means to send their children to higher education institutions. Illiteracy is minimal. Chileans are spending more time at school and the education system provides more services in more parts of the country than ever before. The 2002 Census reports that 2.3 million respondents have attended higher education institutions (21% of the population aged 15 or over), compared to 1.1 million (11.4%) in 1992. When analyzed by age, younger cohorts are not only more likely to have completed secondary education but to have attended one of the three types of higher education institutions.

While Chile has shown impressive economic growth, there is concern that it cannot be sustained without better education and more relevant training. Although there are differences in approach, the broad consensus among policymakers, political parties and educators across the spectrum is that there must be greater investment in human capital for Chile to maintain competitiveness. The labor force changes show increasing educational input. In turn, the expansion of student numbers demonstrates a rational appreciation of Chile's current labor market. On average, university educated and salaried incomes were double those completing secondary technical education.

Other estimates suggest that the university premium is higher, with the average employed university graduate earning 3.68 times more than those completing secondary education.[10] These private advantages are a main justification for Chile's policy requiring students and their families to pay greater proportions of higher education's costs.[11] Moreover, the private rates of return for completed university education are estimated to have grown from 18% to 21% between 1980 and the 1990s.[12] In consequence, higher education credentials have maintained their value, and demand for university education (in particular) has increased. Projections, supported by the Ministry of Education, foresee no decrease in the demand for professionals and technical occupations in Chile.[13]

The entrance examination's importance to student and higher education institutions cannot be overestimated; not only does it determine the university and profession that students might wish to follow but the possibility of financial support. And the exam is equally important for the university, for if a student is ranked among the top 27,500 achievers, the AFI system provides funding and prestige. The entrance examination results thus provide information regarding university segmentation, competitive financing and the quality of secondary schools. The examination is given in December and the results valid for that year's entrance only, so as a consequence, Chile has a thriving pre-university industry of aids, tutors and private preparatory schools and agencies.

Around 70% of students completing secondary education sign up for the entrance examination PAA in the same year, and slightly fewer present themselves for examination. Those that do not take it immediately are likely to take it later as, in recent years, it has been a characteristic that 30% of the total examinees are candidates from

Table 4.   Higher Education: Distribution of Indirect Student Support (AFI)

Institution	1990	1996	2000	2001	2002	2003
Total (thousands of current pesos)	7,326,000	15,006,783	16,106,987	16,509,662	17,021,463	17,021,462
			Percentages			
Universities	92.7	98.8	99.2	99.1	99.2	99.4
CRU	84.1	86.9	85.5	84.0	84.5	82.4
Private	8.7	11.9	13.7	15.1	14.8	17.0
Professional Institutes	6.7	0.9	0.6	0.8	0.6	0.5
With public support	3.7	0.0	0.0	0.0	0.0	0.0
Private	2.9	0.9	0.6	0.8	0.6	0.5
CFTs	0.6	0.3	0.1	0.1	0.1	0.1
Total	100.0	100.0	100.0	100.0	100.0	100.0
Institutions with AFD	87.8	86.9	85.5	84.0	84.5	82.4
Institutions without AFD	12.2	13.1	14.5	16.0	15.5	17.6

Source: Ministerio de Educación, Compendio de Educación Superior. http://www.mineduc.cl.

earlier years. Students must obtain at least 450 points to enter a CRU university and 475 to be eligible for a student loan distributed on a socioeconomic needs basis. The ability to attract good students has financial benefits for higher education institutions and increases their reputation. A university, IP or CFT that offers a place to one of the top 27,500 students, ranked by their test scores, receives a per capita public contribution (AFI).[14] The scheme, which began operation in 1983, was originally intended to promote competition between higher education institutions by making attractive offers to students. Now, as a result of higher education expansion, AFI students make up both a smaller proportion of the student body—falling from 33% (1990) to 21% (2002) of combined university and IP students—and of the receipts of higher education institutions (see Table 4). Nonetheless, AFI students remain important because of the prestige (as much as income) they bring, and no more so than for private universities.

Student Funding and Equality Issues

Today, student funding (loans and scholarships) makes up an increasing proportion of government support to CRU universities, growing from 17.8% in 1995 to 25.2% in 2003 (see Table 3 above). Student credit is funded by the government but administered by each CRU as a separate university-specific fund. Loans rarely cover more than two-thirds of current tuition costs, and although formally based on specific criteria (family income, location, etc.), the universities have considerable discretion. Repayment (and collection) has proved to be one of the major weaknesses of the system, with average rates estimated to be around 55%. In 1994, a law restricted repayments to 5% of gross income over a 12-year period, but with the result that the government has had to replenish the fund annually. In 2004, the government proposed new, stricter repayment rules and a new parallel funding scheme, to be managed through the banking system and open to all higher education students, regardless of institution.

Public funding of scholarships and loans (and the balance between both) represent key policy choices about higher education equity and efficiency. This balance is likely to change in favor of loans as enrollment continues to grow. First, the expansion of university education depends mostly on private universities, which now account for around 40% of first-year student enrollment. If scholarships or loans are not made available to potential non-CRU students, many will not attend or be able to continue. Second, the expense of going to a university is increasing as all universities raise fees to meet costs. Third, the government has become increasingly concerned about the management of student loan funds, their replenishment and poor repayment rates. Partial non-repayment is so widespread that the new stricter rules are unlikely to succeed unless university-based administration is replaced.

However, student finance—its coverage and organization—continues to be a key issue for students, higher education and the government. Without scholarships and subsidized loans, access could become restricted for many—if not the majority—of Chile's students and their families. In fact, university enrollment depends on entrance examination scores and capacity to pay. Opportunities and access are unequal because first, entrance examination scores are closely aligned to the type of school attended by the student, and second, funding is dependent on student or family income.

Students attending private secondary schools have a greater probability of scoring high on the exam than pupils from other schools. Students from private non-subsidize schools, on average, score 75 points higher than private subsidized school students, who in turn are 20 points higher than students at subsidized municipal schools. As a result, in 1998, 43% of students of the top 27,500 (AFI) students were from private paid schools, the remainder divided between the subsidized and public municipal schools.

Cost is the second filter of access to higher education, and it is no surprise that higher education is closely associated with the level of family income, as demonstrated in Table 5.

However, the increases in the lower quintiles—although unsatisfactory—should not be overlooked.[15] Indeed, as this table indicates, access to higher education is spreading downward; each household income quintile in 2000 is higher than the level above in 1990. For example, the second quintile in 2000 is higher than the third quintile in 1990, and so on. These trends have been sustained, according to preliminary information for 2003, with encouraging growth in the lowest quintile of household income.

Institutions: Competition and Change

The rapid adjustment of higher education to accommodate an increasing number of students has been a key factor in the overall system's growth. And within higher education, the driving force has been the creation and expansion of private universities, to which the CRUs have responded. The new opportunities are also a function of higher education costs, which differ by place and institution, but are increasingly related to scale.

Table 5.   Higher Education by Household Income, 1990, 2000 and 2003 (By quintile and total percent)

Household Income Quintile	1990	2000	2003	Change 1990–2000	Change 2000–2003
I	4.4%	9.4%	14.5%	5.2%	5.1%
II	7.8	16.2	21.2	8.4	5.0
III	12.4	28.9	32.8	16.5	3.9
Subtotal I–III	4.9	10.9	13.7	6.0	2.8
IV	21.3	43.5	46.4	22.2	2.9
V	40.2	65.6	73.7	25.4	8.1
Subtotal IV–V	12.3	21.8	24.0	9.5	2.2
Total (I–V)	17.2	32.8	37.7	15.6	4.9

Source: CASEN surveys; for 2003 preliminary.
Note: Income quintile measured as *ingreso autónomo per capita del hogar.*

The expansion of university enrollment—from 53% of total higher education enrollments in 1990 to 71% in 2003 (see Table 2 above)—has impacted both the CFT and IP, albeit for different reasons.

CFTs are characterized by short technical courses for part-time students,[16] with fees one-half to a third lower than other higher education institutions. Yet CFT education is increasingly an outlier of the national system, with its future as dependent on the job market as educational opportunities. Originally conceived as part of a hierarchical system to train students in specific techniques, many CFTs now teach service skills. Both the proportion and number of enrolled students have declined since the early 1990s. In 1990, there were 161 CFTs; in 2001, only 111. CFT enrollment reached its peak in 1993 with over 83,000 students; enrollment declined to 50,000 in 1997, but has recently seen modest increases, to 62,000 students in 2003.

The CFTs' future depends on finding a stable and appropriate market, which has been difficult to do because of competition, costs and quality. First, there are now alternatives more closely aligned to either employment or technical skills. The new secondary technical curriculum is providing a solid education for employment, while firms have greater say and a tax credit with National Training and Employment Service (SENCE)-sponsored short courses. These, according to one calculation (Pollack, 2003, p. 220), helped train over 620,000 workers in 2000, principally managed through commercial firms. Second, this is a market dominated by a few large CFTs; most are small, with relatively simple infrastructure and scarce investment. As a result, staff tends to be part-time and not well-trained, and this in turn affects the quality of the education offered. The most popular courses—in part because they are cheaper to mount—are not in technology but in administration and commerce, catering to the growing service sector. This bias also reflects recruitment, with over 76% coming from the humanistic/scientific secondary stream (1996). Moreover, some universities have re-entered the short course market, with the encouragement of the government, and are creating their own CFTs. A university-sponsored technical certificate

Table 6. Higher Education by Enrollment and First Year Student Size, 2003

	HE Total	CRU	PU	PI	CFT
Total Enrolled Students	567,114	246,750	156,620	101,674	62,070
% Total by sector		43.5%	27.6%	17.9%	10.9%
First year	186,090	60,043	56,353	39,429	30,265
% First year by sector		32.3%	30.3%	21.2%	16.3%
Number of Institutions	215	25	36	48	106
	Institutions with enrollment of 10,000+				
Enrollment (% of Total)	308,835 (54.5%)	68.5%	27.6%	54.7%	43.6%
First year (% of all First year)	90,430 (48.6%)	69.0%	30.3%	47.5%	40.1%
Institutions	19	11	4	2	2
	Institutions with enrollment of 5,000–9999				
Enrollment (% of Total)	111,113 (19.6%)	22.5%	31.0%	6.8%	–
First year (% of all First year)	36,824 (19.8%)	20.9%	36.3%	9.6%	–
Institutions	16	8	7	1	0
	Institutions with enrollment of 1,000–4,999				
Enrollment (% of Total)	111,280 (19.6%)	9.0%	31.0%	27.5%	19.1%
First year (% of all First year)	41,608 (22.4%)	10.1%	29.8%	19.1%	17.6%
Institutions	43	6	19	12	6

Source: Ministerio de Educación, Compendio de Educación Superior, 2004. http://www.mineduc.cl.

offers better facilities and greater prestige. The dual challenges of costs and quality have increased competition for students between CFTs and among higher education institutions.

Professional institutes (*institutos profesionales*, or IPs) have grown steadily, and account for 18% of all higher education students in 2003. Over the last 14 years, the institutional base of this sector has shifted, dominated by two leading institutions. Since 1990, 24 IPs have had their licenses revoked, and others have moved upward to become universities. Of the ten leading IPs in 1990, two became public universities, and four private universities.

In all cases, student expansion has led to (and is created by) economies of scale. Table 6 shows the enrollment size differentiation of Chilean higher education by total enrollment categories together with the equivalent number of new students. The first column shows the total number of students and their distribution across institutions; the second column, reading down, shows the percent of students by category; for example, 54% of all students and 48.6% of first-year students attend institutions with an enrollment of over 10,000. In all, 78 institutions (out of a total 215 throughout the country) enroll over 1,000 students, accounting for 93.7% of Chile's total enrollment and 90.7% of all first-year students.

Enrollments in both CFTs and IPs are highly concentrated in relatively few institutions. For example, two institutions (*Instituto Profesional INACAP* and *Instituto Profesional DUOC UC*) account for 54.7% of all IP-enrolled students, and two

Table 7.   Leading Higher Education Institutions, 2003.

Type	Leading HE institutions (above 10,000 total)	Total	First year	Percent of all students in Chile	
				Total	First year
PI	Instituto Profesional INACAP	33,651	10,023	5.9%	5.4%
CRU	Universidad de Chile	27,601	5,919	4.9	3.2
PI	Instituto Profesional DUOC UC	21,981	8,717	3.9	4.7
CRU	Pontificia Universidad Católica de Chile	19,945	5,056	3.5	2.7
CRU	Universidad de Santiago de Chile	19,252	3,496	3.4	1.9
CRU	Universidad de Concepción	19,099	4,331	3.4	2.3
PU	Universidad de Las Américas	15,918	7,085	2.8	3.8
PU	Universidad Nacional Andrés Bello	15,389	4,296	2.7	2.3
PU	Universidad Mayor	14,828	3,964	2.6	2.1
CRU	Universidad Tecnológica Metropolitana	14,511	4,705	2.6	2.5
CFT	Centro de Formación Técnica Santo Tomás	13,787	5,494	2.4	3.0
CFT	Centro de Formación Técnica INACAP	13,301	6,621	2.3	3.6
CRU	Pontificia Universidad Católica de Valparaíso	12,408	3,115	2.2	1.7
CRU	Universidad de Playa Ancha de Ciencias de la Educación	11,843	3,277	2.1	1.8
CRU	Universidad Técnica Federico Santa María	11,555	3,072	2.0	1.7
CRU	Universidad Austral de Chile	11,367	2,502	2.0	1.3
PU	Universidad Diego Portales	11,040	2,783	1.9	1.5
CRU	Universidad de Valparaíso	10,947	3,731	1.9	2.0
CRU	Universidad Católica del Norte	10,412	2,243	1.8	1.2
	Total	308,835	90,430	54.5	48.6
	Total Percent	54.5%	48.6%		

Source: Ministerio de Educación, Compendio de Educación Superior, 2004. http://www.mineduc.cl.

institutions (*Centro de Formación Técnica Santo Tomás* and *Centro de Formación Técnica INACAP*) account for 43.6% of all CFT students. Further, two IPs are among the largest of all higher education institutions in Chile (see Table 7). Their performance dominates the sector and the fate of other IPs. The same can be said for the CFT sector, such that both are being driven by economies of scale.

Why are economies of scale so important? First, more students mean greater fee income, a stable income source. Attracting more students is the key to current university growth. Although most evident for private universities (with little government support), the CRU relies increasingly on fees and less on government transfers.

Average government transfers, less student support, make up 19.5% of total income, with a range of 7–46.5%. Only five of the 11 universities listed as leading higher education institutions received more than the average in 2002. Over time, this transfer (as a percentage of income) has declined for institutions, while costs have increased and universities have sought other sources of revenue.

Chilean universities, according to the World Indicators Program, rely on fees for 36% of their expenditures, surpassed only by Korea (46%) and Jordan (40%) (Bernasconi & Rojas, 2004, p. 161). Individual examples show that fees have increasing importance (González, 2004, p. 102). A broader analysis, including private universities as well as CRU, shows that between 1995 and 2002, all universities increased their average fees between 36% and 63%. The highest private university fees are, on average, little more than 18% above the eight traditional universities but with wide variations within subgroups. The value of annual tuition costs is around US$2,500 for private autonomous universities and $1,650 for traditional universities, or 59% and 39%, respectively, of Chile's 2002 per capita income of $4,250. All university fees have increased in real terms, led by Santiago-based CRUs (63%), smaller CRUs (around 50%) and private universities (40%). There are wide variations, but two patterns stand out. First, private universities raise fees after they have gained autonomy and, presumably, a solid market position. Second, the growth in CRU fees reflects the demand for education and the knowledge that a high percentage of incoming students will receive either a loan or scholarship (Salas & Aranda, 2004).

In general, private universities are more aggressive marketers. Since the heady days of the early 1990s, there have been a combination of mergers and closures (including the revocation of nine licenses by the Ministry of Education), which have consolidated market leaders and their different orientations. Creating a successful university is a long-term investment which requires funds and educational commitment. Chilean private universities are no exception, and reflect different group interests associated with business, various Church orientations, non-confessional groupings and a variety of mission-based identities. A new phenomenon is the arrival of foreign direct investment, which began when Sylvan Learning (now Laureate Education Inc.) purchased a controlling interest in three leading institutions: the Universidad de Las Americas, the Universidad Andés Bello and a professional institute. While universities may be profitable business—it is difficult to tell with the figures currently available—this group is assuredly looking for a return on their investment.[17]

Learning and Knowledge

What students study is important for their future job prospects as well as the public knowledge platform for the challenges of globalization. The former is handled, more or less, by institutional competition; the latter by policy, which is implicit in Chile. A future challenge is to ensure that incentives are in place to encourage high tech science, where Chile has declared an interest. Evidence of these processes can be glimpsed by an examination of knowledge categories, which (although broad) show the changing profile of undergraduate education and the contribution of universities, professional institutes and CFTs.

Table 8.   Undergraduate Students by Subject Areas: 1990, 2000 and 2003

Undergraduate Enrollments	1990 245,408	2000 435,660	2003 542,580	Percent difference 1990–2000 190,252	2000–2003 106,920
Area	%	%	%	%	%
Technology	27.4	27.8	28.6	0.5	0.8
Administration/Commerce	22.5	15.1	12.6	–7.4	–2.5
Education	10.2	8.3	13.1	–1.9	4.8
Subtotal	60.1	51.2	54.4	–8.9	3.1
Social sciences	9.6	14.2	16.5	4.6	2.2
Agriculture	7.7	6.7	4.8	–0.9	–1.9
Art and Architecture	6.0	7.1	7.4	1.1	0.3
Heath	6.0	6.7	8.5	0.6	1.9
Humanities	4.5	6.2	1.2	1.7	–4.9
Law	3.7	5.5	5.8	1.8	0.3
Basic Sciences	2.4	2.4	1.4	0.0	–1.1

Source: Ministerio de Educación, Compendio de Educación Superior, 2004. http://www.mineduc.cl

The changing profile is illustrated by taking two broad periods, the first decade of the democratic government (1990–2000) and the last 3 years (2000–2003). In the first 10 years, the system coped with an additional 190,000 students, and its dynamism is confirmed by the addition of 106,000 (or 56% of the 10 year total) in the last 3 years. Table 8 provides an overview of students by subject area as well as changes since 1990.

Three areas—technology, education, and administration/commerce—dominated in 1990 (60.1% of all students), a group of subjects that had declined in enrollments by 2000 and then recovered in 2003 because of the increase in education enrollments overall. Strong increases were also seen between 1990 and 2003 in the number of students in social sciences and health. Unlike the earlier 10-year period, 2000–2003 experienced not only proportional changes, but declines in the absolute numbers of students studying agriculture, basic sciences, and the humanities.

These changes are explained by a combination of preferences and/or opportunities. The demand for agricultural experts or technicians is declining as the sector's output and labor intensity alter. However, opportunities have been influenced as much by the changing institutional structure—particularly the growth of private universities—as economic prognosis. The presence of private institutions is changing study opportunities (and, it is presumed, quality) as students move, for example, from technical certificates to professional careers.

Graduate degrees can only be awarded by universities and make up a small but growing proportion of total higher education enrolment. Around 15,000 students (2003) are registered for degree (master's or doctoral) courses, with an equal amount registered for diploma or short courses (*post titulo.*)[18] Postgraduate studies continue to be concentrated in the CRUs, which increased their enrollment from 6,500 to 9,500 postgraduates between 2000 and 2003; private universities also increased from 1,200 to 5,400 in the same period. Almost one-third study education, followed by social sciences, basic sciences and technology. Doctoral studies are in their infancy, with only 147 doctoral graduates from Chilean universities—although there are 1,600 enrolled, of which 448 are in their first year (2002) and over 50% are in the basic sciences. At present, doctoral degrees are offered by only 12 of the CRU, although a small number of private universities intend to open programs soon.

All the indications suggest that postgraduate education will grow quickly, reflecting the increasing number of graduates, the explosion in knowledge and employment requirements for up-to-date information and techniques. Until now, many domestically provided university postgraduate courses have been linked to external partners. While this will continue for certain specialized courses, the boom in diplomas and short courses demonstrates the increasing capacity (and confidence) of Chilean higher education. Although it is not possible to give reliable figures, the leading areas are education, engineering and management. A number of universities have begun postgraduate and online short courses.

Research and Development

Chile spends only 0.6% of its GDP on research, with around 80–85% of identifiable funds provided by the public sector. The National Science and Technology Council, established in 1967, is the principal public agency for science policy and planning, and handles around 70% of public research resources, almost all of which go to universities. Research monies are managed through three competitive funds for university-defined research, links with industry and centers of excellence. Around 60% is spent through the main fund—the National Fund for Science and Technology—which holds annual competitions, open to all subjects. Most important, projects are peer reviewed by Chileans and foreigners, and the experience has provided an important precedent for all later evaluations.[19] CONICYT (*Comisión Nacional de Investigación Científica y Tecnológica*) funds are one of the few components of the higher education budget that has been increasing over the last 20 years.

Chile has a small research community. University research is dominated by the basic sciences, of which the greater proportion is concentrated in three universities.[20] Most universities have, in their search for income, established outreach departments targeting local industries and services. A number have attempted to follow the example of the *Fundación Chile* by establishing institutes for the analysis of scientific potential of natural resources.[21] Research in engineering, forestry, fisheries and mining has helped build local expertise in a number of regions, and the government has been examining tax and credit policies to stimulate this trend further.

Effectiveness and Quality

Higher education's rapid expansion has raised questions about its effectiveness in terms of graduation rates, teaching and quality.

Graduation Rates

If standards have been lowered to attract students, then one would expect that graduation rates as a percentage of total enrollments would have declined. However, between 1995 and 1999, using cohorts and a standard number of years for graduation, there appears to have been little change between institutions, with CFTs (offering shorter courses) being able to retain their students more easily, followed by universities and IPs. Among universities the variation is greater, with CRUs having higher retention and efficiency rates than private universities. Seven of the 17 reserved professions—principally in health and education—show the best results explained by careful selection, a flexible curricula, and university policies which can identify failing students.[22] If the system has remained relatively stable—and perhaps slightly more efficient—there is more concern but less information about first- and second-year dropout rates. Informal surveys suggest that as many as 30% of first-year students do not return to the same course in the second year. Whereas trial and error is sensible for both universities and students, it is expensive for students. University costs are increasingly passed onto students in the form of fees; lower income families or students may not be able to afford to continue without greater public support, which (as noted above) is limited. Also, as a result of rapid and continuous expansion, universities complain about some first year students' poor preparation and study skills for their courses. This is only likely to be overcome when universities pay more attention to the creation of a first-year educational safety net.

Teaching

Professional teaching and university management are becoming more established as a result of better salaries, prestige, educational levels and knowledge demands. There are now 13,000 full-time university teachers, 35% of all 38,000 teachers in universities and IPs. Of this total around 30% have higher degrees, notably among the CRU institutions. In some departments of the leading universities, appointments are no longer made without a doctorate or doctoral studies.[23] Around 15% of teaching staff conduct research.

The growth of part-time teaching—involving an estimated 25,000 faculty (in 2000)—reflects the expansion of student numbers. They are required to keep the system functioning and can be loosely divided into workhorses, professionals and an elite teaching cadre in the learned professions. Professional part-timers could very well teach a full load by giving the same set of courses in a number of universities.[24] There is worry that part-time teachers may not provide necessary quality, and that private universities have not encouraged full-time appointments for cost reasons.

Quality and Evaluation

These issues, together with a growing demand for more public information, have helped the Ministry of Education and Higher Educational Council's push toward a quality evaluation process. In 1999, the government created two commissions to explore and develop undergraduate and graduate program assessments.[25] Unlike the Council, the

Commissions' accreditation process is voluntary, includes both public and private universities, and is based on the work of specialized academic working groups by professional or subject area. By 2004, 108 undergraduate and 175 postgraduate programs had been evaluated, along with 13 universities. The process combines self-evaluation, documentation submitted to specialized groups (agreed upon by the Commission and university), and site visits. The institutional evaluation or accreditation examines institutional self-regulation and the organization and delivery of undergraduate courses, and then one specific feature, chosen by the applicant, which it defines as core to its institutional mission.[26] Although the process has ruffled some feathers, it follows procedures well known to Chilean academics and universities, and has been broadly accepted by the professional academic community.[27] In addition, the government's proposed student loan insurance scheme will only apply to evaluated or accredited institutions.

The effect of this initiative could be far-reaching. Not only will students and parents be able to consult better information, but there will be assumptions that approved institutions or courses are attempting to reach the same level. In the short term, it could broaden the discussion from access to standards, while in the longer term, public and private university prestige will be measured explicitly by program as well as institutional evaluation results. The involvement of both Chilean and foreign senior academics, anxious to preserve the values of their "invisible colleges," should ensure that the process remains rigorous and non-bureaucratic.

Challenges and Opportunities

The Chilean higher education system can best be described as a work in progress. The differentiated levels (university, IP and CFT) and sectors (public and private) are unlikely to change. However, within that structure, lines will become blurred in the university sector, as different universities compete for different markets; quality rankings will alter; research will play a greater role; and universities will choose between niche and mass markets. Given the state of universities in 1990, wilting under the shadow of the military government, the accomplishments made over the last 15 years have been encouraging. The 1990 Commission showed itself to be prescient about both the challenges and policy solutions.

Four challenges—social, economic, academic and managerial—still remain. They will not be decided by government, although it will be an influential factor, but by the messy process of negotiation, student demands, and academic and university leadership.

The principal social challenge is that of inclusion—to what point are higher education institutions willing to develop policies for disadvantaged students, over and above the current approach which reflects secondary education quality as much as capacity and intelligence? And how, given income distribution, are families from lower quintiles to pay for this education, without a broader student support policy?

The economic challenge is twofold. First, can universities contribute to production and services with applied research, particularly to the new, potentially profitable fields of biotechnology, materials science and informatics? Second, if universities are not part of a large conglomerate, how can they generate income consistent with their mission?

The future of smaller universities, catering to regions or providing an entrée for special segments (such as working adults) is not easily assured.

Third, the academic challenge is to reinforce knowledge institutions, their creation and diffusion; a meritocracy requires high academic levels and thus a greater proportion of well-trained academic staff. Finally, both the system and individual institutions will need to develop more flexible mechanisms to permit student transfer; and in some private universities, greater student and staff participation is needed to permit them to become learning organizations as well as degree institutions.

These four dimensions frame the contemporary challenges to Chile's government as well, and may lead it to play a more explicit role in building an active consensus about the value and role of higher education in the service of the nation.

Notes

1. Technical training centers (CFT) are classified by UNESCO's International Standard Classification of Education (1997) as level 5B, Professional Institutes as level 5A and Universities as levels 5A and 6.
2. CRU will be used throughout for universities that are members of the Council of University Rectors, IP for *Institutos Profesionales*, and the Spanish acronym, CFT, for Technical Training Centers.
3. There are in total nine private universities within this group; six Catholic universities and three regional, non-confessional universities.
4. These are law, architecture, biochemistry, dentistry, agronomy, civil engineering, commercial engineering, forestry, medicine, psychology, pharmaceutical chemistry; basic education, secondary education, special needs education (added in 1990); pre-primary education and journalism (added in 1991); and social work (2004). The reserved professions account for 55% of university enrollments.
5. According to the number of students they can attract from a pool of 27,500 who achieve the best scores in an annual national examination for university entrance.
6. University of Concepción (1919), the Catholic University of Valparaíso, (1928), the Federico Santa Maria University, (1931), the State Technical University, (1947), the Austral University (1954), and the Catholic University of the North (1956).
7. The higher education budget fell from 19% to 14% of Ministry of Education funds between 1990 and 2003.
8. The National Commission for the Accreditation of Undergraduate Programs and the National Commission for the Accreditation of Graduate Programs were both established in 1999.
9. Four institutions (Catholic University, University of Chile, University of the Andes and the IP-INCAP) received 46.1% of total donations (1998/2003) and 19 account for 85%.
10. Compared to incomplete technical or university education (1.55) or complete technical education (1.88). See Mizala and Romoguera (2004). Their analysis of occupations shows a strong increase in reported professional monthly incomes and a growing gap between these and other income categories with the exception of directors.
11. According to the OECD's calculation, in the year 2000, 74.7% of funds for tertiary education comes from private sources (OECD, 2003, p. 220), the highest of all non-OECD countries for that year, and similar to Korea (75.6%) the outlier among OECD countries. Total expenditure per student in higher education is given as US $ 7,483 PPP (2000) compared to US $6,118 for Korea (OECD, 2003, p. 197).
12. See OECD (2004, p. 205).
13. In response to concerns about possible market saturation, the government has set up a public observatory to track employment and wage trends. See www.futurolaboral.cl and Meller & Rappoport (2004), where it is claimed Chile has a professional deficit, compared to other emerging economies and OECD countries, and a need to improve quality.

14. The 27,500 students are divided by category according to their score. The basic unit is then provided in multiples of 1, for the first category, then 4, 6, 9 and 12. Thus a top student would contribute 12 times the value of a student at the cut-off point.

15. Income as the sole determinant must be treated with caution and may well be less important than parents' education, family social capital or good schooling; that is, it is necessary but not sufficient.

16. MIDEPLAN & CIDE (2000) report that 49% attended in the morning, 15% in the afternoon and 36% in the evening.

17. With 130,000 students studying in 35 campuses worldwide and online. Since May 2004, the conglomerate has traded on NASDAQ as LAUR.

18. An estimate as not all universities have reported their numbers at the time of writing.

19. FONDECYT spent $16,714 mn pesos for 344 projects (2002). The other funds are FONDEF (Fund for the Promotion of Scientific and Technological Development) to improve applied science and technology for productivity and which requires a private partner to commit 20% of the funds; and FONDAP (Fund for Advanced Research in Priority Areas), which supports centers of excellence in, for example, biotechnology, with scholarships, equipment and research funds. In 2002 FONDEF spent $9,460.7 million on 33 projects and FONDAP $1,342 mn on 404 recipients (2002).

20. The University of Chile, the Catholic University and University of Concepción.

21. An autonomous technology transfer center which pioneered salmon farm fishing, fruit standards and wine processing in Chile. One of its current projects deals with informatics and education.

22. See the discussion of Uribe (2004, p. 161–163).

23. The Catholic University reports 823 of their 1,397 teaching staff have doctorates, the University of Chile, 473 of 1,658 and the University of Concepción 330 out of 1,119 respectively. They account for 55% of all Ph.D.s teaching at Chilean universities in 2002.

24. See the interesting discussion in Bernasconi & Rojas (2004, p. 138–141).

25. CNAP (The National Commission for Undergraduate Accreditation) and CONAP (National Commission for Postgraduate Accreditation).

26. Based in part on the U.K. model.

27. The evaluation techniques build on CONICYT's project assessment, the criteria established for 5% of Direct Financial contributions (AFD) distribution among CRUs, and the procedures used by the Higher Education Council to supervise and accredit new private universities and IPs.

References

Avendaño, M. & Vergara, P. (2003). *Atractividad y posición competitiva. Análisis multivariado de los matriculados en las universidades chilenas del Consejo de Rectores, 1999–2003 (Attraction and competitive position. Multivariate analysis of enrollment at Chilean universities for the Council of Rectors, 1999–2003).* Santiago, Chile: Ediciones Universidad Tecnológica Metropolitana.

Bernasconi, A. & Rojas, F. (2004). *Informe sobre la educación superior en Chile: 1980–2003 (Report on higher education in Chile, 1980–2003).* Santiago, Chile: IESALC-UNESCO and Editorial Universitaria.

Brunner, J. J. (1997). From state to market coordination: The Chilean case. *Higher Education Policy,* 10(3/4), 225–237.

Brunner, J. J. (2003). Nuevas demandas y sus consecuencias para la educación superior en América Latina (New demands on higher education in Chile and their consequences). In Centro Interuniversitario de Desarrollo-CINDA (Ed.), *Políticas públicas, demandas sociales y gestión del conocimiento (Public policy, social demands and the management of knowledge).* Santiago, Chile: CINDA.

Brunner, J. J & Meller, P. (Eds.). (2004). *Oferta y demanda de profesionales y técnicos en Chile: El rol de información pública (Supply and demand for professionals and technicians in Chile: The role of information).* Santiago, Chile: RIL Editors.

Comisión de Estudio de la Educación Superior (Higher Education Research Commission). (1990). *Una política para el desarrollo de la educación superior en la década de los noventa (A higher education development policy for the nineties).* Santiago, Chile: CEES.

Comisión Nacional de Acreditación de Pregrado (National Undergraduate Accreditation Commission). (2003). *Sedes de instituciones de educación superior en Chile (Locations of higher education institutions in Chile)*. Online at: http://www.cnap.cl/estudios/informe%20sedes.pdf. Retrieved September 11, 2004.

González, P. (2004). Una mirada económica de las políticas y de las necesidades de información en educación superior (An economic overview of policies and information needs in higher education). In J. J. Brunner & P. Meller (Eds.), *Oferta y demanda de profesionales y técnicos en Chile: El rol de la información pública (Supply and demand of professionals and technicians in Chile: The roll of public information)*. Santiago, Chile: LOM Editors.

Hunneus, C. (2002). *El régimen de Pinochet (The Pinochet regime)*. Santiago, Chile: Editorial Sudamericana.

Instituto Nacional de Estadística (INE: National Institute of Statistics). (1997). *Ingresos de hogares y personas, encuesta suplementaria de ingresos, 1995 (Household and personal income survey, national supplementary income survey 1995)*. Santiago, Chile: INE.

Instituto Nacional de Estadística (INE: National Institute of Statistics). (2002). *Ingresos de hogares y personas, encuesta suplementaria de ingresos, 2000 (Household and personal income survey, national supplementary income survey, 2000)*. Santiago, Chile: INE.

Meller, P. & Rappoport, D. (2004). Comparaciones internacionales de la dotación de profesionales y la posición relativa de Chile (International comparisons of professionals and Chile's relative position). In J. J. Brunner & P. Meller (Eds.), *Oferta y demanda de profesionales y técnicos en Chile: El rol de información pública (Supply and demand for professionals and technicians in Chile: The role of information)*. Santiago, Chile: RIL Editors.

MIDEPLAN (Ministry of Planning) & CIDE (Center for Educational Research and Development). (2000). *Educación técnica superior en Chile: Reflexiones sobre nueva políticas (Higher technical education in Chile: Views on new policies)*. Online at: http://www.mideplan.cl/sitio/Sitio/ publicaciones/prospectivos/documentos/educsuperior.pdf. Retrieved September 11, 2004.

Mizala, A. & Romaguera, P. (2004). Remuneraciones y tazas de retorno de los profesionales chilenos (Salaries and the rate of return for Chilean professionals). In J. J. Brunner & P. Meller (Eds.), *Oferta y demanda de profesionales y técnicos en Chile: El rol de información pública (Supply and demand for professionals and technicians in Chile: The role of information)*. Santiago, Chile: RIL Editors.

Organization for Economic Cooperation and Development. (2003). *Education at a Glance, 2003*. Paris: OECD.

Organization for Economic Cooperation and Development. (2004). *Review of National Policies for Education: Chile*. Paris: OECD.

Pollack, M. (2003). Más y mejor capacitación para una economía competitiva (More and better training for a competitive economy). In O. Muñoz (Ed.), *Hacia un Chile competitivo: Instituciones y políticas (Toward a competitive Chile: Institutions and policies)*. Santiago, Chile: FLACSO—Chile and Editorial Universitaria.

Salas, V. & Aranda, R.F. (2004). *Estructura de aranceles universitarios en Chile (Structure of university fees in Chile)*. Unpublished Manuscript.

Uribe, D. (2004). Oferta educativa y oferta de graduados de educación superior (Educational and graduate supply in higher education). In J. J. Brunner & P. Meller (Eds.), *Oferta y demanda de profesionales y técnicos en Chile: El rol de información pública (Supply and demand for professionals and technicians in Chile: The role of information)*. Santiago, Chile: RIL Editors.

34

CHINA

Ruth Hayhoe and Qiang Zha
Ontario Institute for Studies in Education of the University of Toronto, Canada

This chapter puts Chinese higher education in the context of modernization and global-ization. It identifies particularities in China's response to these phenomena, with highly developed traditions shaping the modern institutions that emerged under the influences of Western capitalism, then of Western socialism, and finally of globalization. We begin with a historical overview, then provide an analysis of recent developments in three major areas: governance and finance, expansion and differentiation, and international-ization and nationalization.

History

Evolving over more than two millennia, higher education in China is one of the world's oldest systems. Traditional higher education institutions in China can be traced back to the 4th century B.C.E., when Confucius established a private academy (Galt, 1951; Gu, 1964). By the time of the Tang Dynasty (618–907 C.E.), there was a whole range of higher education institutions, headed by the Guo Zi Jian (school for the sons of the Emperors) and the Tai Xue, which took major classical texts of the Confucian school as their curricular content. There were also professional schools for law, medicine, math-ematics, literature, calligraphy, and Daoist studies. In this period, publicly regulated examinations in both classical and professional areas were established, and meritocratic selection for the civil service was institutionalized. In the later Song dynasty (960–1279 C.E.), the Confucian classics were re-ordered to form a knowledge system that had to be mastered by all students aspiring to become scholar-officials in the imperial civil ser-vice. Examinations for professional knowledge fields such as medicine fell into disuse, as these areas became relegated to the category of techniques to be developed under the supervision of the scholar-official class. The imperial examination system thus dom-inated traditional higher education, creating a class of intellectuals who climbed the ladder from local to provincial and finally capital and palace examinations (Hayhoe, 1989a).

　Traditional institutions of higher learning gradually lost their legitimacy and viability in the late Qing dynasty. China suffered humiliation in the face of Japanese and Western

James J.F. Forest and Philip G. Altbach (eds.), International Handbook of Higher Education, 667–691.
© 2006 *Springer. Printed in the Netherlands.*

military incursions. Reform and self-strengthening was essential. The evolution of modern Chinese higher education was thus deeply interwoven with influences from Japan and the West. These came through three major channels: Chinese reformers' efforts, study abroad programs for Chinese scholars and students, and the establishment of Western missionary universities and colleges in China.

The Late Qing Period (1860–1911): The Japanese Influences

Qing dynasty officials launched a self-strengthening movement, which involved the introduction of Western technology for the purpose of national salvation, while keeping intact the basic character of the Chinese empire. Japan was their most important model. The fact that Japan defeated China militarily in 1895 had a devastating psychological impact on China. How had it succeeded in the self-strengthening China so desperately needed? The Japanese model was believed appropriate in cultural terms, since the two countries shared the Confucian tradition (Chen, 2002). Convinced that Western techniques could be absorbed into a revitalized Confucian empire, China modeled its educational reform legislation of 1902 and 1903 closely on the Japanese education system as a pathway to modernization with the preservation of Confucian values (Hayhoe, 1989b).

The Hundred Day Reform (1898) was a first step toward radical reform and one of the earliest modern universities in China—the Capital Metropolitan University, later Peking University—was one of the innovations that lasted. It was patterned after the University of Tokyo, and was supposed to have a supervisory responsibility over all levels of the education system (Hayhoe, 1989b, 1996). A growing number of Chinese students were sent abroad over this period, mainly to Japan. By 1906, there were 7,283 Chinese students and intellectuals in Japan, the majority preparing to be teachers in the newly emerging modern schools (Abe, 1987; Chen & Tian, 1991).

The Republican Period (1911–1927): The European and American Influences

With the Revolution of 1911, the provisional government established by Sun Yat Sen in Nanjing decreed a major reform to instill Republican values. As the first Minister of Education, Cai Yuanpei designed higher education legislation which reflected a European model derived largely from his experience of the German universities of Berlin and Leipzig. The new higher education legislation made a clear distinction between specialist higher education institutions and universities. The arts and sciences were to be the core curricular areas of these Republican universities, rather than the Confucian classics, while professional fields of knowledge such as engineering and law were to be developed in separate higher education institutions. Cai felt that universities had a special responsibility for aesthetic education as a way of building a modern Chinese worldview.

The legislation laid a foundation for academic freedom and university autonomy along the lines of the German university model. These concepts were not to be realized in practice, however, until Cai returned from his second stay in Germany in 1917 and took up the chancellorship of Peking University. Under his leadership, the idea of "professorial rule" provided for in the 1912 legislation blossomed into a transformative cultural movement, known as the May Fourth Movement.

The weakness of China's central government from 1911 to 1927 provided China's higher education with the possibility of vigorous experimentation. By 1921, there were 16 missionary colleges and universities in major Chinese cities, mostly chartered with American state governments and headed by American missionary presidents (Hawkins, 1991; Hayhoe, 1989a). There were also a number of private universities established by patriotic Chinese intellectuals and political figures, as well as a range of national and provincial level public institutions for higher learning. Educational legislation of 1922 and 1924 opened the way for increasing American influences on China's emerging higher education system.

The definition of university was broadened to include most higher education institutions, including specialist professional ones. There was also less emphasis on autonomy, in terms of the rule of professors within the university, and more on social responsibility. Some universities experimented with American-style boards of trustees, which were responsible for finance, planning and major policy decisions. Some adopted a credit system, which resulted in innovative and unregulated approaches to the university curriculum.

The Nationalist Period (1927–1949): The Emergence of a Chinese University Model

As a result of legislation in 1922 and 1924, the number of higher education institutions calling themselves universities burgeoned, from eight in 1917 to 39 in 1930. With the accession to power of the Nationalist Party in 1927, the new government proceeded to develop policies and legislation for higher education that put a strong emphasis on practical knowledge and skills. In the legislation passed in 1928, the aims of higher education were expressed as follows: "Universities and professional institutions must emphasize the applied sciences, enrich the scientific content of their courses, nurture people with specialized knowledge and skills, and mold healthy character for the service of nation and society" (quoted in Hayhoe, 1996, p. 52).

There was considerable concern over academic standards and the lack of clear curricular requirements in many fields. Therefore, the Nationalist government found European patterns attractive due to their greater centralization and standardization. National policy for higher education was influenced by the advice of a delegation of high-level European intellectuals who came to China in 1931—under the auspices of the League of Nations—to study the education system and make recommendations for reform. The recommendations included establishing an academic chair system, clear national procedures for monitoring all academic appointments, and a comprehensive examination at the end of each university program to ensure a basic foundation in each discipline. In the legislation passed between 1933 and 1936, some of these recommendations were adopted, resulting in a greater measure of centralized governmental control.

Generally speaking, this was a period characterized by considerable maturity and independence of educational thought, with eclectic foreign influences being introduced by both Chinese scholars who returned from abroad and Western scholars who came to

China. A wide range of new higher education institutions developed and flourished, in spite of serious problems in economic development and a war with Japan lasting from 1937 to 1945. In the education legislation, it is possible to see European and American influences integrated within patterns that served Nationalist educational goals. Chinese universities went through a process of adaptation and indigenization that might be compared to the development of American universities in the 19th century (Hayhoe, 1996). A contemporary discussion in the Chinese intellectual community has reached the conclusion that Chinese universities in the Nationalist era had developed into mature institutions, achieving a balance between their Chinese identity and their ability to link up to the world community (Chen, 2002; Xie, 2001).

The Socialist Period (1949–1978): The Soviet Influences

At its birth in 1949, the People's Republic of China inherited a higher education system close to the American one in its knowledge patterns. Most of the institutions combined the pure and applied sciences with some social sciences and liberal arts, and were organized into colleges and departments that allowed for the cross-fertilization of knowledge areas. Rather than strengthening the pure and applied sciences within this context, the new government chose to carry out a total reorganization of the higher education system in order to serve a centrally planned economy.

The dominant slogan in China during the 1950s was to "learn from the Soviet Union." According to the official rationale for adopting the Soviet model, "the Soviet Union . . . has a rich experience in socialist construction, and many major departments of science have reached or exceeded the most advanced capitalist countries" (quoted in Hu & Seifman, 1976, p. 44). Based on Soviet experience and advice, the first Five-Year Plan (1953–1957) focused on the development of heavy industry. Plans to reform the higher education institutions so as to emphasize technical education were finalized in 1951. The hallmarks of the Soviet model were "rational" organization based on bureaucratism and modern managerial leadership committed to technological change. The stress was on expertise, a centralized administrative system and a highly formal educational system. Education was viewed as a resource for the system of production.

The new system took shape between 1952 and 1957, with a complete reorganization of old institutions and the creation of new ones around a national plan. Curricular patterns ensured close coordination with the personnel needs of the state as well as a rational geographical distribution of higher education. The country was divided into six major geographical regions, and each of them had an educational bureau that coordinated planning for the region. At the core of the system were three main types of institution that were directly administered by a new national ministry of higher education: comprehensive universities with programs in the basic arts and sciences, polytechnic universities with a wide range of applied scientific programs, and teacher training universities responsible for setting national standards for education. Each region had at least one of each of these three types of institution, and their role was both a national and regional one.

In addition to these core institutions, there was a large number of sectoral institutions in areas such as agriculture, forestry, medicine, finance, law, language studies, physical culture, fine arts, and minority education. They were managed by appropriate ministries and were distributed across the country, taking into account differences of regional emphasis by sector. Each institution was narrowly specialized in its programs, and its role was to train personnel for its specific sector. Each institution offered many more specializations than had been available under the Nationalist system. For example, the discipline of mechanical engineering had sub-disciplinary specializations in machine tools, casting, welding or forging, while thermal power engineering had specializations in boilers, turbines, internal combustion engines, compressors or refrigeration machinery, among others. Specializations matched the precise definitions of manpower needs in heavy industry.

In a situation where the priorities were to build heavy industry as the basis for a modern economy and establish a strong socialist governmental and education system, these patterns worked well at first, as there was a high degree of predictability in personnel planning. However, with a new emphasis on agriculture and light industry during the late 1950s, combined with the rapid growth of secondary education—which increased the pool of graduates competing for entry to higher education—many concerns about the equality of access and the suitability of the system to China's indigenous economic and cultural development came to the fore.

The Great Leap Forward of 1958 represented a bold and idealistic attempt to achieve an accelerated move towards communism. An important concept was "walking on two legs," which meant the simultaneous development of industry and agriculture, national and local industries, large and small enterprises, and the simultaneous application of modern and indigenous methods. Another vital aspect of the new strategy was self-reliance at both national and local levels. It also marked the shift away from a centralized, technology- and capital-intensive economy, and toward a decentralized and labor-intensive economy. A timetable was set up to ensure that within 15 years university education would be available to all young people and adults who wished to continue their education. A radical change in the mission of universities would redirect their priorities toward advancing egalitarian social goals over those of economic production. This reform movement rushed the higher education system into expansion without either a rational plan or the resources to sustain the explosive growth in institutions and enrollments that ensued. By the early 1960s, retrenchment was inevitable, in the face of a faltering economy and the outbreak of severe famine.

The Cultural Revolution of 1966 represented a dramatic attempt at transforming Chinese society as well as the education system. If the education reform during the Great Leap Forward had been a reaction to the Sovietization of the early 1950s, this revolution in education was directed against all foreign education patterns and practices that had been imposed on China. In the destruction of old systems and the repudiation of foreign influences, the intention was to build an egalitarian system of education available to all, and achieve pure communist ideals. For three years, from 1966 to 1969, all regular recruitment to higher education was halted. Between 1971 and 1976, significantly smaller numbers of students were enrolled, selected (without examination) from among the workers and peasants who had practical experience, and who were expected to return to production after a few years' study. Unfortunately, efforts to run open-door institutions and link academic knowledge with social transformation failed. This caused inestimable damage to the economy and society, especially affecting intellectuals and higher education.

The Reform Period (1978–Present): The Open Door Policy

With the death of Mao Zedong in 1976 and the emergence of a new leadership under Deng Xiaoping, a concern for modernization through economic revitalization became paramount. In an important national conference for science and education held in 1978, clear goals of service to economic modernization in the four areas of agriculture, industry, national defense and science and technology were set forth, resulting in dramatic change throughout the 1980s.

In 1985, the Chinese government's *Decision on the Reform of the Education System* emphasized the implementation of a three-level higher education management system at the central, provincial, and major municipal levels. The main rationale for reform given in the *Decision* was "to change the management system of excessive government control of the institutions of higher education, expand decision making in the institutions under the guidance of unified education policies and plans of the state, strengthen the connection of the institutions of higher education with production organizations, scientific research organizations, and other social establishments, and enable the institutions of higher education to take the initiative to meet the needs of economic and social development" (Central Committee of Chinese Communist Party, 1985, p. 186).

An important part of the re-emerging identity of Chinese universities in the 1980s was the role they played in helping China to re-connect with an international milieu after a decade of isolation during the Cultural Revolution. One of the major reasons that considerable support was given to higher education was the leadership's realization of a need for people who could build bridges to the outside world. Now the international relationships were both multilateral and bilateral, as opposed to learning from one specific foreign model in most of the earlier periods.

Among the multilateral interactions, the World Bank projects made the most substantial contributions to Chinese universities. In the early 1980s, the Chinese government was successful in persuading the World Bank to give a primary focus to higher education, and a total of about US$1.2 billion was loaned on concessional terms (Hayhoe, 1996). This funding was crucial to a rapid improvement in academic and scientific standards in Chinese universities. The World Bank also encouraged structural reforms, such as the amalgamation of specialized local colleges into larger and more comprehensive higher education institutions (World Bank, 1997, 1999).

Chinese universities have also been involved in many bilateral projects. These projects are often organized under cooperative agreements between two governments. There are thus cultural dynamics which make possible the creative use of scholarly communities in China that have long historical links with particular foreign countries. Participation in bilateral developmental cooperation—under the auspices of organizations such as the Japan International Cooperation Agency or the Canadian International Development Agency—has also provided applied research and training opportunities that have strengthened the capacity of Chinese universities.

With Chinese higher education now increasingly connected with the international community, the reform of the system in the 1990s can be viewed as part of a global phenomenon. The logic underlying the current restructuring of the Chinese higher education system includes decentralization of the administrative structure and the expansion of university autonomy; diversification of the funding sources for higher education institutions; and the reorganization of universities for efficiency, effectiveness, and reasonable expansion. These trends reflect an international context characterized by a rising tide of human capital theory and "efficiency" movements.

The higher education reforms of the 1990s were derived from the *Decision on the Reform of the Education System*. It was only after 1993, however, when the *Outline for Educational Reform and Development in China* was adopted, that major reforms started to be implemented. This document highlighted China's views on development, which included the belief that education and science are vital to catching up with the most developed countries in the world (Central Committee of Chinese Communist Party & State Council, 1993). The *Program of Educational Revitalization for the Twenty-First Century* took the reform ideas even further (State Council & Ministry of Education of China, 1999). The main points of these documents can be found in the *Higher Education Law* (passed on August 29, 1998, and in effect since September 1, 1999) is the first higher education law to be passed since 1949 (National People's Congress of China, 1998).

Governance Reform: From Centralization to Decentralization

China's educational leadership has been struggling with the issue of centralization and decentralization almost since the founding of the People's Republic of China in 1949. There is a history of experiments with different levels and degrees of decentralization since the 1950s. Early efforts to shift authority from central to local levels were, however, different from the nationwide decentralization seen at present.

As the result of the reorganization in the 1950s, a nationalized system of higher education was organized on a model of state control, i.e., a model characterized by central planning, with all higher education institutions directly run by the state. In May and August of 1950, the (then) Government Administration Council issued the *Provisional Measures of Governance of Higher Education Institutions in Various Administrative Regions* and the *Decision on the Issue of Governance of Higher Education Institutions*, which stipulated the principle of placing all higher education institutions under the jurisdiction of the central Ministry of Education. In October 1953, the Council revised the *Decision*, and stipulated even more specifically the governance of higher education institutions: comprehensive and polytechnic universities were to be under direct jurisdiction of the central Ministry of Higher Education, while specialized institutions were placed under the control of relevant central ministries. Among the 194 higher education institutions in 1955, 75 were administered by the Ministry of Higher Education, 40 by the Ministry of Education, and 79 by other central ministries. None was run by local governments (Liu, 1993; Zhou, 1990).

During the Great Leap Forward, many institutions under the jurisdiction of central ministries were transferred to the control of local governments. Among the 791 higher education institutions in 1958, 86 were under the jurisdiction of the Ministry of Education and other central ministries, and the remaining 705 were under the leadership of local governments (Liu, 1993). From then on a structure emerged that might be described as a combination of "columns" (institutions affiliated to central ministries) and "planes" (provincial institutions). The former tended to be large in size and well resourced, while the latter were small and poorly funded. With the failure of the Great Leap Forward, there was a reassertion of centralized efforts toward economic development. Most power that had been devolved was taken back. By 1966, the institutions directly administered by the Ministry of Education and other central ministries increased to 183, out of a total of 434 (Liu, 1993).

The Cultural Revolution represented another wave of decentralization, when all national institutions were transferred to the control of local governments. Then after 1976 there was a total reversal of these priorities. The university system that was re-established between 1977 and 1980 replicated the model of the early 1960s. The nationally unified entrance examination for higher education standardized enrollment and job assignment plans, unified curricula, and systematized rules and regulations were all restored. This centrally planned system continued to function up to the mid-1990s. In the peak year of 1994, 367 out of the total of 1,080 higher education institutions were under the jurisdiction of central ministries, including 36 belonging to the State Education Commission and 331 administered by 61 sectoral ministries (Hu & Bu, 1999).

The rigidity of this centralized model faced severe challenges in the 1990s, when the establishment of a socialist market economy was clearly the objective of economic and social reforms. This was an ideological as well as a theoretical breakthrough. Along with the shift to a market economy and the growth of diverse elements within that economy, the functions of the ministries of the central government in managing higher education were undergoing major changes. Under the old system of "columns" and "planes," higher education institutions affiliated with the ministries developed in a closed manner. Although colleges and universities were established in local areas, they had few local connections and did not serve local economic development. Such a system was incapable of responding to rapid change and surviving in a market economy.

In the 1990s, a new wave of governmental restructuring aimed to devolve power to the localities. The *Outline for Educational Reform and Development in China* (1993) proposed that higher education institutions be managed on two levels—national and provincial—but with the main responsibility being at the provincial level. Over time, this new direction should result in more effective coordination in a number of areas which are spelled out in a 1995 document, *Some Opinions on Deepening Higher Education System Reform* (Zhou, 2001). These include:

> *Joint Construction*: In this mode, provincial authorities are invited to participate in the sponsorship and management of centrally controlled institutions. There is now a central/local collaboration in institutions which used to be run solely by the central government. By 1999, nearly 200 institutions had been switched to joint investment and administration by central/local governments (see Table 1). The greatest significance of this move lies in integrating the separate "columns"

China 675

Table 1. Administrative Reform in Chinese Higher Education System: Institutions Involved

Year	Joint Construction	Transference[a]	Cooperation	Amalgamation[b]	Total HEI[c]
1991	–	–	8	–	1,075
1992	5	–	11	54(20)	1,053
1993	10	1	109	22(9)	1,065
1994	25	4	58	28(11)	1,080
1995	16	2	50	51(21)	1,054
1996	44	3	39	46(17)	1,032
1997	14	161	50	41(17)	1,020
1998	83	55	–	77(29)	1,022
1999	–	–	–	77(31)	1,071
2000			–	209(85)	1,041
2001				83(38)	1,225
2002				79(35)	1,396

[a]The transference includes such formats as (1) from central sectoral ministries to local jurisdictions; (2) between the central sectoral ministries; (3) from provincial sectoral departments to the education authorities; and (4) from adult to regular institutions.
[b]The numbers in brackets refer to those of the consequent institutions after amalgamations; involved institutions include non-formal (adult) institutions, but exclude a few specialized secondary schools.
[c]Numbers in this column refer to the regular higher education institutions.
Source: Adapted from (Ministry of Education of China, 2001, 2003a, 2003c; Mok & Lo, 2004).

and "planes" of a closed system into an organic and open system. It replaces a one-on-one affiliation relationship with a multiple partnership model. Higher education institutions become closer to the provinces and more active in serving local interests, while the financial burden of the central government is relieved.

Jurisdiction Transference: This occurred when some of the central ministries were dismantled due to administrative restructuring or were reduced in size to enhance efficiency. Higher education institutions under these ministries had to look for someone else to "adopt" them. Transferring affiliation signified a complete change from central ownership to provincial ownership. By 2002, out of the original total of 367 regular higher education institutions administered by the central ministries, nearly 250 had been transferred to local administration (Ministry of Education of China, 2004b).

Institutional Cooperation: This mode can denote various kinds of cooperation between institutions of different jurisdictions and types, on a voluntary basis, with their financial resources remaining unchanged. It is aimed at coordinating the advantages that each institution can offer and allowing intersecting disciplines to improve educational quality.

Institutional Amalgamation: Mergers among higher education institutions are intended to consolidate small institutions into comprehensive universities. Consolidation changes the landscape of the administrative structure of higher education in China. Mergers are seen as a shortcut to producing large, comprehensive and academically prestigious universities. Consequently, university giants have mush-roomed through mergers. By 2002, 597 higher education institutions had been involved in mergers, resulting in 267 new institutions (Ministry of Education of China, 2004b) which are larger in size and more comprehensive in programs offered.

Table 1 reflects how the higher education system has changed between 1991 and 2002, as a result of these four forms of restructuring.

Financial Reform: From Centralization to Diversification

From the 1950s through the early 1980s, higher education institutions received their funding exclusively from a central government appropriation according to a unitary state budgetary plan. All funds were allocated according to rigid norms on a non-fungible line item basis. The budgetary planning horizon was usually a one-year period, and higher education institutions were notified of their budgetary allocation at the beginning of the year. The amount of funds for each was determined by an "incremental approach," which was based on what the institution had received in the previous year. Institutions had no freedom to decide how to spend their budget (Min & Chen, 1994; Wang & Zhou, 1991). This tightly controlled budgetary system provided no incentive for efficiency gains, nor any incentive for institutional initiative.

Since the economic reforms of the 1980s, local authorities have been allowed to retain much of their income and decide their own spending plans. In practice, there has been a demarcation between central and local control of income and expenditure. Since 1994, there has been a further financial reform—taxation. The net effect of the reform is to demarcate between legitimate authorities of taxation, so that both local and central governments have legitimate sources of income. A distinction between local and central taxes has thus emerged.

In conjunction with financial decentralization, local governments have become re-sponsible for investing in local higher education institutions since 1980. Indeed, among the 404 institutions founded between 1980 and 1988, over 300 (74%) were established by local governments. This has resulted in three categories of higher education insti-tutions in terms of investment mechanisms. The first category includes the institutions directly administered and financed by the Ministry of Education. The second group comprises institutions whose budgets and appropriation are taken care of by central ministries. The third are local institutions, which are financially controlled by the provincial governments. Generally, the first two categories of institutions are far better off (Min & Chen, 1994).

Nevertheless, during the rapid expansion between 1977 and 1988, the total num-ber of higher education institutions rose from 598 to 1,075. Along with this rapid growth and development, the Chinese higher education system faced increasing fi-nancial constraints. This situation was exacerbated by inflation in 1988. Universities started to experience serious deficits, as allocations from the government covered only two-thirds of their operating expenses (Johnson, 1989). Inflation led to a situation where government funding covered only basic salary requirements, leaving little for library and program development, equipment acquisition, and general maintenance. Institutions were forced to seek new sources of income, which became indispensable for survival. At some universities, income from alternative sources came to constitute 50% of the total budget (Du, 1992).

There are basically four principal sources of self-generated income: (a) income from university enterprises; (b) income from commissioned training for enterprises, where institutions that offer applied subjects have an advantage; (c) income from research and consultancy, where research universities are in the best position to offer this kind of service; and (d) donations, for which the beneficiaries tend to be prestigious universities with large networks of influential alumni.

Before the reforms of the mid-1980s, university admissions were tightly controlled by the state, with students paying no fees and being assigned jobs upon graduation. The 1985 reform allowed higher education institutions to admit students outside the state plan, as long as they were either sponsored by enterprises or self-financed. In 1989, institutions were allowed to collect fees for accommodation and sundry items. Revenues from tuition and fees at the national level in 1992 accounted for nearly 5% of total revenue in higher education. Starting in 1994, 37 institutions participated in a pilot scheme whereby all students, whether in the state plan or not, were required to pay fees, and the institutions were given the discretion to fix their own fees in accordance with the living standards of their region (Ministry of Education of China, 2003b).

National policy changed in September of 1995, when a reform initiative known as "merging the rails" started to unify the admissions criteria and fee levels for those students within the national plan with those outside it. Since 1997, all higher education institutions have charged student fees. The general tendency is to charge a fee of less than 25% of the recurrent unit cost (Cheng, 1998; Ministry of Education of China, 2003b). Table 2 shows the change in the sources of revenue for higher education over the period 1995 to 2001, with public allocations falling from 73.29% to 51.95%.

Expansion and Differentiation

With the establishment of a market economy, there has been an increasing demand for different types of talents from government, industries and the labor market. At the same time, the newly emerging market economy has increased the income of many families, who in turn seek wider access to higher education for their children. These twin demands have resulted in the rapid expansion of higher education since the 1980s, along with an increasing diversification of the system.

Expansion: From Elite to Mass Higher Education

The issue of expansion has two aspects: the aggregate size of the higher education system, and the average size of each institution. Aggregate size can be proxied by the total number of undergraduate students and the number of regular higher education institutions. The appropriate aggregate size is a matter of policy in relation to the role of higher education in national development. Institutional size is measured by the number

Table 2. Revenue and Sources for the Regular Higher Education Sector (%), 1995–2001

Year	Total Investment	In-Budget	Education Tax	Endowment	Tuition & Fees	School-Run Enterprise Income	Enterprise-Run School Investment	Social Organization Investment	Others
1995	100	73.29	0.29	1.09	11.89	8.30	0.22	0.16	4.77
1996	100	70.37	0.73	1.13	13.66	7.92	0.27	0.17	5.75
1997	100	67.72	0.91	1.50	14.82	7.98	0.31	0.17	6.58
1998	100	61.00	1.36	2.09	13.31	2.05	0.54	0.28	19.38
1999	100	59.63	0.97	2.28	17.04	1.75	0.17	0.46	17.69
2000	100	55.23	0.91	1.66	21.09	1.77	0.26	0.72	18.37
2001	100	51.95	0.71	1.30	24.21	1.38	0.20	0.56	10.88

Source: Adapted from (Department of Finance, Ministry of Education of China & Department of Social Science & Technology Statistics of the State, Statistics Bureau of China, 2002; Department of Finance, Ministry of Education of China, 2001).

Table 3. Scale of Regular Higher Education System in China by National Development Periods

Period	Year	Number of Institutions	Enrollment Size*
Reorganization	1949	205	116,504
	1957	229	441,181
Great Leap	1958	791	659,627
Forward &	1960	1,289	961,623
Adjustment	1965	434	674,436
Cultural	1966	434	533,766
Revolution	1970	434	47,815
	1976	392	564,715
Reform	1978	598	856,322
	1983	805	1,206,823
	1988	1,075	2,065,900
	1993	1,065	2,535,500
	1998	1,022	3,408,800
	2002	1,396	9,033,600

Note: *undergraduate enrollment.
Source: Educational statistics published by the Ministry of Education/State Education Commission of China.

of students in an institution, and reflects the degree of efficiency in the use of scarce educational resources.

The appropriate aggregate size of higher education has been a subject of intense policy debate among Chinese leaders and educators in post-1949 China. Conflicting views on the subject have been associated with large shifts in student enrollment at the tertiary level. At least three episodes of debate and policy change can be identified. The first episode was seen during the period of the Great Leap Forward and the retrenchment that followed. As part of an ambitious effort to realize full communism, the leadership set a policy of rapid expansion and curriculum reform for higher education in September 1958. The goal was that access to higher education would be provided to qualified youth and adults from all backgrounds in about 15 years' time. Based on the approach of "walking on two legs," the government and non-governmental organizations at central and local levels were encouraged to set up different types of postsecondary institutions. The number of institutions increased from 791 in 1958 to 1,289 in 1960 (see Table 3). Student enrollment jumped from 660,000 to 962,000 in the two-year period, an increase of 46%. This rapid increase put a heavy burden on the financial resources of the government and had an adverse effect on the quality of higher education. Retrenchment inevitably followed, and by 1965 the number of institutions was reduced to 434, while student enrollment had dropped back to the 1958 level.

The second large swing in aggregate scale came during the period of the Cultural Revolution. As the higher education system was paralyzed by political activism, there was a big contraction in student enrollment, with a decline from 534,000 in 1966 to about 48,000 in 1970. Over these years, class background prevailed over merit as the important determinant of entry into higher education. In 1970, students from peasant and working class backgrounds were admitted into the university as part of the strategy of ensuring that education served the interests of rural and working class people.

The third episode took place during the reform period. Actually, for many years there has been considerable agreement among leaders in China about the role of higher education in the preparation of highly skilled personnel and in the development of science and technology. During the decade from 1978 to 1988, the aggregate scale of higher education was on an upward trend, with significant increases in both student enrollment and the number of institutions (see Table 3). The expansion was a response to the need for highly skilled personnel in a rapidly growing economy.

The expansion of the aggregate scale of higher education slowed after 1988, and different views emerged regarding the pace of higher education expansion. One view favored a relatively slow rate of expansion, believing the economy might not be able to absorb all the graduates if its growth slowed down, and that the widespread unemployment of university graduates could cause political unrest. This view prevailed during much of the 1990s. Thus, between 1989 and 1998 enrollment grew at only 5.3% per year, and the number of institutions actually declined from 1,075 to 1,022 (see Table 3).

The other view of higher education expansion maintained that the growing national economy, which was increasingly driven by technological change, could absorb more university graduates. It pointed out that there was a strong parental demand for the expansion of higher education, and it would be a wise national policy to direct private consumption into educational investment. The government adopted this view in the late 1990s, and approved a large increase in new entrants into regular higher education in 1999—from 1.08 million in 1998 to 1.53 million in 1999, a 42% increase—despite concerns voiced by educators about the likely negative impact on quality. The government's motivation was largely economic. Since the onset of the Asian financial crisis of 1997, economic growth in China had slowed from an annual average of 9.5% to about 7%. It was assumed that the increase in higher education enrollment could induce additional private consumption and provide a boost to the rate of GDP growth. In the *Program of Educational Revitalization for the Twenty-First Century* (1999), the government announced a plan to increase new enrollment to 12.5% of the age cohort in 2000, and to 15% by the year 2010, the internationally acknowledged threshold of mass higher education.

While the expansion of the 1980s was characterized by a pattern of creating new institutions, which was probably a legacy of the Soviet model of higher education, expansion in the 1990s switched to a more efficient pattern based on increases in institutional size. Confronting the tensions of growth versus quality, and expansion versus cost-effectiveness, the central government sent a clear message to the higher education sector that no encouragement would be given to build new institutions, and that expansion in enrollments was to be achieved through tapping existing resources and expanding existing institutions. Table 4 shows how the average enrollment size of higher education institutions—and by extension, the student/faculty ratio—increased steadily from 1990 to 2002.

Table 4.   Average Size of Regular Higher Education Institutions in China, 1990–2002

	1990	1995	1996	1997	1998	1999	2000	2001	2002
Number of inst.	1,075	1,054	1,032	1,020	1,022	1,071	1,041	1,225	1,396
Average size	1,919	2,758	2,927	3,112	3,335	3,815	5,289	5,870	6,471
Student/teacher ratios		9.83	10.36	10.87	11.62	13.37	16.30	18.22	19.00

Source: Educational statistics published by the Ministry of Education/State Education Commission of China.

Differentiation of the System

Since the mid-1980s, the Chinese government has implemented a new process of restructuring the higher education system, with the goal of task differentiation, rationalization and redefinition of functions (Central Committee of the Chinese Communist Party and State Council, 1993; Central Committee of the Chinese Communist Party, 1985). This recasting of the policies through which the purposes of higher education are construed has profound consequences for the meaning of diversity in this phase of massification.

The government has encouraged the expansion of adult higher education and the emergence of private higher education institutions. The system is thus moving toward a more diverse one, embracing an increasing variety of institutions and programs in terms of prestige, status, mission, emphasis, services and constituencies. Clearly, differentiation is a means through which the massification of higher education is being achieved, as demonstrated in Table 5.

The most dramatic differentiation process can be observed in the university sector, where a rationale for the current reform has been the creation of "comprehensive universities" from the fragmented and specialized institutions of the 1950s. This represents a horizontal differentiation targeted at correcting the reliance on the Soviet model, and reflects the contemporary patterns of knowledge development and institutionalization in the international arena. Differentiation is also occurring vertically; while Chinese universities had long engaged in a systematic hierarchical ranking—by prestige, level of administration and concomitant resources—this hierarchy is being sharpened in the transition to mass higher education, in the name of enhancing excellence and responding to a greater diversity of needs in the labor market.

The reorganization of the higher education system in the 1950s reflected a rigid institutional separation of pure and applied fields of knowledge, and a strong classification in the impermeable boundaries between disciplines and specialties, as noted earlier. Now, by contrast, there is a clear move towards more comprehensive patterns of knowledge, with all higher education institutions seeking to broaden their curricular coverage, and quite a remarkable development of social science and humanities programs in institutions originally designated as highly specialized technical institutes. The whole process could be seen as a dramatic reversal of the reorganization that took

Table 5. Diversity of the Chinese Higher Education System, 2001

Sector	Institutional Diversity	No. of Institutions	No. of Students
Regular higher education	Institutions offering graduate studies programs	411	371,600
	Institutions offering undergraduate programs	597	5,212,000
	Non-degree and vocational colleges: diploma	628	1,978,700
Adult higher education	Broadcasting & TV (open) universities	45	400,300
	Professional training institutions	409	351,100
	Farmers' training institutions	3	800
	Management cadres' institutions	104	153,900
	Teachers' training institutions	122	304,400
	Independent correspondence course institutions	3	15,500
	Correspondence, night and continuing programs affiliated to regular higher education institutions	–	3,333,800
Other types of higher education	Military academies	–	–
	Self-study examination system	–	13,691,300
	Accredited private higher education institutions (offering degree or diploma programs)	89	151,100
	Non-accredited private higher education institutions	1,202	1,130,400
	Religious institutions	–	–

Source: Adapted from (Hao, 2001: pp. 8–9; Ministry of Education of China, 2002).

place during the 1950s under Soviet guidance. Comprehensive universities have developed a range of applied disciplines, while polytechnic and specialist universities have mainly established departments of basic sciences as well as various social science fields and humanities, in many cases.

Since the late 1950s, there has been a select group of elite institutions which are privileged in terms of the resources they enjoy—the key-point universities. The original number was six in 1954, and it was increased over the years to a total of 98 by the early 1980s (Liu, 1993). The selection of these institutions was done by the government, in accordance with its planning priorities and with the expectation that they would perform as leading institutions within the overall system.

In the 1990s, key-point status has been achieved in quite a different way, with higher education institutions taking the initiative rather than the state. In the 1993 reform document, Project 21/1 expressed the state's intention to identify and give special financial support to the 100 best universities by the 21st century. It put aside significant

Table 6. Proportion of Project 21/1 Universities' Major Resources out of National Total

Resource Item	Project 21/1 Universities' Proportion (%)
Library book volume	25.65
Assets of instrument & equipment	38.70
Bachelor's degree & sub-degree student enrollment	18.33
Master's degree student enrollment	69.14
Doctoral degree student enrollment	86.01
International student enrollment	58.19
Ratio of full professors (national average 9.77)	18.85
Ratio of faculty with doctoral degrees (national average 7.14)	19.25
Research funds	70.10
National key laboratories	100.00
National key programs	83.61
Patent registration	72.81

Source: Adapted from Guo, 2003, p. 16.

incentive money so that its limited resources could be concentrated on the very best institutions. Rather than selecting these, as it had done in the past, institutions had to apply for the funds and demonstrate their excellence through institutional strategic plans. The movement has already caused competition among institutions, with some of the mergers noted earlier being made in order to increase their competitive edge. Of the pre-reform key-point institutions, over 72% were successful in getting into Project 21/1, and now account for nearly 73% of the total. Of the 27% of Project 21/1 universities which formerly did not have key-point status, over 42% are from the developed coastal region, 46% from the medium-developed central region, and less than 12% from the underdeveloped region (Zha, 2003). In spite of the open competition, hinterland institutions are thus clearly disadvantaged. Table 6 shows the striking gap in resources and prestige between the universities in Project 21/1 and all the rest.

The latest developments in this saga began in July of 1999, when the government decided to concentrate its investment on an even smaller number of universities (around 10). Project 98/5, given this name because it was approved during the centennial anniversary of Peking University in May of 1998, aims to nurture a small number of universities at a world-class level. The Project 98/5 universities are all institutions that had key-point status before the reform movement.

Privatization and Marketization of Higher Education

Soon after the founding of the People's Republic of China, all education institutions were converted to government institutions by the new leadership. This was aimed at ridding the country of Western influence and reducing social differentiation. Between 1949 and the late 1970s, the collective ideology was dominant, and individual goals were submerged in favor of social goals.

However, the *Decision on Reform of the Educational System* (1985) indicated that the state would diversify educational services by encouraging non-governmental organizations and individuals to voluntarily contribute to developing education by various forms and methods (Central Committee of Chinese Communist Party, 1985, p. 188). In 1987, the (then) State Education Commission issued *Provisional Regulations on Social Forces Running Educational Establishments*, which established guidelines for "people-run" (*minban*) institutions (Zhou, 1995).

Recognizing the fact that the state alone could not meet people's pressing educational needs, the Chinese leadership deliberately devolved responsibility for education to various non-state sectors. In 1993, the *Outline of Chinese Education Reform and Development* stated for the first time the national policy towards the development of non-state-run education as "active encouragement, strong support, proper guidelines, and sound management" (Central Committee of Chinese Communist Party & State Council, 1993, p. 6). In 1995, China's *Education Law* was promulgated, with Article 25 reconfirming that the state would give full support to enterprises, social forces, local communities and individuals to establish schools under the legal framework of the People's Republic of China (National People's Congress of China, 1995, p. 10). On September 1, 2003, the National People's Congress (China's national legislature) officially enacted the *Law on Promoting Private Education*, which finally put the governance of private education on a firm legal basis (National People's Congress of China, 2002).

By 1986, there were altogether 370 private higher education institutions across the nation. This number has been steadily growing ever since, reaching 880 in 1994, 1,219 in 1996, 1,277 in 1999, and 1,321 in 2000. These institutions enrolled more than one million students in 2000 (National Center for Education Development Research, 2001). This resurgence and growth of private higher education indicates that China has already shifted from a state monopoly to a mixed economy of education. Yet only a handful of the private institutions are officially recognized by the government, and most of their students are those who have failed to gain access to state higher education institutions. In terms of the prestige hierarchy, then, China's private higher education institutions are thus clustered at the bottom of the national system.

Internationalization and Nationalization of Chinese Higher Education

The twin forces of internationalization and nationalization are propelling current reforms in Chinese higher education. These reforms are occurring under the influence of globalization, with an evident convergence of reform policies in higher education around the world. China and its higher education system are no longer immune from international forces. In today's Chinese higher education, there is an increasing stress on market-related notions: management efficiency and strong executive leadership; unit cost effectiveness; institutional responsiveness to socio-economic demands; effective

utilization of resources; the tendency of decentralization and devolution; and the introduction of cost-sharing and cost-recovery principles.

Internationalization combines three main elements: international content in the curriculum; the international movement of scholars and students; and international cooperation programs (Harari, 1978). As early as 1983, the architect of the ongoing
reform in China, Deng Xiaoping, put forward his famous call that "education must
face modernization, the world, and the future" (Department of Policy & Legislature
of State Education Commission, 1992, p. 140). The internationalization of curriculum
and research has been characterized by eclecticism, with curricular materials drawn
from diverse Western countries and real efforts made to adapt them to China's own
development needs. Students are being sent to many parts of the world, and collaborative partnerships in academic exchange and socio-economic development have been
established with many countries, allowing for interesting experiments in knowledge
transfer and adaptation. Thus, different strands of China's own evolving traditions are
being linked up with various foreign influences.

Several hundred thousand Chinese students have taken advantage of the open door
to study abroad, with the largest concentration in North America and increasing numbers in Europe, Japan, Australia, New Zealand and elsewhere. Officially published
statistics indicate that 700,200 have been sent abroad since the late 1970s, and to date
only 172,800 have returned (Liu, 2004). Since the mid-1990s, Chinese students abroad
have begun to see new opportunities for a professional contribution in China, both
in higher education and in industry. Thus, the number of returnees has been rising
at an annual rate of 13% during the most recent 5 years (Wei, 2003). As a result,
the faculty in China's top universities are now as internationalized in outlook and
experience as those in major Western universities, if not more so. One recent report
indicates that 78% of the presidents of the universities under the jurisdiction of the
Ministry of Education, and 62% of the doctoral program supervisors in those universities, have had the experience of studying abroad (Liu, 2004). The same report
notes that 81% of academic professionals at the Chinese Academy of Sciences are
returnees.

China's growth as an international power has been accompanied by increasing calls
for the revival of traditional values. The current process of selecting diverse elements
and integrating them within China's own emerging practice is an expression of the
search for national identity and national strength. While in most of the earlier periods
under discussion, there were one or two foreign influences that tended to be dominant,
the current process is neither a matter of all-out negation of traditional Chinese culture
nor all-out westernization. Rather, it represents a transition from critiquing tradition
to critically absorbing tradition, from a holistic copying of foreign patterns to a more
eclectic selection of what is best suited to China.

The combined effects of the deep-rooted strength of Chinese cultural traditions and
the open door policy, with the increasing number of returnees from the West, have
allowed China to offer a unique model of successful East-West academic integration.
With Project 21/1 and Project 98/5, China has set out to make a few of its universities
world-class. As these universities gain the resources needed to pursue world-class

standing, they may well bring new vitality and new cultural resources into the world community.

Conclusion: The State of Chinese Higher Education Today

Major Successes

Looking back to the beginnings of the reform program in China, it is obvious that the Cultural Revolution left a difficult legacy. Nevertheless, the reform of Chinese higher education has achieved notable success. First of all, there has been a successful decentralization process, and a new model has emerged, characterized by the localization of institutions, the diversification of their funding sources, and a dynamic responsiveness to the local economy. Related to this change is the emergence of private institutions. The movements of localization and privatization have further reduced the role of the state, increased the individuality of institutions, and mobilized local initiatives and resources. These trends, in turn, have contributed a great deal to the remarkable expansion of the system.

Higher education in China has expanded tremendously, with over a threefold increase in enrollment (from 2.1 million to 9.1 million) between 1990 and 2002. If part-time students and those enrolled in non-formal and private institutions are included, the student population in 2003 reached 19 million, a figure that represents the largest higher education enrollment in the world, surpassing even the United States (Hayhoe & Zha, 2004). At present, about 17% of China's population between 18 and 22 are enrolled in some sort of postsecondary education (Ministry of Education of China, 2004a), which means China crossed the threshold of mass higher education nearly a decade ahead of its original plan, within an education system that is receiving less than 4% of the government's budgeted expenditure. Another success is the longevity of the reform program despite the controversial nature of some of its goals. Unlike the sudden policy shifts of the past, the essential thrust of the current reform has remained intact for over two decades, despite emerging tensions.

Emerging Tensions

The sweeping changes to Chinese higher education in the reform period have brought problems as well as achievements. The first problem is the paradox of state-led decentralization, which is manifested by the disparities between the policy intention and some of the measures taken in the process of reform. The policy shortcomings of the Chinese higher education reform are somewhat heightened by the paradoxical role of the Chinese government in the reform process: initiating innovations in the universities on the one hand and adopting an instrumentalist approach on the other. As we have noted, a series of policy documents between 1985 and 1999 tended to grant more and more autonomy to Chinese universities, and bring market elements into their management and operations, while the *Higher Education Law* (1998) defined their autonomy and status as legal entities. However, these policy documents have never limited the power of government, which still exercises the right to manage, direct and even punish the university from time to time. The overwhelming policy emphasis has been on higher education as an instrument of economic development, and any discourse on the idea of a modern university has been avoided. The emphasis has been on short-term considerations, with little attention given to the "substantive" autonomy of the university.

Second, the dramatic increases in tertiary enrollment throughout the 1990s were accompanied by disproportional higher education budget allocations. For the period 1993–2002, enrollment in the formal higher education sector increased nearly three-fold, from 2.5 million to 9.1 million, yet the average expenditure per student increased by only 50.6%, and the average public expenditure per student by only 20.2%. While the state's tertiary funding has increased in absolute terms, it has decreased in per capita terms. This is also evident with the fact that governmental appropriations now account for only around 30% (on average) of the institutions' annual operating funds (Tsinghua University Education Research Institute, 2003). This governmental retreat from investment in higher education has forced the universities and colleges to find their own funding—a move that could better integrate them into society, and yet has also forced them to design a market-oriented education to meet the needs of the economy. Rather than being academies for learning, universities have to function as educational enterprises. This has aroused concern over the issue of academic quality.

Third, deep divisions between elite and non-elite institutions, formal and non-formal institutions, and public and private institutions are being aggravated by the decentralization of the system, and by deliberate stratification policies. China is divided into three major economic development zones: the coastal area includes highly developed provinces, the central zone comprises medium-developed provinces and the west is a less-developed region. Higher education development differs in each region due to very different socio-economic conditions. For example, during the 1990s, the vast investments in the eastern coastal area—and the economic, scientific and technological advantages it enjoys as a result—have resulted in increasing disparities between this region and the hinterland. Furthermore, Project 21/1 and Project 98/5 have focused central resources on elite universities, which are mainly located in more advantaged regions. Even in a culture of meritocracy, this phenomenon of increasing inequity has been attracting negative attention.

Last but not least, the hierarchical structure and financial disparities affect university internationalization. Higher education institutions with prestige or in more developed areas are in a much better position to engage actively with foreign partners and gain funding to support these efforts. By contrast, institutions without prestige or in poorer areas often feel helpless when faced with the difficulty of gaining opportunities for international involvement. The increasing differentiation among Chinese higher education institutions means that the elite and better-resourced institutions can take greater advantage of opportunities brought by globalization and internationalization, which then creates a tension for them between maintaining integration with global trends and satisfying local needs.

Chinese Higher Education in the 21st Century

The objective of the current reform journey is to establish a higher education system with "Chinese characteristics" (Yang, 1998). Thus, the future of Chinese higher education depends greatly on the interpretation of "Chinese characteristics." For more than five decades, the Chinese leadership fought over alternative goals and approaches to national development, and the higher education system served as a reactive vehicle for realizing the leadership's development objectives rather than an autonomous institution for social change. For some years to come, higher education will likely remain a "driven" social institution, with the degree of autonomy it enjoys (vis-à-vis the Chinese state) depending on the extent of political reform.

Nevertheless, the decentralization process has begun, and Chinese higher education reform reflects the international context of devolution and marketization. Hopefully, ongoing reforms will nourish an intellectually vibrant and internationally competitive system. Domestically, higher education institutions will provide a foundation for national development based on science, technology, and a comparative advantage in human resources. As knowledge becomes a productive force in its own right, what we are going to see is an incorporation of higher education into the central framework of China's society. Higher education will increasingly function as a promoter of both social and individual development. The large size and multipurpose orientation of most Chinese universities will enhance their capacity to make a transformative contribution to political and social change within China. Internationally, Chinese higher education will be keen to build an international dimension to its knowledge base by pooling wisdom with diverse countries facing similar problems, by using an international template to view domestic development in a fresh light, and by drawing international benchmarks to assess the performance of its own system.

References

Abe, H. (1987). Borrowing from Japan: China's first modern educational system. In R. Hayhoe & M. Bastid (Eds.), *China's education and the industrialized world: Studies in cultural transfer*. Armonk, NY: M.E. Sharpe.

Central Committee of Chinese Communist Party. (1985). Guanyu jiaoyu tizhi gaike de queding (Decision on the reform of the education system). In Department of Policy & Legislature of State Education Commission (Ed.), *Shiyi jie san zhong quanhui yilai zhongyao jiaoyu wenxian xuanbian (Selection of important education policy papers since the third plenary session of the 11th national congress of Chinese Communist Party)* (pp. 182–189). Beijing, China: Jiaoyu kexue chubanshe (Educational Science Publishing House).

Central Committee of Chinese Communist Party & State Council. (1993). *Zhongguo jiaoyu gaige he fazhan gangyao (Outline for reform and development of education in China)*. Available online at: http://www.edu.cn/special/showarticle.php?id=298. Retrieved September 16, 2001.

Chen, P. (2002). *Zhongguo daxue shi jiang (Ten topics on Chinese universities)*. Shanghai, China: Fudan University Press.

Chen, X. & Tian, Z. (Eds.). (1991). *Liuxue jiaoyu (The education of students abroad)*. Shanghai, China: Shanghai jiaoyu chubanshe (Shanghai Education Press).

Cheng, K. M. (1998). Reforms in the administration and financing of higher education. In M. Agelasto & B. Adamson (Eds.), *Higher education in Post-Mao China* (pp. 11–25). Hong Kong: Hong Kong University Press.

Department of Finance, Ministry of Education of China. (2001). *Jiaoyu touru xiangguan jichu ziliao (Basic facts relevant to education investment)*. Beijing: Department of Finance of Ministry of Education of China.

Department of Finance, Ministry of Education of China & Department of Social Science & Technology Statistics of the State, Statistics Bureau of China. (Eds.). (2002). *Zhongguo jiaoyu jingfei tongji nianjian 2001 (China educational finance statistical yearbook 2001)*. Beijing, China: China Statistics Press.

Department of Policy & Legislature of State Education Commission. (Ed.). (1992). *Shiyi jie san zhong quanhui yilai zhongyao jiaoyu wenxian xuanbian (Selection of important education policy papers since the third plenary session of the 11th national congress of Chinese Communist Party)*. Beijing, China: Jiaoyu kexue chubanshe (Educational Science Publishing House).

Du, R. (1992). *Chinese higher education: A decade of reform and development (1978–1988)*. New York: St. Martin's Press.

Galt, H. (1951). *A history of Chinese educational institutions*. London: Arthur Probsthain.

Gu, S. (1964). *Education systems in Chinese dynasties*. Nanjing, China: Jiangsu People's Publishing House.

Guo, X. (2003). Cong daxue gongneng leiji fenbu guilü kan gaodeng jiaoyu zhongdian jianshe (Key building of higher education in the view of the cumulative distribution rule of university function). *Zhongguo gaodeng jiaoyu (China Higher Education), 24*(19), 15–17.

Hao, K. (Ed.). (2001). *Dangdai zhongguo jiaoyu jiegou tixi yanjiu (A study on the structural system of contemporary Chinese education)*. Guangzhou, China: Guangdong Education Press.

Harari, M. (1978). Internationalization of higher education. In A.S. Knowles (Ed.), *The international encyclopedia of higher education*, (Vol. 5, pp. 2293–2301). San Francisco: Jossey-Bass Publishers.

Hawkins, J. N. (1991). Educational reform in China: One step forward, two steps backward. In P. Cookson (Ed.), *Handbook on Educational Reform*. Westport, CT: Greenwood Press.

Hayhoe, R. (1989a). China's universities and Western academic models. In P. G. Altbach & V. Selvaratnam (Eds.), *From dependence to autonomy: The development of Asian universities* (pp. 25–61). Dordrecht, The Netherlands: Kluwer Academic Publishers.

Hayhoe, R. (1989b). *China's universities and the open door*. Armonk, NY: M.E. Sharpe.

Hayhoe, R. (1996). *China's universities, 1895–1995: A century of cultural conflict*. New York: Garland Publishing.

Hayhoe, R. & Zha, Q. (2004). Becoming world-class: Chinese universities facing globalization and internationalization. *Harvard China Review 5*(1), 87–92.

Hu, R. & Bu, Z. (1999). Youhua buju jiegou gaige guanli tizhi (Optimize distributional patterns and reform governance mechanism). In X. Chen (Ed.), *Zhongguo gaodeng jiaoyu yanjiu 50 nian: 1949–1999 (Higher education research in China for 50 years: 1949–1999)* (pp. 1177–1180). Beijing, China: Educational Science Publishing House.

Hu, S. M. & Seifman, E. (Eds.). (1976). *Toward a new world outlook. A documentary history of education in the People's Republic of China, 1949–1976*. New York: AMS Press, Inc.

Johnson, T. M. (1989). The economics of higher education reform in China. *China Exchange News, 17*(1), 3–7.

Liu, N. (2004, March 1). Jin ba cheng jiaoyubu zhishu gaoxiao xiaozhang you guo liuxue jingli (Nearly 80% of the presidents of the universities under jurisdiction of Ministry of Education of China have experience if studying abroad). *Zhongguo jiaoyu bao (China Education Daily)*, p. 1.

Liu, Y. (Ed.). (1993). *Zhongguo jiaoyu dashi dian (The chronicle of Chinese education events)*. Hangzhou, China: Zhejiang Education Press.

Min, W. & Chen, X. (1994). Zhongguo gaodeng jiaoyu jingfei xuqiu yu touzi tizhi gaige (The financial needs of higher education and the reform of investment system). *Jiaoyu yanjiu [Educational Research], 1994*(12), 30–38.

Ministry of Education of China. (2001). *Hezuo banxue xuexiao mingdan (A list of the higher education institutions involved in institutional cooperation)*. Education Administration Information Centre, Ministry of Education of China. Available online at http://www.moe.edu.cn/highedu/gxtz/hzbx.htm. Retrieved November 1, 2001.

Ministry of Education of China. (Ed.). (2002). *Zhongguo jiaoyu nianjian (China education yearbook) 2002*. Beijing, China: Renmin jiaoyu chubanshe (People's Education Press).

Ministry of Education of China. (2003a). *92 nian yilai gaoxiao hebing qingkuang (Higher education institutional mergers since 1992)*. Education Administration Information Centre, Ministry of Education of China. Available online at http://www.moe.edu.cn/stat/gxtiaozheng. Retrieved May 20, 2004.

Ministry of Education of China. (2003b). *Gaoxiao shoufei gaige wenti jianjian (A brief introduction to fees-charging practice in higher education institutions)*. Available online at http://www.edu.cn/20031219/3096236.shtml. Retrieved December 21, 2003.

Ministry of Education of China. (2003c). *Zi 92 nian yilai huazhuan xuexiao mingdan (A list of higher education institutions that experienced transference of affiliation since 1992)*. Education Administration Information Center, Ministry of Education of China. Available online at http://www.moe.edu.cn/highedu/gxtz/hzxx.htm. Retrieved March 4, 2003.

Ministry of Education of China. (2004a). *2003 nian quanguo jiaoyu shiye fazhan tongji gongbao (2003 national education development statistics bulletin)*. China Education and Research Network. Available online at http://www.edu.cn/20040527/3106677.shtml. Retrieved May 27, 2004.

Ministry of Education of China. (2004b). *Survey of the educational reform and development in China*. Available online at http://www.moe.edu.cn/news/2004_01/03.htm. Retrieved February 8, 2004.

Mok, K.-H. & Lo, Y.-W. (2004). Daxue zhengbing yu zhongguo gaodeng jiaoyu zhili bianqian (University merging and changing higher education governance in China). *Jiaoyu zhengce luntan (Education Policy Forum)*, 7(1), 83–100.

National Center for Education Development Research (Ed.). (2001). *2001 nian zhongguo jiaoyu lv pi shu (2001 Green Paper on Education in China. Annual Report on Policies of China's Education)*. Beijing: Educational Science Publishing House.

National People's Congress of China. (1995). Education Law of the People's Republic of China. In Ministry of Education of China (Ed.), *The Laws on Education of the People's Republic of China* (pp. 2–31). Beijing, China: Foreign Languages Press.

National People's Congress of China. (1998). Higher education law of the People's Republic of China. In Ministry of Education of China (Ed.), *The laws on education of the People's Republic of China* (pp. 87–116). Beijing, China: Foreign Languages Press.

National People's Congress of China. (2002). *Zhonghua renmin gongheguo minban jiaoyu cujin fa (The law of the People's Republic of China on promoting private education)*. China Education and Research Network. Available online at http://www.moe.edu.cn/moe-dept/yanjiu/FALV/cujinfa.htm. Retrieved June 13, 2004.

State Council & Ministry of Education of China. (1999). Mianxiang 21 shiji jiaoyu zhengxing xingdong jihua (Program of educational revitalization for the twenty-first century). In Ministry of Education of China (Ed.), *Zhongguo jiaoyu nianjian (China education yearbook) 1999* (pp. 107–116). Beijing, China: Renmin jiaoyu chubanshe (People's Education Press).

Tsinghua University Education Research Institute. (2003). Chuangjian yiliu: Guojia yizhi yu daxue jingsheng de jiehe (Establishing the first-class university: A combination of state will and university spirits). *Zhongguo gaodeng jiaoyu (China Higher Education)*, 2003(12), 16–18.

Wang, S. & Zhou, W. (1991). Woguo putong gaodeng jiaoyu jingfei bokuan jizhi (Regular higher education allocation mechnism in China). *Jiaoyu yu jingji (Education and Economy)*, 1991(4).

Wei, Y. (2003). Chuguo liuxue gongzuo ershi nian (Twenty years work summary of sending students to study abroad). In Ministry of Education of China (Ed.), *Zhongguo jiaoyu nianjian (China education yearbook) 1999* (pp. 45–50). Beijing, China: Renmin jiaoyu chubanshe [People's Education Press].

World Bank. (1997). *China: Higher education reform*. Washington, DC: World Bank.

World Bank. (1999). *The strategic goals of Chinese education in the 21st century*. Washington, DC: World Bank.

Xie, Y. (2001). *Zhongguo xiandai daxue de "zhidu sheji" (The "institutional designing" of modern Chinese universities)*. Available online at http://www.edu.cn/special/showarticle.php?id=5586. Retrieved April 26, 2001.

Yang, R. (1998). A higher education system with Chinese characteristics: Rhetoric or reality? *International Higher Education*, 28(1), 26–41.

Zha, Q. (2003). Stratification trends in Chinese higher education. *Canadian Society for the Study of Higher Education Professional File, 23*(Fall).

Zhou, N. (1995). The evolution and policies concerning NGO-sponsored higher education in China. In T.-I. Wongsothorn & Y. Wang (Eds.), *Private higher education in Asia and the Pacific: Final report, Part I: Seminar papers*. Bangkok, Thailand: UNESCO PROAP and SEAMO RIHED.

Zhou, Y. (Ed.). (1990). *Education in contemporary China*. Changsha, China: Hunan Education Publishing House.

Zhou, Y. (2001). Vital reform and innovation of higher education system. *China Higher Education, 2001*(1).

35

EGYPT

Iman Farag
Research Center for Economic, Legal and Social Studies, Egypt

In 2008, Egypt will likely celebrate the centenary of its first modern university, known today as the Old Egyptian University. Originally established as a private institution in 1908, it became the State University in 1925, was later renamed Fouad the First, in the name of the King of Egypt, and then became Cairo University after the 1952 revolution. There is no doubt that Cairo University—with its remarkable architecture—today constitutes one of Egypt's leading "places of memory," to use a term by the French historian Pierre Nora (Nora, 1997). From national historiography to cinema, from novels to autobiographies, it seems that the university campus has always been seen as an actor in—or at least a witness to—the country's historical events (not to mention the millions of personal lives that the university has significantly changed). Like in most historical commemorations, Egyptians will have mixed feelings (and some bitterness too), when comparing the magnified glories of the past with the university's present situation.

While commemorating the past, no doubt politicians and members of the academic community will point to ongoing reforms. Their aims are to modernize and rationalize the acquisition, transmission and evaluation of knowledge according to global standards, while driven directly by local problems—especially those of employment and employability of higher education graduates. In February 2000, a National Conference on Higher Education endorsed a long-term Higher Education Enhancement Project (HEEP)—funded primarily by foreign donors in concert with local resources—comprising 25 initiatives regarding access, quality assurance, efficiency, relevance and finance of higher education. The first phase of HEEP is to be implemented through 2007, and covers 12 priority components such as quality assurance and accreditation; the reform of faculties of education and of technical institutes; and the improvement of information and communication technologies (Said, 2004).

Today, some 12 state universities (including several branches) are spread throughout Egypt. The country's university landscape also includes al-Azhar University, offering religious as well as secular academic courses; an American University in Cairo, established in 1920 under a special agreement; and nine private universities, established between the 1990s and 2005, enrolling roughly 36,834 students. The higher education system also includes higher and intermediate institutes, both public (around 52)

James J.F. Forest and Philip G. Altbach (eds.), International Handbook of Higher Education, 693–709.
© 2006 *Springer. Printed in the Netherlands.*

and private (90). State universities and institutes are the principal providers of higher education, with the latter enrolling about 22% of Egypt's 18–22 year-old age group (about 1.95 million registered students, according to 2004 official figures). The Ministry of Higher Education and Scientific Research and the Supreme Council of Universities exercise overall control over the system.

While the terms of recent higher education reforms seem to proceed partially from a global agenda, the outcomes will remain local. In preparing for the expected commemorations of Cairo University's centenary, authorities will try to bridge the gap between the past and the future, and will probably explain how the ongoing reforms will make a difference. But will this be the same university? If the time has come for virtual universities, what is the role of the campus and prestigious buildings? Higher education graduates and students constitute a significant part of the population as well as a key factor of the political equilibrium, in a society that is still characterized by a high rate of illiteracy. Therefore, we should expect that higher education's stake will not be reduced to managerial or technical aspects, while sociopolitical considerations are somehow absorbed into academic dimensions. Should we dissociate higher education from what have always been the representations that were associated to the campus as a public space: success, social status and social mobility, the best jobs and salaries, self-esteem and dignity, contentious politics and citizenship? Will higher education remain among the public goods, and who is entitled to define the frontiers of public goods? How can a symbol of national pride become a national burden? How does the State's orientation meet with the individuals' expectations, and how are these multiple and changing expectations affected by a set of socio-political variables, including employment, the social value of knowledge, and new forms of social inequities?

While it is clearly difficult to answer these questions about the future, they frame an intellectual context in which this chapter will examine the socio-historical construction of a set of dilemmas, questions and representations that are associated with the acquisition of the highest form of knowledge. As in other Third World countries, higher education in Egypt has been deeply rooted in a modernization and nation-building narrative. Collective as well as individual dreams for a better future have been encompassed in higher education's promise, although nowadays, it seems to be associated with the counter-narrative of the failure of modernization. Indeed, from the lack of democratic values to unemployment crises and weak industrialization, higher education has been rendered responsible for a series of problems. The first part of this chapter will examine the questions and the conditions of the formative period at the beginning of the 20th century, then turn to the heritage of the 1960s—a period that had long-lasting and decisive effects that are still present in Egypt. Finally, the chapter will focus on three major items of contemporary debate—quality assurance, corruption and privatization—and the ways in which they may introduce changes in the higher education system.

From Philanthropy to State University

Beginning in 1990, severe criticisms were directed toward higher education in the Arab world, lamenting the conditions of knowledge transmission and acquisition in overcrowded campuses; the inadequacy of qualifications with job market prerequisites as well as with fundamental research necessities; the social selectivity of admissions; the geographic disparity of access; the gender gap in student participation; and the imbalance between humanities and science programs (UNDP, 2003). One response was that, compared to the Europeans, universities of the Arab world had a late emergence in an inadequate context, and were designed according to a pattern that was already beginning to face a crisis in its original context. This is at least what is suggested by the Egyptian demographer Nader Fergany, editor of the well-known Arab Human Development Report. According to Fergany, "Higher, especially university, education has already achieved in industrialized countries widespread coverage, at a high level of quality, in an integrated (social, economic, political and cultural) context that was partly made possible through the active contribution of higher education itself. Such societal context is far from complete in Arab countries and, in particular, higher education did not contribute to building such a context yet. Perhaps the most salient feature of modern higher education institutions in the Arab countries is their relatively recent origins" (Fergany, 2001).

Focusing on the case of the Egyptian university at the beginning of the 20th century allows us to formulate significant questions about the stakes of the formative period. For example: Who were the founders? What did they have in mind when they thought about a university? To what models were they referring? And to start with, what was particular about this new establishment and how was it going to fit with the other components of Egypt's educational system at the beginning of the 20th century?

The state system of education was established in the 1820s under the reign of Muhammad Ali, Viceroy of Egypt (1805–1849), who governed the country on behalf of the Ottoman Sultan. A top-down, integrated and selective system of official primary and secondary schools led to prestigious higher schools, according to the needs of the state apparatus, and graduates were systematically oriented to the army or civil servant functions and gained a prestigious social status. They were in essence adopted by the state. Scientific missions, foreign advisors and teachers, and studies abroad were seen as essential parts of this system. Parallel to this was the azhari system, where the aims were different; after a few years of Koranic basic schools, students could have access to al-Azhar University and leave it at any age. The degrees earned through this system were rather authorizations to transmit knowledge and to perform religious rituals. By the end of the 19th century, there was also a set of missionary schools and private Egyptian schools founded by philanthropic elites. This allows us to understand why the founders of the first Egyptian university stressed two particular dimensions—for them, a university meant both all branches of knowledge as well as knowledge that was different from what already existed within the state's higher official schools.

It is worth noting that the political context was first marked by British colonial rule (1882–1922), and that educational policies were among the major grounds in the battle between national elites and foreign domination. For educated elites, this had to do with patriotic feelings as well as social mobility perspectives and political leadership. While a national movement for an Egyptian university was launched in 1907 and raised substantial donations from educated elites and rich landowners, under the patronage of Prince Fouad the First, intellectual debates were addressing the aims of the new establishment and raising questions and criticisms. Since 1890, there had been suggestions about merging the various higher schools into a university, while other debates addressed possible patterns and examples like the Muhammadan Anglo-oriental College (in India) or the Syrian Protestant College of Beirut. These models seemed unsatisfactory to the Egyptians, as these universities didn't teach all disciplines (like Oxford).

When Cairo University was inaugurated on December 21, 1908, initial programs of study focused on history and humanities, particularly western knowledge about Arabs and Islam (or what was commonly known as orientalism), taught mainly by foreign professors. This was something effectively different from what was already taught in higher official schools, and such knowledge was not directed toward preparing for a civil servant career.

A brief description of the university's formative years (Bedayr, 1950) indicates that this modern, secular, somehow mundane yet enlightened institution followed the pattern of al-Azhar, while incorporating some common features of early European universities (such as Heidelberg and the Sorbonne during the Middle Ages) (Le Goff, 1985). The result was an open institution for broad cultural diffusion, embracing knowledge for the sake of knowledge. Among regular students, belonging to several nationalities, there were civil servants, teachers, judges, lawyers and members of other liberal professions (like writers and journalists), and even ladies from high society. However, the majority of students were those who were already students of the high schools or al-Azhar, seeking another kind of knowledge.

It is important to note that between 1908 and World War I, the university sent to Europe about 50 of its students in order to prepare them to assume staff and leadership roles in the university. Among them were many children who were sent to primary education in European schools. This is not to say that the Egyptian society had no modern idea about childhood education, but rather, that the modern civil institutions were perpetuating state practices of the 19th century as well as the Court *habitus*: in fact, young Prince Fouad himself was raised in Italy.

University professors were either Egyptians or Europeans with a variety of profiles and credentials, ranging from azhari graduates to famous orientalists, or "cultivated gentlemen." Years later, the criteria for measuring academic competence were spelled out more clearly, but the cosmopolitan feature was still in effect. Between courses at home and missions abroad, a network of foreign masters and Egyptian disciples developed. Through this system, Durkheim's ideas were diffused through his Egyptian students, while young French teachers at the university became great names upon returning to their home countries—like Alexandre Koyre, the historian of sciences. Under the state university policies and the progressive trend of Egyptianization, there emerged several struggles placing Egyptians in opposition to foreigners (mainly British). However, in other cases, Egyptians had access to professorial positions simply as disciples and successors of their foreign teachers. To this we should add a serious competition between the French and British over the new institution. One should note that with foreign teachers at home and national students abroad, this early internationalization of knowledge, although unequal, did not have to wait for free trade agreements, and in spite of modern facilities, moved across political borders more easily than today. Some researchers raised important concerns about scientific societies in Egypt at that time, particularly regarding the pros and cons of European influences in academe: for example, should we speak about colonial sciences or universal scientific knowledge?

Hybrid practices within the first Egyptian university were balanced by progressive institutionalization: the courses were organized in a faculty of arts, exams were made mandatory, and the university delivered degrees and even doctorates. However, since its establishment there was a critical question related to state recognition and accreditation, and hence, eventual access to public employment. Significantly, the issue was raised when the university began to negotiate official positions for the students who had returned from their missions abroad. An unemployed "Docteur d'Etat" of the Sorbonne was something that no one could accept. Around World War I, the university was characterized by a decline in the number of registered students and by a financial crisis. In 1917, there was another trend toward a state university and the argument was quite similar to that of 1907; higher schools are not enough.

A long process of negotiations between state authorities and the university eventually led to the foundation of the State University in 1925. It is only with this foundation that "academia as a new profession" was established in Egypt (Reed, 1991, p. 83). The originally private philanthropic institution, which was gradually transformed into a Faculty of Arts and a newly founded Faculty of Sciences (based on the previous scientific branch of the Teacher's College), was merged progressively with the state's higher schools (law, medicine, engineering, etc.) under the single banner of Fouad University. It is worth noting that the American University in Cairo was inaugurated in 1920, and that at the time the British representatives in Egypt were not hostile to the State University, although they had been reluctant to accept the philanthropic institution established earlier in the century.

In the mid-1930s, a series of rather independent factors contributed to reshape—for quite a long period of time—the face of the State University. On one hand, students began demonstrating against corrupt political elites who failed to achieve Egypt's national independence. This was by no means their first form of political activism, as they were usually engaged in anti-colonial actions. However, contesting the national political elites revealed a new potential for the students' movement—to serve as a protest movement. What was known in Egypt and other Arab societies as "the youth years" should be considered within the scope of youth movements that emerged in Europe during the same period. On another hand, there was a conjectural employment crisis following economic depression, and the state—the main employer—was unable for a while to provide jobs for graduates. University students were thus demonstrating against both corrupt leaders and the lack of jobs. It is worth noting that although there was no codified state obligation in terms of employment, students' and graduates' claims were considered fully legitimate. At the same time, Egypt was experiencing broad worker unemployment and underemployment (although unemployment among illiterate workers was considered an entirely different phenomena), and while this was treated in the realm of larger social questions and the battle against poverty, delinquency and dangerous class containment, the unemployment of graduates was considered to be merely a political issue (Farag, 1999a, 1999b). It is obvious that as soon as the university was labeled as a state university, it brought heightened employment claims and expectations. While the financial crisis was presented as the main reason for the collapse of the first university, one may wonder about a set of multiple and complementary reasons related to the viability of the pattern; the university could not make it without the state's umbrella, while the state's umbrella was simultaneously translated into legitimate expectations of access to employment.

Toward Mass Universities: The Heritage of the 1960s

When a group of officers launched the July 23, 1952 Revolution and put an end to the monarchy, Fouad the First University was re-named Cairo University. However, some facts about the social and political impetus of Egypt's universities were already well established. A university degree had become a prestigious social asset, providing access to the most distinguished and well paid jobs. Academia was at the heart of intellectual life, and being a professor at the university was seen as the highest level of excellence, giving social prestige, good salaries, political careers, access to the media and the legitimacy that authorized professors to give their opinions on questions far removed from their academic specialties. The campus was a significant component of the polity, and university students were the most visible group acting politically; they constituted properly the wealth of the nation, and hence their demands and claims had a significant political impetus. The campus was thus a very particular and central place, and—despite its lack of autonomy from political power—had its own rules of the game. This was the set of representations that the Free Officers inherited from the Old Regime, which can be summed up in one sentence: if there was a prominent citizen in Egypt, he was a higher education graduate.

Free education began in 1950, starting with the primary education level and then extended to other levels progressively, eventually including higher education in 1962. During these years, the ideal type of a higher educated "son of the revolution" could be described as follows: he belonged to a poor family, his father was a worker who was benefiting for the first time in history from codified working conditions and a secure job in the public sector, or a peasant who had access to land property thanks to the agrarian reform. The young higher educated were mostly represented as an engineer—one of the actors of Egypt's industrialization—or a physician contributing to the well-being and modernization of a backward country. From movies to social realistic paintings, this image of the university graduate constituted the basis for a social contract. It is still difficult to measure how far the representation was effective. Several investigations demonstrate that most of those who benefited from higher education already possessed social assets that enabled their access to free higher education. A majority of them were sons of white-collar families. Urban and middle-class biased social politics comforted social reproduction mechanisms. Still, new social groups had an uneven access to higher education. Most important is the fact that education was established as the main channel for social mobility as well as a means for correcting what has been presented as centuries of injustice and deprivations. Although times have changed, mentalities have not; it is not exaggerating to say that people's expectations still carry this emotional and symbolic charge that associates education with dignity, and knowledge with social power. This can justify in a sense an approach that supercedes classical political chronologies to focus on change and permanence in expectations. In sectors like education or health, it takes years and generations before public policies produce facts, social conducts and representations that validate their reality. As described later in this chapter, a number of changes may have affected the social (as well as political) contract, including changes in value systems, disconnections between wealth (or at least well-being) and knowledge, and what is known in Egypt as the erosion of the middle class.

The 1960s had another major effect on higher education, by consolidating the relationship between education and employment. Under the old regime, this relationship was already well established. During the 1960s, what had been a political norm was consolidated and took the legal form of a formal commitment by the State to secure jobs in the government administration and in the public sector. It was first applied to higher education graduates (in 1961–1962) and then extended to graduates of secondary schools and technical education (in 1964). It should be noted that at the time, private sector employment opportunities were considerably reduced, and in addition to better salaries, employment in the public sector was stable and complemented by a series of social guarantees. In a sense, one can say that guaranteed employment gave a boost to education, at least within some social groups. For about a quarter of a century, solid expectations considering higher education were fostered and deeply rooted.

This state commitment to providing employment has been progressively abrogated since the end of the 1970s; the public sector still does recruit higher education graduates, although in reduced numbers. It is important to note that for those graduates who have limited social capital and nothing to compete with on the job market except their degrees, employment in the public sector and the government remains a first (and yet sometime inaccessible) choice. Despite weak salaries, these positions offer a level of job stability, retirement and health insurance benefits that most of the private sector companies or the informal sector cannot guarantee. Further, most young educated people do not seem convinced of the potential benefits of self-employment. In addition, reduced bureaucratic working hours allow those who work for the government (regardless of their academic qualifications) to hold a second or even third occasional job in the so-called informal sector, which is becoming larger than the formal one. Multiple employment activities have become the norm, and several researchers have demonstrated that young educated people are learning how to live with uncertainty, how to deal with changing circumstances and to develop nomadic working strategies (Tourné, 2003).

However, the expanding private sector has so far been unable to compensate for declining state employment opportunities, while migration opportunities to Gulf States— a strong employment market—were drastically reduced. While trying to earn a living through occasionally, weakly regulated and more or less temporary jobs (that do not correspond to their academic background), most higher education graduates today actually face two competing and complementary prospects. On one hand, small and micro-projects are offered to encourage young entrepreneurs to develop into big entrepreneurs. On the other hand, for a few highly qualified graduates with additional skills, impressive social networks and selective academic backgrounds, there are prospects for highly remunerated positions in certain sectors of the economy related to technological and managerial competencies. Here, the job market is no longer a national one, but is instead tied to global standards.

Contemporary discrepancies of employment in Egypt lead some commentators to speak about the failure of the educational policies inherited from the 1960s. In their opinion, the expansion of higher education was nothing more than an attempt to produce a populist response to people's expectations, and was not preceded by a coherent vision about what to do with the higher educated.

Impact of the Expansion of Higher Education

Were Egypt's higher education expansion efforts a failure or an overt success? A closer look at some of the dynamics related to the expansion and its internal effects on higher education is instructive. In its first academic year (1925–1926), the State University had only 2,027 students. By 1983, enrollment had reached 150,000—even though, according to a UNESCO-sponsored study, Cairo University's buildings were appropriate for only 35,000 (Reed, 1991, p. 221). What goes for Cairo, which benefited from the exceptional historical conditions of its foundation, goes for most of the other 11 universities in the country as well, in terms of limited physical space used by increasing numbers of students, academic staff and administration. This in turn has impacted the conditions of learning and teaching in overcrowded amphitheaters. The already authoritative relationship between professors and students has been reinforced, and magisterial courses tend to replace class discussions. In some departments, students have come to the conclusion that attending courses is relatively useless, and for them the campus remains more of a leisure place where they can at least meet their friends. With growth in enrollment, teaching and learning also rely more heavily on textbooks and notes, amid a scarcity of resources in university libraries, although in some disciplines, private lessons are helping students succeed in their exams.

Further, an already unsatisfactory student/faculty ratio was aggravated during the 1970s by an important wave of Egyptian academic migration to the Gulf countries. This migration has additional social effects, particularly by widening the gap between the standards of living enjoyed by those professors who migrated to the Gulf universities (where they received substantial salaries), and those professors who remained in Egypt, whose salaries appeared insignificant and undervalued by comparison (Reed, 1991, p. 216). Since the 1970s, teaching staff salaries have remained low and particularly incongruent with the perceived social status and prestige of academic positions. Further, while Egypt exported academia to the Gulf countries, it imported several forms of conservatism as well as new lifestyles and modes of consumption.

The expansion of higher education in Egypt was geographic as well. After Cairo (1925), universities were founded in Alexandria (1942); Ain Shams (1950) and Hilwan (1975) near Cairo; Assiout (1952), Minia (1976) and South Valley (1994) in the south of Egypt; and Tanta (1972), Mansoura (1972), Zaqaziq (1974), Menufiyya (1976), and Suez Canal (1976) in the north of Egypt.

The original pattern of a campus—i.e., that of Cairo University, with its impressive physical presence—was still effective, at least as a pale shadow, but the resources were diminishing. The conditions for establishing the newest public provincial universities seem less comfortable. To begin with, most of the recent ones were established as branches of main universities, remaining so until seven faculties met the requirements that enabled them to be gathered under the title of an autonomous university. Today, critics nostalgic for the past still recall that it took seven years to establish Assiout University, and that a comprehensive and integrated body of advanced students was sent abroad years earlier to prepare them to become the academic staff. According to some commentators, it is political pressures and not the ability to satisfy prerequisites that dictate the foundation of universities. Today, the total number of state universities could increase from 12 to 20 simply by decrees merging branches into universities. However, the Egyptian authorities seem reluctant to reform traditional practices. Still, there are campaigns in favor of establishing new universities to absorb the growing number of secondary certificate holders, under identified and fully recognized umbrellas; to rectify geographic disparity, which is seen as a social bias; and to provide deprived provincial centers with new faculties. Overall, despite expansion (primarily during the 1970s), real access to higher education in Egypt remains far below international standards, particularly in terms of the size of Egypt's population and its demographic growth.

The so-called provincial universities deserve particular attention in this discussion. Under the conditions of their establishment, the number of faculty in provincial universities has been historically lacking, and has typically not met the basic requirements of a coherent and integrated foundational education. Although decentralized, they rely heavily on the central universities, especially concerning teaching staff. Over-reliance on the "express professor" (a variant of the "taxicab" professors of Latin America and elsewhere) is surely one of the main reasons for a lack of scientific achievement in many of these universities. Some commentators add that provincial universities are more subject to pressures and interventions from local elites, and are less transparent in terms of management, accountability, and public resource allocation. Paradoxically, some new provincial universities seem to be too close to Cairo's political centrality, while too far from Cairo concerning other aspects of higher education development.

Despite these considerations, if one needs to qualify the relationship between higher education and social change in Egypt, provincial universities constitute an ideal unit of analysis in that they introduced major and radical changes in the dynamics of the provincial cities. Here, as elsewhere, what a campus means socially and politically ranges from a myriad of small shops and coffeehouses to political demonstrations. In the relatively quite conservative south of Egypt, it means much more visibility in the public space for female students. Additionally, recent figures have shown a dramatic reversal of migration patterns away from Cairo and instead contributing to the population growth in middle provincial towns. Universities may have been one of the main factors in this transformation. However, from a social history perspective, there is certainly room for more research on higher education.

In general, universities provide privileged spaces where boys meet girls, and where demonstrations and the collective and public expression of discontent are allowed. Knowing that, any sociological attempt to understand the history of Egypt should consider the role of the university campus. Students coming from different and multiple social backgrounds experience a new environment and face different *habitus*, manners and ways of presenting oneself. Fashion—Western dress versus Islamic veil—offers an arena for confrontation and cohabitation, as does political discourse, reflected in frequent confrontations between university security offices and activists students (either leftists or Islamists).

Focusing on the role of the campus in social change should not lead us to neglect the forgotten and impoverished rural areas, as well as some urban and semi-urban ones. Here, the population is still far from benefiting from adequate basic services, especially in education, health and sanitation. And even if free educational services are said to be available, at certain levels of poverty people cannot benefit from it. In this respect, and despite the expansion of higher education and the growing numbers of university students, Egypt still maintains the social contrasts between illiterates and highly educated graduates.

Students and Graduates of Higher Education

Who are Egypt's highly educated? An examination of the concrete modalities of access to the universities and the way they affect the composition of student cohorts yields interesting findings. Since the mid-1950s, a central administration (the Placement Bureau of the Ministry of Higher Education) has been responsible for providing admission to universities and institutes, within the framework of numerous regulations imposed by the Supreme Council of Universities. Apart from the aptitude tests used to determine access to particular disciplines, admission to all higher education faculties depends on the scores a student achieves on the Secondary Examination Certificate, a nationwide examination which is increasingly taking the form and function of a highly selective and exclusive academic competition. While about 75–80% of applicants are accepted into universities, the remaining portion is distributed among public and private institutes, which constitute an integral part of the higher education system, although they are often socially devalued when compared to the universities.

High scores enable access to distinguished faculties: the better the applicant's marks, the more choices are open for him or her. High scoring applicants usually prefer prestigious faculties, who accept few students, while others are driven towards less prestigious and more numerous ones. Though the rigidity of the system has been the focus of much controversy in recent years, alternative methods of university acceptance—such as institutional evaluation exams—do not seem to be under consideration. Beside orienting students to academic studies that are not corresponding to their wishes or aptitudes, this kind of scientific and practical equity has in fact several kinds of structural limitations. The first is obviously a social and scientific hierarchy between faculties, disciplines and universities; emphasis on elite faculties (including medicine, engineering, and political science) has led to a steady depreciation of humanities and social sciences, while the so-called hard sciences are much more valued (both socially and academically). Scientific faculties recruit far fewer students, while other faculties are open to those applicants who have fewer choices.

This situation is far from being new, as the Egyptian philosopher and specialist of English literature Louis Awad (1914–1990) observed during the 1960s. He criticized the state's overemphasis on technology and technicians, arguing that excellence should be applied to forming creativity and exceptional minds, including in philosophy and humanities, and that knowledge should follow neither job market rules nor the dictates of development and industrialization policies (Awad, 1964). Further, as many critics have noted, elevating certain disciplines to an elite status, and limiting their student enrollment (and by extension, the number of graduates produced), is actually detrimental to the long-term scientific advancement of the country.

This problem has not been unique to Egypt. Indeed, a recent Arab Human Development Report concludes that since the 1960s, the misallocation of human resources in sciences and technology has led to a widening technological gap between the Arab countries and the rest of the world, resulting in a lack of scientific culture as well as having negative effects on economic productivity. Further, according to the Report, overcrowded universities—a situation that applies particularly for Egypt—have been driven by political and populist considerations rather than by an assessment of the country's needs (UNDP, 2003).

Beyond the impact of discipline-based issues of higher education enrollments, one must also consider how the social background of a student influences their access to the university. The great majority of students who obtain high marks on the nationwide Secondary Examination Certificate come from private secondary schools, where they benefited from a better education—or at least better conditions in less crowded classrooms—while their families could also afford to provide them with expensive private lessons. The hierarchy between disciplines was slightly modified according to job market conditions and demands for new qualifications. Beginning in the 1970s, foreign languages gained more importance because of the expansion of the tourism sector and Egypt's open door economic policy (which relied on foreign investors and companies). More recently, computer science has become a top choice for degree-seeking applicants to higher education. Many students who seek eventual state employment attend colleges of education, because teacher recruitment is still important. Such diversity in higher education opportunities (and in a student's access strategies) requires consideration of diverse job markets. If we add to this the other types of cultural and social capital an individual may have, it is obvious that equivalent degrees do not make for equal graduates. Employment opportunities in Egypt are heavily dependent upon such considerations.

Finally, among the heritage of the 1960s we should note a deep differentiation within the body of higher education between universities and the so-called institutes, both public and private. Institutes are less prestigious, because they constitute the last chance for those who were not able to obtain access to state universities. Their relatively low place in Egypt's higher education hierarchy has some impact on the self-image of these institutes and their members. For example, research conducted in one of the particularly well-equipped technical institutes found that symbolic and verbal violence, if not physical, was the main feature of relationships between teachers, students and administrators (Farag, 2004). A number of other differences exist as well. Unemployment among graduates of institutes is much higher than for graduates of universities. For some observers, this has to do with the curricula of the institutes and the abilities of its graduates. Also, in recent years, there has been an uneven expansion in the number of private institutes, resulting in broad criticism towards these institutions, ranging from concerns over the lack of state scientific control to allegations that some institutes make false promises and charge over-exaggerated fees. Thus, some argue, students without access to the universities are paying a lot, not for knowledge but for an under-valued degree.

Significantly, a recent debate deals with the growing number of private higher education institutes, which are designated as "academies." While it is obviously an attempt to by-pass the stigmatizing label of "institute," it appears that there are no clear criteria that allow using this label, which will likely be condemned to stigmatization as well. Far from the prestigious universities, private institutes are often seen as part of a corrupt market, strictly driven by profit and lacking any academic considerations. In essence, as Donald Reid (1991) aptly observed, the legacy of higher education during the 1960s is that a "job was secured by the state, and high university enrollments and widespread illiteracy went hand in hand... the prestige of general academic schools and white-collar employment kept technical and vocational schools anemic, and the slow pace of industrialization pushed the government into becoming the employer of last resort" (p. 186).

Old Debates and New Actors

In a controversial book about the educational institution, a French sociologist noted that education is always under a continuous reform (Milner, 1984). The reason is that concrete realizations remain by definition far from the educational ideal. Contrary to other public policies such as health, transportation or sanitation, it seems that societies are never fully satisfied with their educational systems. While it is surely difficult to evaluate such a general statement, it seems correct in the case of Egypt. Every new cabinet brings new plans. In the newspapers, the debates on education are continuous and often seem to be the most sensible meeting point between state policies and social practices. Reforms also take the particular form of reports that are widely discussed and publicized and which actually constitute the self-history of the educational apparatus. From the 19th century's "Reports to their Royal Highness" to the now-obsolete "Perspectives for the End of the 20th Century," this kind of literature measures progress accomplished and gives us an idea about the way Egypt's rulers think about the future of the society, even if the analysis remains attached to formal aspects and quantitative measurements.

It is also worth mention that official and semi-official critics are sometimes much more severe than informal ones. Interestingly, the American report "A Nation at Risk" (1983) has been widely cited by Egyptian commentators: for them, if the educational situation is so alarming in the most powerful country in the world, what could we say about Egypt? It seems obvious that Egyptian commentators are not familiar with the critics of this report (Gabbard, 2003).

Will the ongoing reforms follow the same path? While it is difficult to estimate their future outcomes, it is clear that most of the identified problems are by no means old ones. It also bears mention that a partly new language—which is both technical and political—is emerging. Finally, in spite of a steady reform scheme, there is a set of new social actors more or less institutionalized, whose interventions will feature prominently in the future of higher education, as well as the formulation of its actual problems.

In recent years, several factors have contributed to transforming the pattern of the relationships between Egyptian higher education and a new set of actors. To begin with, one should mention the growing influence of foreign aid devoted to higher education enhancement—foreign donors are not exercising pressures per se, but there is clearly a lack of solidarity among the interests and points of view between them and their local counterparts in the national bureaucracies and among national experts. One should also mention the key role of some political institutions in giving support to particular reforms, like the prominent "Policies Committee" within the ruling party (National Democratic Party), headed by the son of President Hosni Mubarak. New forms of privatization, involving wealthy businessmen with connections within the state apparatus and the political elite, have also had a significant impact. The formal political arena has seen a renewal of some prominent actors like the Education Committee of the Peoples Assembly, headed by an influential politician (who is also a businessman, while belonging to academia). What seems important to underline is the multiple social identities of those actors who can shift from one formal position to another. We may also mention the pressures coming from beneficiaries and public opinion, provided that we take into account that the latter is not a unified entity. Indeed, the growing diversity (in the forms and institutional frameworks of higher education) has deepened the conflict between multiple and divergent social interests.

Such a multi-dimensional perspective allows us to understand the recent features of higher education that have been discussed as the most salient and urgent. Quality assurance, corruption and privatization seem to focus much of our attention, and this influences the actors that are involved in the reform of higher education in Egypt.

Quality assurance was first introduced into the educational debate as an element of the package called "following global standards." Political endorsement proved to be effective in transforming the slogan into a project. A national independent institution for quality assurance is currently being implemented. Here (as elsewhere) the focus is on the ability to compete on the international level, and there are references to the experience of southeastern Asian countries. Such an institution will not be in charge of solving educational problems but will evaluate quality and conceive differential policies according to quality. Although the pattern is an international one, the Egyptian context poses several questions, such as how to prevent such an institution from becoming a bureaucratic prestigious committee. Another question involves the criteria for determining quality and standards. On one hand, international standards seem too high to apply to any of the components of Egypt's educational system. On the other hand, locally adapted criteria may comfort the status quo and will not be enough to improve the competition for quality between educational establishments, which is among the major aims (Al-Ahram, 2004).

Other questions relate to the political as well as administrative autonomy of a national institution for quality assurance, and how it may curb the scope of action of other institutions, individuals and networks. As it has been proven for comparable bodies, being directly accountable to the presidency or the prime minister (rather than to the ministry of education) does not appear to constitute a sufficient guarantee of institutional authority. Overall, quality assurance constitutes a key term in a partly new vocabulary that allows new agencies to identify some of the problems of higher education.

A similar challenge to quality stems from what has been known as academic corruption. The debate over corruption is far from new; indeed, in 1994 a famous book written by a journalist identified several figures of corruption within the university (Hashim, 1994). However, it seems that there are new voices from inside and outside academia who are willing to confront corruption and are working on new methods to denunciate it. This is partly the content of a Declaration for Reform, signed in July 2004 by more than 100 professors, addressing basically the political autonomy of the university. In the media, regular investigative campaigns periodically uncover more or less anecdotal stories, where students are obliged to purchase expensive textbooks written by their professors as a condition for passing exams or even attending the courses. Such practices are semi-officially tolerated, as they are merely considered as compensatory measures resulting from weak salaries. Private lessons may constitute another type of corruption. In some cases, results of exams have been modified to guarantee success for sons of professors or political personalities. Among academic staff, several cases of plagiarism have been noted. Equally disconcerting is the lack of transparency in the procedures of academic upgrading and promotion of the teaching staff, where personal considerations tend to overcome meritocratic ones. Finally, master's and doctoral studies constitute another field of potential corruption, as advanced students remain under the personal (and sometimes arbitrary) control of their supervisors. We should add that some of these cases have been taken to court, while university authorities deal with others.

It is pointless to ask whether corruption constitutes a series of numerous isolated cases or a nationwide phenomenon. If academic corruption constitutes a system, one must address those components and reciprocal arrangements that allow a system to function. Some commentators note that academic corruption is simply the way universities are influenced by the overall society, while others recall a time when academic ethics were perceived as a model that should be diffused from the university to society.

Finally, new forms of privatization in higher education deserve special attention. Several years ago, partial privatizations were implemented within public universities. State universities introduced foreign language programs for which tuition is charged, allowing students originally from private foreign language schools to follow a curriculum partly in English or French. This ensures a higher quality education and better job prospects for those individuals already endowed with economic and cultural capital. Furthermore, some private schools are authorized to award diplomas from foreign secondary schools. Their students are thus able to avoid the nightmare of the Thanawiyya 'Amma (nationwide final secondary school examination), which simplifies access to the university (Farag, 2000). Since 1998, an Open University Cairo center has been devoted to those who were not able to join the university under standard conditions.

In spite of the numerous forms of privatization, it seems that Egypt's newly-established private universities have been the focus of much recent attention primarily because of political reasons. Although these institutions have gained some amount of political and social acceptance over the last few years, there are still questions under consideration, and it seems that the formative period has contributed to even more questions. What is striking is the fact that within the small number of private universities, there is already a classification that distinguishes among them the "most serious" (in terms of scientific reputation), which are also said to be "the least capitalist." These were established with close relationships to foreign country partners (including German, French, Canadian and British), although all new private universities are strictly Egyptian. Indeed, most of the contemporary criticisms about private higher education concern the other universities that were established during the mid-1990s.

Although six years do not constitute a sufficient period for an evaluation, and looks like a quite arbitrary time horizon, the growing conflicts between the higher education authorities and private universities seem to have accelerated such a critical appraisal. Among different opinions and sources, we can rely here on what seems to be the most substantial one, which is a report of the Education Committee of the People's Assembly (Parliament).

The report first notes growing criticism against private universities in recent years, including accusations that they do not correspond to the needs of the country, nor do they provide new specialties or research and training facilities. In addition, there are flagrant irregularities concerning rates of admission, numbers of admitted students, regulations for exams, and rules of transfer from one university to another. Critics also point to the fact that private universities make profits at the expense of quality. The report also notes the overlap between institutional owners and administration, and the negative effects of this on academia's autonomy. Further, a cursory review of the lists of founders and owners, administrators and even professors and heads of departments, reveals that some universities—not all of them—belong to the "family business" category. Thus, among the recommendations of the report is the necessity of disengaging ownership and administration.

The lack of financial transparency—along with archaic management and budgetary procedures—has been another point of criticism. But perhaps the most critical argument of the report has to do with the initial purpose of the private universities; they were legitimized for years as the sole provider of new and advanced disciplines that public universities could not offer. However, the report notes that the curricula do not differ from those of public universities, and that the mediums are rather traditional. Instead of emphasizing the most attractive disciplines and providing access for those who can afford high tuitions, private universities should work for the future of Egypt, according to the report.

These criticisms speak to the incoherencies of a whole system. Once an official authorization is given to establish a private university, people tend to consider this as a state recognition for the degree, but from the state's point of view, recognition does not mean systematic equivalence; indeed, the latter depends on the Supreme Council of Universities. The same problem is raised for foreign students and the recognition of these degrees in their home countries. In 2003, private universities had about 32 faculties, and some 16 degrees were recognized as equivalent to those of the state universities (Al-Ahram Al-Iqtisadi, 2003).

The case of private universities in Egypt provides an example of the intersection between the political and academic worlds, and involves issues of both political and scientific legitimacy. One could say that the magnitude of this debate has become disproportionate to the small number of private universities or students enrolled in private universities. However, the debate does correspond to the predicable conflicts of interests and the political costs that entail any establishment of private versus public arrangements. Also, it bears mention that an important part of the foundation costs of some of the private universities were covered by loans from the banks. One should also note the social and political power of wealthy families who were able to pay for high tuitions, and have since felt betrayed either by the Egyptian state (for failing to provide quality higher education to its citizens) or by the private universities' promoters (for promising a level of institutional quality that has yet to be delivered), if not both. According to some observers, most of the private universities are nothing but profit-driven projects, which have nothing to do with the values, aims and academic disinterests that motivate such establishments in other parts of the world. One may wonder about such an idealized representation.

To illustrate the scope of the conflict, one can look to an anecdotal but still revealing event; for an entire week, a private university published a full-page advertisement in several daily newspapers—under the title "Address to the Public Opinion"—to claim the innocence of the university against false charges and allegations, and to denounce arbitrary state bureaucratic measures. The climax of this drama came a few months later, with the death of the university's founder.

However, it seems that the private university experience has created the foundations for future forms of privatization, while contributing to new questions and doubts. For example, a debate has ensued about so-called parallel higher education, which consists of admitting a proportion of students to public universities, although their secondary examination scores were below the standards set by those universities, who are required to pay high tuitions. The idea is that they can benefit from the same curricula, same teaching staff, and within the same campus, but during different hours of instruction. This projected system has raised detailed questions about rates of admission and the proportion of admitted students, as well as practical questions about the "time-sharing" system of the campus. However, the basic idea of this two-fold system of higher education (free during the day and privatized by night) must also be questioned. The defenders of the system argue for the resources generated, which can help in enhancing the quality of public universities and supplement academic and administrative staff salaries. On the other hand, critics note that while financial arrangements can help, they do not provide adequate solutions for the complex academic problems faced by Egypt's universities.

Conclusion

In conclusion, it may be said that job market considerations and economic conditions in general have already affected social choices concerning higher education. It is also obvious that the system will have to go through further adjustments, although it is not easy yet to identify precisely the amount of social costs or the victims. The classical dilemma of equity versus quality has to be put in a multidimensional context. Some analysts assume that the decline of knowledge rewards (in terms of job, wealth and social positions) is leading to a devaluation of education. One should distinguish in fact between two kinds of considerations. On the one hand, there is a widening gap between expectations and possibilities; university graduates in Egypt are either fighters or privileged. On another hand, it seems that education as a value remains solid, even (and particularly) for those who cannot have access to it. This is at least what has been proven in the past. Further investigation may confirm it for the future.

References

Al-Ahram, November 2004 (daily).
Al-Ahram Al-Iqtisadi, July 2003 (weekly).
Awad, L. (1964). *Al-jami'a wal-mujtama' al-jadid (The university and the new society)*. Cairo, Egypt: Dirasat ishtirakiyya.
Bedayr, A. A. (1950). *Al-amîr Ahmad Fu'ad wa nash'at al-jâmi'a al-misriyya (Prince Ahmad Fuad and the foundation of the Egyptian university)*. Cairo, Egypt.
Gabbard, D. (2003). A nation at risk reloaded: Part I. *Journal for Critical Education Policy Studies*, *1*(2). Available online at http://www.jceps.com.
Farag, I. (1999a). *La construction sociale d'une éducation nationale: enjeux politiques et trajectoires éducatives. Egypte 1900–1950 (The social construction of a national education system; political stakes and educational trajectories*. Egypt 1900–1950). Thèse de doctorat. Paris: EHESS.
Farag, I. (1999b). Higher education in Egypt: The realpolitik of privatization. *International Higher Education*, 18.
Farag, I. (2003). Al-Mudarissun; masarat wa mumurasat (A great vocation, a modest profession: Teachers' paths and practices). In L. Herrera (Ed.), *Thaqafat al-talim fi Misr (Cultures of education in Egypt)*. Cairo, Egypt: Population Council (under publication in English).
Fergany, N. (2001). *Higher education in Arab countries: Human development and labor market requirements*. Almishkat Center, Egypt. Available online at http://www.almishkat.org.
Hashim, H. (1994). *Suwar min al fassad al jami'i (Figures of the academic corruption)* Cairo, Egypt: Dar al shuruq ed.
Le Goff, J. (1985). *Les intellectuels au Moyen Age (Intellectuals of the Middle Age)*. Paris: Le Seuil, Coll. Points.
Milner, J. C. (1984). *De l'Ecole (About the school)*. Paris: Seuil.
Nora, P. (1997). *Les lieux de mémoire (Places of memory)*, 3 volumes (1st ed.). Paris: Gallimard.
Reed, D. M. (1991). *Cairo University and the making of modern Egypt*, (1st ed.). Cairo, Egypt: The American University in Cairo Press.
Said, M. E-M. (2004). *Role of quality assurance and accreditation in enhancing education efficiency*. Available online at http://www.mans.edu.eg.
Tourne, K. (2003). *Expériences de la vie active et pratiques matrimoniales des jeunes adultes égyptiens dans les années 1990 (Professional activities and matrimonial practices of young adults in Egypt)*. Thèse de Doctorat en Sociologie, Université de Paris I–IEDES.
UNDP. (2003). *Arab human development report: Building a knowledge society*. New York: United Nations.

36

FRANCE

Christine Musselin

Center for the Sociology of Organizations, France

Describing the higher education system of a country always brings to mind how idiosyncratic such systems are and how what seems obvious for local inhabitants may appear strange and lead to difficulties in comprehension for external observers. On the one hand, it is tempting to simplify complexity in order to keep the text readable but, on the other hand, one must go into detail in order to avoid false similarities. It also inevitably leads to somewhat overemphasizing the specificity of each country in order to better characterize it. This chapter will not escape these biases. In the first section, the particularities of the history of universities in French higher education will be stressed. In the second one, the main features of today's French higher education system will be described. In the third section, some reflections and data on the French academic profession and its related academic labor markets will be presented. The final section will deal with the ongoing evolutions and the forthcoming challenges of higher education in France.

A University Framework Inherited from the Middle Ages but with Recent Universities

France has a long university tradition, being one of the first countries where the university was created (around the end of the Middle Ages).[1] But, as argued by the French philosopher A. Renaut (1995), it would be wrong to understand the present higher education system as the direct product of this long tradition. The history of French universities is not one of continuity but of ruptures that sometimes even provoked their disappearance (Verger, 1986). For this reason, French higher education today owes little to the Middle Ages, and instead should first of all be studied in light of the French Revolution. During this period, it was decided to suppress corporations of any kind— including the university corporations—and to foster the development of professional schools (Chevallier, Grosperrin, & Maillet, 1968). This led, for instance, to the creation of the *Ecole Polytechnique* and the *Conservatoire National des Arts et Métiers* in 1794.

For about 15 years, French higher education had no other higher education institutions. It was Napoleon who finally allowed their rebirth, but on a very special basis.

James J.F. Forest and Philip G. Altbach (eds.), International Handbook of Higher Education, 711–728.
© 2006 *Springer. Printed in the Netherlands.*

Instead of rebuilding universities, he created discipline-based structures—i.e., *facultés* (in law, medicine, science, humanities, theology)—independent from one another and all gathered under a national structure, which also included high schools: this structure was called the Imperial University. These events deeply influenced the development of the French higher education system for many years. First, the *facultés* (and especially for sciences and humanities) were no more than a prolongation of high schools; they had very few students, and higher education developed very slowly during the 19th century. This left room for the *grandes écoles* (professional schools) to expand and to become a crucial sector. It also confined the French academic profession to teaching and to the delivery of diplomas, research activities being anything but frequent. Second, this created a national corporation, managed from Paris, instead of the local institutions that existed before the Revolution.

The *Conseil de l'Instruction Publique* (Council for Public Education), composed of Parisian teachers—each responsible for steering his discipline (in terms of teachers' careers, study programs and so on)—became a powerful central body (Gerbod, 1965) managing a vertically and hierarchically structured, as well as discipline-based, academic profession. While the Humboldtian reforms in Germany were promoting the rebirth of universities, and while American higher education was developing through the creation of private higher education institutions (Clark, 1987), the disciplines (i.e., the *facultés*) were becoming the cornerstone of the French university system. The geographical proximity between the ministry and the *Conseil de l'Instruction Publique* (Council for Public Education) favored the development of corporatist co-management between the academic profession and the central public authorities.

The reforms implemented by the end of the 19th century only marginally modified the Napoleonic design. They had a decisive role in promoting the development of French higher education (as shown by the rise in student numbers around 1900 and after; cf. Prost, 1968), and also confirmed the monopoly of universities in the delivery of national university degrees,[2] but they failed in two other respects. First, the attempt to transfer the German model to the French one—and more precisely to promote the development of research activities within the *facultés*—did not succeed (Charle, 1994); French academics remained, first of all, teachers. Second, the re-creation in 1896 of administrative entities called universities, gathering in one institution all the *facultés* of a city, did not weaken the power acquired by the latter during the 19th century.

Three reasons may explain the failure to redistribute power to the universities. First, the successive reforms implemented since 1875 all aimed at giving more prerogatives and more autonomy to the *facultés*; they were thus more powerful than ever when the last round of reforms was promulgated and universities re-created. Second, the newly created "universities" were allowed (by contrast) very small margins for strategic maneuvering and, moreover, their direction was left to high civil servants (called *recteurs*) appointed by the ministry and not by academics. Third, the management of the academic profession by a Parisian discipline-based central body composed of academics was confirmed, preventing the development of direct and dense relationships between the universities and the ministry. As a result, the deans (*doyens* at the head of the *facultés*)—and not the *recteurs*—became the relevant interlocutors for the central authorities and for the lay academics.

To compensate for the low capacity for innovation among each *faculté*, new curricula developed outside the universities, reinforcing the central role played by the *grandes écoles* in the education of the elite and allowing room for new schools to develop. The same process—consisting of externalizing the higher education missions or activities that universities were not able or willing to carry out—led to the creation of the *Centre National de la Recherche Scientifique* (CNRS, National Center for Research) in 1939, and of more specialized research institutions (including the CNES, for space research, and the INRA, for agronomical research) after World War II. Each of these national institutions is oriented towards fundamental research, and recruits and manages their own staff of permanent researchers.

No important reforms occurred until 1968, despite a great deal of criticism against the *facultés* system (cf. Antoine & Passeron, 1966; Colloque de Caen, 1966). But after the "May 68 events" (which started with massive student demonstrations and riots and led to a general strike that paralyzed the French economy for an entire month), the Faure Act (November 1968) suppressed the *facultés* and created new multidisciplinary universities, structured into *Unités d'Enseignement et de Recherche* (UER, Research and Teaching Units)[3] governed by an elected academic (called the "président") and deliberative bodies composed of representatives of teachers, administrative staff, students and "stakeholders."[4] Furthermore, the Faure Act aimed at providing the universities with pedagogical, administrative and financial autonomy. This did not succeed (Cohen, 1978), because the French ministry quickly limited the new margins for institutional maneuvering; it did not modify its traditional practices of co-management with the academic profession; and it did not recognize the new universities as relevant interlocutors. As a result, 1968 is the official date for the rebirth of French universities (as institutions, therefore, they are less than 35 years old), but they remained weak actors on the French higher education scene (Charle, 1994; Compagnon, 1998; Friedberg & Musselin, 1989).

The contractual policy introduced in 1989 somewhat modified this situation (Berrivin & Musselin, 1996; Chevaillier, 1998; Musselin, 1997, 2001 [2004]; *Rapport Frémont*, 2004). Since then, every four years each university gathers data on its activities and collectively decides on future actions, priorities and orientations to be developed. It also prepares a strategic plan and negotiates with the ministry its budget allocation for the next four years. This new procedure, despite the fact it involves no more than 10% of the operating budget[5] (salaries not included), modified the state universities' relationships and favored the emergence of stronger higher education institutions. The preparation of strategic plans, which frequently relies on a participative process, enhanced collective reflection while reinforcing institutional commitments and promoting common objectives.

This resulted in a stronger university management. The presidents became less *primus inter pares*, behaving more as managers and developing a more professional perception of their function (Mignot-Gérard & Musselin, 2002). Nevertheless, these new conceptions are not equally shared. If an alliance is often to be observed between the presidential teams and the university administrative staff—both being convinced by the necessity to run universities more professionally and to develop institutional strategies and policies—there is often a gap between them and the faculty level, where the discipline-based logics and the individual academic autonomy are more valued than institutional development. Nevertheless, it cannot be denied that over the last decade, France has finally recovered its "university institutions."

Main Characteristics of the Modern French Higher Education System

A Differentiated Higher Education System

The French system is first of all segmented into various sectors: university versus *grandes écoles*; long-term general programs *versus* short-term job-oriented curricula; and finally, higher education institutions *versus* research institutions. Moreover, these sectors are less homogeneous than it may initially seem. This is especially true for the *grandes écoles*, some of which (e.g., the top engineering schools) are public and depend on a Minister as well as on the Minister of Education, while others (e.g., business schools) are mostly private. Some are recognized by the state, while others are not. Some are almost free (again, the best engineering schools), and others require high fees. Short-term studies are also varied: they consist of *instituts universitaires de technologie* (IUT, university institutes of technology) programs, located within universities, as well as in *sections de techniciens supérieurs* (STS, vocational training) programs, delivered in *lycées* (high schools).

This differentiated structure is represented in Figure 1, which shows the various possibilities offered after passing the *baccalauréat* (a national exam that completes a student's high school education). One can choose job-oriented training leading to a vocational diploma in two years at either STS or IUT—in both cases, there exist possibilities (often used by the holders of an IUT diploma) to enter the university (at the third year level) or, in fewer cases, to enter a *grande école*. One can enter the university and pass a diploma called the DEUG (after two years), a *license* at

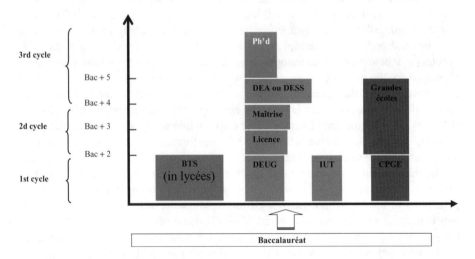

Figure 1. Tertiary education before the generalization of the Bologna process.

the end of the third year, a *maîtrise* at the end of the fourth, and then a DEA (research oriented) or a DESS (job-oriented) diploma. DEA holders can work toward completion of a Ph.D. After each diploma, one can decide to leave the system or to continue (sometimes after passing a selection process). Finally, one can chose to study for the selective examinations required to attend a *grande école* and in this case would first attend the two-year courses offered by some *lycées* and called *classes préparatoires* (preparatory courses). The holders of a *grande école* diploma who want to prepare a Ph.D. must first attend a DEA program of study and obtain this type of diploma from a university.

The complexity of the system is growing, as the frontiers among the sectors are increasingly blurred. As a matter of fact, the best *grandes écoles* still train the French industrial, intellectual, administrative and economic elites, and the universities are frequently "chosen" by default by those who could not enter the *classes préparatoires* (preparatory courses which prepare the student for the selective exams leading to the *grandes écoles*) or the selective short-term studies (IUT or STS). Nevertheless, some rapprochements have occurred between the two sectors. On the one hand, *grandes écoles* are increasingly involved in research activities;[6] some developed doctoral programs or deliver such programs in collaboration with universities; and their teaching staff are increasingly required to have attended the usual academic socialization (e.g., doctoral training) and possess academic credentials (e.g., Ph.D., publications, participation in conferences, and so forth). On the other hand, since the 1970s, universities have diversified their offerings and now provide selective job-oriented curricula, beginning after the first two university years. *Grandes écoles* share more academic characteristics than before, while reciprocally, universities challenge the *grandes écoles* in the domain of training.

A System Mostly in the Public Domain

Until now, however, the trends mentioned above have simply amended the general structure of French higher education without truly transforming it. The divide between universities—which welcome about 80% of the students and are all public—and the *grandes écoles* is still a reality, even if somewhat modified. Further, some of the *grandes écoles* are public; thus nearly 90% of the students attend public higher education institutions, with very low fees. For instance, the fees at all French universities ranged from 141 to 280 euros for most undergraduate and graduate diplomas in 2003–2004, and between 500 and 900 euros at one of the best French engineering schools.[7]

Most of the resources for this public sector come from the state but they remain low,[8] and the contribution per student varies considerably from one institution to another. According to the French Ministry, the average public expense for a university student was 6,850 euros in 2002, but almost 9,100 for an IUT student, 12,000 for an engineering school student in the public sector, and more than 13,000 euros for students attending the *classes préparatoires*.[9] Furthermore, in a recent report, Aghion and Cohen (2004) compared the average 6,589 euros expense for a university student in 2001 with the average 7,879 euros a year for a student in a public high school, and noted that within 25 years the former increased by 25% while the latter increased by 50%. Universities are not the most well-off part of the French higher education system, even if they have the larger proportion of the student population and house a large part of the public research activities (for which they also receive public funding). According to the calculations proposed in a 2001 experts' report[10] written under the direction of A. Frémont on the implementation of the contractual policy in French universities (*Rapport Frémont*, 2004), the operating budget (without the salaries) for research reached 986 million euros. Of this amount, 42.8% was provided by the Ministry of Education or other ministries, 20.3% by the national research institutions, 9.2% by local authorities, 14.3% by firms, 7.9% by the EU and 5.5% by other sources. This means that the public portion (national or local) of these resources reached 85%. If salaries are included, this percentage is close to 94%.

A Mass System of Education

Since the beginning of the Fifth Republic, France has supported a mass system of public higher education. After the *baccalauréat*, access to higher education depends on the sector: *grandes écoles*, university short-term curricula and *lycée* tertiary education (STS) are selective, while traditional university curricula are non-selective as far as access to the first year is concerned. This explains why, even though all sectors expanded, universities absorbed more of the student increase than other sectors during the 1960s. Because the *baccalauréat* (national exam completing a student's high school education) is sufficient for admission to undergraduate programs at the university, the policy launched in the 1950s to broaden access to high schools automatically and mechanically led to an increase in students at the university. This resulted in the first wave of massification in the French higher education system during the 1960s (increasing at a rate of between 11 and 18% a year).

Stability in the rate of the *baccalauréat* holders (at about 25% of an age cohort) during the 1970s (and thus the "decision" not to further expand access to the high schools) slowed down the increase of student numbers in higher education until the 1980s. During this period, the rate of expansion reached 2–4% a year, reflecting the nation's demographical trends more or less. But in the mid-1980s, the creation of new types of *baccalauréats*, and the objective set by the socialist government for 80% of an age cohort to reach the level of the *baccalauréat*, further increased the number of "bac" holders. Between 1988 and 1995, therefore, a second wave of massification occurred, as reflected in Table 1.

Again, the universities were directly affected by this growth, and in absolute numbers attracted most of the new students (over 630,000) but among them the selective short-term curricula (IUT) and those of the engineering schools located in universities registered a sharper increase (respectively 119% and 253%, against an average 72% growth rate for universities). The increasing desire for more selective and more job-oriented curricula during this period was also reflected by the enrollment growth in STS and in *grandes écoles* (including engineering and business schools). In both cases, this expansion was absorbed less by an increase in the number of students admitted in the already existing *grandes écoles* than by the creation of new schools—which, for the moment, do not threaten the prestige of the traditional ones, whose prestige is all

Table 1. Evolution of Student Numbers by Institutional Sectors

	1980–1981	1990–1991		1990–1995		1999–2000	
Universities	871,008	1,199,284	38%	1,571,651	80%	1,501,616	72%
Selective short term	*53,667*	*74,328*	*38%*	*103,092*	*92%*	*117,407*	*119%*
BTS	67,908	201,384	197%	230,239	239%	242,385	257%
% of private	*36%*	*41%*		*30%*		*30%*	
Preparatory classes	42,911	71,478	67%	78,626	83%	80,228	87%
Engineering schools	36,952	57,653	56%	75,640	105%	82,751	124%
Public in universities	*8,330*	*17,325*	*108%*	*24,186*	*190%*	*29,378*	*253%*
Public, not in universities	*20,132*	*26,326*		*32,765*		*35,181*	
Private	*8,490*	*14,002*		*18,689*		*21,192*	
Business schools	15,824	46,128	192%	50,668	220%	56,303	256%
Ecoles Normales supérieures	*2,840*	*2,675*	*−6%*	*3,051*	*7%*	*3,209*	*13%*
Total	1,037,443	1,578,602		2,009,875		1,966,492	

Source: Ministry of Education, 2004.

the more intact because they did not proportionally increase the number of students enrolled.

According to the Organization for Economic Cooperation and Development (2003), 35% of the French population between 25 and 34 years old have attained tertiary education (compared to 40% in the U.S.), as have 29% of those between 45 to 54. However, the democratization project that stood behind this openness of the system has not been achieved. There is indeed an increase in student numbers, but also high dropout rates among university undergraduates, and this more strongly affects the holders of the newly created types of *baccalauréat*,[11] who themselves more frequently originate from lower socioeconomic backgrounds than the holders of more traditional *baccalauréats*. Moreover, a comparison of the socioeconomic backgrounds of undergraduate students with those of doctoral students clearly shows that the selection process at the university is also social. The conclusions are even more dismal when one looks at student recruitment in the more prestigious *grandes écoles*—where, even if most of them charge no tuition fees, the homogeneity of the students socioeconomic backgrounds (mostly upper class) is striking (Euriat & Thélot, 1995).

The French Academic Profession

To fully understand the state of French higher education today, it is important to examine its academic profession. It is all the more necessary given that the structure and the organization of global academic labor markets is probably the main feature differentiating one country from another.

Incomplete Data

The data at hand to describe the French academic profession strictly reflects the complexity of the higher education system described above. Because most *grandes écoles* are either private or public but have their own staff (as they previously were not linked to the Ministry of Education but only to the Ministry for which they trained elite professionals), we lack aggregate figures about their teachers. The statistics gathered centrally by the Ministry of Education mainly concern teachers in universities. They do not include the secondary teachers training STS or *classes préparatoires*, but they include secondary teachers who hold specific positions within universities. There is also no information about the number of "temporary" lecturers recruited to teach a specific course (because of a lack of competent permanent staff to teach it or because there are too many students for the number of permanent staff available). The diversity of the French academic profession, as reflected in Table 2 is therefore very incomplete, as it concerns only the university sector and the institutions managed by the Ministry of Education.

The permanent staff represented in this table consist exclusively of civil servants employed by the state, most of them in permanent positions managed by the state. Those who are not permanent are mostly doctoral students with a ministry fellowship[12] or young doctors on temporary positions. They can apply for *maîtres de conférences* (assistant professors) positions, which are permanent, after the discipline-based central body called the *Conseil National des Universités* (CNU, National University Council) decides they are qualified enough to send applications to the recruiting departments. In sciences and humanities, writing a *habilitation à diriger des recherches*[13] (HDR, literally "agreement to supervise research") is the next step for a *maître de conférences* to be eligible for a professor position. Again, the CNU has to "qualify" the applicant. In other disciplines (including management, economics, law, political sciences, medicine), the *habilitation* is not enough, and there is no qualification from the CNU; instead, the applicants have to pass a highly selective national exam called the *agrégation du supérieur*.

Maîtres de conférences and professors are expected to teach 192 hours a year and to dedicate half of their time to research activities. According to a recent report (CNER, 2003), these university staff members represent 75% of the French public staff engaged in research activity. By contrast, the academic staff in national research institutions (16,430 tenured researchers) have no teaching duties (although individual researchers may teach if they want to).

French Academic Labor Markets

Beyond this formal description, four main features help characterize the way French labor markets operate. First, they always use tournaments—i.e., a procedure in which a few positions are offered and a large number of candidates apply.[14] This holds true for recruitments as well as for merit-based promotions.

Second, access to permanent positions occurs early in the career, shortly after the Ph.D. period—which is considered as an apprenticeship, during which a "disciple

Table 2. Teaching Staff by Status and Institution

Faculty by Status

Tenured				Non tenured			Tenured on contracts		Total
Professors	Maîtres de conférences	Assistants[a]	Sub-total	Specific medical staff	ATER[b]	Moniteurs[c]	Secondary school teachers in universities	Others	
18,991	33,570	1,460	54,021	4,193	5,993	5,168	14,029	421	83,925

Faculty by Types of Institutions

Universities[d]	IUT	Institutions or grandes écoles included in universities	Other institutions managed by the Ministry of education	Total
66,517	9,444	1,141	6,823	83,925

Source: Adapted from Bideault and Rossi (2002).

[a]This category is disappearing as its members retire or become *maîtres de conférences*.
[b]Short-term teaching postdocs.
[c]Doctoral students with fellowships and teaching duties.
[d]Including technological universities.

to master" relationship still predominates. This has remained the case even though the creation of *écoles doctorales* (graduate schools) during the second part of the 1990s led in some cases (with increasing frequency) to the development of doctoral study programs, and sometimes encouraged less bilateral relationships between the doctoral students and their supervisors. On average, the candidates are 33 years of age when they first become *maîtres de conferences*,[15] but access to this first permanent position does not mean autonomy is completely acquired. The *maîtres de conférences* are not considered to have the same competencies and prerogatives as the professors. In some departments, this does not make much difference because there is a rather equivalent allocation of tasks, but in some others there is a clear segmentation: *maîtres de conférences* do not teach graduates students, never give lecture courses, and so forth (Becquet & Musselin, 2004). In principle, socialization and apprenticeship end with access to position of professor.

Third, the French academic labor market is characterized by poor incentive mechanisms (i.e., poor professional regulation as well as poor institutional regulation). Nevertheless, as in some other countries, the best way to "make a career" is to go through competitions and accept institutional mobility until one enters one of the most reputed departments in his or her discipline. Some (few) departments are well-known for recruiting their professors only among top academics. Nevertheless, a lot of French academics remain in the institution where they began: they are recruited, promoted and become professors in the same place.[16] The main point to mention here is that universities have very few incentives to manage this "sedentary" staff. In other words, their internal labor markets (Doeringer & Piore, 1971) are very poorly regulated. Once recruited as *maître de conferences*, it is in theory possible to escape any kind of work assessment. Teaching evaluations are seldom used (albeit they are supposed to be compulsory since the Bayrou Decree of 1997). If the faculty member is not integrated into a research unit labeled by one of the national research institutions or by the ministry (which is the case for about 20% of the faculty), their research production and activity is never evaluated. And if they belong to one of the labeled research units, evaluation occurs only every four years and has no real impact. It is also possible for a *maître de conférences* to never write an HDR (or pass the national selective exam called *agrégation* for the disciplines concerned) and to never compete for a professorial position.

Fourth, the French academic labor market is characterized by a bureaucratic price setting. A system-wide scale determines the salary of each university teacher according to his or her seniority and ranks. Thus, the salary of a *maître de conférences* with no seniority is exactly the same whatever the discipline or the institution. It is fixed at the national level and not by each institution. The only way to get a better salary is to follow a quick career path—i.e., to write the *habilitation* a few years after being recruited as *maître de conférences*, be recruited as a professor and quickly go through the different ranks up to the exceptional class. Academic rewards are therefore more reputation-based and symbolic than monetary. The recognition of one's research unit by one of the national research institutions is a way to get more visibility, more reputation and more resources. Obtaining research contracts through public calls for proposals or with private firms is a supplementary way to increase one's scientific reputation and to get access to more funding. Such processes create some differentiation among academics, but have no impact on the salaries or on the teaching duties of the more talented academics.

Globally, the same holds true for the tenured staff of the national research institutions, even if their activities are systematically evaluated every two years (but also with no impact on salaries). The poor incentive mechanisms, the (not always) compulsory individual assessment, and the narrow reward system are routinely criticized, and there is no doubt that the French academic labor market could be much improved. But at the same time, the heavy workload of many French academics raises the interesting question: how to explain so much work for so little reward and a declining social position within French society?

Recent Evolutions and Future Challenges

Having described the current situation of French higher education, this chapter now turns to highlight the most recent main evolutions and the forthcoming challenges.

The Redefinition of the Relationships Between Public Authorities and Universities

The first point to stress concerns the transformation of the relationship between the universities and public authorities over the last decade. The contractual policy briefly mentioned in the first section of this chapter is part of this process. Universities became seen as a relevant partner for the central administration, weakening the co-management model that had existed between the state and the academic profession. This transformed the nature of the relationships with the universities, introducing negotiation processes as well as the recognition of some differentiation among the various institutions, which in turn resulted in closer relationships between the ministry and all the country's institutions of higher education. It is too often forgotten that the centralized public governance of France is often associated with poor communication and knowledge exchange between the center and the periphery. French higher education did not escape this rule: a study led at the ministry level during the late 1980s showed how poorly informed the central administration was (Musselin & Brisset, 1989). The introduction of contracts somewhat modified this, as the related negotiations forced both partners to share more knowledge and to keep each other better informed. For this reason, the contractual policy can be seen as a more open kind of governance, as well as a more efficient one for the ministry. Nevertheless, it did not improve the "evaluation culture" within the French higher education system. There are in fact a lot of assessment, control, and audit procedures and bodies in the French system (Belloc, 2003), but most of them are *ex ante* rather than *ex post* (or input-based rather than output-based). Thus, the strategic plans receive more attention than their realization. Evaluations are often not linked to resource allocation[17] and some territories remain rather unexplored. There is, for example, virtually no teaching assessment and no evaluation of the quality of student learning.

Parallel to this evolution, leading to more intensive and more institution-based relationships, another transformation occurred in the same period which challenged the bilateral and rather monopolistic interactions existing between the state and universities. Local authorities (especially regional ones) increased their interest in higher education[18] during the 1980s, and some of them developed scientific policies and funded research projects. The regions were also asked by the Ministry of Education to be more involved in planning the university's development as well as financing it for at least as much as 50% of the state funding. This occurred through two contractual processes, U2000 (beginning in the 1990s) and U3M (University of the Third Millennium, launched toward the end of the 90s). Furthermore, the contractual policy which also developed between the states and the regions resulted in the signing of state-region contracts in which higher education topics are very often addressed.

The opportunities offered by the European framework programs for research and development, and the involvement of French academics in such programs, further offered possibilities to relax the traditional monopolistic dependence of French universities vis-à-vis state funding. Nevertheless, while institutional dependence on the central government may have decreased without deeply affecting the bulk of public funding for higher education,[19] these changes must be viewed in context of a much longer and slower evolution toward greater autonomy for French universities (Musselin, 2004).

The European Influence

The concern for European issues is also a recent evolution on the French scene. This influence was almost absent from the transformations mentioned above, which were first of all "national" changes—i.e., reforms motivated by national problems, for which national solutions were developed without looking at related challenges or responses in other countries (Musselin, 2000, 2001[2004]).

The Sorbonne Conference in 1998, which resulted from an initiative launched by Claude Allègre (at that time Minister of Education), introduced what became known a year later as the "Bologna process." Through this, European higher education systems (29 in 1999, increasing to 40 in 2004)—including that of France—are transforming their former structure of study programs into a new one consisting of a bachelor's degree after three years, a two-year masters degree, and the Ph.D.[20]

By 2006, French universities will thus be aligned with others in Europe, as illustrated in Figure 2.[21] The holders of a *baccalauréat* can still chose to attend a STS or IUT and pass a vocational diploma in two years, or to prepare a selective exam to attend a *grande école*, but the study structure at the university is transformed. Universities can still deliver DEUG and *maîtrises* (see Figure 1), but the curricula are now organized in a 3-year program finishing with a bachelor's degree (called "license"), and allows students to attend a 2-year program finishing with a master's degree. These two programs are organized around the accumulation "credits" according to the European Credit Transfer System, in order to favor student mobility from one institution and or (European) country to another. In order to be more visible on the European (international) scene, most *grandes écoles* will deliver diplomas which will be labeled as equivalent to a master's level.

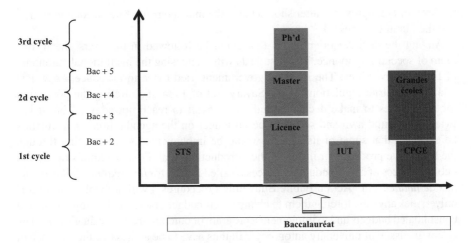

Figure 2. Tertiary education after the generalization of the Bologna process.

This harmonization process of the study programs among European countries is taking place concurrently with an opening of the national French system. French academics, institutions and public authorities are becoming increasingly concerned with the European perspective on higher education. In a way, they are becoming aware of the potential weakening of national borders (a trend expected by some, feared by others) and of the necessity to represent oneself (as individual, institution or public actor) not only as part of a country but also within a larger area (at least the European one, if not also the international one). The global competition for students and academics among higher education systems has thus become a recurrent topic of concern over the last several years, as shown by the numerous papers and declarations about the risk of brain drain (particularly from France to the U.S.) and the declining numbers of foreign students.

Future Challenges

The continual evolution described in this chapter is not to be discounted, but could nonetheless appear rather limited in a few years if some of the potential transformations under discussion were to become true. As a matter of fact, many observers today feel that the French higher education and research systems are in decisive times. The demonstrations and protests that occurred in 2004—launched by researchers against the instability of public funding from one year to another and against the low number of permanent positions opened to the recruitment of young doctors in research institutions and universities—testify to a strong feeling of crisis. But if the unrest revealed a general consensus on the need for change, it also showed a lack of agreement on what and how to change. The numerous documents[22] produced by different bodies or groups of academics in the following weeks clearly express the variety of scenarios and the divergence on issues such as the respective role of research institutions and universities, the level of autonomy the latter should have, the management of the academic staff,[23] and the funding process.

Among the decisive orientations that could be followed in the years ahead, two seem of special importance. The first deals with increasing the institutional autonomy of French universities. The Raffarin government tried twice to introduce a new law relaxing the strict regulations of the Savary Act of 1984 and offering the possibility for universities to make decisions that are difficult to reach nowadays,[24] but it has twice been withdrawn and seems to be no longer on the agenda. It can nevertheless be expected that some of its aspects would be implemented without going through the legislative process. For instance, the introduction in all French administration and public services of a new budgetary process (called LOLF, for *loi organique relative aux lois de finances*, or "Act on Public Budgeting Procedures") will probably "constrain" universities anyway, forcing them to change their budget practices, develop global and consolidated budgets and to implement a program of outcome-based evaluation. By law or not, the issue of university autonomy will thus have to be addressed: the contractual policy launched a move towards more autonomy, but universities are now in midstream. Remaining there is probably the worse that could happen!

The second crucial issue deals with academic careers. The retirement waves which are expected in the near future (Fréville, 2002) are often seen as a good opportunity to modify academic positions and profiles. Regarding positions, the recent (but contested) orientation was to reduce the number of permanent positions in research institutions and to delay access to permanent positions by developing postdoctoral positions and temporary contracts. In terms of academic profiles, the rather simultaneous recruitment of young talent is expected to renew and stimulate the entire profession. But the idea is also to redesign the university-faculty relationship and to give the former the possibility of directly managing the latter.[25] The report written under the direction of the former university president Eric Espéret on academic work and faculty duties (*Rapport Espéret*, 2001) and the report written under the direction of the former university president Bernard Belloc on the status of French faculty members (*Rapport Belloc*, 2003), for example, plead for the recognition of the diversity of academic work and for the opportunity for university presidents to negotiate and sign contracts with each faculty member regarding his or her teaching duties, involvement in research activities, and participation in collective services or administrative tasks. The *Belloc Report* even suggested an incentive bonus system to financially reward differentiated commitments.

Many things are thus on the political agenda for higher education; many of them are quite sensible, and it is indeed very difficult to say, at the moment of this writing, whether the challenges universities are confronted with will be met or not. But it is certain that the coming years will have a decisive long-term impact on the French higher education system and its capacity to be a relevant player in a more open and competitive global environment.

Notes

1. For more on the early history of universities in France, please see the chapter by Harold Perkin in volume 1 of this *Handbook*.

2. This means that the *licence* (diploma that can be passed at the end of the third university year) or the *maîtrise* (diploma that can be passed at the end of the fourth university year) can only be delivered by a university. A *grande école* (professional school) delivers its own diplomas, which can be national if recognized by the French state, but that cannot be called *licence* or *maîtrise*.
3. Since the Savary act of 1984, they are called UFR (Unités de Formation et de Recherche, or Research and Training Units).
4. This is certainly not the vocabulary that was used at that time but the so-called *personnalités extérieures* (individuals who do not belong to the university) were appointed among local industrialists, politicians, etc.
5. The rest being allocated on criteria, such as the number of students, the number of square meters, etc.
6. Many *grandes écoles* had almost no research activities in the recent past.
7. Top French private businesses ask for 7,200 to 7,600 euros a year.
8. According to Aghion and Cohen (2004, p. 33), in 1999, public expenses for higher education represented 1% of the GDP and private expenses 0.1%.
9. French Ministry of Education website: http://www.education.gouv.fr.
10. In France, the President, Prime Minister, one of the Ministers of the Government or some specific institutions can appoint a committee of experts placed under the direction of a French personality (here Armand Frémont, an academic who has had various administrative responsibilities at the Ministry of Education) and ask them to write a report on a specific question. Such reports are then called Rapport X or Commission X, X being the name of the personality chosen to lead the work of the experts. In this chapter, the Rapport Frémont, Rapport Espéret, Rapport Mudry and Rapport Belloc will be mentioned. I shall describe each time precisely what their mission was.
11. Only 45.5% of the students obtain their DEUG in two years (almost 80% if one takes into account those who need five years to obtain this two-year diploma), but only 17.1% of those having a *baccalauréat technologique* (40% in two to five years).
12. In France 11,500 doctoral students received a fellowship from the Ministry (among them 5,168 have teaching duties), but there are 64,170 doctoral students according to the CNER report (2003: 14), not all of them being funded.
13. This is a kind of second Ph.D. The applicant prepares a volume in which he/she presents his/her research program and results over his/her career. He/she provides all his/her publications. A defense is organized and the jury decide whether the applicant is *habilité* (agreed) or not.
14. Satisfying criteria is therefore never enough: one has to be "the best", whatever this means.
15. There is, most of the time, a short period between the end of the Ph.D. and the first recruitment which may slightly vary from one discipline to another, as the average age of access to a *maître de conférences* (tenured assistant professor) position does. In the health sciences, for instance, candidates are expected to do a postdoc after the Ph.D.
16. According to Cytermann, Bideault, Rossi, and Thomas (2003), this concerns 55% of the professors in sciences and humanities. In such a case, the progression from *maîtres de conférences* (tenured assistant professors) to professor, which can only occur if a professorial position is vacant and if a recruitment procedure is launched and an ad published, is obtained by giving priority to local candidates over the external ones.
17. The institutional evaluations produced since its creation in 1984 by the evaluation agency called the CNE (*Comité National d'Evaluation des universities* or National Committee for the evaluation of higher education institutions) are up to now independent from the budget allocations made by the Ministry.
18. This gave rise to the creation of *antennes universitaires* (university branches) for undergraduates in small cities around the town where the university head office is located. Some of these antennas were not even recognized by the ministry and lived on local resources (Felouzis, 2001; Filâtre, 1997).
19. According to the report written under the direction of the former university president Michel Mudry on university budgets (Rapport Mudry, 2004), about 62% of the universities' operating budget (salaries excluded) is public (56.5% funded by ministries, 5.21% from local authorities)

but one should not forget that salaries represent about 60% of the state resources for higher education.
20. For more on this, please see the chapter by Hans de Wit in this volume.
21. Not surprisingly, the IUT are lobbying to offer a three-year curricula.
22. For instance, the report of P. Aghion and E. Cohen (2004) for the CAE, the report published by the Cercle des économistes (Cohen, 2004), the declaration of the University Presidents Conference (CPU, 2004), the report "Du nerf" written by F. Jacob, P. Kourilsky, J.-M. Lehn and P.-L. Lions—all four professors at the College de France—or the report diffused by the president and general director of the CNRS (Larrouturou & Mégie, 2004).
23. The Conference of university presidents, for instance, asks for the suppression of researchers' positions in national institutions and for a unified status, meaning that the latter should all become university teachers.
24. For instance, changing one's university status with a university majority of 50%, where before it should have reached two-thirds.
25. Some ask the positions to be directly managed by each university.

References

Aghion, P. & Cohen, E. (2004). *Education et croissance (Education and growth).* Paris: La Documentation française (Report of the Conseil d'analyse économique, n° 46). Available online at http://www.diderotp7.jussieu.f/2004/01-CAEeducationcroissance.pdf

Antoine, G. & Passeron, J.-C. (1966). *La réforme de l'université (The university reform).* Paris: Calmann-Lévy.

Becquet, V. & Musselin, C. (2004). *Variations autour du travail des universitaires (Variations about academic work).* (Convention MENRT 20022007, ACI: "Travail", monograph). Paris: CSO.

Belloc, B. (2003). Incentives and accountability: Instruments of change in higher education. *Higher Education Management and Policy, 15*(1), 27–47.

Berrivin, R. & Musselin, C. (1996). Les politiques de contractualisation entre centralisation et décentralisation: les cas de l'équipement et de l'enseignement supérieur (Contractual policies between decentralization and centralization). *Sociologie du Travail, 38*(4), 575–596.

Bideault, M. & Rossi, P. (2002). *Les personnels enseignants de l'enseignement supérieur 2000–2001 (Higher Education Staff 2000–2001).* Note d'information 02.42. Paris: Ministère de l'Education Nationale et Ministère de la Recherche (Ministry of Education and Research).

Charle, C. (1994). *La république des universitaires, 1870–1940 (The republic of academics, 1870–1940).* Paris: Seuil.

Chevaillier, T. (1998). Moving away from central planning: Using contracts to steer higher education in France. *European Journal of Education, 33*(1), 65–76.

Chevallier, P., Grosperrin B., & Maillet, J. (1968). *L'enseignement français de la Révolution à nos jours (French education from the Revolution to nowadays).* Paris-La Haye: Editions Mouton.

Clark, B. R. (1987). *Academic Life, small worlds, different worlds.* Princeton NJ: Carnegie Foundation for the Advancement of Teaching.

CNER. (2003). *Evaluation de la recherche publique dans les établissements publics français (Assessment of public research in French higher education institutions).* Paris: La Documentation Française.

Cohen, E. (Dir.) (2004). *Réformer l'enseignement supérieur et la recherche. Un pacte pour une Nouvelle Université (Reforming higher education and research).* Paris: Le cercle des economists (Circle of Economists). Available online at http://www.cercledeseconomistes.asso.fr/cahier_5.pdf.

Cohen, H. S. (1978). *Elusive reform: The French universities, 1968–1978.* Boulder, CO: Westview Press.

Colloque de Caen. (1966). Actes du colloque (Proceedings). *Bulletin quotidien de l'Association d'étude pour l'expansion de la recherche scientifique (Journal of the Association of the Study for the Expansion of Scientific Research),* November 1966.

Compagnon, A. (1998). Pourquoi la France n'a pas d'Université (Why France has no university). *Critique, 611,* 172–192.

CPU. (2004). *Organisation et fonctionnement de la recherche publique en France: situation et avenir (How French public research is organized and functions).* Paris: http://www.cpu. fr/Telecharger/Publi/OrganisationRechercheMai2004.pdf.

Cytermann, J. R., Bideault, M., Rossi, P., & Thomas, L. (2003). Recrutements et renouvellement des enseignants-chercheurs: disparités entre établissements et disciplines (Recruitments and renewal of faculty). Contribution to the RESUP research seminar, 7th of March, Nanterre.

Doeringer, P. B. & Piore, M. J. (1971). *Internal labor markets and manpower analysis.* Lexington: Heath Lexington Books.

Euriat, M. & Thélot, C., 1995. Le recrutement social de l'élite scolaire en France de 1950 à 1990 (Social recruitment of the French student elite). *Revue Française de Sociologie, 36*(3), 403–438.

Felouzis, G. (2001). *La condition estudiantine (Student condition).* Paris: P.U.F.

Filâtre, D. (Dir.) (1997). *Université 2000: Les effets des implantations nouvelles (University 2000: The effects of new university locations).* Report for the DATAR, Vols. 1. & 2. Toulouse.

Fréville, Y. (2002). *Des universitaires mieux évalués, des universités plus responsables (Better assessment of academics, more responsible universities).* Les Rapports du Sénat, no 54.

Friedberg, E. & Musselin, C. (1989). *En quête d'universités (Looking for universities).* Paris: L'Harmattan.

Gerbod, P. (1965). *La condition universitaire en France au XIXè siècle (Academics in France 19th century).* Paris: PUF.

Jacob, F., Kourilsky, P., Lehn, J. M., & Lions, P. L. (2004). *Du nerf! Donner un nouvel essor à la recherche Française (Go ahead! Give a new impulse to French research).* Available online at www.pasteur.fr/pasteur/dunerf.html.

Larrouturou, B. & Mégie, G. (2004). *Notre projet pour le CNRS (Our project for the CNRS).* Paris: CNRS: http://www.cnrs.fr/cw/fr/accu/ProjetPourLeCNRS.pdf.

Mignot-Gérard, S. & Musselin, C. (2002). More leadership for French universities, but also more divergences between the presidents and the deans. In M. Dewatripont, F. Thys-Clément, & L. Wilkin (Eds.), *European universities: Change and convergence* (pp. 123–146). Bruxelles: Editions de l'Université de Bruxelles.

Musselin, C. (1997). State/university relations and how to change them. *European Journal of Education, 32*(2), 145–164. Also reproduced in M. Henkel & B. Little (Ed.), (1999), *Changing relationships between higher education and the state* (pp. 42–68). London: Jessica Kingsley Publishers.

Musselin C. (2000). The role of ideas in the emergence of convergent higher education policies in Europe: The case of France. Working paper series #73. Center for European Studies: Harvard University.

Musselin, C. (2004). *The Long March of French Universities.* New York: Routledge (first published in French in 2001, *La longue marche des universities.* Paris: PUF).

Musselin, C. & Brisset, C. (1989). *Rapport sur les administrations de tutelle des universités en France et en RFA (Report on higher education public authorities in France and Germany).* Study for the Ministère de la Recherche et de l'Enseignement Supérieur (Study for the Ministry of Research and Higher Education). Monograph. Paris: CAFI.

Organization for Economic Cooperation and Development. (2003). *Education at a Glance.* Paris: OECD.

Rapport Belloc. (2003). *Propositions pour une modification du décret 84-431 portant statut des enseignants (Proposals for the modification of the decree 84-431 about faculty staff).* Report to the Ministère de la Jeunesse, de l'Education Nationale et de la Recherche (Report to the Ministry for Youth, National Education and Research).

Rapport Espéret. (2001). *Nouvelle définition des tâches des enseignants et des enseignants chercheurs dans l'enseignement supérieur français (New definition of the workload and duties for university teachers).* Report to the French Ministry of Education.

Rapport Frémont. (2004). *Les universités françaises en mutation: la politique publique de contractualisation, 1984–2002 (French universities in mutation: the contractual policy, 1984–2002).* Paris: La Documentation française.

Rapport Mudry. (2002). *Budget global des universités (Global budget for universities)*. Report for the Conférence des Présidents d'université (Report for the Conference of University Presidents).

Prost, A. (1968). *Histoire de l'enseignement en France 1800–1967*. (A history of French education, 1800–1967). Paris: Colin.

Renaut, A. (1995). *Les révolutions de l'université. Essai sur la modernisation de la culture (University revolutions: Essay on the modernisation of culture)*. Paris: Calman-Lévy.

Verger, J. (Ed.) (1986). *Histoire des universités en France (A history of French universities)*. Toulouse, France: Editions Privat.

37

GERMANY

Barbara M. Kehm
University of Kassel, Germany

German universities have their roots in the development of the European university during the medieval ages. The earliest universities were those of Paris and Bologna, and they served as the basic model throughout the continent long before the foundation of the European nation-states. Already in the medieval ages, universities had the right to regulate their own internal affairs and to award academic degrees. Despite an early differentiation into lower (*artes liberales*) and higher (theology, medicine, law) faculties, the education of students sought to encompass the acquisition of all knowledge available at the time. In order to study at any of the three higher faculties, successful completion of the lower "artistic" faculty was required. Students and teachers formed a community at each university, but it was also normal for both groups to be mobile and to change universities. Mechanisms were in place to recognize academic degrees acquired at any of the European universities (cf. Ellwein, 1985; Stichweh, 1991). Students typically paid their professors for each lesson, and the common language of teaching was Latin.

The first German universities were founded in the late 14th and early 15th centuries, the oldest being Heidelberg, which celebrated its 600th anniversary in 1986. Most universities of the late medieval ages were small. There were two or three professors in each faculty and between 100 and 200 students per university, sometimes fewer. Around the year 1500, the total number of students in the German states and electorates amounted to about 3,000. Only men were allowed to study at this time—the access of women to universities was paved much later, at the beginning of the 20th century during the Weimar Republic. By the year 1700, Germany had about 40 universities serving approximately 8,000 students.

The conceptualization and foundation of Humboldt University in Berlin by Wilhelm von Humboldt—who was head of department and responsible for culture and schools in the Prussian Ministry of the Interior around 1810—marked a decisive point in time for the idea and ideal of the German University which is basically still valid today. Although many experts have argued that neither Humboldt himself nor other responsible actors succeeded in putting the ideal into practice, the main principles laid out in Humboldt's famous memorandum about the "internal and external organization of the higher scientific institutions in Berlin" (cf. Humboldt, 1810 [1993], p. 255) still

James J.F. Forest and Philip G. Altbach (eds.), International Handbook of Higher Education, 729–745.
© 2006 *Springer. Printed in the Netherlands.*

determine the self-understanding of the German university: the unity of research and teaching; academic freedom; the unity of the disciplines under one university roof; the education of character through academic knowledge; a relatively high degree of governmental control coupled with the responsibility to finance the institutions; and the right of universities to regulate their internal and academic affairs themselves. Humboldt's memorandum emphasized in particular that research (and academic learning through research) involves a never-ending search for truth which must be continuously pursued.

Using a modern notion frequently applied within the context of "higher education marketing," it is possible to say that Humboldt's university model became an export commodity. With the exception of the Anglo-Saxon system, most higher education systems in central, east and northern Europe adopted this model for their emerging university systems, as did the United States for its graduate education (although it developed a different direction over the course of time).

The number of students and professors in Germany increased continuously during the 19th century. Universities were internally governed by the chair holders (the full professors), who viewed their institutions as elite—a view which affected a variety of issues related to access, public service, and scholarship. Within the context of German Idealism, the sciences developed and blossomed, leading to a number of important inventions and discoveries. Germany became the most important scientific nation during that time (Ellwein, 1985, p. 131).

Between 1933 and 1945, the time of the National Socialist regime under Hitler, German universities played a rather discreditable role by submitting (to a large degree) to the Nazi ideology. Many teachers, researchers and students—in particular those of Jewish origin—were forced to leave the universities. Access to higher education for women was limited. In the short time span of only 5 years, between National Socialism coming into power and the beginning of World War II, the number of students was reduced by half, from 121,000 in 1933 to 56,000 in 1939 (Peisert & Framhein, 1994, p. 5). Many of the best German scientists emigrated, quite a number of them to the United States. The consequences these events had for German research—especially in the natural and social sciences—can hardly be accounted for even today, but in essence, Germany clearly lost its leading position as a scientific nation. Also, as a result of World War II, the separation of East and West Germany led to the development of two markedly different systems of higher education over the next four decades.

Higher Education, the State and Society after 1945

Higher Education Development in the Federal Republic of Germany

West German higher education policy in the immediate postwar period was under control of the western allied forces (Great Britain, France, and the United States). It focused primarily on the reconstruction of buildings and infrastructure demolished by the war, on de-nazification (i.e., removal of national socialist professors and institutional leaders), and on re-education (i.e., learning democracy). However, in West Germany the notion prevailed that the German higher education system of pre-1933 had been basically sound and should be reconstructed on the basis of Humboldt's idea of the university. With the foundation of the German Federal Republic in 1949, German federalism was reinstated according to the tradition of the Weimar Republic (1918–1933), which meant that the individual states (and not the federal government) were responsible for culture and education. Sixteen universities and nine technical universities became the starting point for the postwar development of the West German higher education system. The resulting development of the system—until the fall of the Berlin Wall in 1989 and subsequent unification of the two German states—can be divided into five phases (cf. Peisert & Framhein, 1994; Kehm, 1999): decentralized reconstruction (1950s); system-wide initiatives (1960s); cooperative federalism (early 1970s); reform and legislative dynamics (mid-1970s); and post-experimental truce (1980s).

The 1950s can be described as a phase of "decentralized reconstruction," guided by federalist principles which were implemented after World War I. However, there was also a growing need for an overall coordination of the educational policy of the West German States. For this reason, the Standing Conference of the Ministers of Culture in the Western Allied zones of Germany had been established as early as 1948. Its task was to assure a certain degree of homogeneity in the West German system of education, including higher education. A federal ministry for education and science was established in 1955, but with limited competency in education. The Science Council, an intermediary body between the federal government and universities, was established in 1957 to advise and recommend on the quantitative, structural and functional development of the West German higher education system.

A second phase of "system-wide initiatives" characterized the early and mid-1960s. After the "Sputnik shock"[1] and Picht's famous essay about the "German educational catastrophe" (Picht, 1964), a new era of higher education expansion began. Plans were made to increase the number of higher education institutions as well as the number of students in order to produce a higher percentage of graduates for the labor market and thus secure future economic growth. Within 10 years, the number of students in West Germany doubled, the number of professors more than doubled, and the number of non-professorial teaching and research staff tripled. Efforts were made to improve equal opportunities for women in higher education, and a system of financial assistance for students from low income families was established by the federal government. In addition, the Federal Ministry for Education and Science acquired some competences in higher education policy by supporting the states with funding for research.

The years around 1970 can be called a phase of "cooperative federalism." In 1969, the West German Constitution was changed to define selected issues in the field of higher education as joint responsibilities of the states and the federal government, in particular the funding of new buildings, the coordination of educational planning and research promotion. For these tasks, joint commissions were established. In addition, debates emerged about a new framework law for higher education, which was finally passed in 1976.

The early and mid-1970s saw a phase of "reform and legislative dynamics." The student movements of the late 1960s and early 1970s had led to a change in government from conservative (via a conservative and social democratic coalition) to a liberal and social democratic coalition government in 1969. Many traditions in higher education were questioned, and far-reaching reforms were demanded. The debates about the role of universities in society were more heated than ever before. The exclusive decision-making power of the professors in the departments and faculties (as well as in the senate) was substituted by a more participative model which included representatives of students, non-professorial and even non-academic support staff in all decision-making bodies of the universities. Furthermore, the basically unitary system of West German higher education—which consisted of universities and technical universities— became a differentiated system with the development of universities of applied sciences (*fachhochschulen*) and, in at least some of the German states, comprehensive universities. Also, new procedures for the development and renewal of curricula were developed, and national curriculum reform commissions were established.

A final phase used to describe the historical development of the West German higher education system lasts from about 1977 until the end of the 1980s, and can be termed a phase of "post-experimental truce." The high hopes for substantial changes had been dampened since the mid-1970s, amid increasing concerns about a growth in graduate unemployment. Demographic prognoses projected a sharp decline in the number of students beginning in the late 1970s. Under these conditions, representatives of higher education institutions and political decision makers arrived at an agreement in 1977 to continue following a policy of open access to higher education for all eligible school leavers without increasing funding and teaching staff. Thus, the institutions were expected to educate an "overload" of students for about a decade until the expected decline in student numbers would re-balance the situation again. In return, political decision makers promised not to start any substantial reforms during the coming period. However, in contrast to these prognoses, student numbers actually increased—continuously and considerably—during this phase, while the numbers of academic staff stagnated. A few legislative changes were carried out—e.g., a change in the higher education framework law in 1985—but generally, this last phase of West German higher education development was clearly less dynamic than those of the previous decades.

Higher Education Development in the German Democratic Republic

Immediately following the end of World War II in 1945, the East German higher education institutions—six universities and three technical universities—picked up their work again generally where they had left off before the War. Throughout the next 10 years, several new institutions of higher education were founded, most of them specialized and mono-disciplinary. The higher education system of the German Democratic Republic expanded altogether earlier than the system of the Federal Republic of Germany. Expansion basically took place by establishing specialized institutions rather than full universities covering the whole spectrum of disciplines. By 1970, the number of higher education institutions in the German Democratic Republic had increased to 54 institutions.

Higher education development in the German Democratic Republic between 1945 and 1989 can also be divided into five phases (cf. Buck-Bechler, 1997; Kehm, 1999): early reforms (late 1940s), nationalization (1950s), expansion (1960s), ideological and industrial focus (1970s), and binary differentiation (1980s). The first phase was dominated by higher education reforms, which were implemented under the military control of the Soviet forces between 1945 and 1949. The state governments still existing at that time were given the task of carrying out the reconstruction of buildings and de-nazification of academic staff. Reforms focused on the creation of adequate structures and conditions to enable access to higher education for young people from families of workers and farmers. To bridge possible gaps between their school qualifications and the level of knowledge required for higher education, so-called workers' and farmers' faculties were created.

A second phase of development began with the official establishment of the German Democratic Republic as a country in 1949, and lasted until the building of the Berlin Wall and the Iron Curtain in the year 1961. This phase was characterized by the in-troduction of socialist educational principles, while Marxism–Leninism became an obligatory part of all degree programs in higher education. In 1952, the five states of the German Democratic Republic were dissolved and a centrally planned economy was introduced. Responsibility for higher education planning as well as the leadership of all higher education institutions became part of the State Secretariat. Higher education institutions lost their traditional institutional autonomy in all academic matters. Fur-ther, students were no longer allowed to study the subjects of their own choice. They were organized into study groups which were increasingly headed by functionaries of the Free German Youth, the only East German youth organization. Work placements in industry and agriculture became integrated parts of each degree program. Finally, the principle of "democratic centralism" was introduced into the leadership and manage-ment of higher education institutions, and research planning was adapted to the 5-year plans of the general economy.

The years between 1961 and 1971 can be characterized as the main phase of higher education expansion in the German Democratic Republic. During this time, ten new higher education institutions were established, and a new higher education law was passed in 1965, regulating the adaptation of higher education institutions to the re-quirements of scientific and technological progress. Applied research and development became more important, while the education and training of students would focus on forming the "socialist character" of students. In addition, greater emphasis was placed on developing and expanding continued education programs and opportunities. The proportion of students in distance learning courses for working people, called corre-spondence courses, increased to one-quarter of the total number of students. Existing planning and management structures in the institutions changed as well—in particu-lar, the traditional division of disciplines or groups of disciplines into faculties and institutes was substituted by a division into sections.

The main phase of higher education expansion ended with the eighth general meeting of the Unified Socialist Party (SED) in 1971, which marked the beginning of a new— more ideologically focused—phase of development, which lasted until about 1980. The general meeting of the SED in 1971 brought about a change in party leadership from Walter Ulbricht to Erich Honnecker. Under Honnecker, ideological education was intensified and the continuous expansion of higher education was regarded as a development in the wrong direction. Beginning in 1972, access quotas were reduced and distance or correspondence courses lost their importance. Relationships between higher education and industry were institutionalized and cooperation was regulated. The curricula of all degree programs were subjected to central planning, which was accompanied by the desire to organize the transition of graduates into the world of work. The annual number of new students was set at 30,000 and remained the same from the mid-1970s onwards. This number was tied to the respective manpower requirement figures of the 5-year plans for the economy. In comparison to West German higher education developments during the same time period, this led to a clearly more favorable student/faculty ratio in East German higher education. However, the proportion of new students among the respective age cohort remained considerably lower (between 10% and 13%) than in West Germany (slightly less than 20%)—in other words, East Germany during this period saw significantly lower levels of access to (and participation in) higher education.

The final phase of this historical review covers the years 1980 through 1989, during which a binary system of higher education was established in East Germany. This consisted basically of universities with a broad spectrum of disciplines and degree programs (on the one hand), and specialized, often mono-disciplinary institutions of higher education (on the other). This differentiation was the result of a targeted access policy which directed student enrollment toward those subjects in which a high demand for graduates existed from the economy (e.g., engineering), or toward those subjects in which central planning saw a need for highly qualified labor to achieve economic progress.

The fifth (and last) higher education conference of the German Democratic Republic, which took place in 1980, aimed at improving the quality of higher education by giving greater emphasis on undergraduate education and the improvement of general and labor market-related contents of study programs. By increasing the flexibility of study plans, students were granted more freedom and autonomy. Finally, the cooperation between higher education and industry was intensified even further by increasing applied and commissioned research.

Effects of German Unification on Higher Education

The fall of the Berlin wall in November 1989 and the subsequent dissolution of the socialist regime in the German Democratic Republic led to the unification of the two German States which had been separated since 1949. The Unification Contract was signed on August 31, 1990 and set off a process of immense change. Political, economic, and social conditions in the five new federal states of East Germany were adapted to West German conditions. Along with many other regulations, the Unification Contract envisioned the adaptation of the basic structure of the West German system of education to East Germany.

Apart from a few specifics, the West German status quo served as a model for the transformation of the East Germany system of higher education (cf. Mayntz, 1994; Buck-Bechler & Jahn, 1994; Schramm, 1993). The task of East German higher education renewal slowed down reforms which had been initiated in the West German system of higher education toward the end of the 1980s. The West German higher education framework law served as the legal basis for the restructuring and transforming of the East German system. The distribution of rights and responsibilities followed the federalist principles of West Germany after the five federal states of East Germany had been re-established. Within higher education institutions, academic self-governance in internal affairs and freedom of teaching and research were reinstated.

Research carried out by the institutes of the East German Academy of Sciences was evaluated by the West German Science Council. Research staff and research structures were reduced, and many institutes and groups dissolved. Those surviving quality assessment and political screening were either re-integrated into higher education institutions or—for the most part—became one of the non-university institutes or research groups of the Gottfried Wilhelm Leibniz Association.[2]

The main activities of higher education restructuring and renewal in East Germany can be summarized in five aspects (cf. Kehm & Teichler, 1996):

(a) *De-politicization*: All departments for Marxism–Leninism as well as all political higher education institutions (party, police, military forces) were closed; political activities of academic staff were evaluated; departments and subjects with close links to the previous political system—in particular law, economics, social sciences, and education—were dissolved and eventually re-established with new (often West German) academic staff.

(b) *Reorganization and evaluation of extra-university research*: Many institutes of the Academy of Sciences, the main organization for basic research, were dissolved; high quality research groups and institutes—the performance of which was positively evaluated—either became part of the Leibniz Group of non-university research or were re-integrated into the universities to strengthen university research in East Germany.

(c) *Establishment of universities of applied sciences (Fachhochschulen)*: The remodeling of previously specialized higher education institutions into universities of applied sciences was coupled with the establishment of a number of new universities of applied sciences.

(d) *Restructuring of subjects and disciplines*: Composition, size and curricula were adapted to West German standards, although with a certain degree of leeway for innovation. The high level of specialization was abandoned.

(e) *Reform of the staff structure*: Staff structures typical for the West German system of higher education were introduced. The political involvement and academic performance of scientific staff were assessed, and in cases of negative outcomes, employment contracts were terminated. In cases of positive outcomes, staff members had the option to either apply to one of the advertised staff positions (thus having to compete with other East German as well as West German academic staff applying for the same position), or to join one of the special research groups of the Leibniz Association. Transition into premature retirement and enforced unemployment were also widespread.

This dramatic German–German "tour de force" required extensive resources in terms of staff and money in order to adapt the East German conditions and structures as much as possible to the West German status quo, although the latter was in dire need of reforms as well (cf. Peisert & Framhein, 1994; Science Council, 1992).

The question of a dual reform of the East German and the West German system of higher education was frequently discussed among experts and political decision makers during that time. Views differ about the issue of whether the West German system of higher education missed a historical opportunity for reforms. However, there was widespread agreement that reforming the West German system—while at the same time restructuring and renewing the East German higher education system—was an impossible mission. Still, the process of German unification has led to unexpected challenges and new questions as well as to new problems and opportunities for both parts of the system of higher education.

Within this context, one cannot underestimate the role which East German higher education has played (and is still playing) as both a challenge and stimulus for reforming the entire contemporary German higher education system. In particular, three factors have contributed to this:

- The process of transformation was seized upon by many East German higher education institutions as an opportunity to introduce innovations in areas like management, teaching and curriculum development.
- The East German tradition of emphasizing teaching rather than research within higher education institutions and providing a favorable student/faculty ratio continues to determine attitudes and self-understanding of academic staff at East German institutions.
- The newly established structures of higher education in East Germany are less consolidated, so that there is generally more openness for experiments and reforms.

Two further challenges and reciprocal influences warrant mention here. First, the rigorous evaluation of the quality of academic work at East German higher education institutions and extra-university research institutes (including the Academy of Sciences) affected West German higher education institutions in a particular way. The resistance of West German professors against any kind of external assessment of their teaching and research performance broke down after they had become involved to a considerable extent in such an exercise in East Germany. Second, the structural transfer of the West German system of higher education did not lead to an identical development in the forms and contents of teaching, studies and research in East Germany. Some of the most interesting and promising innovations in the organization of teaching and study programs came from East German institutions, and serve as models of good practice with which West German higher education institutions can experiment as well. Overall, a new dynamic became visible from the beginning of the mid-1990s onwards, which gradually seized the whole German system of higher education and provided a new thrust for reforms and innovation. This dynamic was later focused on reforming degree structures towards the bachelor's/master's model, triggered by Germany's involvement in the Bologna Declaration.

Structural and Quantitative Developments

In 1989, the starting point of the dramatic structural and quantitative developments described in this chapter, there were 244 higher education institutions in West Germany, categorized by the following six types: 68 universities (including technical universities, special universities, and one distance university); 30 art academies; 121 universities of applied sciences (including those for public administration); 16 theological seminaries and institutions; eight teacher training colleges; and one comprehensive university (cf. BMBF, 2000). In the same year, a total of 70 higher education institutions existed in East Germany, categorized as follows: nine multi-disciplinary universities; 12 technical universities; 29 special institutions (including engineering, teacher training, art, and agriculture); three medical universities; and 17 political institutions (party, police, union, and military).

The process of restructuring and renewal of the East German higher education (including institutional mergers and new denominations) led to 16 universities, 11 art academies, one teacher training college and 31 universities of applied sciences—a type which previously had not existed in East Germany. In addition, 11 theological seminaries and a few private higher education institutions were established. In 2000, 10 years after the signing of the Unification Contract, the German higher education landscape consisted altogether of 350 higher education institutions. An overview of the recent expansion of Germany's higher education system is provided in Table 1.

The German higher education system is characterized as a binary system, with the vast majority of students enrolled in either universities or universities of applied sciences. In 2000, Germany had slightly more than 1.6 million students, the majority of whom (slightly less than 1.2 million) studied at universities. Nearly 46% of all students were women; however, in a number of subjects (e.g., medicine, biology, cultural and social sciences, and languages) the proportion of female students is higher than 50%.

Table 1.   Development of Higher Education Institutions in Germany (1960–2000)

Institutional types	1960	1970	1980	1990	1996			2000		
	(West Germany)				West	East	Total	West	East	Total
Universities	33	41	55	70	73	17	90	78	18	96
Theological seminaries	17	14	11	16	14	2	16	14	2	16
Teacher training colleges	52	51	13	8	6	–	6	6	–	6
Art academies	24	26	26	31	35	11	46	37	12	49
Comprehensive universities	–	–	9	1	1	–	1	1	–	1
Universities for applied sciences*	–	98	115	122	144	32	176	148	34	182
Total	126	230	229	248	273	62	335	284	66	350

Note: * = including *Fachhochschulen* for Public Administration.
Source: Federal Ministry for Education and Research: Basic and Structural Data 2001–2002, Bonn.

The proportion of foreign students was approximately 12% in 2000, although a third of students with a foreign nationality were either born in Germany or had gone to school in Germany. Nearly 214,500 students successfully completed their degree program and finished their final examinations in 2000. Furthermore, Germany produces the highest number of doctoral degree holders among the European countries, namely about 25,000 annually.

German Higher Education in the 21st Century: Challenges and Perspectives

By international comparison, the German higher education system has traditionally been characterized as one of tight state control. In the second half of the 1990s, public and political criticism increased with respect to the quality and attractiveness of German higher education institutions. Political actors in particular thought that German higher education institutions were lagging behind in international competitiveness and had lost their attractiveness to foreign students. The institutions themselves did not accept this criticism but complained instead about chronic underfunding and an overload of students. There was also talk at all levels about a "reform congestion" and about inefficiency, deficits in the quality of teaching, high dropout rates and an overly long duration of studies. Among the many current challenges facing German higher education institutions, these five topics are deemed to provoke the most debate and have the most potential to result in important changes to the system as a whole.

Organizational Management and Market Orientation

In order to address the challenge of "reform congestion," political decision makers proposed a withdrawal of the state from tight control over higher education institutions. Institutions of higher education were allowed to become more autonomous in order to organize their tasks in more efficient and competitive ways. This autonomy was implemented by a far-reaching reform of the higher education framework law in 1998. However, this autonomy was not unconditional. New instruments other than state control were used to enable higher education institutions to react more flexibly to the new demands, including lump sum budgeting instead of the traditional form of line item budgeting. These reforms also included provisions addressing the evaluation of the quality of teaching; accountability; performance-related funding; and contract management.

Within the institutions, internal organizational reforms were expected to contribute to the development of unique profiles and missions, and to a strengthening of the roles of rectors and deans. Although a market orientation has been rather alien for the German system of higher education, a number of initiatives and programs have been launched in recent years to support the export of German courses and programs to students in other countries, and to introduce new competitive activities to market German higher education.

By means of continuous underfunding through the state, institutions are also compelled to try and find an increasing part of their budget from other sources, including the extension of continuing academic education programs (and increasing the price for such programs); the introduction of tuition fees for students who have been enrolled for more than 5 or 6 years without graduating; greater efforts to market research results; a more active acquisition of third party funding for research projects; new attempts to solicit external donors; and the establishment of alumni services. To date, studying in Germany is still tuition free, but this principle is eroding at its margins.

Another important element of organizational reform in German higher education has been the strengthening of institutional management. This includes the gradual dissolution of the traditional collegial model of governance, in which the rector or president is "the first among equals." Currently, more hierarchical models of governance are being introduced which are oriented toward managerial approaches. Increasingly, performance-related contracts are being used to regulate the relationships between the various levels of governance—i.e., between the state government and the individual institution, between institutional management and departments, and between departments and the individual professor or other academic staff members. Higher education institutions in Germany are also increasingly expected to function according to the principles of the market, although there is currently no consensus about the general introduction of tuition fees, so that artificial or "quasi-markets" have to be created.

Reforming the Academic Profession

A second challenge of the reform agenda in German universities has been widely acknowledged for quite some time now: the structure of the academic profession. However, all proposals to improve the situation have met with disagreement. Professors in Germany are life-tenured civil servants, and other academic and non-academic support staff are employees in the civil service, often with tenure, making changes in their employment contracts very difficult.

The introduction of sanctions for low performance was not allowed by unions or professional organizations. Performance-related pay typically involves some extra money, but never less.

The structure of academic staff has become polarized over the years. While professors are tenured for life, other academic staff are predominantly employed on fixed-term contracts of 6 years before the awarding of a Ph.D. degree, and 6 years after that at most. Among the academic staff below the professorship, those with tenure have decreased continuously over the last 10 years. Criticism is mostly directed against the lack of flexibility of this structure. The professional mobility of professors is deemed to be too low and happens only practically within the framework of negotiations for a chair at another university. Another issue is the duration of the qualification process, be it in the framework of getting a Ph.D. or the second formal qualification phase needed to become a professor. In general, junior academic staff are kept employed at the will of their supervisor or the chair holder for too long. Two reforms dealing with staff structure and the pay scale structure were initiated in the years 2001 and 2002, and it is hoped that they might contribute to a change in this situation.

In 2001, the Federal Ministry of Education and Research started a support program of more than six million Euros for the introduction of the so-called "junior professorship." The objectives of the program are to reduce the duration of qualifying junior academic staff until a professorship is achieved (doing away with the habilitation) and provide professorships for highly qualified young academics. Despite continuous skepticism from higher education institutions as well as from some German states (not all German states participate in the program to create junior professorships), a number of institutions are in the process of introducing the new position. Funding from the Ministry provides the resources necessary for the junior professors to get started in their job. Other conditions of employment—e.g., the salary level and teaching load—are determined by the ministries of the respective state.

Junior professors are civil servants on fixed-term contracts. After 3 years, their performance is evaluated and their contract can be renewed for another 3 years. After a second successful evaluation it will be possible to change the junior professorship into a regular professorship, which includes the award of a chair at the institution at which the junior professor has been employed. Traditionally, an academic staff member could not become a professor at the institution at which he or she acquired the habilitation.

The second reform, initiated in 2002, introduced a new salary structure for professors and junior professors. In this structure, elements of performance-related pay will increase, and higher education institutions can determine for themselves the levels of compensation they will offer their faculty. Four instances may lead to a higher income:

- negotiations with the home institution in the case of an offer to become a chair at another institution;
- outstanding performance in teaching, research, art and/or continuing academic education;
- taking responsibility for particular functions in academic self-governance; or
- special funding for teaching and research from third party project funding.

These changes in the organizational culture of German higher education institutions, together with other governmental reforms, reflect a clear trend toward the dissolution of the traditional, non-hierarchical self-governance dominated by the "academic oligarchy." Higher education institutions are being strengthened as organizations in order to be able to react more flexibly to the demands of a changing environment. Further elements to increase flexibility have also been recently introduced: changes in the statutes of institutions, widening the range of resources for funding, and professionalization of institutional management. Amid the changing relationship between higher education and the state, described earlier in this chapter as a shift from state control and regulation to more market elements, changes are being made in the internal organization of institutions, involving a shift from the dominance of professors to a more important role of the organization as a whole. From these shifts, German higher education institutions can become more independent and strategic actors in various societal and political arenas. They will also acquire more power to shape their own development and direction, resulting in greater institutional diversity throughout the system.

Teaching Quality

The third challenge is created by widespread dissatisfaction with the quality of teaching, mainly at (West) German universities, and less so at universities of applied sciences. Criticism with regard to the long duration of studies and high dropout rates had already begun in the second half of the 1980s. But after the participation of West German professors in the evaluation of East German higher education (following the fall of the Berlin Wall and the unification contract), resistance to the assessment and evaluation of teaching quality finally broke down. Since then, most higher education institutions have introduced a regular evaluation of teaching quality, in particular by means of student questionnaires. Only a few universities have implemented more elaborate procedures of evaluation or use external evaluators. External or peer observation of actual class teaching continues to be taboo in German higher education.

All consequences and measures to improve poor results of these evaluations—e.g., seminars for professors and other teaching staff to improve their teaching skills, financial incentives, stricter controls over whether professors actually and regularly teach their classes and whether they fulfill their teaching load, or measures to improve contact with (and advice for) students—have so far been rather vigorously contested. The prevailing skepticism is mainly due to two reasons. First, prestige and career boosts within the scientific community are continuously gained through successes in research and publications, and not in teaching. Second, many professors claim that students today are less well-educated and prepared for studying than in previous times. Therefore, the claim is that higher education institutions should be given the right to select their own students in order to improve the quality of teaching.

Still, during the last 7 or 8 years, efforts have been made to develop and implement appropriate instruments and procedures for the evaluation of teaching in cooperation with universities and their departments and to carry out regular evaluations. Commissions or agencies have been set up either by the respective state ministries or by regional networks of higher education institutions to do this or to support the institutions in carrying out such evaluations themselves. Methods and procedures used have been mostly standardized by now. In these undertakings it became clear that in contrast to a ranking of institutions which is typical for the Anglo-Saxon and American systems of higher education, an institutional ranking in Germany does not make much sense. However, departments (or subjects or disciplines) are being increasingly compared with each other because it is generally assumed that one university cannot be first class in everything.

Results of external evaluations are typically discussed within the respective department and the reports agreed upon with the members of the evaluation commission. Mostly, the reports are not made public. As a rule, the respective department promises to improve upon their weak points, and their success in doing so is re-evaluated after 3 or more years. Most evaluations of teaching quality carried out in Germany are based on the principle of measuring a department against its own goals and objectives. No external standards are imposed apart from procedural ones. Finally, in cases of filling a chair or creating a new professorship, candidates for the position must provide proof of their teaching skills.

Degree Programs

The fourth challenge which is currently making a profound impact on the German system of higher education is the implementation of a tiered system of degrees on the basis of the bachelor's/master's model. When 30 European Ministers of Education signed the Bologna Declaration (1999)—two more signatory states joined somewhat later—they triggered a reform process aiming at the creation of a European Higher Education Area by the year 2010.[3] The Bologna Declaration and the ensuing reform process, called the Bologna process, formulated a number of goals and objectives to which all signatory states committed themselves. The Ministers also agreed to meet every 2 years to take stock of the implementation process. Thus, they met in Prague in 2001, in Berlin in 2003, and will meet in Bergen in 2005. The main goals that are expected to result in a European Higher Education Area are: (1) the introduction of a system of easily understandable and comparable degrees (bachelor's and master's); and (2) the introduction of a system of study programs based on two main cycles (undergraduate and graduate studies). The first cycle should have a duration of at least 3 years, followed by a second cycle of 1 or 2 years, without surpassing a duration of 5 years altogether. When the Ministers met in Berlin in 2003, doctoral education and training was added to this structure as a third cycle of studies.

Since 1999, more than 1,200 bachelor's and master's degree programs have been introduced in Germany. To a rather large extent, universities—as well as universities of applied sciences—are giving up their traditional degrees. Until recently, all new degree programs had to be examined and endorsed by the respective state ministries, a process which could take 2 years or more. With the decision to introduce the new bachelor's and master's degree structure, another important decision was made, namely to establish accreditation agencies. There are currently seven agencies in Germany—some subject-specific, others general—which examine applications for the introduction of bachelor's and master's degree programs according to criteria like quality, consistency and practicability. The application process and the evaluation of the applications have been standardized in order to speed up the accreditation process. The respective state ministries have reserved the right to authorize the legal aspects of the new degree programs—namely, the study and examination regulations.

Currently, the majority of higher education institutions offer the old degree programs parallel to the new ones. This is basically due to the fact that a particular law prescribes that students have a right to finish their degree program on the same conditions they started it. However, it is assumed that within a few years all students will have moved to (or started with) the new degree programs.

One of the conditions for the introduction of bachelor's degree programs was that students would be provided with sufficient key qualifications and professional competences within 3 years, to ensure a reasonable transition to employment; the term used in this context is "employability." Some subjects, however, continue to resist the

introduction of the bachelor's/master's structure (e.g., architects and engineers), arguing that in their field no proper professional qualification can be acquired in 3 years.
Also, potential employers are still unclear about how (and in which positions) the new
graduates can be employed, and what their first salary levels and career paths might be,
because they are unfamiliar with the qualifications, knowledge and competencies of a
person holding a bachelor's degree. Still, the German labor market for graduates from
higher education institutions has always been predominantly determined by supply
rather than by demand, and it is expected that a better marketing of the new degrees as
well as more information will eventually lead to a smooth transition. Overall, political
actors and decision makers hope that the introduction of a tiered degree structure will
achieve a reduction in dropout rates, as well as decreasing the time-to-degree for the
majority of students, thus relieving universities from the "overload" of students about
which they have been complaining since the second half of the 1970s.

Internationalization

The fifth challenge universities are confronted with is further internationalization, in
particular within the context of the General Agreement on Trade in Services (GATS).
Since World War II, the internationalization of German higher education has advanced
in several thrusts. International cooperation and the mobility of students and teaching
staff in the German Democratic Republic was basically restricted to other socialist or
communist countries. Higher education institutions in the pre-1989 Federal Republic of Germany cooperated mainly with other highly industrialized western countries
and the member states of the European Union. Although the European Commission at
first had no competencies in the field of education (which was defined to be a purely
national affair), it succeeded through the ERASMUS program to establish one of the
most successful support programs for mobility and cooperation in the history of higher
education internationalization. Despite the fact that the ERASMUS program has not
achieved its ambitious goal of supporting 10% of all European students for a limited
period of study abroad (usually between six and 12 months), nobody today doubts
the success of this program. But cooperation and exchange of German students and
academic staff is not restricted to ERASMUS and to Europe. Within the framework
of national support programs—which are predominantly administered by the German
Academic Exchange Service (DAAD)—cooperation of German higher education institutions is supported with institutions from non-European countries.

A period of study abroad has almost become a normal option for German students as
part of their degree program. To those students who for various reasons cannot or will not
go abroad for a period of study, students and teachers from other countries at their home
university offer an opportunity to become familiar with foreign cultures and different
styles of teaching and learning. Within the framework of increasing higher education
internationalization since the mid-1990s, a growing number of barriers which tended to
prevent mobility of staff and students have been removed. Throughout Germany, efforts
have been focused on improved counseling and advice for foreign students as well as
a professionalization of the international relations offices. With the help of funding
from the Federal Ministry of Education and Research, special study programs have

been established—most of them taught in English—which are particularly directed at attracting students from abroad.

In sum, internationalization has moved from a marginal to a central position in the activities and policies of many higher education institutions in Germany. Further, the content of studies is becoming increasingly international—be it through an emphasis on international comparisons, a focus on the international aspects of particular issues or the subject matter as a whole, or the development of joint study programs with partner institutions abroad, often finishing with a double degree from both institutions. Above all, the internationalization of study programs and degrees is an important element of the efforts to increase the attractiveness of studying in Germany for foreign students. A competitive advantage is that all bachelor's degree programs and most of the master's degree programs are still tuition free. But apart from the introduction of internationally recognized degrees, the new study programs developed for these degrees are also modularized to a large extent. Credit points are used to indicate successful completion of individual modules, and "diploma supplements"—an account of the subject matter of all degree program modules in the English language—are used to create more transparency in terms of what an individual student has learned.

Conclusion

The efforts of the European Commission and the Ministers of Education of the European countries to create a European Higher Education and Research Area, in order to make Europe the most dynamic and competitive knowledge economy of the world, have triggered far-reaching reforms of the German higher education system that clearly surpass the scope of previous reform phases. Higher education institutions have acquired a new (and for them, a still somewhat unfamiliar) role as autonomous and strategic actors in this process. It is uncontested that higher education institutions are an important element in the emerging knowledge society—not only in terms of their role in the production of new knowledge and in the search for solutions to societal problems, but also in terms of their responsibilities for developing the competencies of an ever-increasing proportion of the population. In order to fulfill these roles and responsibilities effectively, they need to be able to react in a flexible way to the demands of their environment, regardless of whether this environment is regional, national, international, or even global. The first steps have been taken. In the year 2010 or 2020, studying in Germany will clearly be different from today.

Notes

1. "Sputnik shock" is a key term used to denote the lost technological competition of western industrial nations for supremacy in space. In 1957, it was the USSR who first succeeded to launch a rocket, called Sputnik, into space.
2. In this Association, all East and West German extra-university research institutes are organized which are not part of the Max Planck Society (basic research) or the Fraunhofer Society (applied research).
3. For more on this topic, please see the chapter by Hans de Wit in this volume.

References

Bologna Declaration. (1999). Online at: http://www.bologna-berlin2003.de/pdf/bologna_deu.pdf
Buck-Bechler, G. (1997). Das Hochschulsystem im gesellschaftlichen kontext. (The higher education system in its social context.) In G. Buck-Bechler, H. Schaefer, & C. Wagemann (Eds.), *Hochschulen in den neuen Ländern der Bundesrepublik Deutschland: Ein handbuch zur Hhochschulerneuerung. (Higher education in the new states of the Federal Republic of Germany: A handbook on higher education renewal.)* Weinheim, Germany: Beltz, Deutscher Studienverlag, pp. 11–45.
Buck-Bechler, G. & Jahn, H. (Eds.). (1994). *Hochschulerneuerung in den neuen Bundesländern: Bilanz nach vier jahren. (Higher education renewal in the new federal states: A stocktaking after four years.)* Weinheim, Germany: Deutscher Studienverlag.
BMBF (Federal Ministry of Education and Research). (2002). *Grund und strukturdaten 2001–2002. (Basic and structural data 2001–2002.)* Bonn, Germany: BMBF.
Ellwein, T. (1985). *Die Deutsche universität. Vom mittelalter bis zur gegenwart. (The German university. From the medieval ages to the present),* Königstein/Ts., W. Germany: Athenäum.
Humboldt, W. (1993). *Schriften zur politik und zum bildungswesen.* (Works Vol. 4: Writings on politics and education). In A. Flitner & K. Geil (Eds.), *Werke Band 4(4). Aufl.* Stuttgart: J.G. Cotta'sche Buchhandlung.
Kehm, B. M. (1999). *Higher education in Germany. Developments, problems and perspectives.* Bucharest, Romania: CEPES-UNESCO & Wittenberg: Institut für Hochschulforschung.
Kehm, B. M. & Teichler, U. (Eds.). (1996). *Vergleichende hochschulforschung: Eine zwischenbilanz.* (Comparative higher education research: An interim stocktaking.) Werkstattbericht 50. Kassel, Germany: Wissenschaftliches Zentrum für Berufs und Hochschulforschung.
Mayntz, R. (Ed.). (1994). *Aufbruch und reform von oben: Ostdeutsche universitäten im transformationsprozess.* (Uprising and reform from above: East German universities in the process of transformation). Frankfurt/M. & New York: Campus.
Mönikes, W. (1993). *Deutsche hochschulen.* (German higher education institutions). Inter Nationes Sonderheft 9/10. Bonn, Germany: Inter Nationes.
Peisert, H. & Framhein, G. (1994). *Higher education in Germany.* Bonn, Germany: Bundesministerium für Bildung und Wissenschaft.
Picht, G. (1964). *Die Deutsche bildungskatastrophe.* (The German educational catastrophe). Freiburg, Germany: Olten.
Schramm, H. (Ed.). (1993). *Hochschule im umbruch: Zwischenbilanz Ost.* (Reorganization of higher education: Interim stocktaking in the East). Berlin, Germany: Basis Druck.
Stichweh, R. (1991). *Der frühmoderne staat und die Europäische universität.* (The early modern state and the European university). Frankfurt/M., Germany: Suhrkamp.
Wissenschaftsrat (Science Council). (1992). *Empfehlungen zur zukünftigen struktur der hochschullandschaft in den neuen ländern und im Ostteil von Berlin.* (Recommendations for the future structure of higher education in the new federal states and East Berlin). Band 1, Teil 4. Köln, Germany: Wissenschaftsrat.

38

INDIA

N. Jayaram
Tata Institute of Social Sciences, India

India was one of the earliest among the developing countries to have established universities and colleges, and it now has the third largest academic system in the world (behind China and the United States). After a long period of protected expansion with state patronage until the mid-1980s, this system is now experiencing unprecedented change. The adoption by the Government of India in 1990 of structural adjustment reforms has meant the gradual withdrawal of state patronage for higher education and a simultaneous privatization of that sphere. However, with the government dithering about the long-term policy to be adopted in this regard, higher education in India is now passing through a period of stunted growth and uncertain future. Based on an analysis of the development of India's higher education and its contemporary realities, this chapter[1] examines the metamorphosis of a system that was not long ago dubbed as "an immobile colossus" (Dube, 1988, p. 46).

Historical Background

Origin and Growth

The foundation for India's present system of higher education was laid by the British colonial regime in the mid-19th century (Ashby & Anderson, 1966, pp. 54–146). The initial efforts of the Christian missionaries and the East India Company generated a protracted controversy between the "Anglicists" recommending a Western approach and the "Orientalists" favoring an indigenous direction. William Bentinck finally resolved this controversy in favor of the Anglicist orientation, barely a month after Thomas Babington Macaulay had penned his (in)famous *Minute* (on February 2, 1835). Charles Wood's *Despatch* (of July 19, 1854) reaffirmed his policy. Upon the recommendation of the committee appointed on January 26, 1855, the first three universities were established at Bombay (now Mumbai), Calcutta (now Kolkata) and Madras (now Chennai) in 1857.

Modeled after the University of London (established in 1836), these pioneer universities were largely affiliating and examining bodies with very little intellectual life of their own. All the universities that were subsequently established developed in an

James J.F. Forest and Philip G. Altbach (eds.), International Handbook of Higher Education, 747–767.
© *2006 Springer. Printed in the Netherlands.*

isomorphic fashion set on the pattern of the original universities. The British educational implantation in India was conceived to serve the economic, political and administrative interests of the British, and in particular, to consolidate and maintain their dominance in the country.[2] It emphasized English, which not only was taught as a language, but also was made the exclusive medium of instruction in higher education. The content was biased in favor of languages and the humanities, and against science and technology.

It is not as if the British rulers did not realize the problems associated with such an educational implantation or its adverse consequences for the colonized society. Yet it was only during the early years of the 20th century—thanks to the initiative of Lord Curzon, the then Viceroy of India (1898–1905)—that efforts were made to "rescue the original concept of the university from its corrosive narrowness." Several inquiries were instituted during the last three decades of colonial rule, but "hardly any of their major recommendations were translated into university policy or practice" (Tickoo, 1980, p. 34).

Thus, the legacy of higher education inherited by India at the time of her independence in 1947 was already crisis-ridden. As an integral element of colonial underdevelopment, higher education was "anemic, distorted and dysfunctional." Low levels of enrollment, the "liberal" nature of education, "enclavization" of the institutes of higher learning, and spurious modernization were its festering features (Raza et al., 1985, p. 100–109). While the general obsolescence of the inherited system of higher education persisted, the system itself underwent such a phenomenal expansion as never before seen in the world.

In 1947, India had 20 universities and 496 colleges catering to 241,369 students.[3] During the next 55 years, she built up a massive system of higher education: in 2001–02, there were 323 university-status institutions (178 state and 18 central universities, 18 medical and 40 agricultural universities, 52 institutions "deemed-to-be universities," 12 institutes of national importance, and five institutions established under State Legislature Acts), 13,150 colleges, and about 900 polytechnics. The system now employs 350,664 teachers and caters to about 8,275,000 students.

The rapid expansion of higher education in India has taken place within a socioeconomic context in which a substantial percentage of the population is illiterate (34.6% of the over 7-year-old population, according to the 2001 Census), and despite the low rating of education per se in the order of national priorities (the educational expenditure as percentage of the Gross Domestic Product rose only marginally, from 2.80 in 1980–81 to 3.93 in 2000–01). The characteristics of the continuing crisis in higher education in India are directly traced to "over-production of "educated" persons; increasing educated unemployment; weakening of student motivation; increasing unrest and lack of discipline on the campuses; frequent collapse of administration; deterioration of standards; and above all, the demoralizing effect of the irrelevance and purposelessness of most of what is being done" (Naik, 1982, p. 163).

Post-Independence Policy Initiatives

After independence, the Government of India appointed the University Education Commission (1948–49) to examine the development of higher education and make proposals for its future expansion and improvement. The Education Commission (1964–66) was the first commission in India's educational history to look comprehensively at almost all aspects of education, and to develop a blueprint for a "national system of education." Having influenced the two statements on the National Policy on Education (1968 and 1979) and, through them, the policies and programs adopted in the Fourth, Fifth and Sixth Five-Year Plans (1968–83), the Report of the Education Commission (Ministry of Education [ME], 1971) was on the anvil for nearly two decades. However, the Ministry of Education, which processed the Report, obliterated it by treating in a piecemeal fashion selected aspects of what was conceived to be a package deal (Naik, 1982, pp. 31–2).

In 1985, the new government proposed to embark on the complex task of "restructuring the system of education." Toward this end, in August of that year the Ministry of Education (since reorganized as the Ministry of Human Resource Development [MHRD]) presented to Parliament a 119-page document titled *Challenge of Education: A Policy Perspective*. This document placed the utmost emphasis on higher education, since it "can provide ideas and men to give shape to the future and also sustain all other levels of education" (Ministry of Education, 1985, p. 6). Key policy measures it contemplated included the delinking of degrees from jobs; the diversification of courses; placing a moratorium on the expansion of the conventional pattern of colleges and universities; selective admission to higher education based on "scholastic interest and aptitude;" establishment of new centers of excellence; decentralization of educational planning, administration, and monitoring; and depoliticization of academia.

The Program of Action of the National Policy on Education (MHRD, 1986) was reviewed by the Acharya Ramamurti Committee (MHRD, 1991). The recommendations of the Central Advisory Board on Education that considered the review report were adopted by Parliament in May 1992. Still, considering the nature of the constraints that had to be encountered, one could hardly have been too optimistic about their outcome. As with earlier reform policy initiatives, this policy too resulted in ad hoc piecemeal tinkering with the system, rather than its overhaul with grit and determination.

Nature and Scope of the Indian Higher Education System

Definition and Scope

Broadly defined, the label "higher education" in India includes the entire spectrum of education beyond 12 years of formal schooling. Candidates who are successful at the secondary school certificate examination (conducted at the end of 10 years of schooling) have the choice of two tracks of postsecondary education. The first track consists of several vocational, technical, and para-professional courses leading to a variety of certificates and diplomas. The duration of these courses varies from 1 year, as in industrial training or teacher training institutes, to 3 years, as in polytechnics. Of these, only the 3-year polytechnic course leading to a diploma is regarded as "higher education."

The second track, generally described as the "plus-two" stage, is a prerequisite for collegiate education, and is of 2 years' duration. It is offered in two different types of educational settings: junior colleges, which offer this exclusively; and schools, which offer it as standards eleven and twelve. This second track is organized and administered by a separate state-level body. Candidates who successfully complete the "plus-two" stage can take up either a general degree course (such as bachelor's of arts, bachelor's of science or bachelor's of commerce) of 3 years' duration or a professional degree course (such as bachelor's of medicine and surgery [5 years and 6 months], bachelor's of dental surgery [4 years], bachelor's of engineering/technology [4 years], bachelor's of nursing [3 years], etc.). In both these types of courses, a postgraduate degree (master's degree) would entail 2 to 3 years of further education.

After the successful completion of any first-degree course (general or professional), a graduate can pursue a second-degree course such as bachelor's of education, bachelor's of library science or bachelor's of law. Since the mid-1980s, a 5-year "integrated" degree course in law has been introduced by many universities. Another year of postgraduate education would earn the graduate a master's of education, master's of library science or master's of law degree. In all courses, further higher education leading to master's of philosophy (1 to 2 years) and doctor of philosophy (3 to 5 years) is possible.

The post-"plus two" level of education is offered in colleges and/or university departments. Based on the nature of their management, we can broadly identify four types of collegiate-level educational institutions: private unaided institutions, private grant-in-aid institutions, institutions managed by the state government (through the directorates of collegiate education, technical education or medical education), and institutions managed by the universities. While there are internal variations in the principles and practices of management among these institutions, as far as their academic organization is concerned they are all regulated by the university to which they are affiliated.

These institutions offer a variety of courses. If the level of instruction imparted depends on the structural type of institution (i.e., junior college, polytechnic, college, or a university department), the quality of teaching often varies with the basic facilities available in a given institution. This again is determined both by the extent and nature of the resources the administrators can mobilize and their motivation to do so.

Typology of Institutions

As for their structure, the largest number of Indian universities belongs to the *affiliating* type. They have a central campus housing departments or schools of study that offer instruction at the postgraduate level and undertake research. In addition, a large number of colleges generally offering first degree education are affiliated with them. A major task of such universities is to determine and oversee the academic standards of these affiliated colleges and conduct centralized examinations for the candidates enrolled in them. These affiliated colleges may be dispersed geographically, but are under the jurisdiction of a university as determined by law.

The *unitary* type of university, on the other hand, is self-contained, and has no colleges. Most of them offer both undergraduate and postgraduate courses and undertake research. A few universities are in some sense a mixture of these two types. The territorial jurisdiction of the *mixed* type of university (e.g., Delhi University) is usually confined to the city in which it is located. Besides affiliated colleges, this type of university manages its own colleges.

Of the 277 university-level institutions for which data are available, 171 are conventional *multidisciplinary* universities; 96 are *professional/technical* institutions oriented to studies in a few related disciplines like agriculture (including forestry, dairy, fisheries, and veterinary science) (37), health sciences (16), engineering and technology (38), law (4) and journalism (1); and 10 are open universities (Association of Indian Universities [AIU], 2004, p. xi).

The Government of India has conferred upon 12 university-level institutions the status of "institutions of national importance." These include the five Indian Institutes of Technology (IIT), three institutions specializing in medical sciences, and one each specializing in statistical techniques and the Hindi language. These institutions are empowered to award degrees which, according to the University Grants Commission (UGC) Act of 1956, can be granted only by a university. The five Indian Institutes of Management (IIM), which are also national-level institutions, are not vested with the power to award degrees, though their "fellowships" are treated on par with university degrees.

By 2001–02, the central government had recognized 52 institutions as "institutions deemed-to-be universities" under the UGC Act. These institutions either specialize in some area of knowledge or are heirs to a tradition. They are not expected to grow to be multidisciplinary universities of the general type.

Outside the university orbit are research institutes funded by the Indian Council for Social Science Research and research laboratories established under the auspices of the Council of Scientific and Industrial Research or maintained by the Ministries of the Government of India. These institutions are not oriented toward the granting of degrees, though they are recognized as centers for doctoral research work, and many scholars working in them are recognized as guides for doctoral students registered with universities.

The concept of an "open university" to impart "distance education" is yet another landmark in higher education in India. The open university seeks to cater to the educational needs of those who for whatever reasons could not enroll in traditional forms of higher education, or those who want to pursue their studies at their own pace and time. Introduced in 1962, this channel of higher learning was in the beginning under the control of the conventional universities. In addition to 10 open universities, there are 104 institutes of correspondence courses or directorates of distance education functioning under conventional universities, and these cater to about 820,000 students, accounting for 13% of the total enrollment in universities and colleges.

Governance

Universities in India are established by an Act either of the union Parliament ("central universities") or of the state legislature ("state universities"). In some states, all the universities are covered by a common "State Universities Act." While the "institutions of national importance" are established by an Act of Parliament, and those deemed-to-be universities are given that status under the UGC Act. Generally, the President of

India, in his capacity as the Visitor, acts as the Chancellor of the central universities, and the Governor of a state acts as the Chancellor of all the universities established by the state legislature.

Both in central and state universities, the vice chancellor is the administrative and academic head of the university. Statutory bodies such as the *academic council* (which exercises general control over all academic matters), the *senate* or *court* (which exercises general control over statutes and budget), and the *syndicate* or *executive council* (which supervises the executive actions of the university, and is responsible for the general management of the university) govern the universities. The size and composition of these bodies vary from university to university. Nominees of central government or state government, as the case may be, represent the respective governments in these statutory bodies. The institutions of national importance and the institutes deemed-to-be universities are also governed by similar statutory bodies.

Problems and Prospects

Enrollment Rates and Background

The bulk of the expansion in enrollment at the postsecondary level took place during the 1950s and the 1960s, when the rate of expansion was as high as 13–14% per annum. During the last decade or so, the rate of expansion has come down markedly. It was 6.1% in 1982–83, peaked at 7.4% in 1989–90, and has declined to remain stable at 4–5% since then. While this rate of expansion is apparently of a manageable magnitude, the university system has never been tuned to the effects of the earlier expansion of enrollment. The shortages in the infrastructure then have only become magnified now.

Despite the massive growth in higher education, barely 8–9% of the 18–23 year-old age group are currently enrolled in higher education institutions. Unrealistically though, the Tenth Five-Year Plan (2002–07) hopes to raise this percentage to 10% by 2007. Analyzing the data for 2001–02 (Kaur, 2003, p. 366) reveals that those enrolled in arts (46.1%), science (19.9%) and commerce/management (17.9%) together accounted for nearly 84% of the students in higher education. Among the rest, 6.9% were enrolled in engineering and technology, 3.2% in law, 3.1% in veterinary science, and 1.3% in education.

As for gender, women's representation is higher in education (51.2%) and medicine (44%), as compared with arts (38%), science (38%), and commerce (35.6%), and is least in engineering/technology (21.5%) and agriculture (17.4%). Women's representation in higher education has improved over the decades, and they now form about 40% of the total enrollment. They are better represented in higher education in the states of Kerala (60%), Goa (58.6%), Punjab (52.9%) and Pondicherry (52.6%), and the union territories of Andaman and Nicobar Islands (57.8%) and Chandigarh (55.5%). In another 15 states/union territories, their proportions are between 40% and 50%. However, their representation is very low in Rajasthan (32.6%), Arunachal Pradesh (29.7%) and Bihar (23%).

A substantial number of places in institutions of higher education are by law reserved for the Scheduled Castes, Scheduled Tribes and Other Backward Classes. The last of this is a flexible category, and in many states quite a large number of people are covered under it. The number of students belonging to these groups has increased over the years, and in 2002–03, they constituted about 10% of the enrollment. However, their participation in some faculties (like medicine and engineering) is too small and insignificant. While the policy of protective discrimination in favor of these caste groups has created some academic problems, it has without doubt helped these traditionally disadvantaged sections of the population in a substantial way.

India's present system of education can be considered top heavy—that is, secondary and tertiary sectors appropriate about 60% of educational expenditures. As for socioeconomic class, the main beneficiaries of this system belong to the top 30% of the income groups, who occupy about 70–80% of the places in secondary and university levels. Moreover, there is a pronounced urban bias in higher education; about 60–75% of the students in different courses hail from urban areas. In sum, there is an enormously unequal distribution of opportunity and benefits throughout India's higher education system—an issue with significant political, social and economic ramifications.

The Quality Dimension

As is to be expected, rapid expansion of higher education has been at the cost of its quality.[4] The quality of education offered is, no doubt, highly varied. Some institutions, despite the general deterioration of quality, have maintained very high standards, including the Indian Institutes of Technology (IITs) at Chennai, Kanpur, Karaghpur, Mumbai, and New Delhi; the Indian Institutes of Management (IIMs) at Ahmedabad, Bangalore, and Kolkata; the Indian Institute of Science (Bangalore); the Tata Institute of Fundamental Research (Mumbai); the National Law School of India University (Bangalore); and a few exceptional departments in some universities. Some affiliated colleges also have maintained high standards.

The deterioration in quality is most glaring in the state universities in general, and at the undergraduate level in affiliated colleges in particular. This crisis now encompasses the conventional postgraduate (M.A., M.Sc. and M.Com.) courses offered in the university departments, too. These courses are now performing an extended "babysitting" function. This is understandable considering the relatively low unit cost of running these courses, and that the students entering this stream pay absurdly little toward their education—far less than what students in the private-sector primary schools pay. The unregulated expansion of this sector of education has been invariably identified as the main cause of its quality crisis.

What goes on in the name of higher education in many a state university and college is pathetic: in many institutions, the physical facilities are so deplorable and the library and laboratory facilities are so woefully inadequate that they have earned the nickname "academic slums" (Jayaram, 1999, p. 112). While lack of resources—a general refrain heard in this context—is primarily responsible, we cannot blame it alone. What is serious is that even the prescriptions governing the minimum qualifications for the appointment and promotion of academic staff are violated; the minimum number of working days is not met; the calendar of academic activities, if at all, exists only on paper, and the administration has virtually collapsed. All this has adversely affected the quality of education imparted in India's colleges and universities.

The undue emphasis on certification rather than on the teaching–learning process has distorted the orientation of university education. Practically all that takes place in the university system is geared toward examination. Not surprisingly, it is in matters relating to examination and certification that we find a host of problems and scandals. Obviously, many innovations undertaken in the university system relate to examinations—e.g., weighting for internal and external evaluations, grading systems, continuous evaluation, etc.—and the prevention of tampering or faking marks cards and certificates, e.g., the computerization of examination records, insertion of holograms on marks-cards, lamination of degree certificates, etc.

Appreciating the need for a centralized authority vested with the power to provide funds and to set and coordinate standards of higher education, within a decade of India's achieving independence the University Grants Commission (UGC) was established by an Act of Parliament in 1956 (Singh, 2004). Though modeled after the British UGC (established after World War I), the UGC in India is endowed with the responsibility of regulating academic standards. It receives money from the central government and is accountable to Parliament.

The UGC has undertaken several schemes to provide substantial support to universities and colleges in order to strengthen their teaching and research activities. Among the schemes supported by the UGC, the Committee for Strengthening Infrastructure in Science and Technology, the College Science Improvement Program, the College Humanities and Social Science Improvement Program, the Faculty Improvement Program, and the Special Assistance Program deserve special mention. Financial assistance is extended to teachers to do research and to attend seminars, symposia and workshops. Promising young teachers with a research proclivity are offered funds under the Career Award Scheme, and the renowned among senior teachers are given a National Associateship. These schemes have, no doubt, injected a degree of vitality in the system, but the trend toward their ritualization is too apparent to be ignored.

Though the UGC is expected to play a lead role in higher education, it is endowed with very little power. Considering the inordinate number of universities and colleges it is required to oversee, the UGC has been virtually reduced to a fund-disbursing agency, incapable of enforcing its own recommendations. Also, given the diarchy in higher education—with the UGC expected to oversee it and the state governments regulating it in practice—higher education has virtually remained an unbridled horse (Pinto, 1984, pp. 63–107).

The standards of academic performance in professional education are coordinated and regulated by statutory bodies such as the Indian Medical Council, the All India Council of Technical Education, the Bar Council of India, the Dental Council of India, the Pharmacy Council of India, and the Nursing Council of India. The Indian Council of Agricultural Research looks after agricultural education, and the Central Advisory Board of Education is the national level coordinating body for making general policies on education.

As a step in the direction of quality control in higher education, following the National Policy of Education (MHRD, 1986), in 1994 the UGC established an autonomous body called the National Assessment and Accreditation Council (NAAC) (Stella & Gnanam, 2003). Initially, the scheme of assessment and accreditation was voluntary, but the idea of an external institution doing this was not received well by universities and colleges. By March 2004, the NAAC had assessed and accredited only 104 universities and 1,034 colleges. The scheme is now mandatory, and the universities and colleges failing to get themselves assessed and accredited will be deprived of developmental grants. How far this will improve the state of affairs in higher education, even if indirectly, remains to be seen.

The "Shadow Education"

The decline in the standards of formal education has fostered the phenomenon of "shadow education," or private tuition conducted through "coaching classes." With the existing colleges being unable to teach effectively and the students wanting to sharpen their competitive edge, parallel private tutoring has become a vital supplemental industry and is thriving. The competition for admission into reputed institutions and for prized courses—like medicine, engineering and technology—is too stiff, with the cut-off percentages for admission being very high. The alternative to government-subsidized professional education is to join private institutions that charge hefty fees. So, students appearing for various public examinations—including the school leaving certificate and the higher secondary and national-level entrance tests—invariably seek extra lessons or coaching.

Since teachers involved in coaching classes are, by and large, formally employed in colleges on a full-time tenured basis, private tutoring raises the question of professional ethics. On the one hand, their being engaged in private tuition is a reflection of the substandard teaching that their colleagues in the college are doing. On the other hand, since they know that students anyhow go for private tutoring, they themselves do not take their teaching in the college seriously. In brief, the private tutoring industry seems to have caught the teachers and the taught in a vicious circle.

Private tutoring, given by individual teachers or by a group of teachers (coaching classes), is not a new phenomenon. It has now become a money-spinning enterprise and is institutionalized. Institutes offering coaching classes even advertise in the newspapers and claim credit for the success of students in the merit lists of various examinations. Some reputed teachers have taken voluntary retirement or resigned from their jobs in their colleges to engage in this profitable enterprise. The dynamics of this dimension of education are seldom covered in discussions on the privatization of higher education.

The UGC has always been critical of college and university teachers engaging in private tutoring, but has not been able to do anything about it. State governments have been ambivalent about private tutoring. While in principle they are opposed to it, many states have introduced special coaching classes for students belonging to the traditionally indigent sections of the population—the Scheduled Castes, Scheduled Tribes and Other Backward Classes. Some states have formally banned private tutoring and coaching classes, but find it impossible to implement this ban. Teachers' unions are silent over the whole issue.

Distance Education

As compared to conventional university education, the distance mode of education can have better spread and coverage; its recurring expenditure is low; it is cost-effective; and it is flexible, both for the administration and for the students. Some universities initially introduced this mode as an innovation to provide opportunities for employed persons to pursue their studies and to those who, for various reasons, are unable to enroll in traditional programs of study. Its scope was later enlarged to encompass the concept of the "open university." This mode is now institutionalized; many universities have established an office or directorate for this purpose, and states have begun establishing open universities. The Indira Gandhi National Open University (IGNOU), established in 1985, coordinates the educational efforts under this mode at the national level.

The concepts of open university and distance education are laudable, especially in view of increasing the coverage and equalizing opportunities. However, the way open university programs are run in most universities is far from satisfactory. Whipping up unrealistic aspirations combined with the nonfulfillment of promises leaves many candidates in the lurch. Poor quality of study materials, inadequacy and ineffectiveness of the contact programs, and lack of study-center facilities have virtually ritualized such programs. Not surprisingly, the rate of failure is very high for such courses. One wonders why universities should duplicate what the IGNOU is more effectively doing. The bitter truth is that they have found in the open university concept a "cash cow" to supplement their dwindling resources (Jayaram, 1999, p. 114). Plans are on the anvil for the IGNOU's Distance Education Cell to assess and accredit distance education offered by various universities.

Medium of Instruction

The striking feature of the colonial educational transplantation in India was English, which was not only taught as a language but also became the medium of instruction. While the secondary school certificate examination was conducted only in English until 1937, English was almost exclusively used at the university level right through the colonial period. Immediately after independence, the University Education Commission (1948–49) recommended that higher education be imparted through the regional languages, with the option of using other Indian languages as the medium of instruction. The National Integration Council and the Emotional Integration Committee endorsed this recommendation in 1962. The Education Commission (1964–66) emphasized the need "to move energetically in the direction of adopting the regional languages as media of education at the university stage" (Ministry of Education, 1971, p. 527).

A review of the trends in the medium of instruction in higher education (Jayaram, 1993, p. 112) reveals that English is still the predominant medium of instruction. This is especially true at the postgraduate level and in science and professional courses, as well as in the agricultural universities, the institutions of national importance and the institutions deemed-to-be universities. The progress in the switch from English as the medium of instruction, though still insignificant, is relatively better in the Hindi-speaking states than in the non-Hindi speaking states. Even so, such a switch is, by and large, confined to arts, education, and (to some extent) the basic science courses at the undergraduate level.

The Academic Profession

One consequence of the rapid expansion of higher education was the unprecedented demand for teachers. Many postgraduates churned out by the state university system found in teaching an easy employment avenue. The cumulatively adverse consequences of the reckless manner in which teachers were recruited and allowed to function soon became evident. In its nationwide sample survey of teachers and students in higher education and members of the wider community, the National Commission on Teachers (NCT) recorded the "widespread feeling that no profession has suffered such downgrading as the teaching profession" (NCT, 1985, p. 21). The NCT's observations referred to the situation in 1983–85, and there is no evidence suggesting that the situation has changed for the better since then.

Studies on college teachers have invariably stressed the sad deficiency of academic preparation for—and declining commitment to—the profession. The NCT (1985) also bemoaned the fact that most teachers are simply making a living rather than following a vocation. This has, no doubt, a lot to do with the deplorable standards obtained at the postgraduate level education. More important, however, is the fact that for decades most master's degree holders easily found employment in colleges, and even in universities, with absolutely no training in (or orientation to) teaching, and with doubtful aptitude for that vocation.

To arrest this trend, and to ensure proficiency in the subject and aptitude for teaching or research on the part of candidates aspiring to become teachers, the UGC introduced the scheme of the National Eligibility Test (NET). This test is held twice a year. The UGC has permitted many state governments to conduct a State Eligibility Test (SET), which is treated as equivalent to the NET. However, due to various demands in some states, the standard of the SET has been significantly diluted, forcing the UGC to withdraw its permission to conduct the SET in those states.

The Academic Staff College (ASC), instituted in selected universities (51 as of December 2003), is entrusted with conducting programs for properly orienting people entering the profession of teaching, and improving the knowledge and skills of those already in the profession. To instill a sense of seriousness, an element of compulsion has also been introduced—those entering the profession are required to attend an "orientation course" before they complete their probation. Those in service are required to attend two "refresher courses" to become eligible for career advancement or promotion. Unfortunately, as with all initiatives carrying an element of compulsion, the original objectives behind the establishment of ASCs have been lost, and the courses have been ritualized.

The combination of structural adjustment reforms and changing market forces has had a profound impact on academia. Not only has the prospect of employment in the academic profession become dim, but also the security of employment—which was once taken for granted in the academic profession—is increasingly becoming problematic.[5] Most state governments have imposed an embargo on the recruitment of teachers. This has meant a freeze on the establishment of state-supported colleges, downsizing the number of permanent teachers in existing colleges, and optimization of resources by re-deployment of teachers through a policy of transfers. Further, most governments have also introduced "voluntary retirement schemes" (giving incentives to teachers who want to retire from permanent service before they complete their tenure), and some state governments have reduced (or are contemplating reducing) the retirement age for teachers.

The downsizing of the academic profession through freezing of recruitment, re-deployment of excess staff, appointment of guest lecturers, etc. is now a pan-Indian phenomenon. Moreover, it is not confined to the conventional liberal science colleges, and has been strongly advocated in technical education as well. However, in those burgeoning fields where the expansion has been most rapid—such as computer science, information technology, and biotechnology—there is a dearth of qualified teachers. The problem of teacher shortage is most acute in medical education.

Be that as it may, the academic profession does not have much achievement to boast of: most teachers do not avail themselves of opportunities for professional development; the research output of teachers is quite low; with the exception of some universities and the IITs and IIMs, peer review or student evaluation of teachers is virtually non-existent; and "self-appraisal" by teachers, as recommended by the UGC, has either not been introduced or is perfunctorily done and, as such, it has seldom formed the basis of any action.

Interestingly, teachers' unions are not strong anymore. Even the All India Federation of University and College Teachers Organizations does not command the mass support it once did. The strike continues to be the predominant mode of protest by teachers' unions. Still, judging by how the government has dealt with strikes by much stronger unions of employees in other sectors during the last few years, teachers cannot take the material success of their strike for granted. Let alone an all-India agitation, even state-level agitations are running out of steam. It appears that whatever strength teachers' unions manifest is not due to any intrinsic qualities, but due to the soft attitude of the government toward them.

Teachers have often blamed inadequate salaries and unattractive service conditions for the deterioration in the status of the academic profession. With the major revision of pay scales in 1998, following the Rastogi Committee Report, the teachers have received the best deal regarding salary. While the UGC pay package has been accepted in principle all over the country, there are significant variations in its implementation by different states. While some states have postponed the date of implementation, a few have not given arrears accruing from delayed implementation of the scales. Thus, the gross salary of different categories of teachers in terms of their institutional affiliation is not the same across the country. Even so, the increased gross salary of the teachers has practically brought every teacher into the income tax net.

Furthermore, to give adequate and suitable opportunities for vertical mobility to teachers at multiple stages in their career, while noting the new pay package, the UGC has incorporated a career advancement scheme based on the professional development of teachers. Ironically, the improvements in pay scales and service conditions have come at a time when the profession has been declining. Teachers are largely happy with the pay package, but they are also worried about the gradual withdrawal of state patronage for higher education.

Educational Planning and Implementation

In a quasi-federal polity like India, educational planning is a part of the overall national planning. Besides assuming an active participation of the constituent states, the national planning tends to be expenditure-oriented and overwhelmingly macro in perspective. Moreover, since higher education is the concern of more than one government department, the educational plan does not present a coordinated picture. Inevitably, all this adversely affects the implementation of the plan.

Under the Constitution of India, education was largely the responsibility of the states, the central government being concerned only with certain areas like coordination and determination of standards in technical and higher education. In January 1977, the 42nd Amendment empowered the central government to legislate on education concurrently with the states. Though the central government thereby established supremacy over education, the hopes of reform that this amendment aroused failed to become real. With the gradual deterioration of the relationship between the center and some states, no government at the center can confidently take any bold steps in the realm of education.

The absence of a single machinery to look after higher education planning has often been commented on. The responsibility of higher education is divided among various central government departments (e.g., education, finance, health, social welfare and technology), with the state governments' involvement being only peripheral. The state governments pass the buck to the universities which, being totally dependent on state funding, plead their inability to take on this responsibility. Presuming that the state governments can chalk out an excellent plan for higher education, they can hardly be assured of its implementation, as they are humiliatingly dependent on the central government for funds.

Contemporary Scenario

Market Economy and the Changing Demand for Courses

Structural adjustment reforms adopted since the early 1990s have had a significant impact on the demand structure of higher education. At last the expansion of traditional programs of study seems to have outstripped the demand for them by students. While generally the brighter students have always avoided these programs, even the not-so-bright ones appear to be turning their backs on them now, invariably opting for professional programs such as medicine, computer science, information technology, and business management. If they cannot make it into any of these programs, they would rather try their hand at some courses with narrow but specialized job prospects, such as packaging, plastic technology, fabric designing, air conditioning and refrigeration. The fact that good students are no longer taking up basic science courses has seriously affected the academic programs of reputed science institutions such as the Indian Institute of Science (Bangalore), which has now come out with incentive schemes to urge meritorious students to take basic sciences at the graduate level.

The lack of a link between conventional courses and the job market seems to have become too apparent for students and their parents.[6] At best, the employers—not only in the private sector, but also in the government—use the conventional degrees as sieves for filtering the large number of applicants for the limited number of jobs. The unemployment situation, particularly among conventional degree holders, has worsened over the decades, with the government no longer able to absorb them in public employment. Aggravating the situation is the economic liberalization program, which demands knowledge and skills generally not possessed by conventional degree holders. It is only natural that those who have been using conventional courses as waiting rooms are either seeking early entry into the job market at lower levels, with the option of obtaining formal university qualifications later, or entering courses that carry better job prospects. Those who still seek conventional graduate courses are generally the leftovers and dregs, or the first-generation students from rural and indigent backgrounds (the Scheduled Castes and Scheduled Tribes), especially those who are supported by financial assistance from the government.

While the demand for conventional courses has tapered off, the demand for professional and other allied courses has been incessantly increasing, in spite of escalating unemployment even among the professional degree holders. Many educational entrepreneurs are unduly eager to offer such "moneymaking" courses in medicine, dentistry, nursing, engineering and technology, business management, computer science, and education. The latest scandal in the universities concerns the granting of permission to colleges to start these courses. Many of these institutions are inadequately equipped to offer any education, let alone professional education. The gross and brazen violation of the norms stipulated by such bodies as the Medical Council of India or the All India Council for Technical Education is a matter of serious concern.

To enhance their marketability and employment prospects, students taking professional courses try to specialize in a given field or obtain qualifications and skills in some sophisticated courses not generally offered by the universities. A glance at Indian newspapers reveals the number and variety of courses currently offered by various institutions outside the sphere of the university system. These institutions, and the academic entrepreneurs who run them, seem to be extraordinarily sensitive to the variety of knowledge and skills demanded by the changing market economy. They are also extremely flexible, both in what they have to offer and how they go about offering it. While the demand for skills and knowledge is their *raison d'etre*, the maintenance of quality is their badge of success. As in any commodity market, one has to pay more for better-quality education.

It is important to note that in spite of (or essentially because of) the fact they are outside the orbit of the university system, such institutions of higher learning have not only survived but even thrived. Some of them have earned a niche for themselves in higher education, and even recognition from academia and employers abroad. As statutorily established academic entities, the Indian universities have sadly lacked competition, and they tolerate no competition either. With the liberalization of the economy and the state gradually shedding its responsibility for higher education—and with the UGC being no more than a mute witness to the gradual decaying of the university as a public institution—the Indian university system is progressively becoming nominalized and marginalized. Regardless of one's ideological predilections, it is now conceded that the future of higher education in India will be determined by the market economy and the private sector.

Decline of State Patronage

While public expenditure on education in India has always been inadequate for meeting the needs of "education for all,"[7] throughout its history the state has significantly subsidized higher education (Tilak, 2004a). Structural adjustment has meant a drastic cut in public expenditure on higher education: between 1980–90 and 1994–95, the share of higher education in development (plan) expenditures decreased from 12.6% to 6%, whereas the share of higher education in maintenance (non-plan) expenditures declined from 14.2% to 11% (Tilak, 1996). Overall, the allocation for higher education, which had peaked at 28% in the Fifth Five-Year Plan (1974–97), has steadily declined in the successive Plans to just 8% in the Tenth Five-Year Plan (2002–07), which is the same as the allocation in the First Five-Year Plan (1951–56).

The annual growth rate of public expenditure on university and higher education, which was 13.1% between 1980–81 and 1985–86, had fallen to 7.8% by 1995–96 (Shariff & Ghosh, 2000, p. 1400). As a proportion of total government expenditure, the share of higher education declined from 1.57% in 1990–91 to 1.33% in 2001–02. Considering the trends in per student expenditure—from Rs 7,676 (US$154) in 1990–91 to Rs 5,873 (US$117) in 2001–02 (in 1993–94 prices)[8]—the decline in public expenditure on higher education would appear even more drastic (Tilak, 2004b, p. 2160).[9]

Thus, the state, which had hitherto been the dominant partner in funding higher education, is finding it harder even to maintain the same level of funding for higher education. Financial constraint, however, does not affect all sectors of higher education equally: invariably, non-professional courses are more adversely affected than their professional counterparts. Furthermore, the efforts to privatize higher education by encouraging private agencies to establish institutions of higher learning have enjoyed limited success in general education and non-professional courses. Thus, state universities and their affiliated colleges are the ones in financial doldrums.

The gradual decline in state patronage of higher education has been accompanied by its inability to address the need for reforms within conventional higher education. The National Policy on Education (Ministry of Education, 1985), its Program of Action (MHRD, 1986), and their review by the Acharya Ramamurti Committee (MHRD, 1991) were all pre-structural adjustment reform initiatives. Neither the phenomenal fall in the demand for conventional courses in the B.A. and B.Sc. streams, nor the remarkable spurt in the demand for courses in such areas as computer science and information technology, biotechnology, and management studies, was anticipated.

Private Initiatives in Higher Education

The void created by the waning state patronage for higher education is now being filled by private entrepreneurial initiatives. Two types of private initiatives in Indian higher education can be identified. First, there are private colleges and institutes that are formally affiliated with a university. They offer courses approved by a university, and their students write examinations conducted by that university; the successful among them are given degree certificates by the university. While the institutions belonging to the minority communities enjoy certain administrative privileges granted by the Constitution of India, in all academic matters the private colleges and institutes are governed by the university.

Many of these private colleges receive financial assistance to the tune of 80–85% of their expenditures; in addition, they are permitted to collect a small fee from the students to make up the balance. As such, these colleges must observe the grant-in-aid code formulated by the government. At the other end of the spectrum are the unaided private colleges that have to generate their own financial resources. They have considerable leeway concerning administration and the collection of fees from the students.

The concept of a purely private university (of the American type) is new in India. The bill to provide for the establishment of private universities, introduced in Rajya Sabha (the upper house of Parliament) in August 1995, is still pending. While the government is keen on privatization, the private sector is unhappy with some clauses of the bill, such as those concerning the formation of a permanent endowment fund of Rs 100 million (US$2 million), the provision of full scholarships to 30% of the students, and the government monitoring and regulation of the system (Tilak, 2002, p. 12).

Meanwhile, invoking the existing legal provisions (e.g., the UGC Act), several private institutions of higher education have been given the "deemed-to-be university" status. Also, considering that higher education is a concurrent subject under the Constitution, some states (like the newly formed Chattisgarh) have enacted private university acts of their own, and private universities have begun to mushroom in these states. This has, no doubt, attracted the adverse attention of the UGC, which, however, feels helpless. A public interest litigation suit has been filed in the Supreme Court of India challenging the constitutional validity of the Chattisgarh legislation allowing the registration of private universities without providing for even basic educational facilities.[10]

In contrast are the privately owned and managed colleges, institutes and academies conducting courses outside the purview of the universities. Typically, they offer courses in such areas as aviation and pilot training, glass technology, plastic technology, packaging, corporate secretaryship, marketing management, financial management, foreign trade, portfolio management, operations research, hotel management and catering technology, tourism administration, software marketing, computer applications, fashion design, beauty aids, etc. Unlike the diploma courses offered by the polytechnics, some of these courses offered by well-known institutes are accredited with professional bodies in the area, often even outside the country.

Another educational innovation that has come from private initiatives is the concept of the "twinning program." This program involves collaboration between two educational systems, with both systems taking responsibility for teaching and training of students and one of them holding the right to award educational credentials. The program may involve collaboration between an Indian institution and a system abroad (international educational collaboration), or between two systems of education within the country (intranational educational collaboration).

International educational collaboration is slowly gathering momentum. In India, it was originally devised as a way out of the governmental stranglehold on private institutions of higher learning and the enervating rigidity of the university system. Such international educational collaboration is not, however, confined to professional education. To meet the demand for high quality first-degree education, especially in areas such as computer science, some private colleges have entered into twinning programs with universities abroad.

Such international educational collaboration involving twinning programs is significantly different from the more direct marketing endeavors of foreign educational establishments. Several universities—not necessarily reputed ones—in Anglophone countries such as Australia, Canada, New Zealand, the United Kingdom, and the United States of America are enrolling Indian students for their educational programs. Often there is a distance education component, but most of them have arrangements with reputed institutes in the country for offering contact programs for students taking these foreign university examinations. Some of these universities even hold educational fairs in Indian cities to familiarize those interested in pursuing their educational programs.[11]

All this necessarily implies opening the sphere of Indian higher education to foreign educational establishments. For more than a century, the well-to-do in India have been sending their wards abroad for higher education, with the most talented students obtaining fellowships from the Government of India or foreign foundations. Given the globalization of higher education, such facilities are now being brought into the country. This is akin, no doubt, to the operation of multinational companies in industry and business, and as such it cannot be expected to be free of socioeconomic costs.

It is well known that such high-quality education involving multinational arrangements, often involving job placements, is expensive, especially as compared to the absurdly low-cost education offered by Indian colleges and universities. The concept of twinning programs is now taking root intranationally as well. Such programs have effectively combined the advantages of regular and distance modes of higher education. It is also significant that the educational institutions involved are putting their physical, material and human resources to optimum use.

Considering this, it is ironic that the concept of autonomous colleges has not been given the effort that it richly deserves. In light of the current crisis confronting the university system, the need for liberating the best affiliated colleges from their bondage to the university can hardly be exaggerated. The National Policy on Education (1985–86) recommended the granting of autonomy to select colleges and the UGC endorsed this recommendation. By 1990, 500 colleges were envisaged to be given an autonomous status; yet by 2003, only 135 colleges had been granted this status (AIU, 2004, p. xii). Vested interests of the university managers and the political bureaucracy of the state governments have ensured that this innovation remains virtually grounded.

The Uncertain Future

The structural adjustment reforms adopted by the Government of India since 1990 have necessitated a policy of disinvestment of the public sector and open privatization in various spheres of the economy. For higher education, however, the government is hesitant to pursue this policy vigorously. Rather, a different strategy is in operation: there is now a moratorium on the establishment of new educational institutions (especially of the conventional type) under the public sector and an imposition of ceilings on student strength in the existing institutions. The academic profession is being downsized through a freeze on recruitment, reduction in the number of teachers, and rationalization of teachers' work. There is a proposal to introduce the contract system for hiring teachers in the future. At the same time, self-financing colleges (especially in areas of professional education) are encouraged, and the proposal to raise fees in the public higher education institutions is on the anvil. These measures, it is feared, will raise the cost of higher education and make it less accessible to the masses, on the one hand, and—given the government's inability to regulate the private educational institutions—adversely affect the quality of education, on the other (Kumar & Sharma, 2003).

Closely related to these trends is the internationalization of higher education referred to earlier. This is in conformity with the policy of liberalization of education as a service sector under the General Agreement on Trade in Services (Bhushan, 2004). While the requisite legislative provisions are not yet in place, the education sector "opened-up" in April 2004, and foreign universities and educational institutions (especially from the Anglophone countries like Australia, Canada, the United Kingdom, and the United States of America) have begun to offer competition to the existing educational institutions in the country. As observed earlier, there is a fear that this might result in draining resources from India, as well as introduce strong cultural and political influence by foreign countries (Kumar & Sharma, 2003, p. 607).

The lack of a coherent long-term policy perspective is characteristic of higher education in India today. While the Government of India—regardless of the ideological predilections of the party combinations in power—is committed to structural adjustment reforms and liberalization, which necessarily imply gradual withdrawal of state patronage for higher education and the privatization and internationalization of this sector, it appears to be dithering on the issue. Ad hoc policies and the multiplicity of actors—the central and state governments, the UGC, the All India Council for Technical Education, the universities and colleges, and the emergent private sector—dealing with the unfolding needs in higher education in their own way portend a period of stunted growth and uncertain future.

Conclusion: The Challenge in Higher Education

The conventional university system in India, confronting as it is a systemic crisis, has been incapable of introducing any significant educational innovation or effectively implementing any educational reform. Given the mounting pressure for increasing accessibility and over-democratization, the trend in the universities is toward reducing everything to the lowest common denominator or leveling down quality, rather than raising it. The Indian university system is extraordinarily rigid and pronouncedly resistant to change: the impetus for change does not come from within the system. When experiments or innovations are introduced from outside, they are resisted; if enforced, they are ritualized. The fate of such innovations as the merit promotion scheme, faculty improvement program, vocationalization of courses, semesterization of courses, curriculum development center, annual report, college development council, academic staff college and refresher and orientation courses, are too well known to warrant elaboration. It is indeed ironic that higher education, which is expected to function as an agency of change, should itself be resistant to it.

The void created by the paralysis and drift of the conventional university system is being filled by private entrepreneurial initiatives. Thus, significant educational innovations and experiments are currently taking place in institutions outside the university orbit and in the private sector. In view of the rapid expansion of (and increasing variety in) knowledge and skills, there is enormous scope for educational innovations and initiatives. The private institutions have been more responsive to the demands of the economy and industry and the changing employment scenario. They have also shown their ability to match relevance with flexibility both in costs and regulation. This does not, however, mean that all private institutions are necessarily good. Some of them are brazenly commercial establishments out to swindle gullible people looking for better-quality education at affordable prices.

Privatization of higher education is apparently a fledgling but welcome trend: higher education requires it to maintain creativity, adaptability and quality, while the economic trail of liberalization and globalization demands it. Considering the chronic paucity of resources, gradually unburdening itself of the additional responsibility for higher education may be advisable for the government. Instead, it could better utilize the scarce resources for realizing the goal of universalization of elementary education and for improving the quality of school education.

Privatization of higher education, however, is not without social costs. In a polity such as India's, where structured inequalities have been entrenched, privatization is sure to reinforce existing inequalities and to foster inegalitarian tendencies. This necessitates the social supervision of the private sector and effective measures for offsetting imbalances resulting from unequal economic capacities of the population. How to advance equality without sacrificing quality? How to control the private sector without curbing its creativity and initiative? Here lies the challenge for higher education in contemporary India.

Notes

1. In writing this chapter, I have drawn on my earlier work on higher education in India (see Jayaram, 1997, 1999, 2003), and have reproduced portions from my recent work (Jayaram 2004).
2. The British rule gradually supplanted the pre-colonial indigenous system of education consisting of Buddhist *viharas*, Hindu *pathashalas* and *tols*, and Muslim *madrasas* by stopping financial aid. The Indian urban elite, too, welcomed English education as it was viewed not only as an avenue to jobs but also an instrument for social and political regeneration of India (Basu, 2002, p. 168).

3. The statistical data cited in this chapter are drawn from Institute of Applied Manpower Research (2002), Kaur (2003), Ministry of Information & Broadcasting, Government of India (2003), and Association of Indian Universities (2004).

4. Lacking any objective measurement of higher education standards over a period, it is, no doubt, difficult to determine precisely the nature and extent of deterioration. Nevertheless, there is no denying that India's standards compare unfavorably with the average standards in educationally advanced countries. The Education Commission had drawn attention to this as early as the mid-1960s (see ME, 1971, p. 66). No wonder, then, that degrees awarded by Indian universities are not regarded by many foreign universities as equivalent to their degrees. In fact, employers in India, including the government agencies, are wary of these degrees.

5. Only about 70% of the university and college teachers have permanent employment with all statutory benefits. The others are either "temporary" (with no guarantee of continuation) or "*ad hoc*" (appointed against a leave vacancy for a short period) lecturers. Besides, new categories of teachers such as "part-time" lecturers (who teach for a specified number of teaching hours in a week) and "guest" lecturers (who help the college/department "to complete portions of the syllabus") have been added. Such teachers are paid on "hourly basis," and they do not enjoy other privileges that go with a permanent or even a temporary or an *ad hoc* teacher.

6. Being aware of the disorientation of the conventional courses, the UGC had recommended the introduction of job-oriented courses at the first degree level. Many universities have introduced a job-orientation component in their undergraduate curriculum mainly to avail the funds provided by the UGC for the purpose.

7. An international comparison revealed that in a list of 86 countries, India (with an expenditure of 3.8% of the Gross National Product [GNP] on education) ranked only 32nd in terms of public expenditure on education as a proportion of GNP (quoted in Shariff and Ghosh, 2000, p. 1396).

8. In August 2004, Rs 1 = US $0.02 and US $1 = Rs 46.40.

9. It is significant to note that the Government of India's discussion paper on "Government Subsidies in India" (1997) classified elementary education as a "merit good" and higher education as a "non-merit good" warranting a drastic reduction of government subsidies. The Ministry of Finance has since reclassified higher education into a category called "merit 2 goods" which need not be subsidized at the same level as merit goods (Tilak, 2002, p. 12).

10. *Sunday Times of India,* Mumbai, February 01, 2004, p. 6.

11. In its vision document for internationalization of Indian higher education, the UGC's standing committee for the Promotion of Higher Education Abroad recommended holding of Indian International Education Fairs in the Gulf countries, Africa and Southeast Asia, and encouraged Study India Programs and partnership with foreign universities.

References

Ashby, E. & Anderson, M. (1966). *Universities: British, Indian, and African.* London: Weidenfield and Nicholson.

Association of Indian Universities (AIU). (2004). *Universities handbook.* New Delhi, India: AIU.

Basu, A. (2002). Indian higher education: Colonialism and beyond. In P. G. Altbach & V. Selvaratnam (Eds.), *From dependence to autonomy: The development of Asian universities* (pp. 167–186). Chestnut Hill, MA: Center for International Higher Education, Boston College.

Bhushan, S. (2004). Trade in education services under GATS: Implications for higher education in India. *Economic and political weekly, 39,* 2395–2402.

Dube, S. C. (1988). Higher education and social change. In A. Singh & G. D. Sharma (Eds.), *Higher education in India: The social context* (pp. 46–53). Delhi, India: Konark.

Institute of Applied Manpower Research. (2002). *Manpower profile: India—Yearbook 2002.* New Delhi, India: Concept Publishing Company.

Jayaram, N. (1993). The language question in higher education: Trends and issues. In S. Chitnis & P. G. Altbach (Eds.), *Higher education reform in India: Experience and perspectives* (pp. 84–114). New Delhi, India: Sage Publications.

Jayaram, N. (1997). India. In G. A. Postiglione & G. C. L. Mak (Eds.), *Asian higher education: An international handbook and reference guide* (pp. 75–91). Westport, CT: Greenwood Press.

Jayaram, N. (1999). Reorientation of higher education in India: A prognostic essay. In S. Aroni & J. Hawkins (Eds.), *Partnerships in development: Technology and social sciences, universities, industry and government* (Proceedings of the Sixth INRUDA International Symposium on the Role of Universities in Developing Areas, Paris, 8–11 June 1999) (pp. 111–118). Paris: Ecole Spéciale des Travaux Publics.

Jayaram, N. (2003). The fall of the guru: The decline of the academic profession in India. In P. G. Altbach (Ed.), *The decline of the guru: The academic profession in developing and middle-income countries* (pp. 199–230). New York and Basingstoke, England: Palgrave Macmillan.

Jayaram, N. (2004). Higher education in India: Massification and change. In P. G. Altbach & T. Umakoshi (Eds.), *Asian universities: Historical perspectives and contemporary challenges* (pp. 85–112). Baltimore, MD: The Johns Hopkins University Press.

Kaur, K. (2003). *Higher education in India (1781–2003)*. New Delhi, India: University Grants Commission.

Kumar, T. R. & Sharma, V. (2003). Downsizing higher education: An emergent crisis. *Economic and Political Weekly, 38*, 603–607.

Ministry of Education, Government of India. (1971). *Education and national development (Report of the education commission, 1964–66)*. New Delhi, India: National Council of Educational Research and Training (Reprint Edition).

Ministry of Education, Government of India. (1985). *Challenge of education: A policy perspective*. Delhi, India: The Controller of Publications.

Ministry of Human Resource Development, Government of India. (1986). *Program of action: National policy on education*. New Delhi, India: The Controller of Publications.

Ministry of Human Resource Development, Government of India. (1991). *Towards an enlightened and humane society: Report of the committee for review of national policy on education 1986*. New Delhi, India: The Controller of Publications.

Ministry of Information & Broadcasting, Government of India. (2003). *India 2003: A reference annual*. New Delhi, India: Publications Division.

Naik, J. P. (1982). *The education commission and after*. New Delhi, India: Allied Publishers.

National Commission of Teachers. (1985). *Report of the national commission on teachers—II, 1983–85*. New Delhi, India: The Controller of Publications.

Pinto, M. (1984).*Federalism and higher education: The Indian experience*. Bombay, India: Orient Longman.

Raza, M., Aggarwal, Y. P., & Hasan, M. (1985). Higher education in India: An assessment. In J. V. Raghavan (Ed.), *Higher education in the eighties* (pp. 95–173). New Delhi, India: Lancer International.

Shariff, A. & Ghosh, P. K. (2000). Indian education scene and the public gap. *Economic and Political Weekly, 35*, 1396–1406.

Singh, A. (2004). *Fifty years of higher education in India: The role of the University Grants Commission*. New Delhi, India: Sage Publications.

Stella, A. & Gnanam, A. (2003). *Foundations of external quality assurance in Indian higher education*. New Delhi, India: Concept Publishing Company.

Tickoo, C. (1980). *Indian universities*. Madras, India: Orient Longman.

Tilak, J. B. G. (1996). Higher education under structural adjustment. *Journal of Indian School of Political Economy, 8*, 266–293.

Tilak, J. B. G. (2002). Privatization of higher education in India. *International Higher Education, 29*, 11–13.

Tilak, J. B. G. (2004a). Public subsidies in education in India. *Economic and Political Weekly, 39*, 343–359.

Tilak, J. B. G. (2004b). Absence of policy and perspective in higher education. *Economic and Political Weekly, 39*, 2159–2164.

39

INDONESIA

M. K. Tadjudin
National Accreditation Board for Higher Education, Indonesia

At the threshold of the third millennium, public policy decisions regarding higher education must respond to a wide variety of far-reaching changes taking place throughout Indonesian society. Significant shifts in social stratification, enrollment demand, cost containment, consensus on financial support, concerns about quality, and technological advancement will have serious impacts on higher education. Policymakers must recognize that state mandates, regulations and funding formulas stand as major impediments to improving higher education. They provide little incentive for institutions to work together on issues of mutual concern—improvement of lower-division instruction, purposeful growth, and expansion of technology-based education programs. In many ways, they place significant constraints on institutions' ability to cut costs, develop new programs, collaborate with one another and experiment with new ways of doing things. New ways of structuring, governing and financing higher education are needed, such as decentralization and deregulation, performance-based funding models, increased investment in technology, and a greater emphasis on strategic planning, coordination and partnership.

At the same time, the entire nation is facing a critical transition toward a more democratic civil society. After experiencing the worst economic crisis ever, the nation is in a reconstruction period. A new democratic civilian government is in place and community participation is encouraged. After more than three decades under an authoritarian government, however, the credibility of the government and other formal institutions is very thin. In order to truly develop a democratic civil society, it needs a credible moral force as its counterpart. Universities are probably one of very few institutions that can be expected to play the role of a moral force in supporting the nation's democratic evolution. A credible moral force, however, should also have its own house in order, and in this area a critical analysis reveals that fundamental changes are needed in university management.

The objective of the national strategy in higher education system is, therefore, to improve the competitiveness of Indonesia's higher education system by developing institutional credibility through restructuring the nationwide system as well as the internal university system. Universities should be given autonomy, but should also be held accountable to the public, demonstrating high operational efficiency and ensuring

James J.F. Forest and Philip G. Altbach (eds.), International Handbook of Higher Education, 769–780.
© 2006 *Springer. Printed in the Netherlands.*

the quality and relevance of its outputs. An internal management structure that is publicly transparent, and complies with acceptable standards of quality, is also vital to public confidence in the higher education system. As a credible moral force, universities should also contribute by direct involvement in solving the problems of society, and particularly the strategic issues. The higher education sector of Indonesia, in response to these challenges, has introduced a concept of management as its new strategy called the *new paradigm*. The implementation of the concept—which relies on autonomy, merit-based tiered competition, and user participation in planning, transparency, democracy, and higher accountability—has been chosen as the best-suited strategy for higher education. Nevertheless, it must be understood that structural adjustment under this concept is not an objective by itself, since the real objectives involve improvements in the outputs and outcomes of Indonesia's higher education system in the new millennium.

An Early History of Higher Education in Indonesia

Higher education and the development of scholarship started in the Indonesian archipelago 13 centuries ago. Records show that in the year 671 a Chinese scholar (named I-tsing) visited Che-li-fo-che, known to Indonesians as Sriwijaya. He came to Sriwijaya from Guangdong (Canton, China) to study, although he had already spent 14 years at Nalanda in Southern Bihar, India (near Rajargha on the banks of the Ganges), which was one of the premier institutions of higher learning at the time. The university at Sriwijaya existed at least until the year 1023, as records show that at that time a student called Srijnana Dipankara or Atisa studied there in the years 1011–1023 under the guidance of professor Dharmakitri.

The quest for knowledge among Indonesians has ancient roots. Old records from India show the presence of students from Indonesia studying at Nalanda. The records also show that a dormitory for Indonesian students was built around the year 860 as a gift from Balaputradewa. The only way Indonesian students could get to India then was by sea, indicating that Indonesians must have mastered ocean navigation and other sciences like astronomy and geography at that time.

Time spent at Nalanda enlarged the knowledge and vision of the Indonesian students. The beauty and grandeur of the temples built later in Indonesia were based on a number of Indian temples called Silpasastra. Reliefs of famous Indonesian temples like the Borobudur, which was built in the 8th century, showed scenes of teaching and learning, surrounded by fauna and flora common to the Indonesian archipelago.

The History of Modern Higher Education in Indonesia

Modern forms of higher education in Indonesia were introduced by the Dutch as a means to develop qualified manpower for their colonial government. The first of such institutions, the "Sekolah Dokter Jawa" or School for Javanese Doctors, was established in 1851 at Jakarta to obtain qualified manpower for the colonial army and health service. This school was called a "barefoot doctor" school, as the students were not allowed to wear shoes in classes. The languages of instruction were Malay and Dutch.

In 1902, the status of the school was elevated and was named "School tot Opleiding van Inlandsche Artsen," abbreviated to STOVIA or School for the Training of Native Doctors. Teaching was in Dutch and a senior high school program was included in the curriculum.

In 1914, a second medical school was established, called "Nederlandsch-Indische Artsen School" (NIAS) or Dutch East Indies School for Medical Doctors, followed by a school for dentists, established at Surabaya, called the "School tot Opleiding voor Inlandsche Tandartsen" (STOVIT) or School for the Training of Native Dentists.

In 1909, a law school called the "School voor Inlandsche Rechtskundigen," or School for the Training of Native Lawyers, was established in Jakarta to meet the need for government justices and attorneys. In 1922, the name "Native" was deleted and the school became known simply as "Rechtsshool" or Law School. In 1920, a group of Dutch private entrepreneurs established the "Technische Hoogeschool" or College of Engineering at Bandung, to fulfill the need for qualified engineers. In 1924, this college was taken over by the Dutch colonial government. Also during this year, the status of the law school was elevated to that of a law college or "Rechts-hoogeschool," and the STOVIA became a college of medicine, or "Geneeskundige Hoogeschool," at which time both institutions began to enjoy a status equivalent to similar institutions in Holland. The number of native students during the years 1920–1940 in all three colleges (medicine, law, and engineering) was only 1,489 (out of a total number of 3,242 students), while only 230 of the 532 graduates were native students.

During World War II and the occupation of Holland by Nazi Germany, the Dutch opened two other institutions of higher education: the "Faculteit der Letteren en Wijsbegeerte," or Faculty of Letters and Philosophy (founded in 1940 at Jakarta), and the "Landbouwkundige Faculteit," or Faculty of Agriculture (founded in 1941 at Bogor). Calls for the establishment of a university in Indonesia were heard in the colonial parliament or "Volksraad" since 1918, led by (among others) by Dr. Abdul Rivai, a native representative. In 1942, plans were made to combine existing institutions of higher education into a "Universiteit van Nederlandsch-Indie" or University of the Dutch East Indies, but this could not be accomplished because of the Japanese invasion later that year. During the period of Japanese occupation, only two institutions of higher learning were kept open—"Ika Daigaku" (the College of Medicine) at Jakarta and "Kogyo Daigaku" (the College of Engineering) at Bandung. The language of instruction at both colleges was Indonesian.

Following the proclamation of independence on August 17, 1945, the Indonesian government established the "Balai Perguruan Tinggi Republik Indonesia" (BPTRI)— The Republic of Indonesia Institute for Higher Education—in Jakarta, consisting of the faculties of medicine and pharmacy, letters, and law. BPTRI had its first graduation of 90 medical doctors the same year. When the Dutch colonial army occupied Jakarta at the end of 1945, the BPTRI was moved to Klaten, Surakarta, Yogyakarta, Surabaya, and Malang. Meanwhile, the Dutch colonial government, which by 1946 had occupied the big cities and surrounding areas in Indonesia, established a "Nood Universiteit" or Emergency University at Jakarta in 1946. In 1947, the name was changed to "Universiteit van Indonesie" (UVI) or University of Indonesia. In December 1949, the government established a university at Yogyakarta called Gadjah Mada University.

In February 1950, when the sovereignty of Indonesia was officially transferred to the Republic of Indonesia, the government established a state university in Jakarta called Universitet Indonesia, comprised of units of the BPTRI and UVI. The name Universitet Indonesia was later changed into Universitas Indonesia (UI).

In 1950, UI was a multi-campus university with faculties in Jakarta (medicine, law, and letters), Bogor (agronomy and veterinary medicine), Bandung (engineering, mathematics and natural sciences), Surabaya (medicine and dentistry), and Makassar (economics), presently called Ujung Pandang. In 1954, the Surabaya campus became Universitas Airlangga; in 1955, the Ujung Pandang campus became Universitas Hasanuddin; in 1959, the Bandung campus became Institut Teknologi Bandung (ITB or Bandung Institute of Technology), while the School for Physical Education, which was also located in Bandung, became part of Padjadjaran University in 1960. In 1964, the Bogor campus became the Institut Pertanian Bogor (IPB or Bogor Agricultural University), and the Faculty of Education (FKIP) at Jakarta, became IKIP Jakarta.

Since 1950, successive Indonesian governments have increased the number of institutions of higher learning in Indonesia, so that at present there are 98 state tertiary institutions and one open university. There are also about 1,300 private institutions.

The Indonesian National Higher Education System

The Indonesian Constitution says that the government should organize education as a "national education system." Within this framework, the goals of national education in Indonesia are: (1) to educate the people to be agents for development and change with Pancasila traditions; and (2) to develop the human resources needed for national development. A new law on education (Law No. 20/2003) was enacted in 2003, establishing a binary higher education system in Indonesia—i.e., there is an academic stream and a vocational/professional stream. The vocational stream consists of the polytechnics and the *akademi*. Programs offered in this stream are 1-year, 2-year, 3-year, and 4-year diploma programs (D-1, D-2, D-3, and D-4), ranging from accountancy to engineering, information technology, languages, and nursing programs. The practical components of the programs range from 80% in the D-1 programs to 20% in the D-4 programs. Most programs are D-3 programs. D-1 to D-3 programs are terminal programs, although some D-3 programs offer transfer to a D-4 program after graduation. D-4 programs, offered only in a very limited number of subjects, are a continuation of the D-3 programs lasting for a year, and can only be entered by those holding a D-3 diploma.

The academic stream (*sarjana* programs) consists of 4-year undergraduate (S-1), 2-year master's (S-2), and 3-year doctoral (S-3) programs. The academic stream also includes academic professions (labeled specialist programs, or "Sp") like medical doctors or accountants. For certain programs it is also possible to transfer, after graduation, from the vocational stream to the academic stream (D-3 to S-1, D4 to S-1, or D4 to S-2) as reflected in Figure 1.

As in other countries, there are universities and special institutes of higher education for engineering, agriculture and education. The curricular system used is the semester

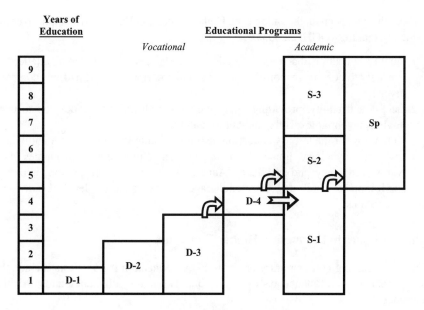

Figure 1.   The Indonesian Tertiary Education Qualifications Framework.

credit system, with a semester duration of 18–20 weeks, depending on the program. The total number of credits for undergraduate studies (or S-1 level) is 144 credits semester units (SKS). For the master's program (or S-2 level), the total number of credits needed is 36–48 SKS, again depending on the program, while for the doctoral programs (or S-3 level) the number of credits needed is 36 SKS.

Indonesian Higher Education: A Vision for 2010

In a globalized world, a nation's competitiveness is defined by its country's economic relationship with world markets, while its products tend to come less from abundant natural resources and cheap labor than from technical innovations and the creative use of knowledge, or a combination of both (Porter, 2002). The ability to produce, select, adapt, commercialize, and use knowledge becomes critical for sustained economic growth and improved living standards. Solow (2001) and other scholars have demonstrated the striking difference in GDP between countries that can be accounted for by their investment in knowledge. Moreover, a nation's competitiveness can only be achieved when its citizens are well-educated and are able to lead meaningful lives. A national higher education system should obviously provide students with a good scientific knowledge. It should also contribute to the process of shaping a democratic, civilized, humane, inclusive society, maintaining a role as a moral force and as the bearer of the public conscience. In the end, higher education should educate students to lead meaningful lives.

From this perspective, the Indonesian Higher Education Vision 2010 emphasizes the following features (DGHE, 2003a):

1. quality education that reflects students' needs, develops students' intellectual capacity to become responsible citizens, and contributes to the nation's competitiveness;
2. access and equity, providing opportunities for all citizens to develop to their highest potential levels throughout life; and
3. autonomy for the tertiary education institutions, coupled with accountability and supported by a legal, financial, and management structure that encourages innovation, efficiency, and excellence. Autonomy also brings a shift in the regulatory environment, which now must encourage innovations at the level of individual institutions.

Current Issues in Indonesian Higher Education

The most pressing contemporary issues in higher education in Indonesia include the need to increase enrollment capacity, equity, quality, funding, efficiency, and curricular relevance.

Enrollment capacity: At present, the 98 state tertiary institutions can only enroll about 100,000 new undergraduate students and 3,000 graduate students each year. In contrast, the private universities can enroll about 250,000 new students. The total number of students enrolled in state tertiary institutions is about one million, while there are about 2.5 million in the private universities, bringing the total number of students in tertiary institutions to about 3.5 million, representing a participation rate of about 14.6% of the college age population in 2004 (DGHE, 2004).

Equity: The economic downturn at the end of the last millennium created a challenge for the nation's efforts to amplify the rate of participation while taking into account equity (gender, social, and regional) in enrollment. The number of students on scholarship of some kind is only around 11% of the total number of students (DGHE, 2004).

Quality: The quality of education is not uniform throughout the system. Usually, the state universities are better than the private ones. An external quality assurance system in the form of a National Accreditation Board for Higher Education is in place. A program review system is used to review about 11,000 study programs now registered. At present, about 80% of all tertiary study programs have been reviewed. The issue of quality is, of course, also related to funding.

Funding: Sources of funding for state tertiary institutions are government budget allocations (60%) and tuition fees (40%). Funding from other sources is very limited. The average amount of funding per year for state tertiary institutions is only about US$1,000 per student, while the real need per year would be about US$2,500 per student. Tuition fees for regular students in state tertiary institutions range from US$50 to $500 per year. Many state tertiary institutions have established special/extension programs with higher tuition fees in order to increase their income. Because of this shortfall, maintenance in many state tertiary institutions suffers. Most private tertiary institutions do not receive government support, so their income is almost exclusively from tuition fees, which range from US$500 to $7,000 per year. With the new policies and shifting role of the DGHE, schemes of financial incentives have been introduced which are open to state and private universities and should steer institutions towards quality, efficiency and equity. These schemes are based on competitive funding among equal institutions or a tiered competition.

Internal and external efficiency: The internal efficiency—especially in the private universities—is still low, causing a shortage of manpower in certain disciplines. In terms of external efficiency, many graduates work in areas outside their area of education. Although some feel that this shows they have been well educated—i.e., they have acquired the ability to work outside their area of education—others feel this demonstrates a waste of resources, especially as there are so many engineers working outside their field. Of course, the state of development and economic situation of the country is also a factor in this matter.

Relevance of the curriculum to the needs of the society: Many university graduates cannot find employment. The curriculum is blamed for this situation as not being relevant to the needs of society. At present, only about 25% of students are enrolled in programs of engineering and science.

Governance: University governance structures at present do not have sufficient autonomy to ensure institutional integrity or to fulfill the responsibilities of policy and resource development. Public universities are treated as part of the government bureaucracy, and private universities as part of the foundations to which they belong. New laws and regulations must be enacted to clearly define the role of leadership in universities.

Quality Assurance in the Indonesian Higher Education System

The basis of quality assurance in the Indonesian higher education system is the basic law on National Education System (Law no. 20/2003) and other government regulations derived from that law. One of the derivatives is the "Higher Education Long-Term Strategy 2003–2010" (HELTS). The goals of the HELTS address the improvement of national competitiveness; the quality of graduates, research, and community/public service; and the internal organization of higher education institutions (i.e., the improvement of organizational health). Strategic goals of the HELTS also address the relevance, quality, and academic atmosphere of institutions; geographic and social equity; and the improvement of higher education management (including dimensions of leadership, efficiency, effectiveness, and sustainability). In order to achieve the goals of the HELTS, a new paradigm of higher education management was introduced for higher education institutions, consisting of increased autonomy, public accountability, and the establishment of internal quality assurance systems and an external quality assurance/accreditation system.

In the context of this new paradigm, accreditation of higher education institutions performs the function of external quality assurance as a component of public accountability. The results of accreditation are used for public certification of the quality of

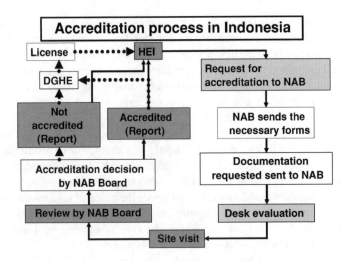

Figure 2. The Accreditation Process in Indonesia.

higher education institutions; to determine eligibility for public funding; and as input for meta-evaluation of the higher education system. Problems for quality assurance in higher education in Indonesia arise from the fact that it is still a new concept for the academic community, and from the attitude of society toward quality education in general. Many people still obtain tertiary education for the credentials rather than for obtaining knowledge and competence.

Accreditation and External Assessment

Figure 2 outlines the process of accreditation for higher education in Indonesia. The process is managed by the National Accreditation Board (NAB) for Higher Education. The board consists of nine members who are appointed by the Minister for National Education for a 4-year period and can be reappointed only once. The system used in Indonesia is program accreditation.

The tasks of the NAB include: organizing the accreditation process; formulating technical directives; establishing evaluation criteria and accreditation status; collecting data; performing evaluations/assessments; publicizing accreditation results; issuing accreditation certificates and recommendations for improvement; helping institutions perform self-evaluation; and reporting periodically to the Minister.

The management paradigm of the NAB involves obtaining accurate results through peer review, accountability, transparency, and cooperation. The methodology used for assessment is predominately quantitative, using structured instruments (Lenn, 2004) that are reviewed every two years. For the purpose of assessment, a variety of key areas, components, and standards are determined. The key areas for assessment are the input (environmental, instrumental, and raw input), process (general management and educational management), and output/outcomes (quality of education, research, public

Table 1. Results of Accreditation of S-1 Programs (as of June 2004).

Type of institutions	Level of accreditation				# of programs accredited	# of S-1 programs	% Accredited
	A	B	C	D			
State universities	350	917	549	79	1,895	1,915	98.9
	18.5%	48.4%	29.0%	4.2%	27.6%	26.2%	
Private universities	309	1797	2004	278	4,388	4,432	99.0
	7.0%	41.0%	45.7%	6.3%	63.8%	61.6%	
Institutes for religious studies	47	264	197	47	555	807	68.8
	8.5%	47.6%	35.5%	8.5%	8.1%	11.2%	
Service institutes	3	20	12	1	36	37	97.3
	8.3%	55.6%	33.3%	2.8%	0.5%	0.5%	
Total	599	2,806	2,607	401	6,476	6,895	95.6%
	9.2%	43.3%	41.2%	7.0%			

Source: National Accreditation Board for Higher Education (NAB), 2004.

service, and competence of graduates) of the educational process. Assessment results are classified into four categories, because of the wide variety in the quality between programs, within similar programs, and even within institutions. These four categories are: (A) equal to international/regional standards; (B) equal to national standards; (C) equal to minimum standards set by the Directorate General of Higher Education; and (D) fail for accreditation. Recent results of the implementation of accreditation processes in Indonesia are provided in Tables 1 and 2.

Standards and indicators are developed in cooperation with peer groups and professional associations, and benchmarked with local, national, regional, international

Table 2. Results of Accreditation of S-2 Programs (as of June 2004).

Type of institutions	Level of accreditation				# of programs accredited	# of S-2 programs	% Accredited
	A	B	C	D			
State universities	10	22	9	0	41	378	10.8%
	24.4%	53.7%	22.0%		54.7%	69%	
Private universities	2	12	15	5	34	136	25.0%
	5.9%	35.3%	44.1%	14.7%	45.3%	25%	
Institutes for religious studies	0	0	0	0	0	37	0
						7%	
Service institutes	0	0	0	0	0	0	0
TOTAL	12	34	24	5	75	551	13.6%
	16%	45.3%	32%	6.7%			

Source: National Accreditation Board for Higher Education (NAB), 2004.

standards. The standards are grouped into (1) standards reflecting components of leadership and institutional development, and (2) standards reflecting components of quality, efficiency, and effectiveness of a program. The standards reflecting components of leadership and institutional development are: integrity, vision, governance, human resources, facilities and infrastructure, funding, and sustainability. The standards reflecting components of quality, efficiency, and effectiveness of a program are: students, curriculum, methods of learning, quality assurance mechanisms, management, and academic atmosphere. Assessment of each of these standards incorporates nine measurement indicators: appropriateness, adequacy, relevance, efficiency, sustainability, selectivity, productivity, effectiveness, and academic atmosphere.

Self-Evaluation and Reviews

In addition to external assessment, higher education institutions are asked to develop internal quality assurance processes, in which self-evaluations are a central part. Self-evaluation reports are also necessary for the accreditation process. The purpose of a self-evaluation exercise is to address a number of important issues, such as: assessment (Where are we now?); improvement (Where can we get to?); accountability (What did we do with what we had?); problem identification (What went wrong?); problem solving (What can we do about what is wrong?); funding (How much money is needed and what are the sources for funding?); and professional accreditation/certification (What do our graduates know, and how competent are our graduates?).

The focus of a self-evaluation review can be structurally vertical, covering the institution as a whole, or on individual departments or programs, the library, an administration office, etc. It can also cover horizontal aspects that transcend the entire institution, such as research, teaching, student support services, community outreach, and disciplines.

Standards in Professional Education

The Dutch colonial government established academic professional education to fill the needs of the colonial administration. The first programs of professional education were established in medicine, followed by law and engineering (as described earlier in this chapter). Professional education in accountancy was established after independence. Standards in professional education are mainly determined by government regulations. "Recognized" universities grant professional degrees. Beginning in 2004, laws have been formulated to give professional associations a dominant role in setting standards in their respective fields and certification. However, licensing would still be in the hands of the related government ministries.

The Impact of Globalization on Higher Education

Although the economic conditions at present are not so good, Indonesia—with its population of 220 million—is still a good market for international education, whether for transnational programs or for recruiting students to study overseas. Many advertisements from institutions engaged in transnational education and in recruiting students for studies overseas appear almost daily in the local newspapers. Many are from reputable institutions, but some come from institutions which are of doubtful reputation (French, 1999). There are no accurate figures, but it is estimated that about 20,000 Indonesians study abroad each year. The number of students taking part in some kind of transnational education within the country is estimated at about 5,000. Compared to the number of students in Indonesia, these numbers are relatively low. On the other hand, the number of foreign students in Indonesia is also relatively low. About half of the foreign students studying in Indonesia come from Malaysia, most likely because of the similarity in language. Students from developed countries usually come to Indonesia to do an elective—usually in Indonesian language or culture—or a research project.

Globalization has also had an impact on the national higher education system and higher education institutions, because globalization means that graduates from Indonesian universities must compete with graduates from overseas universities. At the national higher education system level, the forces of globalization have made the government loosen control on the higher education system, and more autonomy is now granted to higher education institutions. At the institutional level, globalization has forced universities to be more competitive in running their institutions and ensuring quality. Clearly, the public is increasingly demanding that universities deliver more efficient education of a better quality.

In another reflection of globalization, regional cooperation between universities in the region has been established through the ASEAN (Association of Southeast Asian Nations) University Network and within the framework of the SEAMEO (Southeast Asia Ministers of Education Organization) network. Both the AUN and SEAMEO networks have their headquarters in Bangkok, Thailand. With the support of the European Union, the ASEAN University Network (AUN) is promoting mobility within the region, and between the region and Europe, by establishing a regional Credit Transfer Scheme.

Conclusion

Despite all its shortcomings, the development of Indonesian higher education has made giant strides. With only three universities at the birth of Indonesia's independence in 1945, when there were only a few hundred graduates, there are now about 2,000 institutions of higher education and 300,000 graduates. Even so, the demand for higher education is high and funding is limited, forcing universities to be creative in developing programs to meet current and new demands. From the brief historical review of successes and challenges provided here, it is safe to predict that the success of these programs will ensure Indonesia's prominent role in the dynamic higher education landscape of Southeast Asia for many years to come.

References

DGHE (Directorate General of Higher Education). (2003a). *Higher education long term strategy 2003–2010*. DGHE: Jakarta, Indonesia.

DGHE. (2003b). *Higher education sector study*. DGHE: Jakarta, Indonesia.

DGHE. (2004). *Higher education policies and programs*. DGHE: Jakarta, Indonesia.

French, N. J. (1999). Transnational education—Competition or complementarity: The case of Hong Kong. Online at: http://www.edugate.org/conference_papers/Hong Kong,html.htm. Retrieved January 6, 1999.

Lenn, M. P. (2004). *Strengthening World Bank support for quality assurance and accreditation in higher education in East Asia and the Pacific*. Washington, DC: World Bank Education Sector Unit, East Asia and the Pacific Region.

Porter, M. E. (2002). *Building the microeconomic foundations of prosperity: Findings from the microeconomic competitive index*. Davos, Switzerland: The World Economic Forum.

Solow, R. M. (2001). Applying growth theory across countries. World Bank economic review 2001. In *Constructing knowledge societies: New challenges for tertiary education. World Bank Strategy, Volume II*. Washington, DC: The World Bank.

40

IRAN

Abbas Bazargan
University of Tehran, Iran

Higher learning in Iran extends over 25 centuries. The first schools of higher learning were established by King Darius of Persia in the 6th century B.C. (Iranian National Commission for UNESCO, 1977). The first formal university, the University of Gondishapoor (UG), was founded in the 3rd century A.D. (Hekmat, 1972). The UG became one of the most important centers of higher learning during the period. This status was maintained and extended some 300 years after the introduction of Islam into Persia in the 7th century A.D. (IRPSE, 1973).

As Islam spread throughout Iran, religious colleges—called madrasas—became the centers of higher learning. In madrasas, religious leaders provided instruction in topics such as theology, law and medicine. Madrasas were established in major cities around the country and considered the only centers of higher learning until the 19th century.

During the 19th century, attempts were made to introduce modern education in Iran. The first modern institution of higher education, Darolfunun College, was established in 1851. The primary objective of this college was to train technicians for the civil service and military. Darolfunun included seven fields of study: medicine, mathematics, philosophy, mining, military, literature and art (Gol-Golab, 2004). In the early 20th century, some institutions of higher education in fields such as teacher training, agriculture and law were established. Furthermore, the Ministry of Education, Endowment and Fine Arts was established in 1910. This ministry was composed of several offices for general and higher education, endowments, research, evaluation and accounting (IRPHE, 2000).

During the second quarter of the 20th century, the Iranian government began to send students abroad for higher learning, and attempted to establish modern universities. By 1934, six of the existing colleges were combined to form the University of Tehran (UT). In 2002, the UT, as the pioneer in modern higher education in Iran, included about 20 faculties and colleges (IRPHE, 2002).

Between 1947 and 1955, provincial universities were established in Tabriz, Shiraz, Mashad, Esfahan and Ahwaz. After 1960, due to increases in the number of applicants for higher education, privately funded institutions of higher education were established. Among such institutions is the National University of Iran, which was established in

1961. It was re-named Shaheed Beheshti University after the 1979 Islamic Revolution. By 1962, there were seven universities and four higher education institutions, enrolling about 24,000 students.

Before 1950, the University of Tehran enjoyed a considerable level of autonomy. The University council had the right to appoint the chancellor and the deans of the faculties. The UT was given academic, administrative and financial autonomy. The other institutions of higher education followed the bylaws of the University of Tehran, but by 1953—due to socio-political changes—university autonomy was reduced.

In general, the Ministry of Education (MOE) was responsible for higher education institutions. However, in 1967 responsibilities related to higher education were released from the MOE, and the Ministry of Science and Higher Education (MSHE) was established. The MSHE was delegated the following responsibilities: (1) goal setting for higher education and research; (2) policymaking for higher education; (3) monitoring and evaluation of higher education programs; (4) approving the establishment of new higher education institutions; and (5) expansion of science and technology in the country. As a move toward returning administrative and financial autonomy to universities, the MSHE delegated some of its responsibilities regarding decision making to the boards of trustees (IRPHE, 2000). This decision helped the expansion of higher education and the establishment of new institutions, such as the Sharif University of Technology (1966), the largest engineering school in Iran.

By 1967 there were eight universities, 29 higher education institutions, and five centers of higher education, altogether enrolling about 37,000 students. Following the establishment of the MSHE, student enrollment increased to about 68,000 in 1968. A decade later (1979), student enrollment had reached 180,000. One reason for this rapid rate of enrollment increase was the establishment of privately funded higher education institutions, which was in part a direct response to increasing social demand for higher education.

Between 1968 and 1978, innovative projects in higher education were initiated for improving access to—and the quality of—higher education. Among such projects were the Iran Azad (open) University (IAOU) and Bu-Ali Sina University (BASU). The IAOU was designed to be an open learning institution using multimedia and offering distance education. After 1979, the IAOU was merged into a complex of higher education institutions. The BASU was designed as an interdisciplinary university focusing on regional development. The programs of education, research and services of the BASU were planned to be problem-oriented, emphasizing community development. After 2 years of planning, Bu-Ali Sina University enrolled students in 1976. It was considered an effective initiative in integrated higher education, emphasizing problem-based learning related to regional development in environment, health and basic education in Hamadan province. However, the BASU was reorganized as a traditional university after 1979.

In 1979, after proclamation of the Islamic Republic, the Ministry of Science and Higher Education and the Ministry of Culture and Arts were merged into the Ministry of Culture and Higher Education (MCHE). Following this, all university boards of trustees were dissolved. As another move to re-organize higher education, private centers of higher education were turned into public institutions. In 1980, the High Council of the

Cultural Revolution (HCCR) was formed to play a key role in higher education, with an emphasis on centralizing all its affairs. Immediately thereafter, higher education institutions were closed for 3 years, resuming their activities in 1983 (IRPHE, 2000, p. 13).

After 1983, a crucial step in the expansion of higher education in Iran came from the establishment of a non-government university called Islamic Azad University (IAU, 2004). By mobilizing local resources and assistance, the IAU within a short period opened many urban centers throughout the country (Bazargan, 2000, IAU, 2004). In 2002, the IAU system included more than 156 campuses and enrolled more than 58% (904,866) of Iran's total enrollment in higher education. By 2003, the IAU enrollment had increased by about 10%.

In 1985, responsibilities for medical education were delegated to the Ministry of Health, Treatment and Medical Education (MHTME). In this respect, all responsibilities and duties of the Ministry of Culture and Higher Education related to medical education were transferred to the MHTME. Accordingly, faculties of medicine and related fields were detached from the "comprehensive" universities and re-organized under newly established universities of medical sciences. Since then, a university of medical sciences and health services has been established in every one of the 28 provinces. At present, there are more than 30 Universities of Medical Sciences and Health Services in Iran.

In addition to the Ministry of Health, Treatment and Medical Education—which includes affiliated higher education institutions—there are 21 ministries and other government organizations which supervise a variety of specialized institutions of higher education. Examples include the College of Economic Affairs, affiliated with the Ministry of Finance and Economic Affairs, and the College of International Relations, affiliated with the Ministry of Foreign Affairs and providing pre-service and in-service training for their staff (IRPHE, 2002).

After 2000, due to the multiple decision-making bodies in higher education and the spread of higher education institutions under different government organizations, the responsibilities of the Ministry of Culture and Higher Education were re-examined. In order to integrate and coordinate activities related to science and technology, the duties of the Ministry of Culture and Higher Education were streamlined, and it was renamed the Ministry of Science, Research and Technology (MSRT). Since then, university activities have been coordinated by two ministries: the MSRT and the MHTME.

Increasing Demands for Access

In 1996, the population of Iran was 60,055,000 and projected to reach about 74,483,000 by the year 2011 (Taee et al., 2003). The age group of 18–24 year olds fuels the predominant source of demand for higher education in Iran, and is thus of particular interest for this discussion. In 1976, this age group comprised roughly 27.9% (7,797,000) of the total population; it grew to around 10,571,000 in 2001 and is projected to reach about 12,588,000 by 2006 (Taee et al., 2003). More importantly, the average growth rate of this age group, which was 2.4% until 1996, is expected to reach about 11% by 2011. Therefore, the trend of social demand for higher education is going to increase significantly within the next five years, although it is expected to slow down after a decade.

The development of institutions in the first four decades of higher education in Iran was very slow to meet the demand (Bazargan, 2000). The rapid acceleration of higher education commenced after 1985. Between 1979 and 1995, the enrollment rate for the 18–24 year-old age group increased three-fold. In other words, the gross enrollment rate, which was about 5% in 1979, doubled by 1990 and reached about 15% in 1995. Furthermore, the increase in the female enrollment rate has been remarkable during the last decade. The proportion of females in the total student population, which was 27.3% in 1990, reached about 44% in 1999 and grew to 53% in 2002. In other words, female enrollment in higher education is now higher than that of males. This is partly due to the superior performance of female applicants on higher education entrance examinations.

In some fields of study, such as medical sciences, the proportion of female graduates is as high as 60%. This is mainly due to the fact that a majority of students in some fields (such as nursing and midwifery) are female. In 1998, the proportion of female graduates in several fields of study was quite significant, including art (68%), humanities (41%), basic sciences (44%), and agriculture and veterinary medicine (26%) (Gheyassi, 2000). Among the different fields of study overall, engineering tends to graduate the lowest proportion of females.

In 1989, there were 752,000 applicants for admission to higher education in Iran, but only 18% of the applicants were admitted to higher education institutions as first-year students. This proportion was increased to 26% in 1997. The number of applicants for admission to higher education institutions had increased to more than 1.5 million by 2000. However, the proportion of applicants who were admitted as first-year students remained almost the same.

The increase in enrollment was mainly due to the expansion of two large universities: IAU and Payam Noor University (PNU). The PNU was established as a public university by merging several existing higher education institutions in 1997 (Rosokhi, 2001). In 2000, the PNU included more than 160 local study centers around the country and offered distance education programs of study at the bachelor's, master's and Ph.D. levels. In 2002, the PNU accounted for 14% of the total enrollment in higher education. In the same year, the IAU and PNU together accounted for 73% (1,119,675) of the total enrollment (1,538,112) in higher education institutions (IRPHE, 2003). Therefore, the two institutions are considered the largest universities of Iran.

Furthermore, a public institution called the Applied Science University (Elmi-Karbordi) was established in 1991 to offer vocational training and learning opportunities for employed persons in practical fields of study. Access to this university has been expanded to include not only the workers but also other applicants. Applied Science University recently became the first institution in Iran to have designed and implemented a modular program in higher education.

Two centralized assessment processes select applicants for enrollment in higher education. Admission to public tertiary institutions is carried out by Educational Testing Organization (ETO). The Admissions Office of Islamic Azad University (AOIAU) selects applicants for the IAU system. Toward achieving the goals of equity and providing further educational opportunities for applicants from less advantageous backgrounds, special admissions policies have also been implemented through ETO and IAUAO, expanding opportunities for war veterans, applicants from disadvantaged areas of the country and less-advantaged social groups. In this regard, special quotas have been allocated to these groups in the national entrance examinations. However, there is considerable room for improving selection mechanisms that affect access opportunities to tertiary education throughout Iran.

With regard to access, although demand for higher education has doubled in the past decade, the supply has remained proportionally the same and equal to one-fourth of the applicants. It is planned that this ratio will be increased to one-third by 2009 (SOMP, 2003).

Expansion and Accountability

Total enrollment in the public and private higher education institutions of Iran was about 180,000 in 1979, and grew to 1,321,752 in 1997. The average annual growth of the total student population during this period was 9.7%. Public institutions saw a growth rate of 7%, while the growth rate for private institutions was 21% (Tavakol, 1999). In other words, the rate of increase in enrollment at the private institutions was three times higher than that of the public institutions.

In 2002, the distribution of students in the public institutions by major fields of study was as follows: humanities and arts (47%), engineering (23%), basic sciences (12%), medical sciences (11%), and agriculture and veterinary medicine (7%). A longitudinal analysis of the distribution of students by field of study indicates that the humanities and arts have expanded, with a higher proportion than other fields of study at the public institutions of higher education. Further, a look at student enrollment in the private institutions by major fields of study showed similar patterns: humanities and arts (53%), engineering (27%), basic sciences (9%), agriculture and veterinary medicine (6%), and medical sciences (5%). Therefore, the trend of enrollment by fields of study in both public and private institutions of higher education has favored the humanities and arts.

The average annual growth rate of the student population at the non-government (private) institutions during 1989–97 was 20.8%, which was twice the growth rate of enrollment at the government (public) institutions (Bazargan, 2000). In 2002, the total enrollment at the public and private institutions of higher education was 1,538,112 students. They were distributed among 98 universities, about 160 other higher education institutions and postsecondary centers (2-year colleges). An annual increase of about 10% is estimated for the next few years.

During the past two decades, policies of higher education expansion resulted in a wide geographical distribution of higher education in all provinces. As a result, there are now at least two universities in every province. In 2002, among the 28 provinces, the three highest ranking provinces (in terms of student population) were: Tehran (22%), Esfahan (11%) and Khorassan (8%). In other words, Tehran province accounted for more than one-fifth of the country's total enrollment in higher education.

With regard to accountability, there are two centralized mechanisms for academic program approval. Any proposal for initiating a new educational program or institution of higher education should go through an administrative process and obtain approval of at least four councils in hierarchical order. These include: council of department; council of faculty; council of university; and the national Council for Higher Education Development (CHED). Furthermore, the Curriculum Planning Council should be informed about the program changes as well. However, the approval of proposals for establishing new institutions of higher education is solely the responsibility of the CHED. Such a structure has resulted in a highly centralized process of program approval which is not flexible enough to react quickly to the realities of the labor market (Bazargan, 2000). It is intended that during the Fourth Development Plan (2005–2009), the higher education structure will be further decentralized, giving more autonomy to universities and making them more accountable.

The MHTME and the MSRT have recently sought to establish mechanisms to assess the quality of universities. To this end, the MHTME implemented a pilot project for conducting self-evaluation in medical education departments in 1997 (Bazargan, 1999). The results indicated that an evaluation culture could be promoted in higher education through self-evaluation. Furthermore, this experience indicated that the transparency and accountability of higher education at the departmental level could be achieved through ownership of quality assurance by faculty members. After this experience, a self-evaluation process was introduced in non-medical higher education institutions as well. It is planned that an accreditation process, composed of a self-evaluation followed by an external quality review, will be implemented in the higher education system of Iran (Bazargan, 2002). So far, more than 300 departments in about 30 universities have attempted to carry out their self-evaluation reviews.

In order to strengthen quality assurance and accountability, a central council of self-evaluation has been established at the Ministry of Science, Research and Technology to approve necessary policies and give feedback to the process of external quality assessment. But from the viewpoint of organizational structure, there is much room for improvement. It is hoped that program and institutional reviews will be carried out by an authority independent of the government in the near future.

Economic and Financial Issues

Public institutions of higher education in Iran are financed mainly by the government. But private higher education institutions are financed through tuition fees, examination fees, donations, and endowments. The proportion of the total government budget earmarked for higher education was 2.78% in 1979, and reached about 5.14% in 2001. In other words, higher education's share of the government budget has nearly doubled during the past two decades. University research budgets have also increased dramatically over the past decades (Tavakol, 1999).

Differences Between Public and Private Institutions

In Iran, the public institutions receive all their annual support from the national budget. Students in these institutions pay only a nominal fee for enrollment. The majority of private (non-government) higher education institutions, in general, do not receive any funds from the government. Students at these institutions pay for their enrollment and full tuition fees. Between 1989 and 1998, the average growth rate of financial resources (fixed price) for public higher education institutions was 14.8%, and for the private sector was 27.9%, with an average of 17.4% for the whole higher education system (Taee et al., 2003, p. 178).

Curriculum planning for both public and private institutions is centralized and similar for the two sub-systems (private and public). While the Ministry of Science, Research and Technology is in charge of non-medical higher education, the Ministry of Health, Treatment and Medical Education is in charge of medical and health education programs. Public institutions of higher education are expected to endure a long administrative process before establishing new educational programs. The process at private institutions is similar to the public institutions, although it takes less time to approve a new program.

Faculty members in both public and private institutions are classified by the traditional ranks of professor, associate professor, assistant professor, and instructor. The requirements for the rank of professor include a doctoral degree, publication of scientific works (such as research papers, articles and books), proficiency in at least one foreign language, and a minimum of 5 years of teaching and research experience as an associate professor. The prerequisites for the post of associate professor are usually a doctoral degree, publication of research articles, fluency in one foreign language, and at least 4 years of teaching or research experience as an assistant professor. An assistant professor is generally required to hold a doctoral degree and have a mastery of one foreign language. The requirements for the position of instructor are at least a master's degree, adequate knowledge of one foreign language and experience in conducting research. The process of recruiting faculty members for the government institutions is more rigid than the private (non-government) institutions. In the private institutions, many of faculty members are former graduates of the same institutions. The distribution of faculty members by academic rank in public and private institutions in 1999 is provided in Table 1. During the past 5 years, attempts have been made to improve the distribution of faculty members at the public and private institutions of higher education, and the proportion of instructors at the public higher education institutions has recently decreased to less than 50%.

In 1999, there were 37,744 full-time faculty members in Iran's institutions of higher education, of which public institutions accounted for 69% (Taee et al., 2003). In contrast, the student population at private institutions accounted for 59% of total enrollment

Table 1. Distribution of Faculty Members by Academic Ranks, 1999.

Type of institution	Professor	Associate Professor	Assistant Professor	Instructor and others	Total
Public	3.2%	6.8%	36.0%	54.0%	100%
Private	3.3%	2.8%	15.2%	78.7%	100%
All	2.7%	4.5%	25.5%	67.3%	100%

Source: Taee et al., 2003.

in Iranian higher education, while faculty members at these institutions accounted for just 31% of all faculty—in other words, private higher education accounted for nearly two-thirds of all students but only one-third of all faculty members. This major difference in student/faculty ratio accounts for significant variations between the public and private sectors in the educational experiences available to students. In another important dimension separating the public and private sectors, the major public universities (such as the University of Tehran and about 14 other institutions with graduate programs) are placing increasing emphasis on research, while private institutions are comparatively teaching-oriented.

Public institutions are governed by boards of trustees. Major responsibilities of a typical board of trustees are related to administrative procedures, regulations for recruiting faculty members, and budget and financial matters. However, the governance of public institutions of higher education is centralized, falling under the supervision of the ministries (either MSRT or MHTME). There are also several regional boards of trustees for smaller universities and higher education institutions. These boards of trustees make decisions regarding educational and research matters of the institutions under their supervision.

The multi-campus Islamic Azad University is led by a few regional administrative boards across the country, under a somewhat more relaxed governing structure. However, there is a strong board of trustees at the top of the IAU system, which approves organizational structure and administrative procedures, sets regulations, makes decisions about faculty payments, and reviews and approves the chancellor's report.

Graduate Education

In 1979, the proportion of graduate students (master's degree and Ph.D.) within the total student population in public institutions of higher education was 1.3%, growing to about 6.5% in 1993 and 16% in 1997. Across the entire Iranian higher education system, the proportion of graduate students is roughly 10%.

Between 1979 and 1998, the average annual growth rate of master's degree students was 6.6% and for doctoral students was 3.6%—with growth rates of 7% and 6% in the public institutions, respectively (Tavakol, 1999). Considering the average annual growth rate of enrollment in the public institutions in the same period was 4.7%, the growth rate of graduate education in Iran in the past two decades has been higher than the average growth rate of higher education enrollment.

Graduate education is offered in both "comprehensive" (multidisciplinary) universities and specialized universities. In a comprehensive university, colleges or faculties provide undergraduate education in one or more branches of study or professional training (agriculture, basic sciences, engineering, fine arts, etc.). In addition to undergraduate programs, faculties offer graduate programs at the master's and Ph.D. level. There are about 15 such universities which are considered comprehensive. The specialized universities concentrate on a field of study such as medical sciences or engineering. There are 33 universities of medical sciences, of which 29 offer graduate programs at the master's and Ph.D. level, as well as specialized programs for those with first professional degrees (such as specialization in internal medicine).

The University of Tehran provides the majority of undergraduate and graduate education in Iran. In 2002, total student enrollment at the UT was 29,387, and graduate enrollment was 7,751 of which 22% (1,715) were enrolled in Ph.D. programs and 78% (6,036) were enrolled in master's or first degree professional programs. In comparison, Tarbiat Modaress University (TMU), an institution exclusively for graduate higher education, enrolled 4,249 graduate students—1,167 students (27%) in Ph.D. programs and 3,082 students (83%) in master's degree programs. Thus, even though TMU is an institution which enrolls only graduate students, the University of Tehran enrolls more graduate students than any other institution of higher education in Iran.

Challenges Facing Higher Education

As enrollment in higher education institutions expanded during the past two decades, serious questions have been raised with regard to quality and relevance. It is expected that these institutions will be more responsive to the current and future requirements of the country. In this respect, qualifications of graduates vis-à-vis the development needs of the country and also the realities of labor market should be re-examined. For some fields of study, such as engineering, performance of graduates in the labor market is not satisfactory. Results of a survey conducted about the relationship between higher education and manufacturing demand in Iran indicate that graduates are not well equipped to handle the duties related to becoming entrepreneurs (Bazargan, 2000). There have also been indications of serious unemployment among university graduates, even in the fields of medicine and engineering. Another important recent development has been that, in order to develop entrepreneurial skills among graduates and promote self-employment, new courses and programs have been introduced, such as: achievement motivation, business management, and risk taking.

Furthermore, globalization and the move toward a knowledge-based society are posing new demands on higher education. In this respect, colleges and universities in Iran need to be more accountable. There is also a need for promoting a culture of quality assurance. In addition, an ever-increasing social demand for higher education and inappropriate mechanisms for the selection of freshmen have had an undesirable impact on general education. Although procedures have been developed to select capable candidates from among the applicants, so far these procedures have not met the expectations of academics nor the general public. Innovative approaches are required to meet the demand for higher education. In this regard, a major challenge for higher education stems from the policy decision to increase annual enrollment to 36% of applicants by 2010 (Taee et al., 2003, p. 137).

There have also been attempts by several universities to incorporate information and communication technology (ICT) into higher education through the design and implementation of virtual campus programs. However, due to the high costs and requirements for specialized human resources, such programs are in various stages of development. Overall, it is hoped that through the expansion of academic and applied science institutions of higher education, as well as through new distance education programs, more students will eventually have access to higher education.

Retention has also been a significant challenge for higher education in Iran. Pilot studies indicate that the problem of repeaters and dropouts in certain fields of study needs particularly serious attention. A thorough study and reforms are urgently needed to deal with this problem.

One of the most important challenges facing higher education in Iran today is faculty development and management. In 1999, the ratio of students to faculty members in public institutions was nearly 37 to 1, while in private institutions was 64 to 1 (Taee et al., 2003, p. 177). With student-faculty ratios like these, the need for faculty development has been very high. The number and proportion of faculty members with the rank of associate professor and higher have increased during the past few years. However, policies and programs should be designed and developed for improving the recruitment and productivity of faculty members.

The development of university management capacity—particularly in areas of planning, financial management and policy analysis—is also considered an important challenge in Iran. This would help to integrate policies in the private and public institutions of higher education. Finally, although there have been attempts to introduce quality assurance procedures in tertiary education in Iran (Bazargan, 1999, 2000, 2002), there is a need for the consolidation of self-evaluation systems for quality assurance and external quality assessment. In this respect, the creation of a National Board of Evaluation and Accreditation is of high priority.

In sum, the sophistication and vigor with which the government and institutional leaders meet these challenges will rule the fate of higher education in Iran for many years to come.

References

Bazargan, A. (1999). Introduction to assessing quality in higher medical education in Iran: Challenges and perspectives. *Quality in Higher Education, 5*(1), 61–67.

Bazargan, A. (2000). Internal evaluation as an approach to revitalize university systems: The case of the Islamic Republic of Iran. *Higher Education Policy, 13*, 173–180.

Bazargan, A. (2002). Issues and trends in quality assurance and accreditation: A case study of Iran. *Proceedings of the first global forum on international quality assurance, accreditation and the recognition of qualifications in higher education (Paris, October 17–18, 2002)* (pp. 123–128). Paris: UNESCO.

Gheyassi, M. (2000). *A study of female enrollment in higher education in Iran.* Tehran, Iran: IRPHE (in Persian).

Gol-Golab, H. (2004). From medical classroom to medical faculty. *University News (Shaheed Beheshti University of Medical Sciences and Health Services), 11*(36), 74–79.

Hekmat, A. (1972). *Education in ancient Iran.* Tehran: Institute for Research and Planning in Science and Education (in Persian).

Institute for Research and Planning in Science and Education (IRPSE). (1973). *Analytical study on financing of higher education in Iran.* Tehran, Iran: IRPSE.

Institute for Research and Planning in Higher Education (IRPHE). (2000). *Higher education in Iran: A national report.* Tehran, Iran: IRPHE.

Institute for Research and Planning in Higher Education (IRPHE). (2002). *Statistics of Higher Education in Iran, 2001–2002, (and Database).* Tehran, Iran: IRPHE (in Persian).

Institute for Research and Planning in Higher Education (IRPHE). (2003). *Statistics of Higher Education in Iran, 2002–2003, (and Database).* Tehran, Iran: IRPHE (in Persian).

Iranian National Commission for UNESCO. (1977). Iran. In A. S. Knowles (Ed.), *The international encyclopedia of higher education*, (Vol. 5, pp. 2310–2318). London: Jossey-Bass.

Islamic Azad University (IAU). (2004). *IAU database*. General Department of Information and Communication Technology (in Persian).

Rosokhi, M. (2001). *Index of higher education (Iran)*. Tehran, Iran: IRPHE.

State Organization for Management and Planning (SOMP). (2003). *Islamic Republic of Iran fourth economic, social and cultural development plan:2005–2009*. Tehran, Iran: SOMP (in Persian).

Taee, H.; Vahidi, P.; Ghofrani, M. B. (2003). *Trained manpower: Needs assessment and state human resource development policy*. Tehran, Iran: Institute for Research and Planning in Higher Education (in Persian).

Tavakol, M. (1999). Higher education status in Iran: realities and challenges. *Quarterly Journal of Research and Planning in Higher Education (Tehran)*, *6*(4), 1–26.

41

ISRAEL

Yaacov Iram
Bar-Ilan University, Israel

Before exploring the higher education system of Israel, it is first necessary to understand the unique geographic and demographic context of this country. The area of Israel within its 1949 armistice borders is 20,700 square kilometers. In addition, Israel controls "administered territories" of about 7,500 square kilometers (occupied since the 1967 war) from Syria, Jordan, and Egypt, part of which are also administered by the Palestinian Authority following the Oslo accords of the 1990s. (These territories are not dealt with here.) The state is bounded on the north by Lebanon, on the northeast by Syria, on the east by the Hashemite Kingdom of Jordan, and on the southwest by the Gulf of Aqaba/Eilat and the Egyptian Sinai Desert (Israel Central Bureau of Statistics [CBS], Statistical Abstract of Israel no. 55, 246/2004b).

Israel's total population in 2003 was 6,748,400, of whom 5,165,400 (76.5%) were Jews and 1,583,000 (23.5%) non-Jews. Of the non-Jewish population, 1,072,500 were Muslims, 142,400 Christians, 110,800 Druze, and 254,600 others, mainly immigrants and their families who are not registered as Jews in the Population Register (CBS, Israel Central Bureau of Statistics [CBS], Statistical Abstract of Israel no. 55, 246/2004b).

One of Israel's most striking characteristics is the rapid increase in its population. The main source for growth in Israel's population was immigration, accounting for 30% of the yearly increase in the total population and 46.2% in the Jewish population between 1948 and 1988 (CBS, 1989). In the early 2000s, Israel remains a migrant society. Of the 3.4 million Israeli-born Jews, only one-third (33.9%) were second generation Israelis. Of the total Jewish population, only 21.5% were second generation Israelis (CBS, Israel Central Bureau of Statistics [CBS], Statistical Abstract of Israel no. 55, 246/2004b).

Israel is also a pluralistic society. Nationally, there is a Jewish majority and a non-Jewish, predominantly Arab, minority. Linguistically, there are two official languages: Hebrew and Arabic. As a result of national, religious, and linguistic pluralism, separate educational systems emerged: Jewish, Arab, and Druze (Al-Haj, 1991; Mar'i, 1978).

The Jewish majority is diversified ethnically, religiously, culturally, and educationally. Ethnically, in the sense of country of origin, there are *Ashkenazim*—namely, Jews whose origin is in Eastern and Central Europe—and *Sephardim*, or "Orientals"—Jews from the Mediterranean Basin and other Arab and Muslim countries (Patai, 1970; Shama & Iris, 1976). Israeli Jews are also divided into "religious" and "nonreligious"

James J.F. Forest and Philip G. Altbach (eds.), International Handbook of Higher Education, 793–810.
© 2006 *Springer. Printed in the Netherlands.*

(Liebman & Don Yihye, 1984). Culturally, diversity arises from the different ethnic groups who brought from their countries of origin different customs, ceremonies, attitudes, values, and ways of life.

The population density of Israel at the end of 2003 was 305 persons per square kilometer. Three-quarters of the Jewish inhabitants and two-thirds of the non-Jewish population are concentrated in the coastal strip. The northern and particularly the southern district, comprising about two-thirds of Israel's land area, are sparsely populated. More than 88% of the population is defined as urban—that is, residents in localities with 2,000 or more inhabitants. However, the rural-urban division in Israel is of little significance in terms of economic status and educational provision (CBS, 2004a).

Socio-Historical Context

The socio-historical roots of higher education in Israel are connected with the Zionist idea of cultural and national revival (Ben-David, 1986). Thus, the Hebrew University—founded in 1918 and opened in Jerusalem in 1925—was meant to help generate the Jewish cultural revival by becoming an academic center for research in Judaic studies, humanities, and sciences. Its complementary institution, the Technion—the Israel Institute of Technology, founded in 1912 and opened in 1924 in Haifa—was devoted toward realization of the Zionist program of providing the pragmatic technological and technical needs of the *Yishuv*, the Jewish community in Palestine, by training engineers and technical personnel (Ben-David, 1986; Iram, 1983). Thus, the higher education enterprise in Israel was conceived from its beginnings as the responsibility of the Jewish people throughout the world and not only of those in Palestine (and later in Israel). Indeed, the supreme authority of these two institutions—their Boards of Governors—were composed of prominent Jewish individuals in the fields of science, arts, management, and economics, as well as members of societies and friends of Israel in various parts of the world. Today, Diaspora Jewry is represented on the governing bodies of all Israeli universities.

Higher education in Israel shares most of the goals of tertiary systems elsewhere: training manpower, furthering economic development, promoting scientific research, enriching the culture, and transmitting and advancing knowledge in general (Clark, 1983). In addition to these general goals, Israel's higher education institutions are expected to strengthen Jewish scholarship, transmit Jewish culture, and forge cultural links with the Jewish people in the Diaspora. Indeed, the socio-historical roots of higher education in Israel are connected with the Zionist idea of cultural and national revival (Ben-David, 1986; Iram, 1983).

The establishment of the Jewish state produced a growing demand for higher education. Indeed, four new universities were established between 1955 and 1964 (Bar-Ilan, Tel-Aviv, Haifa, and Ben Gurion Universities). The Weizmann Institute of Science was established in 1949 as a research institute, and in 1958 it opened a graduate school to award M.Sc. and Ph.D. degrees. The Open University was launched in 1976, was accredited in 1980, and was authorized to award the bachelor's degree in 1980 (Halperin, 1984). Rapid growth in the number of students became the most conspicuous feature of the expansion of the higher education system, though not the most important feature.

Three of the five new universities founded since 1955—Tel Aviv, Haifa, and Ben Gurion-Beer Sheva Universities—owe their establishment to local initiative; one—Bar-Ilan University—to that of the Zionist religious organization; and one—the Open University—to governmental initiative and philanthropic support (from the Rothschild Foundation). However, despite the diversity in origins of the new universities established during the 1950s and 1960s, they tended to imitate the two veteran higher education institutions—the Hebrew University and the Haifa Technion—by stressing research as a measure of strength and success. Indeed, the longstanding Jewish tradition of the unity of research and teaching is responsible for the growth of research in Israeli universities, their single most important feature (Ben-David, 1986).

Martin Trow's (1984) assertion that "competition accounts for the 'drift' ... of new institutions and sectors toward the academic forms and styles, the curriculum and standards of elite institutions" applies also to the Israeli case. The similarity of Israel's higher education institutions may also be explained by the direct supervision exercised by the Hebrew University and the Technion over the new universities in the initial years of their development, and the indirect supervision exercised by the Council of Higher Education (established in 1958 and led by senior faculty members of the two older institutions and the Weizmann Institute of Science). During the 1950s, two discernible groups exerted decisive influence on the development of higher education in Israel. One group consisted of prominent scientists and scholars who immigrated to Israel during the 1920s and particularly during the 1930s following the rise of Nazism. This group had received its academic training mainly in the authoritarian academic atmosphere of Central European universities. These scholars and scientists became the basis for academic development in the country. In the late 1940s, a second group of scientists and scholars emerged from among the outstanding graduates of the local institutions as well as from England and the United States. The political circumstances at that time (British rule) and the rigid academic norms of the Hebrew University and the Technion combined to limit their academic influence (Iram, 1987). But in the 1950s, this group played a decisive role in the establishment and consolidation of the Weizmann Institute. They brought about a reform in teaching and the adoption of the three-level degree structure at the Hebrew University and the Technion, and were instrumental in the establishment of Bar-Ilan and Tel-Aviv Universities in the 1950s, and Haifa and Ben Gurion Universities in the 1960s.

These developments enabled Israel's universities to conform—in curricula, degree structure, and offerings—to those of the United States and Britain. It also resulted in the increased democratization of research organization and in academic governance. As a result, Israel's higher education became an up-to-date scientific enterprise, and some of its institutions achieved international status. Indeed, the universities' affirmation of research as their supreme goal continues to guide the higher education system even in times of financial constraints. It is estimated that "over 80% of all Israeli scientific research, and almost all Israeli basic research and research training, is conducted within research universities" (The Israel Academy of Sciences and Humanities, 2003, p. 13).

Characteristics of the Higher Education System

"Higher education," as defined by the Council for Higher Education Law, 5718 (1958), "includes teaching, science, and research" that are conducted in universities and other academic degree-granting institutions. The higher education system in Israel is divided into seven distinct groups (Council for Higher Education, 2004):

1. seven universities and the Open University;
2. arts academies (music and dance; arts and design);
3. comprehensive academic colleges, maintaining programs of study leading to the bachelor's degree;
4. academic colleges of engineering;
5. academic programs in regional colleges under university auspices, which are in the process of becoming independent institutions;
6. academic colleges for the training of teachers; and
7. private, for-profit ("non-budgeted") colleges.

The Planning and Budgeting Committee (PBC) of the Council for Higher Education (CHE) is responsible for the budgets of all the institutions in the first five groups, while teacher training colleges are accredited by the Council, but funded by the Ministry of Education, and the "non-budgeted" colleges are accredited by the Council, but not funded by it. Since 1990, the number of higher education institutions in Israel has more than doubled (see Table 1).

Only the universities are authorized to award degrees beyond the bachelor's degree in a variety of fields of study and advanced professional training. The Open University and select "other institutions of higher education" are authorized to award the bachelor's degree, and some of them are authorized to award M.A. degrees in specified fields of study or training. The teacher training colleges are authorized to award the "Bachelor's of Education" (B.Ed.) degree to teachers for primary and junior high schools (K-9). Three years are generally required for the completion of the bachelor's degree and

Table 1.   Institutions of Higher Education, 1990–2004

Type of institution	1990	2003	2004	2005
Universities	7	7	7	7
The Open University	1	1	1	1
Arts academies	2	2	2	2
Comprehensive academic colleges	0	6	6	6
Academic colleges of engineering	2	8	8	8
Non-budgeted academic colleges	2	6	7	8
Academic colleges for training teachers	7	24	26	27
Academic programs in regional colleges	7	7	7	7
Total	28	60	64	66

Source: Council for Higher Education (Planning and Grants Committee), 2003, 2004, 2005.

Table 2.   Students in Higher Education Institutions and Universities

Educational Institutions	1989–90	1999–00	Annual % Change 1989–2000	2001–02	2002–03	Total % Growth 1999–2003
Total	84,464	199,438	8.5%	217,906	228,695	4.7%
Universities	67,201	112,987	5.3%	117,146	120,552	2.2%
Thereof: first degree	46,519	74,194	4.8%	75,247	76,581	1.1%
Academic colleges	3,668	33,709	24.8%	43,492	48,320	12.8%
Thereof: first degree	3,668	33,250	24.7%	42,622	47,015	12.2%
Teacher training colleges	4,618	20,004	15.8%	20,546	21,100	1.8%
The open university	13,007	32,738	9.7%	36,722	38,723	5.8%
Thereof: first degree	13,007	32,400	9.6%	36,110	37,406	4.9%

Source: Council for Higher Education, 2004.

2 years for the master's degree. The Ph.D. degree has minimal formal requirements, and is designed individually according to the candidate's research project.

The number of students at the seven university-level institutions reached 228,695 in 2003, an increase of more than 150% over the last 10 years (see Table 2). Some 60% of the students are studying humanities, social sciences and law, 23.3% natural sciences, agriculture, and medicine, and 16.7% engineering. Some 72% are studying for the first degree (bachelor's), 21% for the second degree (master's), 5% for the doctorate, and 2% for academic diplomas, mainly secondary school teaching diplomas. The 13 non-university institutions of higher education enrolled some 5,800 students. About 13,500 students were enrolled in academic courses at the Open University; this number is approximately equivalent to 2,300 students in full-time study programs at a regular university.

It is difficult to compare the rate of participation in Israel with the rate in Western countries because of variations between university degree programs in different countries. Also, the principal age group attending universities in Israel, ages 20–29, differs from that in other countries due to 3 years of required military service for men and 2 years for women. In Israel, about 20% of the 20–29 year-old cohort received university education, and about 30% of them higher education. This rate is higher than in most developed nations, similar to Japan, but lower than the rate in the United States and Canada.

Governance and Administration of Higher Education

National Administration

When the state of Israel was established in 1948, there were two small higher education institutions (the Hebrew University of Jerusalem and the Haifa Technion) and one research institute. They emphasized research and scholarship (in very few areas), technological training and applied research. They were private institutions supported mainly by foreign donors and run like corporations, following the model of American private universities. Although they were expected to contribute to "the realization of Jewish culture and the Zionist program of building up the country physically" (Ben-David, 1986, p. 105), they safeguarded their autonomy from the Zionist organization that created and supported them, and later (during the 1950s) from the emerging governmental bureaucracy. The universities continued to have full institutional autonomy. Their academic staff enjoyed almost unrestricted academic freedom of teaching and research similar to the British elitist institutions. Academic staff also played a decisive role in administrative matters of the university.

Between 1955 and 1964, four new universities were founded, and the number of students rose from 3,022 in 1950–51 to 18,368 in 1964–65. The academic profession grew from 135 professors and lecturers in 1950–51 to 2,814 in 1968–69. New departments in the social sciences and humanities—as well as professional schools in law and medicine—were established both in the old and new universities. This expansion and the increased demand for public and governmental funds brought to light three interrelated issues: accreditation of new institutions; criteria and means for channeling public funds to the individual institutions; and the issue of governmental control over the system. Indeed, since World War II governments have often intervened in higher education systems in order to democratize access and governance, to make studies more relevant to the economy and careers, and to augment their influence over the magnitude, the cost, and the future direction of the higher education enterprise (Clark, 1983; Trow, 1984). This trend became apparent in Israel in 1958, when the government established the Council for Higher Education (CHE) as a statutory body, serving as "the State institution for matters of higher education in the State" (Stanner, 1963, pp. 244–49). The CHE is the sole authority able to recommend to the government the granting of a permit to open a new institution of higher education, as well as granting academic recognition, accreditation, and the right to confer academic degrees. In an apparent attempt to safeguard academic freedom, Section 4a of the Council for Higher Education Law, 5718 (1958) states that "at least two-thirds of its members must be persons of standing in the field of higher education"—namely, full professors.

The continuous quantitative expansion of the higher education system (see Tables 1 and 2) was accompanied by a massive increase in public expenditure, which rose steadily to 45.5% in 1959–60 and to almost 80% of the ordinary budget in 1974–75. Increased government involvement in financing higher education intensified the basic issue of how to reconcile the inherent conflict between academic freedom and accountability to the public.

The autonomous governing body of each university decided on its development policy without coordination with other universities, the Council for Higher Education, or the government. There was a need to find both a scheme and a mechanism to make universities more accountable to the public, and particularly to work out an equitable system for financing higher education.

In 1974, the Council for Higher Education took charge of planning and appointed the first Planning and Grants Committee (PGC), following the British model of the University Grants Committee (UGC). To safeguard against the intervention of the state, at least four of PGC's six members, including the chairperson, must be full professors appointed *ad person am.* The other two members come from business and industry (PGC, 1985). However, this composition was changed at the last Council to include representation of colleges (CHE, 2003).

The terms of reference for the PGC, as set forth in Government Decision No. 666 of June 5, 1977, are as follows: the PGC functions as a central coordination agency of the Council for Higher Education in allocating governmental and public funds for higher education; it reviews budgetary proposals, both ordinary and developmental, of each institution, ensuring that they are balanced; the PGC is responsible for coordination between institutions; it reviews and evaluates proposals for opening new institutions (or new programs within existing institutions) having financial implications, and submits its recommendations to the Council; and the PGC reports to the Council at the end of each academic year. Although the PGC was meant to guarantee academic freedom and institutional autonomy of the universities, which may negotiate their budgets only with the PGC, in practice the freedom of the individual institution, both in academic and fiscal matters, was eroded considerably.

Indeed, during the 1980s the power of government increased, not directly, but through the Planning and Grants Committee. The PGC became a centralized power in matters of funding, planning, policy initiatives, and evaluation. Thus, the initiatives of the PGC caused it to become a force in the development and regulation of higher education and not just an organ for the channeling of governmental funds. During the second term of the PGC (1979–85), its power and status increased further, as reflected in the change of its name to the Planning and Budgeting Committee (PBC) to better reflect its direct involvement in the budgeting of the higher education system.

Institutional Administration

Higher education institutions in Israel are autonomous, and have academic freedom and self-governance. Section 15 of the Council for Higher Education Law, 5718 (1958) guarantees the autonomy of higher education, not only in its academic conduct but also in its administrative and financial affairs (Stanner, 1963). Although institutions are dependent financially on governmental support and are required to submit to PGC their budgets for approval, "each institution is free to conduct its academic and administrative affairs as it sees fit, within the confines of its approved budget" (CHE PGC, 1988a, p. 15).

The supreme authority of each university is vested in its board of governors and executive committee, a third of which are drawn from prominent Jewish individuals in science, arts, management, and business outside Israel; another third on the executive committees are academic staff. The board of governors appoints a president who is the head of the university. However, the president's main responsibility is for the institution's administrative and financial affairs. The president is assisted by a director general or vice president. The supreme authority in academic matters is the rector, who is a full professor elected for a 2- to 3-year term by the senate, which is composed of all full professors and representatives from other academic ranks, as well as a representative of the student body. The rectors and presidents of all universities have formed a Committee of Heads of Universities, which functions as a consultation and coordination organ. Faculties, institutes, schools and departments elect their heads from their ranks. The power of the rector, the senate and its committees extends beyond academic affairs to administrative matters as well. The board of governors does not usually interfere in academic matters, thus self-governance in academic matters is almost unrestricted.

Because all positions of power are held by temporary academic officials elected by the academic staff from its own ranks, no professional higher education administration has developed in Israel. Constant rotation of academic office holders does not leave time or incentive for staff to become experts in academic administration, politics and planning. Excessive participatory democracies of faculty assemblies have also prevented the emergence of effective academic leadership. Faculty assemblies attend to both routine business (such as appointments) and long-term curricular and research policies, through a complicated system of committees. The support for participatory self-government—and opposition to professional administration—has been based on the principle that universities should be a loose coalition of self-governing departments (Ben-David, 1986). However, others argue that the lack of academic or administrative authority above the department and faculty levels brings to a deadlock any attempt to relocate resources between departments and units in response to changing financial circumstances, research interests, or shifts in employment prospects that require changes in training priorities.

Israeli universities are similar to each other in structure, programs, and aims; they are, or aspire to become, comprehensive research universities. However, two institutions emphasize service to the local community—Haifa University in the north, and Ben-Gurion University in the south—while Bar-Ilan University is committed to religious values and religious education.

Academic work is organized in basic units such as departments, which are based on scientific discipline or field of study and research; schools—usually professional—and institutes comprising both research and instruction; and programs which are interdisciplinary. Departments are grouped in faculties such as humanities, social sciences, natural sciences, engineering, law and medicine. Departments are independent in determining their course of study and admissions requirements, but are responsible to the dean of the faculty.

The Funding of Higher Education

The principal sources of income for the higher education system are: (a) allocations from the government, determined and paid by the PGC; (b) income from current donations; (c) revenue from endowment funds; (d) tuition fees; (e) research contracts and research grants from government and private sources, at home and abroad; and (f) sale of services (including teaching services). The Israeli higher education system depends financially on allocations from the government. In the 1980s, the government—through the PGC/PBC—provided 55–75% of the ordinary budgets of higher education institutions, except for teacher-training institutions and regional colleges, which were financed directly by the Ministry of Education and Culture. In 2003, the PBC allocated US$1.2 billion, which accounted for 45–65% of the higher education institutions' budgets (Grossman, 2004).

The PBC operates through four budgetary channels, including block grant allocation, matching allocations, and earmarked allocations. Through each of these channels, and by determining their relative share in the general budget, the PBC exerts influence over higher education in Israel. The PBC's increased budgetary control is particularly manifest in the changes of the largest item of the government's budget—namely, the block grant allocations to institutions of higher education. This item made up 85% of the total PBC allocations in 2004. It is subdivided into three components: teaching, research and quality of teaching and student services (Grossman, 2004). In this way, the PBC uses the budget to support activities in accordance with its own determined priorities.

The method of—and criteria for—apportioning the block grant allocation between the institutions also reflects the PBC's increased involvement in the evaluation of these institutions. As of 1981–82, budgetary deliberations are conducted in two parallel planes. One team, headed by the PBC's director-general, examines the budgetary proposals submitted by each institution, and the indices on which they are based, such as income, size, and proposed developments. The second team, headed by the chairperson of the PBC, examines data on the "productivity" of each institution: the number of students and graduates by degree level and field of study, the value of research grants, and the scope and quality of research in the institution.

The range of allocation (not a single amount) determined by the two teams is compared and presented to the PBC for discussion and approval. In this way the PBC determines annually the allocation to each institution, based on its work program, proposed development, and research output, as well as on its training of highly skilled professionals.

Universities have questioned the validity of this method. The lack of an established definition of an institution's "productivity" leaves to the PBC the authority to assess the quality of the universities' performance. This policy no doubt weakened the universities' integrity in Israel, a phenomenon which was observed in many national systems during the 1960s and 1970s (Clark, 1983; Perkins & Israel, 1972).

The mid-1970s, early 1980s and late 1990s were marked by severe cuts in governmental expenditure on social services, including education, due to slowdowns in economic growth and inflation (Kop, 1985). Harsh fiscal measures resulted in a major crisis in higher education, with long-term implications. While the number of students increased by some 30% between 1974 and 1983, academic staff decreased by 3% and administrative staffs were reduced by 11%. A definite trend of substantial disinvestment in higher education was reflected in the share of higher education in the national budget, excluding defense expenditures and debt payments, which fell by some 44%.

In times when governmental allocations were cut, time and again, while research funds—national and international—became scarce, particularly during the 1980s, "PGC's authority in the allocation of the higher education budget to the higher education system [was], essentially, unlimited" (Council for Higher Education, 1985, p. 96).

Regulations and Categories of Allocations

Of the 54 accredited and budgeted institutions of higher education in 2003, 24—with 188,000 students—are funded by the PBC; 24 academic teacher training colleges, with 20,700 students, are funded by the Ministry of Education; and six (private) academic colleges, with about 18,500 students, receive no public support. Institutions funded by the PBC must meet the following regulations:

1. New institutions, new units or new academic programs will be opened only after their requests are examined by the PBC from the planning, budgeting and financial perspectives and approved by the CHE. Non-budgeted institutions need the approval of the PBC only in regard to their financial solvency and the approval of the CHE in regard to academic standards.
2. The wages of academic faculty, technical and administrative staff should meet the regulations of the Wages Authority in the Ministry of Finance.
3. Annual budgets must be balanced and approved by the PBC prior to the commencement of the academic year.
4. A public committee appointed by the government every 5 years determines tuition fees.

The PBC's allocations, US$1.2 billion in 2003, account for 65% of the budgets of the universities, 62% of the budgets of Art Academies and Academic Colleges of Engineering, 57% of the budgets of Academic Comprehensive Colleges, and 45% of the budgets of the regional colleges (Grossman, 2004).

Current allocations to institutions of higher education are divided into three main categories: block grant allocations, earmarked allocations, and matching allocations. In addition, institutions can also compete for allocations from the Israel Science Foundation, which is funded separately by the PBC.

Block grant allocation. This is the major source of PBC funds transferred to the institutions of higher education (85%). The block grant consists of three components—teaching, research and quality, each determined by a special model developed by the PGC. The budgeting model has two main objectives:

1. to provide an objective and fair tool for the allocation of public funds to the regular operating budgets of universities for teaching and research, while encouraging efficiency, quality and enhancement of teaching and research outputs; and
2. to enable the universities to plan and budget their teaching and research activities in a way that maintains the academic and administrative autonomy of each institution.

Budgeting for teaching is based on an absolute model, whereas for research it is based on a competitive model. The allocation formulas are based on outputs, the data for which are derived from objective, timely and reliable sources external to the institutions of higher education. Institutions of higher education may use the block grant according to their own internal priorities, on the condition that they maintain a balanced budget.

The *teaching component* of the block grant is calculated as the sum of the number of students in each field of study multiplied by the tariff (per field of study) and by an efficiency factor parameter (calculated by the proportion of graduates to students). Data on students and graduates come from the Central Bureau of Statistics (CBS).

The *research component* of the block grant is allocated only to the research universities, on a competitive basis according to the following four indicators, with their proportional weights:

1. income from competitive research funds (35%);
2. income from non-competitive research funds (20%);
3. scientific publications (15%); and
4. numbers of Ph.D. students (30%).

The *quality component* is currently small, but the PBC is in the process of developing more comprehensive indicators of teaching quality and the quality of student services, as well as mechanisms and tools for the quality control management of both teaching and student services.

Earmarked allocations. The earmarked allocations, as distinguished from the block grant, are used by the PBC to determine the order of priorities in the higher education system. Earmarked programs are generally run for a specified period of time. The earmarked allocations amount to about 10% of the total funds allocated by the PBC to the institutions.

Matching allocations. Matching allocations are based on a historical agreement with the Ministry of Finance. The present matching allocations are based on the level and type of endowment funds each institution had accumulated up to 1987. The matching allocations amount to about 4% of the total funds allocated by the PBC to the institutions.

Allocations to research funds and inter-university activities. The PBC also funds the Israel Science Foundation (ISF), which has developed in recent years to become the largest research fund in Israel. Its competitive allocations are based on scientific excellence and peer review. Between 1997 and 2003, the PBC's allocation to the ISF more than doubled, increasing from US$20 million to US$50 million (CHE, 2005; Grossman, 2004).

Faculty and Students: Teaching, Learning, and Research

Faculty

The academic profession in Israel has grown very rapidly since the establishment of the state in 1948, and particularly during the periods of expansion of the higher education system in the 1960s and 1970s, as well as since the 1990s. The continuous emphasis on research and on the training of researchers at Israeli universities from their inception made it possible to recruit qualified academic teaching staff from among the graduates of the veteran institutions (the Hebrew University and the Technion). Also, cooperation between Israeli and United States researchers facilitated recruitment of foreign—especially American—academic staff who immigrated to Israel. Because of the ample supply of qualified academic staff from these two sources, there was no need to reduce standards of teaching and training in spite of the massive expansion of the higher education system (see Table 2). Nevertheless, the growth of the academic staff was slower than enrollments. Between 1956–57 and 1966–67, the aggregate number of students in higher education multiplied by 4.4 while the academic staff multiplied by 3.4. This increased student/faculty ratios. During the 1970s, it was estimated that the overall ratio was 9:1 (Bendor, 1977). In 1983, the average ratio was about 15:1 in the humanities and social sciences and about 8:1 in the natural sciences, medicine, and engineering. The overall average ratio was about 11.5:1 compared to the desired ratio of 10:1 accepted in England and Wales (PGC, 1984).

The academic staff in the universities consists of assistants "A" and "B," instructors, senior instructors, lecturers, senior lecturers, associate professors, and full professors. Senior instructors and above are required to hold a Ph.D. or another doctoral degree, and only senior lecturers and upward are granted tenure. The academic staff in 1986 numbered the equivalent of some 7,818 full-time positions, with an additional 224 positions in seven non-university institutions of higher education, and a similar number in the seven academic teacher training institutions. In 2003, the number of the academic staff was 10,408 (CBS, 2004b).

Higher education institutions are autonomous in appointing, promoting, and granting tenure to their academic staff. However, the procedures and qualifications for appointments and promotions are similar in all universities. These are based almost exclusively on research qualifications, as demonstrated in publications and evaluated by a committee of professors, and by written evaluations solicited from outside the university—including, as a rule, from foreign referees. This institutionalized procedure throughout the entire system safeguards the academic standards and research tradition of all seven universities as research universities, with research facilities conferring higher degrees in as many fields as possible (Ben-David, 1986). The teaching load of university teachers is six to eight weekly class hours for about seven months of term time. This leaves them ample time for research and publishing. Moreover, from the rank of lecturer upward, academic staff are entitled every seventh year to a full year paid leave of absence. Sabbatical leaves are usually spent abroad in a university or research institute. This provides research opportunities in fields for which facilities and funds are not adequate at the home institution, and encourages Israeli researchers to cooperate with the international community of researchers, thus keeping updated in the most recent developments in various disciplines and fields.

Students

The socioeconomic and geopolitical reality of Israel is responsible for the collective profile of the student body in Israel's higher education system and for some of the distinct characteristics of its students. The majority of students are 2 or 3 years older than elsewhere because of compulsory military service (with no exemptions or deferment for academic studies). About half of them are married at the time of their studies. Although tuition fees are relatively low (about US$2,500–3,000), they are a burden for most students and particularly for those who are married; therefore, most of them are working either full time or part time (CHE, 2004; Globerson, 1978; Silberberg, 1987).

Expectations of university students to fill professional and administrative jobs in the expanding economy and administration were met by universities quite successfully between the 1950s and 1970s, through both the expansion and transformation of their structure, content, and aims. The major changes included the introduction of the 3-year bachelor's degree in 1950 (Iram, 1983), followed by the establishment and growth of professional schools—such as education, social work, and business administration—and changes in disciplinary departments in science, humanities, and social science. These changes also met the aspirations of the students who, after their years of military service, were eager to acquire a marketable proficiency. Indeed, the growth in the number of students in the professional schools and departments, and in "practical" fields of study, is the most conspicuous feature of expanding opportunities for employment in the professions, as shown in the distribution of students (see Table 3).

Approximately 15–18% of the relevant age cohort commences higher education, and a further 20% of the age cohort enters other postsecondary programs of study. Of an entering class of undergraduate students, about two-thirds complete their studies and receive a degree. Four years is the mean length of time needed for completion of an undergraduate course of studies, although the official period of time required is generally 3 years. This is particularly noticeable in the humanities, but is also found in the social and natural sciences.

Table 3. Distribution of Students in Universities

	Students in Universities[a], By Degree							
	1948–49	1959–60	1969–70	1979–80	1989–90	1999–2000	2002–03	2003–04
Total	1,635	10,202	35,374	54,480	67,770	113,010	120,870	124,805
First degree	1,549[b]	9,647[b]	28,053	40,250	46,960	74,210	76,695	78,715
Thereof: first year	405	2,925	9,854	13,510	14,720	22,010	24,620	24,800
Second degree	(2)..	(2)..	5,156	10,050	16,100	30,460	34,695	35,840
Third degree	86	555	1,346	2,930	3,910	6,650	7,980	8,720
Diploma	..	..	819	1,250	800	1,690	1,500	1,530

[a]As of 1969–70 students in special courses not leading to an academic degree are not included. As of 1976–77 data are based on institutions' files, which were prepared close to the time they were received.
[b]Students for second degree are included among first degree students.
Source: Israel Central Bureau of Statistics (CBS), 2004a. Report No. 55, Education 8–58.

A large proportion of undergraduate students study the humanities and the social sciences. However, since the beginning of the 1980s the percentage of students studying sciences and technology has risen (CBS, 2004b; PGC, 1988; Silberberg, 1987).

In 1990, there were 76,000 students in institutions of higher education and an additional 13,000 students in the Open University (where most students study part time). During the 1990s, the system expanded greatly. In 2003, enrollment in higher education institutions reached 189,840, with another 38,620 students in the Open University. The growth of student numbers at all degree levels between 1990 and 2003 was 150%, while the growth in the number of students studying for a bachelor's degree was 161%. Since 2000, students have enrolled in master's degree programs in institutions other than in the seven research universities. In 2003, there were about 2,500 master's students in those institutions, among them 1,210 at the Open University (Grossman, 2004).

Three factors affected the growth in the number of students: the growth in the relevant cohorts of 18-year-olds from 76,500 in 1987 to 105,700 in 1999; an increase in the number of secondary school graduates eligible for a matriculation (*bagrut*) certificate, from 37% of the relevant cohort in 1987 to 55.4% in 1999; and an increase in the rate of participation in higher education of those who obtain a matriculation certificate. In addition, four main factors affected the growth in the rate of participation in higher education: (1) more young men and women recognize the importance of higher education for social mobility and economic progress; (2) the growth, diversification and the geographic dispersion of institutions of higher education (see Table 1 above) provided greater access; (3) developments in various spheres of life, as well as demand, caused the institutions of higher education (new and old alike) to develop programs of study and to offer academic degrees in a wide variety of subjects, some of which were not previously offered in Israel; and (4) the success of Israeli industry, particularly in the fields of advanced technology, increased the proportion of students enrolling in programs in the natural sciences, computer sciences and technology—in fact, enrollment here has grown from 6.7% of the relevant population (aged 20–24) in 1990 to 12.7% in 2003 (CHE, 2004; Grossman, 2004).

However, amid the discussion of expanded student access and enrollment, it should be noted that there is a significant difference in the rate of participation in higher education according to socioeconomic and ethnic background. For example, in 1985 the rate among Israeli-born students whose fathers were born in Europe, the United States, or Israel was 3.8 times higher than those of African or Asian origin and five times higher than those of non-Jews. However, from 1976 to 1985, the rate of participation of students of African or Asian origin increased from 19% to 31% among undergraduate students, while their percentage in the 20 to 29 year-old cohort has changed only slightly, from 43% to 45% (PGC, 1988; Silberberg, 1987).

Further, between 1966 and 1985, the rate of participation of students originating from Asia and Africa has increased two and a half times, while the rate of Arab students quadrupled. The trend of closing the participation rate gap between different ethnically diverse student populations continues (CHE 2004; Silberberg, 1987). Meanwhile, there has been no significant gender difference in the rate of participation in higher education.

In 1986–87, 48.9% of the student population and 49.4% of the degree recipients were women (Statistical Abstracts of Israel, 1988, pp. 640, 644). There are, however, gender differences in fields of studies. About 70% of women study humanities, while only 13% are enrolled in engineering departments (CHE 2004; Silberberg, 1987, p. 29).

The opening of universities and other higher education institutions, especially regional colleges in the north and the south, is probably responsible for the increase in the number of students in peripheral areas, particularly for those sections of the population who were historically underrepresented. However, there are still differences in rates of participation between the populations in peripheral areas of the country—for example, 6.7% in the north, and 15.2% in the south, compared to 31.6% in Tel-Aviv (CHE, 2004).

Conclusion

The expansion of higher learning in Israel that began during the 1980s was among the greatest in the world. Access to higher education was not an important political issue, since both the universities and the government were in favor of providing higher education to all qualified applicants. Thus, since the beginning of the 1980s, the number of institutions more than tripled, and the number of students more than quadrupled. Before the 1980s, higher education in Israel was elitist, selective and monolithic (especially the research universities). However, it has evolved over the past 20 years toward universal access and a differential system, responding to changing demands of the economy and workplace and to different aspirations of the young (CHE, 2005; Grossman, 2004). The percentage of an age cohort attending higher education is comparatively high. As a result, the proportion of college-educated persons in Israel's labor force, whether defined by years of schooling or by occupational classification, is among the world's highest (CHE, 2004; Klinov, 1988). However, more effective steps have to be taken to increase the rate of participation in higher education for certain ethnic and minority groups. The underrepresentation of these groups is inconsistent with Israel's stated social philosophy.

The government provided the lion's share of funding during the expansion of the 1950s and 1960s, regardless of real economic demand, while the universities have demonstrated flexibility in adjusting their programs to accommodate the changing expectations of students and the economy by introducing undergraduate and professional bachelor's degrees. However, the basic commitment of the system to research as a hallmark of excellence continues to characterize both the old and new institutions, thus avoiding an entirely utilitarian approach to higher education. Worsening economic conditions, with drastic reductions in annual allocations to the universities—by 20% between 1982–83 and 1983–84—affected adversely the delicate balance of institutional autonomy and direct governmental control on the one hand, and between the statutory roles of the Council for Higher Education (CHE) and the authority of the Planning and Budgeting Committee (PBC) and the universities on the other. Thus, for example, nationally negotiated wage agreements and tuition rates were imposed on the universities by the Ministry of Finance without consulting individual universities and without commensurate provisions for funding. Indeed, in his 1988 annual report, PBC's chairman noted that the central and vital question is whether the higher education system "is about to lose its independence" (CHE PBC, 1988a, p. 5).

Another development of far-reaching consequences was the change in the composition of funding for higher education: a sharp decline in the government's share, and a rise in both the share of tuition and private funding. The substitution of government funding by private finance resulted in shortages in general purpose expenditures on basic research infrastructure items such as libraries, laboratories, and computers. This trend has adversely affected the quality of instruction and research in the higher education system. To restore the equilibrium of the research infrastructure, additional public funds are required (The Israel Academy of Sciences and Humanities, 1986, 2003). This demand was echoed in the 1987 PBC chairman's annual report: "to repeat previous warnings . . . if higher education does not very soon advance in the national order of priorities, it will no longer be possible to repair the damage that higher education has suffered in recent years" (CHE PBC, 1988a, p. 5). To halt the risk of system-wide deterioration, both in academic standards and in its function of labor force training, the PBC has submitted to the government a plan for increasing the basic higher education budget by 25% in 4 years—an increase which was partially met during the early 1990s. But in the mid-1990s, another financial crisis occurred due to continuous budgeting cuts, and in 2004, the PBC submitted a Five-Year Plan to the Ministry of Finance for the years 2004–5 through 2008–9, to meet both the increasing demand and "to maintain Israeli science at the frontline of world science and technology, to cultivate cultural values . . . and to train vanguard professionals" (Grossman, 2004, p. 8).

On the other hand, demands for accountability proposed that expanding and even existing needs for higher education could be met only by a more efficient and vocationally oriented system. These demands were followed by growing pressure for higher productivity and more efficient or joint utilization of facilities and equipment and interuniversity cooperation in research, as well as demands for academic and administrative restructuring in higher education institutions. University faculties and administrators tend to see some of these demands as a disguise for more direct state control at the expense of institutional autonomy.

The university sector in particular continues to be alarmed over pressures from government intervention in policy issues such as admissions standards, tuition, budgetary cuts, the composition of the Council for Higher Education—namely, a decrease in the universities' representation—and the governance structure of individual institutions. The government's intervention in these issues is seen by the universities as an infringement on institutional academic autonomy, which is considered a prerequisite and essential for the high academic standards of the Israeli academy (Ba'Shaar, 2004; S. Neaman Institute, 2004).

It seems at this point that Israel's higher education system has reached a crossroads. To overcome the crisis, universities, the PBC, the CHE and the government (Ministry of Finance) will have to explore new ways to allow effective planning, financing and policymaking at the university and national levels, taking into account the legitimate public and national interests, academic freedom and institutional autonomy. Overall, more ingenuity will be required by all parties to meet the challenges and exigencies that Israeli higher education is facing today.

References

Al-Haj, M. (1991). *Education and social change among the Arabs in Israel.* Tel Aviv: The International Center for Peace in the Middle East.
Ba'shaar—Academic Community for Israeli Society. (2004). *The status of higher education and research universities in Israel: Warning signs and policy guidelines.* Jerusalem: Ba'shaar.
Ben-David, J. (1986). Universities in Israel: Dilemmas of growth, diversification and administration. *Studies in Higher Education, 11,* 105–130.
Bendor, S. (1977). University education in the State of Israel. In A.S. Knowles (Ed.), *International encyclopedia of higher education* (pp. 2331–2341). San Francisco, CA: Jossey-Bass.
Clark B. R. (1983). *The higher education system: Academic organization in cross-national perspectives.* Berkeley: University of California Press.
Counsil for Higher Education Law, 5718 (1958).
Council for Higher Education. (CHE). (1988). *Higher education in Israel, statistical abstract 1986–87.* Jerusalem: CHE, Planning and Grants Committee (PGC).
Council for Higher Education. (2003). *Annual Reports No. 28/29 Academic Year 2001/02.* Jerusalem: CHE, Planning and Budgeting Committee.
Council for Higher Education. (2004). *Annual Report No. 30/31, Academic Year 2003/04.* Jerusalem: CHE. Council for Higher Education. (2005). *List of higher education institutions (January 24, 2005).* Jerusalem: CHE.
Globerson, A. (1978). *Higher education and employment: A case study of Israel.* Farnborough, CT: Praeger.
Grossman, S. (2004). *Higher education in Israel.* Jerusalem: CHE, Planning and Budgeting Committee, p. 5.
Halperin, S. (1984). *Any home any campus.* Washington, DC: Institute for Education Leadership.
Iram, Y. (1983). Vision and fulfillment: The evolution of the Hebrew University, 1901–1950. *History of Higher Education, Annual, 3,* 123–143.
Iram, Y. (1987). Quality and control in higher education in Israel. *European Journal of Education, 22,* 145–159.
Israel Central Bureau of Statistics. (CBS). (1988). *Statistical abstracts of Israel 1988, No. 39.* Jerusalem: CBS.
Israel Central Bureau of Statistics. (CBS). (1989). *Statistical abstracts of Israel 1989, No. 40.* Jerusalem: CBS.
Israel Central Bureau of Statistics. (2004a). *Higher Education in Israel, statistical abstract No. 55.* Jerusalem: CBS.
Israel Central Bureau of Statistics. (2004b). *Statistical abstracts of Israel 2003, No. 54.* Jerusalem: CBS.
Klinov, R. (1988). Allocation of public resource to education. Discussion paper No.1 in the series *Israel's educational system: Issue and options.* Jerusalem: The Center for Social Policy Studies.
Kop, Y. (1985). Social services in the eighties: A turning point? In Y. Kop (Ed.), *Israel's outlay for human services 1984* (pp. 7–18). Jerusalem: The Center for Social Policy Studies.
Liebman, C. S., & Don Yehiya, E. (1984). *Religion and politics in Israel.* Bloomington: Indiana University Press.
Mar'i, S. K. (1978). *Arab education in Israel.* Syracuse, NY: Syracuse University Press.
Patai, R. (1970). *Israel between east and west: A study in human relations* (2nd ed.). Westport, CT: Greenwood.
Perkins, J. A. & Israel, B. B. (Eds.). (1972). *Higher education: From autonomy to systems.* New York, NY: International Council for Educational Development.

Planning and Budgeting Committee. (PBC). (1986–1997). *Annual Reports Nos. 12–22 Academic Years 1985–1996.* Jerusalem: Planning and Grants Committee.

Planning and Grants Committee. (PGC). (1984). *The higher education system in Israel: Guidelines on the development of the system and its planning for 1988 with a first glance at 1995.* Jerusalem: PGC.

Planning and Grants Committee. (1985). *Higher education in Israel, statistical abstract 1983–84.* Jerusalem: PGC.

Planning and Grants Committee. (1987). *Report No. 2. The Sixth Council 1981–1986.* Jerusalem: CHE.

S. Neaman Institute at the Technion (Israel Institute of Technology). (2004). Transition to mass higher education systems: International comparison and perspectives. International conference, December 5–6, 2004.

Shama A., & Iris, M. (1976). *Immigration without integration. Third world Jews in Israel.* Cambridge, MA: Schenkman.

Silberberg, R. (1987). *Undergraduate studies in the higher education system.* Jerusalem: PGC.

Stanner, R. (1963). *The legal basis of education in Israel.* Jerusalem: Ministry of Education and Culture.

Statistical Abstract of Israel, 1988, pp. 640, 644.

The Israel Academy of Sciences and Humanities. (2003). *Academy Activities 2002/2003.* Jerusalem: IASH.

Trow, M. A. (1984). The analysis of status. In B. R. Clark, (Ed.), *Perspectives on higher education* (pp. 132–64). Berkeley: University of California Press.

42

ITALY

Roberto Moscati
University of Milano-Bicocca, Italy

The Italian system of higher education, through its recent process of transformation, represents a paradigmatic example of the complex difficulties involved in the transition from elite to mass higher education (Trow, 1974). In truth, problems and difficulties faced by the Italian academic enterprise today are not peculiar, and have been grappled with in many other systems around the world. However, the speed of the transformation process in Italy has particularly sharpened the distinctions between an elite and a mass system of higher education.

Generally speaking, higher education in Italy is in the middle of a critical transition to a new era, and yet following a non-linear path whose direction changes according the prevailing side of confronting forces. To explain this peculiarity one must return to the 1960s, when all systems of higher education in Europe where affected by a sudden and consistent increase in social demand. To cope with the new situation, a number of reforms were implemented to diversify the systems, either with the creation of parallel tracks or with the introduction of different stages. In Italy, the response to demand was the introduction of a completely open-door system, abolishing any kind of filter from the secondary to the tertiary level of education. The result was a flood of students coming from different school tracks (some of which were not originally intended to lead to the tertiary level) while the university remained unchanged. As a consequence, the number of university dropouts increased substantially, and the output of tertiary education institutions remained unrelated to changes in the labor market. In short, it is fair to say that the university kept its structure and its operational activity as usual (i.e., as a university for the elite) even if the number of people enrolled reached a level more closely aligned with that of mass higher education systems.

Only during the 1980s did the government (but not the academic world) try to introduce some modernizing adjustments, but this had a very moderate impact on the system. In the 1990s, a sudden decision to accelerate the process of modernization led to a comprehensive reform of the entire system of public education and introduced some dramatic changes in the structure and functions of the university. Importantly, all these changes came from outside the higher education system. The academic world first (in the 1980s) was able to resist, and then (in the 1990s) was driven to accept

James J.F. Forest and Philip G. Altbach (eds.), International Handbook of Higher Education, 811–827.
© 2006 *Springer. Printed in the Netherlands.*

the reforms without really being aware of what they meant. The process of structural reform, imposed by law, in some cases did not produce a change in the attitude of the professoriate and in its related interpretation of the professional role (particularly in some disciplinary fields like the humanities), while in other cases (including the hard and applied sciences) the reforms were accepted and implemented as intended. In addition, the changes of government during the implementation of these reforms created further problems, as new ruling parties opted to modify a process that was already underway without any verification of the initial results. The situation which resulted is still unstable and deserves extensive analysis.

Recent Development of the Italian System of Higher Education

Quantitative Aspects

Increases in the social demand for higher education began in the early 1960s and exploded in the following decade. The open-door policy adopted by the government in 1969 reinforced the expansion phenomenon (see Table 1), but produced a substantial increase in the rate of student dropouts as well.

The increase in the number of students has been strongly influenced by the increase (in percentage and in absolute terms) of women. In 2002, women represented 49% of 19-year-olds in the total population of Italy, and 55% of the first-year university

Table 1.   Students Enrolled by Course of Study and Gender (Selected Years)

Academic year	Traditional Courses ("Laurea")			Short Cycles ("Diploma")			New Courses—First Three Year Level*		
	Male	*Female*	*Total*	*Male*	*Female*	*Total*	*Male*	*Female*	*Total*
1987–88	591,802	539,650	1,131,452	10,713	11,607	22,320	–	–	–
1988–89	622,317	577,618	1,199,935	11,516	12,314	23,830	–	–	–
1989–90	652,121	616,218	1,268,339	11,306	12,310	23,616	–	–	–
1990–91	676,885	660,612	1,337,497	10,777	11,513	22,290	–	–	–
1991–92	730,743	722,496	1,453,239	10,705	11,456	22,161	–	–	–
1992–93	771,623	754,905	1,526,528	21,898	23,797	45,695	–	–	–
1993–94	771,214	800,057	1,571,271	27,203	26,238	53,441	–	–	–
1994–95	766,250	836,691	1,602,941	30,055	28,822	58,877	–	–	–
1995–96	764,558	853,062	1,617,620	34,610	33,691	68,301	–	–	–
1996–97	781,645	912,829	1,694,474	40,260	38,677	78,937	–	–	–
1997–98	724,173	863,376	1,587,549	44,467	44,980	89,447	–	–	–
1998–99	708,213	864,839	1,573,052	52,187	51,463	103,650	–	–	–
1999–00	698,402	871,828	1,570,230	58,260	56,502	114,762	–	–	–
2000–01	673,238	864,278	1,537,516	60,605	63,494	124,099	15.884	9.708	25.592
2001–02	504,953	669,085	1,174,038	34,126	40,650	74,776	205.769	221.255	427.024

Note: In the academic year 2001–02 there were 26,191 students (10,306 males and 15,885 females) already enrolled in the new second level courses (*laurea specialistica*). This table reflects the notable shift in enrollment from the traditional courses to the new ones.
Source: MIUR, 2004.

students. They also tend to perform at the university slightly better then men—in 2002, 56% of graduates were female.

Meanwhile, changes in the population of academic and administrative staff have followed a different trend from that of the students. In fact, the number of academics increased at different speeds throughout the years according to changing rules of faculty recruitment: their numbers grew during the 1970s in response to the impact of the open-door admissions policy (which was introduced at the end of the previous decade), nearly doubling in a single decade. Between 1969 and 1985, the size of Italy's academic profession grew from 20,400 to 42,458. However, since the mid-1980s, the growth of faculty has slowed dramatically due to the bureaucratic implications of a new hiring procedure, reaching only 47,000 in 1994, and 54,000 in 2002 (MUIR, 2004). Further, within the last several years all recruitment of public employees has been completely stopped as a consequence of public debt. As a result, the overall student/faculty ratio has grown from 26:1 (in 1985) to 32:1 (in 2002).

Meanwhile, the number of administrative staff has remained rather stable through the years, and is now at roughly the same level as that of academics (54,000). The distribution of administrators among the universities is rather uneven, and the professional quality is often rather poor—in fact, these kinds of positions are often seen as a haven for "political" hiring (or patronage), and specific training for university administration has never been introduced (although desperately needed).

The number of universities has grown steadily through the years. Beginning in the 1970s, as the number of students increased due to the open-door admissions policy, new branches of universities were created (within the same region), and these branches were eventually transformed into independent new universities. There are currently 77 universities, 13 of them private. When the additional campuses of several universities are accounted for separately, there are over 90 university locations throughout the country.

The largest and most prominent private universities are the Catholic University, with three campuses in Milano, Roma and Piacenza; the "Bocconi" University in Milano; and the *Libera Università Internazionale di Scienze Sociali* (LUISS) in Rome. These last two are lay universities supported by the Italian Association of Industrial Entrepreneurs. All in all, the private universities enroll about 6.2% of all university students (109,351 out of 1,765,418 in the academic year 2002–2003); further, private and public institutions have similar rates of participation in fields like business administration, education science, health, law and social and behavioral science (see Table 2).

Private universities in Italy are legally recognized, which means that the state grants them a right to operate and to give diplomas with legal validity (e.g., equal to those given by the public universities). Recognition comes through a state law—the most recent one (#243), passed in 1991, specifies that the state will give financial support to the private universities, provided that they present each year a budget with the estimated expenditures for the coming year and the actual expenditures of the previous one, as well as statistical data about its structure and activities (enrollment, academic staff and administrative personnel, facilities and different resources, revenues and student fees, etc.). Each year, the national budget includes a total amount of financial resources to be subdivided among the private universities according to various dimensions of

Table 2.   Student Enrollment (First Degree Level) by Field of Study and Gender, 2002–03

Field of Study	All Universities			Private Universities		
		Female			Female	
	Total	N	%	Total	N	%
Agriculture, forestry and fishery	26,813	9,157	34.2%	610	188	30.8%
Architecture and building	93,522	40,390	43.2%	84	17	20.2%
Arts	63,480	44,621	70.3%	5,472	4,233	77.4%
Business and administration	203,216	94,814	46.7%	24,471	9,980	40.8%
Computing	32,053	5,535	17.3%	296	42	14.2%
Education science	88,156	79,615	90.3%	12,117	11,135	91.9%
Engineering and engineering trades	196,017	32,209	16.4%	444	112	25.2%
Environmental protection	11,382	5,810	51.0%	312	116	37.2%
Health	161,609	103,453	64.0%	5,802	3,654	63.0%
Humanities	200,650	152,130	75.8%	12,356	10,243	82.9%
Journalism and information	64,544	40,797	63.2%	11,368	7,880	69.3%
Law	251,163	147,787	58.8%	14,527	7,937	54.6%
Life sciences	66,917	43,318	64.7%	789	501	63.5%
Manufacturing and processing	10,565	5,656	53.5%	390	207	53.1%
Mathematics and statistics	17,232	9,719	56.4%	276	168	60.9%
Personal services	26,705	12,778	47.8%	3,181	1,581	49.7%
Physical sciences	22,611	8,451	37.4%	70	22	31.4%
Security services	1,225	137	11.2%	n/a	n/a	n/a
Social and behavioral science	195,555	121,360	62.1%	14,716	9,004	61.2%
Social services	15,422	13,820	89.6%	1,595	1,439	90.2%
Teacher training	526	297	56.5%	7	5	71.4%
Transport services	3,170	1,578	49.8%	468	361	77.1%
Veterinary	12,885	7,954	61.7%	n/a	n/a	n/a
Total	1,765,418	981,386	55.6%	109,351	68,825	62.9%

Source: EUROSTAT-MIUR, 2004.

size, activity and performance. On average, state financial support covers roughly 15–20% of the budget in the private universities. Both public and private universities are evaluated by the "National Committee for the Evaluation of the University System," with a special individualized analysis of private institutions every 2 years. This latter policy is a rather recent move (a ministerial decree enacted in 2003) related to the progressive strengthening of the evaluation process throughout the entire system of higher education.

Qualitative Aspects: Reform of the System

In mid-1987, a new national government launched an era of reform projects by creating a new Ministry of University and Scientific Research. In essence, this involved the detachment of a section of the Ministry of Education, devoted to the university, and its subsequent transfer to the Ministry of Scientific Research. This move was hotly debated by political forces, particularly its impact on the autonomy of the university. Among supporters, the creation of this new Ministry of Universities and Scientific Research was hailed as a way to unify all programs of scientific research supported by public authorities, and to maximize the efficiency and productivity of the country in several fields where international competition was tougher and more challenging.

Meanwhile, the independence and right of self-governance for every university is expressly mandated in the Italian constitution, although until very recently it did not exist in practice. All details of university organization have been traditionally imposed uniformly by the central authority, not only by means of laws and regulations, but also via circulars and replies to requests through which the Ministry made known its own interpretations of the laws in force. However, in 1993 an amendment to the state general financial law partly changed this procedure by stating that the Ministry of University would now give annually a lump sum to each university according to certain parameters. It would be up to the university to decide how to use this money. This measure, which was never debated and has since almost escaped notice by the university community, represented the first real step toward university autonomy.

Also during the early 1990s, a law was passed creating "short-cycle" programs (*lauree brevi* or *diplomi universitari*) and placing them inside universities as a parallel path to existing programs leading to the traditional *laurea* degree. Admission to these programs was regulated by institutional enrollment capacity, and a variety of 2-year professional programs (in nursing, education, medical technicians, etc.) were transformed into *diplomi universitari*. However, this new university path has had somewhat acceptable success only in the medical fields and in engineering. Aside from the difficulty in matching these programs with specific needs in the labor market, short-cycles were also opposed—at a political level—on the grounds that they would become a second-rate kind of studies, penalizing those enrolling in them. Inside the university, professors expressed a similar position, fearing they would have to teach in second-class institutions (Moscati, 1986, 1991).

The 1996 general election brought into power a political coalition which granted high priority to education. This represented per se a new attitude in Italian modern political history that can perhaps be explained by the growing consensus throughout the EU about the importance of education and training systems. Also, the coalition contained a good number of intellectuals and university professors with direct experience of other systems of education and, in general, an awareness of the unavoidable process of interdependence among European states.

Not surprisingly, the new government therefore launched a comprehensive reform process involving all levels of the education system—from pre-elementary to the university. This reform (*legge quadro*) suggested that postsecondary training should be a task of both the regions and the institutions of secondary and tertiary education. It aimed at (1) establishing for the entire country the prerequisites for competence—at a European level—in related professional activities, and (2) identifying the values of the acquired credits necessary for possible admission to university courses.

This emphasis on reforming the postsecondary level of training can be considered perhaps the most crucial point of the entire modern system of education in Italy. To begin with, vocational training has traditionally been underappreciated in the Italian culture, and in fact it has always been viewed as a form of remedial training for students dropping out from other levels of the system. Secondly, adult education and permanent (recurrent) education in Italy have been largely disregarded; at the very least, they have never been considered as interesting endeavors for higher education institutions. Thirdly, the responsibility of vocational training (assigned to the regions in order to better coordinate supply with demand for professionalization at local levels) proved to be a failure, as regions have not been able in most cases to provide systems of vocational training at an acceptable level of quality.

As for the tertiary level, the first reform measure to be taken addressed the high level of dropouts and the high percentage of students obtaining their degrees after exceeding the expected length of time—the average in many fields then was seven and a half years instead of four. The main effort here was devoted to developing and implementing measures which could increase university "productivity" without introducing the kinds of competitive admissions policies that are strongly opposed by many cultural and political segments of society. The measures foreseen include a better linkage with secondary schools (the reform of which would have in itself supported this attempt). Components of this new policy included orientation in the last 2 years of secondary school; counseling and tutoring during all university courses; an improved student/teacher ratio; and a different way of teaching (more focused on students' real understanding) in the first year of university courses.

Aside from these important reforms, a central component of the new ministerial policy can be loosely defined as improving institutional autonomy, which in essence meant the end of a historically centralized system where all the decisions had been in the hands of the ministry. For a long time, this structural dependence has been both a constraint and an alibi for any autonomous initiative of an individual university. The main consequences have been the domination of disciplinary power inside the academy, and the lack of any real cooperation between university and society. The winds of autonomy seemed to be finally blowing in the Italian university system. This implied a number of consequences, from offering services to the outside world (in order to raise additional financial support), to the introduction of different forms of internal performance evaluation (in order to improve efficiency) and the drive to establish a "brand name" for each university (in order to make individual institutions more attractive to prospective students, research customers, and the like).

The market-oriented tendency of these reforms—which can also be seen in several other European countries—has given rise to a number of opposition groups and general resistance inside the university community at all levels. Nonetheless, the ministry seemed committed—at first, anyhow—to pursue the indicated direction. In fact, while a ministerial ad hoc group was preparing a project for the reform of university curricula, the minister himself—together with his colleagues from France, Great Britain and Germany—took the opportunity of the 800-year anniversary of the Sorbonne foundation in Paris (in 1998) to announce the basis for a policy of homogenization among higher education systems throughout Europe, which a year later became known as the "Bologna process" (Luzzatto, 2001).

An internal drive for the modernization of the Italian university system, combined with the new international policy for the creation of a European model of higher education system, has accelerated the political process of reform in Italy and made the Italian system a more orthodox example of the "three stairs" model (also known as "3/5/8," referring to the standardized number of years involved to earn bachelor's, master's, and doctoral degrees). Other reasons for the acceleration of the reform process were linked to the government's ability to take advantage of an unusually favorable political situation created by the positive feelings between the Minister of the University and Scientific Research (a former rector highly respected by academia) and a substantial portion of the academic world which was aware of the need to keep up with other systems of higher education. In particular, the Italian Conference of Rectors (CRUI) supported the modernizing policy of the minister. At the same time, the government—fearing the delay which a debate in the Parliament would have created—ensured that the reform of curricula was passed at the level of commissions (both in the Senate and House of Representatives). Thanks to all these circumstances, the entire reform process was approved in a very short period of time and without a real extensive debate.

Main Characteristics of the Reform

As mentioned, the new shape of the university experience was based on a three-stair structure: a first level of 3 years, leading to a degree called *laurea*; a second level of two years, leading to a degree called *laurea specialistica*; and a third level, leading to the *dottorato*. This basic change was represented by the subdivision of the traditional 4-year courses into two levels of three and 2 years each. At the same time, the first degree became a necessary step to the second one, and a qualification for the labor market.[1] Curricula may be partly differentiated—in order to orient them more towards further study or towards employability—by varying the mix of basic foundations of disciplines and of applied activities (laboratorial or extramural).

Credits—to be defined according to European Credit Transfer System (ECTS)—became an accumulation system, and not only a transfer system connected to the mobility of students: the credits associated with each course are now seen as the bricks for building a "modular" curriculum. Programs are now defined by their amount of credits, not by their length; the *laurea* is thus seen as a 180-credit program, and the *laurea specialistica,* a 300-credit program. Three (or five) years now merely indicate the time *usually* required to complete those programs for regular full-time students.

Normally, 180 out of the 300 credits needed for *laurea specialistica* are obtained through recognition of credits acquired in a *laurea* program. For the same *laurea specialistica*, more than one *laurea* may have an entirely recognized curriculum; the 120 credits to be added will thus need to be different for students coming from different *lauree*, in order to complement the ones already acquired. Access to a *laurea specialistica* may also be allowed from a *laurea* curriculum that is only partly recognized, which would mean that more than 120 credits have to be added.

Both for *lauree* and for *lauree specialistica*, classes of study programs are determined at the national level. A class is the framework for the study programs offered by universities in the same disciplinary field. Inside each class, there are prescriptions concerning sets of subjects and corresponding credits, and some space is guaranteed for interdisciplinary connections and for extramural work. The legal value of a degree (e.g., in terms of access to regulated professions or civil service) is directly related to the class in which the degree belongs.

Each class is characterized by a description of its general cultural and professional objectives, and through prescriptions concerning no more than two-thirds of the credits required for the degree. The prescriptions assign a certain number of credits to sets of subjects, but not to individual subjects, leaving in any case at least 5% of the credits at the discretion of each student. The determination of the classes, and their characterization, may be revised every 3 years (Luzzatto, 2001).

Within any class, each university may develop one or more study programs. Thus, for each program the university (1) determines precise cultural and professional objectives, in the frame of the general ones indicated for the class; (2) defines the exact title of the degree awarded at the end of the program; (3) assigns a part of the credits by choosing one or several subjects within each set as defined by the national prescriptions; and (4) is completely free in assigning the remaining credits (at least one-third). No university program admissions restrictions are established on a general basis, except for the cases where rules are set by the EU. Instead, universities are allowed to establish some restriction for individual programs, due to limits in existing facilities (classrooms, laboratories, etc.). In 2000, the government defined 42 classes for *lauree* and 104 classes for *lauree specialistica*. Within the somewhat complex framework described above, universities had to reorganize considerably—almost all programs for the new *laurea* began in 2001, and the first programs for *laurea specialistica* were offered in 2002.

Implementation of the Reform

Problems of implementation are almost unavoidable in any reform, but in the case of the Italian higher education system quite a number have come from different origins. Some difficulties have objective reasons, since they originate from the complexity of the reform itself and from the way it has been introduced. Other challenges are derived from the social milieu affected by the reform (primarily from the academic world, but from the national government as well).

Objective Problems

The reform sought to substantially transform the teaching structure, keeping in mind the need to re-establish a coherent relation between supply and demand of higher education. In other words, acknowledging that the student population had changed, the supply was restructured in order to match the needs of a new kind of customers. The declared main purpose was to drastically reduce the rate of dropout and the period spent in the university courses by the majority of students.

To reach these goals, curricula were split in two levels in order to encourage a consistent percentage of students to earn a first degree (*laurea*) and then leave the system after 3 years (instead of staying for seven or 8 years, as had become the norm). Only a minority of students were supposed to continue on to the second 2-year level—largely intended for future members of the elite—while the doctorate was left practically unchanged, remaining the domain of a small number of would-be researchers and academics. In addition, professional education programs of 1 or 2 years—called "master's"—were "permitted" but not specifically established for graduates of either the first or second level.

In fact, the professionalization of the higher education system was and still is a crucial, unsolved problem of the reform. On the one hand, the reform included the introduction of a sort of binary system, with the creation of a professional track that should be administered at the regional level. But this track has never been endorsed at the university level—from either cultural or professional points of view—and thus it has never represented a real alternative to the university. On the other hand, the first level degree was supposed to prepare students for the labor market (and thus have a professionalizing function), while at the same time represent a first stage for the eventual pursuit of a second level degree. However, the responsibility for developing two different disciplinary paths in order to meet these two different purposes was left up to the universities, and has thus far turned out to be too difficult to be implemented.

The reform also had to face many other problems of a different nature. First of all, the government did not allocate an additional sum in the state budget to support the reform. This created a shortage of teachers and (in many cases) of spaces and structures, which has become increasingly evident with the complete activation of the second level of courses. The lack of financial resources prevented the introduction of significant incentives for those among the academic staff willing to give more time to teaching activities, and did not allow institutions to offer part-time engagements to school teachers. Also, a comprehensive orientation program for the students in their secondary school final years, which had been conceived together with the reform project, eventually did not take off for lack of financial resources. This last consequence created a serious mismatch between the cultural backgrounds of prospective university students and the requirements of the new courses (which could be measured in terms of debts of credits). The trouble is that (due to a number of organizational reasons) it is very difficult for universities to offer a large number of remedial courses before or during the first year of study for students who may have chosen their field of study without any serious examination of their background and inclinations.

Another consequence of the weakly supported start of the reform is represented by the delay of the evaluation policy, which has thus far developed with considerable difficulty. To be sure, a National Center for the Evaluation of University Performance (*Comitato Nazionale per la Valutazione del Sistema Universitario* or CNVSU) was created by the Ministry of the University in the late 1990s, and within each university a special section for self-evaluation (*Nuclei di valutazione*) has been established. The *Comitato* (as it is commonly known) requires and collects data from all the universities through the institutional *Nuclei*, which are required to administer a questionnaire to their students in which they evaluate the didactical services of the university. In addition, the Italian Conference of Rectors (CRUI) has launched a program for the evaluation of some courses of study (on a voluntary basis) called "Campus One." All these activities represent a first step which must be completed by a comprehensive evaluation of all university activities, tied to consequences in terms of rewards and punishment. This is particularly relevant for the complete development of institutional autonomy that is supposed to characterize the system. As is self-evident, without evaluation the autonomy of universities will not lead to a true quality system of higher education.

Changes in the government have also undermined the potential of the reform. First, the popular Minister of the University and Scientific Research was replaced, and afterwards the entire government changed following the election results of 2001. These changes certainly did not lead to consistency in how the main elements of the reform project were presented to the academic world.

Second, aside from a few minor initiatives at some universities, the rather complex structure of the reform was never publicly debated. The government was supposed to hold a number of conferences throughout the country, but they have been consistently postponed. Thus, the implications of the reform are still largely unclear to the large majority of the academic staff, and in many cases have been misunderstood. To date, a variety of different interpretations coexist in the university system.

Finally, another aspect of a system based on autonomy that has not yet been fully considered is the adaptation of the university governance to the new demands of individual universities and of the system as a whole. Determining how to lead a self-governing university—competing with others in a market-oriented environment—has been left up to the traditional leadership (rector, academic senate and administrative council), who have for decades functioned in a centralized system. The resulting balance of powers and interests—wherein the power distribution in a given individual university is based upon a balance among different disciplinary fields—has proven to be unproductive when the autonomy of the university stressed the relevance of the internal decision-making process and the need to make decisions in the interest of the institution.

Actors' Attitudes Towards the Reform

The subject of governance also underscores the problems of reform implementation related to the social milieu involved—namely, the attitude of the government and the reaction of those in academia. To begin with, the government which launched the reform changed in 2001, and the new one—coming from a different political orientation—wanted to demonstrate its difference from the previous one in almost all the political and social domains. Thus, in the field of education it stopped the school reform and mandated a new approach, while at the university level it was unable to offer a new alternative and at first allowed the existing reform to continue. However, in several ways the government slowed the reform process, beginning with the reduction of financial resources to support it.

Meanwhile, since the beginning of the reform the ministerial bureaucracy has operated in ways that clearly opposed the idea of university autonomy (a logical response for any government agency trying to prevent a loss of power or control). For them, the principle of a degree's legal value turned out to be a very useful homogenizing tool, reducing the amount of freedom available to an individual university in building its curricula, and *de facto* compelling all faculty to check with the ministry to ensure the acceptability of new programs. A similar situation occurred within the scientific disciplines, where a representative organization—the University National Council (*Consiglio Nazionale Universitario* or CUN)—has traditionally held the power to determine the acceptability of curricula. These structures have continued to undermine the movement toward greater institutional autonomy, as well as (indirectly) the spirit of the reform.

A good example of this dynamic is seen in the creation of the contents of the new curricula. To ensure the autonomy of each university, basic guidelines for the building of curricula were not extremely compelling. As faculty members structured their curricula and organized courses, the traditional habit of leaving each professor free to teach his or her own course (within the discipline for which they had been hired by the university) meant the institution could not compel them to shift from one topic to another (even in the same disciplinary field) nor coordinate the content of his or her course with those of related ones. This obviously led to considerable problems in an institution's capacity to innovate in the structure and content of their curricula.

Thus, in some cases the need to reduce traditional 4- or 5-year programs into 3-year ones—as required by the reform—created a reproduction of existing curricula into smaller versions, protecting all the previous subjects: that is, the same number of courses would be taught, but with abridged content and within a smaller span of time. Very often, this approach resulted in a multiplication of superficial cultural and scientific suggestions submitted to increasingly confused students. On the other hand, the traditional culture of viewing university studies as the final period of organized learning in a person's lifespan has prevented a serious elaboration of lifelong learning activities, which in turn could have been conceived as a way to make a reduction of the first level curricula acceptable.

The response of university professors toward the reform has been far from uniform. Opposing positions have been taken toward the entire project or some of its aspects, with differences arising among (and between) disciplinary fields and members of the same faculty or department. An approximate generalization is that academic staff in the hard sciences (pure and applied) seem to be more in favor of the reform, perhaps owing to their tradition of being more connected with their European colleagues and thus more aware of the need to reduce the gap between the Italian and other European systems of higher education.

It is also fair to say that a large number of university professors—even inside the humanities and the social and political sciences—have accepted the idea of the reform. Support came first from the academic leadership; namely, rectors (through their National Conference, the CRUI), deans and heads of departments. From their roles of collective responsibility, these members of academia were more aware than others of the need for a modernization of Italy's higher education system, and thus began to work toward implementation of the reform.

The traditionally vertical structure of academic power helped to spread a positive attitude toward the reform. As a result, a good number of academic staff became involved in the rather difficult work of transforming the structure of study courses and curricula. Through this collective effort, the new configuration of courses (at least for the first level) was ready in a rather short period of time—in fact, earlier than expected.

On the other hand, groups of professors from the humanities and law developed a somewhat strong opposition toward the innovations implied by the reform. Beyond a general resistance toward innovation and change, the attitude of these members of academia is likely rooted in a traditional interpretation of the university's role in society (and that of the academic staff). Simply put, this attitude views the university as an institution for the formation of the elite, and—accordingly—the role of the university professors as dedicated to the accomplishment of this purpose. This view can be explained only by the traditional independence of the academic world and its relatively exclusive position in Italian society.

The disconnect between systemic change (the movement of the system from elite to mass higher education) and the traditional attitude of a significant portion of the academic staff helps to explain the overall resistance to the reform project. In particular, it highlighted the difference between the task of the first level of courses—the heightening of the country's social capital—and that of the second level, viewed as the training of the elite (Capano, 2002). Thus, for the "traditionalist" in academia, the introduction of the first level simply meant the cultural decline of the university.

Within the context of the governmental reforms, it should be noted that the Italian professoriate is also facing a general reshaping of their careers and the interpretation of their professional role. A revision of their legal status is also under way (after several years of debate). While it is currently difficult to predict what the eventual changes will be, proposed revisions are characterized by increased duties and less career stability, without any increase in benefits or rewards. Further, the reform has implied more administrative and organizational activities for faculty without any real financial return.

In evaluating the relative attractiveness of the academic profession today, several contradictory aspects must be taken into consideration. First of all, it is crucial to consider the relative decline of social prestige due to the expansion of higher education. Being a member of the academic staff is no longer seen as being an educator of the elite. Academics appear to be increasingly valued based on the usefulness of their expertise in realms outside the university. The importance of technical advancement further differentiates the way some faculty are viewed—for example, those in hard and applied sciences appear to be valued more than those in pure sciences.

Economically, the academic profession per se is not very attractive because the initial salary is rather modest and the first steps in a faculty career are neither easy nor rapid. The real appeal of the academic profession—economically speaking—comes from outside sources that some can secure and others cannot. In this respect, the economic environment plays a mixed role: on the one hand, a wealthy city may offer interesting alternatives for prospective researchers; on the other, it may offer opportunities for well-known full-time professors to use their competencies (and thus increase their earning). In either case, such opportunities are clearly less available in peripheral and less-developed areas of the country.

The reform of the higher education system, and particularly the increased autonomy of individual universities, has created a number of financial problems which have had an impact on the recruitment of academic staff and on their careers. It is now progressively raising (a) the possible shortage of academics due to the rapid aging of the profession and insufficient recruitment, and (b) the growing "parochialism" of universities that cannot recruit increasingly costly external faculty members.

The autonomy of individual university budgets plays a crucial role in this process. In financial terms, autonomy of individual universities means that each institution must determine for themselves how best to meet all their different expense items by subdividing income (the lump sum received from the government, the amount received from students fees, and—to a limited extent—possible grants from private sources). However, expenses related to personnel cannot exceed 90% of the total institutional budget. Prior to 1993, the centralized system of university budgeting subdivided institutional income and expenses regardless of university choice, and the possibility of obtaining additional resources for academic staff was a matter of constant negotiation between each individual university and the Ministry of Education.

The Evolving Situation: Initial Impacts of the Reform

Some Positive Results

As described here, the reform of the curricula has encountered many difficulties in its implementation, basically due to the combination of two elements. On the one hand, it was introduced to the academic world from the outside—the political milieu, which argued for a modernization of the higher education system in order to keep up with the main trends developing in Europe. On the other hand, a number of different interests and the lack of a strong political will have also complicated efforts to implement the reform. The introduction of such a comprehensive change with virtually no preparation or experimentation has understandably created a considerable amount of resistance and operational difficulties (Frey & Ghignoni, 2002; Pontremoli & Luzzatto, 2002; De Maio, 2002).

Nevertheless, some positive results of the reform can already be observed. First, it turns out that the new system of university degrees has a strong appeal. The total number of students enrolled in the traditional 4- or 5-year university courses had been slowly declining in recent years, after reaching a peak in the academic year 1996–97 because of the (rather mild) impact of the short-cycle courses. The introduction of the new 3-year courses seems to have changed this trend. Further, the proportion of women enrolling in the university has been a majority in quite a number of fields (including arts, education science, health, humanities, life sciences, law, social services, social and behavioral sciences, and veterinary science). Further, the number of first-year students increased from 310,924 in 2000–01 (the last year before the reform) to 331,368 in 2001–02 (an increase of 6.6%) and to 346,894 in 2002–03 (an increase of 4.7%). Table 3 provides a recent snapshot of first-year students enrolled and the proportion of women among them.

Table 3.   First-Year Student Enrollment by Field of Study and Gender, 2002–03

Field of Study	All Universities			Private Universities		
		Female			Female	
	Total	N	%	Total	N	%
Agriculture, forestry and fishery	6,694	2,271	33.9%	161	58	36.0%
Architecture and building	19,146	7,656	40.0%	40	9	22.5%
Arts	17,328	11,812	68.2%	908	687	75.7%
Business and administration	37,942	17,760	46.8%	4,989	2,099	42.1%
Computing	8,543	1,228	14.4%	160	18	11.3%
Education science	17,763	15,615	87.9%	2,538	2,279	89.8%
Engineering and engineering trades	31,280	4,757	15.2%	114	38	33.3%
Environmental protection	2,690	1,253	46.6%	51	21	41.2%
Health	31,832	21,057	66.2%	1,538	943	61.3%
Humanities	35,300	25,708	72.8%	1,998	1,602	80.2%
Journalism and information	17,741	10,886	61.4%	3,068	1,992	64.9%
Law	39,627	22,544	56.9%	2,495	1,345	53.9%
Life sciences	15,496	10,183	65.7%	253	180	71.1%
Manufacturing and processing	2,691	1,378	51.2%	52	30	57.7%
Mathematics and statistics	2,983	1,520	51.0%	32	20	62.5%
Personal services	8,918	4,337	48.6%	889	456	51.3%
Physical sciences	4,387	1,646	37.5%	16	4	25.0%
Security services	351	50	14.2%	n/a	n/a	n/a
Social and behavioral science	40,270	22,997	57.1%	3,095	1,839	59.4%
Social services	4,857	4,309	88.7%	452	396	87.6%
Teacher training	n/a	n/a	n/a	n/a	n/a	n/a
Transport services	114	19	16.7%	n/a	n/a	n/a
Veterinary	1,207	810	67.1%	n/a	n/a	n/a
Total	347,160	189,796	54.7%	22,849	14,016	61.3%

Source: EUROSTAT-MIUR, 2004.

The impact of the reform can also be seen very clearly among the number of graduates, which increased from 174,197 in 2001 to 198,705 in 2002. In addition, a small improvement has been observed regarding one of the major problems of the Italian university—namely, the dropout phenomenon. Of the students first enrolled in 2001–02, 84% reached the second-year in 2002–03, whereas the matriculation rate had been 80% just 2 years earlier. This should lead to a further increase in the number of graduates. Further, after a declining trend, the percentage of secondary school graduates enrolling in a university is now increasing substantially (from 65% in 2000 to 77% in 2002).

In short, it is fair to say that the reform has shed light on a number of traditional weaknesses in the Italian higher education system. Without efficient systems of evaluation to rectify bad policies, the universities had a serious weakness in the mechanisms of governance. The large majority of them could not rely on the ability of governing structures to deal with the basic problems of administration, especially in terms of coordinating the teaching and research activities among different faculties. Further, university administrators had no model to refer to in the process of adopting policies of fundraising from different sources (other than traditional ministerial ones) and offering various services in order to rebalance the budget.

Nevertheless, the reform did not collapse. On the contrary, it was successfully launched and developed the 3-year first level and the 2-year second level in all universities. The primary reason for this success is based on the positive answer that the top (the reform promoters) received from the bottom (namely, the academics). It seems fair to say that a significant part of the academic staff either felt the old system of higher education had to change or—as suggested earlier—accepted the reform because it was coming from the local academic authority (rector, dean, head of the department, and the like). In any case, a consistent portion of them have become involved in academic business on a regular basis, and this represents a very positive side effect of the reform which will turn out to be crucial for the modernization of the entire system.

The Impact on Academics

Even if the future of the academic profession does not at the moment seem very promising, it cannot be said that as a consequence there is a very significant brain drain phenomenon occurring. On the contrary, a recent study indicates that only 2,678 Italian researchers and 52 doctoral students are abroad—51% of them in Europe, and 35% of them in the U.S. (Moscati, 2003). The study also showed that emigre researchers are mostly working in universities (65.9%) and research centers (23.4%), are predominantly male (67.3%), in their 30s (58.8%) and mainly holding a doctoral title obtained abroad (61.5%).

Financial Problems

The problem of financial resources has always been a serious one in the Italian system of higher education, but recently has been getting worse due to the general financial crisis of the state. In relation to GDP, the expenditures for higher education in Italy (0.8%) have been declining in recent years, and are lower than the average of the European Union (1.2%). One specific aspect has been the relatively lower support given to tertiary education in comparison to primary and secondary education. The state provides the public universities with at least 80% of their budget. Sources are subdivided into different items, with the main one called "the basic fund" (*Fondo Finanziamento Ordinario*, or FFO). In 2001, the FFO exceeded 6.1 million Euros (out of a total budget of over 10 million), as indicated in Table 4.

In the following years, the amount of FFO remained practically at the same level: 6.165 million in 2002, and 6.215 million in 2003. Annual growth in public financing for the universities has declined through the years, and now increases less than 1% per year. In addition, comparatively little support comes from private sources. Both phenomena can be interpreted within the framework of the relatively marginal position given to higher education in the political and economic domain at the national

Table 4.   Financial Sources for the Italian University System, 2001

Sources	Million Euros
FFO for state universities—MIUR	6,163
Private universities—MIUR	107
State funds for system planning	126
Co-financing of research projects—MIUR	126
Incentives to academic staff	74
Fellowships for doctoral studies	157
Regional funds for students	315
State funds for students	129
State funds for university building programs	514
Students fees	1,381
Subsides for research (public and private)	950
Total	10,032

Source: MIUR-CNVSU, 2003.

level. Unfortunately, these funding issues also create a substantial problem for the introduction of new courses within the framework of the Bologna process.

In the 1990s, an additional fund was established in connection with the evaluation of university performance. It was intended to reduce differences among universities through incentives, particularly rewarding positive teaching activities (the number of degrees awarded, number of years spent for a degree, and the like). This additional fund started at a very low level and increased through the years until reaching 7% of the total budget. However, this additional fund has unfortunately been stopped in recent years.

Concluding Remarks

As derived from the number of aspects discussed here, the present situation of the Italian higher education system seems rather unclear and its future highly unpredictable. Failure to recognize changing social and economic needs earlier, and to modify university missions accordingly, helps explain the rapid pace of reform once the political scenario became favorable. As a result, the Italian realization of the "Bologna process" has become the most rapid and comprehensive in Europe, even though it being applied to the most traditional system of higher education. Consequently, a number of severe problems—simmering below the surface for years—have blown open, highlighting the need for a dramatically changed perspective among the academic staff and administrative personnel (both at the ministerial level and at the individual university level).

Perhaps even more striking is that the external source of the initiative has highlighted the fact that only a minority of members—albeit a consistent group—felt the need for system modernization, thus explaining the pervasive resistance to the reform among many in the academy. Members of disciplinary fields who were in positions that allowed them to operate individually (without the support of the institution or the help of colleagues) saw the reform as the beginning of the end of the university. In a way, they are correct, given that their view of the university is largely framed by the model suggested by Wilhelm von Humboldt. In particular, they resent the declining (or changing) role of the intellectuals inside academia. Unfortunately, the rapid pace of reform has prevented any real debate on that complicated matter.

The reform of the Italian higher education system represents an interesting case study of organizational change within a rapidly evolving social and political environment. Often, the need for change is not perceived by those within the organization, and those from outside the environment may not be able to wait for the development of an internal cultural transformation. However, the university is an enduring social institution, and has proven its ability to adapt to change over many centuries. It will thus be most interesting to watch the evolution of the Italian higher education system in the years ahead.

Note

1. There is an exception to this "serial" structure of short-cycle and long-cycle (a central point in Bologna Declaration). In a few cases (e.g., medicine, pharmacy), where prescriptions about degrees and curricula are given by the EU, there are study programs leading directly to *laurea specialistica*.

References

Capano, G. (2002). La riforma universitaria: l'anarchica attuazione di un sistema tecnocratico (The university reform: An anarchist realization of a technocratic system). *Il Mulino, 6*, 1154–1163.

De Maio, A. (2002). *Una svolta per l'università (A turning point for the university)*. Milano: Il Sole-24 Ore.

Frey, L., & Ghignoni, E. (Eds). (2002). *L'importanza della riforma universitaria in corso in Italia (The relevance of the university reform in Italy)*. Milano: Franco Angeli.

Luzzatto, G. (2001). *2001: L'odissea dell'università nuova (2001: The odyssey of the new university)*. Milano: La Nuova Italia.

Moscati, R. (1986). *I "Cicli Brevi" nell'istruzione superiore: Esperienze straniere in una prospettiva italiana (Higher education "short cycles": Foreign experiences in an Italian perspective)*. Milano: Franco Angeli.

Moscati, R. (1991). Italy. In G. Neave & F. van Vught (Eds.), *Prometheus bound: The changing relationship between government and higher education in Western Europe* (pp. 91–108). Oxford: Pergamon Press.

Moscati, R. (2003). Doctoral Degrees in Italy. Paper presented at the UNESCO-CEPES International Seminar on Doctoral Degrees and Qualifications in the Contexts of the European Higher Education Area and the European Research and Innovation Area, September 12–14, Bucharest (Romania).

Moscati, R. (2004). Italy. in J. Sadlak (Ed.), *Doctoral Studies and Qualifications in Europe and the United States: Status and Prospects* (pp. 63–76), Bucharest: Cepes-Unesco.

Pontremoli, S. & Luzzatto, G. (Eds.). (2002). *Università. La riforma è iniziata (University: The reform has begun)*. Milano: La Nuova Italia.

Trow, M. (1974). *Problems in the transition from elite to mass higher education*. Paris: OECD.

43

JAPAN

Akiyoshi Yonezawa
National Institution for Academic Degrees, Japan

Higher education has played an important role in the social and economic development of modern-day Japan. This chapter will discuss a small handful of key themes that contribute to our understanding of the country's higher education system, including access and expansion, finance, privatization, internationalization and quality assurance. Of these, perhaps the most important is the element of expansion, otherwise known as the "massification" of Japanese higher education.

By the mid-1970s, Japan had realized mass higher education based on full partici-pation in senior secondary education. In 2005, 76.2% of 18-year-olds were enrolled in higher and postsecondary institutions—universities (*daigaku*), junior colleges (*tanki-daigaku*), colleges of technology (*koto-senmon-gakko*) and specialized training colleges (*senshu-gakko*) (see Table 1). The massification of Japanese higher education has been realized through the expansion of the private sector, which relies on tuition fees as its main financial resource (Yonezawa & Baba, 1998). Based on the hierarchical structure of the higher education system, graduation from select universities has been regarded as a ladder for a successful life and a source of self-esteem by those working in mod-ern industrial sectors (Dore, 1976; Yano, 1997; Takeuchi, 1997). The heavy financial contribution of Japanese households has made possible an "efficient" mass higher ed-ucation system with limited public finance. However, Japan appears to be suffering as a result of having neglected certain factors along the way. Currently, Japanese higher education is facing challenges (under the pressure of global competition) that demand drastic restructuring.

Origins of the Japanese Higher Education System

The direct origin of the current Japanese higher education system is found in the es-tablishment of a modern university and polytechnic (*senmon-gakko*) system after the Meiji Restoration in 1868. The schools for the *samurai* (warrior) and merchant classes, and later, Western language and science schools had provided various educational programs until the mid-19th century, most of which were closed or else integrated or transformed into the newly established Westernized institutions. Japan developed its

James J.F. Forest and Philip G. Altbach (eds.), International Handbook of Higher Education, 829–837.
© 2006 *Springer. Printed in the Netherlands.*

Table 1. Japanese Higher Education Institutions and Enrollments, 2004

	Total	National	Local Public	Private
Institutions				
Universities	709	87	80	542
Junior colleges	508	12	45	451
Colleges of technology	63	55	5	3
Specialized training colleges	3,443	15	200	3,228
Students				
Universities	2,809,323	624,394	122,864	2,062,065
Junior colleges	233,749	2,975	16,510	214,264
Colleges of technology	58,681	51,729	4,656	2,296
Specialized training colleges	791,540	1,124	28,663	761,753

Source: Ministry of Education, Culture, Sports, Science and Technology, 2004.

higher education system rather independently by combining various Western models, with the German model having the greatest impact in the process of establishing "imperial universities" as prototype Japanese universities (Altbach, 1989; Nakayama, 1989). The Japanese government employed many foreign (Western) academics and experts to help in designing the system and implementing this new form of higher education. Those foreigners, however, were replaced at a very early stage by Japanese experts trained in Europe and North America.

The private sector has played an important role since the beginning of modern higher education in Japan (Kaneko, 1997). The Japanese government began providing legal authorization to private universities in 1919 (Nakayama, 1989), and the number of universities and polytechnics continued to increase even during the Sino-Japanese War and World War II (Itoh, 1999). On the other hand, public money was invested almost exclusively in the public sector, especially in imperial universities, which were treated as a system apart from other institutions.

Access, Expansion and Accountability

The transformation of the education system (based on the American model) after World War II assured wider access to higher education. Most of the former polytechnics were upgraded or merged into the new university system with 4-year undergraduate, 2-year master's and 3-year doctoral degree programs. Two-year junior colleges and colleges of technology (a combination of 3-year senior secondary education and 2-year higher education, mainly in engineering fields) were also established as short-cycle higher education leading to an associate degree; the former have in practice functioned primarily as places of female education (M. Amano, 1997), and the latter have remained an exceptional education track. At the same time, all of the universities—including former imperial ones and private ones—were given the same status as "universities" in principle, although there continued to be a great difference in prestige between institutions with different historical backgrounds.

The public institutions and the top private universities—which, by the 1950s, had become large comprehensive institutions—have been relatively protected from the pressure of expansion since the 1960s. In 1962, the government deregulated the procedure for establishing new faculties and departments (I. Amano, 1997; Kuroha, 2001). This enabled less prestigious demand-absorbing private institutions to meet the increasing need for the training of service and industrial workers, while the government concentrated its investment in the expansion of natural sciences and engineering programs at national universities (Kaneko, 1996, 1997).

The rapid expansion of the private sector, with limited and irregular financial support from the central and local governments, led to a deterioration in the quality and environment at many universities, which became one of the grievances of the student movement which began during the mid-1960s. In order to ensure the quality and accessibility of higher education (including private education) in 1970, the government began providing public funding for the operational expenditure of private institutions. At present, however, these public subsidies cover only around 10% of institutional expenses, the rest being mainly covered by tuition fees. At the same time, the government introduced higher education plans to control student enrollment in each public and private university and junior college (I. Amano, 1997). Through higher education plans and other legal arrangements, the government (until quite recently) virtually prohibited the establishment of new education programs in the big cities, which gave an incentive for the development of new campuses in suburban areas and small cities. At the same time, the non-university 2-year special training colleges were founded to absorb the continuously increasing demand for further vocational education. Presently, some special training colleges are providing advanced vocational training, attracting even university graduates who wish to obtain expertise or qualifications.

The limitation of student numbers and the hierarchical structure of the higher education system strengthened the social function of higher education institutions as a screening device. Entrance to elite universities (not graduation) gave the students a signal of high trainability in the labor market. The enterprises tried to recruit those elite students with potential high ability, sometimes more than a year before their graduation. With the lifetime employment combined with in-house training in large enterprises, those elite students were assured of a successful life (Yoshimoto, 2002).

This system had to be supported by wide participation in the entrance examination based on pure meritocracy. However, the entrance "examination hell" is no longer severe in the new environment of institutional over-supply, along with the rapid decrease in the number of young people in the population and the market deregulation policy of the government (I. Amano, 1997; Yonezawa, 2002). Less prestigious institutions have already started admitting 100% of prospective students, or are actually facing a shortage of applicants. In 2004, 41.0% of junior colleges and around 29.1% of private universities were faced with an enrollment shortfall against the student seats allocated by the government (The Promotion and Mutual Aid Corporation of Private Schools of Japan, 2004). The entrance examination system itself has also changed drastically. Most universities have introduced an American-style "admissions office" system, and have explored various other channels for recruiting a diversity of students, sometimes without any testing (Mori, 2002). The general academic achievement of entrants to higher education is no longer automatically assumed, sometimes even in prestigious institutions, most of which have diversified their recruitment channels. The quality assurance of academic achievement among higher education graduates has become an urgent task for higher education reform (Yonezawa, 2002). The Ministry of Education has even tried to establish guidelines for study hours, GPA, etc. following the recommendation of its advisory committee, the University Council (University Council, 1998).

Economic and Financial Issues

The excess of demand in the higher education market (encouraged by Japan's higher education plans) and the continuous raising of tuition fees by public institutions since the 1970s led to a significant raising of tuition fees in the private sector. The stable expectation of enrollment under the plan and continuing increase in revenue from tuition fees certainly improved the finances of private institutions. The elite private sector in the big cities strengthened their market competitiveness through the 1980s, and the faculty in private institutions have received a higher average salary than those in public institutions since the beginning of that decade.

On the other hand, public institutions experienced financial shortfalls in the 1980s under the strict ceiling of the national budget. National universities started a "poverty campaign" at the end of the 1980s, appealing for help amid a worsening education and research environment caused by the continuous budgetary ceilings. Increased social recognition of the need for science and technology in the knowledge economy led to an expansion of research budgets in the university sector during the 1990s. Most of these research funds are distributed as project or targeted funding, while the share of basic funds for research has been decreasing (Asonuma, 2002). In 2004, the Ministry of Finance unveiled plans to reduce the basic operational budget for national universities by 2% every year.

Faced with the arrival of the second baby boom generation in higher education around 1990, the government allowed a temporary increase in student numbers in both public and private institutions. This brought about a temporary increase in revenue from tuition fees in the private sector. The current over-supply (which began near the end of the 1990s) is clearly having a negative effect on the financial condition of private institutions (Morozumi, 2003). Higher education institutions are trying to develop adult and professional education programs for mature students, although these emerging markets are not likely to contribute financially in the very near future.

The Changing Status of Public and Private Institutions

The heavy reliance on the private sector in Japanese mass higher education is calling the social role of public higher education into question. Traditionally, the role of national institutions had been regarded as fostering elite human resources necessary for national development, and conducting research requiring heavy national investment. However, the improvement in the prestige and academic capacity of top private universities, and the fact that the majority of university students are not receiving public higher education, is creating serious doubts about the justification of the role of national and local public institutions (Yonezawa, 1998, 2001).

Around 2000, there was serious discussion about the "privatization" of public higher education, although it did not become a realistic policy agenda. Instead, a scheme downsizing government organizations through the introduction of an "independent administrative corporation" scheme, under a new public management framework, was applied to the national and most local public institutions (Murasawa, 2002).

In 2004, all the national universities were incorporated as "National University Corporations" (Study Team Concerning the Transformation of National Universities into Independent Administrative Corporations, 2002). The incorporation of national universities enabled more autonomous institutional management under the strong power of university presidents. On the other hand, the government also set up a new control system through performance assessment. All of the national universities are required to publish a mid-term plan and goals every 6 years, in consultation with the Minister of Education. Goal achievement is assessed by the Evaluation Committee for National University Corporation—a senior advisory committee set up inside the Ministry of Education—and the National Institution for Academic Degrees and University Evaluation (NIAD-UE), a third-party administrative organization tasked with university evaluation. Financial allocation is linked to the achievement of an institution's goals (articulated in their planning documents). The new system is still highly unstable, and strongly influenced by an ongoing power game between universities, the government and other stakeholders.

The control of the private sector through quality assurance and financial aid was also strengthened based on the weakening market status of private institutions. Beginning in 2002, the government started direct project-based funding for private institutions, instead of going through the independent Financial Council for Private Higher Education (Yamagishi, 2001). The government also strengthened the role of guidance to the private sector through the amendment of the School Education Law in 2002.

In 2004, for-profit universities in certain districts were officially permitted to adopt a pilot program of administrative deregulation. In addition, the Ministry of Education has announced its basic policy for establishing an official recognition system for branch campuses of foreign universities which are not operated within the legal framework of Japanese higher education (Garrett & Maclean, 2004).

The Impact of Higher Education Reform on the Academic Profession

Traditionally, the status of academics has been strongly protected in both the national and private sectors. A high degree of academic autonomy, especially in personnel matters, was assured under the post-WWII regime, reflecting the negative impact of governmental intervention under the pre-war regime until 1945 (Ogawa, 2002). However, this certainly became an obstacle for the introduction of entrepreneurial management, especially into public institutions and elite private ones. The University of Air, a national broadcasting university established during the 1980s, introduced a fixed-term contract system for all academics, including full professors. The government strongly recommended the introduction of term contract employment, and most national institutions followed this idea. The shrinking higher education market has led to the closing of institutions, schools and departments in the private sector. This situation made the employment of private university teachers unstable, and they started to demand unemployment insurance.

The incorporation of national universities is having a significant impact on the status of the academic profession. A significant number of national universities are planning to introduce performance assessment and a reward system for their academic staff. On the other hand, the national universities have gained more flexibility in regard to raising the salary of excellent academic staff and attracting high quality staff internationally, particularly from the industrial world.

Professional Postgraduate Education

The economic restructuring of the Japanese economy is certainly changing the traditional image of the normal Japanese career; namely, lifetime employment in the same company. Companies are said to be reducing the investment in the in-house training of their employees, and the potential demand from adult learners for professional graduate education is increasing. The government has showed vision in fostering professional graduate education alongside traditional academically oriented graduate education. In the fields of engineering, pharmacy and medical sciences, postgraduate education is no longer dominated by academic programs. The current target is the establishment of law schools and business schools to nurture professionals in these areas. Increasing job opportunities in the foreign companies in Japan are giving incentives for students to enroll in professional education programs, while there appears to be a long way to go before Japanese companies change their attitudes and reward those newly trained professionals in a manner comparable to Western systems.

Internationalization and Quality Assurance

Japanese higher education has developed relatively independent from the global higher education community, partly because of the language barrier, and partly because of its unique system of employment. However, the cross-border flow of students, academics and labor has definitely increased, especially since the mid-1980s. In 1983, the Nakasone cabinet and the Ministry of Education announced a plan to attract 100,000 students from abroad by 2000 (Horie, 2002). This target was achieved in 2003, mainly because of the rapid increase in Chinese overseas students, which has occurred not only in Japan but all over the world. The number of Japanese students studying in foreign countries has also increased quite rapidly within the last two decades, from 15,485 in 1985 to 76,464 in 2001 (Ministry of Education, Culture, Sports, Science and Technology, 2002). There is a big difference between the inflow and outflow of students. Around 90% of the foreign students are coming from Asian countries, especially from China and Korea. On the other hand, the majority of Japanese students abroad are studying in the United States and other English speaking countries, although those studying in China are increasing rapidly.

Around 90% of the overseas students are self-supporting students, and most are working in parallel with their study to meet the relatively high living costs in Japan. Japanese employers sometimes regard these students as cheap labor, and the policy with regard to the student visa closely reflects the immigration policy change (Yonezawa, 2003a).

The proportion of international students tends to be higher in top research universities and some institutions at the bottom in the prestige hierarchy. In the latter case, the institutions cannot attract a sufficient number of Japanese students. Meanwhile, the top research universities are trying to strengthen their support system for international students, including the provision of courses offered in English (Horie, 2002).

The internationalization of academic staff is relatively slow, again because of the language barrier, which especially impacts communication among the administration and faculty. Some universities hold bilingual faculty meetings, and others invite foreign presidents. In most universities, however, the Japanese language is essential for daily academic life. On the other hand, there is little incentive for Japanese academics to leave Japanese universities, mainly because of the relatively good salary and research conditions. However, the increasingly severe competition—especially in the natural sciences and engineering—has led to a greater number of Japanese scholars working actively in institutions abroad.

Foreign branch campuses are in most cases unsuccessful (Altbach, 2002), because it is not easy to find a new market within the very mature Japanese market. Most of the universities which entered the Japanese market are not internationally well known, and most of the best students prefer to study in prestigious Japanese universities, or in the homeland campuses of foreign universities.

The high dropout rates which are common in less prestigious American universities are very difficult for Japanese families to accept. According to the Organization for Economic Development and Cooperation (OECD, 2003), the Japanese higher education system has an extraordinarily high retention rate, over 90%. From an international perspective, this high retention rate may cause serious doubts about the degree standards of less prestigious universities in Japan.

Even inside the government, there are strong arguments about the necessity to open up the Japanese higher education to international competition. At the same time, Japanese universities are trying to establish inroads into the foreign higher education market, not only to give Japanese students learning experiences in foreign countries, but also to attract greater numbers of international students.

The Japanese government is actively supporting the discussion about how to develop an international information network to support both exporters and importers of cross-border higher education (Kimura, Yonezawa, & Ohmori, 2004), while the real influence of cross-border education is still small in Japan.

Beginning in 2004, the Japanese government now requires all of the public and private universities, junior colleges and colleges of technology to submit to a governmentally authorized accreditation review every 7 years, and around 2010 all institutions will submit to the first cycle of the accreditation process.

Conclusion: Fostering Vision Through Higher Education?

In a rapidly changing global context, it is not easy to provide a clear vision of the future of Japanese higher education or of Japanese society itself. The Japanese economy is still heavily supported by the high-tech manufacturing sector, and this enables the Japanese education system to be relatively independent (in terms of both language and the employment system) from the global standard (Yonezawa, 2003a). However, the increasing share of the population in the service industry and the worldwide spread of Japanese manufacturing plants are certainly increasing the pressure to foster a more internationalized labor force.

The role of higher education in providing a clear vision of national development in the global society is also important. Government leaders and higher education institutions are tackling these tasks through drastic system reform, including intensive financial investment in world class research, international educational programs, and improving the quality of education (Yonezawa, 2003b). On the other hand, the change in society and industry's perception of Japanese universities is relatively slow. Japanese universities are still perceived as screening devices rather than value-adding education institutions, and the university-industry relationship is still "under construction" (Hatakenaka, 2004).

The development and quality improvement of higher education in neighboring Asian countries may broaden the alternative future image of Japanese higher education. Direct interaction with the international community is certainly increasing, and the overall future orientation of Japanese higher education is strongly influenced by global trends.

References

Altbach, P. G. (1989). Twisted roots: the Western impact on Asian higher education. In P. G. Altbach & V. Selvaratnam (Eds.), *From dependence to autonomy: The development of Asian universities* (pp. 1–21). Chestnut Hill, MA: Center for International Higher Education, Boston College.

Altbach, P. G. (2002). Japan and international trade in education. *International Higher Education, 29/16* (Fall), 25–26.

Amano, I. (1997). Structural changes in Japan's higher education system: from a planning to a market model. *Higher Education, 34*, 125–140.

Amano, M. (1997). Women in higher education. *Higher Education, 34*, 215–235.

Asonuma, A. (2002). Finance reform in Japanese higher education. *Higher Education, 43*, 109–126.

Dore, R. (1976). *The diploma disease*. London: Allen & Unwin.

Garrett, R., & Maclean, D. (2004). Japanese reforms include recognition of in-country foreign universities and launch of first for-profit universities. *The Observatory of Borderless Higher Education* (April 7).

Hatakenaka, S. (2004). *University-industry partnerships in MIT, Cambridge and Tokyo: Story-telling across boundaries*. New York: Routledge.

Horie, M. (2002). The internationalization of higher education in Japan in the 1990s: A reconsideration. *Higher Education, 43*, 65–84.

Itoh, A. (1999). *Senkanki nihon no kotokyoiku (Higher education in inter-war Japan)*. Tokyo: Tamagawa University Press [in Japanese].

Kaneko, M. (1996). Koto kyoiku taishuka no ninaite (Bearer of mass higher education). In National Institute of Multimedia Education, *Research on the structure and function of mass higher education* (pp. 37–59). Chiba: NIME [in Japanese].

Kaneko, M. (1997). Efficiency and equity in Japanese higher education. *Higher Education, 34*, 165–181.

Kimura, T., Yonezawa, A., & Ohmori, F. (2004). Quality assurance and recognition of qualifications in higher education: Japan. In OECD/CERI, *Quality and recognition in higher education* (pp. 119–130). Paris: OECD.

Kuroha, R. (2001). *Shinban sengo daigaku seisaku no tenkai (Development of postwar higher education policy: 2nd edition)*. Tokyo: Tamagawa University Press [in Japanese].

Mori, R. (2002). Entrance examinations and remedial education in Japanese higher education. *Higher Education, 43*, 27–42.

Morozumi, A. (2003). Daigaku no kyoiku cost (Educational cost of universities) (pp. 27–33). IDE, Tokyo: Minsh-kyoiku Kyokai [In Japanese].

Murasawa, M. (2002). The future of higher education in Japan: Changing the legal status of national universities. *Higher Education, 43*, 141–155.

Nakayama S. (1989). Independence and choice: Western impacts on Japanese higher education. In P. G. Altbach & V. Selvaratnam (Eds.), *From dependence to autonomy: The development of Asian universities* (pp. 97–114). Chestnut Hill, MA: Center for International Higher Education, Boston College.

Ogawa, Y. (2002). Challenging the traditional organization of Japanese universities. *Higher Education, 43*, 85–108.

OECD. (2003). *Education at a glance 2003*. Paris: OECD.

Ministry of Education, Culture, Sports, Science and Technology (MEXT). (2002). *A new image of national university corporations*. Tokyo: MEXT Study Team Concerning the Transformation of National Universities into Independent Administrative Corporations.

Takeuchi, Y. (1997). The self-activating entrance examination system: Its hidden agenda and its correspondence with the Japanese "sarary man." *Higher Education, 34*, 183–198.

The Promotion and Mutual Aid Corporation of Private Schools of Japan. (2004). *Shiritsu daigaku shiritsu tanki daigaku nyugaku shigan doko (Trends of applicants towards private universities and junior colleges)*. Tokyo: Author.

University Council. (1998). *A vision of universities in the 21st century and reform measures: To be distinctive universities in a competitive environment*. Tokyo: Ministry of Education, Culture, Sports, Science and Technology.

Yamagishi, S. (2001). *Daigaku kaikaku no genba he (To the scene of university reform)*. Tokyo: Tamagawa University Press [in Japanese].

Yano, M. (1997). Higher education and employment. *Higher Education, 34*, 199–214.

Yonezawa, A. (1998). Further privatization in Japanese higher education? *International Higher Education, 13* (Fall), 20–21.

Yonezawa, A. (2001). Changing higher education policies for Japanese national universities. *Higher Education Management, 12*(3), 31–39.

Yonezawa, A. (2002). The quality assurance system and market forces in Japanese higher education. *Higher Education, 43*, 127–139.

Yonezawa, A. (2003a). Impact of globalization on higher education governance in Japan. *Higher Education Research and Development, 22*(2), 145–154.

Yonezawa, A. (2003b). Making "world-class universities": Japan's experiment. *Higher Education Management and Policy, 15*(2), 9–23.

Yonezawa, A. & Baba, M. (1998). The market structure for private universities in Japan. *Tertiary Education and Management, 42*, 145–152.

Yoshimoto, K. (2002). Higher education and the transition to work in Japan compared with Europe. In J. Enders & O. Fulton (Eds.), *Higher education in a globalizing world*. Dordrecht, The Netherlands: Kluwer Academic Publishers.

44

KENYA

Charles K. Ngome
Kenyatta University, Kenya

The need to resuscitate the higher education sector in Kenya (as elsewhere in Africa), particularly at the university level, was recognized during the 1990s as an issue of critical priority. Institutions that had once been buoyant centers of academic excellence, were— beginning in the 1980s—reduced to a state of financial insolvency and academic penury. Behind this deterioration has been the economic crisis that has bedeviled the Kenyan economy. The crisis that is afflicting universities in Kenya is being complemented by an emerging awareness that the ability of the higher education system to make a significant contribution to the country's development needs has become increasingly impaired.

Background

Kenya, a former British colony, has a population of about 31 million people (51% females and 49% males). The high rate of Kenya's population growth has been a major constraint on the country's ability to promote human capital formation through education. During the 1980s, Kenya had an annual population growth rate of nearly 4% which has since then dropped to about 2.5%. Some of the basic factors that explain the key challenges facing the education sector today can be seen in the country's basic demographic profile. About 18% of the population is less than four years old, and the age group between five and 14 (which represents the primary school-going age) constitutes 28% of the population. Overall, nearly 67% of Kenya's total population lies within the age brackets of early childhood development, primary, secondary, middle level, college and university education. Catering for the educational needs of this population has compelled the government and other stakeholder groups to expand learning facilities at all levels of the education system.

The colonial government assumed some responsibility for African education during the early part of the 20th century, with the establishment of the Department of Education. It introduced segregation of education along racial lines, ostensibly to preserve respective cultures and prepare individuals for their "appropriate" roles in the society. However, the system contained gross inequalities based on social, racial and religious grounds. The African-focused education had been designed to provide vocational education in order to equip the Africans with the manual skills required on the European

James J.F. Forest and Philip G. Altbach (eds.), International Handbook of Higher Education, 839–865.
© 2006 *Springer. Printed in the Netherlands.*

settler plantations (Standa, 2000). This disadvantaged the Africans to the extent that when the colonial and expatriate personnel departed after Kenya's independence in 1963, very few Africans possessed relevant professional, managerial and technical skills to enable them to occupy vacant and emerging positions in both government and private sectors. This had a bearing on the rapid expansion of higher education in the country, as witnessed in the post-independence era.

Growth of Higher Education

The history of higher education in Kenya can be traced to Makerere University in Uganda, which was founded in 1922 during the era of British colonialism as a technical college for African students from the East African countries of Uganda, Kenya and Tanzania. Although the college offered post-school certificate courses in various fields—including teacher training, carpentry, building technology, motor mechanics, medical care, agriculture and veterinary services—it was only after the publication of the Asquith report in 1949 that the Makerere University Act was passed, thus giving the institution the legal status of a university (Poss, 1992; Mwiria, 1998). As a result, Makerere was re-established as the University of East Africa (and was authorized to offer degrees of the University of London), and admitted its first undergraduate students in 1950. Largely due to nationalist pressures emanating from newly independent Kenya and Tanzania, in 1970 the University of East Africa was broken up into three fully fledged national universities: Makerere University in Uganda, the University of Dar-es-Salaam in Tanzania, and the University of Nairobi in Kenya.

The private university sector in Kenya (like its public counterpart) has also recorded significant progress since 1970, when the United Sates International University (USIU)—the first private university in Kenya—was founded in the capital city of Nairobi. This is mainly due to the insatiable demand for higher education in the country. Despite the number of public universities (which has increased six-fold since 1970), the increasing population base of secondary school graduates seeking access to higher education continues to outstrip the capacity that these institutions can offer. Public universities admit roughly 10,000 students on government sponsorship, while about 5,000 students seek university places outside the country (officially through the Ministry of Education, Science and Technology) and mainly on self-sponsorship to the United States, India, Britain, Canada, Australia, Russia, South Africa, Germany and France (Ngome, 2003, p. 361). It has been estimated that US$192 million is spent annually by Kenyans on university education abroad (Varsity Focus, 1999, p. 6). The provision of higher education in the country therefore continues to be one of the critical challenges facing the government. Unfortunately, the government's expansionary policies undertaken in the last three decades, which have aimed at democratizing access to university education, have only whetted public appetite for more education. As the public continues to expect greater access to higher education, the government's expansion programs in higher education have been halted because of austerity measures that have been introduced following the adoption of the World Bank's and International Monetary Fund's structural adjustment programs. The conditions set by these two Bretton Woods institutions liberalized the economy, devalued the Kenyan shilling and restricted public spending. It was against this backdrop that the Kenyan government has encouraged the establishment of private universities. The private university sector has become a critical component in the country's higher education system. Out of an enrollment of approximately 80,000 university students in the country, over 10,000 (13%) are enrolled in private universities, while 70,000 (87%) attend public universities.

Most universities in Kenya (both public and private) are situated in and around Nairobi. Of the 27 universities in the country, including the four offshore campuses of foreign universities operating in Kenya, only 30% are established outside Nairobi in agriculturally-oriented areas of the country. Most universities have been established in Nairobi for two reasons. First, it is more expensive to establish and manage universities in rural areas. Urban areas (particularly Nairobi, the capital city) has well developed facilities such as roads, schools, hospitals and residential estates which do not have to be provided for the purpose of meeting the needs of universities. Second, higher education institutions have been located in Nairobi because the largest pool of part-time students (who work and attend evening and weekend classes) reside there.

Regulating and Accrediting Private Universities

The Commission for Higher Education (CHE), which is the buffer body between universities and the government, has the overall responsibility of licensing higher private education institutions. CHE categorizes private universities into four main groups: accredited private universities; registered private universities; private universities operating on a letter of interim authority; and offshore campuses. The term offshore campus refers to foreign universities that are running their programs either through mid-level colleges in the country or have established their own campuses. These institutions award certificates of their parent universities. Of the 21 private universities in Kenya, including four offshore campuses, only six are accredited, as indicated in Table 1.

Before accreditation is granted by CHE, a thorough inspection is conducted of the human, physical, technical and financial resources that are available to carry out the operations necessary to achieve an institution's stated goals and objectives. Some of the requirements demanded by CHE for accreditation include the establishment of institutional standards with respect to physical facilities, staffing levels and teaching loads, peer review, visits and inspections of the institutions, internal self-assessment and viability of financial resources on a long-term basis. These conditions are unrealistically too high, and if applied to the letter few universities—including the more established ones like the University of Nairobi—would hardly qualify for accreditation and the granting of a civil charter (Mwiria & Ngome, 1998). Further, some rules and regulations have become obsolete—for example, the requirement that a private university should possess at least 50 acres of land before it can be accredited. Such a regulation was relevant in the past, when universities were meant to be sprawling campuses with high student enrollments. However, with the onset of information technology, approaches to learning have changed, and not as much space is required. Moreover, most of the colleges registered with CHE are theological institutions with enrollments below 100 students. These requirements do not take into account the nature of each institution and put accreditation beyond the reach of many institutions. These stringent conditions

Table 1.   Private Universities in Kenya

Accredited Private Universities
   University of Eastern Africa, Baraton (UEAB), founded in 1992
   Catholic University of Eastern Africa (CUEA), founded in 1992
   Daystar University, founded in 1994
   Scott Theological College, founded in 1997
   United States International University (USIU), founded in 1999
   African Nazarene University, founded in 2002
Registered Private Universities
   East African School of Theology
   Kenya Highlands Bible College
   Nairobi International Bible College
   Nairobi Evangelical Graduate School of Theology
   St. Paul's Theological School
   Pan-African Christian College
Private Universities Operating on a Letter of Interim Authority
   The Aga Khan University
   Strathmore College
   Kabarak University
   Kenya Methodist University
   Kiriri Women's University of Science and Technology
Offshore Campuses of Foreign Universities
   Australian Universities Studies Institute (AUSI)
   The Kenya College of Accountancy Center for the University of
      South Africa (UNISA) in Kenya
   The Kenya College of Communications Technology (KCCT) Center for the Free State
      University in South Africa
   The School of Professional Studies Center for the University of London and Technikon of
      Africa

Source: Commission for Higher Education (2004).

are only applied to institutions that seek to establish full-fledged private universities in Kenya. The offshore campuses that offer programs of foreign universities are not subject to CHE's accreditation model of quality assurance because the Universities Act of 1985, under which it operates, has no legal provisions for offshore campuses.

CHE has also been accused of slowing the expansion of private universities through its process of curriculum review for new programs. It takes between one and three years for CHE to approve new programs in these institutions. Thus, private universities with a dynamic curriculum that seek to respond quickly to the changing socio-economic environment would be constrained by this long gestation period. This contrasts with the approach of the Western Association of Schools and Colleges (WASC), one of several accrediting commissions for senior colleges and universities in United States. WASC allows tertiary education institutions that enjoy its affiliation to launch new programs without consultation (WASC, 1988). Not only does this allow universities some autonomy, it also fosters the development of internal self-regulatory mechanisms.

An encouraging and fair regulatory framework is required to facilitate the growth of private universities in Kenya.

Governance and Management Structures

As universities in Kenya develop and establish programs that are tailored to the challenges posed by the country's socio-economic needs, the question of their instruments of governance and management acquire special significance. Public universities are governed by specific acts and laws of Kenya that provide for their establishment, control and mode of organization. Although governance and management structures in private universities vary from university to university and by type of institution (secular or religious), their institutional charters (for the chartered private universities), history and philosophy define their mission and outline rules that govern their relations with other organizations, and also help in framing some internal rules of operation.

The position of chancellor is the highest governance position in public universities. By Acts of Parliament (which established public universities in Kenya), the president of the Republic of Kenya is the chancellor of all public universities unless he/she decides to appoint other persons to those positions. Until June 2003, when President Mwai Kibaki appointed separate chancellors for each public university in the country, the previous heads of state (Jomo Kenyatta and Daniel Moi) had held this position since 1970, when the country established its first university. Since their appointment in 2003, the role of chancellors has been limited to presiding over annual graduation ceremonies during which they confer degrees, diplomas, certificates and other awards of public universities. The president of Kenya (who is still the chancellor of all public universities according to the country's legal framework) is responsible for the appointment of leadership teams in public universities, including chairpersons, vice chairpersons and honorary treasurers of university councils, and vice chancellors, deputy vice chancellors and principals of colleges.

University senates in public institutions constitute the second level of authority. As supreme bodies with regard to the day-to-day running of public universities, they are composed of vice chancellors as chairpersons, deputy vice chancellors, college principals, faculty/school deans, department heads and other senior university administrators such as registrars and deans of students. Students and faculty members elect their own representatives to the senates. Student representatives, who are elected by their constituents to university senates and councils, spend a very short time in these organizations. This short time span barely allows them to become familiar with the senates' or councils' operations. The time is so transitory that before they settle down to represent their constituents, their term is already finished. It is equally significant to mention that since most senate members (department heads) are appointed by vice chancellors, they tend to support their (vice chancellors') interests, whether they are supportive of the university or not. Consequently, senate deliberations ignore substantive issues and are usually manipulated. As a result, they limit participatory decision making, as the holders of these offices are answerable to chief executives who appoint them and not lecturers that work under their supervision.

In private universities, founders substitute the dominance of university councils by government nominees (which is a major cause of concern among academics in public universities). For example, USIU's Board of Trustees (the institution's highest governing body) has 25 members, 23 of whom are Americans and only two are Kenyans. In private higher education institutions that espouse Christian evangelical philosophies and missions, their governing bodies, faculty and administrative staff are recruited based upon the strength of their Christian beliefs. Another notable departure from public universities is the absence of government influence, except during the process of accreditation. Senior administrators in private universities are usually selected by founders without consulting academic staff and students.

Strategic Planning

The adoption of strategic planning in Kenyan universities is a recent phenomenon. Eight main issues have raised the need for strategic planning by Kenyan universities. First, with higher education having become an international business, foreign universities are aggressively marketing their programs in the country. The marketing is aimed at attracting Kenyan students to join universities abroad or enroll in programs that are provided locally through their offshore campuses based in Nairobi. The competition by foreign universities for Kenyan students has increased following the enactment of the University Amendments Bill 2000, which allows foreign institutions to set up campuses locally without having to go through the various inspections by the Commission for Higher Education. The Australian Universities Studies Institute (AUSI), affiliated with several universities in Australia and established in Nairobi in 2002, is one of the beneficiaries of this legislation. There are also several Kenyan mid-level tertiary institutions that are offering degree programs for the University of South Africa (UNISA), University of London and Technikon University of South Africa. Kenyan universities (public and private) therefore cannot continue to sit on their laurels in the face of emerging competitors. They need to build on their comparative advantage of having been on the scene earlier, and pursue new approaches to research and training ahead of emerging institutions.

A second issue of concern is the local competition between public and private university sectors, as well as among public and private universities themselves. This competition is likely to intensify with the expected establishment of more private universities; the expansion of self-sponsored academic programs and the increasing adoption of innovative modes of tuition delivery made possible by recent technological advances. This competition requires benchmarking—a process whereby a university compares itself with other institutions in terms of their tuition rates and fees, employee salaries and academic programs, among other elements.

Third, strategic planning is driven in part by the problem of reduced public spending on public universities. This raises the need for the generation of supplemental sources of income to augment government resources. Fourth, a growing unemployment rate, especially among university graduates, has put pressure on higher education institutions to demonstrate the relevance of their academic programs to the labor market.

How can Kenyan universities increase their student intake in demand-driven academic programs while optimizing their use of available resources? Fifth, the issue of quality assurance is taking center stage. It is a difficult task to develop programs which are internationally competitive, ensure mobility and employability, and guarantee a high quality of education—all while facing financial constraints.

Sixth, there is an urgent need to mount cost-cutting measures, particularly by eliminating management levels that do not add value to universities, and combining compatible functions in order to reduce layers of management and duplication of efforts. Seventh, there are many problems affecting the research enterprise in higher education institutions. The research in which members of staff engage is limited and driven by personal preferences, and it is not organized to contribute to the teaching or other operations of Kenyan universities. So disoriented are the faculty's research activities that most members of the academic fraternity have no idea of the areas of research their colleagues carry out. This state of affairs is largely attributable to limited financial resource allocations for the support of research programs. In charting a course of action, universities must seek ways of institutionalizing these activities within their core functions and operations, in the belief that the conduct of teaching that is not supported by research activities and intellectual interactions outside the lecture theaters is counter-intuitive.

Finally, the rapid spread of HIV/AIDS in Kenya (as in other sub-Saharan African countries) over the past decade is no longer a health problem but a major cause for the ongoing development crisis. Education is one of the many sectors in the country that are being devastated by the escalation of the pandemic. In the absence of appropriate mechanisms in the universities, the teaching force, non-academic staff and students will be decimated by this epidemic and their output will continue to decline. There is a need to have a better understanding and assessment of the impact of HIV/AIDS on universities in order to design strategies for catering to HIV/AIDS-affected students and staff, and to assist in preventing the spread of the disease.

These challenges require institutions of higher learning to be responsive to the environment in which they exist if they are to be effective and remain relevant. As higher education institutions are accused of being slow to implement change, we must recognize how this can lead to the demise of our universities in an environment characterized by constant change. Thus, strategic planning is a tool that has been embraced to help Kenyan universities plan for current and future challenges.

Access and Equity

Access in higher education is generally meant to describe opportunities available to students who qualify to pursue different academic programs. Equity is deeply interwoven in access, and is seen by some as a creature of access with a specific pointer to some form of balance in the distribution of these opportunities across gender and regional or ethnic lines. Within the realm of access and equity, observers typically discuss university intake requirements, undergraduate enrollments, postgraduate enrollments, and regional and gender imbalances.

University Intake Requirements

Candidates who obtain a minimum grade of C+ on the Kenya Certificate of Secondary Education (KCSE)—or its approved equivalent for university admission in the respective country of applicants from outside Kenya—are eligible for admission. Applicants who wish to attend private universities and privately self-sponsored programs in public universities apply directly to academic registrars in those respective institutions. The Joint Admissions Board (JAB), established during the 1980s, selects government sponsored students for admission into public universities and distributes them into various faculties and schools. JAB's membership is comprised of all six public university vice chancellors, their deputies, principals of constituent colleges, registrars and deans of faculties and schools. It was established on a goodwill basis by vice chancellors and is not recognized under any act. It is, however, recognized by the Commission for Higher Education and Higher Education Loans Board (HELB). HELB provides loans and bursaries to needy students selected to join public universities through JAB. Every year, JAB selects about 10,000 students (out of approximately 250,000 KCSE candidates) to join public universities. These figures show that there is a huge unfulfilled demand for higher education in Kenya.

Although most candidates apply through JAB for admission to public university programs in human medicine, pharmacy, law, engineering, computer science and commerce, because of the immense popularity of these programs, very few are selected. Many applicants are instead placed in arts, education and general science degree courses in which they have no interest. Due to the need for a balanced equation between public universities and degree programs for only 10,000 students, JAB admits students to public universities for courses they never chose. Consequently, most university students on government sponsorship are not even interested in the degree programs for which they are studying at the expense of the public.

Pre-university upgrading or bridging programs have been established in both public and private universities. These programs are intended for students who have completed secondary school education yet do not qualify for direct admission to higher education. The programs thus prepare participants for university education. To be admitted, a student must have scored a minimum of grade C− on the KCSE (or its equivalent). Candidates who complete a bridging program with a minimum cumulative GPA of 2.3 qualify for admission to university degree programs. Several students are thus gaining entrance into degree programs in the public and private institutions of higher learning in Kenya through this path.

Undergraduate Enrollments

The current undergraduate enrollment in both public and private universities (including the privately sponsored students in public universities) is approximately 80,000 (56,400 male and 23,600 female). The regular undergraduate students, whose university education is subsidized by the government, number approximately 40,000, while around 30,000 privately sponsored students also enroll in public universities, and the private universities enroll close to 10,000, as depicted in Figure 1.

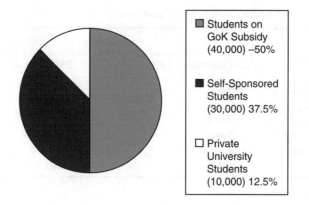

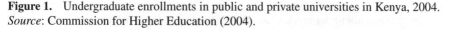

Figure 1. Undergraduate enrollments in public and private universities in Kenya, 2004. *Source*: Commission for Higher Education (2004).

The tremendous growth in student enrollments began after the 1990s, when public universities introduced privately self-sponsored degree programs popularly known as parallel programs. Through the privately self-sponsored programs, candidates who scored a minimum grade of C+ on the Kenya Certificate of Secondary Education or its equivalent—but were not selected by the Joint Admissions Board because of limited capacities in the public universities—can obtain admission. The number of students enrolled in this program at the University of Nairobi has risen rapidly, from 756 students in the 1998–99 academic year to 15,115 during the 2003–2004 academic year, a growth rate of close to 2,000% over a span of six years. Student enrollment in the self-sponsored program at Moi University has increased from 277 in the 1998–99 academic year to 4,000 in the 2003–2004 academic year, an increase of 1,444% over six years. The privately self-sponsored students currently account for 43% of the total undergraduate student population in public universities.

Postgraduate Enrollments

Postgraduate students in public universities have grown as rapidly as the undergraduate category. At the University of Nairobi, postgraduate enrollment is currently standing at about 5,500, having shot up from 1,000 in 1990 (representing a 550% increase). This growth in postgraduate enrollment has been seen at other institutions as well, as reflected in Table 2. The private university sector has also expanded its training at the postgraduate level, although quantifiable data are not readily available.

Gender and Regional Disparities

Gender and regional inequalities have shaped—and continue to shape—the development of education in Kenya. Female students constitute about 30% of the total enrollments in public universities; they pursue less rewarding degree courses in arts and social sciences, and very few are able to continue their education at postgraduate levels. As

Table 2.   Growth in Kenya's Postgraduate Enrollment

Institution	Undergraduate	Postgraduates			Postgraduates/ Undergraduates Ratio
		1990	1994–95	2004	
University of Nairobi	27,000	1,000		5,500	1:5
Kenyatta University	15,000	67		1,200	1:12
Moi University	14,000	70		350	1:40
Egerton University	10,000		2	150	1:66
Maseno University	4,811		1	198	1:24
JKUAT	6,000		10	82	1:75

Source: Ngome (2003).

a result, women are under represented in university teaching, research and administration. Under participation of women in higher education is attributed to the observation that they attend poor quality secondary schools in disproportionately higher numbers, have restricted access to a broad range of curriculum (particularly in the sciences) and are also victims of cultural and religious beliefs that depict women as less competent than their male counterparts—attitudes that influence family investment decisions and place a higher premium on boys than girls. Although JAB has initiated some affirmative action initiatives, helping women to enter the university with lower minimum entry requirements than those of their male counterparts, this action has not yet had much impact.

Gender equity is more apparent in private universities, where 50% or more of the student population is female. At USIU, 52% of the students are female, while Daystar reports that 64% of its population is female. The reason often cited by parents is that they feel their female children are more secure in the private university environment. It may also be related to the fact that most private universities tend to offer programs in the humanities, which are programs female students are likely to select (Brown, 2001, p. 13).

In Kenya—as is the case in other African countries—members of those communities that made the earliest and more stable contacts with European settlers, missionaries and colonial authorities have tended to have more access to formal educational opportunities than their counterparts elsewhere in the country. Thus, it is no surprise that members of the Kikuyu, Luyia, Luo, Meru, Embu, Kisii and Kamba communities—which had the longest association with these entities and inhabit economically higher potential areas of the country (and by extension enjoy the most developed primary and secondary systems)—are over represented in both public and private universities.

Funding Patterns in Public and Private Universities

University Student Loan Scheme

When Kenya gained its independence in 1963, all fees for tertiary education were abolished. This policy was designed to motivate large numbers of students to pursue higher education and to provide adequate middle- and high-level human resource requirements for the economy. In 1974, the government changed the financing of university education by introducing a student loan scheme as a cost-sharing strategy. The cost of a university education was increasing along with the annual increases in student enrollments. The student numbers had grown tremendously, from 600 in 1963 to 6,000 students in 1974, representing a 1,000% increase. The education budget had also grown, from below 29% of total government recurrent expenditures to 34% in 1974. This was occurring against a backdrop of financial difficulties due to the country's adverse macro-economic performance, rapid population growth and the burden of providing basic services like primary education and health. University education therefore faced severe competition from other sectors of the economy for limited government funds.

Through the 1974 student loan scheme, the government transferred some of the costs of university education—particularly catering and accommodation—to the beneficiaries, and hoped to develop a revolving fund to meet such costs in the future. To cushion the poor against the adverse effects of the new policy, loans and bursaries were introduced under the Higher Education Management Board in 1974, which was a section in the Ministry of Education until 1994, when it was dissolved. Due to poor recovery procedures that lacked a sound legal framework to pursue defaulters, the rates of default on these loans ranged from 75% to 80%. The concept of developing a revolving fund from which more students would benefit was therefore thwarted. As a result, the International Monetary Fund (IMF) and the World Bank advised the government of Kenya to establish an autonomous body with the legal framework to enable loan collection and reduce the number of defaulters, with the ultimate purpose of setting up a revolving account from which loan funds could be drawn for supporting needy Kenyans pursuing higher education. This led to the establishment of the Higher Education Loans Board (HELB) in 1995.

Since its inception, HELB has made significant strides in the area of loan recovery, from a 1995 recovery portfolio of US$38,462 per month to the current level of US$641,026 per month (weighed against adverse realities such as limited employment opportunities for university graduates). Consequently, on the current total loan amount of US$14.1 million that HELB awards to university students per year, 45% of it is provided by recoveries from past loans, while 55% is provided by the exchequer. Disbursement to undergraduate students in public and private chartered universities is 98% of the total amount, whereas graduate (master's and doctoral) students receive a paltry 2%. Disbursement to undergraduate students is also skewed against needy students in private chartered universities, who are awarded only 2% (while their counterparts in public universities enjoy 97% of the total disbursement).

This performance notwithstanding, HELB faces a number of challenges. First, HELB charges an annual interest rate of 4% on its loans, against an inflation rate that has averaged at about 8% for the last decade. In other words, for every US$100 that HELB gives to students, it recovers up to US$50. Second, HELB is a widely misunderstood organization, about which students have vehemently complained. Criticism revolves around the amount of money students receive from HELB, which is deemed inadequate. HELB loans, which range from US$513 to US$667 per year, cannot cushion students against the country's high inflation rates. Third, means testing instruments used to identify needy students are not accurate. According to some media reports, HELB has over the years been cheated into giving loans to undeserving students. Over 25% of student applicants have been found to be dishonest with HELB (Odalo, 2000).

The most serious challenge to any means-tested loan system lies in identifying needy applicants. Developing such systems is difficult even in industrialized countries, in which a majority of people annually file income information with the tax authorities. The task is particularly daunting in developing countries like Kenya, where large numbers of families (even the economically able ones) are likely to apply for loans and bursaries and operate in a semi-subsistence mode that makes verifying income and wealth data extremely difficult (Assie-Lumumba, 1994). Fourth, HELB experiences major difficulties in recovering loans from unemployed beneficiaries or those working in the informal sector. The Act of Parliament that established HELB empowers it to collect loans from people who are in formal employment, yet the total share of employment in the informal sector increased from 65% in 1997 to 72% in 2001, whereas the rate of growth in formal sector employment decreased from 2.1% in 1998 to a negative 1.1% in 2001. A fifth challenge is the negative attitude of most beneficiaries of HELB's loans. Even when some of the past beneficiaries are able to repay their loans, some of them regard loans from HELB as "free government money" that should not be repaid. For instance, the 3,262 graduates of the University of Nairobi's Faculty of Law (who attended between 1974 and 2003) are among the few Kenyans doing well economically. Yet, in spite of their economic ability, they owe over US$3 billion to HELB as un-serviced loans and do not show a willingness to pay. HELB will be required to invoke its powers to prosecute loan defaulters and their employers in order to limit instances of defaulting.

Financing in the Public University Sector

Funding of public universities in Kenya (as in most other African countries) is provided by the government. Unlike the period following independence, when universities were the main beneficiaries of government support, recent trends indicate a steady decline in such support as a result of fiscal constraints. For example, budgetary allocations to public universities were cut by 6.6% between the 1995–96 and 1996–97 financial years (from US$57.7 million to US$54.5 million) and then by another 3% in the 1997–98 financial year (to US$52.4 million) (Republic of Kenya, 1997, 1998a, 1998b, 1998c). The reductions in financial outlays to public universities at a time of rising student enrollments has meant that increased enrollment is not being matched with corresponding increases in the provision of physical facilities and equipment to care for their growth. Consequently, the use of existing facilities is over-stretched, while their maintenance has been poor, owing to limited recurrent expenditure funds.

Before 1995, the funding of public universities by the government was based on budgets submitted by each university that were derived from projections of actual needs. The scenario changed drastically in 1995, following the introduction of a unit cost system of financing public universities—defined as the amount of money a university spends on one student per degree program. The current unit cost of US$1,538 consists of tuition (US$897) and catering, accommodation and other incidental costs (US$641).

The government provides US$897 as a grant, while students pay US$641. Students from economically able backgrounds are expected to pay for themselves while those from poor families apply for loans from HELB. Government funding per university is calculated by multiplying the total number of students in the university by US$897. Unfortunately, the unit cost system has been found to be grossly inadequate as a system of funding public universities because of three reasons.

First, the unit cost formula currently in use was based on the 1991–92 audited accounts of universities, and as such does not take into consideration the current inflation rate. Second, the unit cost system does not take into account different costs of the various degree programs. It actually introduces a distortion or inequity in the funding of public universities by the government. Institutions which host expensive science and technology-based degree programs (like the Universities of Nairobi, Egerton, Jomo Kenyatta and Moi) are disadvantaged over those who offer predominantly arts-based programs, like Kenyatta and Maseno Universities. This should not, however, be misconstrued to indicate that Kenyatta and Maseno universities are adequately funded, as the cheapest degree program per student costs US$2,333, while the most expensive is approximately US$6,410.

Third, postgraduate students were excluded while computing the unit cost. As a result, there is no government funding for postgraduate students at present. This undermines the need to enhance postgraduate enrollment to at least 10% of the total undergraduate population and increase research output. The use of a defective unit cost as a basis for providing budgetary allocations to public universities has worsened the already existing problem where these institutions are unable to balance their operating budgets and have thus continued to accumulate debts.

The government under funding of public universities is aggravated by escalating debts and deficits, limited alternative sources of funds, rising payroll and operational expenditures, inefficient fees collection from students and limited returns from full-cost recovery units like catering and accommodation. Reductions in government financial outlays to these institutions has had several adverse effects. Physical facilities in public universities are dilapidated; equipment in critical teaching areas has become unserviceable, with great loss to the quality of teaching; library services are inadequate and disorganized; and all institutions struggle to attract and retain a high caliber academic staff. Meanwhile, revenues from the government of Kenya continue to shrink. On the basis of public policy statements by relevant authorities in the country, there have been strong indications that the government will no longer fully finance public universities. Rather, public universities have been advised to find ways and means of raising additional funds to support their activities. As a consequence of this, public higher education institutions have had to consider various ways of mobilizing resources that include adoption of austerity measures and enhancement of income-generating activities so as to minimize dependence on government funding.

Financing of Private Universities

The private university sector in Kenya is largely self-financing, relying on student tuition and fees for the bulk of its revenue. For example, during the late 1990s, tuition and fees accounted for an average of 100% of the total university income at the United States International University, 74% at Daystar University, 72% at Catholic University of Eastern Africa and 40% at Baraton. Tuition and fees generate most of the income for private universities because it is charged on the basis of full-cost recovery, which puts the cost of private higher education in the country beyond the reach of most people because of the increasing spread of poverty. Tuition and fees in private universities are much more than what public universities charge for both regular and self-sponsored academic programs. The cost of a social science degree program in private universities ranges from US$1,658 per year at the Catholic University of Eastern Africa to US$2,652 at the United States International University, whereas in self-sponsored programs in public universities it ranges from US$1,026 at Moi and Egerton Universities to US$1,538 at the Universities of Nairobi and Kenyatta.

The cost of accommodation and catering is also much higher in private universities than in public universities, where (for example) government-supported students pay US$265 per year at Egerton University and US$334 at the University of Nairobi. Although the rates for self-sponsored students are slightly higher (ranging from US$436 to US$462), they are still much lower than for those at private universities, whose costs range from US$1,153 at Catholic University to US$2,130 at the United States International University. As is the case with tuition, catering and accommodation charges by private universities are on a full-cost recovery basis for all materials, utilities, maintenance and replacement costs expended at the residence halls and kitchens.

Other sources of funds for private universities in Kenya come in the form of auxiliary enterprises (commonly referred to as income generating activities in public universities), student loans, bursaries and scholarships, donations, grants, gifts, endowment and alumni. Baraton University may arguably be said to be the private institution in the country with the most developed auxiliary enterprises. Between 1994–95 and 1999–2000, Baraton raised about 36% of its annual income from auxiliary enterprises (Wesonga, Ngome, Ouma, & Wawire, 2003). In private universities, most development expenditures come from donations, while a good percentage of tuition and other fees go towards recurrent expenditures. This is true for most private universities in Kenya except the United States International University, whose recurrent and development expenditures are largely funded by tuition and fees. The typical donation approach follows a pattern where a project is identified and a proposal is sent to an oversees donor who provides either capital funding or expertise or both (Deloitte and Touche, 1994, p. 92).

Recurrent expenditure in private universities revolves around staff salaries and benefits, purchases of teaching and learning materials, and maintenance of facilities and research. Salaries and benefits constitute the greatest expenditure item, ranging from 36% at Baraton University to 50% at the Catholic University (according to 1994–1995 through 1999–2000 academic year statistics), followed by purchases of teaching and learning materials (ranging from about 3% to 12%). Maintenance of facilities is ranked third (ranging from 0.5% to 2.1%) while research receives the smallest budgetary allocation (ranging from 0.2% to 2%).

The recurrent expenditure patterns in the private sector contrast sharply with the gloomy picture in public universities, where staff salaries and benefits consume as much as 75% of budgetary allocations. This is one of the examples of the relatively efficient and cost-conscious style of administration characterizing most Kenyan private universities. Although research is an important aspect of university education, this is not reflected in the annual allocations. Public universities are also characterized by poor allocations to research activities. For private and public universities to keep up with their mandate of conducting relevant research in Kenya, universities will have to substantially increase money for research.

The financial situation in private universities is healthy. Most of them are solvent and are usually able to post an operating surplus. This encouraging financial condition is due to a number of factors. First, student fees and welfare services are calculated on cost recovery levels. Second, private universities are characterized by the efficient collection and management of fees. Third, the approach of reaching out to the alumni, philanthropists, the private sector and friends of the universities (a standard method of fundraising in leading universities throughout the world) is being followed by private universities in Kenya. Four, the incidence of misappropriation of university funds is low (compared to public universities).

New Modes of Delivery

In addition to utilizing the conventional campus classroom-based teaching approach, universities in Kenya are embracing new delivery mechanisms to expand access to university education in the country. These mechanisms include virtual learning, distance learning, school-based programs and accreditation of middle-level colleges.

Virtual Learning

The rapid and continuing growth and development of information and communication technologies (ICTs) is transforming the ways in which we live, work and learn. In higher education, the effective use of these new technologies offers new ways in which quality, effectiveness and (in particular) flexibility of higher education can be improved. This has made possible the creation of virtual universities, where quality professors, libraries and other utilities can be shared by people and organizations in physically un-connected places. Virtual universities have the advantage of requiring minimum capital investments and operating costs. The concept of virtual learning was popularized in Africa through the African Virtual University (AVU) project. The AVU project—which was started on a pilot basis in 1997 with the support of the World Bank and multilateral donors like the Canadian International Development Agency (CIDA), Department for International Development (DFID) and the U.S. Agency for International Development (USAID)—is a distance learning network with 25 centers distributed across the African continent, with headquarters in Nairobi. Two of these centers are in Kenya, located at Kenyatta and Egerton Universities. Online degree courses are transmitted from different institutions in the U.S. and Australia. These include U.S. institutions such as

Georgetown University, New Jersey Institute of Technology, and Indiana University, as well as Australia's Curtin University of Technology. The AVU sites at Kenyatta and Egerton Universities also offer certificate courses and organize seminars. Between 1997 and 2001, more than 10,000 Kenyans from different professional backgrounds benefited from these programs.

Distance Learning

Although the initial cost of setting up the infrastructure for distance-based learning are high, Nairobi and Kenyatta universities are investing in it because the final costs to learners and institutions are low. Management costs of having residential students and maintaining the physical plant and equipment are reduced. Through its College of Education and External Studies Department, the University of Nairobi offers distance-based academic programs via its regional extramural centers in Mombasa, Kisumu, Kakamega, Nyeri and Nakuru. Kenyatta University has also set up regional centers in seven provinces of the country (Nairobi, Western, Nyanza, Eastern, Northeastern, Coast and Central) to manage its distance education programs. Subject to the availability of funds, Kenyatta University has planned to establish a frequency modulation (FM) radio station to broadcast its programs to students in some of its centers.

School-Based Programs

The innovative development of scheduling courses in the evenings and weekends for privately self-sponsored programs, allowing working people to pursue a university education while continuing to manage their regular responsibilities, has not accommodated teachers at the primary, secondary and middle-level institutions who reside in rural areas. To cater to this category of learners, school-based programs have been initiated by all public universities (except JKUAT, which does not offer teacher-training programs) and one private university, Catholic University of Eastern Africa. Students in these school-based programs attend residential training in April, August and December, as well as during school holidays, and participate in three months of tutorial visits (practicum) by lecturers when schools are in session. Close to 10,000 teachers are currently enrolled in these programs at undergraduate and postgraduate levels.

Accreditation of Middle-Level Colleges

Public universities are extending the opportunity for high-level human resource training outside their walls by collaborating with middle-level tertiary training institutions located in various parts of the country which meet accreditation status. JKUAT has accredited 18 middle-level colleges in both urban and rural parts of the country, and has been the most visible employer of this strategy of enhancing access. Besides accreditation of middle-level colleges, universities that are located far away from towns—such as Egerton, Moi, Maseno and Kenyatta—have been compelled to establish town campus centers nearer to their target populations.

Improving the Status of Information Communication Technology

On a comparative basis, private universities have better information and communication technologies (ICT) facilities than the public universities. Of the private universities, United States International University is on the forefront, with the highest quality Internet connections, electronic database, fax, satellites, CD-ROM databases, mobile phones, and so forth. In 2002, USIU had a computer/student ratio of 1:19, with comparable ratios at Baraton (1:30), Catholic University of East Africa (1:25), and Daystar University (1:22); the average computer/student ratio for all private universities is 1:24 (Wesonga, Ngome, Ouma, & Wawire, 2003).

In contrast, the public universities face a severe shortage of computer facilities. While Internet facilities have reached all universities in Kenya, Kenyatta University and Egerton University have had better equipment owing to the AVU sites that they have hosted. The AVU has enabled these two universities to offer courses via satellite and maintain sophisticated Internet-based digital library of journals, academic studies and textbooks. The University of Nairobi completed a four-phase project in 2002 that was geared toward providing a high-speed backbone infrastructure linking all its campuses and improving Internet service to staff and students. The Kenya Education Network (KENET), launched in 2001, is expected to enhance ICT services at the universities. Daystar University has a communication studio and is preparing to host an FM radio station, much like Kenyatta University. While most of these developments date back to 1997, their early growth was hampered by poor infrastructure and scarcity in capital financial resources; development in this field has also depended on the proximity of an institution to major urban centers. Recent achievements are, however, commendable.

Staffing Challenges and Brain Drain

The effectiveness of a university essentially depends on the efficiency and quality of its academic and non-academic staff. In an economic environment characterized by declining resources and rising enrollments, all universities in Kenya face the challenge of how to do more with less, which involves the recruitment and retention of competent staff. The supply of academic staff to universities, especially at the Ph.D. level, has rapidly diminished over the years due to reduced opportunities for scholarships and the high cost of postgraduate training in view of the diminishing incomes of most families and the poor performance of the Kenyan economy. As a result of this, the number of lecturers who hold Ph.D. degrees has declined throughout the country. At the University of Nairobi—the oldest and biggest in the country, with over 100 academic programs at both undergraduate and postgraduate levels—only 40% of the teaching force hold Ph.D. degrees. Similarly, 33% of the faculty at Kenyatta, 32% of the faculty at Moi and 19% of the faculty at Egerton have doctoral degrees (Ngome, 2003a). Except for USIU, where 46% of its staff hold doctorates, the situation in most private universities is equally grim (see Table 3).

The low quality of academic staff in Kenyan universities is due to poor conditions and terms of service. Over the years, the purchasing power of lecturers in universities has been eroded considerably by inflation. As a result, the title of a university professor

Table 3. Faculty Qualifications in Public and
Selected Private Universities in Kenya

University	Masters	Ph.D.
Nairobi	60%	40%
Kenyatta	67%	33%
Moi	68%	32%
Egerton	69%	19%
USIU	54%	48%
Dayster	88%	12%
Catholic	90%	10%

Source: Ngome (2003).

has lost its financial meaning. The gradual decline in buying power of academic staff salaries over the last 27 years (from 1976–2003) is depicted in Table 4, in which the purchasing power of academic staff is shown to have decreased by over 74%.

As a result, thousands of Kenyan scholars, dissatisfied with the terms and conditions of service, have migrated to places like the United States, Canada, Australia, Europe and throughout Southern Africa (including Botswana, Lesotho, Namibia, Swaziland and South Africa). Rwanda is the latest attraction point owing to the generous pay package that international organizations are offering to scholars that are contributing to the rebuilding of that country. A peer comparison between academics in Kenyan public universities and their peers in Botswana reproduced as Table 5 indicates that, on average, salaries in Botswana are over five times those in public universities in Kenya. It is little wonder that Botswana is one of the preferred destination of Kenyan scholars.

This brain drain phenomenon is impacting negatively on local universities. For example, USIU has advertised for positions in industrial psychology, clinical

Table 4. Decline in the Buying Power of Academic Staff Salaries 1976–2003

	Lecturer		Senior Lecturer		Associate Professor		Professor	
Year	Kshs	US$	Kshs	US$	Kshs	US$	Kshs	US$
1976	3,000	429	4,620	660	6,000	857	7,200	1,029
1986	6,040	288	8,085	385	10,520	501	12,570	599
1997	11,755	203	14,545	251	18,320	327	20,650	368
1998	17,185*	286	21,440*	357	26,855*	448	31,060*	518
1999	17,185*	246	21,440*	306	26,855*	384	31,060*	444
2000	17,185*	226	21,440*	282	26,855*	353	31,060*	409
2003	17,185*	220	21,440*	275	26,855*	344	31,060*	398

Note: *The figures were the minimum entry for the posts.
Source: Ngome (2003).

Table 5. Comparison of Annual Salaries Between Kenya's Public Universities and Those of University of Botswana (in US$)

Grade	Kenya	Botswana
Tutorial Fellow	$2,403	$8,439
Lecturer	2,046	12,744
Senior Lecturer	3,675	24,669
Associate Professor	4,604	30,255
Professor	5,325	34,014

Source: Ngome (2003).

psychology, information technology, finance and marketing at professional levels with limited success for several years. International recruitment is costly and quite often beyond the budgets of most higher education institutions. When international faculty are recruited, it is often for a two-year period or less. The timeframe is too short to transfer skills to a local faculty member. This means that once the resource leaves, the expertise (and often the program) goes with them (Brown, 2001, p. 5). Most departments in Kenyan universities have been so hard hit by brain drain that they are only a pale shadow of their former self.

However, the recent increase (as of July 2004) of academic staff salaries by the government—147% for lecturers, 130% for senior lecturers, 132% for associate professor and 117% for professors—is anticipated to promote competition and lead to the return of many Kenyan scholars from outside the country and the private sector. In fact, Kenyan public universities are now at par with even the most competitive private university (USIU) with regard to faculty remuneration. This may have repercussions for private universities, which have over relied on previously poorly remunerated pubic university faculty.

Quality

Since the 1970s, Kenya enjoyed the reputation of a country that offers some of the highest quality university education in Africa. This reputation has, however, come under attack in recent years by members of the public and by the mass media, particularly represented by commentaries and complaints in the local newspapers. These attacks stem from the challenges in the public university sector posed by an increase in the total number of students without a concomitant increase in resources or the development of the university's infrastructure. The labor market has expressed concern about the mediocre quality of Kenyan university students, particularly regarding their perceived inability to respond flexibly, creatively and competently to the responsibilities that are placed on their shoulders.

University staff are aware of this problem and of the challenges that graduates face, but many of them feel that they cannot adequately prepare their students for their future responsibilities because they are tied (by the students themselves) to a form of

Table 6. Effectiveness of Kenya Public Private and Foreign Universities in Fostering Attributes Most Commonly Reflected in Management Literature

Attributes	Kenyan Public Universities			Kenyan Private Universities			Foreign Universities		
	VE*	MOE*	NVE*	VE*	MOE*	NVE*	VE*	MOE*	NVE*
General competence	17%	73%	10%	28%	72%	0%	57%		4%
Initiative	10%	53%	38%	33%	61%	6%	57%	39%	4%
Discipline	7%	48%	45%	33%	56%	11%	35%	39%	4%
Creativity	10%	62%	38%	17%	61%	22%	48%	61%	4%
Leadership	14%	52%	34%	11%	78%	11%	48%	48%	0%
Adaptability	66%	7%	27%	17%	72%	11%	43%	52%	9%
Responsibility	7%	41%	52%	17%	67%	16%	35%	48%	4%

Note: *VE = very effective; *MOE = moderately effective; *NVE = not very effective.
Source: Deloitte and Touche (1994).

teaching that does not go much beyond expository methods. Students perceive university learning (in both public and private universities) as consisting primarily of the reproduction of poorly assimilated lecture notes, while resources (textbooks, library materials, reproduction facilities, science supplies) are so limited that a teaching style that forces students to think (and penalizes those who do not) cannot in fairness be adopted. This condition is corroborated by CHE's 1994 study of private universities (Deloitte and Touche, 1994), which surveyed many aspects of private tertiary education in the country and also examined employers' attitudes towards Kenyan university graduates. Except for adaptability, graduates from foreign and private universities scored much higher than their public counterparts on measures of general competence, initiative, discipline, creativity, leadership and responsibility (see Table 6).

The quality crisis is further illustrated by university students' inadequate grasp of the English language. One lecturer from the Department of English and Linguistics at Kenyatta University argues that it would be better if students learned no English at all in primary and secondary schools. They are taught so poorly that much of the instructor's time in the university is spent on re-teaching them the foundations of the language (Ngome, 2003b). Since the English language is the medium of instruction in the Kenyan system of education, students' poor command of the language does not bode well for the quality of education. Many students in both public and private universities lack knowledge of basic grammar, such as the rules governing the use of capital letters, and are also incompetent in analyzing the grammatical structure of simple sentences (Indangasi, 1991).

Also identified as a contributing factor to deteriorating quality is the condition of libraries in public universities. Libraries in these institutions (as is the case with other facilities) have been overstretched beyond their limits, and are witnessing unprecedented congestion. Currently, the University of Nairobi library has a seating capacity of 6,000, but is serving a student population of 22,000. Similar patterns hold true for other public universities in Kenya. The services available in public university libraries are generally poor. The bulk of available books and journals are outdated. Acquisitions have not increased to take account of increasing student numbers. Although new degree programs have been initiated in recent years, relevant library resources have not been purchased. It is actually very hard to find out what is in these libraries, as there is no holdings list for journals. Whole catalogues and shelves do not seem to match. The lack of adequate security has led to significant vandalism and theft of books. In essence, libraries are no longer at the heart of teaching and research. However, since lecturers often hold other jobs and have little time to do research or keep up-to-date, and since their methods of teaching do not encourage student reading or project work, there is little reason for library services to improve.

Private universities have comparatively better libraries. Their libraries are financed by a designated portion of the students' fees, as is the provision of textbooks. When teaching staff give their libraries a list of recommended readings, the books are imme-diately purchased because the money is available in the library account. Improvements in the amount of money spent on books and journals (as well as the construction of libraries) by private universities is largely due to pressure from CHE. The standards laid down by this body (with powers to recognize or not recognize a private university) ensure that private institutions of higher learning allocate funding to their libraries (Rosenberg, 1997).

The strain on the existing physical facilities and staff in institutions of higher learning, particularly public ones, due to the dramatic rise in student enrollment—far more than originally planned—has also had a debilitating impact on the quality of education. With the exception of JKUAT, which has benefited significantly from the Japanese government and World Bank donor support, the congestion in public universities is pathetic. Universities are cramming between four and five students into dormitory rooms designed to accommodate only two students. Financial pressure has led some students who are officially accommodated to sublet their dormitory spaces to non-resident students. The incidence of squatting in dormitories is on the increase. Hughes and Mwiria (1990, p. 228) found that lecturers in the Faculty of Education at Kenyatta University are compelled to repeat the same lectures to as many as three groups of students because of a lack of adequate lecture theatres, while in extreme cases some students listen to their lectures through windows.

Private universities have dealt more cautiously with the pressure to expand. They have been reluctant to expand at the cost of quality. While the expansion of opportunities in public universities is meeting excess demand for higher education, this should not be done at the expense of quality. Adequate planning for expansion should be done to ensure that students receive enough attention from their lecturers.

Students and lecturers have also intensified the quality crisis by condoning examina-tions leakages and by promoting lifestyles that are the antithesis of academic pursuits (such as prostitution, drug and alcohol consumption). Both public and private universi-ties are rife with allegations that some male lecturers solicit sexual favors from female students in order to improve their grades, while others extort money from male students in return for leaked examination questions and marking schemes.

Quality Enhancement Strategies

The quality crisis is affecting the ability of Kenyan universities to fulfill their fundamental visions, missions and objectives. This crisis is more evident in the public university sector than in the private universities. These institutions have been forced to respond to the crisis in a number of ways, including the introduction of common units of study, adoption of better teaching and learning techniques, and strengthening of student assessment mechanisms and staff motivation.

Introduction of common units of study: All public universities (and most of the private universities) have introduced common units of study intended to produce multi skilled and responsible graduates. These courses include communication skills, development and gender studies, HIV/AIDS and drugs, introduction to computing and entrepreneurship skills.

Adoption of better teaching techniques and staff motivation: Several measures have been taken to improve the quality of teaching. First, allocation of courses for most of the programs (in both public and private universities) is done in such a way as to ensure that whoever teaches a unit to the regular students also teaches the same unit to the evening and weekend students. Second, large classes are being divided into manageable teaching groups, while at the same time pursuing efforts to revive the tutorial system in public universities, which had collapsed during the 1990s. Third, universities are discouraging the over-reliance on the "talk and chalk" methods of teaching in favor of transparencies and overhead projectors. Along this line, some institutions are considering offering short courses on pedagogical aspects (for lecturers who are not professional teachers) as a way of improving their delivery and effectiveness in teaching. Fourth, lecturers are being encouraged (particularly at Kenyatta University) to post their lecture notes and other supplementary material on the institution's website. Fifth, a system of assessing and reviewing learning and teaching materials has been proposed at the University of Nairobi, particularly at its Faculty of Law, because there has been little evidence to show that contact hours are met across the board or that the content offered meets the requirements of a university curriculum. Sixth, assessment by students (which is a common feature in United States institutions of higher learning) has been introduced at one private and one public university (United States International University and Kenyatta University). At these institutions, students appraise their lecturers at the end of every unit or semester. It is anticipated that once this initiative is fully operational, other universities in the country will emulate it. It is also hoped that student/staff appraisal will not only help assess the productivity of staff but will also motivate performance and identify areas that need further pedagogical training.

Relevance

As pressure mounts for demand-driven academic programs, most universities in Kenya are responding to the challenges by offering courses that are tailored to the labor market. Various universities have developed (and are still developing) partnerships with private sector enterprises to help hone the skills of their students along required dimensions. Jomo Kenyatta University of Agriculture and Technology has initiated a partnership with an international company to help design and review its information and technology programs. At Moi University, the Faculty of Medicine has adopted a system called Problem-Based Learning, where students take a practicum in rural areas to acquaint themselves with typical field situations in the areas where they will work upon graduation. The Department of Medical Microbiology of the University of Nairobi—in collaboration with the University of Manitoba (Canada) and Oxford University, and with support from the International Aids Vaccine Initiative (IAVI)— are carrying out research on HIV/AIDS and generating a wealth of information on the virology of HIV infections.

Kenyatta University's Center for Complementary Medicine and Biotechnology (CCMB) is conducting scientific research on herbal medicine jointly with herbal medicine practitioners as part and parcel of the ongoing national effort by the government of Kenya and the Kenya Medical Research Institute to integrate the use of herbal medicine into conventional medical practice. In this venture, Kenyatta University has been able to benefit from the wealth of experience possessed by herbalists who do not hold university degrees. Except for Scott Theological College, all the chartered universities and those granted letters of interim authority are performing commendably well in the provision of relevant skills. Essentially, relevance is their lifeline. Most of these institutions carry out a market survey before launching new academic programs. Industrial attachments for their students in the world of work form a key training component. These institutions also maintain strong links with business and industry, mainly through their alumni and other stakeholder groups who come to address staff and students regularly. Community-based attachments aimed at instilling a spirit of service are compulsory for degree students at the United States International and Strathmore Universities. These efforts notwithstanding, most academic programs in registered private universities (small biblical colleges) are not attractive to students because they are related to biblical studies and preaching. In public universities, out of the 178 degree programs offered, only 26 are popular to students, 63 are rated as average, and the remaining 89 are seen as unattractive (Daily Nation, 2004).

Conclusions: Impact of Change, Challenges and Lessons Learned

The ongoing reforms in higher education in Kenya have produced positive and negative consequences and also revealed important lessons about the complexities of this process. The most noticeable positive effect of the reforms is enhanced access to university education. The university student population has dramatically grown from about 3,000 in 1970 to approximately 80,000 in 2004. Despite this massive expansion of student enrollments in Kenya, regional, socio-economic and gender imbalances continue to characterize university education in the country. The demands of an expanded student population and the need to generate supplemental income have resulted in the decentralization of the monitoring and administration of the reform process. For example, the University of Nairobi established a new entity called the University of Nairobi Enterprises and Services Limited. Moi University established the Moi University Holding Company Limited, to oversee non-teaching income generating activities, and the Privately Sponsored Students Program Directorate, to manage the self-sponsored academic programs. The other four public universities have similar structures. This decentralization notwithstanding, most of these management units do not have direct access to the funds they generate, since public higher learning institutions' financial transactions are processed through designated university signatories.

The internally generated funds are contributing greatly to the development of public universities. Old buildings have been renovated, plant maintenance improved, stalled projects completed and new buildings are under construction. Procurement of teaching and learning materials is also improving. Staff morale is rising, as individuals are compensated for services rendered through self-sponsored academic programs. Quality improvement measures, enhancement of relevance of demand-driven academic programs, improved efficiency in the use of resources, improved capacity for strategic planning and prioritization of needs—these are other positive consequences of the reform process in public universities. Nevertheless, there are some negative trends that have been engendered by the ongoing changes. First, the pay as you eat (PAYE) system, introduced in the 1990s as one of the cost-sharing measures in the public university sector, has been perceived as being expensive for students; consequently, the majority of students in public universities opt to cook for themselves in hostels, although they are aware of university rules and regulations that forbid cooking in residence halls. Mass cooking by students in hostels has increased the institutions' electricity bills. For example at Kenyatta University, the cost of electricity has shot up from about US$76,923 to over US$512,821 per financial year. Second, cooking in hostels poses a grave danger to the students' lives due to electricity overload. Public university hostels were never designed to accommodate mass cooking. To eliminate this problem, public universities will either have to provide hostels that have kitchens for students or the Higher Education Loans Board may have to pay catering and boarding fees directly to public universities for students who choose to reside on campus.

Third, the quality of education has declined. While increased access to university education and internal generation of funds by public universities is being realized, the quality of education is being sacrificed. Although universities require more financial resources and the country needs more doctors, scientists, lawyers and engineers (among other professionals), these people must be able to handle all the complexities of their respective professions by receiving sufficient education. Adequate planning for expansion has not been done to ensure that public university students receive enough attention from their lecturers.

The reform process has revealed critical challenges and lessons that relate to the internal dynamics of change (and the universities themselves) as well as the prevailing policies and practices of higher education in Kenya. First, the reform process has brought to the fore the fact that Kenya has developed a system of university education with 27 universities—six public, 17 private, and four offshore campuses—and structures of supporting institutions that include the Commission for Higher Education, the Joint Admissions Board and the Higher Education Loans Board. More than in any other country in Eastern and Central Africa, structures exist in Kenya that could provide for a rational and effective development of university education.

Second, the public and private universities are exhibiting interesting interactions in the ongoing transformation of higher education. They are influencing and complementing each other in several ways. The public universities' scheduling of teaching for most of the self-sponsored academic programs during the evenings and weekends, making it possible for working people to pursue university education while managing their regular responsibilities, has been borrowed from the private university sector. Private universities, on the other hand, benefit from public universities by utilizing their academic staff on a part-time basis to bridge their staff shortfall. Competition for students is another dimension of this interaction. That public universities are now attracting fee paying students has created a cut-throat competition not only among public universities, but also with private universities in the country. With higher education having become an international business, foreign universities are intensifying this competition by attracting Kenyan students to their institutions abroad or branch campuses within Kenya.

Third, the development of alternative funding sources by public universities could in the long run bridge the financial shortfalls from the exchequer. Large amounts of debt have been accumulated over the last several years, largely because of gross underfunding and inefficient utilization of the available meager resources. Attempts to reduce this heavy indebtedness through debt servicing have proved futile, thus exacerbating the financial crisis year after year. This debt must be liquidated through a combination of strategies, involving the use of internally generated funds and adoption of realistic unit costs by the government as a basis of funding public universities. It may be instructive to borrow a page from Makerere University in Uganda, where the government has decided on the number of students that it will fully fund (based on the degree programs) while others are charged the full cost fee. This should, however, be accompanied by a firm financial discipline, with a view to seeking improvements in the value for money of all public university functions and activities.

Fourth, although private universities in Kenya are playing a significant role by supplementing the government's efforts in expanding access to higher education at no extra cost to the public, the government has not given them a level playing field to succeed and develop to their full potential, in terms of broadening their higher education spectrum. The Commission for Higher Education employs restrictive regulatory mechanism in accrediting them. The Higher Education Loans Board discriminates against students from private universities. It provides only about 2% of its loans to students in private universities while their counterparts in public universities receive 98%.

Fifth, like other universities in sub-Saharan Africa, public universities in Kenya are struggling to emerge from two decades of crisis, in which financial constraints have resulted in institutional deterioration, loss of vision and mission, brain drain, waning of programmatic relevance and declining quality. A productive re-orientation and transformation process is taking place under the guidance of strategic plans, with a view toward improving efficiency and effectiveness. Enhancement of efficiency has also included the usual double entry solution of reducing expenditures and generating more income. The main strategy for generating more income has been the introduction of demand-driven, self-sponsored academic programs for students who, although meeting the minimum academic qualifications for admission to public universities, could not gain admission due to the competitive selection process that is limited by the university's physical capacity.

Despite these and other challenges discussed in this chapter, one must not end with a sense that all is lost. To the contrary, the future looks moderately bright for higher education in Kenya. The success, or failure, of both public and private universities in the country will clearly depend on thoughtful analysis, strategic planning, fiscal discipline and innovation.

References

Abagi, O. (1999). *Resource utilization in public universities in Kenya: Enhancing efficiency and cost-recovery measures.* Research Paper No. OP/05/99. Nairobi, Kenya: Institute of Policy Analysis & Research.

Abagi, O., & Nzomo, J. (2001). Structural reforms in higher education: Private higher education in Kenya. Unpublished research report, Nairobi, Kenya.

Accrediting Commission for Senior Schools and Colleges. (1988). *WASC Handbook* Oakland: Mills College.

Assie-Lumumba, N. T. (1993). *Higher education in Francophone Africa: Assessment of the potential of the traditional universities and alternatives for development.* Washington, DC: The World Bank.

British Council. (1996). Report on socioeconomic study of access to university education, performance, equity and gender issues. Nairobi, Kenya: unpublished research report.

Brown, F. (2001). The challenges facing private universities in Kenya: The case of United States International University (USIU). Unpublished Paper Presented at the Ford Foundation/Women Researchers of Kenya Seminar.

Commission for Higher Education. (2003). *Re-engineering university education for national development.* A report from the symposium on Kenyan university education. Nairobi, Kenya: CHE.

Commission for Higher Education. (2002). *University-industry linkage in Kenya.* A report of the workshop held in Kenya. Nairobi, Kenya: CHE.

Daily Nation. (2004). *Most courses students take are not popular.* Daily Nation, May 31, 9.

Delloite and Touche. (1994). *The Commission for Higher Education private universities study: Final report.* Nairobi, Kenya. Commission for Higher Education.

Hughes, R. & Mwiria, K. (1990). An essay on the implication of university expansion in Kenya. Higher Education, *19*, 215–237.

Indangasi, H. (1991). From linguistic to literary competency. Unpublished paper presented at a seminar on the Teaching of English and Literature, British Council Hall, Nairobi, Kenya.

Ngome, C. K. (2003a). Higher education in Kenya. In D. Teferra & P. G Altbach (Eds.), *African higher education: An international reference handbook.* Bloomington, IN: Indiana University Press.

Ngome, C. K. (2003b). Public university reform in Kenya: Mapping the key changes of the last decade at Kenyatta University. Unpublished research report, Nairobi, Kenya.

Ngome, C. K., Orodho, J. A., & Wesonga, D. (2003). Financing higher education in Kenya through students' loan scheme: Emerging challenges and prospects. Unpublished report prepared for the Higher Education Loans Board (HELB), Nairobi, Kenya.

Republic of Kenya. (2002). *Economic survey.* Nairobi, Kenya: Government Printers.

Republic of Kenya. (1998a). *Master plan on education and training 1997–2000.* Nairobi, Kenya: Jomo Kenyatta Foundation.

Republic of Kenya. (1998b). *Inter-ministerial committee on unit costs for public universities.* Nairobi, Kenya: Ministry of Education.

Republic of Kenya. (1998c). *Economic survey.* Nairobi, Kenya: Government Printer.

Republic of Kenya. (1997).*Economic survey.* Nairobi, Kenya: Government Printer.

Rosenberg, D. (Ed). (1997). *University libraries in Africa: A review of their current state and the future potential.* London, UK: International Africa Institute.

Saint, B. (1992). *Universities in Africa: strategies for stabilizing and revitalization.* World Bank Technical Paper no. 194. Africa Technical Department Series. Washington, DC: The World Bank.

Standa, E. M. (2000). Report of the Vice Chancellors' Committee on causes of disturbances/riots in public universities. Nairobi: Jomo Kenyatta Foundation.

Varsity Focus. (1999). A newsletter from the Office of the Vice Chancellor University of Nairobi. The 27th Graduation Ceremony. Nairobi, Kenya: The Office of the Vice Chancellor, University of Nairobi.

Wesonga, D., Ngome. C.K., Ouma, D., & Wawire, V. (2003). *Private provision of higher education in Kenya: An analysis of trends and issues in four select universities.* Report Sponsored by Ford Foundation and prepared for the Women Educational Researchers of Kenya (WERK), Nairobi, Kenya.

45

KOREA

Namgi Park
Gwangju National University of Education, Korea

Higher education in Korea can be traced to the 4th century. Higher education comparable to the Western universities and colleges was introduced into Korea at the end of the 19th century. The purpose of this chapter is to briefly introduce international scholars to the history, characteristics, recent challenges and responses, and future direction of Korean higher education.[1] The country faces a number of contemporary challenges, including a shrinking student population for higher education, difficulties in the provincial universities caused by the shrinking population, and developing a robust science and engineering education sector. Korea's government has established policies meant to respond to these challenges and to ensure a better future for Korean society, including a special budget to support higher education. The Korean case can be a good example for developing countries.

History of Korean Higher Education

The history of Korean higher education is closely intertwined with the ebb and flow of Korean culture and patterns of colonial domination by geographical neighbors. This chapter traces important developments in the recent history of Korean higher education.[2]

The first institution of higher education in Korea, Tae Hak (the Great School) of Korguryo dates back to 372 A.D., and is one of the oldest higher education institutions in the world. It was established by the government to educate public officials. There were also private higher educational institutions (Kyoung Dang) that were established somewhat later than Tae Hak. Private schools were established to meet the educational demands of provinces, demands that could not be met by Tae Hak in the capital.

The traditional higher education system, which had a private sector and an elite public university sector, continued to the end of the 19th century. This system worked as an important instrument for the governing classes to maintain their status. Throughout Korean history, those who wanted to be public officials had to pass examinations, and universities provided instruction for students who wanted to pass such examinations. As time passed, access to higher education was widened from a few royal classes to the entire governing class.

James J.F. Forest and Philip G. Altbach (eds.), International Handbook of Higher Education, 867–879.
© 2006 *Springer. Printed in the Netherlands.*

Institutions of higher education, comparable to the universities and four-year colleges of Western countries, have a history of a bit over 100 years in Korea. There were three different streams of influence leading to the establishment of Western-style higher education. The first stream was led by the Western missionaries, who established private higher education institutions such as Ewha Kak Dang (1886) and Sungsil Hak Dang (1897). The second stream was led by the Korean government, which established professional schools to teach Western knowledge such as medicine, telegraphy, industry, mining and agriculture, and languages. The third stream was led by the nationalistic pioneers to teach Western knowledge and to rescue the country from invasion by Japan or Western countries. The third stream continued until Korea was independent from Japanese rule in 1945.

After independence from the Japanese, the modern system of higher education was restructured and reorganized by the United States (1945–1948). At the time of Korean liberation from Japanese rule, there were 19 institutions of higher education in Korea with a total enrollment of 7,819 students and 1,490 faculty members. When the United States armed forces occupied Korea in September 1945, it took a series of significant steps to recognize and expand higher education, acting upon the recommendations of the Korean Committee on Education and the Council of Education. As a consequence, by the end of U.S. government control (1948), the number of higher education institutions had increased by 221% (to 42 institutions) and enrollment had increased by 307% (to 24,000 students).

In the earlier days of the First Republic (1948–1960), colleges and universities continued their growth in terms of student enrollments and the number of faculty. The total number of higher education institutions, however, remained constant, although there were changes in the status of individual institutions. Just before the outbreak of the Korean War, there were four universities, 29 colleges, two community colleges and seven miscellaneous colleges of higher education, with a total of 29,288 students enrolled and 2,049 faculty members.

The Korean War (1950–1953) completely paralyzed the entire system of higher education. Despite the initial setbacks, however, some higher education was carried on in refugee colleges and in the "Wartime Union College." After the war, government policy was tightened, and began to swing in the direction of slowing the establishment of new higher education institutions. The Presidential Decree on the Establishment of College and University Standards, promulgated in 1955, was a significant landmark of this new direction in higher education policy.

Under the Military Government (1961–1963), higher education in Korea went through a series of radical reforms. Enforcement of "rearrangement plans of higher education" involved drastic changes in the status of the existing higher education institutions, causing a great deal of controversy. During this period, the government began to strongly control even private universities and colleges. The government considered higher education as a main source of educated manpower and it tried to merge the "Five-Year Economic Development Plan" with the higher education plan. The main purpose for maintaining control was improving the quality of higher education graduates based on the economic development plan of Korea's emerging economy. Thus, the government enacted the Private College Law in 1963, which transferred many powers of the board of trustees and the president of each institution to the Ministry of Education (MOE). It also enacted the "Rule for Student Enrollment" in 1965, which gave the MOE the right to determine the number of new students to be admitted to higher education. Nevertheless, many private universities admitted more students than the government allowed. At the same time, the government diversified the higher education system through the establishment of more community colleges and vocational higher professional schools.

In the 1970s, the government began to increase the number of new students enrolled in higher education to meet the demand caused by the development of Korea's emerging economy. Thus, from 1973 to 1978, enrollment in higher education was increased by an average 11.8% per year. The major strategy that the government used to increase enrollment was manpower planning. Student quotas (the numbers of students allocated to each area of study) were determined on the basis of manpower demands for heavy industry. In 1973, ten pilot universities (nine private universities and one national university) inaugurated a series of reform projects or programs, such as the reduction of credit requirements for graduation (from 160 to 140). In 1974, the university specialization was introduced, which focused on chemical, electrical, and industrial engineering education. By the end of the decade, pilot institutions had increased to 39, involving most major universities in Korea.

Another important aspect of higher education reform during the 1970s was the revision of vocational higher education. In 1979, the government unified all higher education level vocational schools into vocational colleges (two- and three-year community colleges). Vocational education was divided into three parts: high schools would train craftsman; vocational colleges would train mid-level technicians; and four-year universities and colleges would educate engineers.

In 1979, President Park Junghi—who led the military coup in 1961—was assassinated, and a new military government was established in 1980. The Fifth Republic (1981–1987) reformed many parts of Korean society, hoping to solve social problems and to increase social control. The key policy measures included in the July 30 Education Reform were:

- the unprecedented expansion of enrollments, including a 30% increase in admittance of students by colleges and universities;
- teachers colleges and the National University were upgraded from two to four years, and some junior technical colleges were upgraded to open industrial universities; and
- entrance examinations administered by individual colleges and universities were abolished and replaced with a national exam.

In 1987, the government responded to public demands for democratization in education, and the Ministry of Education proclaimed a new "University Autonomy Plan." The key goals of this plan were: (1) to ensure the autonomy and accountability of university management; (2) to provide for greater participation of faculty in governance; (3) to increase the quality of higher education through extending the rights of the faculty; (4) to increase the autonomy of each institution based on its particular situation; and (5) to protect and foster the autonomy and individuality of private universities and colleges.

During the 1990s, the demand for mid-level technicians increased, caused by the growth of Korea's economy. This demand pushed the government to change the vocational college system. The bachelor's examination program of self-study, recognized as a college education equivalent, was formally launched in 1990. There are now examinations at each stage toward obtaining a bachelor's degree. By providing an alternative path to a bachelor's degree, the self-study system attaches as much importance to social education and the lifelong process of learning as to formal school education. The process of obtaining a bachelor's degree through self-study requires passing four qualifying exams, which include exams in the liberal arts, the basic major, the advanced major, and a final comprehensive exam. From 1992 through 2002, 7,042 bachelor's degrees in 12 specialized fields were granted through this self-study system.

In February 1994, the President established a Commission on Education Reform (PCER), charged with determining the fundamental direction of education for the 21st century and reviewing both short- and long-term educational development plans and the progress of educational reform at the national level. On May 31, 1995, the PCER announced new "Reform Measures to Establish the New Educational System" intended to lead Korea into the age of globalization and the information age. The goals of the measures are to enact a system of "open education and lifelong learning" that emphasizes a learner-centered approach, as well as a diversified and autonomous education. The measures are: (1) broadening the diversity and specialization of higher education; (2) diversification of the criteria for private college foundation; (3) delegation of power to individual institutions to decide admission quotas and matters regarding higher education management; (4) provision of a special supporting system for research; (5) provision for raising the quality of research to world-class levels; and (6) improvement of the connection between university and college evaluation and financial support.

In March of 1998, President Kim Dae Jung succeeded President Kim Young Sam, thereby inheriting the economic collapse of the country. His government followed the basic existing structure for higher education reform designed by the PCER. As part of the effort to continue educational reform, on July 24, 1998, the government established the "Presidential Commission for the New Educational Community." Preserving the fundamental spirit of educational reform upheld by the former regime, the Presidential Commission focused on reviewing and assessing the progress of educational reform, publicizing and offering training for reform, and enlivening civic movements for the promotion of reform. In 1991, the Ministry of Education was transformed into the Ministry of Education and Human Resources Development (MOEHRD), which is headed by the Deputy Prime Minister. The Ministry has tried to innovate the role and function of the university as a new engine for growth. It puts its energy and funds toward elevating the research and development capacity of the university and strengthening partnerships among the industries, universities, and research institutes so that the universities can take the central role in the network of creating and disseminating knowledge.

In 2003, the Roh government announced that "balanced development of the nation" would be its supreme policy mission, and presented "promoting provincial universities" as an important task to buttress the mission. The Presidential Committee on Education

Innovation is currently in charge of formulating recommendations on innovation of the higher education system and human resource development.

Characteristics of the Higher Education System

The characteristics of the Korean higher education system can be summarized as follows (Park, 1995):

1. The private sector has roughly three-quarters of the total enrollment of students (73% in 2003).
2. There has been little financial support for this private sector.
3. All institutions are under the supervision of the Ministry of Education.
4. The ratio of higher education students to the general population is larger than that of any other developing country, but the conditions in higher education institutions are poor by comparison.
5. Students pay for their education. In private universities and colleges, they pay around 80% of their total educational expense, whereas in national institutions they pay around 50%.
6. Higher education has experienced a rapid expansion for the last 50 years.
7. Finally, at the present time, there are seven different types of higher education institutions in Korea: (a) colleges and universities offering four-year undergraduate programs, with some offering six-year medical and other programs as well; (b) four-year teachers' universities; (c) junior colleges—also known as vocational community colleges—offering lifelong vocational education for adults, including programs in fisheries/marine science, nursing, public health, engineering and technology; (d) the Korean National Open University, also known as Air and Correspondence; (e) polytechnics—also known as industrial universities—offering an alternative way of providing wider education opportunities for workers and adult learners to earn their bachelor's degree without leaving their jobs; (f) distance or "cyber" universities; and (g) miscellaneous schools, predominantly in highly specialized fields such as theology or arts, where no degree is offered but completion is considered equivalent to graduation from college and university.

As is the case with many developing countries, Korea has achieved a remarkable quantitative expansion of higher education during the last 50 years. Enrollment in higher education grew from 7,819 in 1945 to 3,558,111 in 2003, as reflected in Table 1.

Table 1. Expansion of Higher Education (1945–2003)

	1945	1960	1970	1980	1990	2000	2001	2002	2003
Schools	19	85	357	556	556	1,184	1,261	1,303	1,390
Teachers and Assistants	1,490	3,808	10,435	20,900	41,920	79,136	83,116	86,441	88,129
Students	7,819	101,041	201,436	601,494	1,490,809	3,363,549	3,500,560	3,577,447	3,558,111

Source: Ministry of Education and Human Resources Development and KEDI (2003), *Statistical Yearbook of Education*.

Because virtually three of every four students in Korea are enrolled at a private college or university, it is important to note that these institutions are highly dependent on tuition. In 2003, student tuition accounted for 77% of the budget at junior colleges, 62% at four-year universities, and 79% at industrial colleges in the private sector (see Table 2). To help alleviate some of the financial demands, the government enacted a law exempting private universities and colleges from taxation in the acquisition and sale of properties. Loans are also provided to help private schools with the expansion and renovation of facilities. And the government's support for research grants, student activities, scholarship and annuities is increasing.

Recent Challenges and Responses

The Shrinking Population for Higher Education

Recently, Korea's student population has been shrinking rapidly. While the size of the age group that reached university admission has diminished, the freshmen quota at the university has increased. The applicants for higher education in 2000 were 867,000, but by 2002 this had declined to 720,000. The ratio between students who apply for entrance examinations and the freshmen quota of universities was 100.7% in 2002—in other words, the seats in universities exceeded actual demand (see Table 3). Demographic trends and forecasts for Korea indicated this phenomenon will continue for some time.

Such a decrease in the number of students is likely to compound the risk factors of Korea's universities. Some institutions in the end may suffer from severe structural vulnerabilities. In 2002, the nationwide average of the unfilled freshmen quotas among four-year universities was 5.5%. The number of universities and colleges with unfilled freshmen quota was greater in provincial institutions than in the Seoul region. This phenomenon is expected to be even more pronounced in the future.

The shrinking population of higher education hits those universities that are highly dependent on student tuition particularly hard, and leads to bankruptcies of (or mergers between) institutions. In order to overcome the difficulty, universities try to find students from overseas, particularly from China and other East Asian countries.

Difficulty in the Provincial Universities

Directly connected with the shrinking population for higher education, provincial universities face considerable difficulties. These include: the difficulty of enrolling students, due to their flocking to the universities in the Seoul region, and the financial difficulty this creates; the difficulty of attracting talented students; the difficulty in employment faced by the graduates of provincial universities; and a weakness in the innovative capacity of provincial universities.

Causes of the crises are categorized into external and internal factors (Lee, 2004, p. 3). The external factors include a concentration of socioeconomic and cultural power in the Seoul region; high school graduates' preference for the Seoul region; and the launching of alternative systems of higher education. The internal factors of the provincial

Table 2.   Source of the Budget for Private Institutions in 2003 (Unit: 1 million Won. 1$ = 1200 Won)

| | Total Revenue | Management Income | | | | Capital and Debt | Unused Balance Carried Forward |
		Tuition	Donation, etc.	Assorted Educational	Non-Educational		
Total	13,847,085	9,066,445	2,520,734	271,127	409,713	885,234	693,832
	100%	65%	18%	2%	3%	6%	5%
Jr. College	3,053,901	2,363,741	140,626	48,184	92,254	136,812	272,284
	100%	77%	5%	2%	3%	4%	9%
University	10,308,097	6,375,550	2,287,608	216,166	307,236	739,926	381,611
	100%	62%	22%	2%	3%	7%	4%
Industrial college	386,458	306,298	33,071	4,868	7,892	4,903	29,426
	100%	79%	9%	1%	2%	1%	8%
Graduate school	92,693	17,717	57,931	1,831	2,268	2,456	10,490
	100%	19%	62%	2%	2%	3%	11%
Others	5,936	3,139	1,498	79	63	1,137	20
	100%	53%	25%	1%	1%	19%	3%

Source: Ministry of Education and Human Resources Development and KEDI (2003), *Statistical Yearbook of Education.*

Table 3. Ratio of High School Graduates and Those Who Applied for College Entrance Test Vis-a-vis University's Freshmen Quota (Unit: Persons, Percent)

Year	Freshmen Quota				High School Grads. (B)	Ratio (A/B)	Applied to National Entrance Exam[b] (C)	Ratio (A/C)
	Total (A)	Jr. College	Univ.[a]	Korea Open Univ.				
1970	54,550	11,360	43,190	–	145,062	37.6	120,580	45.2
1975	94,325	26,685	55,640	12,000	263,369	35.8	223,159	42.3
1980	223,835	84,455	121,380	18,000	467,388	47.9	501,505	44.6
1985	305,450	97,090	174,360	34,000	642,354	47.6	725,861	42.1
1990	388,510	130,520	208,990	49,000	761,922	51.0	–	–
1995	565,750	215,470	282,780	67,500	649,653	87.1	757,488	74.7
2000	712,775	294,175	352,220	66,400	764,712	93.2	868,366	82.1
2001	713,270	292,035	354,835	66,400	736,171	96.9	850,305	83.9
2002	723,283	293,174	363,709	66,400	670,713	107.8	718,441	100.7

Source: Lee, Chong Jae (2004), The cluster strategy for balanced regional development and the policy tasks for provincial universities (p. 4).

[a] "Univ." includes universities of education, universities, industrial colleges, and technical colleges.

[b] "Applied to National Entrance Exam" implies the numbers of the applicants for the "preparatory test for college entrance" from 1970 through 1985, and "college scholastic ability test" starting from 1995.

[c] It is difficult to compute the number of the applicants for the "achievement test for college entrance" for 1990 due to a peculiar application procedure adopted for that year, by which the application term is divided into the early and the late terms and students first applied to college and then applied to the test.

universities include unreasonable increases of student quotas in these institutions; a low capacity for education and research; weak competitiveness of their graduates in the employment market; and a low capacity for self-innovation.

In order to strengthen the innovative capacity of provincial universities, the New University for Regional Innovation (NURI) project was launched in 2004. The aims of this project are ambitious. First, in terms of an overall strategic approach, financial support will be focused upon recovery of the regional identity, decentralization of governance, transfer of resources and authority to provinces, and promotion of provincial universities. Second, the regional development strategy will be implemented based on spontaneous effort of the provinces. Third, in order to create the basis for specialization of provincial universities, the areas of specialization suitable for local development will be selected for focused support, following the "principle of selection and focus." Finally, the selected areas will be connected to internal innovation of the universities to produce an effect of simultaneous restructuring (Lee, 2004, p. 17). For this project, the government plans to allocate around $250 million each year for five years. If this project turns out to be successful, it plans to increase the budget.

Problems of Science and Engineering Education

Another of the challenges that Korea faces involves the need to attract bright students to science and technology majors. Students tend to avoid natural science and engineering majors and flock to a few popular majors. To meet the demands of an advanced techno-intensive higher industrial society, the government has increased scholarships and opportunities for overseas studies for students in those majors. An incentive scheme is expanding financial aid to support faculty participation in joint research, internship programs and seminars. This activates scholarly exchanges with other countries, helping them keep abreast of the rapidly advancing frontiers of technology. At the same time, more resources are being put into the expansion of research facilities of school-industry cooperation.

Future Directions of Korean Higher Education

Distance University Education

Distance university refers to the lifelong education offered in higher education institutions that confer degrees equivalent to those of either junior colleges or four-year universities when students complete a set of credit hours. There are a total 16 distance universities (also called "cyber universities") licensed by the government, 14 for bachelor's degree courses and two for associate undergraduate degree courses. The freshmen quota for them is 200,500. Student supervision by the distance universities varies from one to another; however, in general, it includes Web-based attendance, online participation in quizzes, evaluation of the student's written work, scores on chatting and discussion, and evaluation of the mid-term and final examinations. In 2003, these distance universities only filled 50% of their freshmen quota. This is related to the broader problem of "unfilled freshmen quota" in the traditional universities. However, despite under-enrollment, it is likely that the establishment of distance universities will increase in the long run.

Upgrading the Infrastructure for Academic and Research Information

In 1999, the Korean government founded the Korea Education and Research Information Service (KERIS) as an institution devoted to moving education and academic research into the information age. KERIS investigates and collects data and produces information pertaining to academic research, and runs the information service system for academic research (http://www.riss4u.net), which provides the means for effective distribution of the information produced. This information system provides an integrated search service of the comprehensive index of books stored in domestic university libraries (388 universities had joined as of May 2003). Primary and secondary school libraries will soon be linked and curriculum will be available to encourage the usage of library resources. It also offers an inter-library loan service to support the sharing of data among university libraries, and promotes joint activities to utilize them (331 universities had joined this service as of May 2003). The system also includes a one-stop service for photocopying academic articles from domestic academic associations and university-affiliated research institutes and dissertations from domestic and foreign universities.

Employment Quota System for Female Professors in National and Public Universities

Following an expansion of the opportunity for university education, the proportion of female students in universities has risen. The proportion went up from 22.5% in 1980 to 36% in 2001. In 2002, 48.2% of university graduates were female. The proportion of females among doctoral graduates rose from 8.8% in 1980 to 22.9% in 2001. However, the proportion of female professors in the national and public universities remains at 9.1% as of 2002. Hence, a legal amendment was enacted in 2002 to produce a legal basis for the quota system for female professors in the national and public universities.

Graduate Schools and Brain Drain

Graduate education offers research-oriented facilities for those who need to prepare for academic and professional leadership. There are 142 general graduate schools, 106 professional graduate schools, 596 evening special graduate schools, and 25 independent graduate schools without undergraduate programs.

The minimum requirement for a master's degree is 24 credits, normally achieved in four semesters in the case of full-time students and five semesters for night students. Most doctoral programs require students to take an entrance exam offered by their own schools. The minimum requirement for a doctoral degree is normally 60 credits. Those who complete the required credits and pass two foreign language examinations as well as a comprehensive examination for the doctoral degree are entitled to write dissertations.

One of the major problems that Korean graduate schools have is brain drain at the doctoral level. Excellent students prefer to earn their doctoral degree abroad in such countries as the U.S. or England. Most of them go abroad to study after they complete a master's degree. Except for some good universities, graduate schools have a hard time recruiting excellent doctoral students. In order to solve this problem, the government has launched an ambitious program, Brain Korea 21 (BK 21). It is being undertaken for the purpose of developing graduate school-centered university education at the international level, and includes an emphasis on the basic sciences and an increased number of scholarships in areas of strategic importance. Based on this program, graduate schools are beginning to recruit more excellent students. At the same time, efforts are also being made for doctoral graduates to forego military service in return for working five years in companies or labs acknowledged by the government.

Today, brain drain is not a serious social problem in Korea. In fact, reverse brain drain and brain drain are both occurring at the same time in Korea. Those who found jobs in foreign countries after finishing their studies are coming back to Korea. At the same time there are also people who want to emigrate for better jobs and their children's education. The future of brain drain will thus be dependent on the economic situation of Korea.

Increasing University Autonomy and Enhancing Accountability

The budget accounting system of the national universities, which is currently bifurcated into general accounting and accumulative accounting, will be integrated under a special accounting system to promote autonomous management. As an attempt to raise university accountability—for the purpose of ensuring a university member's right to know and enhancing transparency and trustworthiness in the financial management of private universities—budget making and balance statements of private universities are required to be public. An accounting inspection will be conducted by an external auditor at universities and industrial universities with a freshmen quota over 2,000.

Both professionalism and efficiency of the government-led evaluation of universities has improved, and administrative and financial support for universities is connected to the evaluation of the quality of both the education and research provided by the university in order to enhance the excellence of university education. Accreditation by academic associations or relevant committees—such as accreditation for engineering education or for medical education—is done within the government-led evaluation process.

Also, a university board of trustees, comprised of faculty and non-faculty members, will be established. Currently, presidents of national universities are elected by faculty members. Except in a few cases, most of them are elected from among the faculty members. Recently, administrative staffs have pressured faculty groups to allow their participation in the voting, and in some schools they now hold around 5–7% of the vote. Administrative staffs' participation has awoken the student body, which has begun to pressure schools for their own participation in their president's election. It is expected that in the near future a president's election system will be replaced by a board of trustees' appointing system.

Reunification

One of the significant variables that will affect the future of Korean higher education is reunification with North Korea. There are continual discussions of this possibility, and should it occur, it is likely that there would be an increase in demand for higher education from residents of North Korea. However, this is not seriously considered or prepared for because nobody knows when it will happen. Korea may want to learn from the reunification experience of Germany.

Conclusion

In sum, this chapter has described the history, characteristics, recent challenges and response, and future direction of Korean higher education. The system expanded tremendously after World War II, much like that of many other developing countries, and there are currently several unique characteristics of Korean higher education to consider. First is the size of the private higher education sector, which enrolls nearly three-quarters of Korea's students. Second is the high financial dependence on tuition—around 70% of the budget at private universities and colleges, and around 50% of the budget at national/public universities and colleges, are driven by student tuition. Recently, the government increased its budget for higher education, in order to lower this widespread institutional dependence on tuition and to increase the quality of higher education. Third is the recently upgraded, Internet-based infrastructure which supports academic and research information. Korea is now one of those countries in which the information highway is highly accessible. A new information service system provides an integrated search service of the comprehensive index of the books and journals stored in domestic university libraries, and primary and secondary school libraries will soon be linked to the system. However, despite these unique and exciting advances in higher education, Koreans are still dependent on western universities—especially those in the United States—for awarding doctoral degrees. Current and future government efforts to increase the quality of master's and doctoral programs are expected to decrease this dependence.

Notes

1. The main sources used in this chapter include *Education in Korea* and other data from The Ministry of Education and Human Resource Development's home page (http://www.moe.go.kr); the Educational Statistics System (http://std.kedi.re.kr), published by Korean Educational Development Institute; and *Korean Higher Education*, edited by Weidman and Park (2000).
2. For a discussion on the early history of Korean higher education, please see J. Weidman & N. Park, (Eds.), *Korean higher education: Tradition and adaptation.* (New York, NY: Falmer Press, 2000).

References

Education in Korea. Available online at http://www.moe.go.kr/en/etc/education.html.
Educational Statistics System. Available online at http://std.kedi.re.kr.
Lee, C. (2004). The cluster strategy for balanced regional development and the policy tasks for provincial universities. Paper presented at 2004 KEDI-World Bank International Seminar. Balanced Regional Development and the Role of Tertiary Education in Korea (pp. 1–35). Handong University.
Park, N. (1995). The reformation and changes in Korean private higher education policy. In J. Mauch & P. Sabloff (Eds.), *Reform and change in higher education: International perspectives* (pp. 83–109). New York, NY: Garland.
Park, N. (2000). Higher education in a rapidly developing country: The case of Republic of Korea. In M. McMullen, J. Mauch, & B. Donnorummo (Eds.), *The emerging markets and higher education* (pp. 125–146). New York, NY: Routledge Falmer.
Weidman, J. & Park, N. (Eds.). (2000). *Korean higher education: Tradition and adaptation.* New York, NY: Falmer Press.

46

MEXICO

Hugo Casanova-Cardiel
National Autonomous University of Mexico

With over 450 years of institutional history, higher education has been a constant factor in the cultural and social construction of Mexico. Throughout its existence, higher education has taken a central role in national life. In addition to meeting its substantive responsibilities with respect to teaching, research, and cultural dissemination, the most influential universities have been immersed in a variety of important political and social debates. This participation in public life, which certainly goes beyond the traditional scope and responsibilities of most academic institutions, has also implied a significant contribution of higher education to the complex construction of democracy.

At the beginning of the 21st century, Mexico had a population of some 100 million inhabitants and, according to demographic projections, it will stabilize at between 130 and 150 million toward the middle of the century. The transformation in demographic patterns has meant a narrowing of the base of the population pyramid that will give rise to a reduction in the demand for basic education in a few years. In the coming decade, however, the increase in the population group aged 15 to 24 suggests an imminent growth in the demand for higher education.

Mexico is facing important challenges in economic, political and social terms. The modernization processes of economic factors, entry into the international framework and access to more complex production modalities have had favorable effects for the country, but have also brought unexpected consequences and even new problems, including some that deepen the conditions of social inequality. The political dimension, in turn, is still in a transition phase. The political transformation achieved in 2000 has not been sufficient for the full consolidation of democracy, and it is foreseeable that in the coming years new challenges will appear in the field of national political life.

In social terms, Mexico is subject to dual circumstances—even though some sectors have reached acceptable levels regarding quality of life, the large majority of Mexicans suffer conditions of inequality, inequity and poverty that have not yet been resolved. This is the framework in which higher education operates, and although the solution to such complex conditions is not within the reach of the higher education institutions, it is nevertheless unavoidable that the academic initiatives of these institutions take them into account.

James J.F. Forest and Philip G. Altbach (eds.), International Handbook of Higher Education, 881–897.
© 2006 *Springer. Printed in the Netherlands.*

Higher Education Structure: History and Current Perspectives

Genesis and Historical Development

The first universities in the Americas appeared during the middle of the 16th century, and were steeped in the process of giving shape to colonial society. This is the case of the *Real Universidad de México*, founded by a Royal Decree on September 21, 1551— barely 30 years after the fall of México Tenochtitlan—which began giving lessons to criollos and Spaniards in 1553. Although the establishment of *Real Universidad* (which attained pontifical recognition at the end of the 17th century) offers the most solid historical milestone of higher education in Mexico, the *Colegio de Santa Cruz de Tlaltelolco* (1536) should also be considered among one of the highly significant institutions of the time, offering higher and elementary education to the indigenous population (Ramírez, Pavón, & Hidalgo, 2001).

The 19th century in Mexico represented a break with colonial life and the birth of a nation. Under the reverberations of the Enlightenment, and with the continued struggles between liberals and conservatives, the country began a long defining process that had different effects on higher education. Thus, while new universities (Mérida and Chiapas) were created, the colonial university—after a troubled existence—was finally closed in 1865. Through the 19th century and the beginning of the 20th, different bodies were also created in the country—including institutions devoted to teacher training, and literary and scientific institutes—that were the basis for the creation of new universities (such as Jalisco, Puebla, Oaxaca, and Chihuahua).

In 1910, the National University of Mexico was created, thus uniting the different professional schools. Under the influx of positivist thought, an institution arose in the same year as the revolutionary uprising that paradoxically would be the last creation of the dictatorial regime. The armed struggle represented a complex scenario for the new institution, and its first decades were ones of survival. It was not until the revolutionary institutionalization phase in 1929 that the National University obtained its autonomy and became the most influential institution in the cultural construction of the country. During the first half of the 20th century, other institutions appeared that would give shape to a higher education system: Michoacán (1917), Sinaloa (1918), Yucatán (1922), San Luis Potosí (1923), Guadalajara (1924), Nuevo León (1932), Puebla (1937), and Sonora (1942). It is also important to mention the creation in 1936 (during the Cárdenas administration) of the National Polytechnic Institute, which sought to give opportunities to broader social groups through higher education in technical specialties (Ibarrola, 1986).

Consolidation and Modernization

The 1940s and 1950s represented a modernization stage for higher education. During these years, it is possible to speak of the beginning of governmental policy for higher education, which became manifest in the strengthening of the National Autonomous University of Mexico (UNAM)—the large Mexico City campus, *Ciudad Universitaria*, was opened in 1952—and also in the impulse given to a broader scheme that would give rise to the appearance of new institutions throughout the country. New private institutions appeared during this period, including the Technological and Higher Studies Institute of Monterrey (ITESM), the Autonomous Technological Institute of Mexico (ITAM), and Iberoamericana University (UIA), joining the few private institutions that existed at that time (for example, the Autonomous University of Guadalajara and the Free Law School).

As in other countries, the 1960s were particularly critical in Mexico. The student movement of 1968 expressed a university conflict, but in a deeper sense it also revealed the limits of a political and economic scheme that was inadequate in terms of democracy and equal opportunities. During the 1970s, as the government responded to the social demands of the preceding decade, higher education experienced the most important quantitative expansion and the most intense qualitative diversification seen in its history. During this period, the total number of students multiplied almost eightfold (from 76,000 in 1960 to 565,000 in 1977). A diversification process was also launched, giving rise to innovative modalities at the UNAM and such alternative institutions as the Metropolitan Autonomous University (UAM) (Casanova, 2001).

The 1980s and 1990s represented a modernization stage in higher education, as well as a phase of progressive articulation between higher education and factors of the economy and politics (Díaz Barriga, 1999). Under this panorama, higher education policies were included in a development model following the hegemonic currents of the world economy, with a clear commitment to diverse forms or agreements of a global and regional character (González-Casanova, 2001). Higher education policies also began to respond to the modernization and rationalization process in Mexico's public administration. In this sense, since its introduction in 1982, the so-called "national democratic planning system" has included higher education policies among its programs.

A synthetic balance of these years would have to recognize the introduction of criteria to foster changes in higher education institutions. These changes that, according to official lines, were founded on criteria of quality and efficiency, have achieved advances in the administrative and academic management processes of the institutions. However, they have also generated negative effects, including the predominance of administrative rationality over academic work. In the macro sphere of the system, it is impossible to omit the fact that the modernization policies had other effects, like the contention of university supply and a sharp reduction in public institutional financing. With respect to the growth of private higher education, its positive effects in opening up further options should be mentioned. Nevertheless, it is necessary to point out that, except for the private institutions of historical prestige—including ITESM, ITAM and UIA—most have been deficient in terms of academic quality.

Current Structure

Higher education in Mexico is regulated by a series of normative provisions, the most important of which are: the Political Constitution, the General Education Law, the Law for the Coordination of Higher Education, and the organic laws (in the case of institutions that have autonomy), internal statutes and regulations of different institutions in the system. Institutional coordination typically takes place at the federal level and, where appropriate, the state level.

The higher education system consists of over 1,600 public and private institutions, enrolling 2.2 million students and employing almost 200,000 professors. These institutions include universities, autonomous public universities, technological universities, polytechnic universities, technological institutes, research and postgraduate institutions, teacher training colleges, and higher education schools belonging to the army and the marines, among others. The educational programs include the following levels: higher technical university, associate professional, first degree, specialty, master's degree and doctorate. A significant amount of institutions also offer senior high school level education.

According to the criteria established in 2000 by the National Association of Universities and Higher Education Institutions (ANUIES), institutions are grouped in six subsystems that express the composition of a system in which—because of their quantitative scope and qualitative traits—public institutions predominate:

1) *Public university subsystem*, composed of 45 institutions that include federal and state universities (mainly autonomous). These institutions perform teaching, research and cultural dissemination, and enroll 52% of the national total of first degree students and 48% of graduate students. They carry out at least half of the national research.

2) *Technological education subsystem*, with 147 institutions enrolling 19% of first degree students and 8% of graduate students. This includes prestigious institutions such as the National Polytechnic Institute (IPN) and the Advanced Studies and Research Center (CINVESTAV). Most of these institutions (102) are coordinated by the federal government and the rest by state governments.

3) *Other public institutions subsystem*, including 67 institutions that depend on the federal government.

4) *Technological universities subsystem*, comprising 38 institutions in the year 2000; an innovative model that first appeared in 1991, with just over 1% of the nation's first degree enrollment.

5) *Private institutions subsystem*, composed of 976 institutions, divided into 306 universities, 256 institutes and 434 centers, schools and other institutions, enrolling 27.6% of all first degree students and 36.5% of graduate students (32.6% and 40% in 2002 respectively).

6) *Teacher training colleges subsystem*, covering some 357 institutions (220 public and 137 private) and accounting for 11.5% of the nation's first degree enrollment.

Coordination, Organization and Governance in the Public and Private Sectors

Coordination

During the last 10 years, the modalities for coordinating higher education in Mexico have undergone important transformations in their structure and processes. Regarding structure, the traditional external actors of a public character (the different orders of the public administration, the legislative powers, and the bodies that mediate public administration and the universities) have been joined by a host of internal actors (university directors, academics and students)—although in an incipient way, mainly involving actors related to the student, professional and complementary financing markets, as well as public and private funds for specific projects (Rodríguez, 2003). With some necessary reservation, one can assert that the modalities of coordinating higher education in Mexico—framed in traditional terms within the sphere of the state, accompanied by the presence of academic and intellectual elites—have undergone a diversification process during the last few years. This process has granted a greater presence to external actors, such as those coming from the markets, as well as to new agents from civic organizations, social movements and the media, among other entities.

With respect to the specific bodies that intervene in the coordination of higher education, the Ministry of Education (SEP) plays a central role in coordinating the system, while the National Council for Science and Technology (CONACYT) and ANUIES (formally an agency with a civil character that has come to play a role of mediation between the federal government and the higher education institutions) also intervene. Another intermediate coordinating organization is the Federation of Mexican Private Higher Education Institutions (FIMPES), which articulates the policy concerns of higher education institutions of the private sector. In terms of coordination, the National Coordinating Office for the Planning of Higher Education (COEPES) integrates elements from the SEP, ANUIES and the institutions themselves in order to generate proposals on national plans and programs.

In terms of academic organization, the institutions follow two models: a traditional one, based on separate schools or faculties that are mainly committed to teaching and (to a lesser extent) research (which, when it exists, is developed in other institutional spaces); and the departmental model, which functions as the basic unit of organization for academic work and ideally integrates teaching and research. At present, both models coexist, but it can be sustained that the newly created public and private institutions and those that generate innovation processes have incorporated the departmental model as a form of organization.

Institutional Governance

The field of institutional governance maintains substantive differences depending on the sector (public or private). In public institutions, the collegiate bodies range from university councils and governance boards to technical councils and academic councils. The individual leaders include the rector, directors and department heads, among others. In terms of the distribution of competencies and attributions, it is possible to point out that the collegiate bodies have been favored over individual leaders. Thus, the decisions of individual leaders are limited by the academic rationality established by the collegiate organization. The collegiate bodies of the public institutions usually allow for student organizations that represent the public sector even in the bodies of the highest level and are integrated—although with a limited scope of influence—into the decision-making process.

However, a description of institutional government in the public sector cannot be restricted to its normative dimension. In Mexico, the exercise of institutional governance is highly complex and its praxis surpasses normative and formal limits. Thus, it is possible to find that the individual figures impose their proposals in vertical ways and, on occasions, far removed from collegiate logic. In some cases, the individual figures appeal to collegiate rationality only in order to formalize previously established individual decisions.

In the case of private institutions, collegiate bodies also co-exist with individual leaders. In this case, the individual leaders enjoy full attributions and the collegiate bodies have more of a consultative than decisive role. In this sense, decision making follows a less arduous road. The nature of private organizations does not demand such exhaustive means of legitimization as seen among public institutions, and the individual leaders enjoy broad margins within which to act. In the sphere of the private institutions, the student sector has a less organized presence and its role in institutional life is usually limited to individual ways of expression.

It is important to point out that in practically all Latin America, educational institutions have been encouraged to reform their governance modalities and, in many cases, have introduced processes of change (Brunner, 1991; Casanova, 2002). Mexico has not remained at the margin of these tendencies, and it is possible to mention a transition in governance and management schemes (Ibarra, 2002; de Vries, 2002). This transition is not yet fully defined, and diverse tensions can be observed among managerial modalities that appeal to the strengthening of individual leadership, in comparison with academic management modalities that are set on maintaining a collegiate structure in decision making (Muñoz, 2002). In light of this, it is also important to recognize the lack of programs for the training of higher education directors and managers, and as a result the often minimal levels of professionalization among those who exercise leadership responsibilities in public and private institutions.

One important tension—both historical and contemporary—in the public sphere of higher education governance in Mexico involves institutional autonomy (Levy, 1987). Debate over the roles and responsibilities of the actors involved in higher education—principally the state and government—has been ongoing throughout the last several years, and it is possible to sustain that, with the modernization policies, the traditional margins of autonomy have been redefined, depositing greater responsibilities in bodies external to the higher education institutions (Manero, 1999).

Evaluation and Accreditation of Higher Education

Over the last several decades, governmental educational policies have been based on the criterion of quality as the principal point of reference (Brunner, 1997). In this respect, during the 1980s the specific documents on higher education policies institutionalized evaluation as a mechanism, *par excellence*, to promote quality. In the same way, an attempt was made in the mid-1990s to seek the consolidation of a series of accreditation mechanisms related to the promotion and assurance of quality in public and private higher education institutions (Kent, 2000).

A number of specific bodies have been created in relation to evaluation: the National Higher Education Evaluation Commission (CONAEVA), established in 1989; the Interinstitutional Committees for Higher Education Evaluation (CIEES), formed in 1991; and the National Center for Higher Education Evaluation (CENEVAL), created in 1994. In turn, new entities have been created to promote accreditation, including the Council for Higher Education Accreditation (COPAES), launched in 2000, which—fostered by the ANUIES and the SEP—has the objective of recognizing organizations that accredit public and private academic programs. However, two decades after their introduction, evaluation results do not seem to be proportional to the efforts invested in this area, and there is no evidence to show the impact of evaluation on the effective improvement of quality. With respect to accreditation processes, formalized in 2000 with the creation of COPAES, it is important to note that they are going through an early phase in their implementation and that the number of experiences is of little significance.

Accountability

Proposals with respect to accountability are closely related to the subject of evaluation. Mainly throughout the last decade, the importance of higher education institutions providing reports on their performance has become manifest, not only in financial terms but also in relation to their substantive activities. The subject, however, is complex, and while the government suggests a multitude of modalities and strategies to promote accountability, institutions call for accountability centered on financial and operative themes.

Until now, accountability mechanisms have been centered on the federal government as inspector of institutional tasks. In this sense, extraordinary financial funds have been incorporated for institutional compliance with accountability programs. However, in recent years, the most influential universities—such as UNAM and UAM—have begun to demand that accountability be based on the informational transparency of the institutions themselves, and that it be submitted to instances other than those of the federal government, such as legislative bodies.

Student Enrollment: Access and Expansion

In the decade preceding the modernization of Mexico's higher education policies, there was an important period of expansion that transformed the profile of this educational level. Student enrollment increased almost fourfold, from 224,390 students in 1970 to 853,384 in 1980. This period of rapid growth was followed by a sharp decrease in the rate of expansion, so that by a decade later the system enrolled only 50% more students (roughly 1,245,532). However, by 2002, the student population had reached a total of 2,144,376, representing a significant resurgence in expansion during the 1990s. The main area of growth during this time period was seen among the technological and university first degree students, with 218,637 in 1970 and 1,771,969 in 2002. Also, the number of students in teacher training programs doubled between 1980 to 2000, although the 2002 enrollment in this field indicates a modest decline (see Table 1).

One of the most significant trends in enrollment during the last few decades has been the progressive increase in the private sector (Kent & Ramírez, 2002). Since the 1980s, private higher education has shown an impressive growth rate, explicitly promoted by modernization policies of the federal government, from 13.8% in 1979 to 32.6% in

Table 1.   Student Enrollment in Higher Education

	Student Enrollment University and Technological			Student Population Teacher Training	Student Population Graduate	Total
Years	N	Public	Private	N	N	N
1970	218,637	86.2%	13.8%	–	5,773	224,390
1980	731,291	86.5%	13.5%	96,590	25,503	853,384
1985	961,468	84.3%	15.7%	125,236	37,040	1,123,744
1990	1,078,191	82.6%	17.4%	123,376	43,965	1,245,532
1995	1,217,431	77.5%	22.5%	138,048	65,165	1,421,094
2000	1,585,408	70.6%	29.4%	215,506	118,099	1,962,763
2002	1,771,969	67.4%	32.6%	184,100	132,471	2,144,376

Source: ANUIES (2000), La educación superior en el siglo XXI; ANUIES (2002a), Anuario Estadístico 2002.

2002. It is important to stress, however, that private institutions have developed in a highly differentiated way, and although a small group has stood out in terms of academic quality and demands, these institutions as a group function under modest performance and academic efficiency criteria. The increasing presence of women has also fueled the expansion of higher education in Mexico. During in the mid-1980s, the proportion of women barely reached 33.8% of the total enrollment, but at the beginning of the 1990s it had risen to 42.8%, and to 48.2% by 2002.

Expansion of the system has also been the result of policies developed in response to increasing demand for access to higher education. Thus, the student participation rate has increased from 14.5% of the 20–24 year-old age group at the beginning of the 1990s to 17.7% in 1999. However, geographical diversity is an important issue here, with rates varying throughout the different states of the Republic—in 11 states, the student participation rates are less than 15%; 13 states have rates between 15% and 20%, four states have rates of between 20% and 25%; and four states have student participation rates over 25% (ANUIES, 1999, 2000). In response to this unequal geographical distribution, policies have been implemented over the last several decades to reverse the centralist tendencies in higher education. Thus, in 1970, 52.5% of the student population was located in the Federal District (D.F.), while by 2002 this figure had dropped to 20%. Nevertheless, decentralization has not yet reached the graduate level, as 65% of graduate students can be still found in just five states: the Federal District, Estado de México, Jalisco, Nuevo León and Puebla (ANUIES, 2000, 2002a).

With respect to distribution of enrollment by areas of knowledge, the most recent data indicate a predominance of social and administrative sciences (48.5%), and engineering and technology (33.8%). The remaining percentage is divided in the following way: health sciences (8.7%), education and humanities (4.6%), agricultural sciences (2.4%) and natural and exact sciences (2.0%) (ANUIES, 2002a).

Although important, expansion was not the only facet that characterized the transformation of higher education during the 1970s. Throughout this decade, a broad diversification process was also generated that reached practically all areas of higher education, ranging from the reform of institutional structures to a new conception of higher education in the scenario of government policies. A variety of reform and innovation processes in the pedagogical, organizational and political fields took place in the institutions throughout these decades. Other important changes have included the incorporation of new higher education modalities such as open systems, the development of graduate studies and increasing support given to research.

Graduate Studies

General Aspects

The history of graduate studies goes back several decades and includes significant experiences in different higher education institutions such as UNAM, IPN, CINVESTAV, UAM, the National Anthropology and History Institute (INAH), Colegio de México (COLMEX), and the Center for Economic Research and Teaching (CIDE), among others (Arredondo, 1999). The first wave of growth occurred during the 1970s and 1980s, when graduate enrollment increased from 5,953 to 25,502 students. It bears mention that this increase had a large female component—while the number of men multiplied by 3.6, the number of women multiplied by 8.2 (see Table 2).

As with the other factors in higher education, graduate studies were significantly affected by the modernization policies introduced in the 1980s and 1990s. Growth in this sense was not fortuitous, as higher education policies indicated the need to increase supply at this educational level. Under such a scenario, another modernization trend came into play, reflected in the promotion of the growth of private higher education. Thus, between 1980 and 2000, private higher education institutions increased their proportion of all graduate enrollment from 23% to 40%, while the proportion of graduate students in public institutions dropped inversely (see Table 2).

By 2002, the majority of the graduate student population was enrolled at the master's degree level, with 93,011 students (70.2%), followed by 29,550 students (22.3%) at the specialty level and only 9,910 students (7.5%) at the doctoral level (ANUIES, 2002a). Among graduate students in the specialty level, the largest proportions were in health sciences (54.8%) and social and administrative sciences (31.8%) in 2002.

Table 2. Graduate School Population: Enrollment and Sector

Year	Men	Women	Total Enrollment	Public Sector	Private Sector
1970	5,167	786	5,953	83.3%	16.7%
1980	19,014	6,488	25,502	77.0%	23.0%
1985	26,473	10,567	37,040	79.7%	20.3%
1990	29,792	14,173	43,965	78.3%	21.7%
1995	39,755	25,860	65,615	72.2%	27.8%
2000	67,550	50,549	118,099	60.3%	39.7%
2002	74,435	58,036	132,471	59.9%	40.1%

Source: ANUIES (2002b), Anuario Estadístico 2002.

The majority of master's students could be found in social and administrative sciences (54.1%), with another 21.3% in education and humanities. At the doctoral level, the largest proportions of students were in natural and exact sciences (25.5%), in social and administrative sciences (24.3%) and in education and humanities (17.9%) (ANUIES, 2002b).

Graduate Education and Brain Drain

The problems at the graduate level of education are complex, and not all have received equal attention. Among the most critical matters is the accumulated lag and slow growth rate (barely 12.7% a year). In 2000, barely 1,000 students were enrolled in Ph.D. programs, essential for stimulating research, compared with 5,900 in Spain, and 45,000 in the United States (CONACYT, 2003a). The global brain drain phenomenon, which contributes to the growing polarization between rich and poor nations (and by extension, between strong higher education systems and others that are not) is thus a particularly important consideration in Mexico.

Studies of this problem are currently in an early phase, and few reflections have been made on the matter. Nevertheless, it is known that a large number of Mexican graduate students annually emigrate to the United States and European countries, where they find better academic and personal opportunities. In order to reverse this trend, the CONACYT developed a strategy in the 1990s to attract doctoral graduates in foreign institutions (Licea et al., 2003). This strategy included the creation of a Fund to Retain and Repatriate Mexican Researchers, which—according to official data—has produced some favorable results. Data collected by CONACYT (2003a) indicates around 799 researchers were repatriated between 1990 and 1994, 1,060 between 1995 and 1999, and 392 in the year 2000. However, in spite of these measures, the brain drain problem persists, in part due to continued limitations on higher education expenditures over the last decades, and the insufficient creation of academic positions.

The Academic Profession

General Aspects

As with other dimensions of higher education, the academic profession has gone through profound transformations in recent decades. For example, in the wake of en-rollment growth during the 1970s, the number of professors nearly tripled, from 25,000 in 1970 to 73,000 in 1980. Nevertheless, this growth had unforeseen effects, including the formation of a small homogenous group of academic staff whose academic and professional traits are barely sufficient for effective teaching (Gil-Antón, 2002).

The expansion in the number of academic staff has been a constant trend since 1970, although with considerable contraction during the 1980s, and reached 219,804 academics in 2002. Of these, the highest percentage corresponds to first degree level, maintaining the figures of the 1990s (see Table 3).

The modernization process of the last 20 years also had important effects on academic work. Under the scenario of economic crisis and decline in financing of the 1980s, the

Table 3. Academic Staff in Higher Education

Years	Technological and University First Degree		Teacher Training		Graduate		Total	
	N	%	N	%	N	%	N	%
1980	69,214	93.0	3,558	4.9	1,072	1.4	73,874	100
1985	95,779	85.0	7,849	7.0	9,046	8.0	112,674	100
1990	105,058	81.4	12,488	9.7	11,546	8.9	129,092	100
1995	132,222	84.8	12,730	8.2	10,934	7.0	155,886	100
1999	158,539	82.4	16,836	8.7	17,031	8.9	192,406	100
2002	182,594	83.0	17,676	8.1	19,534	8.9	219,804	100

Source: ANUIES (2000), La educación superior en el Siglo XX; ANUIES (2002a), Anuario Estadístico 2002.

modernizing policies of higher education introduced to the academic corps a series of expectations related to quality improvement. Thus, a variety of programs arose related to the strengthening of the academic profession that covered, among other factors, increases in the academic quality of the professors, in the number of full-time professors, and in faculty productivity. Reflecting an increased emphasis in this area, between 1997 and 2002 the number of faculty with master's degrees doubled (from 11,768 to 22,433), and those with doctorates increased 2.5 times (from 1,840 to 4,513). However, of Mexico's 128,424 academics in 2002, the overwhelming majority (90,321) were graduates of first degree level programs (SEP, 2003).

Modernization also implied a strong impetus for evaluation. Differences among individual academics (in terms of merit and quality) were recognized and rewarded in economic terms. The National Researchers System (SNI) has operated at a national level since the mid-1980s, and programs were introduced at the institutions that promoted differentiation in the faculty salary scale. Specific programs for the training of academics have also been developed, notably the Program for Excellence of Academic Personnel (SUPERA), created in 1994, and the Program for Professor Improvement (PROMEP), created in 1996 (SEP, 2003).

Research

While a comprehensive discussion on science and technology in Mexico would clearly exceed the limits of this chapter, its importance in the higher education framework demands at least a cursory review here. Scientific research is carried out principally in higher education institutions and in centers and institutes belonging to the federal government; in parastatal sector organizations, such as the Mexican Oil Institute (IMP) and the Mexican Social Security Institute (IMSS); and in other private institutions. Of the 25,392 persons engaged in research and development in Mexico, 12,477 are to be found in higher education institutions, 8,069 in government research organizations, 4,587 in productive organizations and 259 in private productive organizations (CONACYT, 2003b).

Over the last few decades, different scientific policy measures have been promoted, with significant effects on higher education. Important milestones include the creation of the SNI in 1984, the Sciences Consultative Council in 1991, and the Program for the Support of Science in 1992 (SEP, 2003). As mentioned above, research is basically performed in the public universities and, according to data from 1997, almost 95% of scientific articles were published by national researchers from public universities (OECD, 1997). One of the explicit objectives of the creation of the SNI was to retain the best academics—through academic and economic recognition—to counter the threat that they would emigrate to foreign institutions.

The SNI has managed to strongly consolidate itself and has grown slowly but constantly since its creation, from 2,276 researchers in 1984 to 9,199 in 2002. The concentration of faculty by primary area in 2002 was the following: physics, mathematics and earth sciences, 19.2%; biology and chemistry, 18.0%; humanities and behavioral sciences, 16.8%; social sciences, 11.9%; engineering and technology, 12.8%; medicine and health sciences, 10.0%; and agricultural sciences, 11.9% (Gobierno Federal, 2003).

Economic and Financial Dimensions

Throughout the last several decades, the one subject of discussion that permeates across the different fields of higher education is economics. This is not solely due to the elementary need of the institutions to have resources available for their operation, but also to the growing role of financing in the definition of higher education policies. In a higher education system with public sector predominance, as is the case of Mexico, the economic dimension is crucial. In fact, since the first decades of the 20th century, higher education experienced diverse funding problems associated (to differing extents) with the national economic crises. However, in historical terms at least two stages of increased financial support for higher education are worth mention: the first, coinciding with the postwar national modernization, included the creation of the University City Campus (the main campus of UNAM); the second, during the 1970s, gave rise to the expansion and diversification processes in higher education, with diverse effects throughout the system.

The criteria for the allocation of financing has changed over the years as well. Before the 1980s, budget allocations were founded on: (a) the size of the student population; (b) the capacity of the university managers to negotiate greater amounts; and (c) the political opportunity represented by public expenditure on higher education institutions (ANUIES, 2003). During the 1980s, allocation criteria were centered around the number of university workers, and beginning in the 1990s, different types of financing were promoted that addressed two dimensions: funds aimed at the operational level of the institutions ("regularizable") and funds aimed at promoting reforms and innovations ("academic performance"). It is not risking too much to sustain that the criteria mentioned in items (b) and (c) (management capacity and political opportunity) have been present to date.

The impact of financing on higher education policies has been manifest throughout these years. In fact, there is evidence to think that the *leit motiv* of the modernization of higher education in Mexico has been the problem of financing. In the 1980s, the conjunction of a series of factors—the national economic crisis, the adoption of neoliberal macroeconomic schemes and a growing confidence in solutions of a technocratic flavor—came to situate the problems to be found in higher education more in the perspective of financial matters than in the sphere of education itself.

Throughout the 1990s and the first years of the 21st century, the effects of economic variables on education have been visible. For example, expenditures per student increased from 18,068 pesos in 1990 to 28,916 in 1994. This was followed by a dramatic decline, from 25,599 per student in 1995 to 22,600 in 1997, and then by a 4-year period of relative stagnation. The situation recovered marginally by 2002, when expenditures per student reached 29,443 pesos. A similar pattern of ebb and flow is observed when assessing the relationship between federal expenditures on higher education and Gross Domestic Product (GDP). Here, too, a rising trend was seen between 1990 and 1994 (from 0.42% to 0.61% of GDP), followed by rapid decline between 1995 and 1997 (from 0.58% to 0.49%), and then a slow increase to an all-time high of 0.67% of GDP in 2002 (ANUIES, 2003).

Over the last few years, some programs of extraordinary funds have been created to encourage institutional achievement and innovation. Some of the most important are the Program for Academic Improvement (PROMEP), the Funds for the Modernization of Higher Education (FOMES), the Integral Program for Institutional Strengthening (PIFI), the Program for University Development, and the Funds for State Universities Investment. There are also different proposals that have been put forward to promote greater rationality in the public financing of higher education. The ANUIES and different university bodies have called for greater institutionality of financing criteria, greater sufficiency of the resources allocated, greater equity among institutions, greater transparency in the mechanisms to distribute resources and greater co-responsibility of institutions in their exercise of the resources, in accountability and in the search for their own revenue (ANUIES, 2003).

Challenges and Perspectives in Higher Education

In the first decade of the 21st century, higher education in Mexico is facing complex problems that can only be resolved through heavy investment in economic, political and social resources. As with other higher education systems, Mexico is facing a series of demands in terms of teaching, research and dissemination that call for greater response and adaptation capacity. Above all, five main challenges are shaping the higher education environment in Mexico:

- *The global challenge.* The forms of articulation in the 21st century are defined using the conjunction of local and global dimensions. The formation of regional blocks and contacts of all types among nations constitutes an undeniable reality (Altbach, 1999, 2004). In this scenario, Mexico faces the choice of integrating itself into this process or remaining on the margin.
- *The challenge of knowledge.* The rationality of our times is, in essence, that of knowledge. The criterion articulating all things social is one of knowledge, and the

institutions where knowledge is produced, transmitted and disseminated acquire greater protagonism (Barnett, 2000).

- *The challenge of the economy.* Economic conditions are a primary determinant for the maintenance and promotion of education. The subject of financing is crucial for higher education in Mexico.
- *The challenge of politics.* The construction of democracy is underway, but it is an arduous process. Solid institutions are required to give certainty to the efforts in educational matters and to permit the proposal of a long-term higher education policy.
- *The social challenge.* Mexico has great social asymmetry. While a small portion of society has acceptable standards of living, most of the population is living in adverse conditions. Social inequality is by far the main challenge to be overcome in Mexico.

For the higher education system, these challenges represent a series of decisions and policies that will define the viability of this educational sphere and its role in the construction of Mexico in the 21st century. From the perspective of Mexico's immediate and mid-term future, five critical dimensions can be identified that will shape higher education's responses to these challenges: quantitative growth; qualitative improvement; coordination and governance; academic mission; and private higher education.

The quantitative growth dimension. One of the dimensions in which haste and precision are demanded refers to access. After two decades of contraction in higher education supply, it is only fair to recognize that rates of student enrollment have started to recover. However, at the beginning of the 21st century, nearly 80% of young Mexicans aged 18 to 24 have been left outside the higher education framework. In this respect, it is essential to put forward a policy that establishes a structural commitment regarding the future in order to overcome historical social inequalities.

The qualitative improvement dimension. In recent decades, enormous emphasis has been placed on the subject of quality, and strategies have been centered around evaluation and accreditation. The results, however, are unequal and there are reservations about the effectiveness of measures taken in this respect. The future demands the incorporation of mechanisms that ensure the quality of higher education, while avoiding the formalist traits of the programs introduced up to now and giving greater consistence to their substantive aspects.

The dimension of coordination and governance. The concurrence of actors from the academic, political, social, productive and economic spheres, among others, requires efficacious, innovative mechanisms that will provide a space in which all can express themselves. Coordination also implies the distribution of attributions and competencies of higher education. The sphere of governance is also demanding forms of representation and decision making that place higher education on the road to progress.

The academic dimension. Even though higher education has to consider proposals coming from different segments of society, the markets and the state, the rationality guiding its development can be no other than academic. This would appear to be the greatest challenge for higher education in Mexico—to recognize and comply fully with the centrality of the academic mission in establishing and meeting future institutional commitments.

The private higher education dimension. In the recent transformation process in the higher education system, one of the most evident traits is the rise of the private sector. Private institutions in Mexico today enroll almost one-third of first degree students and nearly half of the graduate students. Institutional conditions, however, are extremely uneven, and a great deal of effort is needed to generate private higher education of quality. Although there are exceptions, the role of these higher education institutions has been restricted to quantitative attention to demand, and efforts must be undertaken to achieve qualitative improvement and articulation with the rest of the system. In this sense, it is essential to stress the need to consolidate the academic staff, to strengthen the supply of graduate studies, and to generate teaching and research programs.

In sum, the challenges facing higher education in Mexico are highly complex. However, evidence shows that the system has indeed been able to contribute to the construction of the nation. Under the essentially public regime that prevailed until very few years ago, higher education has moved from an elitist, homogeneous scheme to an increasingly broader, diversified modality in which the private sector has a growing presence. As a consequence, public and private institutions have a great responsibility to address the critical challenges mentioned earlier. The long-term development of higher education in Mexico is in their hands.

References

Altbach, P. G. (1999). Patterns in higher education development. In P. Altbach, R. Berdahl, & P. Gumport (Eds.), *American higher education in the 21st century* (pp. 15–37). Baltimore & London: The Johns Hopkins University Press.

Altbach, P. G. (2004). Globalization and the university: Myths and realities in an unequal world. *Tertiary Education and Management,* (1), 3–25. [Note: An updated version of this essay appears in volume 10 of this *Handbook*.]

ANUIES. (1999). *Estadísticas de la educación superior, 1999. Personal docente de los niveles técnico superior, licenciatura y posgrado* (Higher education statistics, 1999. Higher technical, first degree and graduate teaching staff). Mexico City, Mexico: ANUIES. Available online at http://www.anuies.mx. Retrieved on April 20, 2004.

ANUIES. (2000). *La educación superior en el siglo XXI. Líneas estratégicas de desarrollo. Una propuesta de la ANUIES* (Higher education in the 21st century. Strategic development lines. A proposal from ANUIES). Mexico City, Mexico: ANUIES.

ANUIES. (2002a). *Anuario estadístico, 2002. Población escolar. Resúmenes y series históricas* (Statistics yearbook, 2002. Student population. Summaries and historic series). Mexico City, Mexico: ANUIES. Available online at http://www.anuies.mx. Retrieved on April 20, 2004.

ANUIES. (2002b). *Anuario Estadístico, 2002. Población escolar de posgrado. Resúmenes y series históricas* (Statistics yearbook, 2002. Graduate student population. Summaries and historic series).

Mexico City, Mexico: ANUIES. Available online at http://www.anuies.mx. Retrieved on April 20, 2004.

ANUIES. (2003). *Propuesta de lineamientos para una política de estado en el financiamiento de la educación superior* (Proposal of guidelines for a state policy in financing higher education). Document approved in the Ordinary Session of the Public Institutions and Similar Institutions of ANUIES. Mexico City, Mexico: ANUIES.

Arredondo, V. M. (1999). La educación superior: el posgrado (Higher education: graduate level). In P. Latapí (Ed.), *Un siglo de educación en México* (A century of education in Mexico) (pp. 355–383). Mexico City, Mexico: FCE.

Barnett, R. (2000). *Realizing the university in an age of supercomplexity*. Buckingham England & Philadelphia: The Society for Research into Higher Education & Open University Press.

Brunner, J. J. (1991). *Educación superior en América Latina* (Higher education in Latin America). Mexico City, Mexico: Fondo de Cultura Económica.

Brunner, J. J. (1997). Calidad y evaluación de la educación superior (Quality and evaluation of higher education). In E. Martínez, M. Letelier (Eds.), *Evaluación y acreditación universitaria: Metodologías y experiencias* (University evaluation and accreditation: Methodologies and experiences) (pp. 9–44). Santiago, Chile: UNESCO-OUI-USACH-Nueva Sociedad.

Casanova, H. (2001). Expansión y complejidad. La UNAM entre 1970 y 2000 (Expansion and complexity. The National Autonomous University of Mexico from 1970 to 2000). In R. Marsiske (Ed.), *La Universidad de México. Un recorrido histórico de la época colonial al presente* (The university of México. A historical review from the colonial age to the present) (pp. 261–326). Mexico City, Mexico: UNAM-CESU.

Casanova, H. (2002). Políticas y gobierno de la educación superior en América Latina (Policies and governance in higher education in Latin America). In H. Casanova (Ed.), *Nuevas políticas de la educación superior* (New policies of higher education) (pp. 239–264). A Coruña, Spain: Netbiblo.

CONACYT. (2003a). *Programa especial de ciencia y tecnología 2001–2006* (Special program for science and technology, 2001–2006). Mexico City, Mexico: CONACYT. Available online at http://www.conacyt.mx. Retrieved on May 16, 2004.

CONACYT. (2003b). *Informe general del estado de la ciencia y la tecnología 2003* (General report on the state of science and technology, 2003). Mexico City, Mexico: CONACYT. Available online at http://www.conacyt.mx. Retrieved on May 16, 2004.

De Vries, W. (2002). *Políticas federales en la educación superior Mexicana* (Federal policies in Mexican higher education). New York: AHIEPS. Available online at; http://www.nyu.edu/iesp/aiheps.

Díaz Barriga, A. (1999). Contexto nacional y políticas públicas para la educación superior en México, 1950–1996 (National context and public higher education policies in Mexico, 1950–1996). In H. Casanova & R. Rodríguez (Eds.), *Universidad contemporánea. Política y gobierno* (Contemporary university. Politics and governance) (pp. 371–386). Mexico City, Mexico: UNAM-M.A. PORRÚA.

Gil-Antón, M. (2002). Big city love: The academic workplace in Mexico. In P. G. Altbach (Ed.), *The decline of the guru: The academic profession in developing and middle income countries* (pp. 23–51). Boston & New York: Boston College Center for International Higher Education and Palgrave Publishers.

Gobierno Federal. (2003). *Tercer Informe de Gobierno* (Third Government Report). Mexico City: Gobierno Federal. Available online at http://www.siicyt.gob.mx. (14 May, 2004).

González-Casanova, P. (2001). *La universidad necesaria en el siglo XXI* (The university needed for the 21st century). Mexico City, Mexico: Era.

Ibarra, E. (2002, January–April). La "nueva universidad" en México: Transformaciones recientes y perspectivas (The "new university" in Mexico: Recent transformations and perspectives). *Revista Mexicana de Investigación Educativa, 7*(14), 75–105.

Ibarrola, María de. (1986). *La educación superior en México* (Higher education in Mexico). Caracas, Venezuela: CRESALC-UNESCO.

Kent, R. (2000). Reforma institucional en educación superior y reforma del estado en México en la década de los noventa: una trayectoria de investigación. (Institutional reform in higher education and reform of the state in Mexico in the nineties: a research trajectory). In J. Balán (Ed.), *Políticas de reforma de la educación superior y la universidad latinoamericana hacia el final del milenio* (Policies of higher education reform and the Latin American university toward the end of the millenium) (pp. 195–244). Cuernavaca, Mexico: UNAM-CRIM.

Kent, R. & Ramírez, R. (2002). La educación superior privada en México: Crecimiento y diferenciación (Private higher education in Mexico: Growth and differentiation). In P. G. Altbach (Ed.), *Educación superior privada* (Private higher education) (pp. 123–144). Mexico City, Mexico: UNAM-M. A. Porrúa.

Levy, D. (1987). *Universidad y gobierno en México. La autonomía en un sistema autoritario* (University and governance in Mexico. Autonomy in an authoritarian system). Mexico City, Mexico: FCE.

Licea, J., Santillán E., Areuas M., Valles J. (2003). Desempeño de becarios mexicanos en la producción de conocimiento científico ¿de la bibliometría a la política científica? (Performance of Mexican scholarship students in the production of scientific knowledge. From bibliometrics to science policy?). *Information Research, 8*(2), paper no. 147. Online at: http://InformationR.net/ir/8-2/paper147.html.

Manero, R. (1999). Institucionalización, reforma y gobierno en la institución universitaria (Institutionalization, reform and governance in the university institution). In H. Casanova & R. Rodríguez (Eds.), *Universidad contemporánea. Política y gobierno* (Contemporary university. Politics and governance) (pp. 107–153). Mexico City, Mexico: UNAM-M. A. Porrúa.

Muñoz, H. (2002). *Universidad. Política y cambio institucional* (The university. Policy and institutional change). Mexico City, Mexico: UNAM-CESU, M. A. Porrúa.

OECD. (1997). *Exámenes de las políticas nacionales de educación superior. México* (Examinations of national higher education policies. Mexico). Paris: OCDE.

Ramírez, C., Pavón, A., & Hidalgo, M. (Eds.). (2001). *Tan lejos, tan cerca: A 450 años de la Real Universidad de México* (So near, so far: The Real Universidad de México 450 years on). Mexico City, Mexico: UNAM.

Rodríguez, R. (2003). La educación superior en el mercado: Configuraciones emergentes y nuevos proveedores (Higher education on the market: Emerging configurations and new providers). In M. Mollis (Ed.), *Las universidades en América Latina: ¿reformadas o alteradas? La cosmética del poder financiero* (The universities in Latin America: Reformed or altered? The cosmetic of financial power) (pp. 87–107). Buenos Aires, Argentina: CLACSO.

SEP. (2003). Secretaría de Educación Pública (Ministry of Public Education) *Informe nacional sobre la educación superior en México* (National report on higher education in Mexico). Mexico City, Mexico: SEP, IESALC-UNESCO.

47

THE NETHERLANDS

Egbert de Weert
CHEPS, University of Twente, The Netherlands

Looking back over the last two decades, Dutch higher education has undergone several large-scale operations, such as the re-contouring of first-degree study programs in the early 1980s, several retrenchment operations accompanied by enormous budget cuts, a merger and amalgamation process within the nonuniversity sector, and a re-definition in the systems of formal power and authority in universities. In his recent observations of Dutch higher education, Guy Neave expressed amazement at the ability to absorb so much in what, from an institutional standpoint, is a short period indeed (Neave, 2000). This continues with the relatively smooth adoption of the bachelor's/master's degree system as envisaged by the Bologna Declaration in 1999, where countries committed themselves to introducing in Europe a two-cycle system of undergraduate and graduate education. Today, the Netherlands is one of the forerunners in Europe for implementing this in the entire higher education system.

Neave goes on to argue that there are two reasons that account for this adaptation. First, the strategic and deliberative "policy style" and, second, the apparent willingness of higher education to accommodate these reforms. A characteristic policy style is the involvement of as many stakeholders as possible in an attempt to arrive at policy consensus, a practice that has been typified as a "polder model" of decision making. This does not exclude superimposition at some point, but based on the recognition of mutual responsibilities, the relevant stakeholders are given degrees of freedom to shape the process. This became quite clear in the formulation of a new steering conception as articulated in the legendary 1985 governmental paper "Higher Education: Autonomy and Quality." The basic idea is that by increasing the autonomy of higher education institutions, conditions will be created to strengthen their adaptive capacity to respond to the rapidly changing demands of modern society. The paper stated, "We have to find mechanisms that stimulate the flexibility of the system; we have to increase the higher education system dynamics" (Ministry of Education, Culture and Science, 1985). The idea of steering at a distance was meant to move away from the traditional "étatist approach" toward more autonomy and *ex post* evaluation of the performance of higher education institutions.

These reforms have helped the Dutch system to gain efficiency over the years. Since 1992, the number of graduates has doubled and the number of dissertations has tripled,

James J.F. Forest and Philip G. Altbach (eds.), International Handbook of Higher Education, 899–918.
© 2006 *Springer. Printed in the Netherlands.*

while costs per student have declined by 40%. Meanwhile, Dutch scientists have become increasingly prominent in the research community, as reflected by international publication rankings and the two physicists from Utrecht University who won the Nobel Prize in 1999.

However, despite the optimism that such improvements yield, there is a general feeling of discontent. National committees follow one another to explore the issues and present a "grand design" for the innovation of higher education. There are two major concerns. First, public expenditure for universities has decreased steadily in relation to GDP growth, from 35% in 1991 to 25% in 2001. Public investments seem no longer adequate to satisfy the growing demand for higher education. Privatization and marketization—in terms of more private funding by students, more research funding from industry, and performance-based funding—are among the basic trends. The fundamental question stemming from this is how to maintain a publicly funded system that is generally accessible for all citizens.

Second, there is a concern that the Netherlands is losing its competitive edge in Europe, and that higher education is not adequately responding to the needs of the knowledge-based economy. In particular, enrollments in science and engineering subjects are considered too low compared to other countries and, increasingly, foreign students are necessary to fill the gap. Given the ambitions of most European governments to become the most dynamic and competitive economy in the world by the year 2010, both the previous and present Dutch governments have stipulated that the Netherlands should be at the forefront in Europe, and that higher education should play a crucial role in realizing these ambitions.

There is virtually no topic that is not affected by the issue of public funding and the growing Europeanization and internationalization of higher education. At the very least, these two issues permeate all the topics that will be discussed in this chapter, including the current re-structuring of the educational and research system; doctoral education; funding; academic staff; accountability; quality and accreditation; and the relationship between higher education and economy.

The Dutch System of Higher Education

History and Structure

A main feature of Dutch higher education is its binary structure, which separates universities from institutions for higher professional education—*Hoger Beroepsonderwijs* (HBOs). Universities and HBOs developed under very different historical conditions and are based on different rationales and purposes.

The history of universities dates back to the 16th century when the University of Leiden was founded, followed by the Universities of Amsterdam, Groningen, and Utrecht. Because of their age, prestige, and range of subjects they teach, they are the largest universities in the country. Other universities were established during the 20th century, including private universities—founded in reaction to state control of higher education and based on denominational identities—such as the Free University of Amsterdam and the Catholic Universities of Nijmegen, and Tilburg. Despite their private status, however, they are funded by the state under similar conditions as the other Dutch universities. More recently, new universities were established—including the University of Twente (1964) and the University of Maastricht (1976)—as a result of an explicit government policy to further economic activity in the region. In the 1980s, the university sector witnessed two large-scale operations to increase the efficiency and effectiveness of the university sector as a whole, as well as a restructuring of university courses toward 4-year degree programs as a standard (with the exception of engineering, which is a 5-year program).

At present, there are thirteen Dutch universities, nine of which provide teaching and conduct research in a wide range of traditional academic disciplines. Three universities offer courses mainly in science and engineering, and another is primarily for the study of agricultural sciences. In addition to these universities, there are a few university level institutions, mainly in theology and business studies. The main objectives of a university education include training for the independent pursuit of scholarship and preparation for the professions. These goals are to be achieved through teaching and research. The Higher Education and Research Act of 1992 describes an explicit aim of universities as ensuring that knowledge is transmitted for the benefit of society.

The HBO sector dates from the late 1960s, when colleges for higher vocational training were upgraded. Formally, HBOs belonged to secondary education until, in 1986, they were legally acknowledged as a subsector of the higher education system. Because of the sector's fragmented character, the government initiated major reforms in the 1980s. These resulted in the merging of more than 400 smaller institutions into large institutions, currently providing a wide range of vocational courses with a standard period of study lasting 4 years. Today there are around 50 HBO institutions. Their main task is to provide theoretical and practical training with a clear vocational orientation. They also have the important task of transferring and developing knowledge for the benefit of the professions in both the industrial and service sectors. Their role is to support regional and local needs—although, increasingly, they tend to operate nationally and internationally, too. In the context of internationalization, HBOs have adopted the name "universities for professional education."

The relationship between universities and HBOs has been the subject of continuous debate. Although there are overlaps between them and, in principle, courses are of the same duration, the government maintains a basic distinction between the two as a guarantee of institutional differentiation. "Equal but different" is the term which has gained the widest currency. The main difference is the status of research—for universities, this is a main task, but for HBOs it is only permitted where it is applied research or research in the context of professional development. Despite the binary policy, both sectors are incorporated in a single Higher Education Research Act of 1992, encompassing a range of regulations that apply identically to both sectors. There is, however, a tendency to seek more homogeneity in organizational and administrative matters on both sides of the binary line.

In addition to the two main sectors, the Open University (founded in 1984) provides both university and HBO degrees through distance learning. Also, a number of new private providers have entered the higher education market, mainly through distance learning. These providers are not eligible for public funding, but require formal recognition by the Ministry of Education, Culture, and Science through accreditation.

Demand for Access

The Dutch system has in principle an open admission system in the sense that anybody who meets the standard qualifications in secondary education is eligible to enter higher education. The policy objective of "higher education for the many"—articulated during the 1970s—implies the aspiration to make and to keep the higher education system accessible to as many persons as possible.

Entrance qualifications differ for universities and HBOs. For universities, students must have a 6-year preuniversity diploma (VWO). Those who complete the first year of an HBO program are eligible as well. To qualify for HBOs, various routes are possible: the 5-year secondary education (HAVO) is the most common route, but also secondary vocational education and a VWO provides direct access. In order to facilitate the transition to higher education, the secondary education sector has undergone some changes in the last decade. The most notable is that secondary school curricula have been organized around four basic profiles that are optional for pupils: culture, economy, nature and health, and nature and technology. Since access to particular higher education programs requires specific profiles, these profiles have a sorting out function. There are other entrance possibilities, such as the *colloquium doctum* entrance examination and, for HBOs, qualifications acquired elsewhere (for example, through work experience).

For some subjects there exists *a numerus clausus* based on capacity issues or manpower planning, such as in medicine (university) and at health sector-related HBOs. For medicine, the selection of students involves a lottery system, weighted by the average marks of the school-leaving examination. However, when a number of pupils with outstanding marks were unsuccessful in this lottery, the resulting public debate compelled the government to give institutions more freedom in selecting their students. In addition to the central lottery system, institutions are allowed to select up to 20% of their total intake on the basis of other criteria (e.g., individual motivation, talent, or work experience).

In the Netherlands, the overall participation rate of young people in higher education is about 35%. Compared internationally, the proportion of those in the workforce with a higher education degree is slightly below the OECD mean of 26%. The total student population is 514,000, of which 65% are in HBOs (with over 334,000 students enrolled, 80% of them full-time) and 35% in universities (with 180,000 students enrolled, 91% of them full-time).

All students have to pay tuition fees, and the amount has increased steadily up to almost 1,445 euro in 2003–2004 for all institutions and programs. In the last few years, the question of differential tuition fees has been a major issue. As part of the access policy to increase the number of students in science and engineering subjects, attempts have been made to make these subjects more attractive by reducing their tuition fees. So far, the Ministry has been reluctant to use financial incentives to steer enrollment, with the exception of extending the student support system with an extra year for science and engineering students.

The student support system has undergone several changes. The current system is based on a basic grant for all full-time students, a means-tested supplementary grant for a limited number of students (about 30%), and a loans system to be taken up on a voluntary basis, with an interest rate which is lower than the standard rate. Since the early 1990s, the grant is no longer unlimited, and students must demonstrate continual progress in their studies—if they do not pass 25% of their annual study credits, their grants will be converted into an interest-bearing loan.

The present student support system is under review. The basic idea of this revision is that since higher education brings individual students considerable future rewards, students should pay more for the costs of their education. The governmental Central Planning Office (CPB, 2002) advocates a considerably higher loan component as well as a differentiation of tuition fees. However, debates continue on whether such a move would jeopardize the accessibility of higher education for those from lower socio-economic backgrounds.

New Developments: The Bachelor's/Master's System and Institutional Collaboration

The most important development in the last few years has been the adoption of the bachelor's/master's degree system. Following the Bologna Declaration (1999), the university degree distinguishes a bachelor's program lasting 3 years, followed by a specialized master's program of 1–2 years. A new phenomenon in universities is the introduction of two types of master's degrees: a research master's degree, focusing on careers in science; and the professional master's, oriented toward the various professions. For the HBOs, the existing 4-year programs remained virtually unchanged, leading to a bachelor's degree. HBOs also have a tradition of providing professional master's degree programs in various fields, sometimes offered jointly with a university or in cooperation with the professional field.

The Dutch government has been quite eager to adopt this new approach, since this is seen as an essential condition for a modern and internationally oriented higher education system. The aim is to create a flexible system which can meet the needs of students of all ages and an open system which enables Dutch students to study abroad, as well as enabling foreign students to enter the Dutch system (Boezerooy, 2003).

The bachelor's/master's degree system did not emerge all of a sudden. Prior to the Bologna Declaration of 1999, a bachelor's degree program was founded at University College Utrecht, which provides a broad program of study in one of the following areas: humanities, science, or social science. These are highly selective programs for an international group of students. Bachelor's degree holders are eligible to take a more specialized graduate program at any university. Meanwhile, other universities have followed this initiative and established such colleges as well.

There are two other developments worth mentioning here. First, there is a growing collaboration in the form of networks and joint ventures among various universities and between universities and HBOs. For example, the three technical universities have agreed to form a federation aiming at strengthening education and research in the technical fields. A joint graduate school will be established and there will be significant collaboration and tuning between the educational programs at the three universities. The overall purpose is to increase the number of students in technical fields by making programs more attractive in both the bachelor's and master's courses, as well as encouraging more focused and prioritized research with the overall ambition of providing additional impetus to the Dutch knowledge economy.

Another illustration of the growing collaboration during the 1990s has been the mushrooming of partnerships between universities and HBOs. These partnerships are considered beneficial for both sides of the binary line. Collaboration is not limited to joint facilities (such as buildings and libraries) or services, but also includes better student counseling and advising, the development of credit transfer systems across the binary line, and the like. Mergers are not the objective, nor the integration of study programs.

The second development is a widening of participation of nontraditional groups, such as people rejoining the workforce, ethnic minorities, older students, and those who do not opt for a full-time degree course but instead take a course in the context of lifelong learning. Flexible pathways of learning have been created to respond to individual demands, and it is expected that these demands will increase explosively (Leijnse, 2000). Examples are more customized education, assessment procedures (for example, admission to a shortened program based on work experience), e-learning, and cooperative education that combines education and work. The latter form has expanded considerably in Dutch higher education, particularly in the HBOs, while cooperative education is less common in universities, although it is a recognized form.

Research System and Research Training

System and Funding

The research system consists of the universities and research institutes which are attached either to universities, to the Dutch Research Council (NWO), or to the Royal Netherlands Academy of Arts and Sciences (KNAW). The research council plays an important role as it distributes funds across the different disciplinary research areas. This so-called "second flow of funds" supports research programs or individual researchers and consists of 18% of the total research budget of universities. The "first flow of funds" consists of a basic allocation by the government directly to universities, and is the largest (53%). The "third flow" concerns contract research for external constituencies (industry, governmental agencies, and other societal organizations, as well as from the European Union).

This multilevel system of university research funding makes science policy a rather complicated endeavor. The current policy agenda seeks to bring about a more dynamic system by setting research priorities and increasing performance-based funding. One way of achieving these objectives is to divide the basic allocation from government to universities into separate allocations—some that vary according to the size of the university and others under the heading of "strategic considerations allocations."

Regarding the latter, the original plan of the Ministry was to base research allocations on the research quality of a university and an assessment of the societal relevance of their research. However, this plan was never realized because it would entail reallocations between universities, resulting in a major intrusion on the university's autonomy. In the current system, the basic as well as the strategic considerations allocations are not targeted to faculties or departments. Instead, the central management of universities is responsible for distributing these funds across its various faculties and research institutes.

Another way to increase science dynamics is to shift a substantial part of the research budget from the basic allocation to the budget of the research council. This has been an important consideration of subsequent governments. The council would then be able to redistribute the research budget to the most excellent locations in the university system. The performance-based component in research funding would also focus more on specific research areas and those research programs that from a socio-economic perspective are considered desirable. To date, however, universities have resisted this move, but there is increasing pressure on universities to show the outcomes of their research efforts in terms of socio-economic relevance and commercialization of research results.

Other developments regard the growing impact of contract research for external constituencies and the Europeanization of the research agenda. The establishment of "strategic alliances" between universities and industry in the field of research areas has expanded. The participation in large research programs—such as the European Framework Programs—has expanded as well. Several of these programs require that externally awarded research budgets are matched with an equal amount from the university's own budget. This matching requirement claims an increasingly larger part of the university's research budget. Apart from the debate on the perverse effects which contract funding for external constituencies may have, the matching requirement entails that university research is liable to be pushed aside. National advisory councils have taken up the issue as they see the matching requirement as undermining long term, fundamental and risk-bearing research.

The European policy toward a European research area, motivated by a concern about the declining investment in scientific research, stresses the need for more research cooperation and more abundant human resources. University research should become more entwined in larger international networks and larger research consortia in order to be able to effectively take part in framework programs. The Dutch research council is much in favor of establishing thematic research projects on an international basis, as this may yield synergy from which the Netherlands, as a small country, can benefit. In this context, the council advocates the establishment of a genuine European research council, which as a supranational entity would distribute research funds across national borders.

The Emergence of Research Schools

An important development in the last decade has been the emergence of research schools. These schools aim to structure university research and to provide more focused research training. The argument is made that aspiring researchers need further education and training of a sort that can only be provided in an environment of high-quality research. Research schools are an important vehicle for concentrating research in centers of excellence that foster an international research climate with a high mobility of researchers. A strengthening of the research infrastructure and a proliferation of programmatic research frameworks would enhance both an environment for high-quality research and the capacity to compete for research funds.

The structure and role of the research schools are defined by law. The Royal Netherlands Academy of Arts and Sciences (KNAW) is responsible for their accreditation, and an independent committee has been charged with evaluating their performance over a 6-year cycle. At present, 107 research schools have been formally recognized. An important requirement is that the schools have a training program, which contributes to achieving coherence and synergy between research and education at the postgraduate level.

Contrary to research schools (or graduate schools) in other countries—like in the United Kingdom and Germany, where such schools are linked to a faculty, or in the United States, in which a graduate school can cover all the faculties of a university—research schools in the Netherlands are organized on an inter-university basis around particular scientific subject areas. They are affiliated with at least one university, and usually with a number of universities. Thus, research schools are conceived as core entities in a university system rather than as specialized distinctive institutes. They have budgetary responsibilities on the basis of the funds allocated by the participating universities to the research schools.

Doctoral Education

The present graduate education system dates back to 1986, when a formal system was introduced to regulate education and training for doctoral students. Up to that point, research training had been an integral part of the standard university education program amounting to European Research Council 6 or 7 years. Graduates who obtained a position at a university could carry out their own research leading to the award of a doctoral degree.

In shaping doctoral education, two issues in particular played an important role—namely, the structuring and the educational concept. The central question regarding the structuring is whether or not a doctoral program should consist of one continuous period of university research training or of two periods consisting of 1 or 2 years of research-studentship and a 3- to 4-year appointment as an assistant/researcher. In this latter structure, student and employee statuses are separated. With regard to the pedagogical issue, the question is whether or not there should be an educational component (in a strict sense), such as required courses and an explicit training plan during the assistant/researcher period. If there is no educational component, doctoral training could be characterized as a "learning-by-doing-model," suggesting that through the undertaking of research activities, doctoral students can prepare themselves for the award of a doctoral degree.

Questions of structure and of pedagogical concept have been central to the debates on doctoral training to the present day. Subsequent ministers of education have taken particular positions, shifting from a "learning-by-doing-model" to a clear "educational" model, and *vice versa*. The present system bears this double-sided and equivocally felt character of doctoral training in the Netherlands. The so-called *Assistent-in-Opleiding* system (AiO) has the following major features:

- the employment of doctoral trainees (AiOs) on a temporary basis, usually full-time and (in principle) for a standard 4-year period, with remuneration according to a specific salary scale; and
- the drawing up of a legal contract between the university, the supervisor, and each individual research trainee, which specifies a training and supervision plan.

The employment status implies that AiOs hold a distinct academic position. Although they may receive research training and supervision, they are also supposed to contribute to the research output of their faculties. The hybrid character of the AiO position is expressed in the remuneration, which is based on a special salary-scale that includes a built-in deduction for the training and supervision received. Recipients are seen as neither full-time employees nor full-time students.

In general, the AiO system does not require a standard set of courses to be taken by all research trainees. An AiO must devote 75% of his or her total employment time to research. Increasingly the research schools play an important role in doctoral education. However, the research schools are selective, and not all AiOs participate in any of them. The university to which an AiO belongs is the only institution which is eligible to award his or her doctoral degree. The Royal Netherlands Academy of Arts and Sciences advocates a stronger organization of research training. This involves "a curriculum for the aspirant-researcher focused on the specific subject field, to include a structured program for courses and supervision, general and subject-related courses which are linked to a mastery of the subject, and continuous supervision of doctoral students" (Royal Netherlands Academy of Arts and Sciences, 2002).

It is obvious that the embedding of the AiOs in the research schools will lead to a shift from research *training* toward doctoral *education,* in that courses constitute a substantive component of the research training system. The Royal Netherlands Academy and the research council advocate an integral conception of university education, whereby the research-oriented master's and doctoral education should be linked closely. In their view, courses during the master's phase should prepare students for the doctoral program. Universities, however, do not consider the research schools as the guiding principle for the organization of university research, and consider alternative options as well.

One such option is to move away from the classical idea of doctoral education and to design the doctoral process to meet social demand for highly educated professionals. Doctoral education should reflect different career destinations, including the need to incorporate training components which make graduates employable in a variety of employment and professional settings. For example, collaborative arrangements between universities and industry have been established, aimed at incorporating research into industry as a component of postgraduate training. On a cooperative basis, students alternate their research and their professional work in industry with more formal training at universities. Thus, doctoral training is becoming more diversified in terms of its content and location.

Funding

Since the early 1990s, the funding mechanism has included performance indicators in the budget allocation for teaching and research. Regarding teaching, performance is measured in terms of the number of degrees awarded. According to the current "performance-based funding model," which has been operational since 2000, 50% of the core teaching funds are distributed on the basis of the number of degrees granted, 13% on the basis of new entrants, and the remaining 37% as a fixed amount for each university. The rationale for a fixed amount for each university is to guarantee a minimum level of teaching independent of the number of students. The amounts differ across universities and are mainly determined historically. The larger and relatively older universities receive a larger amount compared to the smaller ones. In order to account for differences in the costs of education, a distinction is made between two categories of students and diplomas—roughly humanities, law, and social sciences on the one hand, and natural sciences, engineering and medicine on the other (Jongbloed and Vossensteyn, 2001).

The funding for research was discussed earlier in this chapter. However, it can be added that the relation of performance to research funding concerns the premium for the number of diplomas and Ph.D. degrees awarded. Universities receive an amount proportional to their role in the research school. In addition, a limited number of research schools that are regarded as excellent receive extra funding for a limited period.

The bachelor's/master's structure has provoked a discussion about the extent to which the government is responsible for funding. Since the public investment is no longer adequate to satisfy the total demand for higher education, it was decided that bachelor's degree programs in HBOs and universities, as well as university master's degree programs, are eligible for public funding. In addition, a few HBO master's degree programs are considered first degrees. Furthermore, there is a difference in funding between bachelor's and master's in the sense that universities will receive twice as much for a bachelor's degree than for a master's degree.

The most important criteria for funding are quality and macro-efficiency. In order to limit the ability of institutions to establish new study programs that would be eligible for public funding, a national agency was charged with the task of considering proposals for new programs. This independent, nongovernment committee [the Advisory Committee on the Provision of New Programs (ACO)] assesses new study programs on the basis of quality, transparency, and macro-efficiency. The term macro-efficiency refers to the question of whether a new study program would be desirable given the labor market needs and given the existing regional dispersion of educational provisions. Due to the liberal policy of the last government, however, this committee has experienced a gradual erosion of its capacity to assess new initiatives, resulting in an extensive proliferation of new study programs (ACO, 2003). In 2003, the ACO was discontinued and replaced by a new arrangement. Quality and transparency will now be subject to assessments by the new accreditation organization (described below). The macro-efficiency of initiatives for new study programs will be assessed by the Ministry of Education, Culture, and Science. The criterion for this assessment will be whether a new program contributes to the development of the Dutch knowledge-based economy or labor market needs "in those domains where the government has a specific responsibility." In other words, the Ministry has strengthened its role in approving educational programs that are eligible for public funding.

Challenges Facing the Academic Profession

The university sector employs nearly 42,000 people, of which about 22,000 are academic staff. Academic staff includes three main university positions as well as research assistants and postdocs. Approximately 9,300 members of the Dutch professoriate hold one of three main positions: professor (25%), university main lecturer (24%), and university lecturer (51%). These positions are mostly tenured and are charged with the standard academic tasks of teaching and research. The HBOs employ a workforce of roughly 24,000, approximately 13,500 of whom are academic staff. Here, the academic staff consists predominantly of the ranks of (senior) college teachers and instructors.

An important change during the 1990s has been a decentralization policy through which the central government devolved to higher education institutions the responsibility for determining employment conditions of staff. In 1999, this policy culminated in a practice in which terms and conditions of service are no longer determined by the government, but are settled bilaterally between employers and employees through their representative bodies. The underlying argument for this decentralization was that institutions would be better able to cope with external constraints and to introduce modern instruments for personnel management (De Weert, 2001).

During the process of decentralization, an important debate was whether the civil servant status of the staff should be abolished and replaced by employment contracts under private law. This would be a logical step, and the universities would arrive at a similar position as the three denominational universities as well as the HBOs who are regulated by private law. University managers advocate the privatization of universities, whereby staff are employed by universities as the legal employers. Although the juridical possibilities and consequences of such a transition would not change the nature of universities—universities should remain public institutions—it was decided that for the time being university staff would keep their civil servant status.

In the process of transferring powers and responsibilities from the government to universities and HBOs, a trend can be identified—movement away from uniformity in dealing with staffing issues, and toward the devising of personnel management systems that allow for individual, subject, or market differences and flexible reward systems. An important development is the current implementation of a new system of job profiles for academic staff. This system aims at making explicit the various roles, tasks, and responsibilities that must be carried out in order to achieve the stated objective. Individual development plans become possible, in which different staff roles are to be acknowledged, both vertically and horizontally within the same ranks. Individual staff members can apply for specific roles on the basis of an assessment of their qualifications—for example, to be more involved in either teaching or research. Teaching activities are classified in four specified tasks, such as teaching, curricular development, counseling student projects, and evaluation. Research activities consist of coordination, acquisition of contract research, and participating in research working groups and committees.

The system of job profiles has been designed to function as a basis for advanced personnel management regarding assessment (on the basis of output and competencies), personnel development plans and distinctive career paths. It challenges the traditional view that research performance is the all-determining factor in the career path of an academic. Although in this system teaching and research are intertwined, it distinguishes separate career tracks for academics, giving equal value to excellence in teaching and in research. The challenges facing the academic profession are twofold: first, how to break out of the spiral of the dominance of research and to assess teaching qualifications equally; and secondly, how to guarantee that the diversification of job roles would not result in a fragmentation of academic work tasks, but rather would contribute to a new conception of what academic scholarship is all about.

Another new challenge to the profession is the introduction of the "lectorate" in the HBOs. The lectorate—not to be confused with the traditional rank of lecturer or reader in the Anglo-Saxon world—is considered a highly qualified individual with significant expertise in the subject field and in the professional domain. The leading idea here is that lectors are not appointed as isolated staff members but as leaders of the so-called "knowledge circles," each consisting of a group of 10–15 staff members. A knowledge circle aims to enhance contacts and knowledge exchange with industry and consultancy—for example in the field of applied and developmental research. Through such a circle the lector plays a crucial role in strengthening the linkages between HBOs and industry and other organizations. Lectors are expected to acquire contracts from outside and to develop professional networks in particular fields. With special government funding, HBOs have appointed a considerable number of lectors, and the aim is that in a few years time about half of all teaching staff will belong to some knowledge circle. This initiative challenges the view of HBOs as a "teaching only" type of institution simply conveying the standard canon. By involving staff in broader knowledge networks, it is expected that this will enhance their professional development and keep their teaching up-to-date.

An important concern has been whether higher education still is an attractive working place, especially for the new generation of academics. There are recruitment problems for the research trainee system in several areas of science and technology, due to uncertain and limited career prospects as well as low financial rewards compared to positions elsewhere on the graduate labor market. Also, the relatively low numbers of women is a major concern, particularly among the tenured positions (currently, only 9% of professors are women). A special committee was formed to investigate these issues and to suggest directions for policy (Committee Van Vucht Tijssen, 2000). The committee recommended changes in the financial schemes of universities, special research programs for young researchers and women, and premium payments. Another proposal was to change the rigid formation system into a career principle and to shorten career paths in universities. These proposals are in correspondence with current developments, such as the job-ranking system as described above. Regarding the position of young researchers, a governmental scheme has been established—the so-called "innovation impulse"—which provides young talented researchers with financial opportunities to develop their own research into a research program. At present, scientists in various phases of their career can compete for research funds. In a similar way, women scientists can apply for the *Aspasia* program to develop their research further.

The management of academic staff has undergone a major change, with a new university governance structure introduced in 1997. The purpose of this new structure is to invest deans and university executive boards with clearer managerial authority. The traditional collegiate structure—according to which deans were elected for a fixed period of time as *primus inter pares*—has been replaced by a management model with deans as professional managers. These managers have increased budgetary responsibilities and delegated authority for staffing issues. In this governance model, clear responsibilities have been assigned to deans who can delegate further responsibilities to course directors, who in turn are charged with the organization of the curriculum, and research directors, who are responsible for the organization of research. The new structure puts pressure on academe as a professional work community and constrains its traditional freedom regarding teaching and research, at least formally. However, research thus far indicates that in practice professors still hold a substantial amount of professional autonomy (De Boer, 2003). A contemporary challenge facing the academic profession is whether (and how) the guaranteed right to freely teach and conduct research can be reconciled with managerial authority to determine the duties of staff, to evaluate their performance, and to reward them.

Accountability, Quality Assurance, and Accreditation

The system of quality assessment originated from the government's strategy to strengthen the autonomy of the higher education institutions, presented in the influential policy document "Higher Education: Autonomy and Quality" (Ministry of Education, Culture and Science, 1985). According to this new steering philosophy, autonomy, and quality are closely linked: higher education institutions were given more institutional autonomy in return for their willingness to show that they "deliver" quality. Essential in this view is that instead of *ex ante* control, *ex post* evaluation of quality should be developed. Over time, the government will determine whether the self-regulation of the higher education system yields outputs in an acceptable range (Huisman & Toonen, 2004).

In the development of a quality assurance system, some important themes on the purposes of such a system became apparent which hold true to date. Is the quality assurance system primarily for accountability (control) or should it lead toward the improvement of education and research? Is quality assurance predominantly an internal affair or a matter for some external agency? Should the level of evaluation be the distinct disciplines, the study programs, or the entire institutions? Should these evaluations focus separately on teaching, research, management, and other student support services (like library, administration, and information technology) or would there be some interrelation between these?

In institutionalizing the system, it was agreed by all parties that the Dutch Association of Universities (VSNU) and the HBO council (as the two umbrella bodies of these institutions) would coordinate the procedures. The focus was on accountability, with a special emphasis on dropout ratios and time to degree. At the same time, the government introduced the Inspectorate for Higher Education, charged with the task of evaluating the procedures and outcomes of the quality control system and to advise the minister on the results of follow-up actions by universities.

An essential characteristic is that assessments take place at the program level— that is, the collection of courses leading to the equivalent of a master's degree. On a nationwide level, programs are assessed per discipline in a 6-year cycle. The procedure consists of the following four subsequent phases:

(1) Departments undertake a self-evaluation of their programs on the basis of the guidelines set out by the umbrella organizations. The issues to be covered in the self-evaluation are specified and are intended to indicate the strengths and weaknesses of the program.

(2) External evaluation by a visiting committee consisting of about seven members who are normally sought among peers as well as professional and societal or- ganizations. More than in universities, it is quite standard in the HBOs to have representatives of employers' organizations on board. The committee bases its work on the self-evaluation reports and on their own observations during two-day site visits to each department, interviewing staff members and students. In addi- tion, the committee considers examination papers, syllabi, and a cross-section of master's theses.

(3) The reporting of the results in a national public report, which contains a compara- tive analysis of all the programs as well as a separate discussion of each individual program indicating their strengths and weaknesses. To accomplish the two goals of improvement and accountability, the report of the visiting committee must give an indication to the institutions of the quality of their program and how this is to be improved.

(4) The Inspectorate of Higher Education evaluates the procedures and outcomes of the quality assurance process. Furthermore, the Inspectorate monitors the follow- up of the outcomes of the evaluation by institutions and reports directly to the Ministry.

So far, two complete cycles of the quality assurance process have been carried out. The whole procedure has proven quite satisfactory, although certainly issues have been raised about the administrative investment that is needed for such a procedure, the quality of the reports, and the follow-up. Since the second round began in 1993, the Inspectorate has visited universities to determine whether they are reacting adequately to the evaluation committee's remarks (as provided in a mid-term review 3 years after the initial committee report).

An important element of the Dutch system is that in the spirit of self-regulation, there is no direct link between the quality review reports and funding decisions. It is generally assumed that such a link would harm the operation of the system. Academics and institutions will distrust the external review teams and they will produce self-evaluation studies in compliance with perceived criteria. However, if a study program turns out to be of low quality, and insufficient measure have been taken over a number of years, the government warns the faculty that unless thorough improvements are made soon, the program will be withdrawn from the official register. This would imply that its diploma would no longer be recognized and that it would no longer be eligible for public funding. So far this has occurred in only a few cases.

A question continuously being asked is whether the self-evaluation study (as carried out by the department) is just an information-gathering exercise, or whether it is a genuine, critical self-evaluation. In other words, is the self-evaluation meant simply to meet the requirements of the external visiting committee? Evidence suggests the answer is no: to most in the academy, self-evaluation is not considered to be just a kind of window-dressing to the external world. Rather, it is common that the self-evaluation reports describe the strengths as well as the weaknesses of the program. This is confirmed by the fact that several recommendations of the external visiting committee are in fact drawn from what the faculty itself had concluded in their self-evaluation report. So, in a way the external visiting committee "legitimizes" changes that were already considered desirable from within the faculty. Viewed in this way, the self-evaluation reports function as the cornerstone of the quality assurance system. An awareness of the strengths and weaknesses of the program constitutes a basic condition for quality assurance systems which have a built-in facility for learning and change, even if no external committee were involved. As some commentators put it, "Quality assurance systems need to be able to evolve, while maintaining the delicate balance between the functions of improvement and accountability, even if all other conditions (i.e., external aspects) remain equal" (Jeliazkova & Westerheijden, 2002, p. 434).

Accreditation

The restructuring of higher education systems across Europe toward the bachelor's/master's system implies a quality assurance mechanism that provides transparency and compatibility between national higher education systems. The European ministers who met in Prague (2001) recognized the vital role that quality assurance systems play in ensuring high quality standards and in facilitating the comparability of qualifications throughout Europe. On the European level, initiatives have been taken to arrive at a common set of descriptors or standards that would contribute both to harmonization and to progress in assessment methodology focusing on the output side of the educational process, namely in terms of the competencies of graduates.[1]

From the beginning, the Dutch government was much in favor of international agreements on standards for bachelor's and master's degrees that would be monitored by national accreditation systems. After a committee's recommendations and some experiments in the field, it was decided to add an independent component to the quality assurance system in the form of accreditation. This accreditation will be mandatory for programs that will be eligible for public funding and student financial support.

In 2004, the Dutch–Flemish Accreditation Organization (NVAO) was established to ensure and promote the quality of higher education in the Netherlands and the Flemish part of Belgium. The NVAO has developed a framework existing of six subjects on the basis of which assessment takes place: the objectives of the program; the design and implementation of the program; the program's use of personnel; institutional facilities; internal quality assurance mechanisms; and program results. In order to be accredited, all aspects must be assessed as "satisfactory." It should be stressed that the NVAO does not replace the existing quality assurance system as outlined before. Rather, the accreditation process should be connected as much as possible with the prevailing quality assurance system (Dittrich, Frederiks, & Luwel, 2004). The internal self-evaluation report as such is not part of the accreditation process, as it is argued that in this way there is a better guarantee that the faculty will give a fair self-analysis leading to an internal discussion among all faculty members, which in turn will enhance the chances for improvement. In other words, the improvement function of quality assurance will be maintained in the new emerging system.

The ranking of programs or institutions is not the purpose. The accreditation system is dichotomous. On the basis of an independent assessment process it is determined whether a program meets basic quality standards or not. The NVAO applies a rather broad framework that allows for differentiation of educational programs in terms of distinctive profiles or special quality features. This makes it more difficult to draw up rankings and this is not what the NVAO pursues.

Enduring Issues

In addition to these topics, there are several issues that have permeated higher education discussions in the past and will dominate the debate in the years to come. These include the need to agree upon the way in which higher education should serve the needs of the economy, and determine how to bring about a more differentiated system of higher education.

Higher Education and the Economy

The relationship between higher education graduates and the labor market is an on-going issue. The employment situation of fresh graduates is monitored on an annual basis approximately one and a half years after graduation. The unemployment rate for university and HBO graduates remains relatively low compared to other members of the workforce who have lower educational qualifications. It is expected that the demand for higher education graduates will further increase on an annual basis, with an estimated need for 4.8% more graduates from HBOs and 4.7% from universities (Research Center for Education and Labor Market, 2003).

About 75% of recent HBO graduates work in jobs which require at least their level of education. However, for university graduates the corresponding figure is 65%, although this varies between fields of study. Graduates from economic, technical, and medical studies show a high assessment of the match between their qualifications and their work. Furthermore, over 80% of HBO graduates work in jobs that require either their own or a closely related qualification. This is not surprising, since the HBO is specifically intended to provide vocational training. For university graduates the link between subject field and job is less specific, and graduates from several fields have rather broad employment outlets. Dutch employers overall attach considerable value to the difference between HBO and university graduates in terms of jobs and wages, especially in the earlier phases of a career. Although in some economic areas the difference is less pronounced, employers would not like to see the differences vanish.

Several research findings in the last decade have stressed the growing importance of multidisciplinary knowledge, generic and transferable skills, as well as personal and social skills. In order to enhance the employability of their graduates, universities and HBOs have broadened their curricula with general programs, especially in the earlier phases of the curriculum, with specialist courses in the later study phase.

A relatively new development is competency-based learning. Competencies are derived from work activities, tasks, professional roles, and practices. The future functioning of students in the workplace is taken as a touchstone. Other approaches emphasize the coupling of competencies with personal characteristics or disciplinary contexts, including analytical skills and the ability to integrate and synthesize.

The perceived gap between higher education and society is a continuous topic of debate. Several national agencies and committees in which members of industry have a prominent role have advocated strong linkages between higher education institutions with firms and branches of trade. In a similar vein, the Advisory Council on Science and Technology Policy (AWT, 2001) and the Social-Economic Council (SER, 2003) have advocated a strengthening of knowledge circulation by creating more systematic partnerships between higher education institutions and their external constituencies. Examples of concrete policies include: collaboration on research and educational projects; more working visits and exchange of personnel on either side; more flexible forms of learning (such as cooperative education); and competence-based learning. The most recent initiative to close the gap between higher education and industry *Innovation platform* and to create new partnerships is the launched in 2003 to develop a grand design for the knowledge-based economy. Under the chairmanship of the prime minister, leading figures from the scientific and business communities have been brought together with other constituencies to develop creative ideas for bringing about innovative roles for science in the knowledge-based economy. A larger involvement of industry in university research, a concentration of research in "strategic innovation networks" and the enhancement of knowledge valorization are among the issues discussed. Although this initiative has met considerable skepticism because of its ambitious objectives, it typifies the Dutch feature of bringing together people from various interest groups to arrive at consensus and to increase the commitment to the various measures proposed.

Toward a More Selective and Varied System

In general, the Dutch system can be characterized as very egalitarian, with the exception of the distinction between universities and HBOs (which serves mainly as a clear articulation of institutional differentiation). There is a standard duration for all courses and virtually no differences in quality, while standards of entry and teaching are basically the same. There are also standard tuition fees and standard financial-aid schemes. Because such a system leads to sameness, in the past various attempts were made to move away from this egalitarian principle. It is worthwhile to mention the late Jankarel Gevers, former president of the University of Amsterdam, whose modern version of the "idea of the university" included a differentiation between types of institution—general or specialist, European or regional, more focused on education or research, classical, or technical—yet all labeled as "university" (Gevers, 1998).

Inspired by European developments, the current political climate supports efforts to create greater differences between institutions (in terms of quality), a clear articulation of different characteristics, and different institutional missions. The government's "Higher Education and Research Plan 2004" states that governmental policy aims to achieve both excellence of, and maximum participation in, higher education, "if necessary with non-orthodox measures" (Ministry of Education, Culture and Science, 2004). As students become more internationally mobile, and as international competition consequently increases, Dutch higher education must make an effort to attract the best students and to keep them. Excellence would counter a possible brain drain of Dutch students going abroad and would bring about a brain gain from other countries. In order to achieve this diversity, entrance selection is a condition *sine qua non*. Furthermore, institutions should have more freedom to determine the tuition fees for their courses, enabling them to differentiate the fee for first-class courses as well as for "top-master's" degree programs. A characteristic of these "top-master's" is the quality of the program and the availability of the best academic staff that participate in research groups which have an internationally recognized presence in their field.

It is premature to speculate on how such a stratified system will evolve. In a sense, this policy fits in with some selective programs currently being developed in the context of the bachelor's/master's structure, such as the honors programs for excellent students at different universities, as well as the creation of "top-master's." Also, the accreditation agency can assign credits for a particular profile according to which distinctive features of a particular program are stressed. But if all universities aspire to the pinnacle of excellence and recognition, there will be considerable jostling at the top. Most Dutch universities are claiming the exalted status of research universities, and orient themselves to this single academic ideal. It is not yet clear how this relates to the objective of expanding access and providing opportunities for a wider group of people. Making top-master's a priority may disregard the value of broad undergraduate education which provides educational opportunities for a wider group of people. It may well be that the Dutch sense for realism will assure that maximum participation requires increasingly diverse constituencies, functions and levels of educational preparedness.

Conclusion

Dutch higher education appears to have performed well in the last decade, but the challenges lie ahead. It is clear that individuals will need to take a greater share of financial responsibility for their learning. The question remains how to maintain a publicly funded system that remains generally accessible, not only for the traditional cohorts, but for a larger group of people as well. Another challenge is to bring about a more varied and "dynamic" system of higher education, which allows for differences in education and research and which is better tuned to individual demands and capabilities. More performance-based funding, an increase in external demands for accountability and quality, greater selectivity of students, more differential tuition fees—these all constitute movement toward a "market-driven" higher education system. Such a move has clear advantages, but also bears several risks that as yet cannot fully be understood. The current government has launched various experiments in some areas to explore the possible effects. Finally, international developments are very pressing, and different changes have been adopted in both the education and research system in order to counter these challenges.

Throughout all these changes and daunting challenges, the task remains one of providing excellence in teaching, learning, research, and service. Given this historical review of the Dutch system of higher education, there can be no doubt that academic professionals and institutional leaders will continually rise to meet these challenges with increasing sophistication and success.

Note

1. The Bologna process envisions cooperation in quality assurance, accreditation, and certification and to develop a common framework of reference. An important network is the Joint Quality Initiative, consisting of representatives of various European countries, which aims to improve international cooperation in quality assessment, accreditation, and cross-national benchmarking. A major goal has been to develop shared descriptors of the required competencies of bachelor's and master's degrees. For more on this, please see the chapter by Hans de Wit in this volume.

References

Adviescommissie Onderwijsaanbod (ACO) (2003). *Eindrapport 1993–2003* (*Advisory Committee on the Provision of New Programs, Final report 1993–2003*) Den Haag, The Netherland: ACO.

Adviesraad voor het Wetenschaps- en Technologiebeleid (AWT) & Onderwijsraad (2001). *Hogeschool van Kennis: Kennisuitwisseling tussen Beroepspraktijk en Hogescholen* (*Advisory Council on Science and Technology Policy & Education Council, Exchange of knowledge between professional practice and universities for higher professional education*). Den Haag, The Netherland: AWT & Onderwijsraad.

Boezerooy, P. (2003). *Higher education in the Netherlands. Higher education monitor*. Enschede, The Netherland: CHEPS.

Centraal Planbureau (CPB). (2002). *De pijlers onder de Kenniseconomie. Opties voor institutionele vernieuwing* (*Netherlands Bureau for Economic Policy Analysis, The pillars supporting the knowledge economy. Options for institutional innovation*). Den Haag, The Netherland: CPB.

Committee Van Vucht Tijssen (2000). *Talent voor de Toekomst. Toekomst voor Talent* (*Talent for the future. Future for talent*). Zoetermeer, The Netherland: Ministry of Education, Culture and Science.

De Boer, H.F. (2003). *Institutionele verandering en professionele autonomie* (*Institutional change and professional autonomy*). Enschede, The Netherland: CHEPS.

De Weert, E. (2001). Pressures and prospects facing the academic profession in the Netherlands. In P.G. Altbach (Ed.), *The changing academic workplace: Comparative perspectives* (pp. 105–133). Boston: Center for International Higher Education.

Dittrich, K., Frederiks, M. & Luwel, M. (2004). The implementation of "Bologna" in Flanders and the Netherlands. *European Journal of Education, 39*(3), 299–316.

Gevers, J.K.M. (1998). *De breekbaarheid van het goede* (*The fragility of the good*). Amsterdam: Vossiuspers AUP.

Huisman, J. & Toonen, T. (2004). The Netherlands: A mixed pattern of control. In C. Hood, O. James, G. Peters, & C. Scott, *Controlling modern government: Variety, commonality and change*. Chettenham, England: Edward Elgar, pp. 108–113.

Jeliazkova, M. & Westerheijden, D.F. (2002). Systemic adaptation to a changing environment: Towards a next generation of quality assurance models. *Higher Education*, 44, pp. 433–448.

Jongbloed, B. & Vossensteyn, H. (2001). Keeping up performances: An international survey of performance-based funding in higher education. *Journal of Higher Education Policy and Management*, *23*(2), pp. 127–144.

Leijnse, F. (2000). *Hogescholen tien jaar vooruit* (*Universities for higher professional education ten years ahead*). Den Haag, The Netherland: HBO-Council.

Ministry of Education, Culture and Science. (1985). *Hoger onderwijs: Autonomie en kwaliteit* (*Higher education: autonomy and quality*) (*HOAK paper*). Zoetermeer, The Netherland.

Ministry of Education, Culture and Science. (2004). *Hoger onderwijs en onderzoek plan 2004* (*High education and research plan 2004*). The Hague, The Netherland: Ministry of Education.

Neave, G. (2000). On walking delicately: An outlandish view of higher education in the Netherlands. *Jaarverslag onderwijsraad 2000* (pp. 22–33). Den Haag, The Netherland: Onderwijsraad.

Research Center for Education and Labor Market (ROA). (2003). *De Arbeidmarkt naar opleiding en beroep tot 2008* (*The labor market link between education and profession till 2008*). University of Maastricht: ROA.

Royal Netherlands Academy of Arts and Sciences (KNAW). (2002). *Grenzeloze wetenschap. Enkele gedachten over Onderzoekersopleidingen en de Bekostiging van Universitair Onderzoek* (*Borderless science. Some thoughts on research education and the funding of university research*). Amsterdam: KNAW.

Social-Economic Council (SER) (2003). *Nederlandse kennis- en innovatiebeleid* (*Dutch policy on knowledge and innovation*). Den Haag, The Netherland: SER.

48

NIGERIA

Munzali Jibril
Bayero University, Nigeria

Higher education is defined here as all forms of postsecondary education that takes place in universities, polytechnics, colleges of education, and monotechnic education programs. Over 1.4 million students are enrolled in over 200 such institutions and programs in Nigeria. In 2003, there were 66 colleges of education, with an enrollment of 197,901 students; 55 polytechnics, with an estimated enrollment of 331,466 students; and 55 universities, with an estimated enrollment of 700,000 students. In addition, there were 90 monotechnics (i.e., technical colleges specializing in one area of study such as agriculture or health technology) and about 100 schools of nursing and midwifery and other professional training institutions, with an estimated enrollment of some 190,330 students. Given Nigeria's projected population of nearly 127 million in 2003, the total estimated enrollment in higher education of 1,419,700 represents a participation rate of 1,121 per 100,000 members of the population, which is above the average (in 1995 figures) for developing countries (824) and better than the sub-Saharan African average (328). However, as a gross enrollment ratio for 18- to 25-year-olds (whose population was estimated to be 18 million in 2003), enrollment in Nigerian higher education represents a mere 7.8%.

In terms of graduate education, less than 10% of all Nigerian students are engaged in postgraduate study, and most of these tend to be in the humanities and especially the social sciences, with very few graduate students enrolled in the sciences, engineering, or medicine (Jibril, 2003). Indeed, in some universities more than 50% of the graduate students are enrolled in business administration and related courses, responding to the needs of the labor market. Overall, while Nigeria's higher education sector is among the largest on the African continent, reforms are urgently needed—as this chapter will demonstrate—particularly in terms of curriculum, funding, governance, and access.

Historical Background

The first higher education institution established in Nigeria was Yaba College, which was opened in 1934 by the British colonial authorities to help with the production of middle level technicians (see Ogunlade, 1970). This was followed by the establishment of the University College, Ibadan as a degree-awarding College of the University of

James J.F. Forest and Philip G. Altbach (eds.), International Handbook of Higher Education, 919–934.
© 2006 *Springer. Printed in the Netherlands.*

London in 1948. The Ashby Commission—which the preindependence government established to advise on higher education for the new nation in 1959—recommended the upgrading of the University College to a full-fledged university in 1960, as well as the establishment of a university in the then capital city of Lagos and in each of the Northern and Eastern Regions. The Western Regional Government also proceeded to establish its own regional university at Ile-Ife. Thus, by 1962, there were five universities in Nigeria, which were joined in 1970 by the University of Benin. These six universities constitute what is known as the first generation of Nigerian universities. The second generation of universities consists of seven universities, which were established in 1975–1976 to ensure that each of the then 12 states of the federation had a federal university; two state universities were also taken over by the federal government in 1991 and 1992 to join the second generation club of universities. Although all the regional universities had by 1975 been taken over by the federal government, in 1979 states began to establish new universities of their own. The trend is still continuing, as there are now (in February 2005) 63 universities, of which 26 are federal (including one Defense Academy and one open university), 22 state, and 15 private.

The Ashby Commission Report (Federal Ministry of Education, 1960) also recommended the establishment of four advanced teachers' colleges and polytechnics, which have continued to grow both in number and in enrollment to the levels stated earlier. Of the 66 colleges of education existing in 2003, 21 were owned by the federal government and 40 by state governments, while 5 were privately owned. Similarly, of the 55 polytechnics existing in 2003, the federal government owned 17 and state governments 31, while 7 were privately owned. Most of the 90 specialized colleges are owned by the federal and state governments.

Access

One of the indicators of under-provision in the Nigerian higher education system is the admissions crisis that occurs every year when the season for admitting students to the higher education institutions arrives. Administrators and senior academics in the universities literally go underground in order to avoid meeting desperate parents and guardians of prospective candidates who come visiting to plead for the favor of having their wards admitted for their chosen course. Although the pressure in the polytechnics is also considerable, it is nowhere near the intensity of the pressure in the universities, especially the first generation federal universities and especially where professional courses such as medicine, law, accountancy, pharmacy, and business administration are involved. Although there are well-known criteria for qualifying for admission to these courses, candidates invariably fail to qualify and yet are desperate to be admitted for their course of choice. Sometimes undue pressure is brought to bear on the officers of the university through notes sent by highly placed public officers. Sometimes, too, there are stories of money changing hands, especially where junior academics or members of the administrative staff are in a position to influence the admissions process. A similar phenomenon has been reported in the literature regarding South Korea (NCIHE, 1997) and Eastern Europe and Central Asia (World Bank, 2002).

When admissions are judged against applications, only a small fraction of those who apply manage to get in. In 1997–1998 for instance, of the 419,807 who applied for admission to the universities through the University Matriculation Examination, conducted by the Joint Admissions and Matriculation Board (JAMB) (2000), only 73,432 (17%) were admitted. Similarly, in 1998–1999, only 29,721 (20.5%) were admitted to the polytechnics out of 144,626 candidates who applied for admission through JAMB. In the same year, out of 8,333 candidates who applied for admission to the colleges of education, only 2,824 (33.71%) were admitted.

However, the disparity between the number of applications and number of admission places offered only tells part of the story. The other part is that there is a critical shortage of good candidates. Indeed, many of those offers of admission are not taken up because, although the candidates may have scored highly enough on the matriculation examinations, they may not have the required five credits in the right combination of subjects, without which the universities and other institutions will simply not register them. Statistics of the percentages of candidates who eventually accept the offers made to them are not available, but in 1989–1990, the federal universities were given an admission quota by the National Universities Commission of 62,411, and although 352,544 candidates applied, only 50,928 were offered places, which left 11,483 places unfilled (18%).[1] Similarly, the colleges of education—which were able to admit 12,233 candidates out of the total number of 13,666 who applied (90%) in 1997–1998—could attract only 8,333 applicants in all, a decline of 39% over the previous year's number. The fact that only 34% of these were admitted (2,824) is also indicative of the dearth of good candidates.

The colleges of education and the polytechnics, which are left with the mediocre candidates after the best have gone to the universities, now resort to making up the shortfall in the number of unfilled places by admitting, in some cases, more candidates through the Remedial Course [called Pre-Nigeria Certificate in Education (NCE) and Pre-ND] route rather than through direct entry. According to Isyaku (2000), by 1996–1997, up to 54% of the students admitted to the colleges of education came through the Pre-NCE route. This has serious implications for quality, as the requirement for admission to the Pre-NCE course is simply three passes in the Senior Secondary School Certificate Examination (SSCE). Similarly, five passes are required for admission to the Pre-ND course in the polytechnics. It is doubtful if students admitted with such low entry qualifications (and who are then not subsequently subjected to an external examination after their foundation year course) can measure up to the quality standards that have been set for Nigeria's higher education system.

The Crisis of Access: Some Explanations

The crisis of access to higher education as described above can be explained in several ways. First of all, the secondary school system is itself in crisis and is so inefficient that it can simply not deliver the required quantity and quality of candidates for the higher education system to absorb. The universities require five credit passes in the SSCE, while the polytechnics require four credit passes and the colleges of education require three credit passes plus two ordinary passes in English and mathematics. These

Table 1. Candidates' Performance in the Senior Secondary School Certificate Examination, 1999

Subject	Total No. of Candidates	Score: A1-C6		Score: P7-P8		Fail	
		N	%	N	%	N	%
English	757,233	73,531	9.71	171,098	22.59	491,593	64.91
Mathematics	756,680	138,098	18.25	212,514	28.08	381,029	50.35
Biology	745,102	207,232	27.81	204,214	27.4	312,758	41.97
Chemistry	223,307	69,411	31.08	51,665	23.13	94,347	42.24
Physics	210,271	64,283	30.57	61,772	29.37	77,709	36.95
Economics	717,509	155,418	21.66	245,000	34.14	297,332	41.43

Source: Adapted from Nigerian Economic Summit Group (2000).

credit passes have to be in the right combination of subjects relevant to the desired course of study. In addition, the candidates have to score well enough on the University Matriculation Examination or the Polytechnics and Colleges of Education Examination to qualify for admission. Table 1 provides a summary of the performance of candidates in the 1999 SSCE.

Given that a credit pass in the English language is a requirement for admission to all university courses, it is obvious that less than 10% of the candidates who completed secondary school in 1999 could be eligible for admission to universities. Also, given that a credit pass in mathematics is a requirement for admission to all science-based courses, it is obvious that less than 20% of this cohort could qualify. Overall, the impression conveyed by the data in Table 1 is that the Nigerian secondary school system is operating at an efficiency level below 30%.[2]

It is important to clarify this statement by explaining that there are a few secondary schools whose students are indeed responsible for most of the high scores in the SSCE and whose overall rating (in terms of the proportion of candidates obtaining five credit passes or more) may be up to 90%. These are the federal government colleges, some of the expensive private schools, some of the religious mission schools, and some of the schools established by (and dedicated to) some federal services, such as university staff schools, Army Command schools, Air Force schools, and Navy schools. However, these schools are a minority, as the majority of students study in (state) government secondary schools, community schools, or low-fee private schools. The latter category of schools is usually less well resourced in terms of availability and quality of teachers, laboratories, consumables, and other teaching and learning quality inputs. Unfortunately, the children of the poor usually end up studying in these schools. It is therefore suspected that to some extent the Nigerian middle class is already perpetuating itself by creating favorable conditions for its biological offspring to gain access to higher education while restricting, albeit unwittingly, new entrants into the middle class from the class of the masses.

Another explanation for the access crisis is, of course, the failure of the universities to expand their facilities and teaching staff to keep pace with the demand side of higher education. Another explanation relates to the attitudes of candidates to the nonuniversity institutions—the polytechnics and the colleges of education. Because the employment reward system in Nigeria is university degree oriented, the university is the preferred choice of most candidates. This degree orientation has its roots in Nigeria's colonial history, when members of the British upper and middle classes who were university graduates served as colonial officers in the civil service. Naturally, all privileges were designed to be enjoyed exclusively by them. Technicians and nongraduate teachers were adjuncts in the service and therefore had lower status and restricted career prospects. When independence was achieved, Nigerian university graduates simply stepped into the vacated shoes of the former colonial officers and to this day some of the disparities and inequities still persist. The failed university candidate who goes to the polytechnic or college of education, therefore, still has his or her eyes on the university. Many drop out of the other institutions as soon as a university accepts them. In any case, they are further discouraged from viewing the other institutions as simply alternatives to the university, in part because of the uneven length of the courses in the nonuniversity institutions. For example, a candidate who obtains four credits in the SSCE and goes to a polytechnic spends two years to obtain the Ordinary National Diploma. He has to acquire practical experience for at least one year before he is eligible for admission to the Higher National Diploma (HND) course, which takes him another two years. So, he ends up spending five years to reach the equivalent status of a university graduate, who spends four years of postsecondary study to obtain a degree, admittedly with a higher entry qualification of five credit passes. To make matters worse, the HND holder is still reminded, from time to time, that he cannot rise to the top of his career because he does not have a university degree! In order to come to terms with this situation, HND holders now undergo a post-HND course in some of the polytechnics to qualify them to be rated like university graduates or more precisely, to prepare them for acceptance into master's degree programs in universities.

The failed university candidate who goes into a college of education is up against even more serious obstacles. To begin with, although the Nigeria Certificate in Education (NCE) course was designed during the 1960s—when the Teacher Grade II course (which provided the candidates for the NCE) was a 5-year post-primary one, with the introduction of the 6-year secondary school in 1982—the duration of the NCE course should have been revised to two years. Instead, the entry qualification was lowered to three credit passes. So, the failed university candidate who goes to the college of education spends three years studying for the NCE. Even if he gets admitted into a university immediately after the course, he has to spend, in most cases, another three years to obtain a degree. Invariably, he is required to serve his state government for at least two years before being sponsored to go for a degree course. Consequently, he may end up spending eight years to reach his ultimate goal of acquiring a degree just because he followed the NCE route. Many, in fact, never manage to get a degree because their score on the final NCE examination is unacceptably low for university admission. Many failed university candidates therefore prefer to wait for a year or two, re-taking the SSCE as private candidates, than to go into the long and uncertain route of the nonuniversity institutions.

Distance Education

Distance education in Nigeria can be said to be still in its infancy. There are now (in 2005) some 125,547 distance-learning students in Nigerian higher education. Of these, 93,547 are NCE students enrolled in the National Teachers' Institute's distance-learning program. The other 32,000 students are enrolled in various courses of the newly re-established National Open University of Nigeria. Clearly, this efficient and flexible learning mode has to be considerably expanded in order to reach the envisaged expansion targets of Nigerian higher education.

The Case for the Expansion of the Higher Education System

The structure of the Nigerian education system is skewed, with 24 million pupils at the primary school level, 6.5 million at the secondary level, and only 1.4 million at the tertiary level. Thus, in order to move from a gross enrollment ratio of 5% at the tertiary level, the number of pupils matriculating from the primary to the secondary school levels will have to be substantially increased, and the efficiency of the secondary school level will also have to improve substantially.

The target we should aim at is an enrollment in higher education of at least 20% of the age cohort by the year 2011. According to the National Population Commission (NPC) (1991), the 18- to –25-year-old cohort will be 22.1 million in the year 2010, so 20% of that will be 4.42 million. This amounts to a threefold increase in the size of the higher education enrollment over the next five years. Although this may look ambitious, with the benefit of hindsight, we now know that while the Ashby Commission thought that its enrollment projections were revolutionary, they turned out to be conservative and to have been outstripped by the actual size of the enrollment growth. This may well turn out to be the case here as well.

Given the present size of the secondary school subsector, for the next three or four years only between 900,000 and one million candidates will constitute the potential intake into higher education annually. We should therefore begin to prepare other potential higher education students from outside the secondary schools. There are thousands of secondary school dropouts who have not been able to secure the magical five credit passes in the SSCE or to pass the JAMB matriculation examination. State governments should mount intensive remedial programs for such people immediately. There should be provision for 10,000 such students in every one of the 36 states and the Federal Capital Territory, so that beginning in 2005, there will be at least 740,000 such students in the remedial programs nationwide every year. Some educationally disadvantaged states may not, of course, be able to mobilize up to 20,000 students a year, but then some of the educationally advanced states may be able to mobilize multiples of that number annually, so the numbers should even out overall. State governments should provide this service free to their citizens and should be responsible for the payment of the registration fees for the external examination to be taken by the candidates at the end of the course. It is hoped that at least 500,000 candidates will be successful in both the GCE examination and the JAMB matriculation examination annually, and thus provide additional candidates for the higher education institutions to admit.

The case for the expansion of the Nigerian higher education system is predicated upon the demands of the knowledge economy. At the present time, with only 5% of the relevant age cohort enrolled in higher education institutions, and with only 2.62% of the population having achieved a postsecondary education (NPC, 1991), Nigeria is ill equipped to participate in the knowledge economy. It was predicted as far back as 1977 that for it to survive and grow, every society must provide access to higher education for between 12% and 18% of its relevant age cohort to higher education and that providing access to less than 12% of the cohort to higher education would threaten the future of that society in a globalized and knowledge-based world economy (Perkins, 1977). It has also been suggested (Sadlak, 1988) that within this decade, 40% of all jobs in the developed economies will require at least 16 years of schooling, i.e., higher education. It is instructive that none of the OECD countries had a gross enrollment ratio below 30% by the close of the last century. Indeed, according to UNESCO (1998, p. 6), "In Europe, the gross enrollment ratio almost doubled, increasing from 24.1% in 1980 to 47.8% in 1995. North America, which already had a gross enrollment ratio of 55.7% in 1980, increased further to a ratio of 77.2% by 1990 and to 84.0% by 1995." Similarly, the Asian Tigers had gross enrollment ratios of between 11% (Malaysia) and 43.5% (South Korea) in 1995, according to the Dearing Report (NCIHE, 1997).

The World Bank (2002) has gathered extensive evidence to indicate the strong relationship that exists between investment in higher education, research, and development on the one hand, and economic growth on the other. However, it is emphasized that investment in tertiary education and in research and development on its own may not necessarily translate into higher economic growth. In order for such an investment to yield the required dividend, it must be made within the context of a national innovation system (described as an appropriate macroeconomic framework, innovative firms, adequate infrastructure, and other factors, such as access to the global knowledge base). The extent to which investment in manpower development impacts economic growth, as well as the returns on investment in education for individuals and the society, have been well researched in the economics literature, though there is hardly any unanimity on conclusions.[3]

It has been suggested by some observers that human capital is, in this knowledge economy, more important in contributing to the wealth of nations than produced assets or natural capital. According to Serageldin (2000), human/social capital now accounts for 59% of wealth creation in low-income countries (67% in high-income countries), compared to produced assets (21% low income and 16% high income) and natural resources (20% low income and 17% high income). This dramatic reversal of economic theory has been brought about largely by the role of information and communications technology (ICT) expertise in the knowledge economy. For example, with just 5 million workers representing 4% of the active workforce in the United States, ICT is responsible for one-third of the economic growth of the United States (Glanz, 2001). Meanwhile, the value of Indian information technology exports has been rising consistently in the last 10 years, from $150 million in 1990 to $4 billion in 2000, and is estimated to rise to $85 billion by 2008 (Glanz, 2001). This is particularly instructive for Nigeria, where economic growth is driven largely by natural resources rather than by human/social capital, and where the value of oil exports has yet to exceed $20 billion in any one year.

Thus, while the increasingly knowledge-based economies of countries like India and the United States are estimated (and expected) to rise, Nigeria's is expected to continue to decline owing to a downward trend in oil prices and the possible discovery and development of alternative sources of energy.

It is therefore a global trend that higher education systems are rapidly moving from elite systems, where only a small percentage of the population (usually less than 15%) has access to higher education, to mass systems, where the participation rates range from 15% to 40%.[4] The *massification* of higher education systems is closely correlated to a country's strategic positioning for global competitiveness. However, in view of the linkages between the three levels of education, the expansion of the higher education system has to move in tandem with the expansion of the two lower levels, especially the secondary, from which the higher education system recruits its intake.

The Case Against Expansion

There are valid arguments against the expansion of the Nigerian higher education system. For one thing, it is legitimate to argue that if funding and quality are so poor given the present (relatively small) size of the system, how much worse would they both be in an expanded system? It is equally legitimate to question the rationale for expanding the system further to produce more graduates, when Nigeria's economy already seems incapable of providing employment to the relatively few products of the higher education system.

The arguments put forward earlier in favor of expansion are so compelling that unless Nigeria wishes to postpone its development for another generation, the country's leaders must proceed with a comprehensive reform effort immediately. However, funding arrangements will have to be overhauled to drastically reduce dependence on the public treasury in order to run the higher education system. Quality is, of course, closely related to funding. It can be argued that if the required human and material resources can be mobilized outside the public treasury, it is possible to maintain and even improve quality simultaneously with expansion.

The issue of graduate unemployment can be explained in terms of the political economy of Nigeria. The public sector—which in the first two decades following independence (1960–1980) employed some 80% of the graduates of higher education—is no longer expanding, and is, in fact, contracting. The government is also now withdrawing from large-scale commercial activities and is privatizing or has already privatized, major public utilities such as telecommunications and power. As a consequence, there are very few new openings in the public sector. The private sector, which in other countries is the major employer of skilled manpower, has yet to find its proper bearing in Nigeria. Most of the industries are foreign owned and rather small or are mere assembly plants with only marginal linkages to local producers. Owing to political instability, no substantial new investment has come into the country from outside in the last 15 years, except recently, when the telecommunications sector was deregulated and some foreign companies came to open shop. Also, many wealthy Nigerians who made their money as public officers are afraid to invest the money at home for fear of possible confiscation and/or prosecution. Instead, the funds are hidden in Europe and the United States. But the absence of institutions that can absorb the new graduates of an expanded higher education system should not discourage us from expanding the system.

The example of the Asian Tigers has shown that once a nation empowers its people with the right technical and entrepreneurial skills, they can actually create jobs for themselves and drive the engine for the growth of the nation's economy. This, of course, means that the expanded system will be providing a new type of higher education, quite distinct from what has been on the menu up to this point in time. The question must also be asked: what is the alternative to educating a greater number of the higher education cohort? At present, the dropouts from this cohort provide most of the army of urban unemployed youth who are used by the disgruntled elite to carry out violent intercommunal riots. If the young people had better access to higher education, perhaps they would not be such an easy prey of the mischief-makers.

Funding

Since most of the higher education institutions are owned by state and federal governments, these proprietor governments tend to provide most of the funding for these institutions. In addition to failing to adequately meet the funding needs of these institutions, the governments—especially the federal government—restrict and regulate the institutions' ability to generate revenue from tuition fees and accommodation charges.

From a historical point of view, government funding of higher education in Nigeria has been declining in real terms, owing to the interaction of three key variables: rising enrollment levels, inflation, and the depreciation of the national currency, the Naira. As shown in Table 2, although per student spending grew nominally over the last two decades, enrollment growth and inflation have negated the funding increases—in fact, per student funding has actually declined since 1985 (see Babalola 1988, for instance).

Another yardstick by which we can assess the adequacy of government funding of its higher education institutions is to review the actual funding levels against the requests made by the coordinating agencies on behalf of the institutions—requests that are generally considered realistic appraisals of the minimum funding needs of

Table 2. Declines in Nigeria's Per Student Funding

Sector	Enrollment Growth	Nominal Funding	Adjusted for Inflation
Federal universities	371% (1985–2001)	Increased by 1,740%	Declined by 58%
Federal polytechnics	622% (1985–2001)	Increased by 938%	Declined by 29%
Federal colleges of education	354% (1990–2001)	Increased by 1,270%	Declined by 10%

Source: Adapted from Federal Government of Nigeria (1992), the *Statistical Digest on Colleges of Education in Nigeria* (National Commission for Colleges of Education, 1999, 2000, 2002), the *Digest of Statistics on Polytechnics in Nigeria,* 1998/99, 1999/2000 (National Board for Technical Education, 2000, 2001a, 2001b and 2001c), the *Report of the Committee on the Future of Higher Education in Nigeria* (Federal Government of Nigeria, 1997), Omoregie and Hartnett 1995, Hartnett 2000, National Universities Commission 1992, 2000 and Okebukola (2002).

the institutions. For the period 1990–2001, the recurrent grants released to the federal universities represented, on the average, only 58% of the funding levels recommended by the National Universities Commission. For the polytechnics, the average funding level over the period 1985–2001 was a little better, at 71% of the levels recommended by the National Board for Technical Education.

As a consequence of the restrictions imposed by the federal government on the charging of fees in its institutions, some revenue sources are barely tapped by the universities; for example, student accommodation accounted for only 3.5% of all internal revenue generated by the federal universities in 2000. Similarly, rent on university property accounted for only 2.29% of all internal revenue, while income from consultancies was also poor, at only 5% of all internal revenue.

The Need for Funding Reform

Clearly, the Nigerian higher education system must be reformed to diversify its resource base if it is to deliver the quality output that the country needs to become a respected player in the knowledge economy of the 21st century. The government should deregulate the system and untie the hands of the universities and other tertiary institutions, allowing them to charge realistic fees for both tuition and staff and student accommodation. The government should also improve the public funding of higher education institutions in order to meet the minimum staffing and facilities levels recommended in the minimum academic standards/benchmarks. This funding reform should be implemented in three phases as follows:

- Phase I should involve the full deregulation of staff and student accommodation charges and the re-introduction of minimal tuition fees so that the government's contribution is reduced to 75%; this should take place during 2006–2007.
- Phase II should run from 2008 to 2010 and should involve the raising of fee levels beyond the token levels introduced in phase I; by the end of the phase, the government's contribution should be reduced to 60% while internal revenue should rise to 40%.
- Phase III should run from 2011 onward and should involve a more aggressive revenue drive to reduce the government's contribution (which should continue to rise, nevertheless) to 45%.

Private Participation in Nigerian Higher Education

Currently (as of February 2005), there are 63 universities in Nigeria, of which 15 are private; 55 polytechnics, of which seven are private; and 67 colleges of education, of which nine are private. In the university and colleges of education subsectors, these private institutions account for only 3% and 0.03%, respectively, of enrollment. However, the participation of the private sector has grown from nothing in 1999 to an enrollment of 21,459 presently in the university subsector. Moreover, eight of the 15 private universities have not yet taken off, having only recently secured their licenses. It is therefore expected that in the next five years or so, more will have been registered and those currently struggling to get off the ground will have settled down to serious business.

According to a recent book published by the World Bank, there is a strong positive relationship between the growth of private universities and the charging of fees in public universities. In *Constructing Knowledge Societies* (World Bank, 2002), the authors provide a broad comparative analysis of private growth in the higher education sector.[5] For example, they note that in Portugal, "private universities have expanded in less than a decade to represent 30% of tertiary institutions, and they enroll close to 40% of the student population" (p. 68). In Côte d'Ivoire, "private universities enroll 30% of the student population" (p. 69), while in Iran and Japan, private universities (which were introduced in 1983 and 1991, respectively) now enroll more than 30% and 35% of their respective student populations. The book then proceeds to suggest that in countries like Nigeria, expansion of private institutions of higher learning can be expected only when fees are re-introduced in the public universities.

The Nigerian public has been skeptical about the ability of private institutions to provide good quality higher education. However, given the track record of the private sector at the lower levels of the educational system, this skepticism would appear to be unfair. The regulatory agencies have been attuned to their responsibilities of closely monitoring and guiding these private institutions towards the attainment of acceptable standards. Happily, the indicators coming out of the initial quality assessments of the new private universities suggest that on the whole they are better positioned than public universities to deliver quality instruction. The results of the first accreditation exercise conducted for the private universities by the National Universities Commission show that none of their programs were denied accreditation (compared to the public universities, where 13% of their programs was denied accreditation a few years ago).

The private universities appear to have brought a breath of fresh air onto the Nigerian higher education scene. Because of their small sizes and the fact that tuition and other fees are charged, they have been free from student riots, staff strikes and student violence, which are all disruptive features of the public universities. Their presence on the scene is likely to make it easier for public universities to re-introduce tuition and other fees in order to be able to compete favorably with the private universities in the future.

The governance models and structures of private institutions appear to be different from those of public universities. Although, like their public counterparts, each private university has a vice chancellor and a governing council, that is where the similarity ends. All but one of the seven private universities that are presently operational are owned by individuals (sometimes hiding behind a religious organization) who keep breathing down the vice chancellor's neck and practically making all the major management decisions, much in the same way as the proprietor of a private secondary school renders the headmaster a glorified clerical assistant. The one exception is a university that belongs to a network of 23 other universities around the world owned by the same religious organization. The real battles in higher education will be fought in the future when the proprietors attempt to interfere with academic grading or other aspects of the academic freedom of the faculty.

The Brain Drain and its Impact on Nigerian Higher Education

The loss of highly trained Nigerian professionals to the industrialized economies and other countries that pay higher wages and provide better working and living conditions poses a serious threat not only to Nigerian higher education but to the long-term development of the country as a whole. It has been reported, for instance, that there are up to 3.25 million Nigerians in the United States alone, of whom some 174,000 are information technology professionals, 202,000 medical and allied professionals, about 50,000 engineers, and 250,000 other professionals, including university lecturers.[6] This trend is not unique to Nigeria, as Wolfensohn (2005) reports that only about 20% of sub-Saharan Africans educated abroad return home, the rest staying on in the country of study.

In the Nigerian university sector specifically, only about 36% of the required number of academic staff is actually on the ground, the rest having migrated to Southern Africa, the Middle East or the Western industrialized countries. A survey conducted by the National Universities Commission in 2001, as part of the background information for the negotiations with the Academic Staff Union of Universities, indicated that a full professor in Botswana earned about US$27,000 annually, while in Namibia the post attracted an annual salary of between US$21,000 and US$35,000, and in South Africa the annual salary of a full professor around the year 2000 was in the range of US$18,000–24,000. In Nigeria, despite recent increases in salary, the Nigerian full professor still earns only about US$12,000 per year. This is no doubt an important push factor for the brain drain.

Challenges Facing the Academic Profession

The academic profession in Nigeria faces several challenges. As noted earlier, the most important challenge is that of attracting and receiving adequate remuneration, which can guarantee a decent standard of living for the academic and his family; this should compare favorably with what is obtainable elsewhere in Africa. Although salary levels have increased five times in the last seven years in nominal terms, owing to inflation and the continual loss of value of the Nigerian national currency (the Naira), in real terms the improvement is only about 25% of the 1998 levels. As a consequence of this poor level of remuneration, there is a continuous flood of skilled university teachers out of the country and also into the more lucrative sectors of the Nigerian economy. The internal brain drain to the oil industry and the banking sector by brilliant new graduates—who then earn up to three times what the university would have paid them as graduate assistants—is alarming to the academic profession, as it means that there is no new blood coming into the profession to replace the aging senior academics in the future.

Ultimately, this is but a manifestation of a bigger crisis, the crisis of system funding highlighted earlier in this chapter. Since for the foreseeable future, public universities (especially federal universities) will continue to dominate the system, funding must be reformed and deregulated so as to diversify the resource base of these universities and reduce their dependence on the unpredictable and unreliable public treasury.

One of the consequences of this funding crisis is that equipment and facilities in the universities, colleges, and polytechnics have become obsolete or nonfunctional, while classrooms and laboratories can no longer accommodate the ever-increasing numbers of students. The academic staffing ratios continue to deteriorate below optimum levels (a few years ago the staffing levels were only 36% of what was optimally required). The cumulative effect of all these inadequacies is that the quality of Nigerian higher education continues to decline while academic corruption continues to prosper. Incidents of financial extortion and sexual harassment are on the rise, although few have been brought to public view.

The crisis of governance also looms large on the Nigerian higher education horizon. Although the Nigerian federal government has been singing the melodious song of granting autonomy to its universities, for instance, it is obvious that people in the government are reluctant to let go of their traditional powers of appointment and control in the higher education institutions. Although a bill designed to grant some autonomy to the universities was signed into law by the President in 2003, for some inexplicable reason the previous law is still in operation, and the new one is effectively ignored. The academic staff union is also not comfortable with the kind of autonomy that will compel the universities to be financially independent of the government and to charge appropriate tuition and other fees.

Finally, the problem of student secret cults and the violence their members perpetrate on campuses in some parts of the country is a serious threat to the security of both staff and students on such campuses. Quite a few members of faculty have been killed by such violent students, while student-on-student violence is a daily occurrence in some universities.

Conclusion: The Inevitability of Reform

The Nigerian higher education system needs to be reformed if education is to serve as a tool of development, enabling Nigeria to play its appropriate role as a respected player in the globalized knowledge economy of the 21st century. A comprehensive reform package should have components dealing with the curriculum, funding, and governance, among other issues. The graduates to be turned out into the labor market by the reformed and expanded system will have to be equipped with multiple life skills rather than facts and figures, and will have to be imbued with an entrepreneurial spirit and be ready to create their own jobs rather than expect jobs to be available on demand. This means that institutions of higher learning, especially the traditional universities, will have to come face to face with reality and stop pretending that there is no connection between what they teach and the world of work (or if there is, that connection is none of their business, for they exist in an esoteric world that prides itself on its lack of relationship with reality).

Secondly, it is simply not possible for the system to be expanded, as suggested above, under the current funding and governance arrangements. Already, quality has been declining largely because the government has been unable to discharge its funding obligations fully, and yet has been unwilling to deregulate the system so that other stakeholders can discharge theirs. The federal government, while substantially increasing its per student spending to meet at least 75% of the agreed academic costs of the students in the institutions it owns, should allow the institutions to consult their students, their parents and other stakeholders, and charge reasonable fees to make up for part of the 25% of the academic costs which the government cannot meet. Nonacademic costs should be fully recovered from students but, as a corollary, there should be many scholarships, bursaries, grants and possibly student loan schemes to ensure that students are assisted and encouraged to continue with their education, thus rescuing them from dropping out on grounds of poverty.

Governance arrangements will also have to be overhauled. True autonomy will have to be given to the institutions of higher learning. This will entail the government withdrawing from any active participation in decision making, especially as this relates to the appointment of the chief executives of the institutions. However, the appointment of members of the governing councils should be the joint responsibility of the institutions and the proprietor governments. The institutions should set up transparent processes of generating nominations from the campus and local communities of potential members of such councils who are willing to serve the institutions selflessly, and who will not look upon the institutions as sources of additional income for themselves. Such nominations, which should always be in excess of the number of available vacancies on the councils, should then be sent to the proprietor government for vetting and approval. The Ministry of Education or the relevant regulatory agency should also set up an effective monitoring unit to periodically evaluate the performance of councils and their key members.

Finally, a reform package can only be effective if the right macroeconomic environment exists. In other words, Nigeria must as a nation (and especially as a government) get its act together. The production of highly skilled and entrepreneurial graduates who cannot access microcredit to start off their own enterprises, or who cannot sell their goods and services because of unfair competition from cheap imports that are subsidized in their countries of origin, can only heighten the level of frustration of the country's young people and their anger with society, thus raising the level of violence and insecurity in the land beyond their already unacceptable limits.

Acknowledgments

The research leading to this paper was financed by a grant from the Association for the Development of Education in Africa (ADEA) Working Group on Higher Education.

Notes

1. Admittedly, the universities might have deliberately admitted fewer than they were allowed to by the NUC because the NUC figures are based on approved growth levels, which are not matched by appropriate funding to ensure commensurate growth in staffing and facilities. In this situation, some universities opt for the sensible thing: downsizing.
2. Of course, the six subjects given here do not represent the whole range of subjects taken in the SSCE. But they are among the most critical. Admittedly, scores in subjects such as Islamic Religious

Knowledge, Christian Religious Knowledge, Hausa, Igbo, and Yoruba are higher, sometimes in the region of 90% credit passes.
3. See, for instance, Psacharopoulos (1994), Bennell (1996, 1998), Asplund and Pereira (1999), Cohn and Addison (1998), and Temple (1999, Barro, 1997, Barro and Sala-I-Martin, 1995, Porter, 1990 and Stern et al., 2000). Also, see the chapter by David Bloom, Matthew Hartley and Henry Rosovsky in Volume 1 of this publication.
4. For more on this, please see the chapter by Martin Trow in Volume 1 of this publication.
5. For more on this topic, please see the chapter by Dan Levy in Volume 1 of this publication.
6. See *The Daily Trust* (July 12, 2004, p. 22), where the President of Nigerian Information Technology Professionals in America, Professor Manny C. Aniebonam was quoted as giving these figures.

References

Asplund, R., & Pereira, P. (Eds.) (1999). *Returns to human capital in Europe: A literature review.* Helsinki, Finland: Etla.

Babalola, J. B. (1988). Cost and financing of university education in Nigeria. *Higher Education, 36,* 43–66.

Bennell, P. (1996). Rates of return to education: Does the conventional pattern prevail in sub-Saharan Africa? *World Development,* 24, 183–199.

Bennell, P. (1998). Rates of return in Asia: A review of the evidence. *Education Economics, 6*(2), 107–120.

Barro, R. (1997). *The determinants of economic growth.* Cambridge, MA: MIT Press.

Barro, R., & Sala-I-Martin, X. (1995). *Economic growth.* New York: McGraw Hill.

Cohn, E., & Addison, J. T. (1998). The economic returns to lifelong learning in OECD countries. *Education Economics, 6*(3), 253–301.

Federal Government of Nigeria. (1992). *Higher education in the nineties and beyond: Report of the Commission on the Review of Higher Education in Nigeria (the Longe Commission).* Lagos, Nigeria: Federal Government Printer.

Federal Government of Nigeria. (1997). *Report of the Committee on the Future of Higher Education in Nigeria.* Abuja, Nigeria: Office of the Secretary to the Government.

Federal Ministry of Education. (1960). *Investment in education: The report of the Commission on Post-School Certificate and Higher Education.* Lagos, Nigeria: Federal Government Printer.

Glanz, J. (2001). Trolling for brains in international waters. *New York Times,* April 1, 2001.

Hartnett, T. (2000). *Financing trends and expenditure patterns in Nigerian universities.* Washington, DC: The World Bank.

Isyaku, K. (2000). Teacher education in the 21st century Nigeria: Vision and action (unpublished monograph).

Joint Admissions and Matriculation Board (JAMB). (2000). *Annual Report: 1997, 1998, 1999.* Abuja, Nigeria: JAMB.

National Board for Technical Education. (2000). *Directory of accredited programs offered by poly-technics, colleges of agriculture and similar institutions in Nigeria.* Kaduna, Nigeria: NBTE.

National Board for Technical Education. (2001a). *Digest of statistics on polytechnics in Nigeria (1998, 99–1999, 2000).* Kaduna, Nigeria: NBTE.

National Board for Technical Education. (2001b). *Digest of statistics on monotechnics in Nigeria (1998/1999, 1999/2000).* Kaduna, Nigeria: NBTE.

National Board for Technical Education. (2001c). *Digest of statistics on technical colleges in Nigeria (1998/1999, 1999/2000).* Kaduna, Nigeria: NBTE.

National Commission for Colleges of Education. (1999). *Statistical digest on colleges of education in Nigeria, volume 4.* Abuja, Nigeria: NCCE.

National Commission for Colleges of Education. (2000). *Statistical digest on colleges of education in Nigeria, volume 5.* Abuja, Nigeria: NCCE.

National Commission for Colleges of Education (2002). *Statistical digest on colleges of education in Nigeria, volume 6*. Abuja, Nigeria: NCCE.

National Committee of Inquiry into Higher Education (NCIHE). (1997). *Higher education in the learning society: Main report*. London: Her Majesty's Stationery Office.

National Universities Commission. (1992). *Statistical digest on Nigerian universities 1988–1992*. Lagos, Nigeria: NUC.

National Universities Commission. (2000). *Annual report 1999*. Abuja, Nigeria: NUC.

National Population Commission. (1991). *Nigeria at a glance* (Summary of population census data). Abuja, Nigeria: NPC.

Nigerian Economic Summit Group. (2000). Nigerian Economic Summit Group. *Economic Indicators 6*(2). Lagos, Nigeria: NESC.

Ogunlade, F. O. (1970). *Yaba Higher College and the formation of an intellectual elite*. Unpublished M.A. thesis, University of Ibadan.

Okebukola, P. (2002). *The state of university education in Nigeria*. National Universities Commission.

Omoregie, P. O., & Hartnett, T. (1995). Financing trends and expenditure patterns in Nigerian universities. Washington, DC: The World Bank.

Perkins, J. (1977). Four axioms and three topics of interest in the field of higher education. In *the contribution of higher education in Europe to the development of changing societies*. Bucharest, Romania: UNESCO/CEPES.

Porter, M. E. (1990). *The competitive advantage of nations*. New York: The Free Press.

Psacharopoulos, G. (1994). Returns to investment in education: A global update. *World Development, 22*, 1325–1343.

Sadlak, J. (1988). Globalization and concurrent challenges for higher education. In P. Scott (Ed.), *The globalization of higher education*. London: The Society for Research into Higher Education and the Open University Press.

Serageldin, I. (2000). University governance and the stakeholder society. Keynote address presented at the 50th Annual Conference of the International Association of Universities, Durban, South Africa, August 2000.

Stern, S., Porter, M. E., & Furman, J. L. (2000). The determinants of national innovative capacity. Working Paper no. 7876. Cambridge, MA: National Bureau of Economic Research (http://www.nber.org).

Temple, J. (1999). The new growth evidence. *Journal of Economic Literature, 37*, 112–156.

UNESCO (1998): *World statistical outlook on higher education: 1980–1995*.

Wolfensohn, J. D. (2005). Seizing the 21st century. A video presentation to the Knowledge Economy Forum organized by The World Bank in Abuja, Nigeria, January 30, 2005.

World Bank. (2002). *Constructing knowledge societies: New challenges for tertiary education*. Washington.

49

POLAND

Wojciech Duczmal

Academy of Management and Administration in Opole, Poland

Higher education in Poland has a long and rich history and tradition. The first university, Jagiellonian University in Krakow, was founded in 1364. The two other oldest universities, the University of Vilnius and University of Lvov, were founded in 1578 and 1661, respectively. Warsaw University, the first academic institution located in the capital of Poland (Warsaw), was created in 1816, and the first technical university—the Warsaw Polytechnic—was founded 10 years later in 1826. After World War I, when Poland regained its independence after more than a century of being portioned between Russia, Prussia, and the Austrian Empire, higher education played an important role in restoring Polish culture and science. The higher education system expanded to 32 institutions until the start of World War II. There were five state universities in Krakow, Vilnius, Lvov, Warsaw, and Poznań; three Polytechnics in Warsaw, Lvov, and Krakow; one private university, the Catholic University of Lublin, founded in 1918; and several other private and public higher education institutions in larger cities.

However, the higher education system was an elite system with low enrollment rates, reflecting the society's structure. In the prewar period (1938–1939), there were in total some 120,000 students; almost half of them studied in Warsaw, followed by Krakow, and Poznań (each with 15% of the country's enrollment). The great majority of students came from higher income families, usually from aristocracy and the wealthy class. The costs of study prevented less wealthy students from attending higher education and therefore contributed to (and strengthened) the existing social disparities. The system of state student support was underdeveloped and consisted mainly of student loans. Before World War II, higher education experienced broad academic and institutional freedom, which implied the individual scholar's ability to do research and teach without fear of punishment or loss of employment, and allowed each institution to determine and manage its own internal affairs without state intervention.

Higher education in Poland suffered a great loss during World War II in terms of academics killed and buildings ruined. The invaders closed down all higher education institutions, exterminated almost 40% of the professors, and destroyed most of the institutions' buildings, libraries, and laboratories. After the war, higher education developed from scratch (Poznanski & Kucha, 1992). The first state regulation concerning higher education after the war was the Decree on the Organization of Science and Higher

Education, which was passed by the government in 1947. This decree was relatively liberal in terms of academic and institutional freedom. Higher education institutions functioned within similar institutional arrangements and enjoyed almost the same degree of autonomy as before the war. In order to provide a qualified workforce to restore the country, new higher education institutions were established in Gdansk, Szczecin, Torun, Opole, and Wroclaw, among other cities. Some of them were founded as universities or polytechnics; however, the majority functioned as pedagogical higher education institutions or engineering higher education institutions which were less prestigious, had fewer faculties and at the beginning offered short vocational study programs. They grew quickly, and in a few years, they enrolled the majority of students and offered master's degree programs. In 1946, there were already 54 higher education institutions with some 86,000 students and 11,000 academics. Higher education institutions also offered part-time studies for working students.

The change in the political, social, and economic systems after the war reshaped the higher education structure. The Act of April 26, 1950 subordinated all institutions to the Ministry of Science and Higher Education, which implied a change to the patterns established before the war. The years from 1949 to the mid-1950s can be characterized as the "Stalinist period." The government limited the academic freedom significantly, imposed an ideological criterion for the selection of academics, and isolated the universities from contact with Western countries. In 1949, the government nationalized all private higher education institutions (excluding the Catholic University in Lublin). This transition in effect subordinated all institutional decisions to the needs and requirements of the socialist party. The act also imposed on higher education institutions the responsibility of promulgating socialism throughout Polish society, causing study programs to be modified to meet the needs of socialist ideology. The management system in higher education was based on a single authority—the Ministry, which was responsible in such areas as the goals and directions of higher education institutions; the internal organization of education and research; study programs; and appointment and financial regulations. The socialist party representatives who were present in the collegial organs of higher education institutions oversaw the day-to-day management. Top level positions in the higher education institutions were appointed by the Ministry, whose choices were based on the opinion of the central screening body for academic staff, which took into account not only the academic merits but also the political soundness of the candidate (Sadlak, 1991).

Another consequence derived from the Soviet model was the removal of several disciplines from the universities, including medicine, physical culture, agriculture, and theology, each of which was established in separate higher education institutions. Together with the nationalization of private higher education, tuition fees were abolished and the state took over the financing of higher education. Finally, on top of this policy were personnel repercussions. Academics, ranging from junior assistants to full professors (and especially in the social sciences) were removed from universities and other institutions and replaced by the graduates of the Institute for the Development of Academic Staff, supervised by the Polish United Worker's Party—the only legal political party, which until 1989 played the most important role in shaping and implementing policies in all sectors of the nation's economy.

Despite these negative changes, in terms of the decrease in institutional and academic autonomy, the higher education sector continued to grow. By 1970, there were 85 higher education institutions, with some 330,800 students and 31,000 academics. However, compared with the democratic countries, the growth of higher education in Poland was relatively slow. During the 1970s, higher education experienced significant quantitative growth in terms of student and faculty numbers. The increase was associated with both the economic boom in Poland (stimulated mainly by foreign credits) and the demographic explosion. The policymakers encouraged the expansion of student enrollment in order to respond to manpower needs and to promote the role of higher education as an agent of economic and social change. Student numbers increased from 330,800 in the academic year 1970–1971 to 453,700 in 1980–1981, while the number of faculty rose from 31,320 to nearly 54,700.

However, when the economy stumbled toward the end of the 1970s, the relations between policymakers and higher education became tense and uneasy. In the second half of the 1970s, the government's economic plan failed and state resources spent on higher education were substantially decreased. Insufficient state funds, combined with the strained political relations between the academic community and central governing bodies, brought a set of negative results. Student numbers decreased to some 356,400 in 1988–1989. The most significant fall in student enrollment was seen in engineering, economics, and management studies, where the decline exceeded 50%. During the 1980s, only one public higher education institution was established, compared to the launching of six during the 1970s. The number of graduates fell from 84,000 in 1980 to 49,800 in 1988 (see Table 1).

On the other hand, since the mid-1980s, the government increased the degree of autonomy for higher education institutions. During the second half of the 1980s, the prerogatives of universities and colleges were extended almost every time new legislation on higher education was passed. As a result of ongoing political changes, such as ideological and economic liberalization, the whole system of education underwent a considerable transformation. Pressure grew in many circles for reforms that would

Table 1. Higher Education in Poland, 1946–1991

Year	HEIs	Full-Time Students	Part-Time Students	Total
1946–1947	54	86,500	0	86,500
1950–1951	83	117,500	7,600	125,100
1970–1971	85	209,800	121,000	330,800
1975–1976	89	283,200	184,900	468,100
1980–1981	91	299,100	154,600	453,700
1988–1989	92	272,500	83,900	356,400
1989–1990	97	290,900	87,500	378,400
1990–1991	112	302,600	91,700	394,300

HEIs = higher education institutions.
Source: National Statistic Offices (2003).

create more academic and financial autonomy in Polish higher education. Finally, when the socialist system collapsed in 1989, higher education enjoyed substantive autonomy compared to other sectors of the economy. Higher education institutions were empowered, for instance, to establish their own statutes, plan their programs of research and study, determine the structure of their internal organization, and determine the allocation of funds. Nevertheless, subordination to central governmental bodies was still a part of many crucial institutional activities.

In sum, during the postwar period from 1946 to 1998, the situation of higher education in Poland changed in correspondence to political trends. Political reforms encouraged the quantitative expansion of higher education and increased institutional autonomy, while political reversions (followed by economic crises) cut state subsidies for higher education and imposed more restrictive regulations. It is worth noting that compared to the prewar era of elite higher education, the student body composition during the socialist period was more diverse. Despite the relative failure of the Preferential Points System—which granted additional points for an applicant's social origin, such as working-class or peasant families, during higher education entrance examinations (Sadlak, 1991)—the tuition-free system increased participation in higher education students from lower social and economic backgrounds (Sorensen, 1997).

Reforms and Changes in Higher Education During the 1990s

In general, until 1989 the Polish higher education system was an elite system with very low enrollment rates. A sluggish economy, limited flexibility in the higher education system, resistance to change in the academic community, and poor remuneration and working conditions discouraged many bright graduates from pursuing an academic career. Many academics left the country in search of better job prospects abroad (Sorensen, 1997).

The critical transition period began in 1989. The economic crisis caused a decline in industrial production, an enormous inflation rate (approaching 400%), and soaring unemployment. Against this economic downturn, Poland (and other Central and East European countries) implemented a series of economic reforms, which included the privatization of a number of state-owned companies, elimination of barriers to entry for new private enterprises in almost all sectors of the economy, and the introduction of competitive mechanisms into the economy. The higher education policy was also changed to allow institutions to restructure and adjust to the new economic, social, and political situation. A higher education law passed by the parliament in 1990 provided the basis for far-reaching changes. Major innovative arrangements included the devolution of authority from the government to institutions, the introduction of tuition fees, and the elimination of barriers of entry for private higher education institutions. These changes led to a substantial expansion of the higher education system throughout the 1990s.

Given the low popularity of regulations among academics, the new act on higher education expanded and devolved authority from the government to the institution level. Under the provision of the new law, public higher education institutions had the right to create or transform individual organizational units, create or eliminate fields of study, set their own admissions procedures and the number of student places, fix curricula and study plans, obtain funds outside the state budget, appoint new faculty members, and elect their rectors. This shift of responsibilities represented increased autonomy for higher education providers and reflected the main characteristics of new legislation concerning higher education in Poland at the beginning of the decade.

The most radical change was the permission to establish private higher education institutions. Before 1989, there was only one private higher education institution—the Catholic University of Lublin, established in 1918. Under the new regulations, anyone could establish a nonpublic higher education institution, after meeting the requirements set by the Ministry of Education addressing issues such as the number of professors, curricula, and infrastructure. Since 2001, the Minister must also ask for the approval of a State Accreditation Commission.

The next important change in the regulatory framework was the permission for public higher education institutions to charge tuition fees for part-time students. The "cost sharing" policy was a response to the growing student demand in a situation of limited public resources. At the same time, access to part-time studies was extended to all holders of a secondary school final examinations certificate, without restraining this only to working adults.

Prior to 1989, Polish higher education institutions had an elite status because they educated only a small proportion of society. This conformed with the state's socialist policy, which aimed to maintain the structural majority of the labor class, and was supported by the salary structure, where on average less-qualified people earned more than higher education graduates.

The transition period in the early 1990s reversed this situation by introducing market forces into labor market. High-qualified skills became the condition for having an interesting and well-paid job. A strong correlation between higher education and future work and remuneration motivates secondary school graduates as well as older, less-qualified people to participate in higher education. Never before has higher education in Poland gained such high social and economic motivation (Lewartowska-Zychowicz, 2004). Increased demand for higher education was followed by significant growth in the supply of higher education during the 1990s. Before 1989, the majority of young people (about 74%) attended vocational secondary schools, where they did not (and still today do not) receive the *matura*—a secondary school final examinations certificate, which is a legal and obligatory requirement for access to higher education—therefore practically excluding from participating in higher education. A decade after the reform of the education system, more than 80% of the secondary school graduates received the *matura*, and the majority of them are continuing their education.

In order to satisfy the demand for a high-qualified workforce, public higher education institutions offered new study forms and programs to provide the necessary skills for economic development. In particular, they established student-paid part-time studies in all kinds of fields, and in the form of weekend, evening, and individual study tracks. Higher education institutions introduced an open-door policy and allowed admission to part-time studies for all students holding the *matura*, without entrance examinations. The need for obtaining resources outside the state budget and the great demand for part-time studies produced an enormous growth of student numbers in these types of programs. Between 1991 and 2003, the number of part-time students rose from 92,500

Table 2.   Full-Time and Part-Time Students in Higher Education, 1991–2003

Year	Public Institutions		Private Institutions		
	Full-Time Students	Part-Time Students	Full-Time Students	Part-Time Students	Total
1991–1992	322,000	92,500	4,600	9,100	428,200
1992–1993	350,600	125,200	8,900	11,000	495,700
1993–1994	378,900	170,600	15,800	18,700	584,000
1994–1995	401,800	230,800	21,200	28,400	682,200
1995–1996	421,300	278,800	28,500	60,900	789,500
1996–1997	448,700	330,500	39,900	103,000	922,100
1997–1998	479,300	380,700	55,500	170,900	1,086,400
1998–1999	511,300	426,200	75,800	255,200	1,268,500
1999–2000	543,100	464,300	92,300	326,100	1,425,800
2000–2001	586,600	520,200	101,000	370,400	1,578,200
2001–2002	643,900	559,600	115,100	392,700	1,711,300
2002–2003	706,900	564,800	117,300	411,500	1,800,500

Source: National Statistic Offices (2003).

to 564,800. Full-time student enrollment also increased from 320,000 to 706,900 (see Table 2).

Entrance requirements for full-time study programs at public institutions differ according to the type of institution and study field. In general, entrance examinations are preferred for the most popular programs such as medicine, law, architecture, psychology, and popular linguistic studies at the most prestigious universities. Other institutions usually accept the candidates with the highest secondary school marks (Kaiser & Wach, 2004). Given the limited student enrollment in the free tuition full-time study programs, on average only some 60% of applicants are accepted. The growth of student numbers at the beginning of the 1990s was the highest in economics, administration, and social sciences, while a significant decline was observed in agricultural, medical, and technical sciences (see Table 3). However, in the late 1990s, when the labor market became slowly saturated with the graduates of economics and business studies, enrollment patterns changed, with more students choosing computer science and the natural sciences, such as biology, chemistry, and environmental care. Enrollment in the pedagogic, humanities, economics, and social science fields also decreased, but economics and social sciences have remained the most popular among young people.

To increase the number of public higher education institutions—especially those located in small cities—and to expand the free tuition student places in full-time study programs, the government passed the Vocational Higher Education Schools Act in 1997. Under the new regulations, it is much easier to open a new public higher education institution. The standards for the bachelor's level programs are less demanding than for schools operating under the 1990 Higher Education Act—for example, only two professors are necessary for one study program. New public institutions established after 1997 are registered as vocational higher education schools and can offer only

Table 3. Students in Higher Education Institutions by Discipline (%), 1990–2003

	1990–1991	1993–1994	1997–1998	2000–2001	2002–2003
Pedagogy	14.1	14.4	13.8	11.7	11.4
Humanities	13.2	12.7	10.2	8.4	7.8
Sciences	5.5	5.2	4.3	7.9	9.4
Social sciences	4.3	9.7	11.8	13.9	12.9
Engineering	16.5	19.7	17.6	11.4	11.3
Agriculture	7.0	4.9	3.2	2.0	1.9
Medicine/health	10.1	6.1	3.1	2.4	2.7
Economics and administration	14.8	12.2	20.8	27.7	25.0
Art	2.4	1.6	1.2	1.0	1.0
Law	4.7	6.6	4.9	3.8	3.3
Various disciplines	7.4	6.9	9.1	9.8	13.3

Source: National Statistic Offices (2003).

bachelor's and engineering degree programs, and they cannot apply for master's level courses. In 2002–2003, these institutions enrolled 130,000 students and are situated mainly in smaller cities. New private institutions, established after 1997, are registered as well as new public institutions as vocational higher education schools and can offer only bachelor's degree programs. However, in contrast to public vocational higher education institutions, privates can offer master's degrees, although in order to do so they must first change their status and operate under the 1990 Higher Education Act. For this reason, the newest private higher education institutions have the status of vocational institutions.

A rapid expansion of the private higher education sector began in 1990, when the new state regulations allowed private institutions to enter the higher education market and introduced relatively low legal barriers to entry. In order to became an official higher education provider, a founder must meet certain state requirements. For the first three years, private institutions can offer only bachelor's degrees in a particular field of study. In order to offer courses at the bachelor's level, institutions must employ at least four professors (although such employment could be part-time), develop the curricula according to ministry requirements, and possess the appropriate equipment and buildings. After the initial 3-year period, institutions can apply to offer programs at the master's degree level. The standards for master's level programs are more demanding— a minimum of eight full-time professors as well as relevant curricula and infrastructure. The standards and requirements are the same for state and private institutions, except that public institutions cannot employ professors over the age of 70 (who do not count formally in staff formulas, while in privates they are counted as staff members).

For the first few years under the 1990 Higher Education Act, due to the limited number of professors available, private institutions offered mainly bachelor's programs. However, in the last few years they have attracted more and more professors in order to offer master's level programs and have the authority to confer the Ph.D. While in 1995 only eight private higher education institutions offered master's degrees, in 2002 more than 90 institutions are authorized to offer this type of degree, and four have Ph.D. tracks. The rest (about 150) offer programs at the bachelor's level.

In general, the number of private higher education providers rose from three in 1990 to 280 in 2004, while student enrollment rose from around 6,500 in 1990–1991 to over 528,800 in 2002–2003 (see Table 3). Private higher education institutions exist throughout Poland, although (in keeping with typical patterns cross-nationally) the most prestigious concentrate in and around large cities. Among 280 privates, 137 are located in large cities, with 57 in Warsaw alone. However, many private providers situated in small cities significantly increase higher education possibilities for students from lower socioeconomic backgrounds or from rural areas, thereby earning a measure of social acceptance. Private providers deprived of almost any state support develop mainly "low-cost" study programs (as is the case in most of the region and most of the world), and attract mostly part-time students. Approximately 77% of the private institutions' enrollments are part-time, usually combining study and work in order to pay for higher education. In addition, research conducted in 2000 indicated that most of the students in the private sector are from lower socioeconomic backgrounds and come from rural areas (Ministry of National Education and Sports, 2000). Private providers usually offer programs in business, management, humanities and social sciences, and computer science, as indicated in Table 4. All their students are charged tuition fees, on average between 400 and 700 euro per semester. Private institutions do not receive any direct state support for teaching and research, although the government exempts private higher education institutions (as well as public institutions) from property, sales, and income taxes.

Enrollment in Polish higher education more than quadrupled between 1990 and 2003. Full-time enrollment increased from 322,600 in 1991–1992 to over 824,200 in 2002–2003. Part-time enrollment grew even more dramatically from 101,600 in 1991–1992 to 976,300 in 2002–2003 (see Table 5). In 1989, only about 8% of the relevant age

Table 4.   Students in Private Higher Education Institutions by Discipline* (%), 1991–2002

	1991–1992	1993–1994	1997–1998	2000–2001	2001–2002
Pedagogic	–	8.4	6.6	6.9	9.3
Humanities and social sciences	–	16.8	34.1	26.2	25.1
Sciences	–	–	2.5	2.4	2.5
Engineering	–	2.7	6.1	6.1	5.9
Agriculture	–	–	0.3	1.1	0.7
Medicine/health	–	–	–	0.2	1.1
Economics	100	70.3	50.2	43.1	44.9
Art	–	1.8	0.2	0.2	0.3

Source: Kaiser and Wach (2004).
*Excluding Catholic University of Lublin and other church funded institutions.

Table 5. Growth of Higher Education in Poland, 1991–2003

Year	Private HEIs	Public HEIs	Students in Public HEIs	Students in Private HEIs*	Total Number of Students
1991–1992	12	98	414,500	13,700	428,200
1992–1993	22	98	475,800	19,900	495,700
1993–1994	41	99	549,500	34,500	584,000
1994–1995	56	99	632,600	49,600	682,200
1995–1996	80	99	700,100	89,400	789,500
1996–1997	114	99	779,200	142,900	922,100
1997–1998	146	100	860,000	226,400	1,086,400
1998–1999	158	101	937,500	331,000	1,268,500
1999–2000	174	113	1,007,400	418,400	1,425,800
2000–2001	195	115	1,106,800	471,400	1,578,200
2001–2002	221	120	1,203,500	507,800	1,711,300
2002–2003	252	125	1,271,700	528,800	1,800,500

HEIs = higher education institutions.
Source: National Statistic Offices (2003).
* Including Catholic University of Lublin and other Church founded institutions.

cohort was enrolled in higher education, while in the academic year 2002–2003, this ratio had reached 35% and is still growing. The biggest academic center is Warsaw, with 293,800 students enrolled in 69 higher education institutions. In Warsaw, 57 private institutions enroll 142,100 students. The other important academic centers are Krakow, Katowice, Poznań, Wrocław, Lublin, Łódź, and Gdańsk. Together they educate more than 42% of all students.

The degree structure in Polish higher education consists of two track systems: a two-tier track and a uniform one (Kaiser & Wach, 2004). A two-tier track is formed with two levels: (1) the first level is a *licencjat* (bachelor's) degree, which lasts a minimum of six semesters, or in the engineering studies the first degree is *inynier* degree (engineer), which lasts seven semesters; and (2) the second level lasts four semesters and leads to the *magister* (master's) degree. The second track is called a uniform master's degree program, which lasts nine or 10 semesters and culminates in a master's diploma. There is no formal distinction as to whether the master's degree is obtained in a two-tier track or uniform one, nor whether the bachelor's degree is conferred by academic institutions or by vocational higher education institutions.

The two-tier track system began to develop at the beginning of the 1990s under the new Higher Education Act and is still unfamiliar within the society as well as among academics. Students attending higher education institutions that offer both bachelor's and master's level degrees still prefer the uniform master's track. However, the situation is changing. The two-tier track system gives students more choice and flexibility. In the academic year 2002–2003, some 43% students undertook studies in a two-tier track system.

Academic Staff

As noted earlier, during the 1980s, higher education in Poland suffered from emigration, whereas during the 1990s its main headache was the internal brain drain (Osterczuk, 1996). Academic work is not an attractive career for young higher education graduates, who prefer to work in other sectors of the economy where highly qualified work is better paid and offers more opportunities for future promotions. The higher education policy in Poland during the 1990s was focused mainly on the ways to increase the student places without much increase in the state spending on higher education. Therefore, during the 1990s, the debate about the attractiveness of the academic workplace—which includes such issues as reforming the structure of academic staff, new staff roles and career patterns, differentiation in remuneration, recruitment of younger graduates for an academic career, working conditions, and career perspectives—was absent among policymakers. However, in recent years, facing the problems of enormous growth in student/faculty ratios and a graying senior staff corps (which implies the need for considerable replacement of the senior staff population in the coming years), the employment conditions of academic staff and the attractiveness of the academic career for young generations are of a major concern.

In Poland, major developments affecting the academic workplace include the sharp growth in student numbers, accompanied by the decline in state support for public higher education, a centralized system of employment, and working conditions of academic staff.

The employment conditions of academic staff are determined by the government, in consultation with the sector and labor unions, and articulated in the various acts on higher education and on academic personnel. The acts regulate issues such as pay scales and working hours for each scientific position, as well as function allowances for administrative positions (such as rector, dean, or director); proper appointment qualification requirements and conditions for promotion; performance measurement; and tenure and retirement conditions. While public higher education institutions are bound by all rules established in the acts, privates are confined only to some of them. For example, private institutions have to comply only with the appointment qualification requirements and conditions of promotion. However, in reality they have adopted the majority of the content of employment agreements from public institutions, except for the salary structure and appointment of administrative positions. They sometimes—but not often—award tenure for habilitated doctors and full professors, who have obligatory tenure in public institutions.

Overall, higher education institutions, especially publics, have little possibility to determine and diversify the content of employment agreements. The current law gives public universities little flexibility in creating their own pay scales or incentive/reward systems. Universities thus have limited possibilities for attracting high-performing staff in strategically significant fields or recruiting young scientists in important areas of science. Further, professors have little financial motivation to raise their qualifications or improve their teaching.

The situation differs in the system of research funding. Jongbloed (2004), in his work on the characterization of the funding models in Central European countries, finds the research system and the accompanying evaluation system in Poland to be relatively modern by international standards and classifies it as an output-driven system which bases its decisions on the performance of individual research units within higher education institutions. All research units are evaluated by the State Committee for Scientific Research (KBN), which is a major public agency for research funding in Poland. KBN categorizes the units according to the following criteria: number of publications, number of awarded degrees, and number of patents or research contracts with business partners. The best research units receive the greatest amount of statutory research funds. Secondly, research units can compete for the grants awarded by KBN for a particular research activity. On average, KBN provides twice as much funding for statutory research than for competitive grants. The evaluation criteria are principally accepted by the academics and seem to work well. The major concerns are related to funding levels, which have been declining in recent years. It is worth noting that the average research budget in public higher education institutions accounts only for 16% of the total budget, while the public expenditure on research has decreased from 0.74% of GDP in 1991 to 0.35% in 2003.

As noted earlier, a major issue that affects the academic workplace is the low level of remuneration of academic staff relative to the salaries in other employment sectors. Budget expenditure on higher education in Poland has declined from 1.11% of GDP in 1990 to 0.88% in 2002. The state expenditure per student showed even more dramatic decline over the most recent 10-year period. The negative financial situation in public institutions in particular has a damaging influence on the heart of the university—the academic profession—and the attractiveness of the academic workplace.

Full-time employment in all higher education institutions in 2002 accounted for 80,904 academics, including 20,553 full and associate professors, 44,939 assistant professors (who are required to have a Ph.D.), and 15,412 senior and junior lecturers (who have a master's degree). The number of high-ranked professors is significantly small in relation to student enrollments. While student numbers have increased 4.5 times since 1990, the number of full-time employed academics has increased from some 61,100 in 1990 to 80,904 in 2002. More worrisome is that the increase in the number of scientific staff is not only too slow, but also does not ensure the normal replacement or maintenance of the same number of academics in the coming years. It takes a considerable amount of time to earn a Ph.D. and then to obtain a habilitation (necessary to become a full professor). It usually takes 8 years to obtain a doctoral degree. Between 1998 and 2003, the majority of academics who defended their Ph.D. dissertation were between the ages of 31 and 35. A positive trend is observed in the number of Ph.D. students, which rose from some 2,800 students in 1990–1991 to more than 31,000 in 2002–2003, although only 20% of doctoral studies are completed with conferment of the degree. In 2002–2003, universities granted 5,450 doctoral degrees. Between 2000 and 2003, the average age at which an individual obtained a habilitation was 50.7 years, and they became full professors on average at age 57.

In 2002, the Central Commission for Academic Degrees (which confers scientific degrees) granted 923 habilitated doctoral degrees and 789 academic titles of professors. Projections indicate that in the coming years, the number of professors reaching the retirement age will exceed the number of habilitated doctors that will be appointed to full professor. In addition, salary differences among the different staff categories are quite considerable. For example, the minimum salary of younger staff members with a Ph.D. is half of a full professor's salary, whereas the junior assistant's salary is three times as low. In public institutions, the average salary of a junior assistant is about 350 euro per month, which accounts for 60% of the average remuneration in the Polish economy. In private institutions, the salaries are higher but do not exceed the average for the whole economy. Professors' earnings are much higher—a typical full professor earns up to 1,000 euro in public institutions (and more than that in privates, although there are no precise data from the private sector).

The relatively low salaries in public institutions have prompted many academics to earn additional incomes outside academia (Enders & de Weert, 2004). In Poland, this situation occurs on a large scale, in particular among high-ranking academics who are employed often in two or sometimes more higher education institutions, especially in the field of economics. The staff requirements for establishing a new private or public institution or a new program has led to greater opportunities for professors to hold several different positions in multiple schools, a pattern that is followed by younger academics who are also trying to make a living (Osterczuk, 1996). In fact, the policymakers implementing new higher education policy in 1990, which allowed private institutions to enter the higher education market, were conscious of its effects and tolerated the various employment contracts of many academics.

The "permissiveness" to earn additional income has allowed Poland to increase over-all student enrollment but has limited the number of academic staff and kept academics in relatively poorly paid higher education institutions (Enders & de Weert, 2004). Supporters of this approach argue that academics working at various posts have low marginal costs and high marginal revenues; because they are giving the same lectures in various institutions, they can spend relatively less time for preparation and receive a second salary. In addition, the mobility of academics in general allows them to be more familiar with the new academic environment, as well as new methods of teaching or managing the institution, which can benefit their home university. Moreover, the most common career pattern for academics in Poland is the stationary model, which means that the whole career (from junior assistant to full professor) takes place within one university, so the multiple employment posts can be treated as a surrogate for the more flexible and mobile academic careers essential for higher education in the United States and in many other developed countries (Ratajczak, 2004).

The argument against this approach is that the current system fosters initiative and benefits at a personal level, but may bring negative effects at the institutional level. The overworked academics have little time to bring up-to-date the content of their lectures, and spend less time on research. In general, there is considerable discussion in Poland about the freedom of academics to hold simultaneous positions. Some more prestigious public universities have already restricted this, allowing their professors to have a second position only with the rector's permission, and forbidding them to hold administrative posts in other private institutions. However, the majority of public universities still permit their employees to look for other source of income without permission from the university.

Most policymakers and academics perceive this as an unfortunate effect of low salaries, which lessens the overall quality of Polish higher education. Since 2001, this negative connection between insufficient earnings and quality of higher education has resulted in a relatively high increase of academic salaries (compared to previous years). In addition, in order to make academic careers more attractive for graduates, there is a discussion about simplifying the academic degree structure by dropping the habilitation and leaving only the Ph.D., aligning it with most Western countries. However, most academics argue that this change could reduce the quality of the staff (Kaiser & Wach, 2004).

Contemporary Trends and Policy Issues

Higher education in Poland has gone through a major transformation process since the early 1990s. After the "iron curtain" was removed in 1989, government and academic staff had insisted on a high degree of institutional autonomy, and new regulations devolved authority from the central to institutional level in most higher education activities. In addition, prior to 1989, Poland and other Central European countries were unique for their lack of private higher education. Since then, Poland has created the most developed system of private higher education in Europe, and within a few years the number of students in the private sector had jumped from 0% to 30% of the country's student population.

The rapid massification of higher education and the emergence of 280 new private providers caused concerns about the accountability of Poland's higher education system. Accountability generally means that the state requires the university to demonstrate that it has used public funds efficiently and effectively. Accountability can be provided by a large number of instruments, ranging from financial reports to quality accreditation procedures. Higher education is a typical "experience good" because of the asymmetry of information: it is hard to evaluate the quality of higher education institutions in advance of a student's experience, but only during their study and afterwards. In order to protect the students, as the universities are not able (or not inclined) to gather and disseminate accurate information about themselves in a credible way, there is a role for government to set and enforce adequate regulation about the provision and dissemination of quality information.

In the beginning of the 1990s, the changes in the higher education system did not include sufficient accountability procedures, especially in terms of quality assurance. There were cases where private institutions (as well as publics), after meeting the state requirements for registering, did not employ the minimum number of professors, shortened their curricula, or made it possible for some students to obtain a degree in a shorter period than the state required. For these reasons, questions related to quality control highlighted the need for new accreditation bodies in order to eliminate inappropriate performance among private and public higher education institutions. In 2001, the State Accreditation Commission was founded, whose main purpose is to evaluate the quality of study programs for both public and private providers. Since then, the Commission has evaluated a significant number of study programs at various institutions, and closed down those programs (both public and private) which did not meet the requirements set by the Ministry. In addition, private higher education institutions were (and still are) criticized for having the majority of their students enrolled in part-time study programs, for limiting their offerings to so-called "low-cost" study programs such as business, political science, or pedagogy, and for maintaining low admissions requirements. However, in times of state financial stringency and increasing demand for higher education, providing greater access to higher education for low-income students would be hard to achieve without the private higher education sector. Further, private institutions deprived of any direct state support are not able to offer more expensive study programs in science and technology. On the other hand, the same claims are raised for public providers (in terms of their part-time study programs). Still, the demographic decline in Poland, which has already affected higher education, will increase competition and force private institutions to expand their study offerings and increase their quality. Already, according to various rankings of higher education institutions conducted by popular magazines (such as *Perspektywy*, *Wprost*, and *Newsweek*), some private institutions are seen as leading the country in terms of perceived quality.

Current debates among policymakers and higher education scholars also concern the expansion of state scholarships for all students in the private sector and for part-time students in public institutions. In the Polish higher education system, public student-based subsidies are channeled to students in the form of means-tested and merit-based scholarships as well as in the form of state-supported student loans. In 1998, the Act on Students Loans expanded the system of state aid by making students from both public and private higher education, attending either full-time or part-time studies, eligible for state subsidized loans. However, until 2001, students from private institutions were excluded from both state scholarship systems. In the academic year 2001–2002, students from the lowest category of family income per capita, enrolled in full-time study programs in private institutions, became eligible for state means-tested scholarships. Further, beginning with the academic year 2004–2005, all students attending public and private higher education institutions are entitled to receive state means-tested and merit-based scholarships.

Recently, legislation has been proposed to integrate the various acts regarding higher education, and an act is expected to be passed by the parliament in 2005. This act will probably cover issues such as: simplification of the academic degree structure, by dropping the habilitated doctoral degree; devolution of appointment authority to the institutional level, granting universities more freedom, and flexibility regarding staffing issues; and simplification of the rules concerning tuition fees at public universities. The act is also expected to deal with many other important issues, in essence updating Poland's higher education regulations to accommodate the changing environment and expectations.

Conclusions

Over the last decade, higher education in Poland has experienced enormous growth, changing from elite to mass higher education and facing the problems which are often accompanied with the massification process, such as academics holding multiple teaching posts, a perceived decline in quality, and decreasing public financial support.

In joining the European Union, Poland became part of a large community, which brings both opportunities—for example, more possibilities for international cooperation and for attracting foreign students and research funds—and challenges, including increased competition from universities and colleges from other European Union countries. However, in order to take advantage of these opportunities, Polish higher education institutions will have to develop more attractive curricula, offer more courses in foreign languages, increase the attractiveness of an academic career, and be more active in obtaining research funds outside the state budget, particularly through increased cooperation with business institutions.

Another important issue is the coexistence of the private and public higher education sectors. If Polish private higher education is to play an increasingly significant role in the system, bringing healthy competition for public institutions, the government will have to do more to incorporate the private institutions into the system by implementing market forces to guide the allocation of resources, students, and programs (Zumeta, 1996).

References

Enders, J., & de Weert, E. (2004). *The international attractiveness of the academic workplace in Europe.* Frankfurt, Germany: Gewerkschaft Erziehung und Wissenschaft (GEW).

Jongbloed, B. (2004). Institutional funding and institutional change. In J. File & L. Goedegebuure (Eds.), *Real-time systems: Reflections on higher education in the Czech Republic, Hungary, Poland and Slovenia.* Enschede, The Netherlands: Center for Higher Education Policy Studies, University of Twente.

Kaiser, F., & Wach, P. (2004). Poland. In J. File & L. Goedegebuure (Eds.), *Real-time systems: Reflections on higher education in the Czech Republic, Hungary, Poland and Slovenia.* Enschede, The Netherlands: Center for Higher Education Policy Studies, University of Twente.

Lewartowska-Zychowicz, M. (2004). Masowy student–elitarny uniwersytet. Forum Akademickie, no. 7–8.

Ministry of National Education and Sports. (2000). Report about the accessibility of higher education: Financial and social conditions. Warsaw, Poland.

National Statistic Offices. (2003). *Higher education schools and their finances.* Statistical Yearbook. Warsaw, Poland.

Osterczuk, A. M. (1996). Developments in Polish higher education. *Higher Education Management,* 8(3), 59–69.

Poznanski, K., & Kucha, R. (1992). Poland. In W. Wickremasinghe (Ed.), *Handbook of world education: A comparative guide to higher education and educational systems of the world.* Houston, TX: American Collegiate Service.

Ratajczak, M. (2004). Unia personalna. *Forum Akademickie,* no. 2.

Sadlak, J. (1991). Poland. In P. G. Altbach (Ed.), *International higher education. An encyclopedia.* New York and London: Garland Publishing, Inc.

Sorensen, K. (1997). *Polish higher education en route to the market. Institutional change and autonomy at two economics academies.* Stockholm: Institute of International Education, Stockholm University.

Zumeta, W. (1996). Meeting the demand for higher education without breaking the bank: A framework for the design of state higher education policies for an era of increasing demand. *The Journal of Higher Education,* 67(4), 367–425.

50

RUSSIA

Anna Smolentseva
Center for Sociological Studies, Moscow State University, Russia

Russia is one the most populous nations of the world, and one of the most educated. Nearly 55% of Russians have completed some form of tertiary education, a figure that approaches and even exceeds respective indicators of many developed nations (Poletaev, Agranovich, & Zharova, 2002). The success of Russian higher education is, to a large extent, a product of Soviet educational policy, but a number of achievements have been lost since then. Reforms that began in the mid-1980s, and continued after the demise of the Soviet Union, have constantly tested the national education system, which proved to be both one of the most vulnerable and one of the most inertial social institutions.

This chapter presents an overview of the Russian higher education system, providing some historical background and exploring current issues, challenges and perspectives regarding educational financing, recent and ongoing reform agendas, student and faculty bodies, graduate education, private education, and internationalization. The discussion offers a mostly internal view of higher education, focused on issues of the most serious concern to members of the Russian educational community, but considers some of them from a comparative perspective as well.

Brief History

The history of Russian higher education can be traced to the 17th century, although there is disagreement on which institution should be considered Russia's first. While the earliest institutions of higher learning—Kievo-Mogilyanskaya Kollegia in Kiev and the Slavic-Greek-Latin Academy in Moscow—were founded during the 1600s, these were largely religious institutions (Kinelev, 1995; Avrus, 2001). A prominent milestone in the development of Russian tertiary education was the establishment of a university as an integral part of the Academy of Sciences in St. Petersburg in 1724. The structure affiliating the Academy of Sciences with a university and gymnasium led to the integration of research and education and became a basic organizing principle of Russia's educational system. Aside from these developments, Moscow University— established in 1755—is considered by many to be the first traditional university in Russia.

James J.F. Forest and Philip G. Altbach (eds.), International Handbook of Higher Education, 951–969.
© 2006 *Springer. Printed in the Netherlands.*

Influenced by European models of the university and academic profession, Russian higher education developed largely according to the German experience, focusing on specialized schools for training professionals, rather than on "elite" university education (Petrova, 2000). Russian higher education was also distinguished by its public character: it was founded by state initiative and financed directly from the governmental budget. Thus, it should come as no surprise that the government has consistently attempted to control higher education, from curricula to the social origins of students.

For years, Russian higher education lagged behind Western institutions of higher learning in a number of respects, with the state failing to implement effective educational policies while repressing academic freedom and any reform initiatives. In response to this pervasive governmental pursuit of total control, in the 1860s a non-state higher education sector emerged, allowing women access to higher education. By 1917, Russia had more than 120 institutions of higher education, just over half of which were state institutions (Krukhmaleva, Smolentseva, & Ushakova, 2000).

The revolution of 1917 inaugurated a new era in the history of Russian education. During the Soviet period, state control and the centralization of tertiary education were amplified, bringing faculty repression, the abolishment of certain academic degrees, and the closing of non-state institutions. State policy regulated the number of higher education institutions, the number of students, the range of specialties, the amounts of remuneration and fellowships, the content of curricula and textbooks, graduate employments, and so on.

Simultaneously, the USSR could boast of a number of achievements in higher education. Realizing the importance of education in general, the Soviet government significantly expanded the network of public institutions. By the beginning of the reform period (in 1985), there were 502 Russian higher education institutions, enrolling 2,966,100 students (*Obrazovanie v Rossii*, 2003). Other significant achievements of Soviet higher education included broadening access and instituting a right to tuition-free higher education. The government, striving for equity among its citizens, provided access to higher education for traditionally underrepresented social groups—in particular, workers and members of rural populations. As a result, millions of people gained an opportunity to attend higher education institutions.

Soviet policy emphasized the development of the sciences (particularly physics, mathematics, and chemistry), with a special focus on those disciplines related to the military complex and space exploration, while the social sciences and humanities were under constant pressure to incorporate an ideological dimension to their courses. Science policy concentrated on promoting advanced research in the institutions of the Academy of Sciences. Thus, the growth of scientific research there outpaced developments at higher education institutions, whose capacity to engage in contemporary science degraded over time. Also, a differentiation among Russian higher education institutions regarding research activity was obvious—a small number of top universities were positioned to conduct advanced research and to assemble a qualified academic staff, while most institutions lacked the requisite intellectual environment and equipment. Regional differences were considerable as well: higher education and research institutions were concentrated in the European part of the USSR, and this inequality still persists.

The political reforms announced in 1985 and the downfall of the USSR in 1991 had an enormous impact on higher education. In this transition period, several important legal acts were passed, aimed at countering the negative trends inherent in Soviet education while striving to retain all its positive accomplishments. Changes were primarily directed toward the decentralization of the education system. Major responsibilities were devolved to educational institutions—a step that expanded their autonomy, broadened their rights and governance authority, and empowered them to make decisions on the form and content of education.

Truly, decentralization was the only solution that allowed higher education to survive in a situation of deep economic and political crisis. The diversification of funding sources for educational institutions—a move away from relying solely on state financing—became a necessary change given the permanent decline in state funding. The re-emergence of a non-state sector of higher education was also one of the most important developments in Russian higher education during this period. Other dramatic changes that have been introduced in recent years include an increased emphasis on the humanities in the curriculum, elimination of the bias in favor of engineering specialties, diversification of programs and courses, and an orientation of education toward the needs of the market, society, and individuals.

Legal Framework

The Russian government has designated education as a priority of state policy. The legal base of the policies framing the current operation of higher education includes the following documents: the Law on Education (1992, amended in 1996); the Law on Higher Education (1996); the National Doctrine on Education (2000); the Federal Program of Development of Education (2000); and the Federal Program "Development of Unified Educational Informational Area for 2001–2005." One of the major principles of state educational policy is a principle of unity of the federal educational area. Educational laws have established accessible and free tertiary education on a competitive basis. The requirements for content and quality of education are established in state educational standards, which are based on global norms of education and scholarship. The standards involve federal and national-regional components; the former defines a compulsory minimum content of basic educational programs, a maximum load of students, and the educational outcomes necessary of graduates.

Lifelong learning is another important component of the Russian education system, as individuals may obtain more than one degree/qualification at all levels of education. One can also choose the form of education, including full-time, part-time, distance, and others. Variation in education is seen among institutions by property type–state, municipal, private, and others.

At present, Russian education is on a path of modernization, involving experiments with state unified examinations (EGE), 12-year secondary schools, profile high schools, multi-level higher professional education, the development of information technology in education, and other initiatives to improve the quality of educational practices and to integrate Russia into the global educational arena. The Strategy for the Modernization of Russian Education through 2010, adopted by the government in 2001, indicates the direction of educational development. In addition to emphasizing issues of access and quality, it encompasses new legal, organizational, and economic mechanisms for cultivating and using non-state budgetary resources. Strengthening the links between education and science is also underscored in the documents. The role of the state is also emphasized, as the government serves as a guarantor of the quality of educational programs and services delivered by educational institutions regardless of their legal status.

Responsibility for state policy and governance of Russian education is held by the Ministry of Education and Science (organized by the incorporation of two respective ministries in 2004) and its federal agencies—the Federal Agency of Education and the Federal Control Service in Education and Science (also established in 2004).

Organizational Aspects

Legally, the Russian higher education system includes state standards of higher and postgraduate vocational education, licensed institutions of higher vocational and supplementary vocational education, institutions of scientific research, state authorities, and public/voluntary societies. In Russia, there are three levels of higher professional education, with qualifications of a bachelor's (*bakalavr*), specialist's and master's (*magistr*). This system combines the traditional Soviet 5-year program, leading to a specialist degree, with the Western two-tier model of bachelor's (4-year) and master's (2-year) degree programs. There is also a certificate of incomplete higher vocational education, requiring no less than two years of study at a higher education institution. Currently, the dominant model of study is a 5-year program—among 2002 graduates, 89.4% received specialist degrees, while 9.1% were awarded a bachelor's and another 1.1% received a master's (*Nauka v Rosssii v tsifrakh*, 2004). It should be noted that the prevailing view of most students and employers is that education at the level of the specialist diploma or master's degree is necessary, since a bachelor's degree does not provide a sufficient educational background. Advanced levels of education lead to degrees of candidate of sciences (*kandidat nauk*) and doctor of sciences (*doctor nauk*), described later in this chapter.

The operation of tertiary education institutions in Russia requires state licensing, attestation, and accreditation. There are three types of institutions of higher learning—universities, academies, and institutes. During the Soviet period, the largest category of higher education institutions was made up of the institutes (polytechnic, engineering, pedagogical, medical, etc.). During the 1990s, the majority of them became universities ("subject universities"), mostly as a result of the change in title without a real transformation toward a more "classical" understanding of the university. Today, universities comprise about half of all higher educational institution in Russia.

The organizational structure of higher education institutions in Russia involves faculties (*fakul'tet*) by field of study and departments (*kafedra*) by subject within the field. Broad university governance is provided by an elected representative body—an Academic Council—consisting of the rector, vice rectors, and (upon appointment by the Academic Council) faculty deans. Other members of the Council are elected at a general meeting. Each higher education institution is headed by a rector, elected by secret vote at a general meeting of the Academic Council for a period up to five years and approved by the relevant state authority.

The devastating economic crisis of the early 1990s marked the lowest point in the development of Russian higher education. However, since 1995 Russian higher education has shown some stabilization and development, framed by the stabilization of the economic and political situation in the country. By 2002, the Russian higher education system consisted of 1,039 institutions, of which more than one-third (384) was private. The number of students that year reached 5,947,500, most of which (88%) attended public institutions. Put another way, for every 10,000 members of Russia's population, 414 of them were enrolled in undergraduate and master's level programs. Meanwhile, an additional 140,700 students were enrolled in graduate and postgraduate education at both the candidate's and doctoral levels.

Notable changes have occurred throughout the higher education landscape. In the public sector, between 1990 and 2002 the proportion of students enrolled in science fields decreased by nearly half—from 8.4% to 4.6%—while the share of students in fields of industry and construction also decreased from 40% to 34%. In contrast, the most popular fields of study have been in the humanities and social sciences, where the number of students increased from 11% to 20%. Student enrollment growth in economics and management has been even more impressive (from 12% to 26%). However, these trends in student enrollment and graduation do not yet correspond to the structure of the labor market, and consequently many graduates have not been able to find jobs relevant to their degrees.

Financial Issues

The most serious problem facing Russian higher education today is inadequate government funding. Although the Law on Education mandates an allocation of no less than 10% of the national income to the development of education, this has never been fulfilled. The funding mandates of the National Doctrine of Education—6–8% of GDP—have also never come to pass. In fact, public financing has persisted at the level of 2–4% of GDP. In 2003, all state expenditures on education comprised 3.7% of GDP and are planned for 2004 in the amount of 4.3% of GDP. According to the World Bank classification, Russia belongs to the category of low middle-income countries, and its level of educational financing generally corresponds to the levels of other members of this category (Poletaev *et al.*, 2002).

At public institutions, funding consists of state and non-state (off-budget) resources, which contribute to the institutional budget approximately equally. At private institutions, the majority of funding is expected to come from non-state resources. For both public and private institutions, tuition has become most the important source of funding. According to a survey of selected regions, contributions by the student population comprised 31% of the total income of higher education institutions, or 69.5% of non-state funding (*Ekonomika obrazovania v zerkale statistiki*, 2004). Other non-state funding sources include organizations, foundations supporting science and education, revenues of educational services, and leasing of facilities.

It is important to mention that presently, the tradition of free education established in the Soviet Union has gradually been shrinking, while an increasing number of students pay for their higher education. Legally, the government is bound to provide funding as well as tuition-free education on a competitive basis for 170 students per 10,000 members of Russia's population; yet the demand for higher education has been continually growing, while funding has not increased quite as fast (currently, the government provides funding for 226 student per 10,000). The government also regulates the area of fee-paid education—public institutions are allowed to admit on a fee-paying basis no more than 50% of their students, mostly in the fields of economics, management, law, and public administration. Nevertheless, in 1995 roughly 8.6% of all students in the public sector were paying for their education, whereas in 2002 over 44% were enrolled on a fee-paying basis. Overall, as of 2002 almost 51% of all students enrolled in public and private higher education institutions paid tuition (*Obrazovanie v Rossii*, 2003).

Recognizing the need to design a more effective scheme of public support, the government is striving to reform the system of educational financing. As announced in the Strategy for the Modernization of Education, new organizational and economic mechanisms of higher education are to be devised, moving away from full state funding of higher professional education in favor of investing in it. This scheme is already being implemented in Russia through several experiments, including the introduction of governmental individual financial obligations (GIFO). These are state commitments tied to the results of state unified tests (EGE), thus serving as a performance-based means of funding higher education. This approach is also considered to provide a normative mechanism for achieving the principle of "money following a student." GIFOs, being a kind of voucher, have different categories (presently five). Those students who demonstrate higher scores on the tests receive GIFOs of higher categories (implying higher levels of funding). Reformers believe that this new system lays the foundation for the development of competitiveness in higher education, and will thus stimulate educational institutions to enhance performance.

Experiments with GIFOs have engendered lots of debates in society. Experiments with financing systems are increasingly escalating the debate over whether free higher education will be retained and kept accessible for the majority of the population. Also, the expected competitiveness of higher education institutions will likely be a means of redirecting funding towards the most prestigious institutions and fields, to the detriment of other institutions and fields. But possibly the most important argument regarding the relationship between GIFOs and test scores concerns the potential for exacerbating the risks to more vulnerable social groups—large segments of society who have less opportunity for advanced test preparation, and thus *a priori* unfairly restricting their right for free education.

Students and Access to Higher Education

Since 1993, the number of students in Russia has witnessed a stable growth, increasing more than twice over 10 years. As shown in Table 1, nearly six million students are enrolled in Russia's higher education system, the majority of whom study at public institutions, and more than half study full-time.

Table 1. A Brief Profile of Russian Higher Education

	1985	1991	1992	1993	1994	1995	1996	1997	1998	1999	2000	2001	2002
Institutions (total)	502	519	535	626	710	762	817	880	914	939	965	1008	1039
Public	502	519	535	548	553	569	573	578	580	590	607	621	655
Private	–	–	–	78	157	193	244	302	334	349	358	387	384
Students (total), thousands	2,966	2,762	2,638	2,612	2,644	2,790	2,964	3,248	3,597	4,073	4,741	5,426	5,947
Public, %	100	100	100	97.3	95.9	95.1	94.5	93.8	93.0	91.5	90.1	88.4	87.9
Students, %	–	–	–	2.7	4.1	4.9	5.5	6.2	7.0	8.5	9.9	11.6	12.1

Note: "–" means non-applicable, as the private sector did not exist.
Source: Obrazovanie v Rossii, 2003, 2003; *Nauka v Rossii v tsifrakh,* 2003, 2004; *Vysshee obrazovanie v Rossii,* 2001, 2002.

The quantitative expansion has been accompanied by changes in the socio-demographic structure of the nation's student bodies. Feminization is one of these trends: in 1993, women made up 51.6% of students, whereas in 2002 that figure had reached 57.5%. The research also reveals that over the last several years an increasing number of students have come from the more educated strata of society. The chances for admission to higher education institutions have diminished for children whose parents are engaged in science, culture, education, or health care, while they have increased for children of economists and businessmen. The proportion of students whose parents are employed in the private sector of economics is especially growing. The lowest chances to obtain higher education are found among children of parents working in agriculture (Vasenina & Sorokina, 2002).

There is regional differentiation as well: a decreasing number of students are studying outside their home region, not having a financial opportunity to study in other regions. For example, in 1999 three-quarters of the first-year students at Moscow State University were residents of Moscow or the greater Moscow region (Vasenina & Sorokina, 2002).

The national funding situation is also having a dramatic impact on student enrollment. At public institutions, the number of students receiving governmental fellowships has significantly decreased, as fellowships become more merit-based and need-based: in 1990, 88% of full-time students received financial assistance, while in 2002, this had declined to approximately 43%. Further, the minimal fellowship amount of 200 rubles (roughly US$7) is more symbolic than of significant assistance. This is why a search for additional income has become an important part of a typical Russian student's life. Many full-time students (on average, about 50%) hold regular jobs, simultaneously combining levels of study and work that surely affect their quality of learning (*Ekonomika obrazovania v zerkale statistiki*, 2004). However, motivation for work is not solely based on financial concerns: students also acquire professional experience, which improves their chances of landing a job after graduation.

When speaking of the massification of higher education in Russia, it should be understood that overall the growth in the number of students, as mentioned above, was mainly a result of expanding fee-paid education, which imposes certain restrictions on the provision of broad access to higher education in Russia. Access to higher education is dependent on a number of factors, one of the most essential of which is family income: higher income not only opens doors to the fee-paid forms of higher education at public and private institutions, but also enables a family to invest more in the preparation for admission (in the form of private tutors, special courses of study, or even bribes). High differentiation of quality among secondary schools in Russia is also a factor of inequality. Territorial differentiation has also been observed; higher levels of educational quality are more commonly found in the major cities, while about 30% of students attend rural schools.

Recognizing a need to improve access to higher education, since 2001 the government has conducted an experiment with a unified state examination (EGE), which is aimed to serve both as a final examination at secondary schools and an entrance examination at the tertiary level. Authors of the experiment believe standardized subject tests will provide a unified system of control over education and enable the reform of higher education admissions by enrolling students by merit (e.g., test scores). The exclusion of subjective factors (inevitable at written and oral entrance examinations) allows one to expect an improvement of access. The first unified tests were begun in 2001 in four regions (out of 89); in 2004, the experiment involved 65 regions, and a decision on the future of the EGE was expected by 2005. To receive a public assessment of the experiment, the Ministry will conduct a survey of students, parents, schoolteachers, and educational officials in the participating regions. It is difficult to forecast the results of the survey, as the experiment has generated lots of doubts regarding the EGE testing procedures, methodology, and content. Many agree that a unified system of educational assessment is useful for the nation's education system; but as an instrument of knowledge control, EGE does not seem able to achieve the main goal set by the Ministry—to improve access—and being connected with financial issues (in the form of the GIFO) might even affect access negatively. Generally, this stage of reform requires thorough analysis of the results of experiments before undertaking any implementation of the practices throughout the entire country.

New challenges facing Russian higher education are also related to a temporary demographic decline. According to demographic and sociological projections, stiff competition at universities is diminishing, and by 2009 entrance examinations would have no meaning: during several years, the number of school graduates would be less than the number of places available in public universities (e.g., 1.3 million school graduates and 1.7 million places in higher and secondary professional institutions). All this must be taken into account when formulating Russia's education policy.

The Academic Profession

The academic workplace and academic profession have changed considerably over the last decades as a result of several political and economic transformations in Russia. First of all, Russian academics were liberated from the ideological repression of the Soviet era that restricted their academic freedom to choose topics for research, their access to Russian and foreign scientific literature, and their opportunities to publish papers and collaborate with foreign colleagues. But the negative impact of this transformation has also been striking, particularly in terms of remuneration and prestige. Academics used to be a part of an elite and relatively prestigious social group, but in the post-Soviet reality they have found their social status to be quite low (Smolentseva, 2003).

What has not changed over the last several years is an academic hierarchy of positions: assistant (*assistent*); instructor (*prepodavatel'*); lecturer (*starshii prepodavatel'*); docent (*dotsent*), comparable to associate professor; and professor (full professor). There is no system of tenure or permanent contracts in Russia, and an academic is hired on a contract for a period of up to five years. A contract system was introduced in the 1990s, while during the Soviet era, competition and contracts did not exist—rather, an academic was appointed without stipulation of the term. However, in fact the new appointments system (being competitive only on paper) has not brought any significant change in the system.

Management positions of a faculty dean and a department chair are elective. In public higher education institutions, there is a 65-year age limit for such appointments, which might be prolonged up to 70. The appointments system does not contain any restrictions regarding compulsory retirement at a certain age for regular academic positions.

In Russia, there is a two-tier system of advanced academic degrees, established in 1934 (which replaced the degree system of Imperial Russia, abolished in 1918). The first degree is the candidate of sciences (*kandidat nauk*), considered an equivalent to the doctoral degree (Ph.D.) being granted in other countries. Usually, this degree is awarded after three or four years of graduate study (*aspirantura*), the completion of independent research, writing a dissertation, and its successful public defense. The highest degree is doctor of sciences (doctor nauk), which requires several years of extensive independent research work. The degree is usually earned while the individual is either working in academia or enrolled in postgraduate studies (*doktorantura*). Both degrees are awarded by academic councils, consisting of about 15 members affiliated with different higher educational and research institutions, after a public defense of the dissertation.

Along with the academic degrees, another system of academic ranking is used at higher education institutions: the academic ranks (titles) (*uchenoe zvanie*) of docent and professor. Persons with the rank of professor as a rule hold a doctoral degree; persons with a rank of docent usually have the degree of candidate. All academic degrees and ranks are confirmed by the Supreme Certifying Commission (*Vysshaia Attestatsionnaia Komissiya*), under the Ministry of Education and Science. Since 1993, the number of academics has steadily increased, and by 2002 reached 291,800 (see Table 2). Approximately 11% of faculty at public higher education institutions have a doctor of sciences degree and 46% are candidates of sciences.

Academic staff has experienced a dramatic transformation over the last decades. A massive "brain drain," involving an estimated 2.2 million people (nearly two-thirds of all researchers, by some accounts), drained Russia's intellectual resource base during the 1980s and 1990s (Ushkalov & Malakha, 2000). Some researchers went abroad, while a significant number of others simply quit the academic profession and took jobs in other areas of Russia's economy. Meanwhile, as remuneration in research institutes fell below that of higher education, experts migrated from the institutes to the universities. Through all these changes, the academic potential of Russia's research and higher education institutions was diminished. However, some initiatives are currently underway to establish collaboration with members of the Russian academic diaspora, with invitations to conduct joint research projects and to return as visiting professors to Russian universities.

Unfortunately, low salaries have dented the prestige of the academic profession and forced many faculty members to look for additional sources of income; today, about 50% of Russia's faculty have additional jobs. By law, the average salary of a faculty member must be twice as much as the average salary in industry. However, faculty actually earn less—for example, in 2002 an average faculty salary was around 4,000 rubles (about US$140), which is almost 78% of the average salary in industry (*Ekonomika obrazovania v zerkale statistiki*, 2004). Further, a new stratification of academics by level of income has emerged. This process has not been thoroughly studied yet, but preliminary data show that a relatively small number of academics remain in a high income group that might be a result of their affiliation with more

Table 2. Academic Staff at Russian Institutions of Higher Education (in thousands)

	1985	1991	1992	1993	1994	1995	1996	1997	1998	1999	2000	2001	2002
Public sector	205.0	233.5	239.9	239.8	233.5	239.2	243.0	247.5	249.6	255.9	265.2	272.7	291.8
Doctors of sciences	9.8	14.2	15.7	17.6	18.6	20.1	21.4	22.8	24.3	25.8	28.0	29.7	32.3
Candidates of sciences	103.6	115.1	115.3	117.4	114.5	117.5	118.5	119.1	120.2	122.4	125.4	128.5	135.5
Professors	*	13.7	15.3	18.0	19.4	21.1	22.3	23.5	24.6	25.7	27.0	28.2	30.6
Docents	*	74.8	77.2	81.9	82.2	85.3	86.1	87.4	87.1	89.3	89.8	90.2	94.6
Private sector	–	–	–	4.9	9.7	13.0	17.8	23.6	32.8	42.1	42.2	46.9	47.8
Doctors of sciences	–	–	–	0.7	1.7	2.1	2.7	3.6	4.5	5.4	5.2	6.2	6.2
Candidates of sciences	–	–	–	2.2	4.6	6.3	8.1	10.5	14.8	19.0	19.7	20.9	21.3
Professors	–	–	–	0.6	1.6	2.0	2.8	3.7	4.7	4.7	5.2	5.9	5.8
Docents	–	–	–	1.6	3.7	4.9	6.8	8.3	11.9	13.3	15.2	16.3	15.9

Note: "–" means non-applicable, as the private sector did not exist. "*" means non-available.
Source: Obrazovanie v Rossii, 2003, 2003; Nauka v Rossii v tsifrakh, 2003, 2004; Vysshee obrazovanie v Rossii, 2001, 2002.

prestigious institutions, working in more prestigious fields, or filling top positions in administration.

There are a few other important trends regarding the academic profession. As seen in many other countries, part-time academics are increasingly playing an important role in the structure of an institution's faculty. At public institutions, the proportion of part-time faculty increased from 11% in 1991 to 22% in 2002. At private institutions, part-time faculty comprises the bulk of the academic staff—145% more than full-time academic personnel (as of 2002).

Major transformations have also been seen in the demographic structure of the faculty. Women are increasingly taking positions at public institutions: in 1995, they comprised 44.4%, and by 2002, 51% of the faculty was female. Crucial trends are also observed in the age structure of higher education faculty—the aging of academic staff and insufficient recruitment of younger academics is of particular concern. The average age of Russia's main, full-time academic staff is about 55 years (Belyakov, 2003). It is estimated that most academics with advanced degrees are older than 40 years of age; the average age of a faculty member with a doctoral degree is 62, and the average age of those with a candidate's degree is 54 years. Unfortunately, too few of Russia's promising youth appear interested in an academic career, and there are inadequate numbers of future academics in the graduate education pipeline. These facts amount to a serious challenge for the Russian education system.

Traditionally, low horizontal mobility of Russian academics from town to town (or from university to university) is also worth noting. The opportunity to recruit faculty from other institutions or cities, which existed before, has virtually disappeared as a result of the economic situation in education and in the country as a whole. The new trend of regional limitations on education, both in enrollments and in faculty recruitment, has undoubtedly resulted in the deterioration of educational quality and impacts the future health of universities throughout the country.

And finally, an absence of any real policy on the future of the academic profession in Russia (in spite of the fact that in 1998 academic staff policy was declared a priority for the Ministry of Education) evokes great concern throughout the educational community. But some efforts are now beginning to focus on attracting and retaining junior academic staff, recognizing this as a crucial factor in the long-term development of Russia's education and research institutions.

Graduate Education

With the understanding that a master's level education has only recently been introduced in Russia and currently involves only a minor share of graduate students, a discussion of graduate education can reasonably focus on programs leading to the degree of candidate of sciences (Ph.D.). The focus on education leading to a doctor of science degree seems equally unnecessary, since it is a very specific cohort (involving only about 4,500 people in the entire country). Since 1993, the number of Ph.D. students has increased by 171% on average, reaching 136,242 students in 2002 (see Table 3). This growth was most notable in the fields of economics and social sciences, while the number of Ph.D. students in other fields has not increased as quickly.

Table 3. Graduate and Postgraduate Education in Russia

	1990	1991	1992	1993	1994	1995	1996	1997	1998	1999	2000	2001*	2002†
Candidate's level													
Students	63,072	59,314	51,915	50,296	53,541	62,317	74,944	88,243	98,355	107,031	117,714	128,420	136,242
Graduates	16,355	16,322	14,857	13,432	12,292	11,369	11,931	14,135	17,972	21,982	24,828	25,696	28,101
Graduates with defended dissertation, %	21.3	19.0	21.1	23.8	22.1	22.9	22.9	24.1	25.1	26.1	30.2	24.0	26.4
Confirmed degrees	30,050	28,714	24,121	15,679	12,964	11,553	12,032	13,149	14,558	18,102	23,075	18,976	22,383
Doctoral level													
Students	1,774	1,834	1,644	1,687	1,850	2,190	2,554	3,182	3,684	3,993	4,213	4,462	4,546
Graduates	67	430	617	573	464	464	574	662	821	1,033	1,251	1,257	1,267
Graduates with defended dissertation, %	38.8	35.8	40.0	33.9	36.2	29.5	34.8	34.1	38.0	34.5	38.8	31.6	32.4
Confirmed degrees	5,067	6,326	5,491	4,111	3,185	2,760	3,022	3,278	3,716	4,045	4,592	3,662	4,328

Note: *In 2001, the decrease is due to restructuring of the system of academic councils awarding degrees.
†Preliminary data for 2002.
Source: Obrazovanie v Rossii, 2003, 2003; *Nauka v Rossii v tsifrakh,* 2003, 2004; *Vysshee obrazovanie v Rossii,* 2001, 2002.

Massification of graduate education is not linked to the development of Russian science, and on the contrary is proceeding despite the crisis in the science sector (perhaps explaining why most graduates do not choose the academic profession). Additionally, graduate education is increasingly leaving the walls of research institutes—where science and basic research were traditionally concentrated—and moving into higher education institutions. In the early 1990s, higher education institutions comprised about one-third of all Ph.D. granting organizations; in the late 1990s, this figure had increased to more than 40%. Higher education institutions today enroll the majority (85%) of all graduate students in Russia.

The socio-demographic characteristics of graduate students are changing. Some increase in the share of male students reflects their attempts to avoid compulsory military service by being a student. Meanwhile, in 1993 women comprised 47% of all graduate students; by 1997, this had dropped to 41.6%, but then increased slowly to a level of 44.6% in 2002. The average graduate student is also younger—in 1995, 56% of all graduate students were under 26 years old, and in 2002 this has increased to 73%—suggesting that more students are enrolling in graduate programs directly after completing higher education, instead of accumulating years of work or research experience as was the norm during the Soviet era.

The most important challenge to graduate education in Russia is financial, reflecting the overall conditions in Russian science and its funding. The absence of necessary financing hinders the development of research at universities and research institutes, and thus makes impossible appropriate research training. In addition, the lack of governmental financial support forces full-time students to combine study and work—nearly 70% of graduate students are full-time, but the average fellowship is about 2,000 rubles (roughly US$70). The majority of students thus devote the bulk of their time not to research and writing their dissertation, but to their jobs, contributing to the ineffectiveness of doctoral studies.

Another indicator of challenges in doctoral education is the number of doctoral graduates who defend their dissertation on time, within their term of study. Usually, about a quarter defend their thesis on time, and this proportion reached its highest level (of 30.2%) in 2000. In fact, students might defend their thesis after graduation, but to date there are no statistics on that. Today, much has been said about the generally deteriorating conditions and changing motivation of doctoral students. However, interestingly enough, during the Soviet era the number of graduate students who defended their thesis on time was roughly the same or even less, with a maximum level (of 33.4% for higher education graduates) observed in 1975. This begs the question of whether the doctoral education system established in the USSR has ever been truly effective, and whether a 3-year program of study provides enough time for completing and defending a dissertation.

The issues of graduate education today are discussed quite often, encompassing many essential questions: Who are graduate students or degree recipients? What is their status and where will they be in need? Are they young scholars pursuing academic careers in higher education and research, or are they young people seeking a place among the more educated strata in the age of mass higher education, looking to establish careers not only in academe but also in business, government and other sectors? Despite these and other important strategic questions, state policymaking and regulation have been restricted to mostly quantitative indicators and attempts to limit the number of degrees. For example, a recent reform (2001) sought to reduce the number of academic councils able to award graduate degrees (regardless of the quality of dissertations defended at their institution), and in March 2004, the State Supreme Certifying Commission recommended that the government reduce the number of doctoral students by 20% and close doctoral programs in institutions where the percent of dissertations successfully defended is low.

Another potential innovation suggested by the minister of education in 2004 is an extension in length of doctoral programs up to four years. This initiative might be partly a result of Russia's signing the Bologna Declaration and its interest in joining the European Higher Education Area with compatible degree qualifications. To Europeans, the Russian degree of candidate of sciences currently lacks an educational comparison, and presently only France recognizes this degree. However, the formal extension of the length of study would not really resolve any significant problem of Russian graduate education.

In conclusion, the system of graduate education in Russia is on the eve of change. The question is whether the system will be able to transform and meet the challenges of the changing role of education and science, or will outlive its usefulness along with the devaluing system of academic degrees confirmed by the state commission.

Private Higher Education

One of the most important developments in Russian higher education has been the emergence of a non-state, private sector of higher education, generated by a policy that broke the state monopoly in the field of education. The term "non-state education" appeared for the first time in the 1992 educational law; later, a section of the law on "new educational institutions" was adopted. The development of the non-state sector has been fast: over the first year of its existence (1993), private higher education institutions numbered 78, and had increased to 387 by 2002. However, relatively few students (12%) attend education institutions in the non-state sector.

From the very beginning, non-state higher education has been developed under strict state control. Similar to public institutions, the operation of private ones is regulated by the state and is controlled by the procedures of licensing, evaluation, and accreditation. Only a state-accredited institution is allowed to award degrees and certificates of legal recognition (any institution may award its own degrees and certificates, but only those with legal recognition will lead to opportunities for further education in public institutions, credentials for holding positions at public institutions, etc.).

There is also another dimension of the relationship between the state and private institutions of higher education: state-run organizations, in most cases, are founders of non-state institutions of higher learning. Over half (51%) of non-state institutions have a mixed body of founders (state, non-governmental, and private organizations), 25% are established by one or more legal entities, and 23% by individuals. Among the founders there are state-run authorities (ministries and committees), administrations of different levels, and public higher education institutions (Krukhmaleva *et al.*, 2000).

In particular, certain developmental advantages favor those non-state higher education institutions which were established by major, prestigious public universities and former educational institutions of the Communist party—for example, they are able to draw on the existing infrastructure (plants, facilities, equipment, etc.), academic staff and the reputation of their institutional founders.

Non-state institutions emerged as a reflection of changing socio-economic conditions in Russia. Private institutions try to meet the market demand in a workforce educated in the fields of economics, management, law, social sciences, and humanities, thus occupying a niche in those fields of higher education. Today, a private education institution is usually a small-scale organization training students in the humanities and social sciences, receiving its financing mainly from tuition fees and running as a for-profit organization. Additionally, these institutions expand an academic labor market by providing opportunities for supplementary income for academics employed in public settings.

Non-state institutions (unlike public) attract students with easier admissions, relatively low tuition fees, higher faculty-student ratios, broader programs of study, and opportunities to tailor their curricula or obtain more than one degree simultaneously. Dependence upon material and human resources has defined the unequal distribution of non-state institutions throughout the country—most of them, like public institutions, are located in the major cities of Central Russia.

The most serious challenge for non-state higher education is educational quality. Very few private tertiary institutions in Russia are characterized by high educational standards. That is why most students choosing between paid education at private and public institutions prefer the latter. The student body of most private-sector institutions is drawn from middle-income families whose children could not get into public institutions—in other words, not the most academically gifted students. Similar to public institutions, students of private universities combine work and study, so the majority of them are part-time students (66% as of 2002, in comparison to 43% at public institutions).

Private institutions rely mostly on part-time faculty—in 2002, there were roughly 19,500 full-time academic staff, compared to 28,300 part-time personnel. Private institutions are also an important element in the feminization trend in Russian higher education: the proportion of female faculty increased from 54.0% in 1999 to 58.5% in 2002. The percentage of academic staff with advanced degrees and academic ranks corresponds approximately to that at public institutions and reflects the efforts of private universities to attract more highly qualified staff in order to strengthen their position in the marketplace of educational services.

In addition to a competitive market for tuition-paying students, private education institutions face a variety of other challenges, including the maintenance of adequate facilities, equipment, and libraries; legal matters of operation; state regulations; taxation policies; and questions of property. The development of the non-state sector of higher education is also dependent on its acceptance by the population as consumers of paid educational services. Currently in Russia, an increasingly large group of people are ready to invest in the education of their children, according to their available finances. The question is what form of education they will choose to invest in—public or private.

For non-state institutions, that choice might be critical, since only a few of them are able to successfully compete with the public universities. Governmental policy does not leave behind non-state institutions: in an attempt to achieve a balance between state and non-state sectors, it plans to provide equal opportunities for both types of institutions in competition for state funding awards. So, in the near future, the non-state higher education sector will likely experience further significant changes.

Internationalization

Opening up the USSR in 1985 launched a growing international collaboration throughout higher education, bringing international (mostly U.S. and European) models in content of education and curricula, access to international literature, faculty and student exchanges, joint study and research programs, etc. Major assistance and exchange programs have been funded by the United States, the European Union, foundations and international organizations, and enabled a considerable transformation in Russian higher education.

Another dimension of internationalization in higher education has involved the student body and the delivery of international educational services. For years, the Soviet Union was one of the major providers of higher education for international students. By strengthening ties with countries of the Communist block (along with a number of developing nations), 126,500 foreign students (according to some estimates, up to 180,000) had come to study in roughly 700 institutions of the USSR by 1990 (Sheregi, Dmitriev, & Arefiev, 2002). In post-Soviet Russia, the centralized organization of intergovernmental agreements and a large system of international education were ruined. But in recent years, we have observed substantial growth in the number of international students in post-Soviet Russia. Over the last decade, their numbers have increased to more than 100,000 students, bringing to Russia an estimated US$150 million annually. For most Russian higher education institutions, foreign students mean an important source of non-state financing, but not all institutions are competent enough to participate in this market. The most popular fields of education for international students in Russia have not changed significantly—engineering, medicine, economics, business administration, and humanities.

In terms of expanding international education, Russia's closest neighbors—CIS countries—comprise one of the key regions, and currently students from these countries make up about one-third of all foreigners studying in Russia. Approximately the same number of students come from Asian countries, mostly China. Smaller groups come from Near East and North African countries (approximately 12.8% of all foreign students), with an additional 7.5% from Europe, 5% from Africa, and 3% from Latin America (Sheregi *et al.*, 2002).

Internationalization also involves Russian students going abroad for higher education. Unfortunately, there are no precise statistics, but some estimates suggest that in the mid-1990s about 13,000 Russian students studied outside their country—most of them in the U.S., Germany, France, and U.K. (Ledeneva, 2002). Further, their numbers have been growing—6,238 Russian students were enrolled in U.S. colleges and universities in 2002 (International Institute of Education, 2004). Unfortunately, research has shown that Russians studying abroad are oriented towards an international labor market and do not tend to return to Russia after graduation (Ledeneva, 2002).

In another aspect of internationalization, the government of Russia is planning to increase the export of educational services. Along with oil, higher education is expected to be a strategic export industry of the Russian economy, bringing in billions of dollars. The concept of a federal policy on educating foreign nationals in Russian education institutions was approved in October 2002 by the President of the Russian Federation and launched by the Ministry of Education. The concept implies that Russian institutions of higher learning have traditionally provided higher education for foreign students and still have a potential to be a "key player" in international education. Russian higher education is considered attractive by its relatively high quality, qualified faculty, and comparatively low tuition and cost of living. However, serious challenges must be addressed including the relative incompatibility of Russia's educational structure; the need to meet international standards for equipment and other conditions of study; certain legal hurdles; and insufficient information support.

Another dimension of internationalization is academic mobility. The most important obstacle, which would clearly affect the prospective development of internationalization, is the issue of quality assurance and degree recognition. Signing the Lisbon Convention *de jure* opened possibilities for the recognition of Russian diplomas, but in fact, Russian degrees are generally not recognized in a number of developed and developing countries.

Nevertheless, joining the Bologna Declaration (in 2003) should foster the convertibility of Russian degrees and strengthen the position of Russia in the international education market. Entering the European Higher Education Area has been the most notable event over the last several years and has generated lots of discussion. This process implies a reorganization of the recently established bachelor's/master's system, putting into doubt the system of candidate's and doctor's qualifications, and requires establishing a credit system and devising comparable methodologies and criteria for educational quality assessment. These changes will entail a massive transformation of the entire Russian educational system, and should ensure the competitiveness of Russian higher education, enhancing quality and securing Russia's status as an integral part of the international higher education landscape.

Conclusion

Russian higher education has been constantly changing over the last several decades. The reform agendas have involved many profound and essential issues of national education: the funding of higher education, admissions and access, educational quality, degree recognition, and international integration. Additional challenges faced by Russian higher education include the recruitment of junior faculty and retention of graduate students in academia; the need to strengthen links between higher education and basic research (a new conception of a research university is under review); creating new relationships between higher education and industry; and developing the effective use of information technologies in education. In sum, a variety of exciting transformations are now shaping the future of Russian higher education and warrant careful scrutiny for many years to come.

References

Avrus, A. I. (2001). *Istoria rossiiskikh universitetov. Ocherki* (History of Russian universities. Essays). Moscow, Russia: MONF.

Belyakov, S. D. (ed.) (2003). *Sistema finansirovania obrazovania: analiz effekctivnosti* (The system of educational financing: Analysis of e). Moscow, Russia: Tekhnopechat.

Davydov, V. N. (2001). Modernizatsia v obrazovanii: GIFO—blago ili net? (Modernization of education: Is GIFO a good or not?). *Universitetskoe upravlenie* (University management), 3(18).

Ekonomika obrazovania v zerkale statistiki. Informatsionnyi biulleten' (Economics of education in a mirror of statistics. Information bulletin) (2004). Moscow, Russia: Higher School of Economics, 1(3).

Federal'naya programma razvitiya obrazovania (Federal Program of Development of Education). (2000).

Kinelev, V. G. (ed.). (1995). *Vysshee obrazovanie v Rossii: Ocherk istorii do 1917 goda* (Higher education in Russia: Historical essays up to 1917). Moscow, Russia: NII VO.

Kontseptsiya modernizatsii rossiiskogo obrazovania na period do 2010 goda (Conception of modernization of Russian education for a period up to 2010). (2001).

Krukhmaleva, O. V., Smolentseva, A. Y., & Ushakova, M. V. (2000). *Novye obrazovatel'nye uchrezhdenia v Rossii* (New educational institutions in Russia). Moscow, Russia: NII VO.

Ledeneva, L. (2002). Rossiiskie studenty v zarubezhnykh universitetakh—skol'ko ikh? (Russian students at universities abroad—how many?). *Demoscope*, 55. Online at: http://demoscope.ru/weekly/2002/055/tema01.php. Retrieved May 31, 2004.

Natsional'naya Doktrina obrazovania (National Doctrine on Education). (2000).

Nauka v Rossii v tsifrakh: 2003. Stat. sb. (Science in Russia: 2003. Statistics). (2004). Moscow, Russia: TsISN.

Obrazovanie v Rossii: 2003. Statsbornik (Education in Russia. 2003: Statistics) (2003). Moscow, Russia: Goskomstat.

International Institute for Education. (2004). Open Doors report on international students in the USA. Online at: http://opendoors.iienetwork.org/?p=35933. Retrieved May 31, 2004.

Petrova, T. E. (2000). *Sotsiologia studenchestva v Rossii* (Sociology of students in Russia). St.Petersburg, Russia: Bel'veder.

Poletaev, A. V., Agranovich, M. L., & Zharova, L. N. (2002). *Rossiiskoe obrazovenie v kontekste mezhdunarodnykh pokazatelei. Sopostavitel'nyi doklad* (Russian education in the context of international indicators. A comparative report). Moscow, Russia: Informika.

Sheregi, F. E., Dmitriev, N. M., & Arefiev, A. I. (2002). *Nauchno-pedagogicheskii potentsial i eksport obrazovatel'nykh uslug rossiiskikh vuzov* (Scientific and pedagogical potential and export of educational services of Russian higher education institutions). Moscow, Russia: Center for Social Prognosis.

Smolentseva, A. (2003). Challenges to the Russian academic profession. *Higher Education, 45*(4), 391–424.

Ushkalov, I., & Malakha, I. (2000). "Utechka umov" kak global'nyi fenomen i ego osobennosti v Rossii. *Sociologicheskie issledovania 3*, 110–117. Available in English as Ushkalov, I., & Malakha, I. (2000). The "brain drain" as a global phenomenon and its characteristics in Russia. *Russian Education and Society 42*(12), 18–34.

Vasenina, I. V. & Sorokina, N. D. (2002). Vysshee obrazovanie v sovremennom mire (Higher education in the contemporary world). In *Chelovek i sovremennyi mir (An individual and contemporary world)* (pp. 418–440). Moscow, Russia: INFRA-M.

Vysshee obrazovanie v Rossii: 2001. Stat.sb. (Higher education in Russia: 2001. Statistics) (2002). Moscow, Russia: TsISN.

Zakon. (1992). *Ob obrazovanii (Law on education).*

Zakon. (1996). *O vysshem I poslevuzovskom professional'nom obrazovanii (Law on higher and postgraduate education).*

Zakon. (1996). *Ob obrazovanii (Law on education).*

51

SOUTH AFRICA

Chika Trevor Sehoole
University of Pretoria, Pretoria, South Africa

The Republic of South Africa occupies the southernmost part of the African continent.[1] It has common borders with the republics of Namibia, Botswana, and Zimbabwe on the northern and western sides, and the Republic of Mozambique and the Kingdom of Swaziland in the northeast. South Africa is surrounded by the ocean on three sides—the west, south, and east—and has a long coastline of about 3,000 km.[2] The 2001 census accounted for a South African population of about 44.8 million people. Of these, 35 million classified themselves as African, 4.2 million as white, 1.1 million as Asian or Indian, and 3.9 million as colored.[3] To cater to South Africa's diverse people, the Constitution provides for 11 official languages.

South Africa experienced different periods of colonialism dating back to the 1500s. In 1652, the Dutch East Indian Company (VOC) set up a station at Table Bay (Cape Town) to provision passing ships en route to India. From 1657, European settlers were allotted farms by the colonial authorities in the arable regions around Cape Town, where wine and wheat were the major products. By the early 1700s, the colonists had begun to spread into the hinterland, where they came into contact with some indigenous people. This ushered in a century of warfare, during which the colonists gained ascendancy over the black chiefdoms in the region. In 1795 and 1806, respectively, the British occupied the Cape as a strategic base, controlling the route to India, which led to the integration of the Cape Colony into the dynamic international trading empire of industrializing Britain.

Following the Anglo-Boer/South African War of 1899–1902, the Union of South Africa was established, bringing together the former Boer republics and the British colonies into an independent dominion. Black interests were subsumed by the goal of white nation building across the language divide, thus perpetuating some of the segregationist policies that were already in place. The principles of segregationist thinking were laid down in a 1905 report of the South African Native Affairs Commission and continued to evolve in response to economic, social, and economic pressures from the black people. In 1948, the National Party—with its ideology of apartheid (separation)—came to power following its victory in the all-white elections. Apartheid philosophy was based on a belief in white supremacy and division of people on the basis of race. As such, the South African population became formally segregated into four races,

James J.F. Forest and Philip G. Altbach (eds.), International Handbook of Higher Education, 971–992.
© 2006 *Springer. Printed in the Netherlands.*

namely, white, Indian, colored, and African.[4] These divisions also determined the hierarchy of supremacy and benefits under apartheid, with whites at the top and Africans at the bottom of the social ladder. The racial division of the South African population was bolstered by the passing of a number of laws, including the Population Registration Act of 1950—whereby all South Africans became officially registered according to the government's racial classification—and the Group Areas Act of 1950, which proclaimed residential and business areas for various racial groups. The Group Areas Act initiated the era of forced removals, where black communities were violently relocated because white landowners either did not want blacks living next to them or simply wanted their land. The Separate Amenities Act was also passed, which made it illegal for the different racial groups to share facilities and services, including education. Alongside the development of the legal and institutional settings for the operation of apartheid was the development and formulation of the philosophical base for the operation of this machinery. Education became a strategic sector for the implementation and promotion of apartheid philosophy, since most South African children would be exposed to it to some extent.

It is against this background that the history and evolution of higher education in South Africa need to be understood. The system of apartheid was legally ended in 1990, along with the unbanning of the liberation movement and the release of political prisoners who had fought against the system for over four decades. This was further consolidated with the election of a new democratic government in which the African National Congress, under the leadership of President Nelson Mandela, won the first all-race elections in April 1994.

This chapter analyzes the progress that has been made in the reform initiatives undertaken in higher education in South Africa, from one of the most unequal systems in the world to one that is gradually becoming competitive and staking its claim among the modern democracies of the world. The focus of this discussion is on the interplay of global forces and local realities in shaping the process and content of reform in the first decade of democracy in South Africa. It is argued that following the first term of government in power (1994–1999), which was characterized by the relative weakness of the state as a result of a vacuum in policy and legislation to spearhead transformation, the second term of office (1999–2004) saw a new South African ability to elaborate its policies and put in place policy and regulatory frameworks for a single coordinated system responsive to local realities and global challenges.

The Evolution of Higher Education in South Africa: A Brief Overview

The first institutions of higher education in South Africa emerged during the mid-19th century, with the establishment of two colleges, the South African College in Cape Town in 1829 and Victoria College in Stellenbosch in 1865, followed by the University of the Cape of Good Hope—the first South African university—in 1873. Rhodes University followed in 1904 and in 1918, the South African College and Victoria College changed their names to the Universities of Stellenbosch and Cape Town, respectively. The University of the Cape of Good Hope became known as the University of South Africa (UNISA). The establishment of these universities in the southern part of the country near the coast could be linked to the settlement of white colonialists in the Cape dating back to the 15th century. The South African Native College was established by missionaries in 1916 and became known as the University of Fort Hare in 1951. The School of Mines, established in Johannesburg in 1895, became the University of the Witwatersrand in 1922.[5]

The UNISA was a federal university with a number of university colleges. Over the 30 years following 1930, many of these colleges became full-fledged universities (including the Universities of Pretoria, Potchefstroom, Natal, and the Free State). The Extension of University Education Act (passed in 1959) was designed to bar the entry of black students into historically white institutions (HWIs) and to establish racially segregated universities. The Universities of Durban-Westville, the Western Cape, Zululand, and the North came into existence shortly afterward. Other universities established during the period from the mid-1960s to the mid-1980s included the University of Port Elizabeth, Rand Afrikaans University, the Medical University of Southern Africa, and Vista University. By the early 1960s, South Africa's universities were catering to about 62,000 students, only 5,000 of whom were not white. This racial disparity began to decrease when, in the heyday of separate development in the 1970s and 1980s, universities were constructed in the so-called "independent homelands" of Transkei, Ciskei, Venda, and Bophuthatswana.

This was followed by the gradual "racial opening up" of many of the historically white universities (HWUs), so that by the late 1980s data revealed that in addition to the 150,000 white students studying at the country's universities, there were 120,000 black (African, colored, and Indian) students.[6] Reflecting some progress in building nonracial higher education, today the majority of students in the public sector's 21 universities are black—in 2002 (according to preliminary enrollment figures), there were 149,723 (33%) white students and 311,415 (67%) nonwhite students [Council on Higher Education (CHE), 2004].

Higher education evolved into a binary system made up of well-established university and technikon sectors. The technikons (institutions for technical higher education) emerged from the advancement of technical education and institutions in South Africa, the origins of which can be traced back to the turn of the 20th century with the growth of the mining industry and the subsequent development of a support industry, which led to the need for more technically skilled staff. To address this need, the railway, the Chamber of Commerce, and certain schools initiated part-time classes for teaching technical skills to apprentices. As these classes became more organized, centers for technical training were set up, which finally gave rise to the establishment of technical institutes and colleges. In 1922, an act was passed which instructed technical colleges to offer a theoretical component of the apprenticeship training throughout the country (CTP, 1990–1991).

The debate about the definition of the term "higher education" was brought to a head with the acceptance of the Higher Education Act (HEA) of 1923, which declared some technical colleges higher education institutions (HEIs). These institutions were brought under the control of the Minister of Education and became semi-autonomous state institutions. In 1926, the college councils formed the Association of Technical Colleges to promote cooperation and coordination of the administration and to facilitate control of academic and other matters. Close contact was also maintained between the (then) Department of Higher Education, which examined and certified candidates at the colleges. The four large colleges—Pretoria, Johannesburg, Durban and Cape Town—introduced a new tertiary education phase in 1957, with cooperative courses leading to the National Diploma for Technicians (CTP, 1995). In 1967, four technical colleges were transformed into Colleges of Advanced Technical Education (CATEs) with the passing of the Advanced Technical Education (ATE) Act of 1967. In 1970, the (then) Minister of Education—Minister van der Spuy—stated that CATEs should not be seen as inferior or subservient to universities, but as HEIs with a unique character and function complementary to that of the university (CTP, 1995).

In line with the apartheid policy of segregated education, the provision of technical education was also racially segregated. The development of ATE for other racial groups—colored, Indian, and African—gained momentum during the 1970s. The report of the Committee of Inquiry into the Training of Engineering Technicians (1978) proposed the need for an institutional name change and the acceptance of the fact that the CATEs also had a research function that had to be addressed. The new name, technikon, was accepted and officially changed in May 1979. In 1983, the new law—The Technikon (National Education) Act of 1983—was passed, giving autonomy to technikons and enabling them to take new initiatives and to structure their institutions more in line with the requirements of institutions of higher learning (Hansard, 1983). With the establishment of the Advisory Council for Universities and Technikons (AUT) in 1983, the official status of the technikons was further entrenched. This council was set up to advise the Minister of National Education on joint matters between technikons and universities. These institutions were seen in their own right as being parallel to universities.

A mechanism to give technikons greater autonomy was established in 1986, in the form of the Certification Council for Technikon Education—an accrediting body which gave technikons the right to offer their own examinations—and these institutions finally achieved the status of "degree-awarding" institutions in October 1993. An important milestone in the history of South Africa's higher education system, the Technikon Act of 1993 brought all technikons across racial dividing lines under one legislation. Thus, when the newly elected democratic government took office in 1994, it inherited a well-established higher education system made up of 21 universities and 15 technikons.

The Inheritance of the Apartheid Higher Education System

The change of government in South Africa from an apartheid system to a democratic social order in 1994 ushered in widespread changes throughout higher education. It became necessary to dismantle the architecture of the divided higher education system of the apartheid era and to create a single, coordinated system of higher education. The intention was, among other things, to rationalize the system and to remove the racial inequalities that existed among institutions. However, with the vested interests entrenched in HEIs, restructuring the system would not be easy. This restructuring should be understood in the light of the quest by the postapartheid government to rid its education system of the apartheid past.

Until the early 1990s, education had been a strategic vehicle for the implementation and promotion of the apartheid philosophy. The inequalities in education, and higher education in particular, were accelerated by the passing of the Bantu Education Act of 1953 and the Extension of University Education Act of 1959. The latter was largely based on an attempt to separate the youth of South Africa at the level of higher education on the basis of race, just as was already the case at the primary and secondary school levels. The consequence of that fragmentation was that when the new government came into power in 1994, it inherited a higher education system with the following features:

- The coordination of the higher education system was the responsibility of the Department of National Education, rather than being a line department in the sense of having other education departments or other individual HEIs reporting to it.
- Three Departments of Education (DOE) carried separate responsibilities for universities, technikons, and colleges catering to whites, coloreds, and Indians, respectively.
- The Department of Education and Training was responsible for some universities, some technikons, and some colleges for Africans.
- Six DOEs were responsible for some technikons and some colleges in the six self-governing territories (Bantustans) where Africans were confined.
- Four DOEs were responsible for universities, technikons, and colleges of education in the "independent" states of Transkei, Bophuthatswana, Venda, and Ciskei, serving the Xhosas, Batswana, and vhaVenda ethnic groups, respectively [National Commission on Higher Education (NCHE), 1996].

As the NCHE (1996) noted, these divisions resulted in a gross fragmentation of the higher education system. A consequence was that the effectiveness and efficiency of the system suffered badly through a lack of coordination, common goals, and systematic planning. There was no clear strategy for managing elements such as the size and shape of the system, social and economic needs, overall funds available, growth rates, and the elimination of unnecessary wasteful duplication.

With respect to the institutional landscape, the South African higher education system consisted of 36 public HEIs that were divided along ethnic and racial lines. These institutions included: four English medium universities originally reserved for white students; six Afrikaans medium universities originally reserved for white students; seven technikons reserved for white students; six universities and technikons located in the "Bantustans" and self-governing territories and reserved for African students; two urban universities and technikons reserved for colored and Indian students; two urban universities reserved for black students; and two distance education providers (one university and one technikon) (CHE, 2004, p. 40).

In 1976, the Medical University of Southern Africa (Medunsa) was established, aimed at providing medical training for black students. In 1982, Vista University opened, operating with a number of satellite campuses around black urban townships, but with its administrative offices based in Pretoria. Badat (2002a) identifies the significance of the establishment of Medunsa and Vista as the fact that they were urban-based

Table 1.   1993 Headcount Enrollment by Race

African	191,000	40%
Colored	28,000	7%
Indian	30,000	5%
White	223,000	47%
Total	482,000	100%

Source: Adapted from CHE (2004).

campuses and signaled acceptance by the state of a permanent urban African population in the "white" areas. They could also be seen as part of the state's strategy to enforce a divide between urban African residents and rural and Bantustan African residents. All HEIs were also funded to mirror the apartheid divisions and the different government models imposed on the higher education system.

Student enrollment reflected these racial divisions. In early 1994, 47% of students were white, 40% African, 7% Indian, and 6% colored (Table 1). Participation rates in higher education by gender were similar to those of other countries, with 43% female and 57% male (CHE, 2004, p. 62). Of the African students, 49% were enrolled in historically black HEIs, 13% in historically white HEIs, and 36% in distance HEIs. Until 1983, enrollment of African students in the historically white HEIs required the consent of the Minister of Education, who had to be satisfied that the course(s) for which African students were applying was/were not offered in institutions designated for them (CHE, 2004, p. 62).

The relatively higher number of enrollments of African students was also a result of a recent a phenomenon of the period 1990–1994. As clear signals of the impending changes emerged, all HEIs opened their doors to nondesignated groups. During this period, enrollments showed an overall growth of one-third (more than 130,000). These growth rates were a major contributing factor to the high-growth scenarios envisioned by the NCHE after 1994. This point is explored later in the chapter.

The student profiles of the system also exhibited the racial and gender inequalities of the broader society in terms of access and privilege. Overall, participation rates in the public higher education system remained unsatisfactory.[6] In 1994, the gross participation rates were approximately 17%—higher than in many developing countries, but lower than that of fast-developing and developed countries. Participation rates were highly skewed by race, with approximately 9% for Africans, 13% for coloreds, 40% for Indians, and 70% for whites (Cloete & Bunting, 2000a,b).

In 1994, 69% of students were enrolled in universities and 31% in technikons. Program enrollments were skewed toward the humanities—which constituted 50% of the total—with 25% in science, engineering, and technology (SET), and 25% in business and management courses (Cloete *et al.*, 2002).

Inequalities in staff profiles were more pronounced than student profiles. Just like any other public sector that had to reflect the apartheid policy regarding labor practices and promotion of white supremacy and domination, the higher education system reflected the broader patterns of the apartheid division of labor. As a result, the academic staff and senior administrative staff were overwhelmingly male and white, whereas lower level and service positions were filled predominantly by blacks and women. For example, of about 45,000 staff across the public higher education sector in 1994:

- 80% of professional staff were white, 12% African, 4% colored, and 4% Indian;
- 34% of professional staff were women, and their status was generally lower than that of male professional staff; and
- 52% of nonprofessional staff were African, 29% white, 13% colored, and 6% Indian (CHE, 2004, p. 2).

These are the realities, which the new government had to address, especially the dismantling of the architecture of the divided system of apartheid higher education. According to Jansen (2002), this past had to be resolved through the creation of a single, coordinated system of higher education that purposively dissolved the racial inequalities that existed among institutions. But there was another motivation, though less pronounced in public policy discourse, and that was the need to incorporate the South African higher education system into a fast-changing, technology-driven, and information-based global economy. Thus, it is within the twin logics of the transition that the restructuring and transformation of higher education in South Africa should be understood: the logic of resolving the apartheid legacy in higher education and the logic of incorporating the higher education system into the overall national objective to do well in a competitive, globalized economy.

The New Legislation and Policy Framework for the Transformation of the System (1994–1997)

An important feature of the democratization process in South Africa is how the government and the DOE relied on the use of policy and legislation to steer the system. While the process started slowly as a result of a vacuum in policy during the period 1994–1997, this proved worthwhile since South Africa has now succeeded in laying a solid foundation for the transformation of higher education based on sound policies. While the first five years saw the development of policy and legislative frameworks, the second period of government (1999–2004) saw an elaboration of policies which further enabled the government to get a grip on the levers of power in order to steer the system to not only be able to deal and respond to global challenges, but also to be locally responsive and relevant. This policy and legislative framework for the transformation of higher education in South Africa has been enunciated in the successive development of policy documents: the NCHE (1996) report, the White Paper on Higher Education (DOE, 1997a), the HEA of 1997, the National Plan on Higher Education (DOE, 2001a,b), and Transformation and Restructuring of Higher Education (DOE, 2002). The challenge the government faced was to overhaul the higher education system in order to make it conform to the national development goals underpinned by the values and principles of the emerging democracy (CHE, 2004, p. 2). This discussion will now briefly reflect on the contributions made by successive policy documents produced during this period.

The National Commission on Higher Education

The seriousness with which the new government viewed the transformation of higher education was reflected in the appointment of the National Commission on Higher Education in February 1995 to advise the government on how to transform the higher education system. This was the first Commission to be appointed under the Mandela administration, and it reported to government in August 1996. The work of the Commission laid the basis for the subsequent development of policy and played an important role in putting to rest the history of apartheid in higher education and producing a vision, principles, and values to inform higher education transformation and restructuring. It recommended the following key strategies for transforming the system:

1. A policy of increased participation was required to satisfy the needs of equity, redress, and development. Concomitantly, a single coordinated higher education system was proposed as a way in which the inequities, ineffectiveness, and inefficiency of the existing system could be eradicated.
2. A policy of greater responsiveness was needed to ensure that higher education engaged with the challenges of its social context. This would require changes in the content, focus, and delivery modes of academic programs and research adapted to the knowledge needs of the market and civil society.
3. Cooperative governance, the elements of which included the state in a supervisory role (as opposed to a role of control, or interference); intermediary bodies between the state and the HEIs characterized by internal constituency partnerships; and a set of linkages between HEIs and civil society (NCHE, 1996).

The White Paper on Higher Education

Following its formal response to the NCHE report, through the Green Paper and widespread consultation with the public, the government finally released its policy on higher education in the form of a White Paper in August 1997. The White Paper set out policy in support of the government's intention to transform higher education through the development of a program-based higher education system, planned and governed as a singled coordinated system. This was intended to redress and overcome the fragmentation, inequality, and inefficiency that were the legacies of the past (DOE, 1997a).

The White Paper identified planning, funding, and quality assurance as the three steering instruments for the transformation of South African higher education into a qualitatively improved and more equitable and responsive system. In addition, the requirements of the National Qualifications Framework (NQF) were also stipulated for higher education. The expectations were that the new system and its key instruments would deal comprehensively with the country's historical legacies of exclusion and inequitable development, while also addressing its social and economic needs in an era of globalization and the internationalization of higher education (Singh & Naidoo, 2004). The White Paper further proposed the development of a national higher education plan that would include benchmarks for transformation and a system of 3-year rolling institutional plans. These would facilitate the responsiveness of the system and ensure planned expansion linked to sustainability (DOE, 1997a).

The Higher Education Act

The HEA was passed in December 1997, and put in place formal regulatory mechanisms pertaining to the funding, governance, and quality assurance of the higher education system. These included provisions for the establishment of the higher education branch (with administrative responsibilities) and the CHE, with policy advisory and quality assurance functions. The quality assurance functions of the CHE were to be carried out by the Higher Education Quality Committee (HEQC), which is a permanent body of the CHE (DOE, 1997b).

Discord and Nonalignment in the Restructuring Process

Following the passing of the HEA, it was expected that these instruments for transformation of the higher education system would be put in place to steer the system. However, what became apparent was that in the postapartheid vacuum of policy (1994–1997), there were important developments in the system that suggested some elements of self-regulation that, if left unchecked, threatened the development of a single national coordinated but diverse system of education (DOE, 2001a). The period 1994–1997 was characterized by a high level of optimism among policymakers and institutions, which flowed from expectations that the pressure for access to the higher education system would continue in a postapartheid South Africa. It was assumed that student enrollments in higher education would increase rapidly throughout the rest of the decade. As Cloete *et al.* (2002) point out, the evidence available at the time supported the belief that student enrollment in South Africa was on a steep upward trajectory.

Two important developments took place that threatened to undermine the restructuring and transformation of the system. First, the predicted increase in the enrollment of students in the system did not materialize. Instead, there was a decline in enrollments throughout the system, with historically black universities (HBUs) suffering the most, as there was an exodus of students from these institutions to HWUs (HWIs) and technikons (both black and white) (Cloete *et al.*, 2002). This phenomenon became known as "students voting with their feet." This mass migration of students was ascribed to dissatisfaction with the poor facilities and lower standards of programs in the HBUs, as compared to their white counterparts. On the other hand, the chances of getting financial support were much higher in HWIs as were the prospects of getting employment with qualifications from these institutions (Cloete *et al.*, 2002, p. 154–156).

Concomitantly, some HEIs seized market opportunities: some historically advantaged institutions undertook a range of entrepreneurial initiatives to position themselves advantageously. This entailed introducing distance education programs utilizing "telematic" delivery; partnerships with private providers to tap into expanding markets; and increasing market shares of contract research and consultancies. The net result of

Table 2. Headcount Enrollments in Public Universities and Technikons: NCHE
Projections Compared with Actual Enrollments, 1995–2000

	1995	1996	1997	1998	1999	2000
NCHE projections	571,000	595,000	620,000	650,000	680,000	710,000
Actual	571,000	590,000	599,000	608,000	580,000	600,000

Source: Adapted from Cloete *et al.* (2002).

the unplanned change was a set of HEIs whose differentiation, while overtly linked
to developments in the market, was also directly linked to the differences engendered
by apartheid. This served to exacerbate institutional inequalities with respect to resource opportunities and educational outcomes and to create disparities in institutional
governance capacities (CHE, 2004).

By 1997, student enrollment for the university plus technikon sectors had reached
more than 600,000, an increase of nearly 206,000 (52%) over the total of 1990. The
average annual increase in enrollments between 1990 and 1997 was 4%. The increase in
enrollments also generated expectations in the higher education system that government
funding would grow in future years, particularly because government funds had been
allocated to institutions on the basis of formulae which were given primarily by student
enrollments. However, the predicted growth figures of the NCHE did not materialize,
as reflected in Table 2.

According to Cloete *et al.* (2002), the general decline in student enrollments was a
result of a number of factors, including the productivity levels of the school system.
Between 1995 and 2000, the school system did not produce the number of qualified
school-leavers that had been expected at the time the NCHE was doing its work. The
NCHE had expected one consequence of the rapid end of apartheid in the education
sector to be the rapid growth in the numbers of school-leavers obtaining a university
entrance pass. However, this did not occur. Table 3 shows that over a 6-year period
(1995–2000), 320,000 fewer matriculants were produced by the schools than the NCHE
had predicted.

The other factor that impacted the restructuring process was the growth of private
education in South Africa during the same period. Following the adoption of the HEA,
which gave due recognition to the place and role of private higher education in South
Africa, the system began to experience the mushrooming of private providers, both

Table 3. Projected and Actual Totals of Matriculation Exemptions (University
Entrance Pass), 1995–2000

	1995	1996	1997	1998	1999	2000
NCHE projections	95,000	108,000	118,000	130,000	144,000	158,000
Actual	80,000	80,000	70,000	70,000	63,000	60,000

Source: Cloete *et al.* (2002).

local and international. Before 1997, private higher education was seen by the public HEIs and the Department of National Education as peripheral, unimportant and of low quality (Mabizela, 2004). During the late 1990s, a commonly held view was that a bourgeoning private higher education sector would be needed to deal with levels of access demand that the public sector would not be able to satisfy. The experiences of other developing countries were often cited in this regard: where the capacity of the public higher education sector is limited (the argument went), the development of a new higher education sector funded by private capital should be encouraged by government (Singh & Naidoo, 2004).

With the legal basis for the operation of private providers in place, the system experienced a heightened activity of private provision, which took a number of forms. Private South African companies launched new private HEIs and overseas institutions also attempted to establish satellite operations in South Africa. Partnerships between South African companies and a small group of public universities and technikons seemed to dominate the form in which private providers operated. While the number of private providers at the time was unknown, a survey of 60 private institutions conducted by the Education Policy Unit at the University of the Western Cape found that they enrolled just under 30,000 students (Subotzky, 2002). A study commissioned in order to determine the size of the sector estimated total student enrollment in private education at 500,000, something which proved to be an overestimate.

According to Singh and Naidoo (2004), prior to the establishment of the national DOE private provider registration requirement, there was also an enormous growth in the franchising of qualifications by foreign providers to locally established private institutions. Most of the private providers started through franchise agreements with such foreign providers. Between 1996 and 1999, the DOE received several complaints about the quality of provision from students who were studying at institutions that had franchise arrangements with foreign providers. It became apparent that the franchiser institution often carried out poor oversight of quality arrangements at the local private franchisee. Moreover, national quality assurance agencies from the franchiser's country of origin did not "quality assure" the franchiser's ability to manage the quality of their franchised operations. Also, many franchise arrangements were concluded with foreign institutions (the franchiser) that were perceived as being of poor quality within their home countries (Singh & Naidoo, 2004, p. 22).

As a result of these quality-related problems, the new regulations of the DOE outlawed franchising. This forced foreign providers to establish a physical presence as transnational private providers in South Africa and to take responsibility for the quality of the programs they offered in this country. By 2000, there were only four transnational providers registered with the DOE, whereas during 1996–1999 over 50 foreign providers operated in South Africa through franchise and other partnership arrangements. The termination of the franchising arrangements between the foreign and local private providers gave the impetus for the establishment of local private providers in their own right, as well as a heightened awareness of the need to strengthen the quality of their provision.

The developments in the field that were not in line with policy or that revealed the inadequacy of policy became a source of concern for policymakers. An intervention strategy was required. With respect to public institutions, there was a concern that the "voting with feet" phenomenon was a threat to the viability of HBUs and, given the historical role they have played in the education of the black elite in South Africa, this would be against the goals of preserving national pride. On the other hand, the mushrooming of private providers, some of which offered poor quality programs, necessitated some form of intervention on the part of government.

Consolidation of a Policy and Regulatory Framework: Toward a Single Coordinated System, 1999–2004

With experience gained in government, and the policies and legislation in place, the DOE started consolidating the work done in the first five years by elaborating on policies in order to strengthen their implementation. Consolidation of policy entailed a multiple strategy for putting in place the governance and institutional structures that were legislated by the HEA: securing an amendment of the HEA to deal with policy gaps in both the Act and the White Paper; restructuring the system through mergers; and establishing the regulatory frameworks for a single coordinated system. There are three key documents that served to reconfigure the higher education landscape and put higher education in South Africa on a path toward a single system: the CHE's *Towards a New Higher Education Landscape: Meeting the Equity, Quality and Social Development Imperatives of South Africa in the 21st Century*; *The National Plan for Higher Education*; and the National Working Group's (NWG) report, *A New Landscape for Higher Education and Training*.

Restructuring the System Through Mergers

At the height of the crisis described above (i.e., a system that was self-regulating outside of the policy framework), the newly appointed Minister of Education, Professor Kader Asmal (1999–2004), sought policy advice from the CHE on how to reconfigure the higher education system. The CHE report, *Towards a New Higher Education Landscape: Meeting the Equity, Quality and Social Development Imperatives of South Africa in the 21st Century*, was released in 2000. The report highlighted a lack of meaningful coordination and cooperation within the system, and the fact that the sustainability of the higher education system—including the effective and efficient use of resources—required a reduction in the number of institutions through "combinations." It argued that "the current landscape and institutional configuration of higher education . . . is inadequate to meet socio-economic needs and is no longer sustainable. South Africa does not have the human and financial resources to maintain the present institutional configuration" (CHE, 2000, p. 51).

The key recommendation of the report was a differentiated higher education system based on differential institutional mandates and types. Bedrock institutions would focus on quality undergraduate programs, with limited postgraduate education at the master's level, and research related to curriculum, learning and teaching. A second set of HEIs would focus on quality undergraduate programs, comprehensive postgraduate education up to the doctoral level, and extensive research. A third set of HEIs would provide quality undergraduate programs, extensive postgraduate education up to the master's level, selective postgraduate programs at the doctoral level, and select areas of research (CHE, 2001). The report came under severe criticism from the public, especially because there could not be a reconfiguration of the system, including its shape and size, without the *National Plan*, which was proposed in the White Paper on Higher Education.

In responding to the report, the *National Plan* confirmed that the number of public HEIs could and should be reduced. It proposed two main restructuring strategies. The first was program and infrastructural cooperation, including regional-level rationalization of the provision of costly programs and specialized postgraduate programs. The second strategy was the development of new institutional and organizational forms by means of a process of mergers (DOE, 2001a,b). Accordingly, the NWG was appointed in March 2001 to investigate and advise the Minister on "appropriate arrangements for consolidating the provision of higher education on a regional basis through establishing new institutional and organizational forms, including the feasibility of reducing the number of higher education institutions" (DOE, 2001b, Appendix).

The composition of the NWG reflected the experience, capacity, and sophistication that had been developed within the government. Unlike in the past, where the government relied on outside consultants and experts outside the government for policy development and advice, the NWG was composed of top senior government officials drawn from the Ministries of Finance, Education and the Presidency, and from business and labor. This team represented a phase where the government relied less on external agencies and more on knowledge of macroeconomic realities, availability of resources and the role higher education was to play in development (Sehoole, 2005). The main proposal of the NWG was a reduction of HEIs from 36 to 21 institutions, providing a set of reasons based on a regional analysis of higher education provision in terms of quality, sustainability and equity. It was, however, made clear that the reduction in the number of institutions did not imply the reduction of delivery sites. All the facilities of merged institutions had to be utilized for the purposes of higher education provision.

Following a period of consultation and protracted public and private debate concerning the recommendations of the NWG, the Minister of Education made his final restructuring decisions public on December 9, 2002 (DOE, 2002). The new institutional landscape approved by the Minister consisted of 22 public HEIs (down from 36): 11 universities, five "universities of technology" (formerly knows as technikons), and six "comprehensive institutions" (combining university- and technikons-type programs, and also resulting from a merger of a technikon and a university). Two national institutes of higher education were also approved (CHE, 2004). The mergers would take place in two phases: the first took effect in January 2004, and the second in January 2005.

Regulating the Public and the Private

With respect to competition between the public and private institutions, the plan argued that competition should be regulated within a national framework that promotes and facilitates the sustainability of the higher education system. It further pointed out that the burgeoning private higher education sector requires more stringent regulation to ensure that it complements the public higher education sector and contributes to the overall human resource needs of the country (DOE, 2001a). Quality in higher education should be ensured by auditing the quality assurance mechanisms of HEIs and by accrediting programs of higher education.

In 1999, in the absence of a regulating body and with the challenges that the system was facing with the activities of private providers, the DOE passed a policy that made it a requirement for all private providers to register with the Department. It was hoped that this would give the Department a sense of the size of private provision. Concomitantly, it made the Director General in the DOE a registrar of private providers. This initiative was bolstered by the establishment of the HEQC in May 2001 as a permanent subcommittee of the CHE, whose mandate was to (a) promote quality assurance in higher education; (b) audit the quality assurance mechanisms of HEIs; and (c) accredit programs of higher education (HEQC, 2001a,b).

One of the achievements of the HEQC was the development of a new regulatory and quality assurance framework, which encourages greater planning within institutions, mission differentiation, increased outputs (graduate and research outputs), target setting and attainment, cost efficiency and effectiveness, and the planned use of earmarked funding for student equity and redress. The following are aspects of the framework:

- Private and transnational providers have to (a) operate as a trading company that is registered under the South African Companies Act, (b) sign a declaration of nondiscrimination in relation to students and staff, demonstrating a commitment to advancing the agenda of redress and equity, and (c) be financially viable, with regular monitoring and reporting.
- All qualifications standards have to be assessed by the South African Qualifications Authority (SAQA) and registered on the NQF. SAQA is responsible for evaluating and recognizing qualifications, whereas individual institutions have the right to recognize qualifications for entrance and further study purposes.
- The CHE/HEQC has to assure the quality of all institutions and programs.
- Franchising of programs is not permitted.
- Foreign providers need quality assurance clearance from their country of origin and the qualifications have to be recognized by the parent institution and the country's quality assurance system. Students should be able to transfer from South Africa to the parent institution without losing credits. On application for registration, foreign institutions have to submit proof of the equivalence of qualifications, recognition, and accreditation in their home country (Singh & Naidoo, 2004, p. 20).

The development of this regulatory framework was a milestone in the restructuring process of higher education in South Africa. What is important is the fact that all institutions (private and public) are now subject to the same regulations. This has been exemplified recently in two important reviews undertaken by the CHE. The first involves the registration of private providers and the second is the accreditation of programs.

The HEQC also built on the work of the DOE with regard to the registration of providers. In January 1999, the DOE initiated the process of registration by registering private HEIs, including foreign/transnational providers. In 2000, 14 transnational institutions (11 universities and four colleges) from the United Kingdom, the United States, Australia, and the Netherlands applied for registration. The HEQC was not in operation at the time and SAQA conducted a paper-based evaluation of the proposed programs. In 2001, the DOE registered four foreign institutions: De Monfort University (U.K.), the Business School of the Netherlands, and Bond and Monash Universities (Australia). In 2000, the enrollments at these four transnational institutions totaled 3,165, accounting for 0.5% of the total number of students enrolled at both private and public higher education, and 10% of all private higher education students. However, for reasons that are not clear, enrollments in transnational institutions declined in 2001 to 1,242 (Singh & Naidoo, 2004).

The four transnational providers offer higher education mainly in the fields of commerce and management. Three of the four offer MBAs, while a new transnational institution (Henley School of Management from the United Kingdom) has also applied to offer an MBA. During interviews with HEQC peer review panels, the reasons offered by students for choosing foreign institutions were that they were "international" institutions of a good quality and reputation and provided students with the possibility of international mobility upon completion of their qualifications.

As far as international portability is concerned, the MBAs offered by Australian institutions in South Africa are recognized in Australia. Students can transfer to the parent institution without losing credits or recognition and can enter doctoral programs in management after finishing the MBA. However, MBAs offered by the U.K. institutions abroad are not "fully" recognized in the United Kingdom. Employers have requested that such institutions specify on the certificate that the student graduated in a foreign country and not at the host institution in the United Kingdom.

The Accreditation of Programs[7]

As far as quality is concerned, between 2002 and 2003, the HEQC conducted a national review of all MBA programs offered in South Africa. The first part of the review entailed an accreditation exercise. All MBA programs offered by both the private and public institutions were evaluated by panels of peers and experts against a set of minimum standards. Programs that met the minimum standards were accredited and those that did not were de-accredited and had to discontinue the program.

In 2003, 37 MBA programs from 13 public universities, five public technikons, four transnational providers, and five local private providers were assessed. Of the 18 programs assessed in public universities, seven (35%) were fully accredited, eight (48%) were given conditional accreditation, and three (17%) were withdrawn. None of the programs of public technikons, local private providers or foreign or transnational providers were accredited. The majority of these had their accreditation withdrawn, with a few being given conditional accreditation.

Transnational providers fared the worst among all the institutional provider types. Three of their four MBA programs did not satisfy the minimum requirements and had the recognition of their accreditation withdrawn. The reasons for withdrawal of accreditation were the following:

- The lack of competent and adequate academic staff to deliver the program.
- Heavy reliance on part-time staff from industry. Many of the staff had industry experience, but very few of them had teaching or research experience.
- Dual certification by the local partner and the foreign institution in two cases. In one case, employers in the host country required the certificate to specify that the qualification was obtained in a foreign country. This suggested that employers did not see as equivalent the qualifications obtained in the foreign country as opposed to the ones obtained in the home country of the institution.
- Curricula that were not contextualized to reflect South African needs with regard to management training. The parent institution controlled teaching and learning material rights, with very little room for those academics delivering the programs in South Africa to change and adapt to local conditions (Singh & Naidoo, 2004).

As Singh and Naidoo (2004) point out, the review also demonstrated the importance and need for external validation of the quality of transnational programs, which could be carried out by local national quality assurance agencies or by those local agencies working in partnership with the agencies from the home countries of the transnational providers. International agencies could also be used, although with some caution. In the case of the MBA review, one transnational provider had accreditation for its South African program from such an international agency but was de-accredited by the HEQC. The reason for this was that the international agency focused mainly on the quality of provision in the country of origin of the transnational provider rather than on South Africa as a site of delivery.

Enrollment and Graduate Output Levels

The number and proportion of African students rose dramatically from 191,000 (40%) in 1993 to 404,000 (60%) in 2002. Correspondingly, the number and proportion of white students declined from 223,000 (47%) in 1993 to 182,000 (27%) in 2002 (CHE, 2004, p. 66). However, the number of women students also rose steadily between 1993 and 2002, until they formed the majority in 1999, and reached 54% of total higher education enrollments in 2002.

Enrollments in the humanities and social sciences rose from 269,000 to a peak of 320,000 in 1997, then declined to 277,000 in 1999, followed by a small rise in 2002 to 298,197. Enrollment in science, engineering, and technology (SET) and in business and commerce rose steadily throughout this period, almost doubling in each case. Table 4 shows the rise and decline in enrollment across these fields of study.

As Table 5 demonstrates, there has been a general increase in the number and proportion of university postgraduate enrollments from 1995 (19%) to 2002 (23%). The increases seem to have been evenly distributed across historically advantaged universities, HBUs and distance education programs offered by the UNISA.

South Africa's higher education system has also recently shown signs of internationalization, enrolling 46,687 international students in 2002 (38,492 in universities and 8,195 in technikons) (CHE, 2004).

Table 4. Headcount Enrollments by Field of Study, 1993 and 2002

	Humanities and Social Sciences (%)	Business and Commerce (%)	Science and Technology (%)	Total (%)
1993	57	24	19	100
2002	44	30	26	100

Source: Adapted from CHE (2004).

Graduate output from South Africa's higher education system has grown steadily since 1995, rising above 100,000 for the first time in 2002. About three-quarters of these were from universities and one-quarter from technikons. During the same period, technikon graduates expanded gradually from 20% to 26% of the system's total and, correspondingly, that of the universities dropped from 80% to 74%. At universities, the number and proportion of SET graduates rose from 13,146 (20%) to 16,735 (22%), and those of the business, commerce, and management sciences graduates from 9,203 (14%) to 15,454 (20%) with a corresponding decline in the proportion (but not the number) of humanities and social sciences graduates (from 66% to 57%).

There have also been fluctuations in the number of degrees awarded across all levels since 1995, with a decline among undergraduate degrees from 44,029 in 1995 to 40,812 in 1998, and a decline among "lower" postgraduate degrees from 48,584 to 47,944. The causes of these declines warrant further research. Meanwhile, university master's degree graduates increased sharply between 1998 and 2002, from 3,952 to 6,667. The number of doctoral graduates produced by the system was just under 1,000 in 2002—up from 801 in 2001, but still very low in comparative terms, constituting only 1% of all undergraduate and graduate degrees awarded that year (CHE, 2004).

As an indicator of the fundamental relationship between higher education and employability, a Human Sciences Research Council (HSRC) study of graduates between

Table 5. Distribution of University Headcount Enrollments by Qualification Level and Institutional Type: 1995 and 2002

Qualification Type	HAU	HBU	UNISA	Total
1995				
Undergraduate	100,857 (72%)	98,640 (89%)	99,161 (83%)	298,657 (81%)
Postgraduate	39,131 (28%)	11,641 (11%)	19,599 (17%)	70,372 (19%)
Total	139,988 (100%)	110,281 (100%)	118,760 (100%)	369,029 (100%)
2002				
Undergraduate	156,049 (69%)	76,529 (84%)	124,201 (87%)	359,779 (77%)
Postgraduate	70,675 (31%)	14,049 (16%)	18,935 (13%)	103,659 (23%)
Total	226,724 (100%)	14,049 (100%)	18,939 (100%)	460,439 (100%)

HAU, historically advantaged universities; HBU, historically black universities; UNISA: University of South Africa (distance education programs).
Source: Adapted from CHE (2004).

1991 and 1995 found that 59% of respondents surveyed were employed immediately after obtaining a degree, and a further 25% within 1 year, although with wide variability between groups of respondents. The most successful in finding employment were graduates in the medical sciences (91%) and engineering (77%); least successful were graduates in the humanities and arts (34%), law (40%), and natural sciences (48%). While 67% of the graduate respondents from HWUs found employment immediately, only 28% of their counterparts from HBUs were as fortunate; 34% of colored graduates immediately found employment, as did 56% of Indian graduates (Cloete & Bunting, 2000a,b; Maharasoa & Hay, 2001).

Research

Higher education research in South Africa is part of the national system of research and development (R&D). The R&D system is a subset of the national science and technology (S&T) system, which is in turn a subset of the national system of innovation—that is, all institutions and individuals directly and indirectly engaged in formal innovative activities. Under apartheid, there was fragmentation of higher education institutional research agendas, leading to skewed patterns overall. The science councils operated obliviously of each other, government departments conducted research operations independent of science councils, and universities and private sector laboratories were isolated. This resulted in a disjuncture between the science system and the challenges of development, and the failure of the system to complete the cycle of innovation. Another example of the impact of the apartheid state on national and higher education research programs is that the social sciences became marginalized under the pressure of the academic boycott, and tended to be insular in research (Bawa & Mouton, 2001). Furthermore, the apartheid-related missions of HBUs largely precluded research development and that meant that research and teaching functions became separated.

The CHE (2004) report indicates that R&D undertaken by South African HEIs was in relatively equal share with government and industry. HEIs received 40% of state spending on R&D, which totaled around 0.8% of gross domestic product (GDP) between 1989 and 1994. Funding for research was directly allocated to universities through the Department of National Education on the basis of numbers of students and research publications, with different weightings for the natural and human sciences (technikons did not receive direct research funding). Research funding was also indirectly allocated via contracts from government departments and science councils. The business sector was the source of just under 10% of the R&D income of HEIs. South Africa was undertaking approximately 0.5% of the world's scientific research in 1994, with the majority favoring social sciences and humanities rather than natural sciences. Universities performed 98.7% (by expenditure) of the academic research, with the balance produced by technikons. While universities produced 70% of South African indexed research publications, nearly 80% of those were concentrated in five institutions—Cape Town, Natal, Pretoria, Stellenbosch, and Witwatersrand.

Since 1994, there has been a restructuring of funding sources aimed at innovation in research strategies and a redress of past funding and research practices. This includes the merging of the Foundation for Research and Development and the Center for

Science Development into the National Research Foundation (NRF). The NRF has a consolidated funding agency function for the human and natural sciences and has drawn together university/technikon-based research funding. It is also required to distribute funding within the focus that reflects the development, equity, and capacity-building priorities of the state and to this extent it is responsible for a fair amount of influence in terms of setting higher education research priorities.

The other source of government funding for higher education (and other) research is the Technology and Human Resources for Industry Program (THRIP), managed by the NRF for the Department of Trade and Industry (DTI). THRIP was introduced in 1991 and participates in matching grant schemes between research entities in public HEIs and the private sector—that is, contributions to approved projects are made by private sector partners, the DTI and the participating HEI. Of importance is the fact that THRIP provides incentives for the participation of graduate students historically excluded from S&T (black and women students). The DTI budget for THRIP increased from R3 million in 1994 to R96.5 million in 1999, with private sector expenditure increasing from R6 million to R105 million in the same period (CHE, 2004, p. 111).

A study conducted by the HSRC revealed several important developments and shifts since 1994. Total R&D expenditure for 2001 was 7.5 billion rand. In percentage terms, gross expenditure on R&D was relatively steady between 1993 and 2001 at around 0.75% of GDP. The challenge remains to reach the goal of 1% of GDP in 2005, as set by the National R&D Strategy. By comparison, Sweden spends 4.27% of its GDP on R&D; the United States, 2.82%; the European Union member states, on average, 1.93%; and Australia, 1.5%. South Africa closely follows China (1.09%) and Spain (0.96%), but with higher research intensity than most other developed countries (Department of Science and Technology, 2004).

South Africa distributed its 2001 expenditure of R&D by major research fields as follows: natural sciences (22%); engineering sciences (20%); applied sciences and technology (15%); computers and ICT (13%); social sciences and humanities (11%); medical and health sciences (10%); and agricultural sciences (9%). By type of research, 2001 gross expenditure on R&D was as follows: applied research (40%); experimental development (33%); strategic basic research (15%); and pure basic research (12%) (CHE, 2004).

As an indicator of the availability of research skills, the number of full-time equivalent (FTE) researchers per 1,000 employed in 2001 was 0.9—up from 0.71 in 1997. These figures indicate that the South African research community remained small compared to the FTE figures of other countries, like Australia's 7.2, Malaysia's 7.0, South Korea's 6.4, Spain's 5.0, Argentina's 2.0, and China's 1.0. Women researchers made up 35% of the total research community in South Africa, compared with Argentina (49%), Russia (44%), Spain (35%), South Korea (11%), and Japan (10.7%). Overall, the nation's R&D is produced by industry (54%), higher education (25%), and government and science councils (20%) (CHE, 2004).

In general, higher education faces the challenge of finding sustainable ways of reproducing its capacities and traditions in new generations of knowledge producers. As the CHE (2004) report shows, despite the success of targeted funding strategies in promoting responsiveness, the goals of supporting the development of young, black and female researcher seems far from being achieved. It further highlighted the "frozen demographics" of an aging research population, the causes of which are multiple— including the high rate of change in the first 10 years of democracy, which has not provided stability critical for fostering research and has drawn resources away from research; the institutional cultures of the HEIs, which are not yet fully able to satisfy the aspirations of a diverse set of young scholars; postgraduate scholarships and fellowships, which are thin on the ground; and the fact that HEIs may offer unattractive remuneration and turbulent work environments in contrast to the private sector. The "brain drain" may also be a factor (Badat, 2002b). However, despite these weaknesses, South Africa's national research and innovation system remains the best developed and resourced on the African continent.

Overview and Conclusion

In sum, the higher education system in South Africa has transformed considerably during the first 10 years of democracy, from one of the most unequal and uncoordinated in the world, to the one now operating as a single coordinated system. The South African government has relied on the development of national policies as a basis for transforming the system, but the pattern of development during this period also shows that change is not exclusively driven by the state and national policy. Indeed, it has also been propelled from within the higher education sector (e.g., stakeholders acting to pursue self-interests based on varying interpretations of policy) and by the economy and society (as market forces and shifting social demand for higher education came to bear). While the DOE used its legislative and policy tools to steer the system in the desired direction, the CHE argues against reliance on policy alone. Such an approach would run the risk of succumbing to rationalist assumptions about the efficacy of policy as the principal (and even the sole) driver of change. However, as the CHE rightly suggests, acknowledging the intricacy and uncertainty, change and policy outcomes neither render national policy redundant and ineffectual nor diminish the state's responsibility for driving equitable and effective change toward stated policy goals (CHE, 2004). This analysis thus offers important implications for understanding the "system," system change, policy and the policy process, and how these are approached in practice.

An important development in higher education policy during the first decade of democracy in South Africa is that it not only dealt with national policy issues, but also addressed the challenges posed by transnational providers, as exemplified in the registration of private providers and the accreditation of MBA program initiatives. Currently, South Africa is said to be one of the few if not the only country that has developed a comprehensive regulatory framework that is able to deal with the challenges of transnational and cross-border education. This should also be able to assist the country as it develops its policy on the General Agreement on Trade and Services (GATS). The significance of this also lies in the fact that the development of a GATS policy will be based on empirical evidence on the behavior of transnational providers in South Africa.

Notes

1. Stretching latitudinally from 22°S to 35°S and longitudinally from 17°E to 33°E, with a surface area of 1,219,090 km^2.
2. SA Year Book 2001/02.
3. Statistics South Africa, Digital Census 2001 Atlas. Available at http://www.statssa.gov.za/census2001/digiAtlas/index.html.
4. The term black will be used to refer to all the racial groups that were oppressed under apartheid, namely, Indian, colored, and African.
5. South African Universities Vice Chancellors Association (SAUVCA). Available at http://www.sauvca.org.za/highered/uni/.
6. Per international norm, this is calculated as the total number of enrolled students divided by the total population in the age range of 20–24 years.
7. This section draws heavily from the paper by Singh and Naidoo, who work for the CHE HEQC and were involved in the accreditation process.

References

Badat, S. (2002a). *Black student politics: Higher education and apartheid from SASO to SANSCO: 1968–1990*. New York: RoutledgeFalmer.
Badat, S. (2002b). Reproducing and transforming and the next generation of South African scholars and researchers: Promoting and challenges. Paper presented at the Academy and Science of South Africa Consultative Forum on Promoting South Africa S&T Capacities for the 21st Century: From Policy to Reality, Roodevallei, Pretoria, South Africa, 2002.
Bawa, A., & Mouton, J. (2002). Research. In N. Cloete, R. Fehnel, P. Maasen, T. Mojo, H. Perolel, & T. Gibbon (Eds.), *Transformation in higher education: Global pressures and local realities*. Lansdowne, South Africa,: Juta.
Cloete, N., & Bunting, I. (2000a). *Higher education transformation: Assessing performance in South Africa*. Pretoria, South Africa: Center for Higher Education Transition (CHET).
Cloete, N., & Bunting, I. (2000b). Increased and broadened participation. In N. Cloete & I. Bunting (Eds.), *Higher education transformation: Assessing performance in South Africa*. Pretoria, South Africa: Center for Higher Education Transformation (CHET).
Cloete, N., R. Fehnel, P. Maasen, T. Mojo, H. Perolel, & T. Gibbon (Eds.). (2002). *Transformation in higher education: Global pressures and local relations in South Africa*. Lansdowne, South Africa: Juta.
Committee of Technikon Principals (CTP). (1990–1991). *Chairman's report for the year 1990–1991*. Pretoria, South Africa: CTP.
Committee of Technikon Principals (CTP). (1995). *Report to the National Commission on Higher Education*. Pretoria, South Africa: CTP.
Council on Higher Education (CHE). (2000). *Towards a new higher education landscape: Meeting the equity, quality and social development imperatives of South Africa in the twenty-first century*. Council on Higher Education Size and Shape Task Team. Pretoria, South Africa: CHE.
Council on Higher Education (CHE). (2004). *South African higher education in the first decade of democracy*. Pretoria, South Africa: CHE.
Department of Education (DOE). (1997a). *Education White Paper 3: A program for the transformation of higher education*. Pretoria, South Africa: DOE.
Department of Education (DOE). (1997b). *Higher Education Act (Act No. 101 of 1997)*. Pretoria, South Africa: DOE.
Department of Education (DOE). (2001a). *National plan for higher education*. Pretoria, South Africa: DOE.
Department of Education (DOE). (2001b). *The restructuring of the higher education system in South Africa*. Report of the National Working Group to the Minister of Education. Pretoria, South Africa: DOE.

Department of Education (DOE). (2002). *Transformation and restructuring: A new institutional land-scape for higher education.* Government Gazette No. 23459. Pretoria, South Africa: DOE.

Department of Science and Technology. (2004). *South African national survey of experimental research and development (R&D) (2001–2002).* Pretoria, South Africa: Government Printers.

Higher Education Quality Committee. (2001a). *Founding document.* Pretoria, South Africa: CHE.

Higher Education Quality Committee. (2001b). *Quality assurance in the 21st century: Lessons for a new QA agency.* Pretoria, South Africa: CHE.

Jansen, J. D. (2002). Mergers in higher education: Theorizing change in transitional contexts. In J. D. Jansen *et al.* (Eds.), *Mergers in higher education: Lessons learned in transitional contexts.* Pretoria, South Africa: UNISA Press.

Mabizela, M. (2004). *Recounting the state of private higher education in South Africa.* Paper prepared for the Policy Forum on private higher education in Africa, 2002–2003 (November, 2004), Accra, Ghana.

Maharasoa, M., & Hay, D. (2001). Higher education and graduate employment in South Africa. *Quality in Higher Education, 7*(2), 139–149.

National Commission on Higher Education (NCHE). (1996). *National Commission on Higher Education report: A framework for transformation.* Pretoria, South Africa: NCHE.

Sehoole, M. T. (2005). *Democratizing higher education policy: Constraints of reform in post-apartheid South Africa.* New York: Routledge.

Singh, M., & Naidoo, P. (2004). *National regulation of transnational higher education: A South African case study.* Pretoria, South Africa: CHE.

South African Government, Communication and Information System. (2001). *South Africa Year Book, 2001.* Durban, South Africa: Universal Printers.

South African Parliament, House of Assembly. (1983). *Debates of the House of Assembly (Hansard),* 19(9312). Cape Town, South Africa: Government Printer.

Subotzky, G. (2002). The nature of private higher education sector in South Africa: Some quantitative glimpses. *Perspectives in Education, 20*(4), 1–14.

52

SPAIN

José-Ginés Mora

Technical University of Valencia, Spain

Higher education in Spain consists almost exclusively of universities. Currently, there are 70 universities—50 public and 20 private. There are 1.6 million students enrolled, only 8% in private institutions. Formally, all universities have a similar structure and scope as a consequence of rigid state regulation. In principle, all may deliver programs of any level and are engaged in research activities, though in practice there are relevant differences among institutions.

The Spanish higher education system experienced rapid growth in the last three decades, and has transformed into a mass higher education system enrolling a high proportion of secondary school graduates. Very recently, the system has entered a period of enrollment stability due to the nation's overall population decrease. During this period of growth, a complete legal and structural revolution deeply transformed the entire higher education system. This chapter will focus especially on these last decades, the most important in the history of the Spanish universities.

A Brief History

Spanish universities are among the oldest in the world. The University of Salamanca in the Kingdom of Castile and Leon was founded in the earliest years of the 13th century, and the University of Lleida in Catalonia was established in 1300. Universities of that time bear little resemblance to current institutions. They were small institutions focused on fields such as law, philosophy, and theology. Kings and the Church played a relevant role in the functioning of the institutions, though some universities—like the University of Valencia, founded in 1500—was under the tutorage of the city, being the first "citizen university" in Spain.

In the 16th century, 10 of Spain's current universities were already established. In the same century, the first universities in the Spanish American colonies were founded in Santo Domingo, Bolivia, Mexico, and Peru. This situation did not change significantly for almost four centuries. Remarkably, only three of the currently 50 public universities in the country were founded between the 16th century and 1968. Although the Industrial Revolution did not result—as it did in many other countries—in the flourishing

James J.F. Forest and Philip G. Altbach (eds.), International Handbook of Higher Education, 993–1001.
© 2006 *Springer. Printed in the Netherlands.*

of new institutions, the 19th century was nevertheless a critical era for Spanish universities. At the beginning of the 19th century, liberalism—stemming from the French Revolution—changed the structure of the state. Under the Napoleonic system of higher education adopted by Spain, the universities were organized as state agencies that were totally regulated by laws and norms issued by the state at the national level. Universities had no specific budgets, and expenditures were regulated by the state (down to the smallest detail). Until very recently, academic programs were identical in all institutions—they had the same curricula, and there were no differences even among course syllabi. This strictly regulated higher education system was also an elitist system whose main goal was to prepare the ruling group of the modern state, especially the civil servants. Consequently, Spanish universities had (and to some extent, still have) a strong professional orientation. The teaching process was focused on the transmission of skills essential to the development of professions, many of which were part of the state structure.

Nevertheless, it should be kept in mind that the new liberal state was the shield for all citizens against the aristocratic and ecclesiastic oligarchy in the Ancient Regime. This change brought (though not without fierce resistance and periods of reaction) the concept of the university as an institution of the state, and the state eventually replaced the church as the monopoly of authority (García-Garrido, 1992, p. 664). The state monopoly over higher education originated in Spain, as in other European countries, as a mechanism to protect universities against the social sectors which opposed academic freedom and independence of knowledge. However, in contrast to other countries—where private ownership of the universities was the guarantee of freedom and independence from external powers—in Spain the state became the guarantor of freedom for both teaching and the administration of universities.

Recent Developments

The situation described above began to change during the 1970s, when the system started to shift from elite to mass higher education. Legal changes helped trigger a complete renovation of the higher education system. After the restoration of democracy and the promulgation of the new Constitution in 1978, the transformation of the universities was one of the main political objectives of both academics and political parties. Thus, the first major change in the educational system was the reform of higher education. In 1983, the University Reform Act (*Ley de Reforma Universitaria*, hereafter referred to as LRU) was passed, resulting in a profound transformation in the Spanish higher education system. The LRU formed the basis for emancipating higher education from the control of the state, as occurred in other European countries during this decade (Neave & Van Vught, 1991). The main changes introduced by this act were (Garcia-Garrido, 1992; Mora, 1997a):

- universities became autonomous entities with the capacity to establish their own programs and, to some extent, the curricula;
- professors were no longer part of a national body and began to "belong" to each university;

- responsibility for universities was transferred to regional governments;
- institutions began to receive public appropriations as a lump sum, and to have wide-ranging capabilities in allocating funds internally; and
- private universities could now be established (where before, only Catholic Church universities were allowed).

It is worth mentioning that currently 17 regional governments now have responsibility for their universities in financial and organizational matters. Nevertheless, the Napoleonic tradition of "national diplomas" and civil servant staff has remained, and the central government still has the capacity to establish general rules for curricula and staff salaries or duties (across all public universities), and bears the responsibility of accrediting the study programs.

Another remarkable consequence of the LRU was the strong democratization of the internal structure of universities. The power over crucial decisions was transferred to collegiate bodies, where non-academic staff and students were present in a considerable number (roughly, one-third of the members). The University Senate had considerable power, including the election of the rector (president). Boards with large numbers of members made the decisions on faculties and departments and elected deans and heads of departments. The Social Council (patterned after boards of trustees in American universities) was also established as an external body representing the wide interests of society in the university. However, the real influence of this body is quite small.

In the dawn of the new millennium, Spanish universities face a new operating environment, involving:

- a new legal framework, which was drawn up by the central government towards the end of 2001 (*Ley de Ordenación Universitaria*, hereafter referred to as LOU);
- the agreement among all European governments for transforming the structure of higher education in European countries (the Bologna Declaration); and
- the decreasing number of students as a consequence of the dramatic decline in the nation's birth rate.

The LOU made only small changes to the legal structure of higher education. Among the most noteworthy features of the act were: (a) the incorporation of some lay persons in the running of a university (always a minority group); (b) election of the rector by direct vote (as opposed to an indirect vote by the senate); (c) an increase in the representation of tenured professors in the collegial bodies; (d) a requirement that academic staff must obtain national accreditation before being appointed by universities; and (e) the obligatory *post hoc* accreditation of study programs by the new National Agency for Quality Assessment and Accreditation.

In general, the act gives universities and autonomous regions more independence to organize themselves as they wish. This is a positive feature because it allows both universities and regions to change their own legal regulations and adapt them to the new political, social, and economic environment. This will allow the differentiation and improvement of those universities which fulfill two conditions: their heads must be interested in promoting change, and they must be located in an autonomous region whose leaders are also concerned about the competitiveness of their universities. While it is still too soon to comment on initial results, it can already be seen that some regions are doing more than others on this front.

Curricular Structure

There are four basic types of university programs: short-cycle programs, which are more vocationally oriented and run 3 years; long-cycle programs, which last 5 or 6 years; second-cycle programs, which last 2 years (a first program is required); and doctoral programs, which add two more years of course work and require the preparation of a research-oriented thesis after a long-cycle degree. Doctoral programs are pursued primarily by students interested in an academic career. Generally speaking, people with greater economic resources or intellectual capabilities traditionally have preferred long-cycle university programs.

The Bologna Declaration, which is to be implemented in Spain within the next several years, established a cyclic structure that will change the current model in next years. Nevertheless, because the Spanish system was already partially cyclic, this reform will not result in as much of a dramatic structural change as in other European systems. The main change will be the split of the traditional long-cycle programs into two consecutive cycles.

More important than structural changes are the changes that have been developed in curricular content and in approaches to teaching and learning—in both cases with the intention of achieving real improvement. Traditionally, courses in Spain have been strongly based on theoretical knowledge, to the detriment of practical, methodological or other formative aspects. Adaptability to society's needs, to students' curricular demands and to the variability of labor market demands substantial reform in the curriculum.

A process of reform began during the late 1980s, when basic national criteria for new curricula were established. The aim of the curricular reform was to adapt the system to the new operating environment, introducing a new teaching and learning style which was to be more focused on practical lectures and tutorials, more flexible and more suited to social needs. Consequently, the new curricula have a modular structure, courses are mostly delivered in semesters, the proportion of optional courses has increased and practical content has been extended in every course.

Each university established *ad hoc* committees to develop these guidelines for each of their degree programs. However, conflict often arose within these committees between what was in the interest of academics (e.g., keeping and developing courses related to their field of expertise, personal interests, or merely their routines) and the necessity to adapt curricula to new requirements. In most cases, academics eventually imposed their own interests. In addition, when the new curricula started to be implemented, most academics did not fully realize that the old model of teaching and learning was obsolete, and they viewed the reform as a mere re-organization of old programs. The result of this process is that new curricula are better than the old ones, but are still far from meeting the new demands of the knowledge society.

After the relative failure to implement the new syllabi—as a result of the academic staff's refusal to take the aims of the reform to heart—adaptation to the new European common space for higher education is considered to be an excellent opportunity to point the system in the right direction. This is probably the most important challenge that Spanish higher education must face in the next several years. A positive result in this endeavor will make a tremendous difference for the future.

Higher Education Demand

The real growth of Spain's higher education system began in the early 1960s. Throughout that decade, the number of students doubled; it doubled again within the next 12 years, and once again before 1995. During the mid-1990s, enrollment increases stopped abruptly, and in the last decade the number of students has stabilized at around 1.6 million. This stability is largely the consequence of the dramatic and continuous decrease in Spain's birth rate since 1975, which has only recently stabilized at a very low level. Thus, while the number of students enrolled has stabilized, the participation rate in the higher education system has increased considerably. It can be estimated that roughly 60% of the nation's secondary education graduates are now entering higher education.

In 1970, the proportion of women among all higher education students was just 26%, but by 1986 the proportion had reached 50% and continued increasing throughout the following years, now holding steady at around 54%. Women's access to higher education is particularly high in fields such as health sciences (especially in short-cycle programs), social sciences, and humanities.

By fields of study, social sciences (where economics and business are the most popular disciplines) and law currently account for half of Spain's university students. Traditionally, engineering has been in high demand, but the number of places offered has been scarce and the level of difficulty for students very high. Recently, the establishment of new programs—especially short-cycle programs—and the increasing participation of women have increased the share of engineering students to 25%.

Access to higher education is quite open. After finishing academic secondary education, students must pass an entrance exam if they wish to enter long-cycle university programs. The main goal of this entrance exam is to control standards of educational achievement in the secondary schools, public and private. This exam is organized by the universities at the regional level. After passing the entrance exam, students are allowed to apply for any university program, generally at a university in the same region. Students who pass the exam receive a total score (selectivity score) that is used to assign students to programs depending on their preferences and the availability of places.

To have a more accurate portrait of the Spanish university system, it is important to note that students spend considerably more time finishing their degree programs than formally required. Therefore, the yearly number of graduates is low when compared to the large number of people enrolled at the universities. This low percentage is explained by the high number of dropouts and students who fall behind in their studies.

It is surprising that the remarkable growth of higher education in Spain has never been accompanied by any explicit governmental statement recommending or supporting access to higher education. Moreover, it seems that most people in political and academic spheres have considered the growing number of students in universities as something undesirable but inevitable. Nevertheless, central and regional governments have implemented *de facto* policies to satisfy the strong demand for higher education. The growth of higher education has clearly been a demand-driven process. The supply of places and the resources committed to universities have increased dramatically, though always with some lag behind increases in demand, and usually with a lack of planning. This growth in resources has been especially remarkable since 1984, when the autonomous regions started the process of taking over universities and the "political value" of universities thus increased.

Financial Resources

In 1985, the total funding for higher education was only 0.54% of GDP, and in 2000 reached 1.2% of GDP (OECD, 2003). However, while this represents an important increase in resources made available to the universities, there are special features that should be clarified to understand how this amount of money is distributed. First, there is a relative importance placed on resources set aside to fund new infrastructure. During the 1990s, greater efforts were made to invest in the higher education system in order to solve one of its key problems: the shortage of buildings and equipment. As an example, in 2000, Spain assigned 20.6% of total spending to capital investment (compared to the OECD average of just 11.6%).

Second, most of the current expenditures in Spanish higher education institutions pay for staff. As mentioned previously, this is one aspect of expenditure which universities have little control over, since salaries are set by the central government and, to a lesser extent, by regional governments. This is an important characteristic because it means that only a small percentage of current resources are set aside for expenses other than staff—in particular, funds to purchase goods and services which allow universities to develop quality policies.

Third, the role of private sector funding for higher education increased during the 1990s. In 1991, approximately 20% of university funding came from the private sector; by 1999, this had increased to 25.8%. From a comparative perspective, it is important to mention that during this period of growth in Spain, private funding in other EU countries decreased. Whereas in 1995 the average private sector funding in EU countries was 15.6% of total expenditures, in 1999 this figure had fallen to 13.8%. Finally, an important (and controversial) feature of higher education funding in Spain involves the lack of resources set aside to provide financial aid to students—in 1999, only 0.08% of the GDP was allocated for student grant expenditures.

The Academic Staff

The LRU brought significant changes for Spain's academic staff (Mora, 2001). The main structural changes were as follows:

– departments, with several professors working together and sharing teaching and research activities, replaced the former system of individual chairs;

- professors became members of a university, and could only move to other institutions by open competition; and
- academic staff salaries were increased, making an academic career more attractive from an economic point of view.

The current structure of academic staff in Spain was also deeply shaped by the legal changes implemented during the 1980s. Their effects amounted to that of an earthquake shaking the traditional structure of Spanish universities. The hierarchical system, based on the individual power of the chair-holder, and the excessive influence of the national guild of chair-holders collapsed. The old academics claim that the profession has lost prestige and social recognition. This is probably true, but it is mostly due to the simple fact that the number of professors has grown enormously as a result of the move towards a mass higher education system.

Nevertheless, the LRU did not change the legal status of the academics. Academics in tenured positions (around 70% of the total) are still civil servants and members of national bodies. There is thus a deep contradiction between the status of academics and the autonomy of universities. Personnel matters are a perfect example of the conflicts that result from this dilemma. On one hand, the central government decides on general personnel policies (basic structure, workload, and salaries), while regional governments are responsible for financing universities and, indirectly, for the payroll in public universities. Yet academics are mostly civil servants, with salaries and working conditions defined by the central government. In addition, universities can establish their own personnel policies, such as the number of staff in each category or the actual workload of personnel. In fact, decisions are made in universities by the staff through their collegiate boards. Eventually, decisions on staff numbers (made by universities) and decisions on salaries (made by the central government) have direct implications on the costs that regional governments must meet. It is obvious that such a complex, four-level structure of decision making on university personnel issues is inevitably a permanent source of conflict and discord. Fortunately, though these conflicts are permanent, they are less virulent than one may expect of such a potentially conflictive structure. As expected, the recently enacted LOU has maintained the same civil servant structure, although it allows regional governments to create new positions for professors without civil servant status.

Quality Assurance and Accreditation

Generalized assessment of individuals and institutions began in the early 1990s. Teaching and research activities of academics are now evaluated on a regular basis, while promotion and some salary increases depend on the results of these assessments (Mora, 2001). Nevertheless, several years passed before this principle started to be implemented in study programs. In 1993, the "Experimental Program for Assessment of the Quality in the University System" was launched. This program evaluated teaching, research, and institutional management in several universities. As an experimental project, the primary purpose was to try various methods and make proposals for change based on the experiences gained (Mora, 1997b).

After these pilot projects, the Council of Universities established the National Pro-gram for Assessment of Quality in Universities in 1995 (Mora & Vidal, 1998) with the aim of introducing a systematic assessment of universities. This program fueled the spread of a culture of quality among the Spanish universities. After only a few years, Spanish universities have established new offices to support quality assurance programs, and thousands of people are participating in self-assessment activities and external visits around the country.

The LOU established that programs must undergo assessment, certification, and accreditation. The management of quality assurance may be carried out by the newly created National Agency for Quality Assessment and Accreditation (ANECA) or by regional agencies in their own territories. The LOU also obliges study programs to undergo a process of accreditation in order for their degrees to be considered as official qualifications. This represents an important innovation in regulating the Spanish higher education system. Previous requirements have always had to be met in order to obtain official approval, but no further checks were made afterwards. The accreditation of study programs is currently in an experimental design phase, and it will be at least several years before it is introduced.

A Last Challenge: University Governance

As mentioned earlier, a consequence of the LRU was the strong democratization of the internal structure of universities. At that moment, after leaving behind nearly a half-century of political dictatorship, those developments were considered a positive and necessary move for everybody. In terms of governance, the main responsibility for managing institutions lies among the academics. Although some institutions hire professional managers for some managerial positions, they are always in dependent positions, while most of the decision-making power lies in the hands of academics who are temporarily occupying a managerial post. Unfortunately, there is no evidence that academics have enough knowledge or training to be effective as university managers. On the contrary, in general they have no experience in the management of any type of big organization. The results are normally far from being a model of good practice.

The move from direct state intervention to institutional autonomy should be accom-panied by other mechanisms, such as competitiveness (for students, staff, funds and reputation), diversification of resources, and increasing client power and social respon-sibility of institutions. These trends have not been sufficiently followed in Spanish universities for several reasons, including: (a) the lack of a tradition of serving the community—coming from a bureaucratic model, universities and staff (mostly civil servants) consider themselves more as belonging to a branch of the public administra-tion than as part of an institution at the service of the community; and (b) the lack of governmental policies on higher education—regional governments, with few excep-tions, have not been able to define policies for higher education, establish goals for public institutions, or require universities to achieve some objectives.

By the end of the 1990s, all academic analysts and political parties were aware of the need for changes in the legal structure of higher education, in the sense of introducing a more professional governance style. Nevertheless, the new LOU made only slight changes in the legal structure of universities, as we mentioned before. Although these were not major changes, they were not at all well received by most university and student leaders, who considered these measures to be an attack on university autonomy and university democracy. However, the act altered such minor aspects of the system—and the reforms had such a lack of ambition—that it did not attract the support of those parties most interested in change. The act was eventually passed, but all the experts agree that it does not reach far enough. The overall impression is that it will make very little difference to the Spanish higher education system.

References

García-Garrido, J. L. (1992). Spain. In B. R. Clark & G. Neave (Eds.), *Encyclopedia of higher education* (Volume 1). Oxford: Pergamon Press.

Mora, J. G. (1997a). Market trends in Spanish higher education. *Higher Education Policy, 10*(3/4), 187–198.

Mora, J. G. (1997b). Institutional evaluation in Spain: An on-going process. *Higher Education Management, 9*(1), 59–70.

Mora, J. G. (2001). The academic profession in Spain: Between the civil service and the market. *Higher Education, 41*(1/2), 131–155.

Mora, J. G. & Vidal, J. (1998). Introducing quality assurance in Spanish university. In J. Gaither (Ed.), *Quality Assurance in Higher Education: New Directions on Institutional Research.* San Francisco: Jossey-Bass.

Neave, G. & van Vught, F. (1991). *Prometheus bound.* Oxford: Pergamon.

Organization for Economic Cooperation and Development. (2003). *Education at a Glance.* Paris: OECD.

53

TURKEY

Hasan Simsek
Middle East Technical University, Turkey

The world's higher education systems are in the process of a profound transformation. While to varying degrees the general pattern of trends and developments is the same for both developed and developing countries, this profound transformation has become more challenging for the higher education systems of the developing world. In particular, many new forms of inequalities seem to separate the richer nations of the North from the poorer nations of the South, where educational systems—including higher education—are paralyzed by the demands of local and national needs, such as increasing population rates (accompanied by pressures for greater access to basic and further education) and by the demands of a globally competitive environment.

"Any discussion of globalization cannot avoid the deep inequalities that are part of the world system of higher education. Globalization has added a new dimension to existing disparities in higher education" (Altbach, 2004, p. 6). The Turkish higher education system is no exception. With a population of 70 million, approximately half of it being under the age of 20, the entire education system is beset by a complex array of issues and constraints, the most fundamental one being the need to address a growing demand for educational opportunities of all kinds. Higher education is one of the most pressing educational issues. In 2004, 1.7 million students took the centrally administered University Entrance Examination, but only about 15–20% of them will be placed in a 4-year degree program (excluding the nonformal/distance higher education sector, which is largely seen as being of low quality and is not demanded much by many able students).

The purpose of this chapter is to provide an overview of the current status of Turkish higher education. The following section will briefly introduce the reader to a short history of the Turkish higher education system by emphasizing key turning points in its evolutionary pattern. Following the history section, key issues, constraints, dilemmas, and opportunities for the current Turkish higher education system will be addressed.

Turkish Higher Education System: A Brief History

According to Guruz, Suhubi, Sengor, Turker, and Yurtsever (1994, p. 151), when the Turkish Republic was founded in 1923, the Turkish higher education system and its

James J.F. Forest and Philip G. Altbach (eds.), International Handbook of Higher Education, 1003–1018.
© 2006 *Springer. Printed in the Netherlands.*

institutions (except the Istanbul Technical University) had not evolved naturally from their antecedent institutional conditions as a result of experiences and sometimes struggles for over hundreds of years. Many institutions were merely transplanted from the European system by the Revolution's reformist leaders.

The Period of Forming (1773–1946)

Observers of Turkish history do not see a deep tradition of higher education in the Ottoman Empire. The madrasa (Islamic boarding school) equivalent of the Western medieval university was first founded by Seljuk Turks in Baghdad in the 11th century. It later served the Turkish Empire (the Ottomans) in the form of learning and interpretation of knowledge in the fields of religion, canon law, rhetoric, philosophy, mathematics, astronomy, and medicine. Contrary to their counterparts in the Western world, the madrasas later became the primary sources of resistance to change and modernization (Council of Higher Education, 2004a, p. 1).

The first higher education establishment of the Western tradition was founded in 1773 as a military institution in engineering for the Navy (the Imperial Naval Engineering College) right after the defeat of the Ottoman Navy by the Russians. "Subsequently, in 1795, the Imperial Military Engineering College was opened. These two institutions represent the first diversion from the traditional education of the madrasas, and were later merged to form the roots of today's Istanbul Technical University" (Council of Higher Education, 2004a, p. 1). Considering the fact that prototypes of modern European higher education institutions were founded in the 11th and 12th centuries (University of Bologna in 1088 and University of Paris in 1160), the foundation years of these two establishments indicate that Ottomans lagged 700 years behind Europe in creating the prototype of a modern university (Guruz *et al.*, 1994, p. 151).

Numerous attempts were made to establish other institutions of higher education between 1827 and 1900. The Imperial Medical College was founded in 1827, followed by the establishment of the Imperial Military College in 1834. The Ottoman University (its original name being the Ottoman House of Sciences) was founded in 1900, containing programs in law, medicine, religion, literature, and biology. The decision to establish it was actually made in 1846; after 17 years of preparation, it was inaugurated in 1863, but was closed down twice because of resistance mainly from the teachers of madrasas, which by that time had become the bastions of reactionary activities and antimodernist movements (Council of Higher Education, 2004a, pp. 2–3). The institution was firmly reestablished in 1900 and, after the Revolution of 1923, was reorganized under the name of Istanbul University.

Under the French influence, several other state institutions—similar to the *grandes écoles* of France—were founded toward the end of the 19th century: the School of Public Administration (1877), the School of Law (1878), and the Higher School of Commerce (1882). These institutions formed the roots of some of today's universities, such as Istanbul Technical University, Marmara University, Mimar Sinan University, and Yildiz Technical University in Istanbul (Council of Higher Education, 2004a, p. 2). Reflecting a separate influential model, Robert College was founded by the American missionary Cyrus Hamlin in 1863 in Istanbul. It was first opened as a liberal arts college under the ordinance of the State of New York. In 1912, engineering departments were added to the College's academic programs. On the original campus of Robert College, Bosphorus University was founded in 1971.

As Guruz *et al.* (1994) note, it is proper to mark the emergence of the modern Turkish higher education system with the Independence War that took place between 1919 and 1923, and particularly by the proclamation of the Turkish Republic on October 29, 1923. Until this date, all higher education establishments were located in Istanbul, and there was no single higher education institution in the rest of the country. After Ataturk (the war hero and the first president) designated Ankara as the Capital City of the Republic, the School of Law (now Faculty of Law under Ankara University), Gazi Institute of Education (now Faculty of Education under Gazi University), and School of Agriculture (now Faculty of Agriculture under Ankara University) were established in 1924, 1926, and 1930, respectively.

A Swiss professor, Albert Malche, was invited to Turkey to evaluate the status of Istanbul University in 1932. The reform efforts of the government, based on Professor Malche's report, marked an important turning point in the Turkish higher education system. Professor Malche raised the need for a body that would be responsible for the university, as well as pointing out that the university was distant and isolated from the society. Following the evaluation of this report, Law 2252 was legislated in the parliament in 1933 to reform the higher education system in a number of ways: organization and administration, teaching, research, academic programs, and operations. Some new terms such as "rector" (president), "dean," and "faculty" were used for the first time (Kisakurek, 1976, pp. 18–19). "The 1933 reform is indeed the beginning of the history of the modern university in Turkey" (Guruz *et al.*, 1994, p. 153).

Between 1933 and 1946, three new faculties were founded in Ankara, namely the faculty of Language, History, and Geography (1937), faculty of Science (1943), and faculty of Medicine (1945). Between 1923 and 1946 (that is, during the forming years), there was a clear and significant impact of the Continental European model of higher education systems, mainly French and German, on Turkish higher education.

The Period of Normalization (1946–1973)

The year 1946 is considered another turning point in the history of Turkish higher education. Law 4936 was enacted in 1946, granting universities autonomy in governance and giving them the authority to elect rectors and deans. After the 1950 elections, the Democratic Party came to power in the Turkish government. Contrary to the more welfare-oriented policies of the People's Republican Party, the Democratic Party followed a host of relatively more market-oriented economic policies. After World War II, Turkey had to make a choice between the path of establishing a strong alliance with the West or to deal with Stalin's threats alone from the North. Turkey preferred the Western, chiefly American alliance and was admitted to NATO in 1950. With the accession of the Democratic Party to power, Turkish higher education fell under a clear influence of the American higher education model, leaving the Continental model aside.

The new government opened four new universities after the American Land Grant model, with the belief that high-quality technical personnel needed by the Turkish economy would be better educated within the framework of this model. These universities—Egean University (1955), Black Sea Technical University (1955), Middle East Technical University (1956), and Ataturk University (1957)—were designed to be campus universities. However, except for the Middle East Technical University, these later evolved much like other typical Turkish universities—being placed under the governance of the Ministry of Education and being supervised and sponsored in the foundation years by the academic personnel of Istanbul and Ankara Universities, which were traditional and conservative. Only the Middle East Technical University has successfully evolved consistent with the original idea, and it is now one of the several prestigious universities in the country (Council of Higher Education, 1996a,b, p. 3). Until 1976, it was governed by a board of trustees.

Following the fall from power of the Democrats in 1960, a new constitution was prepared in which university autonomy was effectively defined as the right of faculty members to elect rectors and deans (Council of Higher Education, 2004a, p. 5). In 1967, Hacettepe University in Ankara was founded as a hybrid model "between the Anglo-American model of the Middle East Technical University and the Continental European model of the other state universities" (Council of Higher Education, 2004a, p. 6).

In order to avoid uncoordinated and unplanned growth, Law 1750 was legislated in 1973, which established the Council of Higher Education to coordinate and plan the higher education system. The law did not say anything about funding and internal administrative structures of universities, which were largely old and archaic. In this sense, its primary concern was the regulation of the higher education system in terms of administration, coordination, control, and planning at the national level.

The Period of Unregulated Growth, Tumult, and Chaos (1973–1981)

Although the Law 1750 was initially put in effect to coordinate and regulate the higher education system, efforts were not successful for various reasons. The Council of Higher Education as a coordinating board was seen as a threat to academic freedom by faculty and was strongly resisted. On the other hand, "because the Council of Higher Education was chaired by the Minister of National Education and included lay members, it was soon found unconstitutional by the Supreme Constitutional Court, on the grounds that the presence of such members violated university autonomy" (Council of Higher Education, 2004a, p. 6).

Between 1973 and 1981, the system continued its unplanned growth. For example, 10 new universities were opened outside of three big metropolitan cities (Istanbul, Ankara, and Izmir). At this point in time, each university was administering its own admissions procedures. The increased number of universities in different provinces of the country as well as variations in admissions criteria and procedures became a serious problem for students. They had to travel from university to university, and from province to province to apply for admission and examinations. To solve this, a Student Selection and Placement Center was established in 1974.

Over the years, this uncontrolled growth created a serious problem for the higher education system, containing various kinds of institutions of higher learning with different goals, durations, and status. Four major categories of institutions were observed in this period (Guruz *et al.*, 1994, p. 156):

1. 4-year undergraduate programs provided by faculties in universities;
2. 4-year undergraduate programs provided by Academies of Engineering and Architecture, Academies of Economics and Commerce, and Academies of Art (these were independent establishments which had no relation with universities);
3. 2-year higher vocational institutions and 4-year academies of sports, supervised by various ministries and by the Ministry of Education; and
4. 3-year teacher-training institutions run by the Ministry of Education.

This was apparently a confusing picture of the higher education system, suggesting the need to regulate and consolidate the system; this was how the 1981 reorganization came into effect.

The Period of Regulation and Consolidation (1981–1997)

Turgut Ozal came to power in 1983, following two years of military rule. He was quick and successful in implementing his right wing, new liberal policies—especially focusing on the economy, banking, telecommunications, transportation, and other sectors. Within less than a decade, the face of the country had dramatically changed (to the surprise of many foreign agencies and individuals). However, despite this national transformation (and in contrast to his counterparts in other nations), education and higher education had never been a priority in his reform agenda, with the exception of several loan agreements with the World Bank concerning tertiary education and the establishment of the Council of Higher Education to coordinate activities of higher education institutions in the country.

During the 1980–1981 academic year, only 5.9% of the relevant cohort age were enrolled in higher education—far behind many developing countries. For example, the higher education enrollment rate was 37.7% in South Korea, 27.0% in Greece, and 17.8% in Syria in the same year.

On the other hand, only 17 of every 100 university students were able to complete their university education, with large proportions of students dropping out throughout each academic year. It was thus widely recognized that universities were not being used to their full capacity. Further, there was a seriously unequal distribution of academic staff among the universities, and they were functioning without any clear visions for the future needs of the country, as well as being detached from each other (Council of Higher Education, 1991, p. 1). The need was clear and strong. Reform initiatives which had been blocked earlier by faculty under the guise of academic freedom and autonomy had a stronger chance of success this time because of the 1980 military takeover. In 1981, the Higher Education Law 2547 was put into effect.

The Higher Education Law 2547 was considered one of the most comprehensive higher education provisions since the 1933 reform. The Law 2547 related to many domains of higher education, such as revitalizing the Council of Higher Education as an intermediary body to regulate and coordinate the system; creating some new concepts such as graduate schools, a department-based academic organization, and academic promotions based on research and international publication; allowing nonprofit foundations to establish higher education institutions as well as making some structural changes, such as the consolidation of 166 different higher education establishments under nine new universities; and making teacher-training institutions 4-year faculties under universities.

With the reform, a unified system of higher education was introduced and a coherent and interrelated pattern of institutional diversity created. All the academies, teacher training institutes and vocational schools were reorganized; while some of them were, where viable and convenient, amalgamated to form new universities, some were transformed into new faculties and affiliated to the universities in their own regions. Thus, with the establishment of nine more state universities in 1982 and one foundation university in 1984, the total number of universities rose from 19 to 28. In 1992, 24 new state universities were established in different regions of the country (Council of Higher Education, 1996b, p. 2).

By 1998, the total number of universities was 68, of which 11 were private (or more accurately called "foundation") universities. Within a decade—from 1981 to 1991—the number of students enrolled in 4-year university programs increased fivefold, from 41,574 to 199,571. Participation rates increased from 5.9% to 9.6% of the relevant age group. The number of teaching staff increased by 65%, from 20,917 to 34,469, and the number of assistant, associate, and full professors increased by 126%, from 4,905 to 11,070. At the same time, the reform positively impacted the quality of higher education in terms of the number of students per teaching staff and the graduation rate. The number of students per teaching staff was 84 in 1978, 46 in 1981, and (despite a substantial increase in enrollment) dropped to 39 in 1991. Meanwhile, the graduation rate increased from 50% to 80% in science and engineering, and from 70% to 90% in health sciences.

The Period of Expansion of the Private Sector and a Political Siege of the Universities (1998–Present)

The expansion of the system has continued since 1998, this time in the private sector. Between 1998 and 2004, 16 new universities have been founded by nonprofit foundations in different parts of the country, 13 of which are in Istanbul alone. The Turkish higher education system currently comprises 53 state and 23 private universities. Two of the state universities are entirely English medium (the Middle East Technical University in Ankara and the Bosphorus University in Istanbul), and one is French medium (Galatasaray University in Istanbul). Virtually all (22 of 23) privately founded universities are English medium and one is German medium (Council of Higher Education, 2004c, p. 1).

Besides these numerical indicators of expansion, higher education has been in the spotlight of the public and politics since the elections of November 2002. With the accession to power of the Justice and Development Party (the majority in parliament), the Turkish higher education system, and (as its apex organ) the Council of Higher

Education, are under fire. The Islamic background of the party founders and extremist factions within the party declared an open hostility toward the bastions of modernism and secularism, the university, and the Council of Higher Education. The roots of this animosity date back about a decade, during which (through the strong leadership of the Council of Higher Education) university presidents and administrators became staunch supporters of the Republic's secularist ideals, refusing to allow the use of religious symbols such as headscarves within the university campuses and curbing the admission of secondary Imam and Preach School graduates into regular 4-year university programs other than the Faculties of Theology. The government has recently passed a law that allows the Imam and Preach School graduates into any university program as well as changing the structure of the Council of Higher Education in order, as many critics proclaim, to ease political intrusions into the decision-making processes and procedures. Turkish universities are all now on guard to defend their autonomy and to protect the secularist ideals of Kemal Ataturk, the founder of the modern Turkish Republic. As a result of a strong, organized reactionary campaign by NGOs, business and media—led by very prominent universities of the country—the government has recently been forced to move the issue to the backburner, "to be reconsidered again at an unknown date in the future," as the Prime Minister declared.

System Review

Overall System Characteristics

Higher education is defined as all postsecondary programs with a duration of at least two years. The system consists of universities (53 state and 23 foundation) and nonuniversity institutions of higher education (police and military academies and colleges). Each university consists of faculties and 4-year schools, offering bachelor's level programs, the latter with a vocational emphasis, and 2-year vocational schools offering prebachelor's (associate's) level programs of a strictly vocational nature. Anadolu University in Eskisehir offers 2- and 4-year programs through distance education. (As will be discussed later, Turkish higher education comprises one of the largest distance/nonformal education systems in the world.) The diversity of postsecondary programs is striking: there are presently 2,835 bachelor's programs (of 468 different types), and 3,336 prebachelor's programs (of 267 different types) operating in Turkish universities (Council of Higher Education, 2004c, p. 1).

Access

Admission to higher education in Turkey is centralized and based on a nationwide single-stage examination administered by the Student Selection and Placement Center (OSYM) every year (Council of Higher Education, 2004c, p. 1). Although the Turkish higher education system has achieved an impressive expansion in enrollment, there is still an increasing demand for higher education. Within roughly two decades—from 1983 to 2002—the number of applicants for higher education increased from 361,158 to 1,823,099. This figure shows that the total number of university applicants has increased almost five times. On the other hand, the number of students enrolled in higher education programs increased from 105,246 to 614,125 between 1983 and 2002 (328,730 students were placed in 4- and 2-year programs, and 285,395 were placed in the Faculty of Distance Education at Anadolu University). From these numbers, the admissions rate in the year 2002 was 33.8% for the entire higher education system, including the distance programs (Council of Higher Education, 2003, pp. 32–33). The ratio of total applicants to the ones admitted to formal, day programs is 18%, the remaining 15% being in the nonformal, distance education programs.

According to the population estimates prepared by the State Institute of Statistics and the Ministry of National Education, the 18–21 age cohort tended to decline between 1995 and 2000, but has shown an increase since then. According to the estimates, there will be 4,194,143 students at the secondary education level (who will be seeking higher education opportunities after graduation). The secondary education schooling rate was 32% in 1986, 37% in 1991, 57% in 1999, but will be estimated to be 80% in 2006. In 2006, there will be about two million secondary education graduates who will be seeking admission to university programs (Council of Higher Education, 2003, p. 30). This means that the expansion pressure for the Turkish higher education system will continue in the coming years.

Although the private/foundation higher education sector has shown a phenomenal growth in the last decade, the enrollment capacity created by these institutions was only about 7% in 2002 (with 23,281 students enrolled in private university programs) (Council of Higher Education, 2003, p. 34). In the near future, this sector is not expected to hold more than 10% of total higher education enrollments. Because of this, the pressure will still be felt to a great extent by state universities.

There are four possible ways to address the increasing demand for access to higher education: increasing the number of higher education institutions, including in the private sector; enlarging the capacity of current higher education institutions; increasing the capacity of nonformal and distance education; and increasing the number of 2-year programs, including 2-year postsecondary vocational and technical schools.

Concerning the creation of new universities, the number of institutions in Turkey increased from 28 to 76 (including the private sector) from 1984 to 2003. Establishing new universities has far from remedied the problem because, according to Dundar and Lewis (1996), "supply side policies" have inherent problems; in particular, they cause internal inefficiencies because most of the newly established universities in the country have higher costs of instruction as well as higher unit costs per student than the older universities.

Regarding the capacity increase in current higher education institutions, Guruz *et al.* (1994, p. 168) reported a decade ago that "the Turkish higher education system has already exceeded the optimal capacity at the four-year, undergraduate level." As will be discussed later in this chapter, many university programs in the state higher education sector are seriously understaffed. That is, any further push for capacity increase in formal higher education will, no doubt, damage quality. On the other hand, diversifying higher education by increasing the share of private and nongovernmental institutions should be seriously considered. Today, the share of these institutions in the total higher education enrollment is about 7%. However, since these institutions currently aspire to play an elite role, a sudden jump in their enrollment scheme is not expected in the foreseeable future. So, the burden for capacity increase will substantially remain on the public higher education system in the near future.

Expanding the capacity of nonformal/distance education can be another alternative for increasing enrollment in higher education. Nonformal education has grown phenomenally since the 1981 reform. For example, from 1983 to 1993 the number of students admitted to higher education programs increased from 105,246 to 324,402, and the proportion enrolling in nonformal education during this period jumped from 14.2% to 47.8%. However, while 285,395 students registered in nonformal education programs in 2002, the demand for nonformal/distance education programs has declined steadily over the last decade. Moreover, the proportion of nonformal education in postsecondary enrollment has always been very high in Turkey, by global comparison ranking second only behind Thailand (Council of Higher Education, 1996a, p. 21; Guruz *et al.*, 1994, p. 168). In this sense, the likely advantages of further increasing the enrollment in nonformal education are slim, particularly considering the fact that demand for nonformal education is in decline.

The last alternative to be explored for enlarging the capacity of Turkish higher education is to increase the number of 2-year postsecondary vocational and technical schools. The number of students attending 2-year vocational-technical postsecondary institutions was 126,347 in the 1995–1996 academic year. This sector's share of the country's total higher education enrollment is 15%, which is one of the lowest compared to other comparable national systems. For example, this ratio is 22% in South Korea and 63% in Singapore (Council of Higher Education, 1996a, pp. 20–21). Many observers of Turkish higher education generally agree that a substantial increase in the share of the 2-year vocational and technical postsecondary enrollment is the only viable solution to expand the capacity in formal higher education (Dundar & Lewis, 1996; Guruz *et al.*, 1994). Indeed, when the Council of Higher Education removed the exam barrier for students who wish to continue their education at a 2-year vocational school, the enrollment rate increased by 127% in 2002—approximately 145,330 students enrolled in these schools without experiencing any exam trauma. This trend should continue, considering the fact that there is still a great potential of growth for the share of this sector in the higher education system.

Governance

Organizationally, at the top of the Turkish higher education hierarchy resides the Council of Higher Education—a corporate public body of 22 members responsible for the planning, coordination, and supervision of higher education within the provisions set forth in Higher Education Law 2547 (Council of Higher Education, 2004b, p. 1). The Higher Education Council's General Assembly is the main policymaking body, led by an Executive Committee of nine members (elected by the Council and appointed by the President of the Republic). This committee ensures the execution of policies adopted, carrying out day-to-day functions, and the implementation of resolutions passed by the General Assembly. Moreover, in order to maintain close cooperation and collaboration with the universities, an Interuniversity Council and a Rectors' Committee contribute to the coordination and planning of higher education policies. "The Interuniversity Council is an academic advisory body, comprising the rectors of all universities and one member elected by the senate of each university. The Minister of National Education represents higher education in the Parliament and can chair the meetings of the Council, but has no vote. Neither decisions of the Council nor those of the universities are subject to ratification by the Ministry" (Council of Higher Education, 2004b, p. 1).

Appointment to executive positions in the Turkish higher education system (such as rectors, deans, and chairpersons) involves a mix of the Continental European model of collegiality (based on elections) and the Anglo-American tradition of appointment. For a presidency, six names are identified through a general election within each university by the faculty members who are above the rank of assistant professor (assistant, associate, and full professors). The names are presented to the Council of Higher Education, who reduces the list to three and is free to re-rank the candidates independent from the votes they received from their university faculty. The Council presents this three-name list to the President of the country, and the President is free to appoint any of these three candidates independent from the ranking of the Council.

Deans are appointed by the Council of Higher Education. An election is held in each college (faculty), and the three names who received the highest votes from the faculty are presented to the Rector. The Rector is free to re-rank the candidates independent from the votes they received from the faculty. The appointment is finalized by the Council of Higher Education.

Department chairs are appointed by deans and approved by the president of the university. Although there is no such rule in the Law 2547, generally a voting process takes place in the department and the process is finalized by the dean and the rector, respectively.

The overall organizational and governance pattern of Turkish higher education has evolved since the 1960 Constitution, when a purely collegial approach was the accepted norm for universities and the appointment of rectors and deans was carried out through elections. Some call this organizational pattern "an academic oligarchy" (Clark, 1983). For decades, and especially between 1973 and 1980, Turkish universities did not respond effectively to changes in the society, becoming highly inert, introverted, and isolated. The 1981 reform accepted the principle of appointment of rectors and deans rather than elections. However, through an amendment to the Law 2547 in 1992, election was formally established as the initial stage of appointment.

As will be discussed later in this chapter, the financing pattern of higher education involves heavy state involvement in institutional and college level operations. This, in turn, explains another aspect of Turkish higher education—overt domination by state authority, or what Clark (1983) described as the "bureaucratic model." In general, Turkish higher education can thus be described as a system which is framed by both state authority and academic oligarchy (Guruz *et al.*, 1994). However, drawing on Clark's "coordination triangle" (through which a third dimension of activity is tied to the market or society, creating what he called an "entrepreneurial university"), a number of observers have proposed that the direction in which the Turkish higher education system has to move is the market or an entrepreneurial university model.

There are examples of this trend among other higher education systems; indeed, many national higher education systems which were traditionally dominated by both state authority and academic oligarchy (such as in France, Sweden, Austria, and Italy) have developed reforms in the areas of decentralization and institutional diversification, to make their university systems more aligned with market forces. There are several points that almost all similar reform initiatives uniformly accept. First, primarily through flexible funding patterns, universities are given more autonomy in institutional and financial operations. Second, while shifting a great deal of decision making to institutional levels, intermediary bodies are created to make the institutions more accountable to the society by various forms of coordination, supervision, planning, and control. Third, to weaken the classical public dominance in higher education (which has led to inefficiencies), institutional diversification is strongly sought either through privatization or permitting the private and nongovernmental institutions to enter into the higher education sector.

All three of these provisions are being seriously considered in Turkey today. First, there are legislative proposals to make Turkish higher education institutions more autonomous in spending the appropriated public funds as well as to have them diversify their income sources. Second, the Council of Higher Education will function as an intermediary body to develop performance and accountability measures and to oversee the system based on social priorities. This requires redefinition of the role of the Council of Higher Education, which is currently distracted by unnecessary bureaucratic matters. Third, institutional diversification has also been on the rise, making the total number of private/foundation universities 23 and enlarging their portion of enrollment rate from 1.7% in the early 1990s to 7% in 2003 (Council of Higher Education, 2003, p. 34).

Finance

In Turkey, the major source of income for public universities is state funds. Universities prepare their annual budget for the coming year, which is presented to the Council of Higher Education. These budget requests are consolidated by the Council and sent to the Ministry of Education. The Minister defends these budget requests in the Parliament as a component of all education appropriations.

Turkey is one of the few OECD countries that allocates less than 5% of GNP for education (others include Italy, Japan, Argentina, India, and Greece). The OECD average for educational spending is 5.9% of GNP. In Turkey, this figure stayed below 3% between 1981 and 1991, and has only increased since then to 3.83% in 2003. The share of higher education within the education budget hovered around the 25% level between 1981 and 2003 (25% for three consecutive years of 2001, 2002, and 2003). Higher education's share of GNP has increased steadily since 1989 (when it was 0.45%), reaching its highest level of 0.96% in 2003 (Council of Higher Education, 2003, pp. 120–122).

Besides these direct state funds, universities have two other sources of income— revenue from services provided by the university, such as patient care and contract research, and student contributions, which are collected in a separate fund to be used for highly subsidized student services. For a typical university, 59% of university income is derived from the state budget, 35% from income generated by the institution, and only 4% is from student contributions. "Only 27% of the income from student contributions was spent for education, with the rest going to very highly subsidized meals, lodging, and medical services provided to the students, and to financing extracurricular activities. Thus, there are no real tuition fees in Turkey" (Council of Higher Education, 2004c, p. 11).

Financing of higher education in Turkey involves a terribly inefficient funding scheme based on negotiated, incremental line-item budgeting. It hardly provides opportunities for wise and efficient use of resources, and greatly reduces accountability. For example, in 1993, in a typical institution's budget, 62% went to personnel salaries, 10% to other recurrent expenditures, 23% to investments, and 5% to transfers (Guruz *et al.*, 1994, p. 201). Researchers who have studied the financing pattern of Turkish higher education claim that the funding mechanism for public higher education (negotiated, incremental line-item budgeting) in Turkey needs to be changed to make the system more efficient and accountable. The findings of the Dundar and Lewis study (1996), based on an extensive analysis of the system, indicated that Turkish higher education is highly inefficient. They suggested that the Turkish higher education system must get away from a highly inefficient funding scheme of negotiated, incremental line-item budgeting. Instead, they propose that university budgets should be simplified by eliminating unnecessary details through a "lump sum" appropriation scheme. Through this, university administrators will become the owners of their own budgets, which would lead to much wiser resource use under some accountability measures supervised by an intermediary body, such as the Council of Higher Education (2004c, p.14) (Guruz, 2001, p. 220; Guruz *et al.*, 1996, p. 252).

Faculty

In the academic year 2001–2002, there were 70,012 teaching staff in the Turkish higher education system, including 9,396 professors, 5,367 associate professors, 11,190 assistant professors, and 25,864 research assistants. The average student/faculty ratio in formal education was 25:1 in 1980, 24:1 in 1994, and 31:1 in 2002. It is thus clear that the system has expanded in terms of enrollment rates but this expansion has not been accompanied by a corresponding expansion in the number of faculty members. This is an alarming case for the higher education system, given that Turkey lags behind countries like Thailand (where the ratio is 29:1). In comparison, the student/faculty ratio in other countries that year was 12:1 in Brazil, 18:1 in France, 15:1 in the United States, 10:1 in the United Kingdom, and 7:1 in Japan (Dundar & Lewis, 1996, p. 19; Guruz *et al.*, 1994, p. 183).

Furthermore, the situation is worse for some higher education programs, including many areas of teacher-training programs (where the student/faculty ratio in preschool education programs was 437:1; in classroom teaching, 363:1; and in physical education and sports, 135:1), as well as economics (83:1), management (67:1), computer engineering (52:1), and electrical and electronics engineering (43:1), according to the Council of Higher Education (2003, pp. 50–53).

Three strategies could be used to solve the problem of faculty shortage: joint graduate programs between advanced and newly established universities within the Turkish higher education system; providing scholarships for students to earn their degrees abroad; and changing the mission of some high-ranking universities into elite research institutions in order to supply more Ph.Ds.

As to joint graduate programs between advanced and newly established universities, the Council of Higher Education amended a regulation in 1983 to make the higher education system more flexible and to allow interuniversity degrees and programs. Under this regulation, research assistants—especially those working at newly established universities—are allowed to enroll in the graduate programs of more advanced universities. However, the policy has not been successful due to several reasons, including the lack of necessary material conditions—for example, there is no support mechanism designed for students' residences in host universities. Since all advanced universities are located in the largest metropolitan areas of Turkey, it is very costly for students to pay high rents. Further, there are no financial aid resources for students' thesis expenses. Plus, instruction in two of the advanced and most desirable universities (the Middle East and the Bosphorus Universities) is in English, and students thus need to reach a level of English proficiency, but there is no provision in the regulation on who would pay expenses for English preparation. Finally, there are no mandatory provisions in the regulation ensuring the availability of this to graduate students. As a result, in many newly established universities, research assistants are assigned courses to teach and administrators are reluctant to provide such joint graduate degree opportunities to their research assistants.

Concerning scholarships for degrees abroad, the Council of Higher Education initiated a policy in 1987 to provide master's and Ph.D. scholarships to research assistants, especially in the above-mentioned fields where the shortage is alarming. However, the approximate monthly cost of a student studying abroad is about $1,800 (where the cost is about one-quarter of this in a good Turkish university), which equals to an annual cost of $42 million (Council of Higher Education, 1996a, p. 39). This is, no doubt, a very high cost, and the Council of Higher Education is now considering how to better utilize domestic sources—for example, a number of high-ranking institutions are being provided certain institutional incentives such as a reduction in undergraduate student population, as well as extra funds for research and graduate education (Council of Higher Education, 2003, pp. 71–72).

Research and Knowledge Production

In Turkey, the net research funding allocated to higher education institutions in 2001 was about $31.6 million (0.64% of the consolidated budget). However, R&D spending per person was $39.2 for Turkey, compared with $460.9 for European Union (EU) countries, $962.8 for the United States, and $106.6 for Greece (Council of Higher Education, 2003, pp. 115–116). Despite the relatively scarce resources allocated for research, the number of articles by Turkish academics has shown a steady increase since the 1980s. While Turkey ranked 41st in the Science Citation Index country listing in 1980, it was ranked 22nd in the 2002 listing. From 1999 to 2002, the publication rate of Turkish academics increased much faster than that of academics in Israel, Belgium, Taiwan, or Poland (Council of Higher Education, 2003, p. 114).

These comparative data suggest that although its universities receive considerably lower levels of research appropriation from public resources, Turkey has a strong potential for research and for its international dissemination. A number of strategies have been proposed to further strengthen Turkish universities' research capacity, such as increasing the percentage of research allocation to at least 1% of the general budget; significantly increasing the number of R&D personnel in both universities and private firms; increasing the share of the private sector contribution to R&D activities to at least 50%; and finally, rather than spreading the R&D resources thinly, focusing on (and substantially funding) critical and high-potential areas (Council of Higher Education, 2003, p. 116).

Turkey's Candidacy for Full Membership to the EU and Its Potential Impact on Turkish Higher Education

From its establishment through the early 1990s, the EU did not have an explicit educational policy. However, especially since the mid-1990s, common economic policies of the EU have spilled over to other sectors such as education and higher education. The EU has four forms of involvement in higher education (de Witte, 1993): the right to provide higher education, in that individuals or organizations can establish higher education institutions and offer educational services throughout the EU; the right to work for higher education institutions—that is, any person who resides in an EU country and works as an educator (including researchers) has the right to live and work in another EU country without any restrictions; the rights of students, including nondiscrimination on the grounds of nationality, and free movement for seeking educational opportunities; and finally, the right to the recognition of diplomas by member states.

To facilitate these rights, the EU has established the National Academic Recognition Centers (NARIC), with liaison offices in each member and candidate country. A unit within the Council of Higher Education serves as a liaison office in Turkey. Turkish universities are also obligated by the Council of Higher Education to prepare Diploma Supplements for all university graduates that will allow students to use their earned credentials in other EU universities through the European Credits Transfer System (ECTS). Also, in order to facilitate the free movement of students among the institutions of higher education of member countries, the EU now has a program called ERASMUS that also comprises direct financial support for students. ERASMUS was established in 1987 to support a network of universities and direct financial support for students pursuing a period of study in another EU member country. According to Neave (1995), all these measures and policies to create a European space for higher education increasingly resemble a higher education system of the Anglo-American tradition.

The EU and its higher education policies are seen by many as providing a good opportunity to integrate the majority of Turkish universities into the world system of higher education. Several state universities have made significant progress in this area, including the Middle East Technical University in Ankara, the Bosphorus University and Istanbul Technical University in Istanbul, and most of the recently founded private/foundation universities. Integration with the European higher education space, many believe, will eventually lead to major curricular and administrative reform in the Turkish higher education system.

Conclusion

Overall, the Turkish higher education system has shown impressive improvements in many respects, especially in the last two decades. In contrast to Europe's aging population, Turkey has one of the world's youngest populations, with significant need for educational opportunities of all kinds, and particularly higher education. It is estimated that the number of students who will seek admission to a higher education program in 2006 will be around 2 million, but only about 20% of these students will have a reasonable chance of enrollment (excluding the low-demand, low-prestige open university or distance learning programs). No matter what the prospects might be for some traditional solutions (such as increasing the share of 2-year vocational-technical institutions within the higher education system), the Turkish higher education system must clearly expand in order to respond to the demand for access from a growing youthful population.

However, many believe that the Turkish state universities are lacking strategic governance because the finance of higher education is strictly in the hands of the government organs, primarily the Ministry of Finance and the State Planning Institute, the latter controlling and appropriating the investment budgets. Many university rectors are complaining that the line-item budgeting process creates unnecessary intrusions into the autonomy of universities in terms of limiting the strategic uses of appropriated public monies by university administrations.

Although there is a tuition policy within Turkish higher education, the tuition and fees are so low that, for some, higher education is almost free in Turkey—revenues from student tuition cover less than 3% of total costs to the state of the higher education system (Dundar & Lewis, 1996). Since it is a politically sensitive issue, the reform of higher education has been on the agenda of almost all governments in the last 15 years, but this funding inequality has yet to be addressed.

As mentioned above, there is continuous pressure on Turkish higher education to grow because of high student demand, and there is also a critical shortage of faculty in many university programs. This critical faculty shortage can be solved by both utilizing degree programs abroad and expanding the capacity (and increasing the quality) of graduate programs in Turkey, especially in the advanced older universities.

Faced with these challenges, it seems that Turkey's candidacy for full membership in the EU provides the greatest opportunity for a major transformation of the Turkish higher education system. Turkish universities have recently been granted the right to fully utilize higher education opportunities and privileges provided for full EU members, such as ERASMUS and ECTS. The success of Turkey's response to this impetus for change will depend on several strategic decisions over the next several years, decisions which demand careful analysis by both government and institutional leaders, as well as by the members of the academic profession.

References

Altbach, P. G. (2004). Globalization and the university: Myths and realities in an unequal world. Online at: http://www.bc.edu/bc_org/avp/soe/cihe/publications/pub_pdf/Globalization.pdf. Retrieved May 17, 2004. (An updated version of this essay appears in volume 1 of this *Handbook*.)

Clark, B. (1983). *The higher education system: Academic organization in cross-national perspective.* Berkeley, CA: University of California Press.

Council of Higher Education. (1991). *Ten years in higher education (1981–1991): The 1981 reform and outcomes (in Turkish).* Ankara, Turkey.

Council of Higher Education. (1996a). *Turkish higher education system: Developments from 1994–95 to 1995–96 (in Turkish).* Ankara, Turkey.

Council of Higher Education. (1996b). *Turkish higher education system and institutions (in Turkish)* (2nd ed.). Ankara, Turkey.

Council of Higher Education. (2003). *Current state of Turkish higher education (in Turkish).* Ankara, Turkey.

Council of Higher Education. (2004a). The Turkish higher education system (Part 1: History). Online at: http://www.yok.gov.tr/english/part1.doc. Retrieved April 21, 2004.

Council of Higher Education. (2004b). The Turkish higher education system (Part 2: Governance). Online at: http://www.yok.gov.tr/english/part2.doc. Retrieved April 21, 2004.

Council of Higher Education. (2004c). The Turkish higher education system (Part 3: Current status). Online at: http://www.yok.gov.tr/english/part3.doc. Retrieved April 21, 2004.

De Witte, B. (1993). Higher education and the constitution of the European Community. In C. Gellert (Ed.), *Higher education in Europe* (pp. 186–202). London: Jessica Kingsley.

Dundar, H., & Lewis, D. R. (1996). Equity, quality and efficiency effects of reform in Turkish higher education. Paper presented at the annual meeting of Association for The Study of Higher Education, Memphis, TN.

Guruz, K. (2001). *Higher education in the world and in Turkey: History and current management systems (in Turkish).* Ankara, Turkey: OSYM Publications.

Guruz, K., Suhubi, E., Sengor, A. M. C., Turker, K., & Yurtsever, E. (1994). *Higher education, science and technology in Turkey and in the world (in Turkish).* Istanbul, Turkey: TUSIAD Publications (Publication No. TUSIAD-T/94, 6-167).

Kisakurek, M. A. (1976). *Innovation in our universities (in Turkish).* Ankara, Turkey: University Faculty of Education Press.

Neave, G. (1995). On living in interesting times: Higher education in Western Europe 1985–1995. *European Journal of Education, 30*(4), 377–393.

54

UNITED KINGDOM

Michael Shattock

Institute of Education, University of London, UK

The origins of the UK university system lie in the Middle Ages. Oxford University came into being as an organized association of masters and students about the end of the 12th century or the start of the 13th. Based on the characteristics of the University of Paris, the scholars formed a guild of masters and, ultimately, an organized *universitas*. In about 1209, a group of scholars migrated to Cambridge and formed a corporation within the diocese of Ely. At Oxford, the office of Chancellor has been held in continuous succession since 1221 and at Cambridge from 1226. In both universities, licensed halls were developed to provide accommodation for students, and those grew into colleges, which came to be endowed by wealthy benefactors. Thus, in the 13th century University College, Oxford was endowed by William of Durham; Balliol, by John de Balliol and his wife; and Merton College, by Walter de Merton, who made over his estate at Maldon to a community of scholars that by 1270 had settled permanently at Oxford. The Bishop of Ely, Hugo de Balsham, founded Peterhouse at Cambridge in 1284. The two universities have remained collegiate in character, with the creation of additional colleges being the natural route to the growth of the institutions. In 2004, Cambridge announced its intention to build three new colleges in the next 15 years.

In Scotland, a group of Scottish masters—most of whom had graduated in Paris—began to teach at St. Andrews in 1410 and acquired recognition from their bishop two years later. A university was founded in Glasgow in 1451 and in Aberdeen in 1494. The three universities were organized into "nations" rather than colleges, and were each under the charge of a rector. While these first universities in Scotland were authorized or founded by bishops, the university in Edinburgh was created in 1583 by town councillors. These universities are now known in the Scottish higher education system as the Ancient Universities.

At the beginning of the 19th century, Oxford and Cambridge—like Trinity College in Dublin (Ireland was then under British rule)—restricted entry to members of the established church, the Church of England. (No such restriction applied in Scotland.) This led to various dissenting academies being established from time to time, but the first to survive was London University which, founded on the site of what is now University College, London on Gower Street, was financed by a joint stock share issue in 1825. Criticized as the "godless college" because it required no religious affiliation

James J.F. Forest and Philip G. Altbach (eds.), International Handbook of Higher Education, 1019–1033.
© 2006 *Springer. Printed in the Netherlands.*

for entry, a rival in Kings College, London was established in 1829 in the Strand. These two were to come together as separate colleges of the University of London in 1836, which was later to incorporate Imperial College, the London School of Economics, and a range of other colleges and specialist institutes. A further English university, the University of Durham, was founded by the chapter of Durham Cathedral in 1837.

These new institutions were forerunners of a significant movement later in the century to establish colleges in large industrial cities—like Manchester, Liverpool, Leeds, Sheffield, Bristol, Birmingham and Newcastle—which were to emerge in the first years of the 20th century as the new civic universities. These universities, all founded on the basis of civic enthusiasm and funding, were (like their predecessors) entirely independent of the state, had strongly vocational missions rooted in the economic character of the cities or regions in which they were located; none of them was established on a collegiate basis. Following in their wake were a further group of university colleges— Exeter, Hull, Leicester, Reading, Nottingham and Southampton—which offered University of London degrees and which, over the period up to and including the 1950s, acquired full chartered university status (with, of course, independent degree awarding powers).

These two groups of universities are often collectively described as the "red brick" universities after an influential book of that name published in the 1940s by Allison Peers (a professor of Spanish at Liverpool) under the pseudonym of Bruce Truscott (Truscott, 1943). Another important development that deserves mention is the evolution of the University of Wales. In 1852, a limited right to award degrees was granted to St. David's, Lampeter, and several colleges were created over the next 30 years in Aberystwyth, Bangor, Cardiff and Swansea. Towards the end of the century, these all were combined to form a federated University of Wales. This followed the model of the National University of Ireland, originally based on colleges in Belfast, Cork and Galway, and founded in 1848 by the British Government to provide an alternative to the Protestant Trinity College and the proposed Catholic university, in Dublin.

It is important to note that none of the English, Scottish or Welsh universities and colleges was founded by the state or received regular funding from government sources up to World War I, although sums of money were allocated from time to time to support particular functions. In 1919, however, the contribution of the universities to the War effort, the recognition of the existence of national qualified manpower needs and the actual state of the institutions in the aftermath of the War persuaded the UK government to establish a University Grants Committee (UGC) with the purpose of deficiency funding those universities and colleges that had been identified to be on an approved grants list. The UGC functioned as a committee of H.M. Treasury, well out of the sphere of influence of the Board (later Ministry) of Education, and comprised a group of senior persons—mostly from an academic background, including some serving on the staff of universities—whose task was to review university plans and allocate resources to supplement their existing income, while not interfering with the universities' legal autonomy. In practice, in specialist vocational areas like medicine, agriculture and veterinary science, and in technology, the UGC more or less steered the system because of the growing recognition for funding purposes of the national economic and public importance of the disciplines. But over the inter-War period, the UGC contribution to university and college budgets was no more than one-third (on average), with the remaining two-thirds of the institutions' funding coming from student fees and from private funds (mostly interest on endowments). However, one by-product of UGC funding and the way it was administered was that there was no pressure to create private universities, and even Oxford and Cambridge—which had substantial private wealth—saw no grounds for breaking away from the UGC. The year 1919 also saw the creation of the UK Committee of Vice Chancellors and Principals (CVCP), with a permanent secretariat in London, which was to be the representative body for UK universities and the main channel for the expression of university views in discussions about policy with the UGC and with the government.

Not surprisingly, the universities did not prosper during World War II and were ill-equipped to face the challenge of admitting the numbers of ex-servicemen who sought university places in 1945–46 and whom the government was willing to fund to do so. Some institutions had suffered bomb damage, some London colleges had been moved out of the capital, and all had lost staff whom they had been unable to replace. The CVCP reached an agreement with the Ministers under which, in effect, it would accept more direction from the government in return for a major investment in staff and capital facilities. The proportion of state funding rose from a third to over 90%, and the terms of reference for the UGC were re-drawn to give it greater planning and steering powers. Nevertheless, in the first issue of the new *Universities Quarterly* (in 1948) its founder, Lord Simon, wrote that there was no such thing as "a higher education system" in the UK, just a heterogeneous set of institutions. This was to continue until the Robbins Commission on Higher Education—a body established to inquire into the future of higher education—published its report in 1963. One new institution—the University College of North Staffordshire (later Keele University)—was established in 1949, but by the mid-1950s concern was being expressed in the UGC that the existing universities, which were reluctant to expand, would not be able to cope with the expansion in the number of 18 year-olds caused by the "bulge" in the birthrate at the end of the War, and the increasing numbers of children staying on at secondary school after the age of 16. The UGC therefore initiated the founding of seven "new" universities—Sussex, East Anglia, Essex, Kent, Lancaster, Warwick and York (sometimes known as the Shakespearean, or "the plate glass" universities)—to take up the expansion overflow in the late 1960s. Two additional new universities (at Stirling in Scotland and Coleraine in Northern Ireland) were added subsequently. In 1955, the Ministry of Education took the first major step to establish higher education outside the universities when it created eight colleges of advanced technology (CATs), based on the advanced work carried out in local technical colleges, and established a National Council of Technological Awards (NCTA) to award a Diploma of Technology to students in the CATs (which was intended to be a degree equivalent qualification). These colleges were planned to be strictly vocational, as compared to the universities, and were expected to meet the growing demands for high level technically trained personnel.

The Robbins Report represented a watershed in UK higher education: not only did it have the status of a Royal Commission, whose main recommendations the government had little choice but to accept, but it also published a series of statistical appendices which provided the basis for the future maintenance of a high quality database on

UK higher education. During the inter-War years, enrollment in higher education had grown slowly from 61,000 to 69,000 students, but had expanded much more quickly during the post-war years to reach over 200,000 by the time of the Robbins Report, and the Committee forecast a rise to 700,000 by the late 1980s (a figure that in reality was far exceeded). In 1961, the age participation rate (APR) was 7%, but Robbins forecast a doubling by 1980. It recommended firmly that the government had to make financial provision for this expansion. It also recommended that the CATs should become universities (together with two colleges in Scotland which were to become Heriot Watt and Strathclyde Universities) and that sometime in the next decade provision should be made for a range of technical colleges to be upgraded to university status.

This set a pattern for the future—the natural route to university status was via upgrading institutions rather than, as had been the case during the 1960s, establishing entirely new universities. There were to be two exceptions to this: the Open University and the University of Buckingham (see below). One result of the Robbins Report, though not one of its recommendations, was that the UGC was transferred from the Treasury to the new Department of Education and Science (DES) with the aim, it was said, of providing a closer integration with educational policies generally.

Two years after Robbins, the new Labor Government announced a dramatic shift in policy. Robbins had assumed that, if not coterminous, the future of the university sector and of higher education was indissolubly linked. The Labor Government was not satisfied, however, that the freedom traditionally accorded to the universities—for example, to provide whatever degree programs they thought appropriate—should be permitted to circumscribe what the government saw as public interest in higher education issues, and in 1965 announced the foundation of 30 polytechnics in England and Wales (later balanced by the creation of four Scottish Central Institutions and a further polytechnic in Northern Ireland), which were to be vocational and which were to grow according to "natural need." These institutions were to be developed out of existing regional colleges of technology and were to remain under local (municipal) authority control. This automatically created a second sector of higher education and led to the so-called "binary line" between the universities and local authority-led higher education. The NCTA was abolished and replaced by a Council of National Academic Awards (CNAA), which was to be the degree awarding authority for the polytechnics. The legislation creating the CNAA specified that the degrees (first degrees and higher degrees) were to be of similar standard to university degrees (universities had historically enjoyed the power to award their own degrees).

This left one further sector of higher education, the teacher training colleges, untouched. Robbins had recommended that the two-year teacher training colleges should extend their courses to three years and be put under the control of the universities. The three-year recommendation was accepted, and in practice it was the universities that validated the B.Ed. degree, but in a significant move in the second half of the 1970s the DES rationalized the colleges, closing some and encouraging the merger of most of the rest with the polytechnics, thus further reinforcing what became known as "the public sector" of higher education.

In a further important development, the Open University—conceived and planned by Harold Wilson's Labor Government—accepted its first students in 1971 as a part-time distance learning institution which was "open" in the sense that it did not demand academic entry qualifications and which was also expected to undertake research in the broad range of disciplines it taught. The Open University proved to be immensely popular and in 2003–04 enrolled over 200,000 students. As a model it has been widely copied internationally. A few years later, a privately financed initiative led to the establishment of the University of Buckingham. Founded out of dissatisfaction with the UGC system, the University gained recognition from Mrs. Thatcher's government to award degrees on the basis of two years intensive study rather than the three years normal in England, Wales and Northern Ireland and four in Scotland. The UK's only private university has, however, remained small at about 1,000 students, more than half of whom are from overseas.

The creation of the binary line—with the public sector on one side and the universities on the other—led to widespread debate over issues of policy. To the university sector, it seemed clear that the DES favored the polytechnics because, through the local authorities, they had a greater measure of control over them. In fact, the DES exercised little control, and the local authority "pool" funding arrangements encouraged polytechnics to broaden their mission to establish humanities and social science programs which overlapped with what was offered in the university sector, a development which came to be described as "academic drift" (Pratt & Burgess, 1974). The polytechnics, for their part, envied the more favorable student/faculty ratios in the universities—the result of the funding they received for research—and were critical of the comparatively favored status they enjoyed in respect to facilities and salary distribution, as well as, of course, their status with the public as universities.

The arrival of the government of Mrs. Thatcher in 1979 brought sharp reductions in funding for both sectors, and presaged far-reaching changes. In 1980, the subsidy for fees for overseas students was removed, and higher education institutions (HEIs) were required to charge full cost fees to all foreign students (although this has subsequently been reversed for students from European Union countries because of the provisions of the Treaty of Rome). In 1981, with government funding still running at about 90% of institutional budgets, an overall cut of 17% over four years was announced. The UGC decided to allocate the reductions differentially, on the basis of internal assessments of institutional quality and to ensure that the measure of per-student resources, which had declined in the 1970s, would be protected. This led to some universities receiving cuts of over 30%, and nearly all universities being required to reduce student numbers in some areas.

The UGC's action became a political issue, and raised questions about its powers vis-à-vis those of the Secretary of State. Cuts were also imposed by the government on the public sector of higher education, but because the polytechnics and other public sector higher education institutions were financed almost entirely against student numbers under the "pool" funding arrangements, the reductions attracted less public attention. These budget reductions were followed by the introduction in the university sector of the Research Assessment Exercise (RAE) in 1986. This was a peer review mechanism employed by the UGC to assess institutional research performance and redistribute recurrent funding for research support toward the most research-active university academic departments. This signaled the beginning of a drive to concentrate research funding in the most research-intensive universities. Initially introduced only for the university sector, this mechanism has become a fundamental element in the structure and management of UK higher education.

In 1988, the Education Reform Act replaced the UGC with a Universities Funding Council (UFC) and created a Polytechnics and Colleges Funding Council (PCFC) to cover the public sector institutions in England and Wales, which were simultaneously removed from the local authority control. (The Scottish public sector institutions remained under the control of the Scottish Office). The new Funding Councils were deliberately established as "funding" (not "planning") bodies to emphasize the greater use of market forces to determine the future character of higher education. Funding was to be by formula against student numbers; policy was to be in the hands of the Secretary of State, rather than a government "quango." The period between the mid-1970s and the mid-1980s had seen a slow increase in the age participation rate from 14% to 18%, but in 1988 a national change in mood accompanied by the Funding Councils' encouragement for market-driven expansion led to a doubling of student numbers between 1988 and 1995 from 800,000 to 1.6 million, and to an increase in the age participation rate to 35%.

But in 1992, further structural change was imposed by the Further and Higher Education Act, which abolished the UFC and the PCFC and established—as part of a general political decision to devolve governmental responsibilities—separate funding councils for England, Wales and Scotland, with Northern Ireland higher education to be managed by the Northern Ireland Office. Even more radically, the English and Welsh polytechnics and the Scottish Central Institutions were refashioned as universities with degree awarding powers, and the CNAA was abolished. In Northern Ireland, the polytechnic was merged with the "new" university at Coleraine. These events brought an end to the binary line and merged the two sectors, and in 1992, the former public sector of higher education was offered the opportunity to enter the RAE.

The results of the 1992 RAE confirmed a research ranking which placed the post-1992 universities below the pre-1992 universities, but also continued the process of differentiating between the research-intensive and less research-intensive pre-1992 universities. Further RAEs in 1996 and 2001 reinforced these divisions in spite of investments in more research-orientated staff—mainly recruited from the pre-1992 universities—on the part of the post-1992 institutions. The system became significantly extended in terms of research concentration, with eight universities receiving 33% of recurrent funding for research; 75% of research funding was distributed among the top 25 institutions.

These divisions in the UK system of higher education—both regional and in research intensity—were given added substance with the translation of the CVCP into Universities UK, with separate but closely linked Universities Scotland and Higher Education Wales, and by the emergence of three other bodies: the Russell Group, formed by a group of the most research intensive universities; the '96 Group, made up of smaller pre-1992 universities; and the Coalition of Modern Universities, made up of the former polytechnics. A further body, the Standing Committee of Principals (SCOP), signaled the emergence of a group of higher education colleges, some of which had acquired degree awarding powers and many of which saw themselves following the polytechnics to full university status. In the process of the transformation from an elite to a mass higher education system, some important differentiation of functions had begun to emerge between institutions which required separate representation at the national level.

The 1992 Act also charged the Funding Councils with the responsibility for assuring the quality of teaching in the higher education system. This led to the establishment of a national Quality Assurance Agency (QAA), which set up a Teaching Quality Assessment (TQA) process to review all higher education programs, discipline by discipline (described later in this chapter).

In 1996, the government established the National Committee of Inquiry into Higher Education (1997) (the Dearing Committee) which reported its findings and recommendations in 1997. The background to the appointment of the Committee was the decline in funding per student in real terms of 45% over the previous 15 years, leading universities to press for the ability to charge "top up" fees over and above the funds made available by the government. The Dearing Committee produced a wide-ranging report, entitled *Higher Education in the Learning Society,* which emphasized disparities in levels of access to higher education and the importance of the provision of lifelong learning, while recommending a new structure of means-tested fees and student loans. As a result, fees at the level of about £1,000 per annum were introduced on a means-tested basis in 2001 across the entire landscape of higher education. However, it was quickly recognized that this was an inadequate response to the needs, particularly at the most competitive end of the UK higher education institutional market, where universities argued for much higher levels of funding if they were to be able to retain their internationally competitive position.

In 2003, a White Paper—*The Future of Higher Education*—recommended the abolition of up-front fees and the introduction of a Graduate Contribution Scheme (to be launched in 2006), under which HEIs could charge fees of up to £3,000 per annum, student loans would be provided, and graduates would repay the loans upon reaching an earnings threshold of between £10,000 and £15,000. This was an extremely controversial proposal, not only from the point of view of students but because of the possibility of variable fees being charged to reflect an institutional market position. Some institutions opposed fees altogether, while others demanded the ability to charge much higher fees than those proposed. The scheme was also controversial in Parliament, and at second reading was passed by only five votes, with the government agreeing to review it within three years of the introduction of the new system. The new system will only, however, apply in England and Northern Ireland, the Scottish Parliament having rejected the introduction of fees and the Welsh National Assembly having not yet decided to implement the measure.

Higher education in the UK has therefore entered a new phase, where not only has a new system been introduced in England and Northern Ireland, but Scotland and Wales are also diverging from a previously unified model. In Scotland, the Scottish Funding Council—which is being merged with its Further Education equivalent, reflecting the fact that 25% of Scottish higher education is provided in further education colleges—funds 14 universities and seven other HEIs. Scotland has an age participation rate of over 50%, as compared with England at about 40%. In Wales, the Welsh Funding Council—which is also closely linked to its Further Education counterpart—funds 13

HEIs, of which some are linked through the University of Wales. In England, HEFCE funds 131 HEIs, of which 77 are universities, 14 are general higher education colleges and 40 are specialist HEIs, while other forms of post-16 education are funded through a national Learning and Skills Council.

The UK can claim to have a very successful higher education system: it carries out 4.7% of the world's research and produces 7.6% of the world's scientific publications and over 9% of the citations of scientific papers. It is the second largest host country for international students (after the US), and its share of international students is rising among OECD countries (IMHE/OECD 2004). The overall age participation rate in the UK is currently 43%, while the proportion of graduates who do not complete their courses is lower than all but three OECD countries. In addition, studies have shown that this high output of graduates has been readily absorbed by the labor market. The major contemporary problems for the UK higher education system involve resolving its funding issues, achieving the government's stated APR target of 50%, and maintaining a group of "world class" universities, without causing detriment to the quality of the higher education system as a whole.

Legal Status

HEIs are independent bodies and are neither structurally part of the government nor regarded as part of the public sector. When they borrow, their borrowing does not count as part of the government's borrowing requirement. The autonomy of the pre-1992 universities—with some exceptions, where institutional constitutions are governed by an Act of Parliament—is individually guaranteed by the award of a charter and statutes by the Privy Council. The post-1992 universities and higher education colleges are designated in the 1992 Further and Higher Education Act as Higher Education Corporations (HECs). In both cases, academic freedom is guaranteed for academic staff by law.

The Department for Education and Skills (DfES) is the government department responsible for higher education. Neither the DfES nor, for example, its Scottish and Welsh equivalents, have a direct relationship with the HEIs, but set strategic objectives and funding priorities for intermediary bodies—the Funding Councils—which themselves devise the funding mechanisms for institutions. HEIs are responsible for their own admissions policies, the appointment of staff, the control of courses and their curricula, the examination of students and—in the case of universities and some higher education colleges—the awarding of degrees. On the other hand, they are accountable to their Funding Council, under the terms of a Financial Memorandum which they are required to sign, for the proper expenditure of government monies. Further, the head of the institution, together with the chief executive of the appropriate Funding Council, may be liable to be summoned before the Public Accounts Committee of the House of Commons in the case of financial mismanagement.

Another way in which institutional autonomy is somewhat constrained involves the power of an institution to award degrees. Following the 1992 Act, HEFCE and the other Funding Councils were given a statutory duty to ensure that the quality of teaching was assessed through a Quality Assurance Agency (QAA). Initially, the QAA launched both full institutional reviews and a Teaching Quality Assessment (TQA) for individual disciplines conducted at an institutional level but on a sector-wide basis. The TQA exercise provoked widespread concern because of the academic time it consumed, and after the completion of the first run-through was replaced by a more selective "lighter touch" approach that relied on external reviews of institutions' own quality control procedures. The principle said to underlie the new approach is "intervention in inverse proportion to success." The approach continues to reflect the public interest in ensuring that HEIs provide higher education, awards and qualifications of both an acceptable quality and an appropriate academic standard; exercise their legal powers to award degrees in a proper manner; and provide public information to inform student choice.

Governance and Management

The two oldest universities, Oxford and Cambridge, have retained some of the forms of governance of their mediaeval origins—in particular, their governing bodies are made up primarily (in the case of Oxford) or exclusively (in the case of Cambridge) of representatives of the academic community. Both retain a meeting of all academic staff—Convocation at Oxford and the Regent House at Cambridge—as an integral part of their governance structure, and at Cambridge the Regent House remains legally the governing body of the university. Both universities have a chancellor, a largely honorary figure; a vice chancellor, who is a permanent full-time officer; and a registrar (registrary at Cambridge), as well as a number of pro vice chancellors.

The predominant model for other pre-1992 universities is for there to be a council (court in Scotland), which is the governing body and is made up of a majority of external (lay) members, one of whom chairs it. In addition to the council, which is responsible for matters of management and finance, each institution convenes a senate which, according to the statutes of most of the universities, is the "supreme academic authority" and is made up of academic members and chaired by the vice chancellor, who is recognized as the "chief executive" of the university.

The post-1992 HEIs have a rather different structure, as their governing bodies are restricted to 25 members—of whom only two or three will be academics—and are entrusted both with the managerial and financial authority of the pre-1992 universities as well as with determining the "educational mission" of the institution (on the recommendation of the vice chancellor). The post-1992 HEI academic boards, while responsible for all academic matters, do not have the statutory powers of the pre-1992 senates. The vice chancellor (or principal) in the post-1992 HEIs is seen much more by the academic community as the "chief executive" than would necessarily be the case in the pre-1992 universities, and will normally have established a "directorate" or "senior management team" of full-time permanent officers (pro vice chancellors, director of finance, director of human resources, etc.) to run the institution. The post of registrar (or secretary) that persists in the pre-1992 universities, serving as secretary to all the statutory bodies and responsible for much of the administration of the institution, has been reduced in scope in most post-1992 HEIs to being little more than the secretary to the governing body. All HEIs will have student membership on governing bodies and senates or academic boards. Students in the ancient universities in Scotland retain the right to elect a rector who may claim the right to chair the court of the university, although in practice such a right is rarely claimed. The growing interest in governance issues has led to the creation of the Committee of University Chairmen (CUC), which produces a *Guide* on governance issues (intended for members of governing bodies) and offers development programs for new and existing members.

The 1980s and 1990s have seen a shift in the way HEIs—and even the pre-1992 universities—have been managed, under the pressures of size, financial stringency and the requirement for greater accountability. This has led to HEIs becoming less collegial and more managerially-led institutions. At the same time, there has been pressure (through the Dearing Report and through the Lambert Report of 2004 on links between HEIs and industry) for the pre-1992 universities to review their councils or courts and to reduce them in size to that of the post-1992 institutions, with the aim of strengthening their strategic capacity. More universities are appointing full-time deans, often from outside the institution, and devolving financial decision making to faculties or departments on New Public Management principles. A Leadership Foundation has been established with HEFCE funding to strengthen the leadership capacity in higher education, and the Institute of Education in London has set up an MBA program in Higher Education Management. Much greater attention is given than before to the appointment and training of heads of academic departments, who will be expected to prepare their departments for the RAE and for QAA visitations.

Financing

The sources of total income for English HEIs in 2001–02 are shown in Figure 1 below. This shows that on average about 60% of a HEIs income comes from state sources and 40% from non-state sources. However, the ability to generate non-state income

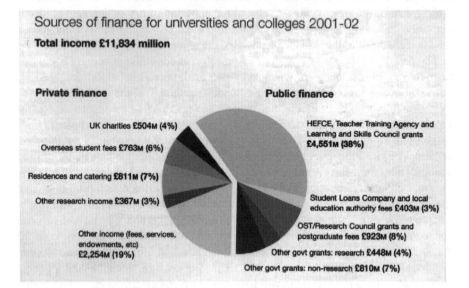

Figure 1.   Sources of Finance for English Universities and Colleges, 2001–02 *(Funding amounts indicated are for England only).*

is unevenly spread across institutions. Twenty-five institutions (the most research-intensive) generate more than 50% of their income from non-state sources, while 35 generate less than 30%, and a further six less than 20%. If the funding for research grants and contracts from Office of Science and Technology (research council) sources were transferred across to non-state sources (because they are awarded competitively against individual applications), the extremes in the differentiation of funding would be much greater. This differentiation may be expected to increase after 2006, when the new student fee system is introduced.

Funding for Research

Public funding for research comes from two main sources, through the Funding Councils via the RAE and from the research councils (humanities, social sciences, science and engineering, medical, particle physics and the natural environment), in what is known as the "dual support system." Funding Council allocations (known as quality-related funds) are intended to support research infrastructure, the salary costs of permanent academic staff, facilities, libraries and IT costs, as well as "blue skies" research, while the Research Councils provide funding for specific research programs. Table 1 provides an overview of the sources of research income for HEIs in 2001–02.

The effect of the RAE system has been to concentrate research support in fewer institutions. Although the RAE methodology has varied over the years, the essential features are that institutions may submit staff research performance over a stated period of years under prescribed disciplinary headings, to be reviewed by panels appointed by HEFCE (acting for all the Funding Councils). These panels rate the performance by discipline using the following scoring: 5*, 5, 4, 3a, 3b, 2 and 1. After the 2001 RAE, funding was weighted broadly at 3.3 for 5*, 2.7 for 5 and 1.0 for 4 (each Funding Council adopted slightly different approaches), using the staff numbers in each subject submission as a volume measure. Because the scoring was subject-based, it was distributed—on a fully transparent basis—to a wide number of institutions, but

Table 1. Sources of Research Income for UK HEIs 2001–02 (in £ Millions)

Source	Amount (£)
HE Funding Bodies	888
Research Councils	668
UK Charities	504
UK Central Government/Local Health and Hospital Authorities	318
Other Grants and Contracts	287
UK Industry	209
Total	2,874

Source: HESA Finance Statistics Return (p. 23, Figure 3), 2001–02.

the failure not to weight 3a and 3b scores (which had received funding following the 1996 RAE) served to concentrate research funding to a greater extent than ever before. It is the intention of the current government to increase research funding substantially while continuing to concentrate it on successful departments.

Research Exploitation and Knowledge Transfer

Public policy suggests that one of the keys to future economic success is innovation achieved through research, and HEIs are seen as key drivers. In 2002, a White Paper—*Investing in Innovation: A Strategy for Science, Engineering and Technology*—published jointly by the DfES, the Department of Trade and Industry and H.M. Treasury, set out the case for increased research funding and the need to give greater attention to knowledge transfer, including contract research, consultancy, training and professional development, as well as the exploitation of basic research (or technology transfer). Mechanisms have therefore been established to encourage regional collaboration among institutions, aimed at economic development; funding has been awarded on a competitive basis to establish investment vehicles to support spin-off companies; and so-called "third stream" funding has been allocated by the Funding Councils to HEIs in order to stimulate links with industry and with regional development agencies. Many universities have established science or research parks, both to provide a base for companies linked to departmental research and to contribute to local economic regeneration. It has been claimed that the most famous of these, at Cambridge, together with the magnet effect on other technology-based industries, has added £8 billion to the nation's GDP.

Access

The slow transition from an elite to mass higher education system in the UK has not benefited social classes equally. In the 1930s, the UGC calculated that one person in 60 was admitted to a university, but the ratio had moved to one in 31 by the early 1950s. The Robbins Committee showed, however, that children from manual labor backgrounds, with the same levels of measured ability and in the same educational environment as children from non-manual labor backgrounds, were less than half as likely to attend a university. The growth in the APR rose dramatically first in the early 1960s, leveled off for more than a decade, and then rose sharply again during the 1980s (Figure 2).

However, this increase did not significantly change the social class composition of the student body. It was expected by many that the polytechnics, which were primarily planned to meet local demands for access, would eventually broaden the social class distribution. However, recent research has shown that in 1977, half the public sector student population was still from social class I and II (which comprised only 25% of the overall population) and was not very different in socioeconomic composition from the student populations at the universities. In essence, "social drift" accompanied "academic drift" (Archer, Hutchings & Ross, 2003).

These issues were re-addressed in the Dearing Report, which published an analysis of participation rates by socio-economic group (Figure 3):

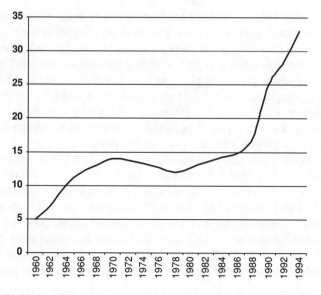

Figure 2. UK Higher Education Age Participation Index. *Source*. Dearing (chart 3.5), 1997.

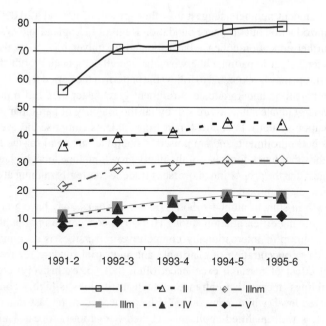

Figure 3. Changes in the Age Participation Index for each Socio-economic Class, 1991–95 England. *Source*. Dearing (chart 3.8), 1997.

These and other trends considered by Dearing clearly demonstrated that the beneficiaries of the growth in the APR since 1960 have been primarily the middle classes, and that the rate of growth for lower social classes, while steady, has been much slower. This issue became politically important with the publication of the 2003 White Paper, and the government is putting in place an Office of Fair Access and requiring that HEIs prepare strategic plans as to how they will address access issues, with the proviso that permission to charge up to £3,000 fees will be conditional on such plans being approved. Such plans are expected to provide statements as to bursary schemes that HEIs will create to support widening participation rates.

In some other respects, however, the changes in the APR can be shown to have increased equity. In 1938, it has been estimated that the age participation rate for women was about 0.5% compared to 3.5% for men. The APR between the sexes became equal in 1992 and by 2001 women had taken a 5% lead over men. While there remains a disproportionate number of men in certain subjects—like physics, chemistry, engineering, medicine and dentistry—women made up 10% of the overall student population in 1960 and 53% in 1999. During the period 1984 to 1993, mature student numbers (full-time and part-time) doubled and more than doubled again by the year 2000.

Prospects for the UK Higher Education System

Forecasts of student numbers suggest a further growth of around 120,000 (10%) by 2010. The introduction of two-year Foundation Degrees in England and Wales, mostly taught in further education colleges but validated by universities, may also have the effect of widening participation. Otherwise, the overall composition of the UK student body of the future may be expected to follow the pattern of the period from 1996 to 2001, wherein the part-time undergraduate enrollment grew faster than full-time (although full-time undergraduate students are still by far the majority of participants in the UK higher education system). In contrast, part-time students comprise the overwhelming bulk of graduate enrollment, and are poised to continue this trend for the foreseeable future. On the other hand, forecasts of the likely growth in the global higher education market suggest that the proportion of overseas students, currently running at 10%, could very well increase significantly.

This growth in student numbers, both UK and overseas, may have a dramatic impact on the growing differentiation among HEIs. The concentration of public research funding in a group of internationally competitive universities is accompanied by a complementary concentration of charitable and industrial funding for research. The reputational effect of research excellence, often (but not exclusively) coupled with historic buildings, means that entrance to such institutions is highly competitive at the first degree level, while many other HEIs are dependent on last-minute decision making by less well qualified applicants. United Kingdom/European Union student number targets must be agreed upon by each institution and its Funding Council, and any agreement to allow these institutions to expand numbers can disadvantage the others, especially in areas (like some science and technology subjects) where there are fewer applicants. The lack of research funding in many post-1992 universities and their necessary concentration on local, socially disadvantaged students creates a significant differentiation between them and the research intensive universities.

It remains to be seen whether the 2003 White Paper recommendation for a category of "teaching only" universities will be realized, possibly from the upgrading of some of the higher education colleges. However, the disparities of funding between the two "ends" of the system seem likely to make generalizations about the system more difficult as the years go by. Similarly, the different policies employed in Scotland and Wales from those in England are likely to produce new kinds of differentiation within the United Kingdom. The higher education system thus seems to be on a path towards less homogeneity, a greater influence from the market, and a continued separation of function between higher education institutions.

References

Archer, L., Hutchings, M., & Ross, A. (2003). *Higher education and social class*. London: Routledge-Falmer.

IMHE/OECD. (2004). *On the edge: Securing a sustainable future for higher education*. National Study, England. Paris: OECD.

The National Committee of Inquiry into Higher Education. (1997). *Higher education in the learning society* (the Dearing Report). London: The Stationary Office.

Pratt, J. & Burgess, T. (1974). *Polytechnics: a report*. London: Pitman.

Robertson, D. & Hillman, J. (1997). *Widening participation in higher education for students from lower socio-economic groups and students with disabilities*. Report No. 6 for the National Commission of Inquiry into Higher Education. London: The Stationary Office.

Truscott, B. (1943). *Redbrick university*. London: Faber and Faber.

55

UNITED STATES

Peter D. Eckel and Jacqueline E. King
American Council on Education, USA

U.S. higher education borrows its structure from both the British undergraduate college and German research university, but its character is profoundly influenced by three major philosophical beliefs that shape American public life.[1] Shaped by the Jeffersonian ideals of limited government and freedom of expression, states, religious communities, and individuals established and maintain a range of higher education institutions and continue to protect these institutions from the levels of government control seen in most other countries. The second set of influences is capitalism and belief in the rationality of markets. American colleges and universities vie for students, faculty, and funding under the assumption that diversity and high quality are best achieved through competition rather than centralized planning. The final major philosophical influence on American higher education is a widespread commitment to equal opportunity and social mobility. Higher education was an elite activity for much of its history, excluding individuals based on gender, religion, race/ethnicity, and social class. However, during the 20th century, economic and social changes transformed higher education into a primary gateway to the middle-class, and women and minorities made inroads against long-standing exclusion from mainstream higher education. Americans came to view broad access to higher education as a necessary component of the nation's ideal as a "land of opportunity." Higher education responded by broadening access. Indeed, the one uniquely American type of institution—the community college—was founded in the 20th century to ensure open access to higher education for individuals of all ages, preparation levels, and incomes.

Guided by these beliefs, U.S. higher education reflects essential elements of the American character: independence, suspicion of government, ambition, inclusiveness, and competitiveness. This chapter will describe the major characteristics of American higher education and important issues that challenge it, linking back as appropriate to these essential philosophical underpinnings.

The Distinctive Characteristics of U.S. Higher Education

Because American higher education is so diverse and complex, any description of "standard practice" inevitably misstates much about individual colleges and

James J.F. Forest and Philip G. Altbach (eds.), International Handbook of Higher Education, 1035–1053.
© 2006 *Springer. Printed in the Netherlands.*

universities. Indeed, important exceptions to most of the characteristics described in this chapter exist. Nonetheless, this section provides an overview of how most colleges and universities are governed and financed, their students and faculty, and the nature of the curriculum and student life.

Size and Composition of U.S. Higher Education

In addition to diversity, autonomy, competition, and accessibility, size is a distinguishing feature of U.S. higher education. The U.S. Department of Education counts 6,500 postsecondary institutions that participate in its student financial aid programs, including 4,200 colleges and universities that award degrees and 2,300 institutions that award vocational certificates. These 6,500 institutions enrolled approximately 16 million full- and part-time students, including 14 million undergraduates and 2 million graduate and professional students, in the fall of 2001. The 4,200 colleges and universities awarded more than 2.4 million degrees in academic year 2000–2001. In addition, an untold number of other institutions offer postsecondary instruction of some type but do not choose to participate in the federal student aid programs and therefore are not counted by the federal government (U.S. Department of Education, 2003).

Degree-granting institutions are typically divided into four major groups, and a considerable amount of diversity exists within each group.

Community colleges. America's 1,100 public 2-year institutions, or community colleges, enroll the largest share of undergraduates (6 million students in 2001). These institutions award associate degrees (which are typically completed in two years) in academic and vocational fields, prepare students for transfer to 4-year institutions, and serve their communities by providing a wide array of educational services. These services range from specialized training for large employers, to English language instruction for recent immigrants, to recreational courses. Almost four million students attended community colleges part-time in 2001. The U.S. government does not track enrollment figures for noncredit adult education or recreational courses, but the American Association of Community Colleges estimates that an additional five million students enroll in these types of courses at community colleges every year.

Public colleges and universities. There are only 630 four-year public colleges and universities in the United States (meaning they award bachelor's degrees, which are typically completed in four years, although many of these award graduate degrees as well). But these institutions—which include regional comprehensive universities that concentrate on undergraduate teaching and graduate preparation in professional fields such as teaching and business, as well as research universities that offer a comprehensive set of undergraduate, graduate, and professional degree programs—enrolled 6.2 million students in 2001. This figure includes five million undergraduates and slightly more than 1 million graduate students.[2]

Private colleges and universities. Private not-for-profit institutions are extremely diverse, including research universities, 4-year liberal arts colleges that focus on

Table 1. U.S. Postsecondary Institutions and Enrollments: Fall 2001

	Public	Private Not-For-Profit	Private For-Profit	Total
Institutions	2,099	1,941	2,418	6,458
4 year	629	1567	324	2,520
2 year	1,165	269	779	2,213
Less than 2 year	305	105	1,315	1,725
Enrollment	12,370,079	3,198,354	765,701	16,334,134
4 year	6,236,486	3,120,472	321,468	9,678,426
2 year	6,047,445	63,207	241,617	6,352,269
Less than 2 year	86,148	14,675	202,616	303,439

Source: U.S. Department of Education, National Center for Education Statistics.

undergraduate teaching, a small number of 2-year institutions, faith-based institutions that maintain strong links with religious denominations, women's colleges, historically black colleges and universities, and specialized institutions that focus on a single field such as nursing or performing arts. Private not-for-profit institutions enrolled 3.2 million students in 2001, including 2.3 million undergraduates and more than 700,000 graduate students.

For-profit institutions. For-profit institutions primarily offer vocational programs that result in certificates rather than degrees.[3] Of the more than 2,400 for-profit institutions counted by the U.S. Department of Education, 500 offer 2-year associate degrees and 320 offer bachelor's and/or graduate degrees. In total, for-profit institutions enrolled more than 750,000 students in 2001, all but 50,000 of whom were at the undergraduate level.

Table 1 provides an overview of enrollment in each of these four sectors. This large number and wide range of institutions offer both access and choice—two hallmarks of American higher education that respond to the previously described value placed on opportunity and faith in the market.

Governance

Another of the philosophical underpinnings of U.S. higher education is the Jeffersonian notion of limited and, whenever possible, locally controlled government. Based on this model, the U.S. Constitution reserves for the states all government functions not specifically described as federal. Among those functions is education. As a result, each of the 50 states is responsible for governing public colleges and universities (which enroll 75% of the nation's students), rather than the federal government. The degree of control by the states varies tremendously. Some institutions, such as the University of California and the University of Michigan, enjoy constitutional autonomy as separate branches of state government. At the other extreme, locally elected boards of trustees govern some community colleges. In some states, a governing board appointed by the governor and/or legislature oversees all institutions, setting funding levels, establishing accountability measures, setting policies, and approving new academic programs. In others, the state board plays only an advisory function and has little direct authority over institutions. In many others, a state agency is poised between the institutions and state government, implementing statewide policy but also attempting to insulate institutions from ill-advised or overly intrusive state policies.

Some public universities are part of statewide multi-campus systems in which an additional layer of oversight exists between the campus and state government. System administrators may oversee campus budgets, set policies such as admissions standards, coordinate degree programs, and facilitate credit transfer and articulation between the state's public colleges and universities. They additionally, and importantly, advocate to the legislature on behalf of public colleges and universities. In some states, more than one multi-campus system exists, such as California's distinct systems of community colleges, comprehensive state colleges and universities, and research universities.

Because of the constitutional restriction on the federal role in education, the United States has never had an education ministry, such as those found in most other countries. With the important exception of the Morrill Land Grant Act of 1862, which donated federal territory to the states for the establishment of public universities, the federal government played almost no role in higher education until the middle of the 20th century, when World War II necessitated the establishment of federal funding for scientific research at colleges and universities to build U.S. military capacity. In 1944, President Franklin Roosevelt signed the GI Bill of Rights, which granted returning veterans funding to attend college as a way to integrate servicemen back into the U.S. workforce. As the Civil Rights movement took hold in the 1960s, the federal role in supporting students expanded to include grant and loan programs for low- and moderate-income students. Since that time, federal support has expanded so that it is now the primary financer of both scientific research and student financial aid.

While the federal government generally does not provide direct operational support to colleges and universities, this special-purpose funding is an extremely important revenue source and, in turn, has increased the ability of the federal government to influence colleges and universities in areas outside research and financial aid. For example, in order for institutions to participate in the financial aid programs, they must comply with a wide range of federal reporting requirements on topics ranging from teacher preparation to gender equity in intercollegiate athletics. However, despite the growing influence of the federal government, its role is still limited and has not yet intruded into core academic decisions, which are generally left to the institutions and, in the case of some public institutions, the states.

Two sets of voluntary organizations act as bulwarks against excessive government control of higher education: accrediting organizations that monitor quality assurance, and membership associations that represent institutions to the federal and state governments. Accrediting organizations are composed of volunteers who work at colleges and universities and agree to assist other institutions by providing evaluation through peer review. There are three types of accrediting organizations: regional organizations, that review the quality of entire institutions and focus almost exclusively on public and private not-for-profit degree-granting institutions; national organizations, that monitor the quality of for-profit and non-degree-granting institutions; and specialized accrediting organizations, that evaluate academic programs within a specific field such as medicine, law or teacher education.

American accreditation differs from the type of quality assurance conducted by governments in most other countries. Federal and state governments can and do impose their own accountability requirements on institutions, but they generally have left the assessment of academic quality to institutions themselves through the self-study and peer review processes of accreditation. The federal government, in particular, relies on recognized regional and national accreditation organizations to determine whether institutions are of sufficient academic quality and managerial soundness to merit inclusion in the federal student financial aid programs. When the U.S. Department of Education officially recognizes an accrediting organization, it certifies that the organization adequately monitors quality in areas mandated by the federal government, such as fiscal soundness and managerial competence, fair admissions, and recruiting practices, and evidence of student success.

Accrediting organizations establish minimum standards that institutions must meet in a range of areas such as the curricula, faculty qualifications, student learning outcomes, co-curricular students services, and financial health. Accrediting organizations do not, however, mandate how institutions go about meeting those standards. Further, because accreditation measures institutions against a set of standards, it generally does not provide a gauge of how well an institution is performing relative to other institutions. Accreditation is accomplished through institutional self-study and a peer review process to determine whether the institution has met the organization's standards. Accreditors typically review institutions on a 3- to 5-year basis (Eaton, 2000).

Membership associations, which can have either institutions or individuals (such as business officers) as members, represent the interests of colleges and universities to the federal government and, in some cases, state governments. Many colleges and universities also employ their own staff to advocate for them, but in most cases, those staff work only on issues of concern to the individual institution, such as state appropriations or federal research contracts for the institution. Membership associations champion those public policies that are in the collective best interest of either all or some major segment of higher education. In Washington, DC, colleges and universities are represented by hundreds of organizations, which also provide networking and professional development opportunities for their members.

Finance

Colleges and universities are financed in ways consistent with both the Jeffersonian ideal of limited government and the belief that market competition tends to improve quality and efficiency. While government plays a very important role in financing, American colleges and universities are supported further by diverse revenue sources that reflect the market choices of students and parents as well as other consumers of the goods and services that institutions provide. The major sources of revenue include tuition and fee payments from students and families (including the government-backed financial aid that students use to pay tuition); appropriations, grants, and contracts from federal, state, and local governments; private gifts; endowment and other investment earnings; and sales from auxiliary enterprises and services.

Some of these sources are more important to some types of institutions than to others. For example, local governments account for 18% of revenue at community colleges but 1% of revenue at private not-for-profit institutions. Similarly, private gifts contribute 14% of revenue to private not-for-profit institutions, but only 1% of revenue to community colleges (U.S. Department of Education, 2003). While the revenue sources of American institutions are diverse, two sources are of particular importance to most institutions: state appropriations, particularly for public institutions, and tuition and fees. These two sources (along with local appropriations at community colleges and federal research grants and contracts at research universities) provide the bulk of funds for general operating expenses. One of the perennial questions in American higher education finance is how much of the cost of education should be borne by government, and how much by students and families.

Traditionally, state appropriations have made up the bulk of institutional revenue at public institutions, but they are diminishing both as a share of state expenditures and as a percentage of institutional revenue. In response, state governments and public institutions have raised tuition, shifting the responsibility from taxpayers to students. In most states, higher education is the third largest item in the budget, after health care and elementary/secondary education. Because health care costs are escalating rapidly and voters demand that spending on elementary/secondary schools be protected, higher education falls logically into legislators' sights when they're forced to make budget cuts. Not only does higher education represent a significant portion of state budgets, but (unlike other programs such as prisons) it has a natural alternative source of revenue—tuition payments from parents and students. Typically, in good economic times, states will raise appropriations to colleges and universities and demand that, in return, institutions keep tuition increases low. When the economy is in trouble and state tax revenue falls, states cut spending on higher education and expect institutions to make up the difference through tuition increases.

Private donations from individuals and corporations provide another source of revenue for American colleges and universities that is typically not found outside the United States. Total voluntary support for higher education, encouraged by the U.S. tax structure, surpassed $23 billion in fiscal year 2003, of which $11 billion was donated by individuals (Council for the Aid to Education, 2004). To this end, many colleges and universities construct sophisticated approaches to fundraising, and college and university presidents dedicate much of their time to raising private gifts.

A significant and growing set of expenditures at many private not-for-profit institutions is institutional financial aid, sometimes called "tuition discounting." Private colleges have a long tradition of providing financial assistance to low-income students. In addition, most of these institutions (and, increasingly, many public institutions as well) have turned to institutional financial aid to attract students who may be able to pay the full price but who are unwilling to attend without a discount. For some institutions, tuition discounting is a way to compete with other institutions for the "best and brightest." For others, it is a necessary practice that fills enrollment places that otherwise would remain vacant. In either case, these discounts contribute to increases in the posted or "sticker price."

All institutions face real increases in the cost of providing education. Technology and equipment costs are rising, as are the prices of journals and books, health care for employees, and building maintenance. Institutions are working to update and expand facilities and services to meet student demand for state-of-the-art technology, small class sizes, and world-class academic and recreational facilities.

In the face of these increased costs and reduced revenue from states and other sources, universities and colleges have three options. They can cut back, improve efficiencies, and/or generate new revenue. For the most part, institutions are engaged in some combination of all three. They cut back by reducing staff travel and equipment purchases, postponing salary increases, leaving vacant faculty, and administrative positions, reducing administrative and support staff, and postponing building and renovation. Rarely do institutions cut academic programs.

Institutions also strive to become more efficient. Much of this effort focuses on administrative and student service functions, such as lowering electrical usage, streamlining purchasing and procurement processes, and altering financial systems. Some institutions are pursuing efficiencies in academic areas, such as using technology to reach more students, increasing class size, and hiring adjunct instructors. However, most efficiencies are being sought outside the classroom. Finally, American colleges and universities are pursuing many efforts to diversify and expand their revenue streams, such as developing online education and niche-oriented degree, and non-degree academic programs, expanding research capacities, engaging in licensing and sponsorship agreements, and pursuing auxiliary enterprises, such as managing real estate and running conference centers. Because a primary source of additional revenue is student tuition and fees, over the past 20 years they have risen at twice the rate of inflation, outstripping increases in both family income and financial aid resources.

The implications of increasing prices for students and families are a matter of constant policy debate. Despite tuition increases, demand for higher education continues to increase. Further, a wide array of government and private financial aid programs provide assistance to students, based on both financial need and academic merit. Financial aid to students totaled more than $105 billion in 2002–2003, including $71 billion in federal grants, loans, and tax credits; $6 billion in state grants; and $20 billion in grants provided by colleges and universities, as well as private organizations (College Board, 2003). Despite these resources, access and success in higher education continue to be stratified according to income, with students at the upper end of the income spectrum far more likely to attend college and earn a degree than those from disadvantaged backgrounds. Of course, many factors play into college access and success, not the least of which is students' level of prior academic preparation. Because the quality of U.S. elementary and secondary schools varies widely depending on the wealth of communities, tuition prices alone cannot be blamed for disparities in educational opportunity. However, even if low-income students are able to overcome the academic and financial barriers to enrolling in college, their ability to succeed once enrolled can be impeded because they must work and attend part-time in order to pay their tuition, suggesting that financial matters play a crucial role.

Students

Despite increases in the price of attending college, the American student population continues to grow rapidly both in size and diversity. As noted previously, there are more than 16 million individuals seeking degrees at U.S. postsecondary institutions, and an estimated 5 million additional students enrolled in noncredit courses. American college students are diverse in age, race/ethnicity, gender, socioeconomic status, and academic interests. The majority of undergraduate students are women, and one-third are racial or ethnic minorities. More than 40% are age 25 or older (U.S. Department of Education, 2002b). About 20% come from families with incomes at or below the federal poverty level (King, 2004). Three out of four American college students are considered *nontraditional*—that is, they possess one or more of the following characteristics: they are age 25 or older, have delayed entry into higher education after completing high school, did not earn a traditional high school diploma, are married, attend part-time, work full-time, or have children (U.S. Department of Education, 2002a). Approximately 80% of students work during the academic year. Half attend part-time (U.S. Department of Education, 2002b).

In part because most nontraditional students juggle college attendance with work and family responsibilities, it is becoming increasingly unusual for students to enroll at one institution and remain there for their entire undergraduate career. Nearly 60% of bachelor's degree recipients attend more than one institution. In about half of these cases, the student formally transfers from one institution to another. The most common form of transfer is from a community college to a 4-year institution. In the remaining half of these cases, students may maintain their primary enrollment at one institution but also take classes at other institutions, sometimes attending two different institutions simultaneously. Students also may move among multiple institutions, often suspending enrollment (or "stopping out") for some period before enrolling at a new institution.

This student mobility is possible because the American system of higher education uses a common "currency" to measure academic progress—the credit. Students earn credits toward their degrees by completing courses. These credits can then typically be transferred to another institution if the receiving institution agrees that the academic rigor and material in the courses is roughly equivalent to its own similar courses. Many institutions develop transfer or articulation agreements to help facilitate student mobility, determining in advance which courses are of equivalent value. Institutions struggle to balance the goal of expanding access by allowing students to take classes where and when they want with the need to maintain the academic integrity of their degree programs and capture much-needed tuition revenue.

Although American college students enjoy a level of mobility unknown to most of their peers around the world, they still must compete for admission to the more selective colleges and universities. American higher education includes institutions with a wide range of admissions selectivity, from open-access 2- and 4-year institutions that admit all students, to highly selective research universities and liberal arts colleges that admit only a small fraction of those who apply. Many students apply to more than one college or university and enroll in one from among those that offer them admission. Admissions decisions at selective institutions are based on a fixed set of academic criteria, including high school coursework, grade point average and class rank, and admissions test score, as well as a more flexible set of nonacademic characteristics, such as demonstrated leadership ability, creativity, and community service. Because the United States has no national secondary school curriculum or high school exit examination, colleges rely on two privately developed admissions examinations—the SAT and ACT. These tests, while important, are only one criterion among many that institutions consider. Indeed, the admissions decisions at highly selective institutions are so complex and consider so many factors that wealthy families often hire private admissions counselors to help them anticipate which factors a given institution is likely to weigh most heavily and to help their child craft an application that best meets those criteria.

Consistent with American faith in the market, institutions compete heavily to attract the most talented students. While this competition spurs improvements in quality and keeps institutions focused on meeting student needs, it also can have negative effects, sometimes prompting institutions to make academic and financial choices that may improve student recruitment but that are inconsistent with the institution's mission, the best interests of the public, or the long-term financial health of the enterprise.

The Curriculum and Degrees

Five types of degrees exist in the United States. Two-year colleges (community colleges) and a small number of 4-year institutions grant associate degrees, typically awarded after the completion of 60 credits. Associate degrees may represent a terminal degree in a vocational field or may prepare students to complete a bachelor's degree at a 4-year institution. The bachelor's degree is by far the most common type of degree awarded, preparing students for most jobs that require a college degree and for further graduate study. Three degrees exist at the graduate level:

(1) The master's degree is the most common type of graduate degree. About 75% of graduate students are enrolled in master's degree programs, divided roughly evenly among students in education, business administration, and all other fields (U.S. Department of Education, 2002c). A master's degree may have either a professional or theoretical focus and usually requires a comprehensive examination and/or thesis or other original piece of work. The master's degree either prepares graduates for future advanced study at the doctoral level or is itself a terminal degree.

(2) Professional degrees provide access to advanced professions in fields such as law and medicine.

(3) The doctoral degree is the highest academic award and recognizes the graduate's ability to conduct independent research. The most common degree of this type is the doctor of philosophy (Ph.D.), but it also includes the doctor of education (Ed.D.).

No national laws govern the titles of degrees, although each state typically regulates the level of degree that institutions located within its borders can award. Each institution has the autonomy to determine its own program requirements, typically following broad degree guidelines set by the states or by specialized accrediting agencies.

The undergraduate curriculum typically consists of two components—general education and the major field of study (the major). The purpose of general education is to provide students with broad knowledge and prepare them to be engaged and informed citizens. General education is delivered predominantly through either a core curriculum, in which all undergraduate students take the same courses, or an elective or distributive format, in which students choose courses from a pre-specified list representing a range of topics (such as science, art and aesthetic appreciation, mathematics, humanities, etc.). General education requirements typically constitute between one-quarter to one-half of a student's courses, depending upon the institution and the student's major. The other courses include those related to the major. Students choose their major (depending on their institution's policy) either upon enrolling or after completing their first or second year of studies. Students may change their majors if their interests change and still use most of their credits earned toward the completion of their degree.

Although most institutions continue to rely on a traditional nine-month (two semesters) academic calendar, many colleges and universities are innovating with their academic calendars, and additionally offer short month-long courses, overlapping semesters, and courses in a condensed weekend format, as they try to create programs that meet student needs and schedules.

Faculty and Their Appointments

More than 1 million academic staff (faculty) work at American colleges and universities. Faculty appointments may be full-time or part-time and may be tenured/tenure-track or nontenured track. Tenure is an academic employment arrangement, granted after a probationary period, that ensures holders a series of rights, including academic freedom and participation in institutional governance. It often implies continuous employment, barring dismissals for cause or financial exigency. However, not all academic positions carry tenure. See Table 2 for a list of faculty titles in the tenure and nontenure tracks.

Faculty responsibilities typically fall into three basic categories: teaching, research, and service to the campus and/or community. However, faculty jobs are by no means

Table 2.   Faculty Rank and Titles by Tenure/Nontenure Track

	Tenured/Tenure Track	Nontenure Track
Full-time	Professor	Lecturer
	Associate Professor	Instructor
	Assistant Professor	Professor of Practice
	Research Professor	Research Professor
Part-time	Professor Emeritus	Adjunct Professor
		Lecturer
		Instructor

uniform, and the time and attention that faculty devote to these three roles depend upon the mission of the institution at which they work, their academic discipline, and their rank and career stage. For example, faculty at community colleges more often tend to teach and be engaged in service activities, while many senior faculty at research universities spend more time engaged in research than in the other two areas.

Approximately 38% of all full-time faculty are women, but women hold only 21% of full professorships. At the assistant professor rank, 46% of full-time faculty are women. However, women's larger presence at the junior ranks does not guarantee future proportionality at senior ranks. The number of full-time faculty from racial/ethnic minority groups almost doubled over the last 20 years, yet only 14% of all full-time faculty are racial/ethnic minorities. The largest minority group is Asian American/Pacific Islander, comprising 6% of the total full-time faculty population, with African Americans at 5%, Hispanics at 3%, and Native Americans at less than half of 1% (Harvey, 2003).

In 1999, according to an American Council on Education study (Anderson, 2002), approximately half of all faculty were employed part-time and/or in nontenure-track positions. These faculty include those who are qualified for and seek full-time, tenure-track appointments yet do not obtain them, as well as individuals who do not have doctorates and/or teach in addition to other professional responsibilities. Debate and discussion continues to focus on the increasing use of part-time and nontenure-track faculty. Much of this growth accommodates increasing student enrollments. Another important reason for hiring part-time and nontenure-track faculty is to reduce personnel costs and increase institutional flexibility in course offerings, as these faculty can be hired and fired as interest in their academic fields ebbs and flows. However, critics charge that reliance on part-time and nontenure-track faculty has hidden institutional and educational costs while also lowering quality, as these individuals do little student advising and research and do not participate in non-instructional activities such as faculty governance.

University Administration and Governance

Although the internal organization and structure of U.S. institutions vary based upon size and mission, some common elements exist. Lay boards of trustees who tend not to be academics govern most college and universities. These boards are the legal agents for the institution and are responsible for ensuring and monitoring its financial health, setting strategy to fulfill its mission, and evaluating both institutional and presidential performance. The size, structure, and appointment of boards vary. For example, some boards of private nonprofit institutions can exceed 50 members. Public institution boards tend to be much smaller, consisting of seven or eight members. For most public institutions, the state government typically appoints board members, often after nomination by the governor and approval by the legislature. However, in some states and at many community colleges, board members are chosen through general elections. For private institutions, boards select their own members (called self-perpetuating boards). The length of board members' terms varies from 4 years to as long as 12 years. In some cases, board members can be reappointed to additional terms.

Boards hire and delegate much of the administrative responsibility for running the institution to the president (sometimes called a chancellor). The president is responsible for providing overall leadership to the institution, managing its finances and budget, developing and executing the institution's strategic plan, and establishing systems of accountability and performance. However, much of the president's work lies outside the institution. The president advocates for the institution's needs and seeks support from legislative and other external audiences, meets with alumni and prospective students, develops relationships with corporations and community groups, and provides the public persona of the institution. The president serves either at the pleasure of the board or on a fixed-term contract, eligible for renewal.

Beyond the president, other senior administrators provide the leadership for the institution's various divisions. The typical structure includes academic affairs, responsible for academic programs and research; student affairs, overseeing student services and student life; business and administration, accountable for the financial operations, auxiliary services, and campus facilities; and development, focusing on fundraising and alumni relations. Within each division, a variety of deans, directors, and department chairs complete the administrative structure. Figure 1 provides an overview of a typical college or university administrative structure (American Council on Education, 2001).

Although presidents have primary responsibility for the institution, most rely upon a system of shared governance between faculty and administrators for key institutional decisions. The primary organizational structure for shared governance is the faculty senate. The senate is responsible for recommending academic decisions and policies, such as those affecting new curricula and courses, degree requirements, and academic hiring and workloads. Its members typically include full-time faculty, although students, administrators, staff, and part-time faculty sometimes participate as well. At some institutions, the senate has the ability to make final decisions; at others, the senate makes recommendations for administrative or board action. In smaller institutions, all faculty typically participate in the senate. In larger institutions, senators are elected, frequently representing particular departments or colleges.

Student Life and Athletics

The U.S. collegiate experience is strongly shaped by a residential tradition, although today more than half of undergraduate students are older and/or enrolled part-time, and less than 20% of all undergraduates live on campus. Building upon the foundations of the British residential college, U.S. institutions have developed an expansive infrastructure to meet the needs of students. Most 4-year colleges and universities provide housing for students during the academic year. These residence halls, in addition to providing food service and sleeping rooms, provide programming to students on a variety of topics, both academic and social, such as HIV/AIDS awareness, alcohol abuse, and study skills. Colleges and universities additionally provide a range of student support services, including personal counseling, career placement and advising, recreation and physical fitness, child care, transportation, banking, health care, and tutoring.

Beyond these services, colleges and universities host various student organizations and clubs, including academically focused groups—such as the National Society of

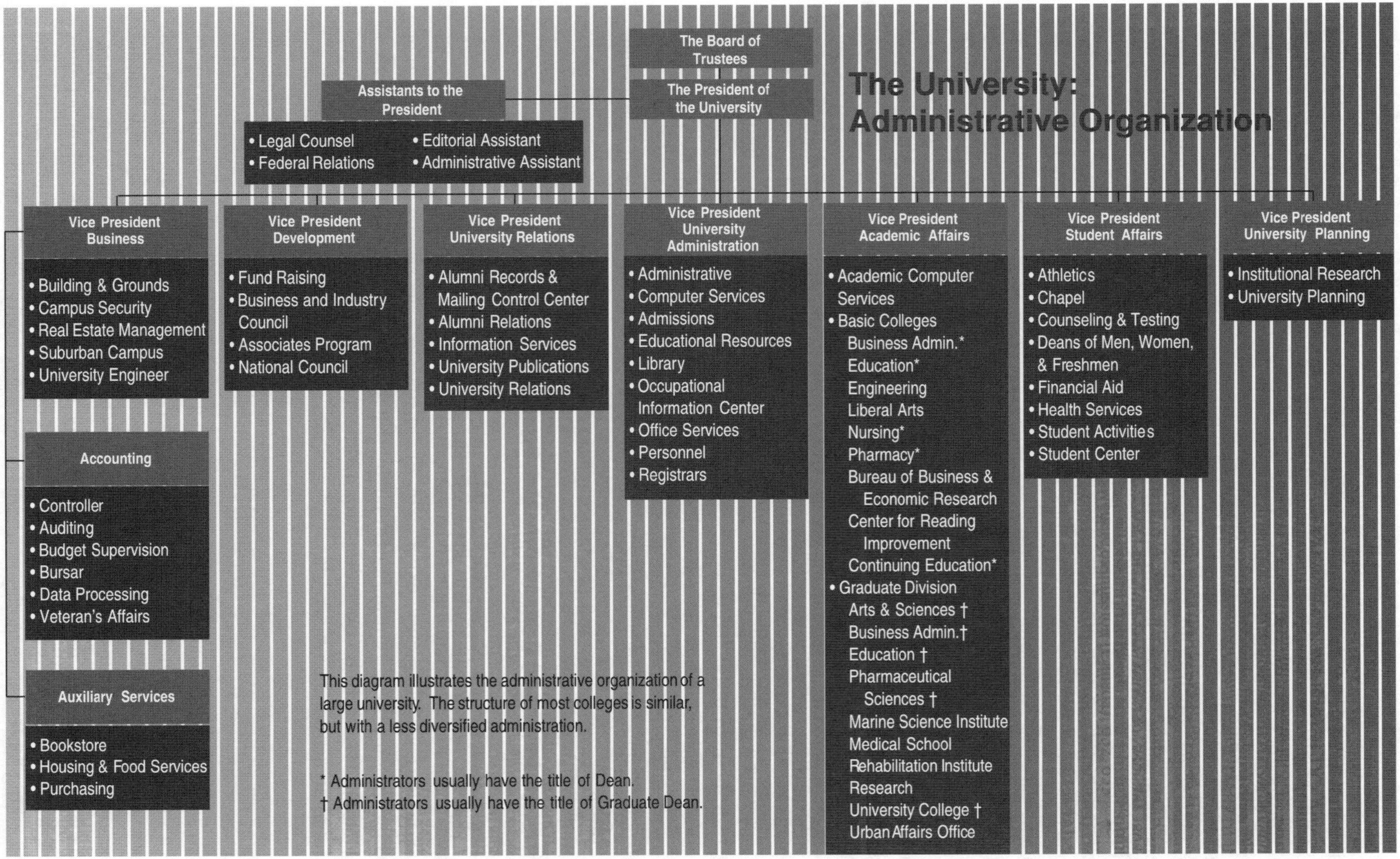

The University: Administrative Organization

The Board of Trustees

The President of the University

Assistants to the President
- Legal Counsel
- Federal Relations
- Editorial Assistant
- Administrative Assistant

Vice President Development
- Fund Raising
- Business and Industry Council
- Associates Program
- National Council

Vice President University Relations
- Alumni Records & Mailing Control Center
- Alumni Relations
- Information Services
- University Publications
- University Relations

Vice President University Administration
- Administrative
- Computer Services
- Admissions
- Educational Resources
- Library
- Occupational
- Information Center
- Office Services
- Personnel
- Registrars

Vice President Academic Affairs
- Academic Computer Services
- Basic Colleges
  - Business Admin.*
  - Education*
  - Engineering
  - Liberal Arts
  - Nursing*
  - Pharmacy*
- Bureau of Business & Economic Research
- Center for Reading Improvement
- Continuing Education*
- Graduate Division
  - Arts & Sciences †
  - Business Admin.†
  - Education †
  - Pharmaceutical Sciences †
- Marine Science Institute
- Medical School
- Rehabilitation Institute
- Research
- University College †
- Urban Affairs Office

Vice President Student Affairs
- Athletics
- Chapel
- Counseling & Testing
- Deans of Men, Women, & Freshmen
- Financial Aid
- Health Services
- Student Activities
- Student Center

Vice President University Planning
- Institutional Research
- University Planning

Vice President Business
- Building & Grounds
- Campus Security
- Real Estate Management
- Suburban Campus
- University Engineer

Accounting
- Controller
- Auditing
- Budget Supervision
- Bursar
- Data Processing
- Veteran's Affairs

Auxiliary Services
- Bookstore
- Housing & Food Services
- Purchasing

This diagram illustrates the administrative organization of a large university. The structure of most colleges is similar, but with a less diversified administration.

* Administrators usually have the title of Dean.
† Administrators usually have the title of Graduate Dean.

Figure 1. A Typical College or University Administrative Structure.

Black Engineers or the Public Relations Student Society of America—as well as athletic (such as rugby and water polo clubs), cultural and religious (such as the Muslim Student Society or Association of Asian Students), and social organizations. A familiar type of student social organization is the Greek-lettered fraternity or sorority. Another important student organization is student government, which is the formal, recognized student advocacy body on campus. However, for the most part, its influence is limited and its agenda constrained, particularly when compared with similar student governments or student unions in Latin America and Europe.

Finally, any discussion of student life at American colleges and universities must include athletics, which plays a major role on many—but not all—campuses. The influence of athletics on campuses tends to be disproportional to the small number of student athletes. At institutions with "big-time" sports programs, the athletics budget can reach millions of dollars, dwarfing those of academic departments, and coaches of men's basketball and football teams are frequently the university's highest paid employees. At these institutions, athletic teams are divided into revenue sports (football, men's and increasingly women's basketball, and in some cases, ice hockey) and non-revenue sports (for example, track and field, swimming, wrestling, golf, tennis, field hockey, and soccer).[4] The majority of student-athletes participate in the non-revenue sports. The revenue sports tend to be highly commercialized, garnering national television coverage and athletic apparel endorsement deals. Athletics on U.S. campuses is a double-edged sword. In some situations, it can provide a unifying catalyst for the institution and its community and teach its participants valuable lessons. In other situations, it has been described as an unstoppable "arms race" exemplifying a winner-take-all attitude, spurring scandal, academic dishonesty, excessive commercialization, abuse of student-athletes, and distraction from the institution's academic priorities.

Current Challenges Confronting U.S. Higher Education

The introduction to this chapter described the fundamental belief systems that shape the character of American higher education and distinguish it from higher education in other countries. This section expands on that discussion, describing how the inherent tensions among these central beliefs have created serious challenges for U.S. higher education. The section concludes with a short overview of additional issues on the national higher education agenda.

The Marketplace (Not Government) As Key External Driver

Many believe that the marketplace has overtaken government as the dominant external force shaping (and reshaping) American higher education, even for public colleges and universities. As noted earlier, government support is not keeping pace with educational expenditures. Thus in many ways, the market is having more bearing on higher education than government. To create more flexibility, many public colleges and universities are asking for less government regulation and oversight. In some instances, they are even asking for less state money in return for more autonomy. Their argument is that the current structures and accountability requirements impede their capacity to be effective and efficient. The ability to set tuition, seek block-grant funding, and secure freedom from state policies and regulations in areas such as purchasing and building represent just some of the additional autonomy that public institutions are seeking. Many are pressing for new legislation to provide this freedom through a range of innovations, including public corporations, charter colleges, state enterprise status and performance contracts.

The result is that activities and research in certain fields and disciplines (such as engineering, applied natural science, and agricultural science) become higher institutional priorities because they have stronger market value than do other programs (such as humanities). Institutions create new programs, alter academic calendars, and pursue different financial aid policies to capture more and better students—particularly those who can afford to pay high tuition prices. For instance, executive master's of business administration (MBA) programs are increasingly popular. Institutions seek contracts and partnership agreements, and enhance research programs with practical applications that have large financial payouts. They are changing their institutional structures—for example, by adding new units that focus on generating external grants and bringing new technology to market, by building conference centers, and by creating for-profit subsidiaries. The implications of the growing privatization are that academic research is increasingly focused on marketable knowledge, entrepreneurial priorities are taking precedent, services are being outsourced, and students are carrying an increasing burden to pay higher tuition and fees for their education.

Administrators see little option except to respond to the marketplace, for if their institution doesn't react effectively, it will not have the necessary resources to offer high-quality and diverse academic programs. Institutions unable to compete may face trying circumstances as public support continues to fall, students become better-informed consumers, and advances in technology and new entrants into higher education widen the number and reach of competitors. In turn, the ability to compete—for students, resources, faculty and prestige—becomes a driving strategic force. At its extreme, competition can overtake more traditional academic values such as unfettered inquiry, access and choice for a diverse student population, and critical social commentary. The downside of pursing market goals without appropriately balancing them against the public good is that institutions will no longer be able to uphold their part of the social compact to produce a well-educated citizenry and face the threat of losing their privileged place in American society as they resemble more closely other market-driven organizations.

Higher Education As an Engine of Mobility

Since World War II, U.S. higher education has been engaged in a process of "massification," that is, expanding to serve students from all walks of life. Motivating this effort is a widespread belief in the power of education to create social and economic mobility and in the morality and social value of making higher education accessible to everyone. Longitudinal data bear out public perceptions: young people from low-income backgrounds who complete a bachelor's degree have income and employment characteristics after graduation equivalent to their peers from more affluent backgrounds (Choy, 2002). Education truly can be "the great equalizer."

Despite widespread public faith in the value of higher education, the process of massification has not been without its detractors, and progress has been slow and uneven. Higher education did not admit significant numbers of racial and ethnic minorities until after the Civil Rights movement of the 1960s forced change. Further, despite significant expenditures on financial aid, minority and low-income individuals are still less likely to attend college than whites or students from middle- and upper-income families—although these gaps have narrowed somewhat. Despite progress in narrowing the access discrepancies, large gaps remain between completion rates. Low-income students come to college less prepared, are concentrated at community colleges and other large public institutions that do not have the resources to offer students much individual assistance and attention, and must balance student demands with work and family responsibilities.

Finding ways to increase the enrollment rates of low-income students and encourage their success once enrolled are two of the most important problems facing American higher education. One of the challenges to meeting these goals is that they can conflict with the other central tenets of American higher education: market competition and resistance to government control. For example, institutional competition for the most academically talented students is likely to foster increased use of tuition discounting for students without financial need, which could divert resources away from need-based financial aid for low-income students. Similarly, institutions may seek to distinguish themselves in the academic marketplace by becoming more selective in admissions decisions, thereby reducing the number of low-income students admitted. A primary role of government in the United States is to mediate the potentially negative effects of competition by insisting that institutions adhere to their missions, providing need-based financial assistance to students, and holding institutions accountable for their performance. Institutional resistance to government control provides a useful check on the ambitions of government, pushing policymakers to focus on ends rather than means and leave core academic decisions largely in the hands of institutions. Nonetheless, a constant preoccupation of American higher education is this tension between the competitive, ambitious nature of institutions and the interests of government in promoting important public goals, primary among them broad access and widespread success for all students.

Current Issues

This section explores some of the other challenges currently facing American higher education. This list is not inclusive, but rather reflects some of the key issues creating sleepless nights for academic leaders.

The blurring of institutional types. American higher education is known for its institutional diversity. However, the characteristics that make many types of institutions distinct are fading. For instance, in some states, community colleges are seeking to offer 4-year degrees to meet growing demand for higher education. Public colleges and universities are in many ways becoming private, as the percentage of state funds in their budgets is dropping—in some cases, to less than 20%. They are soliciting gifts and working to build endowments in ways similar to their private counterparts, and are seeking more procedural autonomy from state oversight. At the same time, for-profit institutions are vying for public funds previously reserved only for nonprofit institutions.

Documenting student learning. American colleges and universities are facing increased external scrutiny of the effectiveness of undergraduate education. As budgets become tighter and tuition continues to rise, taxpayers and policymakers—as well as students and their families—are asking the extent to which their investment is producing real educational results. Simply put, they want to know what and how much students are learning. Outside pressure is mounting on institutions to document student learning, in much the same way that the elementary and secondary education sectors document learning through assessments linked to standards of what students should know and be able to do. Of course, the challenge of demonstrating student learning is much more difficult in higher education because of the diversity of the curricula. Nonetheless, higher education leaders are being challenged to find some way to show that real learning takes place at their institutions.[5]

Internationalizing the undergraduate experience. Many U.S. colleges and universities are making a concerted effort to make their institutions and curricula more international and to provide experiences for students that broaden and deepen their understanding of other cultures. At the same time, U.S. institutions continue their efforts to train and educate foreign students, both by bringing them to campus but also through distance education and satellite programs abroad (although we do not know the extent of U.S. involvement in such cross-border education). However, recent U.S. immigration policy changes coupled with an increased desire by foreign universities to recruit abroad means that the U.S. share of the international student market is shrinking. Institutions from England, Australia, Canada and New Zealand, for instance, are establishing a presence abroad and benefiting favorably from their government's policies. The effect is slowed growth in the number of international students enrolling in American colleges and universities.

Increasing productivity and efficiency. Because of increasing pressure to reduce costs, keep tuition increases small, and serve more students, institutions are seeking ways to improve their productivity and efficiency. They are creating administrative efficiencies, such as by streamlining business processes. They are innovating with technology-based teaching to reach more students both on campus and in the broader community through distance education. Many institutions are also beginning to view collaboration as an important strategy. Partnerships include (among other things) joint research, collaborative purchasing arrangements, shared financial services, and inter-institutional academic programs. These alliances allow partners to extend capabilities; develop research, courses, and services more quickly; generate greater economies of scale; share costly investments; gain access to knowledge and skills; and reduce expenses.

Conclusion

In many ways, the American system of higher education is unique in the world. In its size, diversity of institutions and students, freedom from government controls, and reliance on market forces, it is without peer. However, higher education systems around the globe are struggling with many of the same issues as the United States and are exploring similar strategies, such as imposing tuition to create greater access while instituting student aid programs, creating a credit system to facilitate student mobility, and standardizing degree programs. Other nations wrestling with these challenges may benefit by understanding the philosophical beliefs that shape U.S. higher education—distrust of government, faith in markets, and reliance on education as a gateway to social mobility—and the ways in which the United States continually struggles to balance market forces, government intervention and access to high-quality education.

Notes

1. In the United States, several important terms differ in meaning from most of the rest of the world. The term *college* refers to an institution that typically awards only undergraduate degrees. The term *faculty* can refer to either an individual professor or to all instructors (e.g., "The Harvard faculty approved a new degree program").
2. The number of graduate and undergraduate students does not add to the total number of students because some students may take courses outside a formal degree program and, in other cases, the degree level of students was not reported.
3. For more information on for-profit higher education, please see the chapter by Kevin Kinser and Dan Levy in volume 1 of this *Handbook*.
4. Much debate exists as to whether or not these sports ultimately generate actual revenue, given their expenditures.
5. For more on this topic, please see the chapter by Elaine El-Khawas in volume 1 of this *Handbook*.

References

American Council on Education. (2001). *A brief guide to U.S. higher education*. Washington, DC: American Council on Education.

Anderson, E. (2002). *The new professoriate: Characteristics, contributions, and compensation*. Washington, DC: American Council on Education.

Choy, S. (2002). *Access and persistence: Findings from 10 years of longitudinal studies of students*. Washington, DC: American Council on Education.

College Board. (2003). *Trends in student aid: 2003*. New York: College Board.

Council for the Aid to Education. (2004). *Charitable giving to higher education stabilizes in 2003: Gifts from alumni rebound after a sharp one-year decline*. Santa Monica, CA: RAND Corporation Council for Aid to Education. Online at: http://www.cae.org/content/pdf/2004FullPressReleaseVSE2003.pdf.

Eaton, J. (2000). *An overview of U.S. accreditation*. Washington, DC: Council for Higher Education Accreditation.

Harvey, W.B. (2003). *Minorities in higher education: Annual status report*. Washington, DC: American Council on Education.

King, J.E. (2004). *Choice of institution: Changing student attendance patterns in the 1990s*. ACE Issue Brief. Washington, DC: American Council on Education.

U.S. Department of Education, National Center for Education Statistics. (2002a). *Findings from the condition of education 2002: Nontraditional undergraduates.* Washington, DC: Government Printing Office.

U.S. Department of Education, National Center for Education Statistics. (2002b). *Profile of undergraduates at U.S. postsecondary institutions: 1999–2000.* Washington, DC: Government Printing Office.

U.S. Department of Education, National Center for Education Statistics. (2002c). *Student financing of graduate and first-professional education, 1999–2000.* Washington, DC: Government Printing Office.

U.S. Department of Education, National Center for Education Statistics. (2003). *Digest of education statistics: 2002.* Washington, DC: Government Printing Office.

ABOUT THE EDITORS

Philip G. Altbach is Director of the Center for International Higher Education and the J. Donald Monan, SJ, Professor of Higher Education in the Lynch School of Education at Boston College. Professor Altbach has extensive experience in the field of comparative and international higher education. He is editor of *The International Academic Profession* (1997), co-editor of *American Higher Education in the 21st Century* (1997), former editor of the ASHE journal, *The Review of Higher Education*, and the editor of *International Higher Education: An Encyclopedia* (2 volumes). He is author of *Comparative Higher Education, Higher Education in the Third World*, and other books. His most recent book is *Asian Universities: Historical Perspectives and Contemporary Challenges* (2004). He also co-edited *In Defense of American Higher Education* with Patricia Gumport and Bruce Johnstone, published in 2001. Professor Altbach holds a doctoral degree from the University of Chicago. His research interests include comparative education, history and philosophy of higher education, international education, student political activism, the academic profession, and knowledge networks.

James J.F. Forest is a civilian faculty member at the U.S. Military Academy, West Point. He has held research and administrative positions in several higher education and government organizations, and most recently served as Assistant Dean for Academic Assessment at West Point. His current research covers issues of individual and organizational knowledge transfer, technology, globalization, non-state actors and international relations. His publications include the 2-volume *Higher Education in the United States: An Encyclopedia* (co-edited with Kevin Kinser, 2002), *I Prefer to Teach: An International Study of Faculty Preference* (2001), and *University Teaching: International Perspectives* (1998), as well as several book chapters and articles in journals such as the *Cambridge Review of International Affairs*, the *Journal of Political Science Education, International Higher Education*, and *Connections: The Journal of the New England Board of Higher Education*. Dr. Forest holds undergraduate degrees from De Anza College and Georgetown University, and graduate degrees from Stanford University and Boston College.

ABOUT THE CONTRIBUTORS

Abbas Bazargan is Professor of Research Methodology and Statistics in the Faculty of Psychology and Education, University of Tehran. He has previously served as Vice Chancellor of Bu-Ali Sina University (Hamadan, Iran) and Vice President of the Institute for Research and Planning in Higher Education (Tehran). He has been an international consultant with UNDP and UNESCO in Asia and Africa, and is a member of the editorial board of the *Higher Education Policy Journal*.

Svava Bjarnason is Director of Research and Strategy at the Association of Commonwealth Universities (ACU) based in London. She also serves as the Director of the Observatory on Borderless Higher Education—an international strategic information service which is an initiative of the ACU and Universities, U.K. A citizen of Canada, she worked as an independent research consultant in higher education from 1994 until she joined the ACU in 1998.

David E. Bloom is the Clarence James Gamble Professor of Economics and Demography at the Harvard School of Public Health and a faculty research associate at the National Bureau of Economic Research. He was formerly Deputy Director of the Harvard Institute for International Development and before that, Chair of the Economics Department at Columbia University. His current research interests include economic growth and development, labor, education, health, and demography. He has also served as Co-Director of the Task Force on Higher Education and Society, a body convened by UNESCO and the World Bank.

José Joaquín Brunner is Professor of the Government School, Universidad Adolfo Ibáñez in Santiago, Chile. His research focuses on comparative education policies and higher education systems. As a consultant to the World Bank and other international organizations, he has worked in more than 20 Latin American, African and Central and Eastern European countries. He is the author or co-author of several books, including *Oferta y demanda de profesionales y técnicos en Chile: El rol de información pública* [Supply and demand for professionals and technicians in Chile: The role of public information] (co-edited with Patricio Meller, 2004).

Hugo Casanova-Cardiel is Professor in the Center for Studies on the University at the National Autonomous University of Mexico, and a member of the National Research System of Mexico. He has been a visiting scholar at the Institute of Latin

American Studies (University of Texas at Austin) and a visiting professor at the University of Barcelona. His research has focused on policy and comparative issues in higher education.

Egbert de Weert is Senior Research Associate at the Center for Higher Education Policy Studies (CHEPS), University of Twente, The Netherlands. His major fields of research concern higher education and employment, human resource policies in higher education, and the academic profession. He is co-editor of the *Dutch Journal for Higher Education*.

Hans de Wit is Senior Advisor International at the University of Amsterdam, the Netherlands. He is the Editor of the *Journal of Studies in International Education*, and has published widely on strategies for internationalization of higher education in Europe, North America, Asia/Pacific and Latin America. He is active as an international higher education consultant for such entities as the OECD Program on Institutional Management in Higher Education, the World Bank, the European Commission, UNESCO/CEPES and the Salzburg Seminar. He is also a co-founder and past president of the European Association for International Education.

Wojciech Duczmal is a lecturer at the Academy of Management and Administration, a private higher education institution in Opole, Poland, and a doctoral student in the Center for Higher Education Policy Studies at the University of Twente, the Netherlands. He completed his earlier graduate studies at the Faculty of Economics in the Warsaw School of Economics, and his current research interests address market dimensions of higher education, private higher education, and financial accountancy.

Peter D. Eckel is the Associate Director for Institutional Initiatives at the American Council on Education. He currently directs a set of projects addressing the challenges of increased competition and changing fiscal realities, and is the primary architect of a new program for newly appointed chief academic officers. His papers appear in many of the leading higher education journals, and he is the lead author of two ACE occasional paper series *On Change* and *The Changing Enterprise*. His most recent books include *Taking the Reins: Transformation in Higher Education* (with Adrianna Kezar, 2003); and *Changing Course: Making the Hard Decisions to Eliminate Academic Programs* (2003).

Elaine El-Khawas is Professor of Education Policy at George Washington University. She previously served as Professor of Higher Education at the University of California, Los Angeles and as Vice President for Policy Analysis and Research at the American Council on Education. A sociologist who earned her master's and doctoral degrees at the University of Chicago, she is a former president of the Association for the Study of Higher Education and a member of the board of trustees of Emmanuel College, and currently serves on the editorial boards of *The Review of Higher Education, Higher Education Management and Policy*, and *Quality in Higher Education*.

Jürgen Enders is Professor and Director of the Center for Higher Education Policy Studies at the University of Twente, the Netherlands. He is a member of the board and Secretary of the Consortium of Higher Education Researchers, and a member of the editorial board of the book series *Higher Education Dynamics* and the journal *Higher Education*. His research interests are in the areas of the sociology of education and the professions, organizational studies, governance and management of higher education and research, higher education and the world of work, and the academic profession.

Iman Farag is Researcher in Political Sociology at the *Centre d'Études et de Documentation Économique, Juridique et Sociale* (Research Center for Economic, Legal and Social Studies) in Cairo, Egypt. His fields of interest concerns the construction of public debates, forms of political mobilization and historical sociology of education.

Ana M. García de Fanelli is Senior Researcher at the National Commission for Scientific and Technological Research, and coordinates the Higher Education Research Department at the Center for the Study of State and Society, Buenos Aires, Argentina. She is also Professor of Argentine Social Structure at the University of Buenos Aires and Professor of Finance in Higher Education at the National University of Mar del Plata and Palermo University.

Grant Harman is Emeritus Professor of Educational Management at the University of New England (Australia), where he has specialized in studies of higher education management and policy. He has special interests in research policy and management, university-industry research links, and intellectual property and the commercialization of research outputs. At the University of New England, he has held the positions of Chair of the Academic Senate and Pro Vice Chancellor (Research). He is also Coordinating Editor of the journal *Higher Education*, published in the Netherlands by Springer.

Matthew Hartley is Assistant Professor of Education at the University of Pennsylvania's Graduate School of Education. He received his doctorate from Harvard University's Graduate School of Education in 2001, where he served as a research assistant, teaching fellow, and co-chair of the *Harvard Educational Review*. His research examines academic governance, organizational change and civic engagement efforts at colleges and universities. His publications include *A Call to Purpose: Mission-Centered Change at Three Liberal Arts Colleges* (2002).

Arthur M. Hauptman has been an independent public policy consultant and author since 1981. He is an internationally recognized expert and has written extensively on issues relating to student financial aid, college costs and higher education finance generally. In the United States, he has consulted with many federal and state agencies, colleges and universities, and associations on policy issues relating to higher education. Internationally, he has worked with governmental and institutional officials in more than a dozen countries to help develop higher education financing strategies. He holds a B.A. in Economics from Swarthmore College and a M.B.A. from Stanford University.

Ruth Hayhoe is Professor at the Ontario Institute for Studies in Education, University of Toronto, and President Emerita of the Hong Kong Institute of Education. Her recent books include *Education, Culture and Identity in Twentieth Century China*, co-edited with Glen Peterson and Yongling Lu (2001), and *Knowledge Across Cultures: A Contribution to Dialogue among Civilizations*, co-edited with Julia Pan (2001).

Linda Herrera is Editor of the *ISIM Review*, a journal of the International Institute for the Study of Islam in the Modern World (a consortium of 4 Dutch universities). An educational anthropologist who specializes in education systems and Islam in the Middle East, her research projects cover topics such as the privatization of higher education and Islamic schooling in Muslim societies. She received her Ph.D. from Columbia University, her M.A. from the American University in Cairo, and her B.A. from the University of California at Berkeley.

Yaacov Iram is Professor of Comparative and International Education at Bar-Ilan University, Israel. He has served as President of the World Association for Educational Research, the Israel Educational Research Association, the Israeli Comparative Education Society, and the Israeli History of Education Association. He currently holds the Dr. Josef Burg Chair in Education for Human Values, Tolerance, and Peace/UNESCO Chair. His research on social issues, multiculturalism and higher education has been published widely in American and European scholarly journals, book chapters, and encyclopedia entries.

N. Jayaram is Professor of Research Methodology at the Tata Institute of Social Sciences, Mumbai, India. He is on the Steering Committee of the International Network on the Role of Universities in Developing Areas and the Editorial Advisory Committee of the Indian Council of Social Science Research. He is Managing Editor of *Sociological Bulletin* (the Journal of the Indian Sociological Society) and Editor of the *ICSSR Journal of Reviews and Abstracts: Sociology and Social Anthropology*. He has published extensively on the sociology of higher education in India, and his books include *Higher Education and Status Retention* (1987), *Sociology of Education in India* (1990), *Social Conflict* (co-edited with Satish Saberwal, 1998), and *The Indian Diaspora* (2004).

Munzali Jibril is Executive Secretary of the National Universities Commission in Nigeria. He holds a master's degree from the University of Leeds, U.K., and a Ph.D. from the University of Lancaster, U.K. He was formerly Dean of the Faculty of Arts and the Postgraduate School at Bayero University, and Provost of the Nigerian Defense Academy in Nigeria.

Glen A. Jones is Professor of Higher Education and Associate Dean (Academic) at the Ontario Institute for Studies in Education, University of Toronto. His research interests focus on higher education systems, government policy and institutional governance. He recently co-edited *Creating Knowledge, Strengthening Nations: The Changing Role of Higher Education* (2005).

Barbara M. Kehm is Professor of Higher Education at Kassel University and Managing Director of the Center for Research on Higher Education and Work. She has previously worked as a senior researcher at the Institute for Higher Education Research in Wittenberg (East Germany), and taught German language and literature at Sussex University (U.K.). Her fields of specialization include issues of internationalization in higher education and higher education governance. She has published numerous books and articles and is a member of the editorial board of four internationally renowned journals in the field of higher education research. She has also served two terms of office on the Executive Committee of the European Association of Institutional Research (EAIR).

George Keller is an education consultant and writer, one of America's leading scholars of higher education, a noted strategic planner, and award-winning editor. He has held senior faculty and administrative positions at Columbia University, the State University of New York system, the University of Maryland system, and the University of Pennsylvania's Graduate School of Education. His publications include *Academic Strategy: The Management Revolution in American Higher Education* (1983), *Transforming a College* (2004), and more than 100 articles and reviews. He also edited the journal *Planning for Higher Education* from 1990 to 1997. He received his undergraduate and graduate degrees at Columbia University.

Jacqueline E. King is the Founding Director of the Center for Policy Analysis at the American Council on Education (ACE). She is the author or co-author of numerous reports, articles, and book chapters including the ACE status reports on the Pell Grant and federal education loan programs, *Gender Equity in Higher Education: Are Male Students at a Disadvantage?* (2003) and *Crucial Choices: How Students' Financial Decisions Affect their Academic Success* (2002). She is also editor of *Financing a College Education: How it Works, How it's Changing* (1999), and co-editor of *Changing Student Attendance Patterns: Implications for Policy and Practice* (2003).

Kevin Kinser is Assistant Professor of Education in the Department of Educational Administration and Policy Studies at the State University of New York at Albany. He received two master's degrees and a doctorate from Columbia University's Teachers College and has taught in the higher education programs at Teachers College and Louisiana State University. His research on non-traditional and alternative higher education has been published in the *Journal of Personnel Evaluation in Education, International Higher Education* and *Innovative Higher Education*, and his recent publications include *Higher Education in the United States: An Encyclopedia* (co-edited with James Forest, 2002), a comprehensive two-volume overview of American postsecondary education since World War II.

Jane Knight is Adjunct Professor at the Ontario Institute for Studies in Education, University of Toronto, where her research and professional interests are focused on the international dimensions of higher education. In addition to her involvement with regional comparative studies of international education (in Latin America, Asia Pacific,

North America, Europe) with OECD and the World Bank, she is currently examining key policy issues such as trade agreements, brain drain, strategic alliances and immigration. She is a member of the editorial board for the *Journal of Studies in International Education* and the *Indian Journal on Higher Education: Policy and Practices.*

Lisa R. Lattuca is Assistant Professor of Higher Education and Research Associate in the Center for the Study of Higher Education at the Pennsylvania State University. In addition to journal articles on curriculum and learning in higher education, she is the author of *Creating Interdisciplinarity: Interdisciplinary Research among College and University Faculty* (2001), co-author (with J. Stark) of *Shaping the College Curriculum: Academic Plans in Action* (1997), and co-editor (with E. Creamer) of *Advancing Faculty Learning through Interdisciplinary Collaboration* (2005).

Molly N.N. Lee is the Coordinator of the Asia-Pacific Program of the Educational Program for Development and Program Specialist in Higher and Distance Education at UNESCO's Asia and the Pacific Regional Bureau for Education in Bangkok. Prior to joining UNESCO Bangkok, she served as Professor of Education in the University of Science, Malaysia. She holds a Ph.D. and a master's degree from Stanford University, and a master's degree from the University of London Institute of Education. She has published extensively on issues and topics relating to education in Malaysia, higher education, teacher education, gender issues, globalization and education.

Daniel Levy is Distinguished Professor in the Department of Educational Administration and Policy Studies at the State University of New York at Albany, where he directs the Program for Research on Private Higher Education (PROPHE). His eight books and over a hundred articles concentrate on higher education policy globally, related nonprofit sectors, or Latin American politics. He has lectured at nearly all the top-ranked U.S. universities and on six continents, and has also consulted for many leading international agencies.

Simon Marginson is Professor of Education and Director of the Monash Center for Research in International Education at Monash University, Australia. He has published widely and participated in policy discussions on higher education in Australia, and is funded as an Australian Professorial Fellow with a research program focused on comparative and international higher education in the context of globalization. He chaired the International Forum of the Association for Studies in Higher Education in 2004–05, and is actively involved in the Conference of Higher Education Researchers (in Europe), the American Educational Research Association, the Comparative and International Education Society, and the Society for Research in Higher Education.

Marcela Mollis is Full Professor of the History of Education and Comparative Education, and serves as the Director of the Research Program on Comparative Higher Education, a program of the Research Institute of Education in the School of Philosophy and Literature at the University of Buenos Aires. She is also the Latin American coordinator for the research group on "Society and University" of the Latin American

Center of Social Sciences (CLACSO). Two of her latest books are *La Universidad Argentina en Tránsito: Un Ensayo para Jóvenes y no tan Jóvenes* [The Argentine University in Transition: An essay for young and not so young readers] (2001), and *Las Universidades en América Latina: Reformadas o Alteradas?* [The Latin American Universities: Reformed or Altered?] (2003).

José-Ginés Mora is Director of the Center for Higher Education Management (CEGES) at the Technical University of Valencia (UPV). He is the President of the European Association of Institutional Research (EAIR) and a member of the governing board of the OECD Program on Institutional Management in Higher Education. His recent publications and research have addressed the economics of education, labor market, higher education and quality assurance.

Roberto Moscati is Full Professor of the Sociology of Education at the University of Milano-Bicocca, and has held faculty positions at the University of Trieste, the University of Catania, and Milano State University. He is a member of the editorial boards of the *European Journal of Education, Inchiesta, Scuola Democratica, Università e Scuola*, and *Tertiary Education and Management*. He is also a member of the Committee for the Study of Human Resources for Science and Technology (CORUS) at CNR (Italian National Research Council), and has been a member of the Italian governmental Committee for University Reform. He holds degrees from the Catholic University of Milan, Northwestern University and Harvard University.

Christine Musselin is Senior Researcher at the *Centre de Sociologie des Organisations* (Center for the Sociology of Organizations), a research unit of the Sciences-Po university and the CNRS (National Center for Scientific Research). She leads comparative studies on higher education systems and primarily deals with university governance, public policies on higher education and research, state-university relationships and academic labor markets. Her latest book, *La Longue Marche des Universités Françaises* [The Long March of French Universities] (2001) was recently re-published in English (2004).

Charles Kibani Ngome is a lecturer at the School of Education, Kenyatta University, Kenya. He is also the Deputy Director of the Institute for Research and Development at Kenyatta University. He holds a Ph.D. in education, and pursues research on contemporary educational issues.

Namgi Park is a professor in the Department of Educational Studies at Gwangju National University of Education and a member of the Advisory Committee to the Minster of Education and Human Resource Development in Korea.

Harold J. Perkin, Professor Emeritus of History at Northwestern University, passed away on October 16, 2004 at the age of 77, shortly after submitting his chapter for this volume. A British social historian, his nine books include *The Origins of Modern English Society, 1780–1880, The Rise of Professional Society: England since 1880*, and

The Third Revolution: Professional Elites in the Modern World. He also edited a series of books, *Studies in Social History,* founded the Social History Society and served as its chairman (1976–85), and served as president of the Association of University Teachers. In 1997, he retired from Northwestern and returned to London, where he published his final book—an autobiography entitled *The Making of a Social Historian* (2002).

Henry Rosovsky is the Lewis P. and Linda L. Geyser University Professor Emeritus, and the former Dean of the Faculty of Arts and Sciences at Harvard University. He has been a Professor of Economics at Harvard since 1965, and has served as the Chair of Harvard's Economics Department and Associate Director of the East Asian Research Center. He is the author of numerous articles and books, including *The University: An Owner's Manual* (1990)*, Capital Formation in Japan* (1961), and *Quantitative Japanese Economic History* (1961). He was co-chair of the Task Force on Higher Education and Society, a body convened by UNESCO and the World Bank, and has been active in promoting new ideas about higher education in developing countries.

Peter Scott is Vice Chancellor of Kingston University in London and was formerly Pro Vice Chancellor and Professor of Education at the University of Leeds. Until 1992, he was Editor of *The Times Higher Education Supplement.* He is a member of the Boards of the European Universities Association (EUA) and the Higher Education Funding Council for England (HEFCE). His research interests include the governance and management of universities, the globalization of higher education and the development of new paradigms of research and knowledge production.

Evanthia Kalpazidou Schmidt is Associate Professor at the University of Aarhus, Denmark. She has published widely on higher education and research organization and policy, European research and technological development, innovation, European evaluation policy and the sociology of science and society. She is the Danish national coordinator of the project MORESS (Mapping of European Social Sciences and Humanities), initiated by the European University Association, and her latest work is connected to the 5-year assessment of the 5th and 6th European Framework Programs for Research and Technological Development.

Simon Schwartzman is a Brazilian political scientist at the *Instituto de Estudos do Trabalho e Sociedade* (Institute for the Study of Work and Society), Brazil. He has served as President of Brazil's Statistical and Geographical Institute, and has worked in the areas of comparative politics, science and technology, higher education and social policy. His books include *Bases do Autoritarismo Brasileiro* (1982); A Space for Science: *The Development of the Scientific Community in Brazil* (1991, re-published 2001 in Portuguese); *The New Production of Knowledge* (with Michael Gibbons, Camille Limoges, Helga Nowotny, Peter Scott and Martin Trow, 1994); and *El Futuro de la Educación Superior en America Latina* (1996).

Chika Trevor Sehoole is Senior Lecturer at the University of Pretoria, South Africa, where he teaches Education Policy Studies. He holds a Ph.D. degree from the

University of the Witwatersrand, Johannesburg. During the 2003–04 academic year, he was a visiting postdoctoral fellow at the Center for African Studies, University of Illinois at Urbana Champaign. His research interests are in higher education policy and globalization, especially in relation to the General Agreement on Trade in Service (GATS) and transnational education.

Juma Shabani is Director of the UNESCO Harare Cluster office and Representative to Botswana, Malawi, Zambia and Zimbabwe. A professor of mathematical physics, he has also served as Vice Rector of the University of Burundi (1988–1992), Deputy Secretary General of the Association of African Universities (1992–1996) and UNESCO Senior Specialist for Higher Education in Africa (1996–2002).

Michael Shattock is currently Visiting Professor in the Center for Higher Education Studies at the Institute of Education, University of London, and was previously Registrar of the University of Warwick. He has published widely in higher education, including *The UGC and the Management of British Universities* (1994) and *Managing Successful Universities* (2003). A further book *Entrepreneurialism and the Transformation of Russian Universities*, is forthcoming. He is also editor of the journal *Higher Education Management and Policy*. He was educated at the University of Oxford and holds honorary degrees from the Universities of Reading and Warwick. He has served as an adviser or consultant on higher education issues in the U.K. and around the world, and led the OECD review of Irish higher education in 2004.

Hasan Simsek is Professor of Education in the Department of Educational Sciences at the Middle East Technical University in Ankara, Turkey. His research focuses on educational administration, leadership and higher education. He has also served as a consultant to the World Bank, the Turkish Ministry of Education and the Turkish Higher Education Council.

Anna Smolentseva is Research Fellow at the Center for Sociological Studies at Moscow State University. She holds a Ph.D. in Sociology from Moscow State University and has been a NAE/Spencer Postdoctoral Fellow. She is an author of nearly 30 articles contributed to *Higher Education, International Higher Education* and a number of Russian scholarly journals and books. Her research interests involve the sociology of education, globalization and internationalization in higher education, transformation of the academic profession, doctoral education, higher education and the labor market.

Barbara Sporn is Associate Professor of Education at the Vienna University of Economics and Business Administration in Austria. She was recently appointed Vice Rector for Research, International Relations, and External Affairs at the same institution. Her empirical work is based on extensive field studies in the United States and Europe, and she has held various positions at Stanford University, New York University, the University of Michigan, and the University of California at Berkeley. She has published her work widely in journals and monographs, addressing topics such as environmental forces and organizational responses shaping higher education systems, and serves as editor of several European journals of higher education.

Muhammad Kamil Tadjudin is Chair of the National Accreditation Board for Higher Education in Indonesia. He is also Professor Emeritus of Medical Biology at the University of Indonesia, and Dean of the Faculty of Medicine and Health Sciences at the State Islamic University. He is a member of several national and international scientific institutions, and at present is also a member of the UNESCO Southeast Asia Regional Forum for Higher Education. He graduated from the Faculty of Medicine Universitas Indonesia in 1962, where he served as Rector from 1994–1998.

Damtew Teferra is Assistant Professor (research) of Higher Education and founding Editor-in-Chief of the *Journal of Higher Education in Africa* at the Center for International Higher Education, Boston College. His recent publications include *Scientific Communication in African Universities: National Needs and External Support* (2003) and *African Higher Education: An International Reference Handbook* (co-edited with Philip Altbach, 2003). He holds a bachelor's degree from Addis Ababa University (Ethiopia), a master's degree from Stirling University (U.K.), and a Ph.D. from Boston College.

Anthony Tillett is currently an independent consultant in Chile, and has worked with various development agencies and universities in the U.K., Canada, the U.S. and Mexico. Previous positions include serving as the Regional Director, Latin America and the Caribbean regional office of the International Development Research Centre (IDRC). His publications and conference presentations have addressed a variety of issues related to social and economic policy in Latin America.

Martin Trow is Professor Emeritus in the Goldman School of Public Policy at the University of California. He has published widely on various topics in the sociology of politics and comparative higher education, and particularly the history, sources and consequences of the expansion and diversification of higher education in advanced industrial societies. Publications include *Union Democracy* (with Seymour M. Lipset and James Coleman, 1957), *Problems in the Transition from Elite to Mass Higher Education* (1973), and *University and Society: The Social Role of Higher Education and Research* (with Thorsten Nybom, 1991). He is a Foreign Member of the Royal Swedish Academy of Science, a Fellow of the American Academy of Arts and Sciences, the National Academy of Education, and the Society for Research in Higher Education in Great Britain, and has served as Chairman of the Academic Council of the University of California.

Akiyoshi Yonezawa is Associate Professor of the National Institution for Academic Degrees and University Evaluation (NIAD-UE). He is a comparative sociologist of higher education, whose research focuses on quality assurance, private higher education and social class issues. He has held professional positions at the University of Tokyo and Hiroshima University, and has been involved in various projects conducted by

OECD and UNESCO-CEPES. He is a member of editorial advisory board of two journals, *Higher Education Management and Policy*, and *Higher Education Research and Development.*

Qiang Zha is currently a Ph.D. candidate in Higher Education at the Ontario Institute for Studies in Education, University of Toronto, Canada. He has worked for the Chinese government in educational administration at both provincial and national levels, and taught at the university level for three years. As a Chevening Scholar, he received a degree of master's degree from the University of London Institute of Education, and in 2004 he was awarded the Palgrave Prize in Higher Education Policy Research by the International Association of Universities for his comparative study (co-authored with Daniel W. Lang) on entrepreneurialism in Canada and China.

INDEX

AAHE (American Association of Higher
Education), 355, 367, 369, 372
AAU (Association of African Universities), 91,
415, 498, 577, 579, 1065
Abelard, Peter, 162, 201, 202
Aberdeen, 168, 1019
ABET (Accreditation Board for Engineering and
Technology) (U.S.), 61
academic
capitalism, 144, 146, 157, 242, 321, 328, 511,
515, 641, 645
council, 404, 455, 752, 885, 954, 955, 960, 963,
965, 975, 1066
credits, 55, 551
discipline, 4, 28, 247, 315, 326, 348–350, 370,
592, 608, 617, 901, 1045
drift, 10, 1023, 1030
freedom, 6, 7, 11, 12, 15, 21, 41, 83, 130, 159,
161, 163, 170, 177, 189, 199, 201, 258, 409,
414, 416, 420, 432, 433, 452, 455, 550, 565,
566, 604, 668, 730, 798, 799, 809, 929, 936,
952, 959, 996, 1006, 1008, 1007, 1026,
1044
and autonomy, 565, 1007
and teaching, 6, 11, 12, 15
in a global context, 836
leadership, 12, 18, 65, 78, 124, 125, 143, 145,
147, 148, 150, 151, 153–155, 226, 237, 238,
240, 241, 249, 251, 252, 257, 259, 270, 273,
284, 294, 349, 363, 403, 412, 430, 439, 457,
511, 520, 531, 596, 615, 663, 668, 670,
672–674, 679, 683, 684, 688, 695, 696, 733,
775, 778, 800, 821, 843, 858, 876, 886, 972,
1009, 1028, 1043, 1046, 1065 see also
administration; management
major, 48
migration, 129, 700
profession, 3, 5–19, 76–79, 200, 281, 284–286,
347, 349, 350, 358, 361, 370, 372, 393, 396,
397, 403, 439, 446, 453, 455, 456, 535, 539,
541, 550, 563, 579, 580, 584, 606, 650, 685,
711–713, 717, 718, 721, 739, 757, 758, 764,

772, 778, 798, 803, 813, 822, 825, 833, 834,
890, 891, 909–911, 917, 930, 945, 952, 959,
960, 962, 964, 1018, 1057–1059, 1065
see also faculty
and academic freedom, 11, 12
and governance, 141–157
and research, 284–286
and technology, 377–390
and tenure, 12–13
and traditions, 7, 10, 16
centers and peripheries of, 16, 17
changing roles and expectations of, 6–9
history of, 159–205
international dimensions of, 16, 17
working conditions of, 12–16
senate, 397, 620, 820, 1059
standards, 111, 124, 216, 218, 244, 248, 252,
257, 258, 265, 446, 452, 456, 528, 669, 750,
754, 802, 804, 808, 928, 1027
traditions, 17, 122, 542, 557
Academie des Sciences (France), 173, 178
Academy of Finland, 526
Academy of Sciences (Russia), 178, 951–952
access, 1–4, 8, 9, 17, 26, 46, 50, 52, 83, 98, 101,
112, 115, 116, 124, 125, 129, 130, 132,
134–137, 142, 152, 178, 179, 196–198, 225,
243, 244, 246–248, 251–267, 269–271,
274–278, 281–284, 288, 290, 294, 306, 309,
321, 323, 341, 377–387, 389, 415–417,
445, 447, 449–453, 457, 467, 476, 485, 487,
488, 494, 496, 497, 500, 504, 510, 511, 517,
521, 523, 526, 528, 529, 531, 539, 540,
543–546, 548, 552, 558, 561, 563, 566, 574,
575, 594, 596–598, 604, 615–618, 621,
623, 629, 630, 634, 636–638, 643, 647, 648,
655, 663, 671, 677, 679, 684, 693, 695–698,
701–704, 706, 707, 716, 718, 720, 721, 724,
725, 729, 730, 732–734, 774, 782–785,
789, 798, 806, 807, 818, 829, 830, 840, 845,
848, 853, 854, 861–864, 867, 881, 887, 888,
894, 902, 916, 919–922, 925–927, 932,
939, 948, 952, 954, 956, 958, 959, 967, 968,

1094   *Index*

reforma, the (Latin America), 336, 994
Reformation, the, 6, 42, 43, 160, 161, 163, 164,
168, 172, 200
regionalization, 10, 211, 462
relationships, student-teacher, 43, 44, 245,
248–250, 254, 255, 286, 348, 361, 700, 703,
720
relevance, 8, 49, 76, 89, 112, 174, 214, 219, 223,
319, 357, 383, 483, 496, 497, 500, 508, 518,
524, 541, 543, 552, 553, 647, 693, 765, 770,
774, 775, 778, 789, 820, 844, 860–863
relevant age group, 2, 188, 192, 195, 245–248, 252,
253, 262, 266, 504, 805, 925, 942, 1008
religious institutions, 286, 288, 577, 682 *see also*
historical background; private higher
education
funding sources of, 288
religious organizations, 282, 333, 334, 344, 795,
929
religious private universities, 282
remedial courses, 819, 921
Renaissance, the, 42, 124, 159, 162, 169, 312, 390,
410
Renardus, 383, 384
research activities, 88, 129, 267, 277, 309–311,
313, 314, 326, 478, 480, 491, 492, 494, 566,
577, 580, 582, 588, 592, 594, 608, 643, 712,
715, 716, 718, 724, 725, 754, 802, 825, 845,
853, 906, 910, 945, 952, 993, 998, 999
research:
and centers and peripheries, 125, 284, 311, 312,
314, 315, 318, 320, 321, 324, 326, 397, 402,
491, 492, 494, 553, 578, 606, 640, 651, 693,
825, 884, 914, 1047, 1059, 1064
and donor agendas, 50
and intellectual property, 325
and publishing, 320–322
and scientific communication, 322–326
and teaching loads, 232
and technology, 322–326
and the Internet, 322–326
assistants, 72, 77, 397, 909, 1014, 1015, 1059
commercialization of, 92, 104, 211, 397, 905,
1059
competitive funding mechanisms for, 319
dependence on donors, 304
facilities, 15, 72, 235, 268, 491, 492, 804,
875
faculty, 146, 234, 563, 803
funding councils, 315
funding for, 309–326
inadequate infrastructure for, 309–313
income from, 316–318

industry funding for, 320–322, 608
infrastructure, 315, 324, 563, 595, 607, 608, 808,
906, 1029
institutes, 6, 41, 46, 55, 74, 125, 160, 175,
177–179, 191, 232, 234, 235, 239, 278, 314,
317, 318, 325, 326, 400, 437, 467, 490, 520,
521, 533, 609, 614, 618, 622, 687, 713, 714,
716, 718, 720, 721, 723, 724, 736, 744, 751,
794, 797, 804, 861, 870, 876, 904, 905, 952,
960, 962, 964, 1015, 1062
institutes and centers of, 61, 322–326
-intensive universities, 309, 310–313, 322, 326,
604, 1024, 1033
laboratories, 78, 277, 314, 751
links with industry, 309, 320–322, 661, 1030
methods, 45, 395, 398, 1057, 1060
-oriented universities, 67, 72–74, 77, 125
priorities, 88, 316, 318–320, 904, 989
priority setting for, 8, 309, 316, 318–320, 326
productivity, 142, 312, 347, 542
public funding of, 309, 316–318
quality, assessments of, 145, 317, 523, 905
role of the state in directing, 314–316
role of universities in, 210, 309, 398, 535, 650
the role of the state in, 147, 149, 309, 314, 432,
456, 548, 686, 954
universities, 6, 10, 16, 44, 47, 50, 67, 78, 117,
122, 125, 174, 175, 177, 184, 191, 231, 251,
256, 270, 273–275, 277, 278, 312, 313, 317,
324, 445, 510, 545, 609, 619, 620, 632, 641,
677, 795, 800, 803, 804, 806, 807, 835, 916,
968, 1035, 1036, 1038, 1040, 1042, 1045,
1047
residence halls, 7, 234, 385, 852, 862, 1046
residential, 41, 43, 45, 47, 230, 244, 250, 255, 256,
331, 344, 590, 841, 854, 972, 1046
residential colleges, 41, 43, 45, 47, 590, 1046
resource allocation, 35, 145, 146, 148, 150, 151,
154, 222, 304, 318, 521, 532, 621, 701, 721,
845, 949
Resource Development Network (U.K.), 383
retention, 52, 57, 94, 234, 352, 364, 398, 593, 662,
790, 835, 855, 968, 1060
retrenchment, 626, 671, 679, 899
revenue, sources of, 84, 378, 546, 659, 677, 1039
Robbins Commission on Higher Education (U.K.),
1021
Robbins Report (U.K.), 246, 1021, 1022
Rockefeller Foundation, 567
Romania/Romanian, 25, 110, 171, 337, 425, 426,
428, 430, 439, 468
Rome, 159, 164, 166, 168, 169, 172, 173, 464, 813,
1023